THRESHOLDS
LITERATURE-BASED COMPOSITION

THRESHOLDS
LITERATURE-BASED COMPOSITION

J. STERLING WARNER

Evergreen Valley College

Harcourt Brace College Publishers

Fort Worth   Philadelphia   San Diego
New York   Orlando   Austin   San Antonio
Toronto   Montreal   London   Sydney   Tokyo

Publisher	CHRISTOPHER P. KLEIN
Executive Editor for English	MICHAEL ROSENBERG
Developmental Editor	MICHELL PHIFER
Project Editor	LOUISE SLOMINSKY
Senior Production Manager	KATHLEEN FERGUSON
Senior Art Director	DON FUJIMOTO

Cover photo: Copyright © Jeffrey N. Becom; photo 20-20.

Harcourt Brace College Publishers may provide complimentary instructional aids and supplements or supplement packages to those adopters qualified under our adoption policy. Please contact your sales representative for more information. If as an adopter or potential user you receive supplements you do not need, please return them to your sales representative or send them to: Attn: Returns Department, Troy Warehouse, 465 South Lincoln Drive, Troy, MO 63379.

Address for Editorial Correspondence:
Harcourt Brace College Publishers
301 Commerce Street, Suite 3700
Fort Worth, TX 76102

Address for Orders:
Harcourt Brace & Company
6277 Sea Harbor Drive
Orlando, FL 32887-6777
1-800-782-4479, or 1-800-433-0001 (in Florida)

Library of Congress Catalog Card Number: 96-76634

Printed in the United States of America

ISBN 0-15-501977-5

6 7 8 9 0 1 2 3 4 5 016 9 8 7 6 5 4 3 2 1

Preface

Thresholds, a combination rhetoric, reader, and research guide, ideally suits the needs of today's composition student. Featuring a wide selection of authors from many cultural viewpoints, *Thresholds* targets many pressing issues: writing skills (reader-response), critical thinking skills, the research process, and cultural literacy. Topics and issues relevant to our lives and the world in which we live appear in various literary genres in *Thresholds* and serve as a stimulus for rhetorical discussions, formal and informal evaluation, analysis, and argumentation. The diverse genres of literature in *Thresholds* also function as a forum for word study. For instance, poems offer an excellent resource for studying word use in its most compressed form through effective diction (literal and figurative language; concrete, visual, and sensory images; denotation and connotation).

Some of the thematic readings *fit* in more than one chapter. Indeed, any single literary work yields numerous possibilities for discussion and analysis. The dominant theme for a chapter works like a lens and offers readers a focal point, but not a boundary excluding other possibilities or relationships. Depending on a reader's focus, for example, Dick Gregory's essay "Shame" could provide a lively discussion of "Identity" instead of "Dreams and Disillusionment." In "Good Country People," class discussions could focus on the theme of "Relationships: Friends, Family, and Lovers" rather than "City and Country: Urban, Suburban, and Rural." Louise Erdrich's poem "The Woods," which was presented in chapter 1 under the *mini theme* of "loss," might lend itself to consideration under several chapters, including "Identity," "Relationships: Friends, Family, and Lovers," "Dreams and Disillusionment," and "Sacrifice and Fulfillment." Since people do not share a universal set of values and experiences, they relate to topics and issues differently. Thus, in *Thresholds* student response is emphasized; writers are encouraged to consider *a* theme instead of *the* theme and to engage in readings that are representative of *an* aspect of a topic, rather than *the* narrowly perceived "core" of a theme.

Thresholds consist of three major sections: (1) "The Writing Process and Literature," (2) "Thematic Readings: Essays, Fiction, and Poetry," and (3) "The Research Paper." My goal has been to couple innovative with traditional methods of writing instruction to provide flexibility for different approaches to teaching and learning.

Part 1 of *Thresholds* is a rhetoric including information on active reading strategies, the composition process (prewriting, drafting, revising, and editing), as well as critical and creative approaches to argumentation and exposition. Part I of this text, "The Writing Process and Literature," provides a base to return to when moving from one thematic group of readings to another. In addition to being a review of how major forms of discourse—

particularly exposition and argumentation—pervade all types of literature, Part I briefly discusses how rhetorical modes might be used to develop and revise compositions. (Since literature-based composition emphasizes that methods of development overlap, the first section of the book is the logical and convenient place to refer to developmental techniques.) The first part of *Thresholds* also features the following:

- An essay, poem, and short story that exemplify the mini theme of "loss" and demonstrate the different ways of reading and responding to texts.
- Active reading strategies.
- Collaborative activities (called *Collaborative Reflections*) on the writing process that reinforce dominant ideas and concepts discussed in their respective chapters.
- Checklists for reading essays, fiction, and poetry critically.
- Methods and techniques for revising essays.
- A basic summary of each rhetoric chapter: *(1) Strategies: Reading and Responding, (2) Strategies: Drafting the Essay, (3) Strategies: Revising the Essay, (4) Strategies: Editing the Essay.*
- Information pertaining to the development of precision of word choice, voice, and style in writing.
- A checklist for the final draft of an essay. The rhetoric section concludes with a revised final draft of a student essay that was formerly presented during the drafting stages of writing (chapter 2).

Part II of *Thresholds*—the reader—gives a brief introduction to each thematic unit, including references to the forthcoming essays. The chapter introductions further include information on *Rhetoric at Work* in the chapter and a checklist for writing about each thematic unit. Biographical sketches prior to readings also provide contextual information on the work that follows. The postreading apparatus deals with the reading/writing process, subdivided into *Writing Log/Journal Assignments* (questions inviting exploration of one's personal, cultural, or historical knowledge), *Individual and Collaborative Considerations* (content comprehension and rhetorical structures questions), and *Writing Assignments.*

Additional Topics and Issues for Writing and Research conclude each chapter. They are then followed by a list entitled *Starting Points for Research*. These lists were compiled through several sources, including the Library of Congress. Since modern technology has changed the face of the research process, *Starting Points for Research* is particularly useful when accessing information on CD-ROM and online indexes and directories, not to mention computer services and computer networks.

Part III of *Thresholds* is a section on the research paper. This part of the text offers an overview of modern techniques of literary research (CD-ROM and online catalogs) as well as traditional, hard bound indexes. The two research chapters include the following:

- Information on how to document sources and format a list of works cited.
- Sample parenthetical documentation and a list of works cited.
- Material on the process of writing research papers using online databases, indexes, computer services, and computer networks.
- An annotated list of works cited.
- A sample student research paper.

In short, *Thresholds* is not just another anthology of literature. Rather, it is a collection of excellent poetry, fiction, and essays particularly accessible to the writing classroom. By responding to ideas and issues presented in literature rather than engaging in literary analysis, writers remain focused on the task at hand—improving composition skills. This is the heart and soul of literature-based composition.

Since I began writing *Thresholds*, I have greatly benefited from frank, insightful reviews by Samantha Morgan, University of Tennessee, Knoxville; Kim Flachmann, California State University, Bakersfield; Jennifer Hicks, Massachusetts Bay Community College; Mary Frances Hodges, University of Arkansas, Little Rock; Maureen Hoag, Wichita State University; Pauline Uchmanwicz, Wayne State University; Linda Palumbo, Cerritos Community College; and Susan Fitzgerald, University of Memphis. I am likewise indebted to many friends and colleagues for their constructive criticism and encouragement: Rose Anna Higashi, Evergreen Valley College; Martha Henning, Portland Community College; Reginald Lockett, San Jose City College; Jean Embree, Evergreen Valley College, and Bruce Henderson, Fullerton College.

I would also like to thank the numerous people at Harcourt Brace College Publishers for their assistance, beginning with Stephanie Surface, Harcourt Brace Regional Manager, who was there when the concept for *Thresholds* originated over lunch; Michael Rosenberg, Executive Editor for English, who stood by me as the manuscript evolved; Michell Phifer, Developmental Editor, who helped me to complete the text in a timely manner—never too busy or tired to answer a question; Louise Slominsky, Project Editor, who patiently worked with me on production matters as *Thresholds* went from galleys to page proofs; Ilse Wolfe West, Marketing Manager, who oversaw the promotion of the text; and the production team of Don Fujimoto, Art Director and Kathy Ferguson, Production Manager. Finally, I want to thank both John Malone, Angus McDonald, and all the other individuals who championed *Thresholds* at one point or another during its development.

J. Sterling Warner

Contents

Essays

What is a cultural collision? How does one develop a sense of self when caught between two cultures? When Mai Nguyen made plans to move in with a girlfriend and "to continue working at a public policy institute on campus where she had been a statistical researcher" before graduating with honors at UC–Berkeley; "Her parents refused vehemently. . . . Like many traditional Vietnamese families, they expected their children to live at home until married, except for time out for school."

Cisneros had a childhood passion for disappearing into the monkey garden to play with her friends. The special moments in the garden gave way to change however—first with her friends and then with herself. Cisneros laments the reality that one day, "the garden that had been such a good place to play didn't seem mine either."

How do people "identify" with others as we move into the twenty-first century? Ellen Goodman concludes that "If our offices are our new neighborhoods, if our professional titles are our new ethnic tags, then how do we separate our selves from our jobs? Self-worth isn't just something to measure in the marketplace. But in these new communities, it becomes harder and harder to tell who we are without saying what we do."

Fiction

"Sargeant didn't see the snow, not even under the bright lights of the main street, falling white and flaky against the night. He was too hungry, too sleepy, too tired." All doors seemed to close on him, but when he reached a church, "Sargeant for once had no intention of being pulled or pushed away from the door."

As she reflects on her aunt who shamed and was not recognized by her family, Maxine Hong Kingston states that "I do not think she always means me well. I am telling on her, and she was a spite suicide, drowning herself in the drinking water. The Chinese are always very frightened of the drowned one, whose weeping ghost, wet hair hanging and skin bloated, waits silently by the water to pull down a substitute."

Shifts in point of view, role reversals, and mental metamorphosis, all play an integral part in "Axolotl." From observer to the observed,

Cortázar's protagonist exchanges traits of the axolotl in the aquarium and finds himself drawn to the world that invites reflective thought rather than movement.

Poetry

Essays

mother felt such matters were not important and put Walker and her sisters at a disadvantage.

Fiction

The plumber who stood before the astronomer's wife was a man of action and directness—something she found intriguing. "But whenever the astronomer gave voice to the thoughts that soared within him, she returned in gratitude to the long expanses of his silence."

With all the horses sold and her brothers moving on, Mabel seemed quite alone, but Jack Fergusson was more than just a country doctor; he too was frightened and fascinated by love: "She lifted her face to him, and he bent forward and kissed her on the mouth, gently, with the one kiss that is an eternal pledge. And as he kissed her his heart strained again in his breast. He never intended to love her. But now it was over. He had crossed over the gulf to her, and all that he had left behind had shriveled and become void."

"She let herself be caressed, drops of sweat in the small of her back, her body exuding the scent of burnt sugar, silent, as if she divined that a single sound could nudge its way into memory and destroy everything, reducing to dust this instant in which he was a person like any other, a casual lover she had met that morning. . . ." He was different, however; they shared a mutual secret.

Poetry

She wanted "a little room for thinking" for an hour in the middle of the day, "but she saw diapers steaming on the line, / a doll slumped behind the door"; even at night she would think about the hour and "place that was hers" alone.

Speaking from the persona of "Circe," the enchantress who for all her magic could not tempt Odysseus to stay with her, H. D. explores the passion and torture of an unrequited love.

dream ends and another begins. He speaks of a time when "Things fall apart; the centre cannot hold; / Mere anarchy is loosed upon the world, / The blood-dimmed tide is loosed, and everywhere / The ceremony of innocence is drowned. . . ."

Essays

Fiction

Poetry

11. Conflict and Resolution   357

Essays

Fiction

adventure'—signifies that destiny has summoned the hero and transferred his spiritual center of gravity from within the pale of his society to a zone unknown."

Although Letty Cottin Pogrebin considers herself a rational person, there are some things like "superstitions" beyond the confines of logic that are meaningful to her; she says, "My superstitions are my mother's superstitions, the amulets and incantations she learned from *her* mother and taught me."

The shadows in the room became shapes—women—and they began singing, "Singing and dancing in the ancient steps of the women, the Spider." She understood that "those women, so long lost to her, whom she had longed and wept for, unknowing, were the double women, the women who never married, who held power like the Clanuncle, like the power of the priests, the medicine men. Who were not mothers, but who were sisters, born of the same mind, the same spirit."

Fiction

As the barber prepared to shave Captain Torres, he considered the captain's reputation and the power he held in his hand: "Murderer or hero? My destiny depends on the edge of this blade. I can turn my hand a bit more, press a little harder on the razor, and sink it in. The skin would give way like silk, like rubber, like the strop. There is nothing more tender than human skin and blood is always there, ready to pour forth."

To escape the "dead ends" of his life in Dublin, a young boy engages in a quest—to attain something from Araby—for a woman. "At night in my bedroom and by day in the classroom her image came between me and the page I strove to read. The syllables of the word *Araby* were called to me through the silence in which my soul luxuriated and cast an Eastern enchantment over me."

Poetry

Motherhood presents Sylvia Plath with a ritualized pattern of behavior as she waits at night to hear and respond to her child's cries that "rise like balloons."

and creates his masterpiece, she tells him "Giving me your soul must have made me very beautiful."

knotted, big, spidery, and rough, with sensitive fingertips good at dealing cards."

How reliable is a personal confession? In what way might point of view flavor one's testimony regarding a murder victim? Akutagawa presents a case of homicide and allows his readers to deduce what really occurred in the grove.

Despite the lack of life forms around it, on the hour, the fully automated house kept up its programmed tasks. "This was the one house left standing. At night the ruined city gave off a radioactive glow which could be seen for miles."

Poetry

Harlem Renaissance poet / author Paul Laurence Dunbar writes that to disguise all true fear, pain, and suffering, "We wear the mask that grins and lies, / It hides our cheeks and shades our eyes—."

A bus traveling westward passes a panorama of sights and sounds, and when it stops, the driver points out that the moose that has just stepped out of "the impenetrable wood" was "perfectly harmless"; meanwhile, a "sweet sensation of joy" overcomes the passengers.

Rhetorical Contents

VII. Comparison and Contrast

VIII. Division and Classification

IX. Exposition (Combined Strategies)

X. Argumentation and Persuasion

PART I

The Writing Process and Literature

1

Literature-Based Composition: Essays, Fiction, and Poetry

Works of literature are written to be read, enjoyed, and related to your own life. As such, the themes and motifs in literature frequently reflect the rituals and realities of day-to-day life: love and hate, victory and defeat, life and death, freedom and oppression. In *Thresholds*, you will be focusing your attention on rhetoric—word use—and style, preserving the inherent enjoyment to be had in both reading and writing while you acquire new or develop unrealized communication skills. As you explore the possibilities of essays, fiction, and poetry with the goals of composition in mind, each will function as a lively stimulus for a writing topic; each genre has something to offer a writer in the never-ending quest to master the written word.

The active reading, responding, and writing strategies outlined and illustrated in Part I of *Thresholds* will transfer to all your reading and composition assignments as you move from analyzing topics in fiction and responding to word use in poetry, to critiquing diction, dialects, and themes in short fiction or essays. In every instance you will engage in some form of prewriting, organizing materials and planning the essay, drafting your composition, revising your draft, editing your work, and preparing a final draft. In most instances, the focus of your individual and group activities will be an intensive study of the writing process and the power of rhetoric. Questions and activities following readings will range from conceptualizing ideas or taking positions on topics presented in a literary work to expressing them in writing. Additionally, ongoing development of your critical thinking skills will be an important part of every postreading question or activity.

ACTIVE READING STRATEGIES: MARKING THE TEXT

Preview   You can use previewing strategies to note your initial impressions of an essay, a short story, or a poem. First, browse quickly through the piece of literature before reading it in depth. Notice the title or any headings which may guide your reading by indicating the forthcoming theme or issue.

Identify Patterns   Looking for patterns of development can establish clear relationships and lead to coherence. Do certain words appear again and again, or are particular phrases in italics or underlined? How might the repetition of images establish a theme or attitude towards a topic (e.g., images projecting anger, tenderness, respect)? You might also search for patterns indicating the *controlling idea* of a literary work, traditionally recognized as the "thesis" in an essay and understood through images, actions, theme, and characterization in poetry and fiction.

Anticipate or Predict Next, take the time to anticipate what the work will be about. As a result of your browsing, who or what do you imagine will be the focus of the piece? Predict what may happen on the basis of a poem's, essay's, or short story's title, subheadings, or other features catching your attention. The act of anticipation can open your critical and imaginative abilities, leading to greater comprehension and appreciation of a work. What, for instance, might you anticipate or predict about a story entitled "The Pomegranate," a poem called "To an Athlete Dying Young," or an essay called "Living Like Weasels"?

Highlight After browsing, anticipating, and predicting the content of a literary work, read it over once for enjoyment. Then reread the work, highlighting key words and phrases (those which strike you as particularly meaningful or important, usually words or phrases echoing major points or themes), repetitive images, and main ideas or concepts. As a general rule, underline words you do not know when you highlight and then look them up; they may be crucial to the overall comprehension and appreciation of an author's plot, theme, or thesis. When you reread your work, reassess your anticipations, predictions, and general impressions from a first reading. What sorts of new things are you aware of the second time you read a work?

Respond Jot down insights and perceptions in the margins of the text. Since no one will read your annotations, do not worry about making profound statements or witty remarks. Respond to anything striking you as important, provocative, or appealing (your perceptions are as good as the next person's, anyway).

Question Actively dialogue with the text, asking *Who? What? When? Where? How?* and *Why?* about words and phrases. As a question pops in your head, write it in the margin. If you think something was very nicely phrased, say so. When you read something that seems sheer nonsense, jot down "Yeah, in a pig's eye!" or any other expression that captures your attitude towards something ridiculous or improbable. A piece of literature speaks to you from the page, so talk back to it. Be a definite presence, an active person as you read.

Connect Connect situations, people, and places—as well as themes and motifs found in literary works—to your own life experiences, to other literature you have read, and to the world at large.

Discuss Talk with other people about your insights into an essay, a short story, or a poem. What dominant impressions did they have of a work? When, where, and how did your observations concur and differ?

Stay Involved Ongoing active involvement in the reading process will not only promote your understanding of a literary piece, but also help you make meaningful connections between what you read and your own life experiences.

Notice how active reading strategies and *marking the text* are at work in the following short story, "The Pomegranate" by Yasunari Kawabata; initial impressions of the story are frequently followed by commentary based on the reader's own experiences and first-hand knowledge of human behavior.

※

The (Pomegranate) — A fruit whose seeds are eaten

Yasunari Kawabata

In the high wind that night the pomegranate tree was stripped of its leaves. *Why a tree*

The leaves lay in a circle around the base. *"naked in the*

Does this Symbolize something? Kimiko was startled to see it <u>naked in the morning</u> and *morning"?* wondered at the flawlessness of the circle. She would have expected the wind to disturb it.

There was a pomegranate, a very fine one, left behind in the tree.

5 "Just come and look at it," she called to her mother. *Similarity*

"I had forgotten." Her mother glanced (up) at the tree and *between* went (back) to the kitchen. *pomegrante's*

existence and

It made Kimiko think of <u>their loneliness. The pomegran</u>- *their own...* ate over the veranda too (seemed lonely and forgotten.)

Two weeks or so before, her seven-year-old nephew had come visiting, and had noticed the pomegranates immediately. He had scrambled up into the tree. Kimiko had felt that she was in the <u>presence of life.</u> *Whose life?*

Why?

"There is a big one up above," she called from the veranda.

10 "But if I pick it I can't get back down."

It was true. To climb down with pomegranates in both hands would not be easy. Kimiko smiled. He was a dear.

Until he had come the house had forgotten the pome- *Forgotten life?*
granate. And until now they had forgotten it again.

Then the fruit had been hidden in the leaves. Now it stood
clear against the sky.

How is fruit strong? There was strength in the fruit and in the circle of leaves
at the base. Kimiko went and knocked it down with a bam-
boo pole.

15 It was so ripe that the seeds seemed to force it open. They
glistened in the sunlight when she laid it on the veranda,
and the sun seemed to go on through them.

She felt somehow apologetic.

Upstairs with her sewing about ten, she heard Keikichi's
voice. Though the door was unlocked, he seemed to have
come around to the garden. There was urgency in his voice. *Why the r*

"Kimiko, Kimiko!" her mother called. "Keikichi is here."

Kimiko had let her needle come unthreaded. She pushed
it into the pincushion.

20 "Kimiko had been saying how she wanted to see you
again before you leave." *Drops her task for something more important*

Which war? Keikichi was going to war. "But we could hardly go and
see you without an invitation, and you didn't come and
Who won? didn't come. It was good of you to come today."

Who lost? She asked him to stay for lunch, but he was in a hurry.

"Well, do at least have a pomegranate. We grew it ourselves." She called up to Kimiko again.

He did not come to eat He greeted her with his eyes, as if it were more than he
could do to wait for her to come down. She stopped on the
stairs. *Urgency builds (could not wa*

25 Something warm seemed to come into his eyes, and the
pomegranate fell from his hand.

They looked at each other and smiled. *Tears?*

When she realized that she was smiling she flushed. Keikichi got up from the veranda. *Embarrassed*

"Take care of yourself, Kimiko." *Aware of the shortness of life*
"And you."

30 He had already turned away and was saying good-by to
her mother.

Kimiko looked on at the garden gate after he had left.

"He was in such a hurry," said her mother. "And it's such
a fine pomegranate."

He had left it on the veranda.

Apparently he had dropped it as that warm something came into his eyes and he was beginning to open it. He had not broken it completely in two. It lay with the seeds up.

Tears again (Keikichi = reluctant to leave)

Her mother took it to the kitchen and washed it, and handed it to Kimiko.

Kimiko frowned and pulled back, and then, flushing once more, took it in some confusion.

More embarrassment

Keikichi would seem to have taken a few seeds from the edge.

With her mother watching her, it would have been strange for Kimiko to refuse to eat. She bit nonchalantly into it. The sourness filled her mouth. She felt a kind of sad happiness, as if it were penetrating far down inside her.

Opposites (How do they relate to the story?)

Uninterested, her mother had stood up.

She went to a mirror and sat down. "Just look at my hair, will you. I said good-by to Keikichi with this wild mop of hair."

Hair = messy image

Kimiko could hear the comb. *Sound of hair tearing*

"When your father died," her mother said softly, "I was afraid to comb my hair. When I combed my hair I would forget what I was doing. When I came to myself it would be as if your father were waiting for me to finish."

Memory? Where's her father? (Dead? — At war also?)

Kimiko remembered her mother's habit of eating what her father had left on his plate. *Mother = not picky*

?? She felt something pull at her, a happiness that made her want to weep.

Her mother had probably given her the pomegranate because of a reluctance to throw it away. Only because of that. It had become a habit not to throw things away.

Like her mother, she fears

Alone with her private happiness Kimiko felt shy before her mother.

Happiness that comforts but does not remove one from an isolated lifestyle

She thought that it had been a better farewell than Keikichi could have been aware of, and that she could wait any length of time for him to come back.

She looked toward her mother. The sun was falling on the paper doors beyond which she sat at her mirror.

She was somehow afraid to bite into the pomegranate on her knee.

Already she is sharing with her mother

Responding to a text from the first word until the last will prepare you to move from the role of a reader to that of a writer. Your highlighted material

---

Active Reading Checklist

1. *Preview* your reading.
2. *Identify patterns* leading to coherence (development).
3. *Anticipate and predict* what will happen.
4. *Underline/highlight* the piece of literature.
5. *Reread and reassess* the work.
6. *Jot down notes* in the margins.
7. *Question* the content; comment about it (remain in an active dialogue).
8. *Discuss* your insights with others.
9. *Connect* what you read to your own life experience—past and present—to other pieces of writing and to the world at large.

---

and marginal notations will provide you with something to "spin off of" as you create a composition which *is different from yet similar to* the stimulus literature.

THE CREATIVE WINDOW

The importance of creativity must never be underestimated in the writing process, regardless if you are writing your doctoral thesis or an informal essay. Remaining creatively receptive to "possibilities" rather than responding the same way to topics and issues enables you to make fresh connections between them. When you mark texts, it is always important to balance your critical annotations and insights with creative intuition. In *Thresholds,* you will nurture your creative responses and strengthen active reading skills by working with haiku poetry.

A haiku poem will appear in the introduction to each of the thematic chapters in Part II of *Thresholds.* There you should mark the haiku in the manner the student annotated and highlighted Yasunari Kawabata's "The Pomegranate," looking for symbols, meaningful images, and thematic ideas. The following haiku by Yosa Buson provides an excellent example of this:

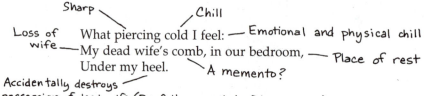

At first this process may be difficult, but as you continue the activity, you will find it easier to make intuitive responses to the haiku, exploring topics creatively, building trust in your own convictions. In addition, you will have constant practice marking a text—a skill you will be able to apply to all your readings in *Thresholds*. To make the best use of the *creative window,* you also may want to write a haiku poem of your own from time to time; the study and practice of writing haiku build sensitivity to word use, point of view, and rhetorical structures.

WRITING LOGS AND JOURNALS: RESPONDING TO IDEAS, TOPICS, AND ISSUES

Since most writers do not immediately assess material or generate essay topics after reading a work of literature, keeping a writing log or a journal as a resource for ideas is most advisable. Both writing logs and journals perform similar functions because they record information for later reference. Sometimes the two are distinguished according to the focus of your material. A writing log usually contains information pertaining to academic notes, responses to readings, and topics for writings. Responding in her writing log to multiple readings and discussions about "addictions," Andrea Sisneros wrote:

> Drugs are not always the obsession of an addict. I am addicted to something few people could ever imagine to be the focus of an unhealthy, mind-wasting, body-deteriorating needful desire. I am addicted to lipstick. A trivial item to most women, it is unnecessary in completing their lives. Personally, I think they're too scared to try it; they're too scared to get hooked.

These few notes were the seeds of an entire personal narrative—seeds that had been planted in a writing log and brought to fruition in an essay.

Journals differ from writing logs because their contents are more personal and often take the form of diaries, recording daily events, hopes, and dreams (literally and figuratively). In the following journal, Troy is more engaged in freethinking than specifically responding to anything:

> Hard to believe some people. Jason's such a nerd. Nerd! Now there's a word, slang. As I walked down the street on my way home today I heard people cursing at each other in slang. Funny, I could never understand all the terms they were using — not literally but I think their big voices told me lots. When I got home, I called some friends. Everybody is doing something tonight but me. So I'm writing about angry people who use slang. Why do people use slang? I guess it's more civilized — or should I say, civ?

Though the journal entry is a randomly arranged collection of thoughts, it records and communicates information, which is the purpose for keeping a journal. More importantly, Troy's "stream of consciousness" journal entry, which freely associates ideas without concern for overall coherence, presents a good example of creative exploration. For some reason, slang was on his mind; eight out of eleven sentences he wrote dealt with it. By recording such personal thoughts, Troy has an impressionistic record to refer to if and when he would like to use it as a starting point for a formal essay.

Writing logs and journal entries might also be *guided;* that is, you may have to respond to a specific topic or writing assignment. You might be asked, for instance, to jot down your impressions of a photograph, to evaluate a recent motion picture, or to respond to a specific question your instructor asks. Whatever type of writing you do in your writing log, journal, or hybrid of the two (perhaps there is no need to distinguish them at all), the important thing is constant practice in expressing yourself.

THE DIALECTICAL JOURNAL: TAKING AND MAKING NOTES

Dialectical inquiry uses reasoning and discussion in the form of a dialogue as a method of intellectual investigation. The dialectical process which attempts to resolve the conflicts between contrary or opposing ideas can be quite useful when applied to journal entries. Writing in a dialectical journal provides you with a chance to both take and make notes about assigned readings. Each page of a dialectical journal is divided in half, and on the left-hand side of the page, you *take notes;* that is, you copy down quotations or paraphrase the ideas of the author from the day's reading assignment. Then, in the right-hand column, you *make notes* by commenting on what you find particularly significant or moving and why. There are no wrong answers, just inquiries, observations, and perceptions—things you find interesting and meaningful. Finally, at the end of the dialectical entries, you might summarize the entire essay, story, or poem. Keeping a dialectical journal can help you to remember facts and details in context. Moreover, the original impressions you record might lead to topics or issues for writing assignments. Binh Ngo wrote the following example of a dialectical journal entry in response to Richard Rodriguez's "Aria" (chapter 15).

"It is not possible for a child — any child — ever to use his family's language in school."	When I first read this, I thought that the author was ashamed of his native language. For this reason, it did not give me a good impression of him. Later, when I realized that his own language gave him a sense of security, I appreciated him more.
"My mother and father were more annoyed than intimidated by those two or three neighbors who tried initially to make us unwelcome."	I'd feel annoyed too, if my neighbors made me feel unwanted. Who are they to judge us so harshly ???

"Our house stood apart"

Maybe he's just a bit paranoid about being a foreigner.

"They began to connect my behavior with the difficult progress my older sister and brother were making"

It seems the older ones have a worse time trying to learn English than the younger ones. My parents say it's because the older ones have "hard tongues" that are hard to teach to curl in new directions. Huh?

"Intimate sounds no longer rushed to the door to greet me."

I felt sad for the author because it seemed that he lost his family when his family language "no longer existed."

"Aria" Summary

Richard Rodriguez's "Aria" is a story about the childhood of the author himself. He called it "an essential myth of my childhood—inevitable pain," and as we read through his touching autobiography, we see his statement to be true. He was fighting between a comforting language and a language only used *in public. Rodriguez also explained that with his new public identity, he felt he was an American citizen and free to "seek the rights and opportunities for full public individuality."*

An additional example of active reading and responding strategies to essays, stories, and poems in the form of a writing log / journal entry, a dialectical journal entry, or a marked text will appear following the sample piece of literature for each genre. "The Brown Wasps" by Loren Eiseley, an essay, will appear annotated (marked); "Northern Lights" by Joy Harjo, a short story, will be followed with a writing log / journal entry; and "The Woods" by Louise Erdrich, a poem, will offer a dialectical journal entry. Regardless of the genre you are reading, marking the text and writing journal entries will be valuable and useful in establishing a connection between reading and writing, leading to your critical written response in the form of an essay.

THRESHOLDS AND THEMES

The literary selections in this book are loosely arranged according to topics and experiences we all share: the ongoing quest for individual, cultural, and social identity; the aspiration towards high ideals and the disappointment in settling for less; the dynamics of living in a multinational society in an ever-changing world; and the interaction with art forms, observance of rituals, and intensity of initiations. We constantly cross new thresholds or re-explore old ones: thresholds of dreams, thresholds of pain, thresholds of adventure, thresholds of creativity, thresholds of love, thresholds of disillusionment. We frequently become aware that many of the topics and issues we discuss might be identified or classified under a broad theme. We have all had experiences of "loss and gain," the general theme of a mini "thematic unit" in this chapter. In Loren Eiseley's essay, "The Brown Wasps," for instance, memory preserves the lost things in life. Whether it is the pigeon's loss of a food source in the abandoned rail station, the mouse's loss of a home, or Eiseley's loss of a tree and the significance he associated with planting it, Eiseley says, "We cling to a time and place because without them man is lost, not only man but life."

Joy Harjo's story, "Northern Lights," implies the significance of loss or losses in Whirling Soldier's life on many levels: loss of control, loss of self-esteem, loss of sense of self. Hope also exists for a future not defined by strife or dysfunction. Whirling Soldier's loss or losses can be viewed as positive because he is "letting go" of the "violence that chased him from fight to fight," opening up and "talking to a spirit who had never been a stranger but a relative he had never met."

The transformation of the narrator in Louise Erdrich's poem, "The Woods," also illustrates a theme of "loss and gain." Unlike the strong sense of loss in "The Brown Wasps," or the implied promise of renewal in "Northern Lights" (there's a ray of hope that Whirling Soldier will be able to change the violent lifestyle he has led), "The Woods" clearly celebrates the *gains* achieved through change: a transformation of character. The speaker's losses in the poem—the lifestyle and persona she had formerly assumed with her lover—are thoroughly outweighed by her gains as a fully independent woman.

Obviously, a single theme can be found in quite varied pieces of writing, from *loss* in the most literal sense—"the harm or privation resulting from loss or separation," as illustrated in Eiseley's essay—to considering "loss or separation" from someone or something as a positive action, as suggested in both Harjo's short story and Erdrich's poem. Similarly, your own responses to topics, issues, and themes in the following literary works will be varied, depending on how you view a person, situation, or thing, and your purpose for writing about it in the first place.

Essays

Strictly speaking, the essay is a nonfiction work dealing with a limited topic. Sometimes you will critique someone's speech, and other times you will write an argumentative paper to validate a position on an issue. From the informal writing of narrative remembrances of childhood to formal writing in term papers, you will constantly be setting forth opinions, placing insights and perceptions into written language. Whether an essay is presented informally or formally, however, will depend entirely on your audience, your purpose, and your occasion for writing.

Audience Knowing your audience facilitates clear communication. Your language will be appropriately familiar, and thereby informal, when addressing friends and relatives—people you know well. Audience awareness is important whether you are writing an entire essay or just dedicating a gift to another. An inscription on a pocket watch reading "To John, love Jean," would be an informal dedication. The word "love" suggests some degree of familiarity between the two people. If the recipient were a mere acquaintance—an employee, perhaps—the inscription might formally read "To John, from Jean." The single word "from" keeps the two individuals at a respectable distance, implying no intimacy. What seems cold and unfeeling to a familiar audience might be perceived as quite suitable to another. Any way you look at it, word selection can make the difference between connecting or alienating your intended audience.

Purpose   The reason you are writing defines your purpose and whether an informal or a formal approach is in order. Are you trying to sell something? If so, formality rather than familiarity might serve your purpose best. A letter of apology, on the other hand, would be more effective written in an informal, sensitive manner. The major question to ask yourself is *How can a formal or informal format advance my purpose?*

Occasion   There are many different occasions for writing. On birthdays, anniversaries, and holidays, your writings probably would be festive and informal, in the spirit of celebration. In contrast, your prose would be more formal for a written examination, an article for a professional journal, or an inauguration speech. Perceiving the appropriateness of formality or informality to a given situation is crucial when writing on different occasions, and common sense can be a valuable guide. It would be inappropriate, for instance, to write a funeral eulogy filled with sarcasm and backhanded compliments. A funeral or memorial service is not an occasion to disparage and degrade the dead but an occasion to sincerely and respectfully reminisce about them. Though sometimes audience, purpose, or occasion taken in isolation can indicate the nature of a composition, it is a good practice to consider and address all three.

An extremely wide array of nonfiction prose has come to be recognized and referred to as the essay. Although references to nonfiction and the essay may be used interchangeably in this text, it would be a mistake to think that all essays are the same. A documented research paper and a personal essay, for instance, are about as much alike as an opera and an MTV video. However, the term *essay* provides a common umbrella for the different kinds of nonfiction (the personal essay, critical analysis, research papers) just as the word *poetry* classifies both an epic poem and a sonnet as *verse*.

Where do you think Loren Eiseley's "The Brown Wasps" would fit under the essay umbrella? As you read through the essay, notice how he presents the theme of "loss." Then reflect on what Eiseley says in "The Brown Wasps" and attempt to make connections between his material and your own life experiences. Also, note how the marked text exemplifies the ongoing dialogue between Eiseley, the author, and a reader.

--------------------------------- ❋ ---------------------------------

The Brown Wasps

Loren Eiseley

1   There is a corner in the waiting room of one of the great Eastern stations where women never sit. It is always in the

shadow and overhung by rows of lockers. It is, however, always frequented not so much by genuine travelers as by the dying. It is here that a certain element of the abandoned poor seeks a refuge out of the weather, clinging for a few hours longer to the city that has fathered them. In a precisely similar manner I have seen, on a sunny day in midwinter, a few old brown wasps creep slowly over an abandoned wasp nest in a thicket. Numbed and forgetful and frost-blackened, the hum of the spring hive still resounded faintly in their sodden tissues. Then the temperature would fall and they would drop away into the white oblivion of the snow. Here in the station it is in no way different save the city is busy in its snows. But the old ones cling to their seats as though these were symbolic and could not be given up. Now and then they sleep, their gray old heads resting with painful awkwardness on the backs of the benches.

Why the distinction between travelers?

A symbol of life?

Oblivion = state of being forgotten

Life's meaning = held in the seats "old ones" cling to?

2 Also they are not at rest. For an hour they may sleep in the gasping exhaustion of the ill-nourished and aged who have to walk in the night. Then a policeman comes by on his round and nudges them upright.

3 "You can't sleep here," he growls.

4 A strange ritual then begins. An old man is difficult to waken. After a muttered conversation the policeman presses a coin into his hand and passes fiercely along the benches prodding and gesturing toward the door. In his wake, like birds rising and settling behind the passage of a farmer through a cornfield, the men totter up, move a few paces and subside once more upon the benches.

Ritual = a series of actions & procedures followed in a ceremonious fashion

Colloquial expression (To give the person money)

5 One man, after a slight, apologetic lurch, does not move at all. Tubercularly thin, he sleeps on steadily. The policeman does not look back. To him, too, this has become a ritual. He will not have to notice it again officially for another hour.

6 Once in a while one of the sleepers will not awaken. Like the brown wasps, he will have had his wish to die in the great droning center of the hive rather than in some lonely room. It is not so bad here with the shuffle of footsteps and the knowledge that there are others who share the bad luck of the world. There are also the whistles and the sounds of everyone, everyone in the world, starting on journeys. Amidst so many journeys somebody is bound to come out all right. Somebody.

Sleeper = like wasps

Journeys (Is someone bound to get somewhere?)

7   Maybe it was on a like thought that the brown wasps fell away from the old paper nest in the thicket. You hold till the last, even if it is only to a public seat in a railroad station. You want your place in the hive more than you want a room or a place where the aged can be eased gently out of the way. It is the place that matters, the place at the heart of things. It is life that you want, that bruises your gray old head with the hard chairs; a man has a right to his place.

Rather die with a "place in the hive" than be "eased out" of life

8   But sometimes the place is lost in the years behind us. Or sometimes it is a thing of air, a kind of vaporous distortion above a heap of rubble. We cling to a time and place because without them man is lost, not only man but life. This is why the voices, real or unreal, which speak from the floating trumpets at spiritualist seances are so unnerving. They are voices out of nowhere whose only reality lies in their ability to stir the memory of a living person with some fragment of the past. Before the medium's cabinet both the dead and the living revolve endlessly about an episode, a place, an event that has already been engulfed by time.

We cling to time & space

Voices stir memories & create realities

Eternal struggle

9   This feeling runs deep in life; it brings stray cats running over endless miles, and birds homing from the ends of the earth. It is as though all living creatures, and particularly the more intelligent, can survive only by fixing or transforming a bit of time into space or by securing a bit of space with its objects immortalized and made permanent in time. For example, I once saw, on a flower pot in my own living room, the efforts of a field mouse to build a remembered field. I have lived to see this episode repeated in a thousand guises, and since I have spent a large portion of my life in the shade of a nonexistent tree, I think I am entitled to speak for the field mouse.

Need to immortalize objects (something to return to?)

Mouse & flower pot = quest for the familiar

10   One day as I cut across the field, which at that time extended on one side of our suburban shopping center, I found a giant slug feeding from a runnel of pink ice cream in an abandoned Dixie cup. I could see his eyes telescope and protrude in a kind of dim, uncertain ecstasy as his dark body bunched and elongated in the curve of the cup. Then, as I stood there at the edge of the concrete, contemplating the

slug, I began to realize it was like standing on a shore where a different type of life creeps up and fumbles tentatively among the rocks and sea wrack. It knows its place and will only creep so far until something changes. Little by little as I stood there, I began to see more of this shore that surrounds the place of man. I looked with sudden care and attention at things I had been running over thoughtlessly for years. I even waded out a short way into the grass and the wild-rose thickets to see more. A huge black-belted bee went droning by and there were some indistinct scurryings in the underbrush.

Contemplates slug

Suddenly more thoughtful and reflective

11   Then I came to a sign which informed me that this field was to be the site of a new Wanamaker suburban store. Thousands of obscure lives were about to perish, the spores of puffballs would go smoking off to new fields, and the bodies of little white-footed mice would be crunched under the inexorable wheels of the bulldozers. Life disappears or modifies its appearances so fast that everything takes on an aspect of illusion—a momentary fizzing and boiling with smoke rings, like pouring dissident chemicals into a retort. Here man was advancing, but in a few years his plaster and bricks would be disappearing once more into the insatiable maw of the clover. Being of an archaeological cast of mind, I thought of this fact with an obscure sense of satisfaction and waded back through the rose thickets to the concrete parking lot. As I did so, a mouse scurried ahead of me, frightened of my steps if not of that ominous Wanamaker sign. I saw him vanish in the general direction of my apartment house, his little body quivering with fear in the great open sun on the blazing concrete. Blinded and confused, he was running straight away from his field. In another week scores would follow him.

Even discoveries are just transitory

?? Eiseley seems glad thinking those who destroy will also be destroyed

What is an "archaeological cast of mind"?

12   I forgot the episode then and went home to the quiet of my living room. It was not until a week later, letting myself into the apartment, that I realized I had a visitor. I am fond of plants and had several ferns standing on the floor in pots to avoid the noon glare by the south window.

13   As I snapped on the light and glanced carelessly around the room, I saw a little heap of earth on the carpet and a scrabble of pebbles that had been kicked merrily over the edge of one of the flower pots. To my astonishment I discovered a full-fledged burrow delving downward among

Sound

the fern roots. I waited silently. The creature who had made the burrow did not appear. I remembered the wild field then, and the flight of the mice. No house mouse, no *Mus domesticus*, had kicked up this little heap of earth or sought refuge under a fern root in a flower pot. I thought of the desperate little creature I had seen fleeing from the wild-rose thicket. Through intricacies of pipes and attics, he, or one of his fellows, had climbed to this high green solitary room. I could visualize what had occurred. He had an image in his head, a world of seed pods and quiet, of green sheltering leaves in the dim light among the weed stems. It was the only world he knew and it was gone.

(marginal notes: Memory (much of this essay = remembered events); Lost = life the mouse knew = gone)

14   Somehow in his flight he had found his way to this room with drawn shades where no one would come till nightfall. And here he had smelled green leaves and run quickly up the flower pot to dabble his paws in common earth. He had even struggled half the afternoon to carry his burrow deeper and had failed. I examined the hole, but no whiskered twitching face appeared. He was gone. I gathered up the earth and refilled the burrow. I did not expect to find traces of him again.

(marginal note: Mouse's efforts = tireless)

15   Yet for three nights thereafter I came home to the darkened room and my ferns to find the dirt kicked gaily about the rug and the burrow reopened, though I was never able to catch the field mouse within it. I dropped a little food about the mouth of the burrow, but it was never touched. I looked under beds or sat reading with one ear cocked for rustlings in the ferns. It was all in vain; I never saw him. Probably he ended in a trap in some other tenant's room.

(marginal note: Why does he watch the mouse at work? (What fascinates him?))

16   But before he disappeared, I had come to look hopefully for his evening burrow. About my ferns there had begun to linger the insubstantial vapor of an autumn field, the distilled essence, as it were, of a mouse brain in exile from its home. It was a small dream, like our dreams, carried a long and weary journey along pipes and through spider webs, past holes over which loomed the shadows of waiting cats, and finally, desperately, into this room where he had played in the shuttered daylight for an hour among the green ferns on the floor. Every day these invisible dreams pass us on the street, or rise from beneath our feet, or look out upon us from beneath a bush.

(marginal note: Smell (what does an autumn field smell like?))

17   Some years ago the old elevated railway in Philadelphia

was torn down and replaced by a subway system. This ~~an~~ El = an ~~cient El~~ with its barnlike stations containing nut-vending ~~elevated~~ machines and scattered food scraps had, for generations, ~~railway~~ been the favorite feeding ground of flocks of pigeons, generally one flock to a station along the route of the El. Hundreds of pigeons were dependent upon the system. They flapped in and out of its stanchions and steel work or gathered in watchful little audiences about the feet of anyone who rattled the peanut-vending machines. They even watched people who jingled change in their hands, and prospected for food under the feet of the crowds who gathered between trains. Probably very few among the waiting people who tossed a crumb to an eager pigeon realized that this El was like a food-bearing river, and that the life which haunted its banks was dependent upon the running of the trains with their human freight.

[margin notes:] Pigeons associate the sound of "change" with vending machines and food

El = lifeforce; food from river ceased "to flow"

18
19
    I saw the river stop.

The time came when the underground tubes were ready; the traffic was transferred to a realm unreachable by pigeons. It was like a great river subsiding suddenly into desert sands. For a day, for two days, pigeons continued to circle over the El or stand close to the red vending machines. They were patient birds, and surely this great river which had flowed through the lives of unnumbered generations was merely suffering from some momentary drought.

[margin notes:] Anticipation

River = like a desert (sterile and barren)

20
    They listened for the familiar vibrations that had always heralded an approaching train; they flapped hopefully about the head of an occasional workman walking along the steel runways. They passed from one empty station to another, all the while growing hungrier. Finally, they flew away.

21
    I thought I had seen the last of them about the El, but there was a revival and it provided a curious instance of the memory of living things for a way of life or a locality that has long been cherished. Some weeks after the El was abandoned, workmen began to tear it down. I went to work every morning by one particular station, and the time came when the demolition crews reached this spot. Acetylene torches showered passers-by with sparks, pneumatic drills hammered at the base of the structure, and a blind man who, like the pigeons, had clung with his cup to a stairway leading to the change booth, was forced to give up his place.

[margin notes:] Memory of all living things

Where does the blind man go when he's given up his seat?

22 It was then, strangely, momentarily, one morning that I
witnessed the return of a little band of the familiar pigeons.
I even recognized one or two members of the flock that had
lived around this particular station before they were dis-
persed into the streets. They flew bravely in and out among
the sparks and the hammers and the shouting workmen.
They had returned—and they had returned because the
hubbub of the wreckers had convinced them that the river
was about to flow once more. For several hours they flapped
in and out through the empty windows, nodding their heads
and watching the fall of girders with attentive little eyes. By
the following morning the station was reduced to some
burned-off stanchions in the street. My bird friends had
gone. It was plain, however, that they retained a memory
for an insubstantial structure now compounded of air and
time. Even the blind man clung to it. Someone had provided
him with a chair, and he sat at the same corner staring sight-
lessly at an invisible stairway where, so far as he was concerned, the crowds were still ascending to the trains.

Power of observation

Sounds convince pigeons the river will flow once again

Memory of El= intact in pigeons

23 *Tree* I have said my life has been passed in the shade of a
nonexistent tree, so that such sights do not offend me. Pre-
maturely I am one of the brown wasps and I often sit with
them in the great droning hive of the station, dreaming
sometimes of a certain tree. It was planted sixty years ago
by a boy with a bucket and a toy spade in a little Nebraska
town. That boy was myself. It was a cottonwood sapling and
the boy remembered it because of some words spoken by
his father and because everyone died or moved away who
was supposed to wait and grow old under its shade. The
boy was passed from hand to hand, but the tree for some
intangible reason had taken root in his mind. It was under
its branches that he sheltered; it was from this tree that his
memories, which are my memories, led away into the world.

Eiseley = one of the brown wasps clinging to a dream

Tree not rooted in reality — — just in his mind

24 After sixty years the mood of the brown wasps grows
heavier upon one. During a long inward struggle I thought
it would do me good to go and look upon that actual tree.
I found a rational excuse in which to clothe this madness. I
purchased a ticket and at the end of two thousand miles I
walked another mile to an address that was still the same.
The house had not been altered.

Eiseley's age?

25 I came close to the white picket fence and reluctantly,
with great effort, looked down the long vista of the yard.

There was nothing there to see. For sixty years that cotton- *Sixty years of*
wood had been growing in my mind. Season by season its *growth in*
seeds had been floating farther on the hot prairie winds. We *his mind*
Special had planted it lovingly there, my father and I, because he
moment had a great hunger for soil and live things growing, and
in time because none of these things had long been ours to protect.
!! We had planted the little sapling and watered it faithfully,
and I remembered that I had run out with my small bucket
to drench its roots the day we moved away. And all the
years since, it had been growing in my mind, a huge tree
that somehow stood for my father and the love I bore him.
I took a grasp on the picket fence and forced myself to look
again.

26   A boy with the hard bird eye of youth pedaled a tricycle *Innocent*
slowly up beside me. "What 'cha lookin' at?" he asked cu- *Curiosity*
riously.

27   "A tree," I said.

28   "What for?" he said.

29   "It isn't there," I said, to myself mostly, and began to
walk away at a pace just slow enough not to seem to be
running.

30   "What isn't there?" the boy asked. I didn't answer. It was
obvious I was attached by a thread to a thing that had never
been there, or certainly not for long. Something that had to
be held in the air, or sustained in the mind, because it was *Like field and*
part of my orientation to the universe and I could not sur- *El station, the*
vive without it. There was more than an animal's attachment *Symbolic tree*
to a place. There was something else, the attachment of the *no longer existed*
spirit to a grouping of events in time; it was part of our *in real time*
morality.

31   So I had come home at last, driven by a memory in the *Home in*
brain as surely as the field mouse who had delved long ago *memory does*
into my flower pot or the pigeons flying forever amidst the *not match home*
rattle of nut-vending machines. These, the burrow under the *in reality*
greenery in my living room and the red-bellied bowls of
peanuts now hovering in midair in the minds of pigeons,
were all part of an elusive world that existed nowhere and
yet everywhere. I looked once at the real world about me
while the persistent boy pedaled at my heels.

32   It was without meaning, though my feet took a remembered path. In sixty years the house and street had rotted
out of my mind. But the tree, the tree that no longer was,
that had perished in its first season, bloomed on in my in-

dividual mind, unblemished as my father's words. "We'll [Rooted tree = like a rooted family] plant a tree here, son, and we're not going to move any more. And when you're an old, old man you can sit under it and think how we planted it here, you and me, together."

[33 Who might] I began to outpace the boy on the tricycle.

[34 the boy represent? (The world?)] "Do you live here, Mister?" he shouted after me suspiciously. I took a firm grasp on airy nothing—to be precise, on the bole of a great tree. "I do," I said. I spoke for myself, [Lives there in spirit] one field mouse, and several pigeons. We were all out of touch but somehow permanent. It was the world that had changed. → [* People & animals = same / * World around us changes]

As you read through the essays in *Thresholds*, note how an author's intentions in a composition determine everything from tone and diction to style and organization. The following checklist offers a few additional *critical reading strategies* particularly relevant to the essay. After you consider Eiseley's purpose for writing "The Brown Wasps," for example, reflect on how his choice of words and examples complemented and advanced his thesis. Sometimes you want to think about your thinking (metacognition). Thinking about observations of a thesis or plot, bringing what you already know to a text, is just one example of metacognition—critical thinking.

Reading Essays Critically: A Checklist

- Identify the essay's main idea or thesis.
- Pay attention to diction (word choice). How does it help establish the tone of the essay?
- Question how well examples illustrate or argue the essay. Are the examples and arguments representative, reliable sources of information?
- Make note of devices unifying the essay.
- Assess the reasons for and effectiveness of paragraphs and sentences of varying length.

Fiction

When studying and responding to ideas in literature orally or in writing, we typically analyze such things as plot, characterization, setting, and point of view. Even when the primary thrust of a course is to develop good composition skills, considering conventions of a genre can be quite fruitful. You might study the *plot* of a story to build an understanding of a general theme, one you could examine in an analytical or exploratory essay. The way an author develops personalities through *characterization* in a story may offer an insight into individual behavior and human nature in general. Understanding the possible significance of *setting* in fiction might build your sensitivity to the background of a topic or issue you write about. Questions regarding *when* and *where* the story takes place, as well as *why* or *how* the location of the story is significant to the plot are frequently just the starting points of such essays.

Point of view is also interesting when assessing a story and may refer to an author's attitude towards his or her subject. More often, however, point of view refers to the perspective from which an essay or story is written. In formal writing, point of view is expressed in first or third person. As Ellen Goodman illustrates in "A Working Community," the *first-person* narrator participates in the action and creates an intimate relationship with readers using the familiar pronoun *I:*

> I have a friend who is a member of the medical community. It does not say that, of course, on the stationery that bears her home address. This membership comes from her hospital work.

Third-person narrators such as Gabriel García Marquez in "A Very Old Man with Enormous Wings" distance themselves from the work, often presenting information from a limited point of view, using the pronouns "he," "she," or "it" to talk about others and relate events:

> Sea and sky were a single ash-gray thing and the sands of the beach, which on March nights glimmered like powdered light, had become a stew of mud and rotten shellfish. The light was so weak at noon that when Pelayo was coming back to the house after throwing away the crabs, it was hard for him to see what it was that was moving and groaning in the rear of the courtyard. He had to go very close to see that it was an old man, a very old man, lying face down in the mud, who, in spite of his tremendous efforts, couldn't get up, impeded by his enormous wings.

The following short story by Joy Harjo, "Northern Lights," is told from a predominantly third-person point of view, although Harjo occasionally provides a first-person insight (e.g., "I noticed Whirling Soldier beneath the garish lights of the auditorium"). Note how *point of view* assists her narrative development.

Northern Lights

Joy Harjo

Northern lights were sighted above Lake Superior as we danced concentric circles around the drums at Ashland, each step bringing us through the freezing. Bells, the occasional sacred flute like wind beneath an eagle, and the drum marking more than time, rather outlining ancestors, a pipeline into the earth to the mother of volcanoes. I noticed Whirling Soldier beneath the garish lights of the auditorium. He trusted nothing, still broke swords with angry gods. His war scars were evident in the way his eyes flinched and burned with gunpowder, from the recurring horror of his decapitated ditch-mate draped on the trees, spilled across him. We talked wild rice, modern fiction, and of his daughter who was hitting eighteen, sober after drinking away adolescence, and we were proud to watch her dance by us, her eyes on fire with the intimate knowledge of survival from the abyss. She carried her niece, his grandmother laughing, to see so many grandmothers, so many relatives.

He had returned from the war, from Wichita with a spirit feather pressed against his heart. The killing wind chaffed his lips. There were no prayers anymore. All he knew was he was leaving Nam, and approaching the destruction of his people by laws.

The northern lights were reminiscent of mercy gathering on the horizon. Sometimes he thought he saw them in Nam, or was it fire from the unseen enemy, which could have come from the Ohio boy in the foxhole next to him, or the gook rattling the bush who appeared as his cousin Ralph, an apparition making an offering of the newest crop of rice.

He was killing himself, he thought, each shot rigged his spine to hell. There was no way to get out. He was in it, and knew the warrior code had said nothing about the wailing of the children in the dark. The sacrifice reminded him of his mother stuffing wood into the stove, cooking potatoes in the gray before dawn, before she went to clean houses. They never had enough to eat. He always went to find his father, instead of going to school with his sisters, his stomach warm with potatoes and coffee, sometimes with fresh deer meat, when they were lucky.

5   Suddenly he was in Vietnam, a man like his father had been when he had found him floating on ice in the lake. His father had been fishing for redemption when his heart gave out. The empty bottle skudded away, slipped into the river, an epitaph read by fish drinking in the lake.

Under fire, the image of his father on ice often took hold through the scope, and his teeth would chatter in the hot, damp jungle as if he were freezing, but he couldn't put his rifle down. And nothing killed the image, kept it from growing on its own. Soon it was spring and the lake thawed and his father sunk to the bottom. Deer stopped to drink. Clouds surfaced in the blue. He made it through the summer, was shot clean through, missed the shinbone while flying on heroin making volcanoes of the bush. By then he couldn't see through to the surface of the water. He was lucky to be able to walk, climb up the muddy bank, make it to Wichita, after the blur of San Francisco, Oklahoma City, on his way home.

In Yuma, in the hangover of a dream of his mother beading a blanket in his honor he tore the medals from his pack and pawned them for a quart. He snuffed his confusion between honor and honor with wine, became an acrobat of pain in the Indian bars of Kansas.

One of those mornings no different from any other except for the first taste of winter, reminded him of the beginning of the world and he imagined his mother wrapping a deer meat sandwich in a plastic bread wrapper. When he opened the door his breath took the form of question marks, imitated clouds over water. His father sat up on the sagging bed, coughed, asked him where he was going. But he didn't hear the question until years later, as he staggered up some state road north of Wichita, with a pint of Seagram's tucked in his pants, the staccato of machine guns still stuttering in his memory.

What must have been the Head Crow laughed from a stiff telephone wire, swung back and forth beneath the sun, blinking his eyes at the sleeping pitiful world. Whirling Soldier muttered, his voice broke off in waves. He wished he had a cigarette. The eye of a dried sunflower reminded him his baby would be two, but she, too, had probably disappeared in the azimuth of forgetfulness.

10   He unscrewed the cap of his final fix. His last fight did not involve the clockwork of artillery, but a punch that shattered the mouth of a man who looked like his brother. He staggered away from the man who whimpered like a child into the shiny black blood pool, and threw up in the weeds breaking the sidewalk. Suddenly the high winds of violence that chased him from fight to fight found him north of Wichita, at dawn, talking to a spirit who had never been a stranger but a relative he had never met.

I can't tell you what took place beneath the blessing sun, for the story doesn't belong to me, but to Whirling Soldier who gifted me with it in the circle of hope. After the dance, we all ran out onto the ice to see the northern lights. They were shimmering relatives returned from the war, dancing in the skies all around us. It was an unusual moment of grace for fools.

Sample Writing Log/Journal Entry for Joy Harjo's "Northern Lights"

Northern lights. Aren't they the same thing as the Aurora Borealis? I'm not sure of the relationship between northern lights and the theme of the story. Webster's dictionary says something to the effect that the northern lights are a luminous phenomena- streamers of light that arch across the sky— particularly in the Arctic circle. Might not the circle of hope mentioned in the story correspond to the arches of light? The story made me think. Whirling Soldier is sure messed up, but then I can under- stand how he became what my psychology instructor would refer to as a dysfunctional person. He's a real stressed guy. The odd thing is he is partly to blame for his mental and physical pain. What light does he see at the end of the story? Perhaps none. On the other hand, I can't help but to think that there is a connection between the northern lights, "shimmering relatives returned from the war," dancing in the sky and Whirling Soldier who has also returned from war and a life of strife and turmoil.

Description often plays a crucial role in establishing time and place. The *dance* in "Northern Lights" was significant because it gave the speaker of the story hope, but for what? Harjo's detailed account of who attended the dance, particularly Whirling Soldier who "unscrewed the cap" of a bottle of liquor for his "final fix" and had his "last fight," clarifies the conflict in her story and shows the reader why she had reason for hope and renewal— despite the "destruction" of her people "by laws."

Studying fiction in a composition class offers more than a source for writ- ing assignments when you creatively and critically analyze the nature and use of language in context. That is, reading and enjoying fictional stories may not only activate your imagination but also stimulate your analytical skills as you make creative associations, envision an author's *settings*, and picture the evolution of characters through dialogue and descriptive

---

Reading Fiction Critically: A Checklist

- Note how characters evolve. In what way do words provide initial exposition, build on conflicts, reach a climax, and conclude with some sort of resolution?
- From whose point of view is a story told? Does this *point of view* enhance or decrease the credibility of the tale?
- Look for motives behind characters' actions.
- Consider the role ethics, logic, and emotions play in the story.
- Reflect on the dynamics of the plot with respect to larger social, political, economic, ethnic, and gender concerns in the world today.

---

narrative. The checklist above contains items you may wish to consider while reading the fiction selections in *Thresholds*.

Poetry

Since Aristotle's *Poetics*, written 2,300 years ago, there have been numerous attempts to define poetry. Though definitions have varied from the "imaginative expression of strong feeling" (William Wordsworth) to the "rhythmic, inevitably narrative, movement from an overclothed blindness to a naked vision" (Dylan Thomas), most definitions agree on some common properties of poetry: the rhythmic expression of emotions, the imaginative shaping of ideas, and the quest for beauty and truth. The rhythmic nature of poetry may well have something to do with its roots in dance and song, perhaps recording great events in primitive societies in the oral tradition. The subject matter of modern poetry still emphasizes topics and themes of intense personal and social concern: love, protest, disillusionment, nature, spirituality, and so on. Yes, modern poetry continues the ancient tradition of recording of great events in verse.

Poetry often stimulates deep feelings of pity, sorrow, or tenderness in a reader. These emotional properties, along with figurative speech, frequently convey experiences difficult to express literally. Here, also, imagery and form distinguish poetry from prose. Actually, poetry is often like essay in miniature, for in its compact use of language and effective employment of images to express thoughts and ideas, a poem can accomplish in a few stanzas (groups of lines in a poem) what would take five pages in a composition. Poems will offer an excellent resource for studying word use in its most compressed form (e.g., effective diction, use of tone, concrete visual or sensory images).

The quest for beauty and truth in poetry has much to do with the age-old notion that the primary purpose of poetry is to delight and create pleasure. Even though all poets do not agree on what precisely constitutes "beauty" or what is the "truth," there is more agreement than one might expect. Granted, "beauty" is a relative quality which can hardly be enumerated or measured. However, if we consider that an honest, intense exchange of ideas is a primary objective of poetry—whether the subject matter is treated seriously, humorously, angrily, or sarcastically—then successfully conveying material will indeed be beautiful and most definitely reflect truth.

A great deal can be learned and transferred to the expository or argumentative essay by observing how words are employed in poetry. As you read through the following poem, "The Woods" by Louise Erdrich, (1) jot down some images you find powerful or effective, and (2) compare the two types of language (figurative and literal) present in the poem.

The Woods

Louise Erdrich

At one time your touches were clothing enough.
Within these trees now I am different.
Now I wear the woods.

I lower a headdress of bent sticks and secure it.
5   I strap to myself a breastplate of clawed, roped bark.
I fit the broad leaves of sugar maples
to my hands, like mittens of blood.

Now when I say *come,*
and you enter the woods,
10   hunting some creature like the woman I was,
I surround you.

Light bleeds from the clearing. Roots rise.
Fluted molds burn blue in the falling light,
and you also know
15   the loneliness that you taught me with your body.

When you lay down in the grave of a slashed tree,
I cover you, as I always did;
this time you do not leave.

Sample Dialectical Journal Entry for Louise Erdrich's "The Woods"

NOTETAKING	NOTEMAKING
"At one time your touches were clothing enough."	Enough what? "Enough" to provide the speaker with satisfaction and warmth?
"... now I am different. / Now I wear the woods."	A change or transformation in character seems to have taken place. It seems that the woods have played a large role in bringing about change, for it is within the trees of the woods that the speaker becomes "different."
"I lower a headdress of bent sticks..."	The speaker is obviously adorning herself (himself?) with objects of nature — the woods.
"I strap to myself a breastplate of clawed, roped bark."	Interesting image of the wild. Could the "clawed bark" have received its distinctive markings from a bear?
"I fit the broad leaves of sugar maples / to my hands, like mittens of blood."	Sugar maple leaves cover her hands completely—fine. But why are they like mittens of blood? If blood is an essential part of life, might we conclude that "mittens of blood" are analogous to mittens of life?
"Now when I say come,"	Why is the word "come" italicized? Perhaps this refers to "invitations" or "entreaties" the speaker formerly made.

"hunting some creature like the woman I was,"

This line suggests that she was once treated like a "creature," but she is no longer that "creature" — a woman without a sense of self. This was the first indication of the speaker's sex in the poem.

"I surround you."

Is she implying she is no longer someone who can be controlled or put in a narrowly defined place or role?

"Light bleeds from the clearing. Roots rise."

Bleeding light — nice image, very visual. Since roots "burrow" rather than "rise" in order for something to grow, could the speaker be suggesting that ties to her former relationship have been released — that she has let loose one lifestyle from her past in favor of another in the present? On the other hand, a rising root could be a phallic symbol ...

"and you also know / the loneliness that you taught me with your body."

It seems we are exchanging "realities" and their ramifications here. The speaker found "loneliness" (and perhaps lack of personal fulfillment) in her mate. In her new reality as part of the woods, he, now the stranger, will learn the meaning of "loneliness."

"When you lay down in the grave of a slashed tree"

Has her former lover/ mate literally or figuratively died? (He seems to lie "down in the grave.")

"I cover you, as I always did; / this time you did not leave."

What has happened? The speaker indicates that she is still somewhat of a "nurturer" or "caretaker" with the line: "I cover you as I always did." This much of her character has not changed. Has her companion left her before? Has he died?

"The Woods" Summary

"The Woods" begins with the speaker reflecting on the past, noting that there was a time when the physical interaction, the "touches" of another, were enough for her, but she goes on to say that now she has changed. As the speaker moves on to the second stanza, the sort of change which has occurred becomes obvious: She has returned to the "woman who runs with wolves," that is, she now personifies the "wild woman archetype." Phrases like "headdress of bent sticks," a "breastplate of clawed, roped bark," and sugar maple "mittens of blood" all attest to such an interpretation. Now when she beckons her lover/mate to "come," she does so as a changed person. In her transformed self, the speaker — who finally identifies gender with the line "hunting some creature like the woman I was." She — like the woods — will then surround the male who is searching for her discarded persona (the person she was). The reference to the "roots" that "rise" no doubt indicate her freedom from the past. That is, she is no longer "rooted" to people, places, and things like she once was. The final three lines present somewhat of a puzzle. On the one hand, it seems as though her mate could have literally died and she, being the "nurturer" and "caretaker" she is, covers him one last time. Apparently he will remain in her domain. On the other hand, these lines could be entirely symbolic, and the "grave" could be part of the "realities" wherein the speaker was but a "creature," someone who satisfied him sexually. In the woods, home of the speaker and the "wild woman's abode," his realities are dead and may never again return to life.

Reading Poetry Critically: A Checklist

- Look for images and symbols.
- Observe how words are presented. In groups? In individual lines? And how do stanzas (groups of lines separated by space) organize material?
- Search for word groups establishing rhythmic patterns. How does rhythm affect the poem?
- Determine the purpose for any rhyme schemes present in the poem.
- Notice when and where people, places, and things are referred to figuratively rather than literally. Where do word sounds echo the subject under discussion?

The subject matter of the poems offered in *Thresholds* may vary from chapter to chapter, but one thing will remain constant: word study. From literal and figurative language to the denotative and connotative meaning of words (all discussed in detail in chapter 4), we will remain focused on how and why diction can aid or undermine the objective of our compositions. The checklist on page 33 for *reading poetry critically* offers some additional reading strategies you might apply to the verse (poetry) in *Thresholds*.

STRATEGIES: Reading and Responding

1. *Scan* your readings; highlight main titles and headings.
2. *Question* the reliability, truth, or strength of the facts you have at hand.
3. *Identify* patterns that lead to coherence (e.g., words that indicate progression).
4. *Analyze* contextual clues—diction, setting, and point of view—which lend themselves to an understanding and appreciation of an author's intentions in a work.
5. *Reread* and *reevaluate* the essay, story, or poem you have read.
6. *Underline* key words and phrases and jot down notes in margins.
7. *Respond* to works of literature by recording impressions in a writing log or journal.
8. *Write* dialectical journal entries, engaging in "notetaking" and "notemaking" as well as summarizing pieces of literature.
9. *Review* your journal entries and notes frequently; establish or confirm relationships.
10. *Expand* journal entries into full-length essays, critiques, short stories, or poems.

Collaborative Reflections

After assembling in your groups, select one of the literary works, "The Pomegranate," "The Brown Wasps," "Northern Lights," or "The Woods," presented in this chapter and then read it aloud to each other. Once you have finished, discuss active reading strategies in general and how you *did* or *could have* applied them to your group's selection. Next, apply one of the methods of responding to a written work to your group's literary piece. Finally, present the method your group used to actively respond to a written work to the rest of the class.

2
Drafting the Essay

Few people can sit down and write an essay straight through from beginning to end. Writing is a process, a matter of (1) prewriting, (2) drafting, (3) revising, and (4) editing, and each stage contributes to the success of a composition. Planning and starting essays are among your biggest challenges when writing. Chapter 2 will focus on these challenges as it addresses *prewriting*—generating writing topics and supporting details and focusing thesis statements—and *drafting*—organizing, shaping, writing, and developing essays. (Chapter 3 examines revision strategies and chapter 4 considers editing techniques and style.)

PREWRITING: GENERATING TOPICS AND EXPLORING ISSUES

To avoid the frustration of being unable to "produce" a well-written essay off the top of your head, begin your composition by prewriting. What is prewriting? Simply put, prewriting is any activity or combination of activities that gives you an opportunity to generate and explore ideas about a topic or issue *before* writing them in essay form. The dominance of a particular attitude or group of facts in your prewriting might then give you a definite direction to take with your topic—your controlling idea or thesis statement. Prewriting is a creative activity; you never have to worry about *prewriting off target*, since you will not know what your topic is until you have completed the process. There is no "best way" to prewrite essays; however, there are several strategies you may draw from to develop a method of prewriting that works best for you.

Freewriting is one of the most common methods of prewriting. Just writing freely, associating and connecting ideas without concern about grammatical and mechanical errors, can be a liberating exercise for any writer. In addition to "stream of consciousness" writing where one thought leads to another with no particular design or direction, you might also want to *freewrite with focus*, so that the ideas you generate revolve around a limited topic or theme. For instance, after reading two poems, Robert Hayden's "Those Winter Sundays" and Emily Dickinson's "Because I Could Not Stop for Death," and two essays, E. B. White's "Once More to the Lake" and Loren Eiseley's "The

Brown Wasps,'' the student focused her freewriting on the topic of aging, expressing everything she could think of.

Old people are lovable and relaxing to be around, as long as I am not one of them. People tell horror stories about old people becoming senile. Old age. I am afraid of growing old. When I see youthful photographs of my grandparents, it's hard to believe they are the same people. I love them to death, but I don't want to be like them. Their complexion has changed. They have gray or no hair, and wrinkles covering their faces. Old age makes people lose speed; they tend to take longer doing everything. They even tend to drive slower! I think the worst-case scenario would be to grow old alone with nobody around who cares for you.

By freewriting with focus, the student considered a wide range of possible topics about aging. Changes in physical appearance (complexion), mental stability (senility), and lifestyle (leading lonely, solitary existences) are just a few issues the student associated with being old. Ultimately she decided that since the fear of growing old was the dominant theme in her freewriting, it was worth pursuing in a full-length composition entitled "Do Myths Enhance My Fear of Aging?"

Brainstorming or *listing* are also common methods of generating ideas. Here, once again, you will freely associate words and ideas. You might list one word after another, seeking some sort of relationship between opposing as well as similar qualities and images. For instance, after reading Edwin Arlington Robinson's poem "Richard Cory," you might make a list of words or word groups—much like the list Lydia, a student, wrote—that describe Cory. As you read through the poem, note how the speaker associates dignified images with Cory, reflecting and reinforcing the townspeople's perception of him as *the person who seems to have everything.*

Richard Cory

Edwin Arlington Robinson

Whenever Richard Cory went down town,   *people— look with awe*
We people on the pavement looked at him: *gentleman*
He was a gentleman from sole to crown,   *sole*
Clean favored, and imperially slim.

5 And he was always quietly arrayed,   *quiet*
And he was always human when he talked;   *human*
But still he fluttered pulses when he said,   *glittered*
"Good-morning," and he glittered when he walked.   *rich*

And he was rich—yes, richer than a king—   *king*
10 And admirably schooled in every grace: *admirably schooled / grace*
In fine, we thought that he was everything   *he was everything*
To make us wish that we were in his place.   *work*

So on we worked, and waited for the light,   *light / without meat*
And went without the meat, and cursed the bread;   *cursed bread*
15 And Richard Cory, one calm summer night,   *calm summer night*
Went home and put a bullet through his head.   *bullet through his head*

Lydia found she had three categories of words in her prewriting list: observations from a distance (gentleman, quiet, human), details and images suggesting royalty (glittered, rich, king, grace), and disenchantment (the townspeople's lifestyle—and Cory's suicide). The list in its entirety suggested a broad notion to Lydia: *appearances can be deceiving.* This notion in turn became the focus—the thesis—of her paper. In order to recall personal experiences, observations, and readings to illustrate her thesis, Lydia wrote two more lists, using "appearances" and "deception" as the headwords. When she finally composed her paper, she had three reference lists containing resource words and concept relationships.

Clustering words in order to "picture" or "visualize" the relationships between ideas associated with a topic has become a popular, effective method of prewriting. To cluster, begin with a topic or stimulus word, freely associating words and ideas around the topic. Circle each word and draw connections between your responses. Eliminate associations and details which have little bearing on the major recurring theme—a theme you will focus and develop in a composition. In the following piece of prewriting, Aaron, a student, clustered the word *poverty* and came up with five major subgroups surrounding the word.

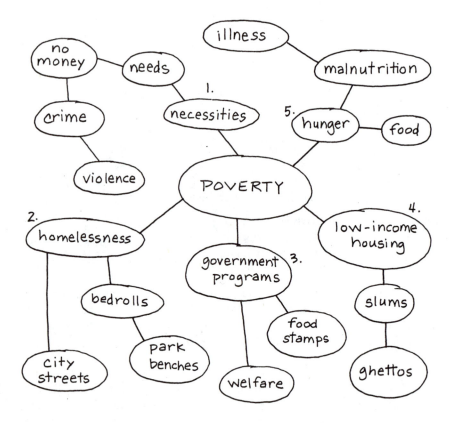

Though Aaron could have gone in five different directions—(1) necessities, (2) homelessness, (3) government programs, (4) low-income housing, and (5) hunger—he narrowed his exploration of poverty to "homelessness." Like "poverty," however, "homelessness" was too broad a topic for a short essay, and so he clustered "homelessness" to consider possible directions he could take, to narrow his focus, and to brainstorm details. Looking over his next cluster, what ideas would you have added?

Most of the items in this new cluster dealt with reasons people become homeless. Therefore, Aaron crossed out all clustered words which did not have a direct bearing on his dominant impressions. His remaining clusters supported his tentative thesis: *Homelessness results from any combination of causes: substance abuse, unemployment / no money, a lack of affordable housing, or insufficient support systems.* When he jotted down a quick scratch outline to consider the best order for development, however, he realized the cluster on "insufficient support systems" already had four major supporting points (friends, family, churches, and government programs). Therefore, he narrowed his focus once more and rewrote his tentative thesis: *Homelessness results from any combination of causes, one of the most underacknowledged of these being insufficient human support systems.* Aaron then demonstrated how each point supported his claim. The number of times you cluster a topic is up to you. Like freewriting, brainstorming, and listing, clustering offers a prewriting method taking you from a general topic to a focused thesis.

THESIS STATEMENTS: BROAD AND NARROW

A standard piece of advice given in most composition texts is to avoid thesis statements too narrow to develop or too broad to cover in a given assignment. Admittedly, once you begin to draft your essay, your controlling idea might ramble a bit—which is not unusual. After all, writing is a process, an exploration of sorts, not a product. (In subsequent drafts of your essay, once the dominant thrust of your essay becomes apparent, you will be able to focus more explicitly on your subject and less on essay formula.) Nonetheless, avoiding a thesis that is too broad or too narrow to begin with can be helpful. To determine if the topic you generated is too narrow for thorough development, ask yourself, "What else can be said or argued about the thesis?" Does the intended thesis make a statement complete in itself like *Neil Armstrong was the first human being to step on the moon?* If so, then your thesis is too narrow. Similar to the old cliché "you can't squeeze blood out of a turnip," you cannot develop or argue a nonexisting thesis. On the other hand, if you add "focusing words" to the sentence, you might discover something to argue or explain about the subject. *Several contributing reasons led Neil Armstrong, the first human being to step on the moon, to become a public recluse.*

Jotting down a brief scratch outline (just the thesis and major discussion or supporting points) is also useful in deciding whether your topic is either too broad or too narrow for development. The broad topic will have too much to say in very little space, whereas the narrow topic will offer nothing to develop. The second cluster on poverty (homelessness) led to the following tentative thesis before Aaron realized he needed to narrow his controlling idea further:

Thesis: Homelessness results due to any combination of causes: substance abuse, unemployment/ no money, a lack of affordable housing, or insufficient support systems.

    I. Lack of affordable housing

    II. Substance abuse

        —alcohol

        —narcotics

        —chemicals

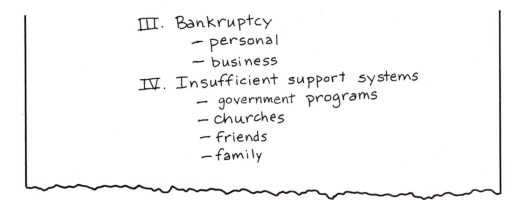

III. Bankruptcy
 — personal
 — business
IV. Insufficient support systems
 — government programs
 — churches
 — friends
 — family

The revised, manageable thesis as seen through a scratch outline:

Thesis: Homelessness results from any combination of causes, one of the most underacknowledged of these being insufficient human support systems.
 I. Government programs
 II. Churches
 III. Friends
 IV. Families

Had Aaron constructed a thesis like *Many homeless people sleep on park benches,* inspired by the cluster "park benches," his scratch outline would have quickly illustrated the topic's limited potential for development. His scratch outline probably would have looked something like this:

Thesis: Many homeless people sleep on park benches.
 I. Joe
 II. Eva
 III. Fabian
 IV. Susanne

After identifying a few homeless people who do sleep on park benches, what else could be said here? Not much. In fact, all the information could have been presented in a single sentence: *Many homeless people—including Joe, Eva, Fabian, and Susanne—sleep on park benches.* Scratch outlines can be helpful in deciding whether topics are too limited or too broad for development. As the outline on park benches illustrates, however, people, places, events, and things listed as major discussion points are not always what they appear. Give yourself time to reflect for a moment on tentative supporting points; ask yourself, "What more can I say about them?" before you attempt to write something that looks marvelous in an outline, but does not lend itself to realistic development.

DRAFTING ESSAYS

Whether you are writing about a personal experience, responding to the theme of a poem, or arguing a position presented in a short story or an article, you will be presenting your ideas in some form of an essay. How long is an essay and how is it structured? First of all, an essay should be as long as necessary to fully develop a topic or argue an issue. That may be the last answer a developing writer wants to hear, but there is no sense denying the truth; writing to communicate does not neatly fit a formula (e.g., an essay consists of five paragraphs).

Compositions traditionally include an introductory paragraph that leads to a thesis, supporting or body paragraphs that justify or illuminate the thesis or controlling idea, and a concluding paragraph that places major discussion points back into focus with your thesis and brings a note of finality to your investigation, analysis, argument, or exposition. No one would dispute the need for a beginning, middle, and end to an essay. Writers run into difficulty when they believe that merely because they have written an introductory paragraph, followed it with three body paragraphs, and concluded with a single paragraph, they have satisfactorily structured and developed a topic or an issue.

Explicit and Implied Thesis Statements

Terminology can often confuse as well as clarify. Whether you call a thesis statement the controlling idea, the main idea, or simply "a thesis" in an essay, its function never changes. Your thesis presents a reader with the "big picture," or purpose of your writing; it takes a definite position on a topic or an issue and defends or explains it. Traditionally, an *explicit thesis* statement follows the "lead-in" sentences in your introductory paragraph and is the sort of thesis used for most of your college writing. An *explicit thesis* specifically states your intentions and identifies the ideas you plan to develop in the body of your paper. With a definite sense of direction and purpose provided by your thesis, you will find breaking down supporting points into smaller units—paragraphs—for detailed discussion much easier.

As you develop your writing skills, you may occasionally want to use an *implied thesis*, especially for narrative and descriptive essays written for purposes and occasions that do not always lend themselves to an explicitly stated thesis statement. The following introductory paragraph from E. B. White's "Once More to the Lake" *implies* that the speaker went to "revisit old haunts" to recapture a moment in time, although he never specifically says so:

> One summer, along about 1904, my father rented a camp on a lake in Maine and took us all there for the month of August. We all got ring worm from some kittens and had to rub Pond's Extract on our arms and legs night and morning, and my father rolled over in a canoe with all his clothes on; but outside of that the vacation was a success and from then on none of us ever thought there was any place in the world like that lake in Maine. We returned summer after summer—always on August 1 for one month. I have since become a salt-water man, but sometimes in summer there are days when the restlessness of the tides and the fearful cold of the sea water and the incessant wind that blows across the afternoon and into the evening make me wish for the placidity of a lake in the woods. A few weeks ago this feeling got so strong I bought myself a couple of bass hooks and a spinner and returned to the lake where we used to go, for a week's fishing and to revisit old haunts.

White carefully constructs his narrative so readers can intuitively understand the implied thesis—his purpose for writing. The first three sentences of his essay nostalgically reflect on how his family would go to a camp in Maine for a month every August, sharing the belief there was no "place in the world like that lake in Maine." The fourth sentence informs readers that he now has become a "salt-water man," but it also notes how he frequently wishes "for the placidity of a lake in the woods." By the fifth sentence, readers have a profound sense that White returned to "the lake" for more than a week of fishing; he came to relive a treasured past.

Introductory Paragraphs and Lead-in Sentences

The effective writer will usually "lead" into his or her thesis rather than simply beginning a composition with a thesis statement. Why use a *lead-in* sentence? For one, you want to "hook" your reader's interest in your essay immediately. For another, you need to prepare your reader for your thesis by introducing a topic in general before you say anything specific about it. In other words, well-crafted lead-in sentences can ease readers into your thesis. You might begin an essay with a *quotation* and lead to your controlling idea, or you could state some alarming *facts* and *statistics* to get your reader's attention. *Rhetorical questions* frequently raise issues you intend to explore and address. Sharing *anecdotes* and *personal experiences* can also announce a subject and lead to the controlling idea or thesis. The point is, no matter how provocative a thesis statement might be, effective lead-in sentences give a boost to most introductory paragraphs. The following introductory paragraphs by professional and student writers illustrate various types of lead-in sentences concluding with explicit thesis statements in italics.

A Startling, Ironic, or Disturbing Fact

Mai Nguyen's graduation from college was the worst day of her life. *Mai, a straight-A student in high school in Milpitas and an honors graduate in math from UC–Berkeley, had expected congratulations, flowers and love from her parents. Instead, she was disowned.*

T. T. NHU

Personal Experience (Anecdote)

I just spent two days with Edward T. Hall, an anthropologist, watching thousands of my fellow New Yorkers short-circuiting themselves into hot little twitching death balls with jolts of their own adrenaline. Dr. Hall says it is over-crowding that does it. Overcrowding gets the adrenaline going, and the adrenaline gets them hyped up. And here they are, hyped up, turning bilious, nephritic, queer, autistic, sadistic, barren, batty, sloppy, hot in the pants, chancred-on-the-flankers, leering, puling, numb—the usual in New York, in other words, and God knows what else. Dr. Hall has the theory that overcrowding has already thrown New York into a state of behavioral sink. Behavioral sink is a term from ethology, which is the study of how animals relate to their environment. *Among animals, the sink winds up with a "population collapse" or "massive die off." O rotten Gotham.*

TOM WOLFE

Rhetorical Question

Did Junichiro Tanizaki secretly wish that he had been a podiatrist instead of a novelist, or did he perhaps have an unresolved Oedipus complex, which many psychologists feel is the source of a fanaticism *such as his?* When most people think of feet, they conjure images of bunions, Dr. Scholls, and the dreaded open-toed shoe. To many the foot is a symbol of the ordinary, the inconspicuous, and the mundane. *It is not surprising, then, that most people cannot understand the prevalence of feet in the writings of Tanizaki; what is it about feet that so captivates his attention?*

ROBIN FADDEN

Quotation

"The first time she drowned in the cold and glassy waters of Lake Turcot, Fleur Pillager was only a girl." With these opening words, Louise Erdrich sets the stage for her story where the active imaginations of people on the reservation—and then later in Argus—piece together happenstance, accusing Fleur of creating and controlling destructive natural forces and events around her. *Despite the extraordinary events which seem to follow and connect her to life, a close study of*

Fleur's independent character reveals only one thing: she is a victim of vicious gossip and public innuendoes, not an initiator of supernatural actions.

LIEN NGUYEN

Definition

A euphemism is commonly defined as an auspicious or exalted term (like "sanitation engineer") that is used in place of a more down-to-earth term (like "garbage man"). People who are partial to euphemisms stand accused of being "phony" or of trying to hide what it is they are really talking about. And there is no doubt that in some situations the accusation is entirely proper. For example, one of the more detestable euphemisms I have come across in recent years is the term "Operation Sunshine," which is the name the U.S. Government gave to some experiments it conducted with the hydrogen bomb in the South Pacific. It is obvious that the government, in choosing this name, was trying to expunge the hideous imagery that the bomb evokes and in so doing committed, as I see it, an immoral act. *This sort of process—giving pretty names to essentially ugly realities—is what has given euphemizing such a bad name. And people like George Orwell have done valuable work for all of us in calling attention to how the process works. But there is another side to euphemizing that is worth mentioning, and a few words here in its defense will not be amiss.*

NEIL POSTMAN

Often writers wait until they have drafted their entire essay before constructing the lead-in to their thesis so they will know what they are introducing. This approach makes sense when you consider that a first draft of an essay is based on a tentative thesis, one which may change form or direction during the course of writing. Attempting to make an essay "fit" an inappropriate introduction is like trying to slip your size-nine foot into a size-three shoe. In both situations you are forcing an unrealistic "fit." Therefore, if you feel yourself getting bogged down with a "lead-in" to your thesis, move on to the body of your paper and return to the introduction later.

Developing Essays: The Body Paragraphs

Developing your material is the next step in drafting an essay. Once you have determined the controlling idea or thesis for your composition, place it—along with supporting points—in a scratch outline. Next, write out your composition as fully as possible. You may frequently want to refer to a scratch outline to make sure you have not drifted off the topic; however, allow yourself to explore your topic and maintain the momentum of your argument. Some authors, for instance, write out an entire essay before committing themselves to a thesis. (Often freewriting during the prewriting stage can accomplish the same purpose in a lot less time!)

Most readers will be interested in learning how and why you came to your conclusions. Generally speaking then, back up your general points with specific facts, details, and analysis. As you glance over your scratch outline, ask yourself the six journalistic questions: *Who? What? When? Where? Why?* and *How?* for each supporting point. Look for spots in your prose where questions beg to be answered, and jot down any explanations, associations, or arguments that come to mind. Insights gleaned from answers to such inquiries may become useful details as you move beyond "narration" and "telling" to an analysis of a topic or an issue.

Evidence and Examples   Supporting evidence or examples range from personal experience and observations to testimonies and readings. Examples share a common thread: They illustrate the validity of your sentences and substantiate your arguments. Your topic, audience, purpose, and occasion will all play a role in determining appropriate supporting materials. *Personal testimony* comes from your immediate experiences and is often used in narratives. Although you should never undervalue the merit of your personal experiences, remember that readers are "convinced" better by several representative examples than an example from a single perspective. (For an interesting discussion on the reliability of personal testimony, read "In a Grove" in chapter 15.) *Observations* of the world around you can also supply a multitude of examples. As an observer, you might exert more objectivity in a composition since you are not directly involved in the action. *Professional, authoritative testimony* becomes essential when you are trying to establish credibility about a topic outside the area of your expertise. Allowing the validity of your thesis to rest on one authority's opinion, however, is also inadvisable. For the best results, check your source by locating an esteemed authority who corroborates the testimony. This applies to all professional areas, whether you are a tree surgeon or a supreme court judge, a carnival barker or a dentist.

The *media*, a term referring to any means of transferring, conveying, or presenting information, is a constant source of information and examples, including magazines like *Time* and *Newsweek, Omni, Ms., Ebony, Mother Jones,* and *Rolling Stone;* television talk shows, tabloid news shows, legitimate new programs, news networks; movies; newspapers; radio, and so on. *Readings* include forms of mass media, but also nonfiction, short stories, novels, poetry, and drama. Allusions to literary themes and motifs and quotations followed by commentary and analysis are other ways readings can illustrate and explain your material. *Statistics* and *polls* can establish facts, support points, and persuade readers. A statistic is only as good as its source, however. One would place more belief in a survey done by *Time* or *Forbes* than *Star* or a tabloid magazine. Like professional testimonies, it is a good practice to corroborate your statistics with findings from similar studies.

Topic Sentences and Paragraph Unity   Topic sentences, sometimes referred to as discussion points, sum up material in paragraphs and often appear at the beginning of them. Like the focusing words in a thesis statement, the focusing words in topic sentences are extremely important to writers, too, because they provide them with specific *guidelines* for paragraph development. The golden rule of development might be this: "When you make a point, stick to developing that point and don't wander." That way your work will be *unified*. If you stated, "In 1994, illegal immigration into the United States became a hot election campaign issue," then the remainder of your paragraph should explain *how, why,* and *with whom* illegal immigration became a "hot election campaign issue." You would "miss the mark" if you talked about someone living in the United States illegally, for you would not be addressing the issue summarized by your topic sentence. The latter sentence would *disunify* your material.

Concluding Paragraphs

Concluding paragraphs should do more than simply restate your thesis in different words. True, it is often helpful to pull together the parts of an essay by reiterating major discussion points and placing them back into focus with your thesis. Still, you should go beyond reiterating ideas to leave a lasting impression on your reader. One way to do so is to offer readers satisfying concluding or "clincher" statements. To give your composition a powerful or significant sense of closure, you might (1) add comments reflecting on the subject; (2) use a rhetorical question or a statement that asks the reader to consider the larger implications of your essay; (3) provide a call to action (something must be done); or (4) offer an anecdote or a quotation to reiterate the main idea of your essay. The following concluding paragraphs illustrate some ways you might bring a composition to an effective close.

Commentary on the Larger Implications of a Topic or Issue

One of our most visionary politicians said that he envisioned a time when the United States could become the brain of the world, by which he meant the repository of all of the latest advanced information systems. I thought of that remark when an enterprising poet friend of mine called to say that he had just sold a poem to a computer magazine and that the editors were delighted to get it because they didn't carry fiction or poetry. Is that the kind of world we desire? A humdrum homogeneous world of all brains but no heart, no fiction, no poetry; a world of robots with human attendants bereft of imagination, of culture? Or does North America deserve a more exciting destiny? To become a place where the cultures of the world crisscross. This is possible because the United States is unique in the world. The world is here.

ISHMAEL REED

Reflection

My aunt haunts me—her ghost drawn to me because now, after fifty years of neglect, I alone devote pages of paper to her, though not origamied into houses and clothes. I do not think she always means me well. I am telling on her, and she was a spite suicide, drowning herself in the drinking water. The Chinese are always very frightened of the drowned one, whose weeping ghost, wet hair hanging and skin bloated, waits silently by the water to pull down a substitute.

MAXINE HONG KINGSTON

Suggestion/Call to Action

One could hardly ask for more important evidence of the dangers of considering persons as split between what is "inside" and what is "outside" than that interminable half-comic, half-tragic tale, the oppression of women. How easy it is to start off by defining women as caretakers of the surfaces, and then to disparage them (or find them adorable) for being "superficial." It is a crude trap, and it has worked for too long. But to get out of the trap requires that women get some critical distance from that excellence and privilege which is beauty, enough distance to see how much beauty itself has been abridged in order to prop up the mythology of the "feminine." There should be a way of saving beauty *from* women—and *for* them.

SUSAN SONTAG

Quotation

Taken at face value, MUDs (Multi-User Dimensions) are a game. Looking deeper, they present an interesting form of communication where words and "actions" are the sole form of communicating, understanding and learning. People are not judged on MUDs by their skin color, hair style, or clothing, but by their personality and "actions." MUDs can certainly evoke "real life" emotions, so does that mean that MUDs are a game or an extension of real life with game-like qualities? Regardless of the answer to that question, MUDs have certainly laid the groundwork for an interesting future. Already, corporations and research organizations are using alter MUDs to train employees, hold meetings and conduct interviews. *As stated by* WIRED Online: "*With each new [MUD], a new community begins and new cultures emerge to socialize a place where anything is possible. The Big Surprise of the Information Age is what people use their computers for: to communicate.*"

ROBBIE SINCLAIR

ALTERNATE METHODS OF ESSAY DEVELOPMENT

Nonfiction traditionally has been divided into four major categories called rhetorical modes: narration, description, exposition, and argumentation. Though sometimes rhetorical modes are taught with the intent of expanding your awareness of and ability to use a variety of strategies to explain and argue topics and issues, they are frequently mistaken as "absolute" methods of development. A dominant method of development in one essay may play a minor role or none at all in another essay! The objective of your paper should remain the most important consideration when you write, and rhetorical modes that assist you in development—but are not an end in themselves—should be kept in perspective. Rather than look towards narration, description, exposition, or argumentation as strict models to emulate, use whatever mode of development seems natural and appropriate for your first draft. Then when you revise your paper, you can use strategies derived from a basic understanding of the rhetorical modes to develop your paper in greater detail. (This will be discussed further in chapter 3.) Since authors often blend a variety of rhetorical techniques to develop essay topics, a review of the four categories of composition is next in order.

Narration

Of the four forms of nonfiction, narration—telling a story—is the most accessible because relating a tale or recounting an event comes naturally to us. Our daily lives as well as a large portion of literature tend to include narrative elements. Gossip tends to be narrative. Sermons tend to be narrative. Lectures tend to be narrative. Poems tend to be narrative. Epics tend to be narrative, and song lyrics include narrative. In short, narratives are all around us. Chronology, the placement of events in time and space, also is important in a narrative. Time transitions such as "first," "second," "third," and "finally" guide the reader from the start to the conclusion of a narrative. Spatial transitions indicate relationships with words such as "above," "below," "inside," "outside," "here," "there," and "beyond"; they explain where something takes place.

Description

Though usually subordinated to other types of writing such as narration, description has a distinct purpose: to enable a reader to visualize a setting, situation, or person. To present vivid details and examples, writers select words or word groups that appeal to one or more of the five senses: sight, sound, touch, taste, and smell.

Exposition

In theory, exposition, meaning *to expose,* is a distinct form of composition; however, it is frequently a combination of various rhetorical modes at work (e.g., comparison and contrast mixed with description). Expository essays attempt to explain an idea or issue. There are many methods of developing an expository essay: illustration and example, process analysis, definition, cause and effect, and classification. An essay's purpose and thesis will determine what mode (form) or combination of modes would do the best job in developing and explaining a subject. If the purpose of an essay were to explain "how to" do something, you could use process analysis to naturally and effectively accomplish the task. On the other hand, process analysis would hardly serve any author well if he or she wanted to examine the contributory causes of inner-city violence. (See the glossary for a brief review of modes and how they can apply to exposition and argumentation.)

Argumentation and Persuasion: *Ethos, Logos, Pathos*

Argumentation and persuasion have the same goal: to convince or persuade a reader to a new way of thinking. The two do have differences though, differences which can be easily explained by noting whether authors appeal to their audiences ethically, emotionally, or logically. Argumentative essays, for instance, will appeal to a reader's sense of logic (*logos*). Such an appeal is rational. Writers who establish themselves as ethical, knowledgeable, and incorruptible use the ethical appeal (*ethos*) to convey the fact that their rationale, motives, and conclusions are noble, fair, and trustworthy. When ethics are coupled with an appeal to logic, writers appear to be persons of *sound mind* and *good will*. As they develop their argumentative or persuasive essays, they will attempt to maintain particular images in order to sustain the ethical appeal.

Argumentative reasoning has been discussed, traditionally, in terms of inductive logic, deductive logic, and common sense. Admittedly, *common sense* could be considered a subjective term because precisely what constitutes common sense to one person might be misunderstood or overlooked due to another's cultural experiences. Inductive and deductive methods of reasoning, however, are a bit easier to explain.

Inductive logic moves from several specific facts to a general statement or conclusion based on those facts. The more facts you can gather and assess before making a generalization, the less a reader must accept a conclusion just because an author "says it is so." Why? Consider the following generalization: *Young teenage girls have the best chance of winning a medal in gymnastics at the Olympics.* The validity of such a conclusion will depend on the number of particular facts—teenage girls who have won medals at the Olympics—that lead to your generalization. Merely pointing out that Nadia Comaneci was fourteen when she won four gold medals at the 1972 Olympics proves nothing. There are exceptions to most things, and her victory at such a young age may have been an extraordinary achievement. On the other hand, the writer who researches the ages of female gymnasts who have won medals at Olympic games over the past twenty years would have a substantial basis for his or her generalization.

Deductive logic follows a process of evaluating general points, divided into major and minor premises (information and evidence), which lead to some sort of conclusion. The validity of your deductive conclusion depends on the truth of its premises. For instance, if you reasoned that all English instructors teach Shakespeare (major premise), and Nancy is an English instructor (minor premise), then you might conclude (deduce) that Nancy teaches Shakespeare. Such a conclusion would be faulty because not "all" English instructors teach Shakespeare. What is missing here, of course, is a qualifying word such as "most" or "many" before *English instructors.*

Do people really think deductively and inductively before passing judgments and reaching conclusions? Indeed, we frequently consider the weight of evidence (premises) to deduce who is telling the truth about an event or issue. Unfortunately, many times we are less likely to act upon a logical argument than an emotional appeal. The absence of emotionally charged reasoning in argumentation clearly distinguishes argumentation from persuasion.

Persuasion, like argumentation, attempts to convince a reader about a topic, issue, product, and so on. In addition to appeals to logic and ethics, though, persuasion also appeals to a reader's emotions (*pathos*). Why emotions? Because passion or emotions, no matter how illogical they may be, prompt people to do, say, and think things. An emotionally charged word, in fact, is more likely to influence a person's choice of food in a restaurant or to convince someone of a political candidate's sincerity than a well-reasoned, logical argument.

Emotionally charged words frequently address our hopes, dreams, fears, wants, wishes, likes, dislikes. Of course, few people are going to place much faith in someone who uncontrollably "oozes" his or her emotions across the paper. Excessive flattery, denigration, and protests tend to become suspect. To counter the possibility of excess leading to a lack of credibility, a writer will want to employ the standard elements of argumentation—deductive and inductive logic—in a persuasive essay. A combination of *ethos, logos,* and *pathos* will make most emotionally driven arguments seem logical and based on verifiable facts.

In sum, narration, description, exposition, and argumentation, and the subgroups or rhetorical modes of development—illustration, process analysis, definition, cause and effect, comparison and contrast, and classification—appear in all forms of literature. Since you are interested in seeing how methods of development are used effectively in context, rather than searching and observing pure models of each rhetorical mode (if, indeed, pure examples of each rhetorical mode even exist!), the diverse readings in part II coupled with the postreading apparatus for writing activities will simplify studying composition.

Sample Student Essay: First Draft
"The Wild Woman Archetype"

In the following student essay, Robin Fadden blends argumentation, analysis, and illustration and example to support her claim that women throughout history have been labeled as "disobedient" for wanting to maintain their own identity and their own sense of dignity, and that the price of being "disobedient women" was often to become an outcast, even die, because their desire for independence threatened the existing social order. Using several pieces of world literature as samples, Fadden analyzes representative instances of women who have suffered in one way or another for "finding and preserving their inner identities and spirituality," regardless of the outward price they had to pay.

To prewrite about her topic, Fadden brainstormed and listed words she associated with the phrase "Wild Woman Archetype." In addition to coming up with some major focal areas to discuss in her essay, she also generated numerous examples of the Wild Woman Archetype drawn from written works.

ASSOCIATIONS

individuality
needs
wants
progressive / threatening
defiance
disobedience
obligation
    to self
    to others
self-preservation

CONCRETE EXAMPLES

Eve
Fleur Pillager ("Fleur")
Tita (Like Water for Chocolate)
Lilith
Speaker ("In the Woods")
Inanna (Sumerian mythology)
Kingston's aunt ("No Name Woman")
Estés (Women Who Run with Wolves)

Next, she looked for a pattern or reoccurring theme, a common thread running through her prewriting list. The causes and effects of disobedience among women jumped out at her, yet she still had no controlling idea. Therefore, she began to ask herself a series of questions: *What may my audience know about my general topic? How might I focus my thoughts? Is there a particular conflict I could use to frame my controlling idea?* By addressing the last question with another (*why have women been ashamed of their true nature?*), and then addressing her rhetorical question (*the answer may lie in the many examples of the disobedient women who have been used to admonish the reluctant into submis-*

sion), Fadden arrived at a tentative direction for her paper. By drawing examples from her list of the Wild Woman Archetype in literature which she (1) had recently read about and (2) could relate to each other and analyze, Fadden was able to focus her attention on the purpose of her essay rather than spending time trying to make examples *fit* her discussion points. Finally, before Fadden began to write, she organized her information by making a brief scratch outline—a tentative plan of development for her essay.

I. Thesis: Why have women been ashamed of displaying their true nature? Ironically, the answer may lie in the many examples of the disobedient women who have been used to admonish the reluctant into submission.

II. Supporting paragraphs 2 and 3: definition of terms (Estés)
   a) identity and the Wild Woman Archetype
   b) spirituality and the Wild Woman Archetype

III. Wild Woman Archetype and Eve (disobedience)

IV. Wild Woman Archetype and Kingston's aunt (identity and spiritual unrest)

V. Wild Woman Archetype and Sita (bonds of tradition)

VI. Conclusion: common link between women reestablished

Fadden 1

Robin Fadden
Professor Burns
English 1A
12 Sept. 1996

The Wild Woman Archetype

Over the years, it would seem that a confusion has been created between how a woman perceives herself and how her society perceives her. This confusion is the rift that separates women from the outward persona they feel obligated to convey and the inner self which they have historically felt ashamed to show. Why have women been ashamed of displaying their true nature? Ironically, the answer may lie in the many examples of the disobedient women who have been used to admonish the reluctant into submission.

The more a woman focused on her inner identity, the more her inability to fit comfortably into the restrictive patriarchy which had previously had autonomous rule over her seemed to become problematic. The historical "woman in progress" was seen as a threat to society because she was able to connect with that which is most essentially "woman," most recently referred to in Clarissa Pinkola Estés' work, Women Who Run with the Wolves, as the "Wild Woman Archetype." She was labeled "disobedient" because this would reinforce the idea that she needed to be punished for trying to disrupt the societal norms the Wild Woman nature displaces. While these "disobedient women" were to be made the examples of conduct that was not acceptable to the rest of the established society, they also, somewhat ironically, served as the largely misunderstood testimony to the importance of keeping the essential spirit of the "essential woman" intact and unstoppable.

These women reinforce the idea that, wherever the spirit of this Wild Woman is being restricted or enslaved, women must strike out at the enemy that attacks them, and protect themselves from becoming a forgotten myth. When this Woman could not be contained within the context of her restrictive society, she was punished under the pretext of "reestablishing order." However, the Wild Woman's actions were determined by a much more necessary motivation—the need for self-preservation. What prompted these women to abandon the safety of the monotony of their narrow existences? They must have felt the need to protect their almost extinct inner nature. Their disobedience was, therefore, not only defiance, it was the conservation of their identity. It was the fight to preserve the Wild Woman in them all.

In the story of the Fall of Man, from Genesis, Eve is punished for eating from the tree of knowledge, therefore causing the original sin. Eve strikes out at the obstacle which separates her from understanding her true self and eats the fruit. To the patriarchy of the Christian church, her act has been interpreted as being one of willful sin. As seen through the eyes of the Wild Woman, Eve is merely acting out of self-preservation. Eve has ultimately gained far more than she has lost when one compares the outcomes of a life of self-negation and ignorance in the Garden of Eden, to her ultimate knowledge of her true self, which satisfies a far more basic need than any physical fulfillment could offer. Her disobedience is what has allowed the first "essential woman" to survive.

In Maxine Hong Kingston's novel, The Woman Warrior, Kingston also deals with protecting one's identity in the chapter called "No Name Woman." In it, she tells the story of her aunt who, after having an illegitimate daughter, is ostracized by her family and, after having her farm totally destroyed by a mob of villagers as punishment for her "extravagance," she finally kills herself and her daughter as a kind of last hope of retaining some kind of dignity. Interestingly enough, she chooses to commit suicide by drowning herself in the family's well, therefore, polluting their only supply of drinking water. Although part of her punishment was to be totally ignored by her family, she does manage to paradoxically achieve some kind of lasting memory as a precautionary tale told to the author by her mother to dissuade her from similar behavior. It would seem that, although she was severely punished by her family and her society, Kingston's aunt still manages to retain some sense of inner identity, even in her death. By choosing to pollute her family's well, she takes a last stab at their superiority, reinforcing her disobedience, but she also reinforces her inability to totally submit to their unfair values and mores. She retains some of the Wild Woman spirit by choosing to retain some dignity by killing herself (suicide has traditionally been seen as more honorable in Asian cultures than in Western society) rather than having to endure the continued punishment she, and her daughter, would have to face if they were to have lived. She subconsciously asserts that she respects herself and her daughter too much to allow themselves to be tortured by her village's traditions. She becomes the family's taboo; the unspoken spirit of the Wild Woman.

The character of Tita in Laura Esquivel's novel, Like Water for Chocolate, also experiences being branded as the "disobedient woman" for wanting to preserve her own identity. From the moment she was born, she was destined to never marry, so that, as the youngest daughter of her family, she would carry on the tradition of being the one to take care of her mother until her mother's death. However, Tita does not agree with the tradition she had been forced into. The majority of the rest of Tita's life is spent in forced compliance with her mother's wishes. Every day she would have to endure the suffering of watching the man she loved marry her sister, so that, by doing so, he could remain close to Tita, and the tyrannical rule of her mother. One day, Tita finally snaps under the years of repressed anger and frustration she has held inside. The death of her nephew sparks a terrible fight between Tita and her mother, in which she blames her mother for causing the death of the child whom she had raised as her own.

Finally Tita has broken the tradition of which she had been the unwilling victim for so long. It is because she could no longer stand to ignore her individuality that it was necessary for her to disobey her mother. For her punishment, she is forced to leave the ranch and fend for herself. Ironically, this is exactly what Tita wants. Now she has the freedom to experience her true individuality. She can allow herself to grow and mature without the limitations of her mother's irrational traditions. She finally can allow herself to focus on her inner identity, and begins the search for her own true nature. Her disobedience was necessary if she was to save any aspect of her true self. She was conserving the spirit of the Wild Woman which would not let her be resigned to a fate of servitude.

All these women are linked by more than just their common gender. They were considered outcasts, or threats to the stability of some preestablished order they could never agree with. While they all differ in their attempts to retain some aspect of their inner personality that has beenthreatened, all these women manage to reassert the tenacity of the Wild Woman Archetype. They continue the pattern of behavior which marks their inner focus. They are all, in some way, unable to coexist with the societal rules the archetype displaces, and therefore, must be punished if the society with which they disagree with is to retain its strict sense of order. However, regardless of time or space, these women show that the Wild Woman still exists; she must if women are to retain their unique individuality and sense of inner peace. These women are a part of a heritage in search for the inner sanctity only the Wild Woman can offer. They are a testimony to her own eternal longevity, which lives in every one of these misunderstood martyrs.

Works Cited

Esquivel, Laura. Like Water for Chocolate. Trans. Carol
    Christensen and Thomas Christensen. New York:
    Doubleday, 1992.
Estés, Clarissa Pinkola. Women Who Run with the Wolves:
    Myths and Stories of the Wild Woman Archetype. New
    York: Ballantine, 1992.
Kingston, Maxine Hong. "No Name Woman." The Woman
    Warrior. New York: Knopf, 1975.

At this point, if you peer edited Robin's paper, what "common sense" revision suggestions might you offer her and why? What questions ran through your mind as you read her paper? Did she seem to overlook some vital connections between her material? Were her examples general or specific? How did her exposition or analysis of subject matter clarify and illustrate her thesis? After considering such questions, jot down a few notes in your writing log or journal and take a look at them before reading the revised version of Robin's essay which appears following a discussion of the next two stages in the writing process: revision and editing.

STRATEGIES: Drafting the Essay

1. *Prewrite* in order to generate writing topics: freewrite, cluster, brainstorm, list; use any form or combination of forms of prewriting that work for you.
2. *Move* from a broad topic such as "the rights of biological parents" to a tentative, limited thesis that says something about your topic (e.g., "the concept that biological parents have inherent rights over their children should be reexamined"). Your focusing words should unmistakably define your thesis or controlling idea.
3. *Organize* and *shape* the ideas you have generated into a progressive form, beginning with an introductory paragraph, moving to supporting paragraphs in the body of the essay, and ending with a final paragraph that brings your essay to a satisfying, definite conclusion.
4. *Write* your first draft; keep referring back to your thesis to ensure continuity of development.
5. *Reread* your work and note areas that seem to need more support areas by asking *Who? What? When? Where? Why?* and *How?*

Collaborative Reflections

Assemble into groups of three or four and choose one of the following topics to write about in a group (collaborative) essay: advertisements, AIDS, sports, video games, higher education, or virtual reality. Using one of the prewriting strategies in this chapter, everyone should then write a tentative thesis statement on the topic. Next, select *one* of the thesis statements your group generated to function as the thesis of a collaborative essay. Working together, break down the thesis into major topic sentences (discussion points), and then develop each point in detail. Choose a recorder, someone to write down the information from your group's collaborative efforts. Have the recorder also make photocopies of the collaborative activity: (1) the group thesis statement and (2) supporting paragraphs. Then distribute them to group members at the next class meeting. For homework, review the different methods of "leading-in" to a thesis statement and write an original "lead-in" (your own) for the group essay. Also, construct a concluding paragraph placing all of the major discussion points into focus with your thesis statement. Make use of some sort of clincher statement. Finally, reassemble with your group and share the ways you all chose to lead into the same thesis and to "conclude" the identical essay.

3

Revising the Essay

As you move from drafting to revising an essay, your task shifts from creating to reshaping and reworking it. Revising material to make it more comprehensible and effective is a must; however, revision is a lot more than correcting mechanical or grammatical errors. All areas of a composition, from its title to the last sentence in the concluding paragraph, are targets during the revision stage of writing. When you revise, you will assess and rework (1) the overall unity and coherence of your composition; (2) the clarity of your introductory paragraph (lead-in sentences and thesis statement); (3) supporting paragraphs; (4) sentence constructions (sentence variety, sentence combining, topic sentences, and concrete nouns and active verbs); and (5) concluding paragraphs.

With each new revision, you will examine the "big picture"—the thesis of your essay—and determine how well you supported and explained it. In so doing, you will think about the variety and types of examples you used to support what you say. Here you may also want to pause and reflect on how you structured your examples. Did they seem to build on each other?

Every time you revise a draft, strive for rhetorical effectiveness (how well something is said) not just grammatical correctness. Often, for instance, repeating sentence patterns becomes monotonous and therefore boring. In fact, using the same structure to convey different information may make your information seem repetitive—even if it is not. To create greater interest in what you have to say, go through your composition and combine related material, condensing where possible. Eliminate words that do not advance an argument or clarify an explanation. Wordiness may make readers stop to reread material. In doing so, you may lose the rhetorical impact—the momentum—of your presentation.

METHODS AND TECHNIQUES: REVISION

Distance Yourself from Your Work   After writing the rough draft of a composition, and all subsequent revisions, set it by for a while to distance yourself from it. Then, read it from the start to finish, noting areas that "read" awkwardly. A major objective here is to assist you in revising your essay with the "reader's" rather than the "writer's" eye. The difference between the two is the writer's awareness of facts and details unknown to the reader.

Ask Yourself the Journalist's Questions   To determine if your paragraphs are sufficiently developed, ask yourself the six journalistic questions: *who, what, when, where, why,* and *how,* in context; *Who* am I talking about? *What* am I talking about? *When* am I talking about (past, present, future) a topic? *Where* does my topic take place? *Why* am I writing about a topic (what is my objective)? And *how* did I support what I said about my topic? Your answers to such questions support and strengthen an argument or clarify information in an exposition. Add specific facts, details, and verifiable examples to illustrate and develop your topic sentences. Finally, make sure all your examples explain and support your topic sentences to maintain paragraph unity.

Read Your Work Out Loud   Place some sort of mark in the margin of your paper to alert yourself to sentences and passages you will want to rewrite for greater clarity. A variation of this revision activity would be to read the last sentence first and the first sentence last in your essay, judging each sentence on its own merit. (Sometimes reading sentences out of context reveals structural or grammatical problems overlooked when reading material chronologically.) When you get to your initial sentence, read the paper once more chronologically—also out loud. Reading your work out loud also builds your sensitivity to the rhythm of sentence constructions, the importance of diction, and the rhetorical power of words as you take time to listen to your sentences. If you tend to write comma splices, sentence fragments, and run-ons, or unreasonably assume reader knowledge, you will find this latter revision strategy particularly useful.

Address Your Annotations   Once you have read your essay, return to your marks and marginal notes indicating awkward, imprecise sentences, underdeveloped paragraphs, and other information. Before you begin to rework your constructions, ask yourself what you intended to say, and if possible, express the point in different words than you used in your original draft. Clinging to a particular word or construction can result in an equally awkward revised sentence. Your content may seem forced, unnatural, unfocused, or muddled if you insist on a *form* you are fond of instead of one that effectively conveys your point.

PEOPLE AND PURPOSES: APPLYING MODES IN REVISION

The rhetorical modes in revision, just as in drafting a composition, can provide strategies—methods for explaining, describing, or arguing a topic or an issue. This applies to essays where you write about literature (e.g., analyzing *voice, imagery,* and *tone* in two poems such as "The City Planners" by Margaret Atwood and "Impressions of Chicago: For Howlin' Wolf" by Quincy Troupe) or develop a thesis generated from topics and issues discussed in fiction, nonfiction, or poetry (e.g., arguing a thesis about the real significance of personal identity after reading "Becoming American Is a Constant Cultural Collision," an essay by T. T. Nhu; "Axolotl," a short story by

Julio Cortázar; "Queen Victoria and Me," a poem by Leonard Cohen; and "Fleur," a short story by Louise Erdrich). Modes are helpful in establishing recognizable patterns or by offering rhetorical strategies that might lend themselves to a successful analysis of your topic across the curriculum.

By asking yourself questions with a sound sense of audience and the ultimate purpose of your composition in mind, the modes can assist you in selecting the writing methods that will do the best job at achieving your objectives. Put yourself in the place of your reader and ask yourself questions about the essay's content. If you come up with questions that ask "why" something happens or results, you might answer the query by using causal analysis—the most natural method for explaining "why." Perhaps in going through a paper written for a science class, you question "why" burning objects radiate heat. Examining the cause–effect relationship between combustion and warmth would answer your question and provide your reader with important information. In another paper, sentences raising the question "how" might indicate the appropriateness of "process analysis" to explain how fake identification cards are made and distributed (explanatory process analysis). To address a topic or issue requiring evidence, factual data, or proof, you would make use of argumentation, asking yourself questions like "Are facts up to date?" and "Have I offered several representative, reliable examples?"

LOGICAL FALLACIES AND REVISION

A fallacy is an incorrectly or falsely reasoned fact. Since a fallacy is neither logical nor defensible, it can undermine an argument and alienate your audience. As you revise your work, review and assess argumentative points, eliminating logical fallacies and replacing them with solid evidence and sound reasoning. The following are some of the fallacies most likely to occur and weaken an argument.

Ad Hominem ("To the Person")   This fallacy shifts and distorts the focus of an argument by attacking the person who made it rather than arguing the issue at hand. In other words, a person guilty of *ad hominem* often spends time trying to convince readers that an opponent is disreputable rather than refute an argument.

False Dilemma (Either/Or Fallacy)   The false dilemma fallacy oversimplifies issues by assuming that there are only two alternatives in an argument. Thus, instead of exploring possibilities, readers are forced to choose between two extremes when other choices may exist.

Faulty Sampling   This fallacy occurs when you attempt to influence an audience by presenting them with misleading, unrepresentative statistics.

An argument asserting that ninety percent of United States citizens watch tabloid news shows for five hours a day, for instance, carries little weight if you based the statistics on ten responses received from individuals in the same geographical area. Make sure your examples are representative and samplings are broad enough to serve as evidence to support your argument.

Post Hoc/Ergo Propter Hoc   The Latin phrase literally translates as "It happened after this; therefore, it happened because of this." However, just because one event follows another does not produce a logical, valid cause–effect relationship. There is no true causal relationship expressed in a sentence like *Every time I wash my truck it rains.* Washing the truck did not cause rainfall to occur.

Stereotyping   Stereotypes weaken rather than strengthen an argument because they inaccurately represent people, places, and things. Base your arguments on verifiable examples rather than narrow prejudices and assumptions.

Hasty or Sweeping Generalizations   This fallacy in reasoning occurs when the gap between evidence and a conclusion becomes too great. To avoid hasty or sweeping generalizations, use qualifying words and phrases such as *usually, often, most, some, several,* and *many,* and avoid absolute phrases like "Nowadays, everybody owns color television sets." (Only one person who owns a black-and-white television set would invalidate your entire point.)

CONCRETE WORDS AND ACTIVE VERBS

After sharpening general or vague topic sentences by adding "focusing words," consider how concrete words and active verbs can strengthen your sentence structures. As a general rule, *concrete words* may stand by themselves and be understood because they are perceived through the five senses: touch, taste, sight, smell, and sound. For instance, we can touch, see, hear, and smell a dog; therefore, the word "dog" is concrete. On the other hand, the dog's *hunger* would be *abstract* since it is perceived only through its relationship with another word. Abstract words define ideas, concepts, and attitudes (love, hate, ethics, indifference, honesty, pride, and so on) and tend to be subjective in their interpretation. Using concrete words can keep your reader from wandering into a blur of information. Rather than say, "He left his *things* at the door because Ariadne didn't approve of that sort of thing," identify your vague words. An improved sentence might read: "He left his *buck knife and shotgun* at the door because Ariadne did not approve of *hunting.*" In the revised sentence, your reader definitely knows "things" referred to a buck knife and a shotgun, and "that sort of thing" referred to the act of "hunting." When guesswork is eliminated, there is less chance of being misunderstood or misinterpreted.

"Show" rather than "tell" your reader about a topic or an issue whenever possible; doing so will bring life into your writing. Replace *linking verbs* (particularly forms of *to be: is, are, was, were*) with *active verbs*. Linking verbs often just connect a subject (noun) with a quality (adjective). For instance, in the sentence *Anne is conscientious,* the verb *is* tells—but does not show—readers that a relationship between *Anne,* the subject, and *conscientious,* the object, exists. Without undermining the author's intention, the same information could have been conveyed by placing the adjective in front of Anne ("conscientious Anne"). Then, by adding an active verb, the author could show Anne's conscientious nature: *Conscientious Anne paid all her bills, wrote up a report, reread her literature homework, and studied for a philosophy exam before she went to sleep last night.* In fact, the revised sentence expresses Anne's conscientiousness so fully, the adjective *conscientious* prior to Anne's name is unnecessary.

Active verbs that show rather than tell can add a great deal to your writing. Note the difference between the following sentences with linking verbs which tell and the revised constructions which show:

TELLING:	Susan is a Grateful Dead fan.
SHOWING:	Susan attends every Grateful Dead concert in Oakland, owns all of their records/CDs, wears "deadhead" T-shirts, and sings Grateful Dead songs wherever she goes.
TELLING:	Sylvester was tired.
SHOWING:	Sylvester laboriously jumped onto the couch, curled into a ball, and slept for five hours without moving.

INCREASING COHERENCE: TRANSITIONS AND LINKING DEVICES

The first step towards increasing coherence in an essay is checking the organization of its parts: paragraph and sentence order. Do your paragraphs work together to promote a single, unified effect by supporting your thesis? Make a scratch outline of your most recent draft and then ask yourself how each discussion point contributes to your thesis. Eliminate paragraphs that relate to your topic but have no bearing on your thesis (e.g., a paragraph on pedigreed dogs in an essay arguing that large dogs make better pets than small dogs).

Reorganizing material is an important task while revising an essay. Begin by referring to your scratch outline once again, rearranging material as needed. Generally speaking, save your strongest evidence until the end of the paper. Doing so will allow you to build your case or analysis and avoid making the rest of your supporting evidence seem anticlimactic by comparison. The importance of organizing and reorganizing material in each draft you revise cannot be emphasized enough. Sometimes the simple lack of chronology—or the assumption your readers understand your intentions—is enough to throw them off track.

When you "revise" a piece of writing, you "re-visit" the work, "re-seeing" (re-*visioning*) it in a different light. Review your use of connecting words and add transitions and linking devices to clearly establish relationships between words, phrases, clauses, and entire paragraphs. In addition to smoothing out material as you move from one point to the next, effective transitions will also improve coherence in your writing since they offer special signals indicating relationships to your readers. The following is but a partial list of transitional expressions and linking words. (Some transitional expressions may signal more than one kind of relationship to a reader, depending on its context in a sentence or paragraph.)

Forms of Transitions

ADDITION:	First of all, secondly, third, finally, last of all, in addition, moreover, furthermore
SPATIAL:	Above, below, inside, outside, here, there, and beyond, behind, between, over, under
TIME:	First, second, third, then, next, after, as, before, while, during, now, finally, meanwhile, subsequently
CHANGE OF DIRECTION:	But, consequently, however, yet, in contrast, otherwise, still, on the contrary, on the other hand, nevertheless, nonetheless
CONCLUSION:	Therefore, consequently, thus, as a result, then, in summary, in conclusion, last of all, finally, in short
ILLUSTRATION:	For example, for instance, specifically, such as, as an illustration
EMPHASIS:	Furthermore, moreover, most of all, principally, especially, most importantly, especially significant

Adverbial conjunctions (sometimes referred to as conjunctive adverbs) function partly as adverbs and partly as joining words; as such, they make excellent transitional words.

The Most Common Adverbial Conjunctions

additionally	furthermore	nonetheless
consequently	however	regardless
eventually	moreover	subsequently
frequently	nevertheless	therefore

By their very nature, adverbial conjunctions are extremely strong joining words and are used to "lead-off" constructions, connecting ideas between separate sentences as well as the second clause in a compound sentence punctuated with a semicolon. Always follow adverbial conjunctions with a comma; precede them with a semicolon when you have two independent clauses.

EXAMPLE: The weather caster warned citizens of the approaching tropical storm; **nonetheless,** Dwaine parked his car in the street and left his car windows and the sun roof open.

SENTENCE VARIETY

Sentence revision might well begin with a review of basic sentence patterns (see the glossary for specific patterns). Such a review may "refresh" your memory about the many sentence structures available for conveying information. Of course, dependence on any one sentence pattern will limit rather than expand the possibilities of presenting your information in an effective, memorable fashion. In addition to reorganizing paragraphs to obtain coherence and unity, and mixing simple, compound, complex, and compound/complex patterns to achieve sentence variety, you can use several other devices to gain the same ends in revision.

Adverbial Sentence Openers

Adverbial openers provide a refreshing way to vary your sentence patterns. Whereas your adverbial opener might be one of the adverbial conjunctions discussed, you might also use adverbial phrases (an adverb and its modifiers) to begin a sentence.

EXAMPLE: *Reverently,* the child placed fresh flowers on his parents' graves.

EXAMPLE: *Very quietly,* James walked through the house in the early morning.

EXAMPLE: *Furthermore,* Mary did not need peer approval to give her the confidence to cultivate her talent.

Appositive Phrases

Appositive phrases present yet another method to add variety to your sentence structures. An appositive phrase consists of a noun or a pronoun used to rename another noun. You can use appositive phrases effectively at the beginning, in the middle, and at the end of sentences. Note how an appositive phrase can be lifted from a sentence without changing its general sense.

Appositive Openers

EXAMPLE: *A race horse*, Secretariat was the last "triple crown" winner.

Appositive within Sentences

EXAMPLE: Norma, *my Irish friend*, returned to Dublin after completing her college education in California.

Appositive Concluding Sentences

EXAMPLE: The Blackfords paid $300 for their new puppy, *a Dalmatian*.

Prepositional Phrases

A *preposition* plus a *noun* or a *pronoun* constitutes a prepositional phrase. When revising sentences in general, prepositional phrases offer a concrete method of clarifying information by expanding thoughts and adding details that answer the questions *who, what, when, where, why,* and *how.*

EXAMPLE: **On** top **of** *the kitchen cabinet*, Peter kept the stubs **to** *his paychecks* **in** *a round tin can.*

For sentence variety, open an occasional sentence with a prepositional phrase followed by a comma.

EXAMPLE: **Under** *the sink*, Carmen placed a mousetrap.

A Brief List of Prepositions Well Worth Remembering

aboard	around	between	except	of	toward
above	as	beyond	for	off	under
according to	at	but (except)	from	on	underneath
across	because of	by	in	out	until
after	before	concerning	in addition to	past	up
against	behind	contrary to	in place of	since	upon
along	below	despite	inside	through	with
along with	beneath	down	in spite of	throughout	within
amid	beside	due to	like	to	without
among	besides	during	near		

STRATEGIES: Revising the Essay

1. *Assess and rework* introductory paragraphs (lead-in sentences and the thesis statement).
2. *Reread* your creation; read it out loud to an audience if possible and *listen* to your word use.
3. *Practice reading* your work using the "reader's eye" rather than the all-knowing "writer's eye."
4. *Maintain paragraph "unity"* by making a point and sticking to its development.
5. *Logically organize* your material; work towards spatial and chronological coherence.
6. *Unify* your material; when you make a point, stick to developing it.
7. *Develop* general points with specific representative facts, details, examples, and reasoning.
8. *Increase "coherence"* by using transitions and linking words to clearly establish the intended relationship between words, phrases, sentences, and complete paragraphs.
9. *Use* rhetorical modes like comparison and contrast to assist you in exposing and explaining topics and issues to your readers.
10. *Ask* yourself journalistic questions like *who, what, when, where, why,* and *how* as you read through your work to locate sentences and paragraphs needing further explanation.
11. *Replace* vague nouns and passive verbs with concrete nouns and active verbs; allow your sentences to *show* rather than *tell.*
12. *Sharpen* the focus of vague or imprecise topic sentences to guide your reader clearly and effectively through your supporting paragraphs.
13. *Restate the essay title,* as needed, in order to capture the full essence of your paper with as few words as possible.
14. *Condense* and *combine* awkward, wordy sentences to add variety and interest to your constructions.
15. *Peer edit* a colleague's paper and vice-versa before returning to subsequent drafts; you might adapt the peer-editing exercise at the end of this chapter to any such activity.

Collaborative Reflections

Begin by exchanging your group's collaborative essay (Collaborative Reflections assignment for chapter 2) with another group's essay in class. Carefully proofread and edit your peer (group) essay, asking questions and suggesting places where additional details and development would make the essay more effective. Here are some of the areas you should consider:

1. *Content:* Do the authors thoroughly develop the essay's thesis?
2. *Structure:* Is your peers' essay clearly structured? Does it have a specific,

interesting introductory paragraph(s), well-developed body paragraphs, and a definite conclusion?

3. *Coherence:* Are your classmates' paragraphs unified and coherent? What would you suggest they should do to improve the relationship between essay parts?

4. *Evidence/Support:* What facts, statistics, and details do the authors of the collaborative essay offer? Are the authors' examples truly representative of the subject? How do the authors use concrete illustrations and logical reasoning in the essay?

5. *Sentence Constructions:* Check for illogical statements; unclear points; run-ons and comma splices; fragmentary thoughts; clichés and trite, worn-out phrases; and repetitive sentence structures.

On a separate piece of paper, write a one-page critique of your peers' collaborative essay in your group, noting its strengths and weaknesses. You might begin your critique by analyzing the effectiveness of the introductory and concluding paragraphs and make suggestions for improvement. If you liked a particular part of the essay—great! Do not forget to explain to your readers *what* you liked and *why* you liked it. Bringing positive points to the attention of authors can reinforce confidence in what writers *think* they do well and what readers *know* they do well. Finally, return the collaborative compositions to their authors. Then, participate in rewriting your own group's collaborative essay in view of the constructive criticism you received. Remember, as an author, you "write to be read," and each member of the class is a valid reader!

4

Editing for Precision and Style

By the time you reach the editing stage in the composition process, you will have written and revised your work countless times, and a good portion of it will be in final form. Your final editing will polish what you have written through *proofreading:* locating and correcting careless grammatical and punctuation errors which could affect coherence and understanding. Editing is also a time to polish your style.

Editing is not the same as composing or revising, so you should not attempt to edit and create, or to edit and revise simultaneously. True, it is ultimately important to punctuate your writing correctly and to restate awkward, grammatically incorrect sentence structures. If your words are imprecise or ungrammatical, it is quite likely that what you express will fall short of your intentions. Nonetheless, editing (a mechanical act) while writing and revising (creative and critical acts) can often result in convoluted sentences and writing blocks.

APPLIED GRAMMAR AND MECHANICS

The real importance of grammar and mechanics can be seen when applied to the writing process rather than studied independently of it. Certainly, a knowledge of the basic parts of speech, such as nouns, verbs, adjectives, adverbs, prepositions, articles, and conjunctions, can be helpful to writers, but becoming walking, talking dictionaries of grammatical terms or identifying word forms as parts of speech does not enable people to write. Identifying and applying are two different activities. As a writer yourself, you will be largely concerned with the latter, grammar as it applies to a composition, since the correct application of grammatical skills will help you to clearly and effectively convey ideas and information. Sentences like *Monica throw all her clothes into a washing machine and started it* create problems, so correcting faulty grammar to improve understanding is essential. A reader's first question might be, ''Did Monica put the clothes in the washing machine in the past or at this very moment?'' As the writer, you must make sure your time references are consistent. If your verb tense is in the past, then for agreement in tense (and coherent placement of events in time), you need to change *Monica throw* to *Monica threw.* If you want to place the sentence in the present tense, you will not only need to change *started* to *starts,* but also

Monica throw to *Monica throws* so that your subject (*Monica*) agrees with your verb (*throw*) in number.

Your interest in applied mechanics is similar to your interest in applied grammar: assistance in promoting clear written communication. When editing, locate sentences needing signals. A sentence like *Marlon a daredevil squeezed into his helmet hopped on his motorcycle kicked against the starting stick raced across the plateau and jumped over Snake Canyon* confuses readers because several things are happening in a progressive order, but there is no separation of activities. By adding a pair of commas to indicate an appositive phrase and a set of commas to divide the items in the series, the unclear sentence becomes coherent: *Marlon, a daredevil, squeezed into his helmet, hopped on his motorcycle, kicked against the starting stick, raced across the plateau, and jumped over Snake Canyon.* (A brief overview of punctuation marks you are likely to apply to your writings appears under "Effective Punctuation.")

EFFECTIVE WORD CHOICE: DENOTATION, CONNOTATION, AND TONE

The tone of a written work usually indicates an author's attitude towards the subject or the audience and is reflected through the words the writer selects. Here is where precise use of language becomes so important; similar words may carry quite different associations, sometimes marked positive and at other times negative. The word *defendant* presents an excellent example of this. Any person arrested and indicted for a crime in a court of law in the United States is referred to as *the defendant,* rather than *the accused* because *the accused* has negative—suggestive—connotations. The word *defendant* is a more neutral term which presumes innocence until proven otherwise. The news media, by contrast, will use words like *the accused,* constantly reminding its audience of the supposed crime because it is less interested in a fair, impartial reference to a person than offering its readers or viewers a "good story." Imagine the effects of word choices on your audience when you write. Calculate reader response. All in all, you want your readers to infer neither more nor less than you intend from your words. Thus, to polish your diction during the editing stage of writing, building a sensitivity to the denotative and connotative meanings of words, becomes essential.

The denotation of a word is the most literal, dictionary meaning of the word, understood without emotional influences or associations. The connotations of a word are people, places, meanings, and implications we have come to associate with a particular word that extend beyond its literal definition. Whereas the definition of a *jalopy* would be a car, a *jalopy* suggests a particular kind of car: a piece of junk. The noun *college* is defined as an institution of higher education, yet it also carries the emotional associations of stress, hard work, expense, and prestige.

A sensitivity toward the denotation and connotation of words goes beyond "political correctness." As you edit your final draft, take out any discriminatory language, particularly language carrying negative connotations about someone's sex, race, or age. For instance, to avoid implying an exclusion of women in the workplace, political arena, or social ladder, use "chair" in place of "chair*man*," "synthetic" instead of "*man*made," and "human beings" or "people" rather than "*man*kind." To avoid masculine pronoun references (*The artist becomes concerned when nobody attends **his** exhibitions*), recast your sentences using the plural form of the pronoun and its antecedent (***Artists** become concerned when nobody attends **their** exhibitions*). Show respect for your readers—do not insult them! What you want in clear communication is accurate word choice and fair representation; what you want in memorable writing is style!

EFFECTIVE PUNCTUATION

Punctuation marks offer readers important signals, promoting the clear comprehension of your material. **Periods** indicate the completion of one thought and the beginning of another: *Al never questioned why he was fired. He just cleaned out his desk and walked out the door.* **Commas** (1) separate items in a series: *The dogs, goats, pigs, and chickens ran across the barnyard when I stepped out of my truck;* (2) introduce quotations: *As Lin-chi once said, "In Buddhism there is no place for using effort";* (3) separate two independent clauses when followed by one of the seven coordinating conjunctions: *Alex quit college, and he began his career at Pacific Valley Bank;* (4) separate everyday material (dates, cities and states): *On October 4, 1995, Glenda drove to Fort Worth, Texas;* (5) set off sentence openers: *After work, Jackson dropped by a tavern to watch a ballgame;* or (6) punctuate sentence interrupters (commas here are used as a pair): *Brad, my auto mechanic, always gives me a discount when he tunes-up my car.* **Semicolons** (1) separate two complete sentences: *The moon was full; therefore, we stayed up most of the night telling werewolf stories* or (2) separate items in a series when there are commas within individual items: *Pat has lived in San Jose, California; Jacksonville, Florida; and Las Vegas, Nevada.* **Colons** indicate "this follows": *I have two sisters: Deborah and Colleen.* **Exclamation points** indicate emphasis: *Fred had never met anyone so mean!* **Question marks** are used after inquiries—questions, rhetorical and otherwise: *Why are we even arguing?* An **ellipsis** signals the omission of words or word groups: *"Baptism by blood, water, or desire . . . is necessary for salvation."*

STYLE

Diction and Syntax

Style, the way you arrange your material and express your ideas, might also be explained as the relationship between subject matter and the form it takes.

What makes one person's style stiff and boring and another person's style fluid, vivid, and engrossing? Choices—choices of words, sentences, paragraph length, punctuation—anything to move an essay forward and arrive at a definite destination. "Good" and "bad" are relative terms regarding style; the real question is, "What works, what doesn't work, and why?" Style is the intricate connection of words and word groups. What might you deduce about John's "style" from the following short excerpt?

> The creature had thin fleshy pieces of skin for lips which barely covered its massive teeth from which the putrid stench of carnivorous breath spewed forth and made me gag.

Although John's sentence has a "definite style," is it one that you or anyone else would really want to emulate? Probably not. **Style is more than a flamboyant or pretentious display of vocabulary; style is rhetorical and works to further an effect or reach a response.** John seems to exert little control over his subject. On the contrary, John's subject matter—a creature—seems to dictate *what* he will write about (descriptive details) and *how* (stacking adjectives and adverbs, and modifying words in general). As a result, he becomes a slave to his style rather than directing it, and the potential rhetorical boost his style might have given his writing is nonexistent. Use your rhetorical tools! Make them work for you!

Punctuation

Punctuation also lends itself to stylistic application and effective presentation of phrases, clauses, and sentences. A well-placed dash in place of a comma, for instance, can draw attention to a specific person, place, thing, or point quite effectively.

COMMA TO DASH:	Last year, the Johnsons finally bought their first house for $412,000, a lot of money by anyone's standards.
	Last year, the Johnsons finally bought their first house for $412,000—a lot of money by anyone's standards.
PERIOD TO SEMICOLON:	Nothing happens without a reason. My past made me the way I am.
	Nothing happens without a reason; my past made me the way I am.

Like John's overuse of descriptive words in the "creature" sentence, excessive use of any punctuation mark (outside of periods and necessary indication of dialogue and questions) can diminish its rhetorical effectiveness. Thus, avoid the temptation to use a dash in every other sentence. Also, use exclamation marks, semicolons, and semicolons followed by adverbial conjunctions sparingly. Finally, if your sentence calls for a question mark—fine. However, do not fall into the following writer's habit of piggy-backing punctuation marks in hopes of capturing multiple effects: *Considering all the work I did for her, why shouldn't I be upset when Maria refused to invite me to her party??????!!!!!!!!* For one thing, more than one end punctuation mark of any sort does not make your information more emphatic. Multiple punctuation marks—five periods, four question marks, or fourteen exclamation points—serve no purpose; everything they signal can be conveyed with a single punctuation mark. Placing an exclamation mark after another type of end punctuation (a period, a question mark) is also superfluous. Make a decision. What do you want to do? Indicate a question? Emphasize a point? Call attention to the end of one complete thought and the start of another?

FIGURATIVE LANGUAGE AND STYLE

To convey a point dramatically and express the content of your writing distinctively, you may choose to employ figurative language. Why figurative language? Figurative language may enable any reader to picture an abstract quality or situation more easily. "Love," for instance, is a rather difficult concept to *literally* describe to another. If someone has never known the pleasure of love, the meaning of the term will be elusive. With the assistance of figurative language such as metaphors and similes, however, writers can attempt to convey what love "is" or what love "is like." Both metaphors and similes creatively express connections or similarities between unlike things. However, metaphors state comparisons directly whereas similes make comparisons and establish connections with the use of "like" or "as." By using a metaphor, you could figuratively explain what love *is*: "Love is a priceless jewel." In contrast, by writing a simile, you communicate what love *is like*: "Love is *like* a priceless jewel." The description of a topic or an issue—figuratively or literally—may be essential to accomplishing the goal of an essay. The ability of figurative language to convey abstract concepts, therefore, will be a valuable tool in your writing; it increases the possibilities of connecting with your audience accurately and effectively.

Clichés and Dead Metaphors

A cliché might be described as a trite, worn-out expression or a "dead metaphor" that either becomes a stereotype or is meaningless in its original context. The phrases "dumber than a doorbell," "clumsy as an ox," or "happy as a lark" are neither fresh nor imaginative ways of expressing one's self. Instead, overuse has *conventionalized* such phrases, and the images such phrases might once have vividly conveyed are lost on individuals in modern society—many of whom have never seen an ox (and therefore do not relate to its clumsy nature) or have never distinguished the songs of wild birds outside (and therefore cannot relate happiness to the song of the lark). In the initial stages of writing, you may capture a particular thought by resorting to a cliché or dead metaphor; however, as you move through successive stages of revision and editing, you will want to replace clichéd responses with language that is fresh and thought provoking.

Slang and Jargon

As mentioned earlier, the occasion, purpose, and audience you write for plays a major role in determining the accuracy and appropriateness of your vocabulary. Since new words or a specialized use of old words—slang and jargon—constantly find their way into the English language, however, precise word selection is not always easy. Generally, unless you are writing for a narrowly defined audience who use and understand your terms, avoid slang and technical jargon.

Slang differs from other colloquial (casual, common) language because it carries a sense of group identification. Individuals indicate that they belong to a particular social, economic, or occupational group by using its slang. The trendy nature of slang, however, definitely affects its enduring usefulness in formal writing. For the most part, slang expressions become overused and often experience perpetual transformation. Indeed, an audience familiar to one slang expression may not recognize it in an altered form. The expression "chill out" evolved from the earlier colloquialism "cool off" (relax, get your anger under control), and "chill" eventually replaced "chill out." Similarly, the slang "hangin'" (stay around) developed from "hanging out," only to be superseded by "hang." Many people who read and write English simply do not keep up with trendy or regional slang. Ten years from now would you still know what an author meant by *Lisa had a "wet"* (Lisa had a drink) or *Phil wanted to "fig up" his horse* (Phil wanted to use artificial means to liven up his horse)? Probably not. Therefore, in order to reach a wide audience in formal compositions, substitute slang with the word it originally replaced. Doing so will promote clarity and effectiveness in your prose.

In many discussions today, technical or scientific jargon is appropriate—if not essential. However, unnecessary jargon becomes ludicrous in its application, especially when comprehension requires readers to translate your meaning from its standard context. The clause *We are golden* (ready to go) makes perfect sense if talking about software, but it has limited use in formal writing or colloquial speech. Jargon such as *Let's double-click on that* (open up an issue for examination and discussion) creates amusement on the one hand and confusion on the other. Not everyone is familiar with Macintosh or Windows from which the term originated. Instead of writing *Before he interfaced with his brother, Greg "booted up" with a cup of Java*, be direct; say what you mean (i.e., *Before he talked to his brother, Greg drank a cup of coffee*).

In addition to avoiding slang and jargon, try not to clutter your papers with pretentious, pompous words. Though you may associate long words with sophistication, they often muddle your material and distract or alienate readers. Sentences like *The fortuitous marriage gave citizens an opportunity to perambulate around the Governor's mansion and to momentarily forget the social inequities of inner-city stratification* exemplify this point. Certainly, large words serve important functions in communication, but if usage muddles and obscures information, they lose their practical purpose and rhetorical effectiveness. Overall, it is well worth your time to go back through your essays and eliminate imprecise diction—including slang and jargon—to ensure clarity, advance your purpose for writing, demonstrate a sensitivity towards your audience, and present an unmistakable understanding of your topic.

The division between editing and revising is not always as sharp or distinct as writing instructors would like; overlapping definitely exists. When you "re-visit" your writing during the editing stage of the writing process, however, it is hard to overlook that you are engaged in a more linear, mechanical process than revision. The word *proofread*, which is often synonymous with *revision*, suggests "clean-up" or "correct" rather than "create anew." A way to remember the differences between revision and editing would be to note their respective interests in grammar and rhetoric. *Revision* is concerned with the rhetorical effectiveness of sentences (how something is expressed), whereas *editing* is focused on the grammatical correctness of constructions (when sentence punctuation and grammar conform to established conventions of usage).

STRATEGIES: Editing the Essay

1. *Fine-tune* your diction (word choice); consider the denotation and connotation of words and their contribution to the "tone" of a composition.
2. *Replace* clichés with fresh, original expressions.
3. *Proofread, locate, and correct grammatical errors* which muddle thoughts and confuse the reader: subject–verb agreement, pronoun agreement in person and number, consistent verb tense, prepositions (faulty use or lack thereof), articles, adjectives, and adverbs.
4. *Consider* the stylistic advantages one punctuation mark may have over another on occasion—perhaps a dash instead of a comma.
5. *Proofread, locate, and correct mechanical errors* which obscure meaning: faulty or omitted commas, hyphens, dashes, end punctuation (periods, exclamation points, question marks), apostrophes, semicolons, quotation marks, colons, and so on.
6. *Eliminate* sexist or racist language.
7. *Omit* wordiness; often, words like *which* and *that* clutter more than clarify sentences.

8. *Incorporate* figurative language, especially metaphors and similes, into your writing for variety and style.

Collaborative Reflections

Gather in small groups and discuss what elements contribute to the "tone" of a piece of writing. Share each other's understanding on how authors create a mood and reflect their attitudes towards their subject matter. You might select an essay written by a classmate or one of the professional authors in *Thresholds*. Read the essay chosen by your group out loud, identifying as

---

Checklist for Your Final Draft

1. Does your essay title succinctly capture the essence of your thesis and point of your essay?
2. Has your thesis been clearly identified and sufficiently limited? Does your introductory paragraph begin with "lead-in" sentences and end with your thesis statement?
3. Have you organized your paragraphs in a logical, coherent fashion? Does one major discussion point lead to the next, and do they all back up your thesis?
4. Do you support your thesis with a wide variety of representative examples? Are argumentative points well reasoned?
5. Have you read your work out loud, singled out careless spelling and punctuation errors, and corrected them?
6. Have you located and corrected comma splices, run-ons, and fragmentary thoughts?
7. Have you checked your end punctuation marks? Did you use exclamation points and question marks sparingly in order to maintain their rhetorical effectiveness?
8. Do your pronouns agree in number and person to maintain clarity and coherence?
9. Do your verbs agree in number and tense?
10. Have you eliminated any sexist or racist language from your work?
11. Have you polished your diction? Do your words express exactly what you intend?
12. Does your final paragraph draw your essay to a natural and satisfying conclusion?

---

many instances of slang, jargon, or clichés as you can find. Discuss the effect of jargon and slang in a serious composition, considering the denotations and connotations of words and their currency. In what ways do they strengthen or weaken your assertions? Why? Next, evaluate how grammar and punctuation lend themselves to the writer's sense of style. Lastly, share your group findings in a short forum on "editing, diction, and style" during class.

Revised and Edited Student Essay: Final Draft
"Disparity and the Wild Woman Archetype"

Before Robin Fadden wrote the final draft of her essay, she used a modified form of the revision and editing strategies and techniques outlined in chapters 3 and 4. For one, she set her paper aside for a while to distance herself from it. This way she would approach it freshly, as her readers eventually would. Then, she read her paper silently *and* out loud, from the last sentence to the first, and then the first sentence to the last, locating phrases, clauses, and entire paragraphs which would benefit from further work. She also annotated sections of her paper where additional development and analysis could strengthen her examples. To get feedback prior to her final revision of sentences and paragraphs, she had a colleague edit her paper, using many of the peer-editing techniques discussed in "Collaborative Reflections" on the preceding page. By comparing Robin's final paper to her initial draft (pp. 54–57), you will be able to identify several of her major and minor revisions.

The Thesis Paragraph   Fadden began her revision of "The Wild Woman Archetype" by narrowing the scope of the essay's title. She settled on "Disparity and the Wild Woman Archetype," since it more precisely summarized the focus of her essay than her broad working title. Next, after considering a peer's comment that the relationship between the essay title and "disobedient women" lacked clarity, Fadden turned her attention to her thesis and sharpened it by following "disobedient women" with an appositive phrase, *Wild Woman Archetype* (the key focusing word of her essay).

Supporting Paragraphs   After revising the topic sentences in paragraphs 2, 3, 6, and 9 for accuracy and clarity, she proceeded to clarify supporting details, eliminate wordiness, and rearrange syntax throughout her essay. In paragraph 3, she inserted quotations to serve as examples and reference points for further exposition, and she added transitional expressions to establish clear relationships between words, clauses, and entire paragraphs. Robin improved paragraph 4 by expanding her analysis, explaining Eve as the Wild Woman Archetype. Since there seemed to be a gap between her discussion of Eve and Maxine Hong Kingston's aunt—the original focus of paragraph 5—Robin decided to add another supporting paragraph. This paragraph discussed the Wild Woman and spirituality, using the speaker in "The Woods," a poem by Louise Erdrich, as a bridge between the other two discussion points. She then divided paragraph 6 dealing with Kingston's aunt into two separate paragraphs, expanding the second paragraph about her (paragraph 7), adding more details, evidence, analysis, and support. Although she was happy with the content in paragraph 8, she decided to prune unnecessarily wordy sentences and improve coherence by inserting transitions and linking devices between words and phrases. With the exception of her first two sentences, which she rewrote, she also felt the structure of paragraph 9 was pretty good; therefore, she did not spend a lot of time "fixing something that was not broken."

Concluding Paragraph Since her objective here was to relate major issues discussed and to put them into perspective with the essay's thesis, she began by replacing her general reference to "all these women" with a specific reference to "Eve, the speaker in 'The Woods,' Kingston's aunt, and Tita." Then she added some expository comments. Finally, Robin rounded off her concluding paragraph with a quotation—a quotation echoing the controlling idea of her thesis.

Fadden 1

Robin Fadden
Professor Burns
English 1A
24 Sept. 1996

Disparity and the Wild Woman Archetype

Over the years, it would seem that a disparity has been created between how a woman perceives herself and how her society perceives her. This disparity is the rift that separates women from the outward persona they feel obligated to convey and the inner self which they have historically felt ashamed to show. But why have women been ashamed of displaying their true nature? Ironically, the answer may lie in the many examples of the

Lead-in sentences move to a rhetorical question and thesis

*Point #1:
definition
of terms,
reasoning,
and
analysis
(Estés)*

disobedient women, the "Wild Woman Archetypes," who have been used to admonish the reluctant into submission.

The more a woman focused on her inner identity, the more her inability to fit comfortably into the restrictive patriarchy—which previously held autonomous rule over her—seemed to become problematic. Because she was able to connect with what is most essentially "woman," Pinkola Estés' work, Women Who Run with the Wolves, as the "Wild Woman Archetype," the historical "woman in progress" was seen as a threat to society. She was labeled "disobedient" because this would reinforce the idea that she needed to be punished for trying to disrupt the societal norms the Wild Woman nature displaces. While these "disobedient women" were to be made the examples of conduct that was not acceptable to the rest of the established society, they also, somewhat ironically, served as the largely misunderstood testimony to the importance of keeping the essential spirit of the "essential woman" intact and unstoppable.

*Point #2:
further
definition
of terms,
reasoning,
analysis*

These "disobedient women" reinforce the idea that, wherever the spirit of this Wild Woman is being restricted or enslaved, women must strike out at the enemy that attacks them and protect themselves from becoming a forgotten myth. When this Woman could not be contained within the context of her restrictive society, she was punished under the pretext of "reestablishing order." However, the Wild Woman's actions were determined by a much more necessary motivation—the need for self-preservation. What prompted these women to abandon the safety of the monotony of their narrow existences? Invariably, they must have felt the need to protect their almost extinct inner nature. Their disobedience was, therefore, not only defiance, but also the conservation of their identity. It was the fight to preserve the Wild Woman in them all.

In the story of the Fall of Man, from Genesis, Eve is punished for eating from the tree of knowledge, therefore causing the original sin. It is interesting that, upon closer analysis, Eve can be blamed for no more than wanting the knowledge of good and evil. To the Wild Woman, a life of ignorance would be nothing more than a pleasant euphemism for a life of sterility. To her, it would have been the same if Eve had never been created. Eve, therefore, strikes out at the obstacle which separates her from understanding her true self and eats the fruit. To the patriarchy of the Christian church, her act has been interpreted as being one of willful sin. However, as seen through the eyes of the Wild Woman, Eve is merely acting out of self-preservation. Eve has ultimately gained far more than she has lost when one compares the outcomes of a life of self-negation and ignorance in the Garden of Eden to her ultimate knowledge of her true self, which satisfies a far more basic need than any physical fulfillment could offer. Her disobedience is what has allowed the first "essential woman" to survive.

First extended supporting example of a Wild Woman Archetype drawn from a written work; reasoning, and analysis (Bible)

In "The Woods," a poem by Louise Erdrich, ideas similar to Eve's self-preservation are apparent in the actions of the poem's speaker. As she says in the first two lines of the poem, "At one time your touches were clothing enough/within these trees now I am different" (23). She had to choose between continuing to honor established—albeit unfair—social practices and her own spiritual growth and selects the latter. She refuses to conform to the shallowness of a corporeal existence. Indeed, she has spiritual justifications for her actions, and when she asks for him to "come," and "surrounds him," she explains that he too will soon know "the loneliness" that he taught her with his own "body" (23). The Wild Woman recognizes the importance of retaining some sense of spirituality, for that is what gives the soul

Second extended example of a Wild Woman Archetype drawn from a written work; reasoning, analysis, and details (Erdrich)

meaning. Because the speaker in "The Woods" feels a stronger spiritual obligation to uphold than one of compliance with an unjust law and stifling social practice, she disobeys and ignores her significant other, on the one hand, losing him and the lifestyle she knew, but on the other, ensuring him that her identity remains intact. She can feel confident that her eternal soul will not be damned for sublimating her duty to her self to that of her former self. Her fight takes on the role of being one of spiritual self-preservation instead of merely physical self-preservation. The speaker has higher priorities than her lover; in her own words, he is still "hunting some creature like the woman I was." Understandably, she has gladly given up the life of "some creature" to ensure the longevity of her soul.

Third extended example of a Wild Woman Archetype drawn from a written work; reasoning, and analysis (Kingston)

In Maxine Hong Kingston's novel The Woman Warrior, Kingston also writes about protecting one's identity in the chapter called "No Name Woman." In it, she tells the story of her aunt who, after having an illegitimate daughter, is ostracized by her family. After having her farm totally destroyed by a mob of villagers as punishment for her "extravagance," she finally kills herself and her daughter as a kind of last hope of retaining some kind of dignity. Interestingly enough, she chooses to commit suicide by drowning herself in the family's well, therefore polluting their only supply of drinking water. Although part of her punishment was to be totally ignored by her family, she does manage to paradoxically achieve some kind of lasting memory in a precautionary tale told to the author by her mother to dissuade her from similar behavior. It would seem that, although she was severely punished by her family and her society, Kingston's aunt still manages to retain some sense of inner identity, even in her death. By choosing to pollute her family's well, she takes a last stab at their superiority, reinforcing her disobedience, but she also reinforces her inability to totally submit to their unfair values and mores.

Kingston's aunt retains some of the Wild Woman spirit by choosing to retain some dignity by killing herself (suicide has traditionally been seen as more honorable in Asian cultures than in Western society) rather than having to endure the continued punishment she, and her daughter, would have to face if they were to have lived. She subconsciously asserts that she respects herself and her daughter too much to allow themselves to be tortured by her village's traditions. Somewhat like Erdrich's speaker in "The Woods," she retains some kind of spiritual inner dignity even though she will become an outcast, even among the spirits of the dead. However, she will be an outcast that is not ashamed of herself because she was never contrary to her inner identity. Her only crime will be that she was a victim of circumstance. She becomes the family's taboo, the unspoken spirit of the Wild Woman.

Expanded analysis of Kingston, her aunt, and the Wild Woman Archetype; details and analysis

The character of Tita in Laura Esquivel's novel <u>Like Water for Chocolate</u> also experiences being branded as the "disobedient woman" for wanting to preserve her own identity. From the moment she was born, she was destined to never marry, so that, as the youngest daughter of her family, she would carry on the tradition of being the one to take care of her mother until her mother's death. However, Tita does not agree with the tradition she had been forced into.

Fourth extended example of a Wild Woman Archetype (Esquivel)

> Tita lowered her head, and the realization of her fate struck her as forcibly as her tears struck the table. . . . Still Tita did not submit. . . . For one thing, she wanted to know who started this family tradition. It would be nice if she could let that genius know about one little flaw in this perfect plan for taking care of women in their old age. If Tita couldn't marry and have children, who would take care of her when she got old? (Esquivel 11)

Reasoning, analysis, and details

Much of the rest of Tita's life is spent in forced compliance with her mother's wishes. Every day she would have to endure the suffering of watching the man she loved marry her sister, doing so simply so he could remain close to Tita, and the tyrannical rule of her mother. One day, Tita finally snaps under the years of repressed anger and frustration she has held inside. The death of her nephew sparks a terrible fight between Tita and her mother; Tita blames her mother for causing the death of the child whom she had raised as her own.

> Tita felt a violent agitation take possession of her being. . . . "Here's what I do with your orders! I'm sick of them! I'm sick of obeying you! . . . You killed Roberto!" (Esquivel 99)

Closing discussion; necessary disobedient acts; analysis and reflection

Finally, Tita had broken the tradition which had victimized her for so long. Because she could no longer stand to ignore her individuality, it became necessary for her to disobey her mother. For her punishment, she is forced to leave the ranch and fend for herself. Ironically, this is exactly what Tita wants. Now she has the freedom to experience her true individuality. She can allow herself to grow and mature without the limitations of her mother's irrational traditions. She finally can allow herself to focus on her inner identity, and she begins the search for her own true nature. Her disobedience was necessary if she was to save any aspect of her true self. She was conserving the spirit of the Wild Woman which would not let her be resigned to a fate of servitude.

All these women, Eve, the speaker in Erdrich's poem, Kingston's aunt, and Tita, are linked by more than just their common gender. They all share the ability to connect with the essence of womanhood in some way. For finding and preserving their inner identities, they were branded as "disobedient." They were considered outcasts, or threats to the stability of some preestablished order they could never agree with. While they all differ in their attempts to retain some aspect of their inner personality that has been threatened, all these women manage to reassert the tenacity of the Wild Woman Archetype. They continue the pattern of behavior that marks their inner focus. They are all, in some way, unable to coexist with the societal rules the archetype displaces, and therefore, must be punished if the society with which they disagree is to retain its strict sense of order. However, regardless of time or space, these women show that the Wild Woman still exists; she must if women are to retain their unique individuality and sense of inner peace. These women are a part of a heritage in search of the inner sanctity only the Wild Woman can offer. They are a testimony to her own eternal longevity, which lives in every one of these misunderstood martyrs. As Clarissa Pinkola Estés once wrote:

> We are all filled with a longing for the wild. There are few culturally sanctioned antidotes for this yearning. We were taught to feel shame for such a desire. We grew our hair long and used it to hide our feelings. But the shadow of Wild Woman still lurks behind us during our days and in our nights. No matter where we are, the shadow that trots behind us is definitely four-footed. (Estés xiii)

Concluding paragraph; discussion points are placed back into focus with Robin's thesis

End quote echoes thesis

Works Cited

Erdrich, Louise. "The Woods." <u>Jacklight</u>. New York:
Henry Holt, 1984.

Esquivel, Laura. <u>Like Water for Chocolate</u>. Trans.
Carol Christensen and Thomas Christensen.
New York: Doubleday, 1992.

Estés, Clarissa Pinkola. <u>Women Who Run with the
Wolves: Myths and Stories of the Wild Woman
Archetype</u>. New York: Ballantine, 1992.

Kingston, Maxine Hong. "No Name Woman." <u>The
Woman Warrior</u>. New York: Knopf, 1975.

PART II

Thematic Readings: Essays, Fiction, and Poetry

5

Identity

Do not resemble me—
Never be like a musk melon
Cut in two identical halves
MATSUO BASHO

Essays

Fiction

Poetry

Creating an identity can be a matter of distinguishing yourself from the movement of the masses, and yet it is much more than that. The simple word *identity* suggests all sorts of relationships and possibilities. An identity might be an individual's sense of belonging or a group's sense of being. When you identify with social values, political preferences, or religious beliefs, you share concerns with others. In Leonard Cohen's poem "Queen Victoria and Me," for instance, he is not actually writing a love poem to Queen Victoria (Queen of England from 1837 until her death in 1901). Instead, his invocations to her are those of a kindred soul; the two of them share something in common: "an incomparable sense of loss" with respect to their loved ones. Prince Albert, Queen Victoria's husband, died very young, and Cohen's lover has left him.

Identity might be linked to one's vocation: dentistry, sales, engineering, education (teaching), aviation, gardening. Identity could result from what one does: lead a nation, play music, build clocks, sail boats, raise thoroughbred horses, or play professional sports, but, as Ellen Goodman points out in "A Working Community," this focus could also have its drawbacks when vocation eclipses other parts of your personality.

Developing your personal identity and recognizing your heritage cannot help but create conflicts. As Basho states in his haiku poem, a person should strive to attain personal identity, a sense of self, rather than being like a musk melon "Cut in two identical halves." Again, if you take Basho's advice and do not spend your life trying to "resemble" others (friends or family) in mind and spirit, you could eliminate a lot of problems. In real life, however, as T. T. Nhu illustrates in "Becoming American Is a Constant Cultural Collision," the evolving sphere of a personal identity and career (becoming American) tends to exclude many values held by traditional Vietnamese families. Unfortunately, Mai's parents force her to choose between the two value systems.

Sometimes identities go through a metamorphosis, and distinctions between characters become difficult to distinguish. Julio Cortázar's story "Axolotl" exemplifies such a metamorphosis. Here the character himself takes on the traits of the axolotl in the aquarium and presents readers with an interesting shift in point of view. The piece brings to life the notion that "we know who we are but not what we may become." In the twentieth century, subconscious or unconscious energies have been frequently used by psychologists like Dr. Carl Jung to identify personal and universal archetypes leading to self-discovery. Nikki Giovanni's poem "Ego Tripping," for instance, presents her sense of personal consciousness as the universe personified as a human, a timeless being enriched through an identification with significant people and places from the past.

The theme of identity takes many twists and turns, some anticipated, some unexpected. In the search for one's identity, questions like "Who am I?" and "What am I?" often lead to a fully realized sense of self. Recognition as a unique individual is frequently crucial to identity. This need is why many people resent the fact that they seem to mean nothing more than a number in modern society. In Maxine Hong Kingston's "No Name Woman," she writes about her aunt who lost all sense of recognition from her family. Kingston's writing about her aunt creates the first link between aunt and family for decades, and yet the outstretched hand may be as much a curse to Kingston as a blessing to her aunt because she's "telling" everyone about her aunt's "spite" drowning.

Sargeant does not question who he is in Langston Hughes' short story "On the Road," but he is tired of being denied the status of a human being; he is fed up with hypocrisy of those individuals who should open rather than close doors on fellow human beings. In contrast, Sandra Cisneros is going through a period of change in "The Monkey Garden" and is reassessing her sense of "self" as she comes to the realization that people and priorities change. In a search for self, she is no longer interested in answering the question "Who am I?" but, rather, "What have I become?"

RHETORIC AT WORK

The search for identity invites discovery. In a similar fashion, the ongoing quest for word recognition and vocabulary development leads to new understanding—a discovery of sorts. At this time, begin a personal vocabulary

---

A Checklist for Writing about *Identity*

1. Who or what am I writing about? Is the nature of my essay self-discovery? Would a narrative provide the best format for expressing my material? Why? Why not?
2. What am I trying to illustrate? Am I attempting to explain how something or someone came to be?
3. If I am searching for my own identity in an exploratory essay, what is my starting point? How do I perceive my "self"? At what point do I question, "Who am I?" Where do I show my recognition and acceptance of my new identity?
4. What concrete details demonstrate my topic best? Am I discussing an identity crisis? If so, what sort of diction did I select to infer a troubled mind?
5. Did I examine the cause–effect relationship between my immediate environment and my ultimate identity? What did I conclude? Why?
6. How did my use of transitions and linking devices lead readers through my transformation in character or identity?

list consisting of unfamiliar words that come up in the following essays. In addition to looking up the definitions for words on your vocabulary list, note why you think the author selected the word to begin with. (Keep up this vocabulary log throughout the course.)

❋

Becoming American Is a Constant Cultural Collision

T. T. Nhu

Born in Hue, Vietnam, in 1947, Tran Tuong Nhu (also known as Nhu) grew up in Europe, Asia, and the United States and speaks French, Vietnamese, and English. After graduating from the Dalton School, she completed undergraduate and graduate studies at the University of California at Berkeley in Anthropology and Asian Studies. She then won enough money on *Jeopardy* to make a trip around the world before returning to live and work in Vietnam. During the Vietnam War, Nhu became a social worker and worked for NBC News. She was the principal researcher of the documentary *Sins of the Father*, which depicted the plight of "Amerasian" children abandoned by GI's, and distinguished herself in 1981 by winning the *San Francisco Examiner*'s Investigative Reporting Prize for the best three-part series: *Vietnam by the Bay*. A former editor for American Friends Service Committee and Lancaster-Miller Publishers, Nhu has also written for the *San Francisco Chronicle, Cuisine, Parenting, West, Image,* and the *Civil Rights Digest*. Since 1987, Nhu has been writing for the *San Jose Mercury News*. Originally a member of the Editorial Board, she is now a Living columnist and writes on a wide range of subjects, especially about changing communities and mores in California. The following essay first appeared in the *San Jose Mercury News* on Friday, May 19, 1989, and it explains Mai's conflict when she was forced to choose between two value systems: the one of her parents and the one of her adopted country.

1   **M**ai Nguyen's graduation from college was the worst day of her life. Mai, a straight-A student in high school in Milpitas and an honors graduate in math from UC–Berkeley, had expected congratulations, flowers and love from her parents. Instead, she was disowned.

2   It started when she announced that she was planning to continue working at a public policy institute on campus where she had been a statistical re-

searcher. She was going to move into an apartment with two girlfriends while figuring out what to do next.

3   Her parents refused vehemently. They said they had tolerated her four years away because it was necessary for her to acquire a degree from a prestigious university, but now it was time for her to come home. Like many traditional Vietnamese families, they expected their children to live at home until married, except for time out for school. If she insisted on taking her own apartment and living independently, she would be on her own—permanently.

4   The day ended in tears and recrimination. Mai was devastated because her decision to cut loose had resulted in her life being broken in two.

5   "I was always taught to obey my parents, no matter what happens. They wanted me to become an American, learn perfect English and do well in school. After I learned to be an American, they took it all back and wanted me to be Vietnamese again. I sort of knew that they wanted me to stay Vietnamese, but academically and professionally, they wanted me to be more American than American."

6   Mai has Asian friends—the children of immigrants—who are also in her situation. They are rebelling against an older generation and asserting themselves with newly acquired attitudes which emphasize individual rather than traditional collective concerns.

7   "My friends and I compare our families with the families of our American friends and we ask: 'Why do we have to obey everything you say? You know, sometimes, you could be wrong.' "

8   By American standards, Mai's desire to live on her own is reasonably normal. From the perspective of an immigrant family, it is not only unfilial and heretical, but so . . . so American.

9   Compared with other Vietnamese, Mai sees herself between two extremes. "I'm pretty much in the middle," she said.

10   "I'm more Vietnamese than half of them and more American than the other half. I know some people who have become so completely American they barely understand Vietnamese. Except for food, they reject everything about Vietnam, as if they have left it all behind. Then there are others who are just Vietnamese-Vietnamese. They hang around only Vietnamese, at school, in cafés and clubs. They listen to Vietnamese music, read only Vietnamese books and newspapers."

11   Mai decided to go it alone although it meant that she would not be part of her family, and by extension her society, anymore. It has been three years since her parents forbade her to come home.

12   When she wants to see her beloved little grandmother, she has to sneak in the house while her parents are out. Although her grandmother misses Mai, she stands by the parents' decision.

13   Mai's siblings visit her away from home because no one is allowed to bring up Mai's name.

14   This notion that she is no longer a member of a family, clan and society is what is most painful for Mai. When she thinks about the noisy celebrations

at New Year and family holidays, the memories sharpen her loneliness. She knows nothing will make her parents change their mind short of her giving up her new identity.

15   Accompanying this are the questions regarding what kinds of friends she should have, who she should marry, and what kind of life she wants to lead. Her life, she feels, need not be ordained by family, duty and marriage.

16   When she had boyfriends in college, she would not think of introducing them to her parents. Communication was never free enough for her to discuss male friends without the subject of marriage intruding. Dating was an emotional and dangerous subject, best left unmentioned.

17   All these are thorny issues [which] complicated the difficult process of growing up, while becoming an American.

18   The threat of disownment is a familiar ultimatum in Vietnamese families, although it's not always effective in this country. The way her parents can see it, they have been flexible with their children, blending the best of both worlds. But Mai was ostracized when she adopted the independent attitudes fostered by the American way of life.

19   Dr. Allen Seid, a psychiatrist and founder of Asian-Americans for Community Involvement in San Jose, has often seen this dilemma caused by the disruption of assimilation. He wonders if bi-culturalism—the integration of two cultures—is something that a person can turn on and off.

20   Can Mai, who has grown up in two different worlds, be expected to have one set of values at home and another outside?

21   "This process of assimilating must be started early on," cautions Seid, "even before having children, a couple must be comfortable with both worlds so that the children will not be faced with this 'either or' prospect and can grow up into an integrated self."

22   For the time-being, Mai is resigned to exile. The situation could change. Her parents have already come a long way and she is ready to meet them half-way any time.

Writing Log/Journal Assignment

Describe one of the worst days in your life, a day that forced you to consider who you are, what you have done, and/or where you may be (or who you may be) as a result of your future sense of identity. As a starting point, consider what you expected to happen as opposed to what did occur on this day.

Individual and Collaborative Considerations

1. What is the basic conflict in Nhu's article? Why is becoming an American a "constant cultural collision" for Mai?

2. How does Nhu's word selection (diction) reinforce the magnitude of Mai's decision?
3. Paraphrase then analyze the author's examples of two extremes of a bi-cultural individual. What does each offer in the way of personal identity?
4. Exactly what sort of attitude must a person adopt to become "more American than American"? In your opinion, is there a recognizable American "persona"? If so, what is it?
5. Although the "threat of disownment is a familiar ultimatum in Vietnamese families," why isn't it always an effective means of controlling their children in America?

Writing Activities

1. Take one of the many statements in this article (e.g., the "process of assimilating must be started early on") and defend it in a fully developed essay using a variety of concrete, verifiable evidence to support your position.
2. Have you ever tried to be like someone else (parents, friends, movie stars, rocks stars, and so on)? What did you hope to achieve? Were you successful? Why? Why not? Write an essay discussing the *importance* or *danger* of modeling behavior and values after other people or social and cultural groups.

✳

The Monkey Garden

Sandra Cisneros

An author of fiction and poetry, Sandra Cisneros has led workshops in acting and in creative writing and has received two National Endowment for the Arts Creative Writing Fellowships, one in 1982 and the other in 1988. Additionally, she received the Before Columbus Book Award in 1985. Her works include *Bad Boys* (1980), *The House on Mango Street* (1984), *My Wicked Ways* (1987), and *Woman Hollering Creek and Other Stories* (1991). Although she was born in Chicago, her mother took the family back to Mexico City on a regular basis. She now writes about Latino culture and how it may differ from the ethnocentric experiences of many of her readers. The following narrative is an excerpt from *The House on Mango Street*.

1 The monkey doesn't live there anymore. The monkey moved—to Kentucky—and took his people with him. And I was glad because I couldn't listen anymore to his wild screaming at night, the twangy yakkety-yak of the people who owned him. The green metal cage, the porcelain tabletop, the family that spoke like guitars. Monkey, family, table. All gone.

2 And it was then we took over the garden we had been afraid to go into when the monkey screamed and showed its yellow teeth.

3 There were sunflowers big as flowers on Mars, and thick cockscombs bleeding the deep red fringe of theater curtains. There were dizzy bees and bow-tied fruit flies turning somersaults and humming in the air. Sweet sweet peach trees. Thorn roses and thistle and pears. Weeds like so many squinty-eyed stars, and brush that made your ankles itch and itch until you washed with soap and water. There were big green apples hard as knees. And everywhere the sleepy smell of rotting wood, damp earth and dusty hollyhocks thick and perfumy like the blue-blond hair of the dead.

4 Yellow spiders ran when we turned rocks over, and pale worms blind and afraid of light rolled over in their sleep. Poke a stick in the sandy soil and a few blue-skinned beetles would appear, an avenue of ants, so many crusty ladybugs. This was a garden, a wonderful thing to look at in the spring. But bit by bit, after the monkey left, the garden began to take over itself. Flowers stopped obeying the little bricks that kept them from growing beyond their paths. Weeds mixed in. Dead cars appeared overnight like mushrooms. First one and then another and then a pale blue pickup with the front windshield missing. Before you knew it, the monkey garden became filled with sleepy cars.

5 Things had a way of disappearing in the garden, as if the garden itself ate them, or, as if with its old-man memory, it put them away and forgot them. Nenny found a dollar and a dead mouse between two rocks in the stone wall where the morning glories climbed, and once when we were playing hide and seek, Eddie Vargas laid his head beneath a hibiscus tree and fell asleep there like a Rip Van Winkle until somebody remembered he was in the game and went back to look for him.

6 This, I suppose, was the reason why we went there. Far away from where our mothers could find us. We and a few old dogs who lived inside the empty cars. We made a clubhouse once on the back of that old blue pickup. And besides, we liked to jump from the roof of one car to another and pretend they were giant mushrooms.

7 Somebody started the lie that the monkey garden had been there before anything. We liked to think the garden could hide things for a thousand years. There beneath the roots of soggy flowers were the bones of murdered pirates and dinosaurs, the eye of a unicorn turned to coal.

8 This is where I wanted to die and where I tried one day, but not even the monkey garden would have me. It was the last day I would go there.

9 Who was it that said I was getting too old to play the games? Who was it I didn't listen to? I only remember that when the others ran, I wanted to

run too, up and down and through the monkey garden, fast as the boys, not like Sally, who screamed if she got her stockings muddy.

10   I said, Sally, come on, but she wouldn't. She stayed by the curb talking to Tito and his friends. Play with the kids if you want, she said, I'm staying here. She could be stuck up like that if she wanted to, so I just left.

11   It was her own fault too. When I got back, Sally was pretending to be mad . . . something about the boys having stolen her keys. Please give them back to me, she said, punching the nearest one with a soft fist. They were laughing. She was too. It was a joke I didn't get.

12   I wanted to go back with the other kids who were still jumping on cars, still chasing each other through the garden, but Sally had her own game.

13   One of the boys invented the rules. One of Tito's friends said you can't get the keys back unless you kiss us, and Sally pretended to be mad at first but she said yes. It was that simple.

14   I don't know why, but something inside me wanted to throw a stick. Something wanted to say no when I watched Sally going into the garden with Tito's buddies all grinning. It was just a kiss, that's all. A kiss for each one. So what, she said.

15   Only how come I felt angry inside. Like something wasn't right. Sally went behind that old blue pickup to kiss the boys and get her keys back, and I ran up three flights of stairs to where Tito lived. His mother was ironing shirts. She was sprinkling water on them from an empty pop bottle and smoking a cigarette.

16   Your son and his friends stole Sally's keys and now they won't give them back unless she kisses them and right now they're making her kiss them, I said all out of breath from the three flights of stairs.

17   Those kids, she said, not looking up from her ironing.

18   That's all?

19   What do you want me to do, she said, call the cops? And kept on ironing.

20   I looked at her a long time, but couldn't think of anything to say, and ran back down the three flights to the garden, where Sally needed to be saved. I took three big sticks and a brick and figured this was enough.

21   But when I got there Sally said go home. Those boys said, leave us alone. I felt stupid with my brick. They all looked at me as if *I* was the one that was crazy and made me feel ashamed.

22   And then I don't know why but I had to run away. I had to hide myself at the other end of the garden, in the jungle part, under a tree that wouldn't mind if I lay down and cried a long time. I closed my eyes like tight stars so that I wouldn't, but I did. My face felt hot. Everything inside hiccupped.

23   I read somewhere that in India there are priests who can will their heart to stop beating. I wanted to will my blood to stop, my heart to quit its pumping. I wanted to be dead, to turn into the rain, my eyes melt into the ground like two black snails. I wished and wished. I closed my eyes and willed it, but when I got up my dress was green and I had a headache.

24   I looked at my feet in their white socks and ugly round shoes. They seemed far away. They didn't seem to be my feet anymore. And the garden that had been such a good place to play didn't seem mine either.

Writing Log/Journal Assignment

Describe a place where you and your friends liked to retreat to during your adolescence or youth. What sort of things did you do at your retreat? Why was it "special" or unique to you? When did you stop visiting your retreat and why?

Individual and Collaborative Considerations

1. When did Cisneros and her friends take over "the garden," and what were some of its distinctive features? List a few of the details she provides to give readers a visual picture of "the garden."
2. Occasionally, Cisneros omits the use of conventional punctuation marks (especially quotation marks around dialogue) in her memoir. To what extent does her omission of recognizable symbols which guide a reader affect the coherence and overall readability of the piece?
3. What situation came about making Cisneros feel "angry inside" and how did she deal with it?
4. At the end of her memoir, Cisneros feels she had to run away and hide in the jungle part of the garden. Why did she want her "blood to stop" and her "heart to quit its pumping"?
5. Games are mentioned throughout this essay—games played by children as well as games played by adolescents. How do these games relate to the development or maintenance of individual identity?

Writing Activities

1. Reread your journal response for "The Monkey Garden" and fashion a thesis out of the last part of the assignment, making it applicable to the human experience in general rather than to you in particular. For instance, you might arrive at a thesis stating that no matter how fond people are of special "haunts" or "secret retreats," sooner or later they will abandon them. Develop your essay with specific representative examples and analysis.
2. Write a brief anecdote about a time in your life when a major misunderstanding of people and their actions led to embarrassment or disappointment. Perhaps you were viewing a situation from a naive point of view, judging human behavior as it would apply to "the games of innocence," only to find out—like Cisneros—your friends were now interested in

behavior appropriate to their newly adopted "games of experience."
What did you do when you came to your new understanding?

---------------------- ※ ----------------------

A Working Community

Ellen Goodman

A featured columnist for the *Boston Globe* since 1972, Ellen Goodman
worked as a reporter for the *Detroit Free Press* and *Newsweek* prior to joining the *Globe* staff in 1967. In 1979, she became a commentator on the *Today Show* and received a Pulitzer Prize for journalism in 1980. In addition
to her book *Turning Points* (1979), Goodman has published three collections of her columns: *Close to Home* (1979), *At Large* (1981), and *Keeping in
Touch* (1985)—the source of the following essay. Her writings frequently
make astute observations of traditional American morals and manners as
well as changes in gender roles. In "A Working Community," Goodman
wrestles with the problem of identifying with other people as the twenty-
first century draws near because, more and more, "it becomes harder and
harder to tell who we are without saying what we do."

1   Boston—I have a friend who is a member of the medical community. It does
not say that, of course, on the stationery that bears her home address. This
membership comes from her hospital work.

2   I have another friend who is a member of the computer community. This
is a fairly new subdivision of our economy, and yet he finds his sense of
place in it.

3   Other friends and acquaintances of mine are members of the academic
community, or the business community, or the journalistic community.

4   Though you cannot find these on any map, we know where we belong.

5   None of us, mind you, was born into these communities. Nor did we move
into them, U-Hauling our possessions along with us. None has papers to
prove we are card-carrying members of one such group or another. Yet it
seems that more and more of us are identified by work these days, rather
than by street.

6   In the past, most Americans lived in neighborhoods. We were members
of precincts or parishes or school districts. My dictionary still defines community, first of all in geographic terms, as "a body of people who live in one
place."

7   But today fewer of us do our living in that one place; more of us just use it for sleeping. Now we call our towns "bedroom suburbs," and many of us, without small children as icebreakers, would have trouble naming all the people on our street.

8   It's not that we are more isolated today. It's that many of us have transferred a chunk of our friendships, a major portion of our everyday social lives, from home to office. As more of our neighbors work away from home, the workplace becomes our neighborhood.

9   The kaffeeklatsch of the fifties is the coffee break of the eighties. The water cooler, the hall, the elevator, and the parking lot are the back fences of these neighborhoods. The people we have lunch with day after day are those who know the running saga of our mother's operations, our child's math grades, our frozen pipes, and faulty transmissions.

10   We may be strangers at the supermarket that replaced the corner grocer, but we are known at the coffee shop in the lobby. We share with each other a cast of characters from the boss in the corner office to the crazy lady in Shipping, to the lovers in Marketing. It's not surprising that when researchers ask Americans what they like best about work, they say it is "the shmoose [chatter] factor." When they ask young mothers at home what they miss most about work, it is the people.

11   Not all the neighborhoods are empty, nor is every workplace a friendly playground. Most of us have had mixed experiences in these environments. Yet as one woman told me recently, she knows more about the people she passes on the way to her desk than on her way around the block. Our new sense of community hasn't just moved from house to office building. The labels that we wear connect us with members from distant companies, cities, and states. We assume that we have something "in common" with other teachers, nurses, city planners.

12   It's not unlike the experience of our immigrant grandparents. Many who came to this country still identified themselves as members of the Italian community, the Irish community, the Polish community. They sought out and assumed connections with people from the old country. Many of us have updated that experience. We have replaced ethnic identity with professional identity, the way we replaced neighborhoods with the workplace.

13   This whole realignment of community is surely most obvious among the mobile professions. People who move from city to city seem to put roots down into their professions. In an age of specialists, they may have to search harder to find people who speak the same language.

14   I don't think that there is anything massively disruptive about this shifting sense of community. The continuing search for connection and shared enterprise is very human. But I do feel uncomfortable with our shifting identity. The balance has tipped and we seem increasingly dependent on work for our sense of self.

15   If our offices are our new neighborhoods, if our professional titles are our new ethnic tags, then how do we separate our selves from our jobs? Self-worth isn't just something to measure in the marketplace. But in these new

communities, it becomes harder and harder to tell who we are without saying what we do.

Writing Log/Journal Assignment

Assume that everyone belongs to multiple communities and discuss in detail the communities of which you are a part. What are the common bonds in each community? How enduring does your "membership" in them seem to be?

Individual and Collaborative Considerations

1. How has a sense of "community" changed over the years? What presently creates "a sense of belonging"?
2. What emphasis do people tend to put on "labels" and why?
3. Where is the "realignment of community . . . most obvious"?
4. In what way does Goodman argue her case? How complete are her examples? To what extent does she (a) emotionally, (b) rationally, and (c) ethically appeal to her reader?
5. In what way would the "bi-cultural collision" as discussed by T. T. Nhu in "Becoming American Is a Constant Cultural Collision" (pp. 92–94) be similar to a loss of community?

Writing Activities

1. Write an essay in which your thesis either agrees (and supports) or disputes (and disproves) the final line in Goodman's essay: "But in these new communities, it becomes harder and harder to tell who we are without saying what we do."
2. Construct an essay showing how joining a particular group or community can offer you a sense of *identity* or *selfhood*. You might want to consider how and why you continue to redefine your sense of *self* long after being accepted by your peers.

※

On the Road

Langston Hughes

Born in Joplin, Missouri, in 1902, Langston Hughes (he dropped his first name, James) became a merchant seaman at a young age, lived in Paris and Rome—and traveled a great deal throughout the United States, Russia, and Europe. Regardless where he went, however, he identified with the poor people he met. Indeed, as illustrated through the character of Sargeant in Hughes' story "On the Road," the poor and their concerns were frequent subjects in his writings. During his life, Hughes compiled twenty-eight anthologies of African American folklore and poetry, and he became a key figure during the Harlem Renaissance in the twenties and thirties—a time period in New York when many African American artists, poets, writers, and musicians seemed to emerge. Extremely prolific, Hughes wrote several plays: *Mulatto* (1936) and *Simply Heavenly* (1963); collections of poetry: *The Weary Blues* (1926), *The Negro Mother and Other Dramatic Recitations* (1931), *Lament for Dark Peoples and Other Poems* (1944), and *Selected Poems of Langston Hughes* (1959); short stories: *The Ways of White Folks* (1934), *Laughing to Keep from Crying* (1952), and *Something in Common* (1963); and novels: *Not without Laughter* (1930) and *Tambourines to Glory* (1958). *A Langston Hughes Reader* (1958) gives readers an idea of the scope of his writing, its richness and variety.

He was not interested in snow. When he got off the freight, one early evening during the depression, Sargeant never even noticed the snow. But he must have felt it seeping down his neck, cold, wet, sopping in his shoes. But if you had asked him, he wouldn't have known it was snowing. Sargeant didn't see the snow, not even under the bright lights of the main street, falling white and flaky against the night. He was too hungry, too sleepy, too tired.

The Reverend Mr. Dorset, however, saw the snow when he switched on his porch light, opened the front door of his parsonage, and found standing there before him a big black man with snow on his face, a human piece of night with snow on his face—obviously unemployed.

Said the Reverend Mr. Dorset before Sargeant even realized he'd opened his mouth: "I'm sorry. No! Go right on down this street four blocks and turn to your left, walk up seven and you'll see the Relief Shelter. I'm sorry. No!" He shut the door. Sargeant wanted to tell the holy man that he had already been to the Relief Shelter, been to hundreds of relief shelters during the depression years, the beds were always gone and supper was over, the place was full, and they drew the color line anyhow. But the minister said, "No," and shut the door. Evidently he didn't want to hear about it. And he *had* a door to shut.

The big black man turned away. And even yet he didn't see the snow, walking right into it. Maybe he sensed it, cold, wet, sticking to his jaws, wet on his black hands, sopping in his shoes. He stopped and stood on the sidewalk hunched over—hungry, sleepy, cold—looking up and down. Then he looked right where he was—in front of a church! Of course! A church! Sure, right next to a parsonage, certainly a church.

5   It had *two* doors.

Broad white steps in the night all snowy white. Two high-arched doors with slender stone pillars on either side. And way up, a round lacy window with a stone crucifix in the middle and Christ on the crucifix in stone. All this was pale in the street lights, solid and stony pale in the snow.

Sargeant blinked. When he looked up, the snow fell into his eyes. For the first time that night he *saw* the snow. He shook his head. He shook the snow from his coat sleeves, felt hungry, felt lost, felt not lost, felt cold. He walked up the steps of the church. He knocked at the door. No answer. He tried the handle. Locked. He put his shoulder against the door and his long black body slanted like a ramrod. He pushed. With loud rhythmic grunts, like the grunts in a chain gang song, he pushed against the door.

"I'm tired . . . Huh! . . . Hongry . . . Uh! . . . I'm sleepy . . . Huh! I'm cold . . . I got to sleep somewheres," Sargeant said. This here is a church, ain't it? Well, uh!"

He pushed against the door.

10   Suddenly, with an undue cracking and screaking, the door began to give way to the tall black Negro who pushed ferociously against it.

By now two or three white people had stopped in the street, and Sargeant was vaguely aware of some of them yelling at him concerning the door. Three or four more came running, yelling at him.

Hey!" they said. "Hey!"

"Uh-huh," answered the big tall Negro, "I know it's a white folks' church, but I got to sleep somewhere." He gave another lunge at the door. "Huh!"

And the door broke open.

15   But just when the door gave way, two white cops arrived in a car, ran up the steps with their clubs, and grabbed Sargeant. But Sargeant for once had no intention of being pulled or pushed away from the door.

Sargeant grabbed, but not for anything so weak as a broken door. He grabbed for one of the tall stone pillars beside the door, grabbed at it and caught it. And held it. The cops pulled Sargeant pulled. Most of the people in the street got behind the cops and helped them pull.

"A big black unemployed Negro holding onto our church!" thought the people. "The idea!"

The cops began to beat Sargeant over the head, and nobody protested. But he held on.

And then the church fell down.

20   Gradually, the big stone front of the church fell down, the walls and the rafters, the crucifix and the Christ. The whole thing fell down, covering the cops and the people with bricks and stones and debris. The whole church fell down in the snow.

Sargeant got out from under the church and went walking on up the street with the stone pillar on his shoulder. He was under the impression that he had buried the parsonage and the Reverend Mr. Dorset who said, "No!" So he laughed, and threw the pillar six blocks up the street and went on.

Sargeant thought he was alone, but listening to the *crunch, crunch, crunch* on the snow of his own footsteps, he heard other footsteps, too, doubling his own. He looked around, and there was Christ walking along beside him, the same Christ that had been on the cross on the church—still stone with a rough stone surface, walking along beside him just like he was broken off the cross when the church fell down.

"Well, I'll be dogged," said Sargeant. "This here's the first time I ever seed you off the cross."

"Yes," said Christ, crunching his feet in the snow. "You had to pull the church down to get me off the cross."

25 "You glad?" said Sargeant.

"I sure am," said Christ.

They both laughed.

"I'm a hell of a fellow, ain't I?" said Sargeant. "Done pulled the church down!"

"You did a good job," said Christ. They have kept me nailed on a cross for nearly two thousand years."

30 "Whee-ee-e!" said Sargeant. "I know you are glad to get off."

"I sure am," said Christ.

They walked on in the snow. Sargeant looked at the man of stone.

"And you have been up there two thousand years?"

"I sure have," Christ said.

35 "Well, if I had a little cash," said Sargeant, "I'd show you around a bit."

"I been around," said Christ.

"Yeah, but that was a long time ago."

"All the same," said Christ, "I've been around."

They walked on in the snow until they came to the railroad yards. Sargeant was tired, sweating and tired.

40 "Where you goin'?" Sargeant said, stopping by the tracks. He looked at Christ. Sargeant said, "I'm just a bum on the road. How about you? Where you goin'?"

"God knows," Christ said, "but I'm leavin' here."

They saw the red and green lights of the railroad yard half veiled by the snow that fell out of the night. Away down the track they saw a fire in a hobo jungle.

"I can go there and sleep," Sargeant said.

"You can?"

45 "Sure," said Sargeant. "That place ain't got no doors."

Outside the town, along the tracks, there were barren trees and bushes below the embankment, snow-gray in the dark. And down among the trees and bushes there were makeshift houses made out of boxes and tin and old pieces of wood and canvas. You couldn't see them in the dark, but you knew they were there if you'd ever been on the road, if you had ever lived with the homeless and hungry in a depression.

"I'm side-tracking," Sargeant said. "I'm tired."

"I'm gonna make it on to Kansas City," said Christ.

"O.K.," Sargeant said. "So long!"

50   He went down into the hobo jungle and found himself a place to sleep. He never did see Christ no more. About 6:00 A.M., a freight came by. Sargeant scrambled out of the jungle with a dozen or so more hobos and ran along the track, grabbing at the freight. It was dawn, early dawn, cold and gray.

"Wonder where Christ is by now?" Sargeant thought. "He musta gone on way on down the road. He didn't sleep in this jungle."

Sargeant grabbed the train and started to pull himself up into a moving coal car, over the edge of a wheeling coal car. But strangely enough, the car was full of cops. The nearest cop rapped Sargeant soundly across the knuckles with his night stick. Wham! Rapped his big black hands for clinging to the top of the car. Wham! But Sargeant did not turn loose. He clung on and tried to pull himself into the car. He hollered at the top of his voice, "Damn it, lemme in this car!"

"Shut up," barked the cop. "You crazy coon!" He rapped Sargeant across the knuckles and punched him in the stomach. "You ain't out in no jungle now. This ain't no train. You in jail."

Wham! across his bare black fingers clinging to the bars of his cell. Wham! between the steel bars low down against his shins.

55   Suddenly Sargeant realized that he really was in jail. He wasn't on no train. The blood of the night before had dried on his face, his head hurt terribly, and a cop outside in the corridor was hitting him across the knuckles for holding onto the door, yelling and shaking the cell door.

"They musta took me to jail for breaking down the door last night," Sargeant thought, "that church door."

Sargeant went over and sat on a wooden bench against the cold stone wall. He was emptier than ever. His clothes were wet, clammy cold wet, and shoes sloppy with snow water. It was just about dawn. There he was, locked up behind a cell door, nursing his bruised fingers.

The bruised fingers were his, but not the *door*.

Not the *club* but the fingers.

60   "You wait," mumbled Sargeant, black against the jail wall. "I'm gonna break down this door, too."

"Shut up—or I'll paste you one," said the cop.

"I'm gonna break down this door," yelled Sargeant as he stood up in his cell.

Then he must have been talking to himself because he said, "I wonder where Christ's gone? I wonder if he's gone to Kansas City?"

Writing Log/Journal Assignment

Literally, "On the Road" deals with *who Sargeant is:* a Black man in the South during the Depression, who encounters racial prejudice and its effects in one situation after another. Surreally or fantastically, the story also indicates *what he could be:* a liberator for Jesus Christ. Write a short journal entry describing who you really are (you might consider hobbies, talents, likes, dislikes, and occupation) as opposed to who or what you would like to be. Regardless of what you say, be sure you address the question "why?"

Individual and Collaborative Considerations

1. List as many symbols as you can find in this story. Which are most significant? What symbols tend to "reappear" throughout the story, perhaps in slightly altered forms?
2. What is the major conflict in Hughes' story? In what way is nature, in addition to other people, antagonistic towards him?
3. In paragraph 5, what might have been Hughes' strategic purpose for placing *two* (in *two* doors) in italics? Analyze the importance Sargeant places on "doorways."
4. At what point in the story do you begin to suspect the reliability of the narrator? Why? How does "point of view" affect your perception and acceptance of information in the story?
5. Explain the purpose of the conversation between Sargeant and Christ. What bearing does it have on the main theme of the story? Where does each character ultimately seek refuge?

Writing Activities

1. Analyze the role of symbolism in "On the Road" in a well-developed, thoroughly explained essay. What would the story lose by omitting the symbolism?
2. Write an essay of your own about people presently "on the road": the homeless. Prewrite on your topic until you arrive at a particular focus which will help you shape your thesis. Relate the social prejudices the homeless face today to Sargeant's plight in Hughes' story whenever you can.

✳

No Name Woman

Maxine Hong Kingston

The daughter of Chinese immigrants, Maxine Hong Kingston was born in Stockton, California. Her articles and stories have appeared in publications such as *Ms.*, *The New York Times*, and *New West*. Kingston's books include *The Woman Warrior: Memoirs of a Girlhood among Ghosts,* which won the National Book Critics Award in 1976; *China Men,* winner of the American Book Award in 1981; and *Tripmaster Monkey* (1990). The following narrative was taken from *The Woman Warrior.*

"**Y**ou must not tell anyone," my mother said, "what I am about to tell you. In China your father had a sister who killed herself. She jumped into the family well. We say that your father has all brothers because it is as if she had never been born.

"In 1924 just a few days after our village celebrated seventeen hurry-up weddings—to make sure that every young man who went 'out on the road' would responsibly come home—your father and his brothers and your grandfather and his brothers and your aunt's new husband sailed for America, the Gold Mountain. It was your grandfather's last trip. Those lucky enough to get contracts waved good-bye from the decks. They fed and guarded the stowaways and helped them off in Cuba, New York, Bali, Hawaii. 'We'll meet in California next year,' they said. All of them sent money home.

"I remember looking at your aunt one day when she and I were dressing; I had not noticed before that she had such a protruding melon of a stomach. But I did not think, 'She's pregnant,' until she began to look like other pregnant women, her shirt pulling and the white tops of her black pants showing. She could not have been pregnant, you see, because her husband had been gone for years. No one said anything. We did not discuss it. In early summer she was ready to have the child, long after the time when it would have been possible.

"The village had also been counting. On the night the baby was to be born the villagers raided our house. Some were crying. Like a great saw, teeth strung with lights, files of people walked zigzag across our land, tearing the rice. Their lanterns doubled in the disturbed black water, which drained away through the broken bunds. As the villagers closed in, we could see that some of them, probably men and women we knew well, wore white masks. The people with long hair hung it over their faces. Women with short hair made it stand up on end. Some had tied white bands around their foreheads, arms, and legs.

5   "At first they threw mud and rocks at the house. Then they threw eggs and began slaughtering our stock. We could hear the animals scream their deaths—the roosters, the pigs, a last great roar from the ox. Familiar wild heads flared in our night windows; the villagers encircled us. Some of the faces stopped to peer at us, their eyes rushing like searchlights. The hands flattened against the panes, framed heads, and left red prints.

"The villagers broke in the front and the back doors at the same time, even though we had not locked the doors against them. Their knives dripped with the blood of our animals. They smeared blood on the doors and walls.

One woman swung a chicken, whose throat she had slit, splattering blood in red arcs about her. We stood together in the middle of the house, in the family hall with the pictures and tables of the ancestors around us, and looked straight ahead.

"At that time the house had only two wings. When the men came back, we would build two more to enclose our courtyard and a third one to begin a second courtyard. The villagers pushed through both wings, even your grandparents' rooms, to find your aunt's, which was also mine until the men returned. From this room a new wing for one of the younger families would grow. They ripped up her clothes and shoes and broke her combs, grinding them underfoot. They tore her work from the loom. They scattered the cooking fire and rolled the new weaving into it. We could hear them in the kitchen breaking our bowls and banging the pots. They overturned the great waist-high earthenware jugs; duck eggs, pickled fruits, vegetables burst out and mixed in acrid torrents. The old woman from the next field swept a broom through the air and loosed the spirits-of-the broom over our heads. 'Pig.' 'Ghost.' 'Pig,' they sobbed and scolded while they ruined our house.

"When they left, they took sugar and oranges to bless themselves. They cut pieces from the dead animals. Some of them took bowls that were not broken and clothes that were not torn. Afterward we swept up the rice and sewed it back up into sacks. But the smells from the spilled preserves lasted. Your aunt gave birth in the pigsty that night. The next morning when I went for the water, I found her and the baby plugging up the family well.

"Don't let your father know that I told you. He denies her. Now that you have started to menstruate, what happened to her could happen to you. Don't humiliate us. You wouldn't like to be forgotten as if you had never been born. The villagers are watchful."

10   Whenever she had to warn us about life, my mother told stories that ran like this one, a story to grow up on. She tested our strength to establish realities. Those in the emigrant generations who could not reassert brute survival died young and far from home. Those of us in the first American generations have had to figure out how the invisible world the emigrants built around our childhoods fit in solid America.

The emigrants confused the gods by diverting their curses, misleading them with crooked streets and false names. They must try to confuse their offspring as well, who, I suppose, threaten them in similar ways—always trying to get things straight, always trying to name the unspeakable. The Chinese I know hide their names; sojourners take new names when their lives change and guard their real names with silence.

Chinese-Americans, when you try to understand what things in you are Chinese, how do you separate what is peculiar to childhood, to poverty, insanities, one family, your mother who marked your growing with stories, from what is Chinese? What is Chinese tradition and what is the movies?

If I want to learn what clothes my aunt wore, whether flashy or ordinary, I would have to begin, "Remember Father's drowned-in-the-well sister?" I cannot ask that. My mother has told me once and for all the useful parts.

She will add nothing unless powered by Necessity, a riverbank that guides her life. She plants vegetable gardens rather than lawns; she carries the odd-shaped tomatoes home from the fields and eats food left for the gods.

Whenever we did frivolous things, we used up energy; we flew high kites. We children came up off the ground over the melting cones our parents brought home from work and the American movie on New Year's Day— *Oh, You Beautiful Doll* with Betty Grable one year, and *She Wore a Yellow Ribbon* with John Wayne another year. After the one carnival ride each, we paid in guilt; our tired father counted his change on the dark walk home.

15   Adultery is extravagance. Could people who hatch their own chicks and eat the embryos and the heads for delicacies and boil the feet in vinegar for party food, leaving only the gravel, eating even the gizzard lining—could such people engender a prodigal aunt? To be a woman, to have a daughter in starvation time was a waste enough. My aunt could not have been the lone romantic who gave up everything for sex. Women in the old China did not choose. Some man had commanded her to lie with him and be his secret evil. I wonder whether he masked himself when he joined the raid on the family.

Perhaps she encountered him in the fields or on the mountain where the daughters-in-law collected fuel. Or perhaps he first noticed her in the market place. He was not a stranger because the village housed no strangers. She had to have dealings with him other than sex. Perhaps he worked an ad-joining field, or he sold her the cloth for the dress she sewed and wore. His demand must have surprised, then terrified her. She obeyed him; she always did as she was told.

When the family found a young man in the next village to be her husband, she stood tractably beside the best rooster, his proxy, and promised before they met that she would be his forever. She was lucky that he was her age and she would be the first wife, an advantage secure now. The night she first saw him, he had sex with her. Then he left for America. She had almost forgotten what he looked like. When she tried to envision him, she only saw the black and white face in the group photograph the men had had taken before leaving.

The other man was not, after all, much different from her husband. They both gave orders: she followed. "If you tell your family, I'll beat you. I'll kill you. Be here again next week." No one talked sex, ever. And she might have separated the rapes from the rest of living if only she did not have to buy her oil from him or gather wood in the same forest. I want her fear to have lasted just as long as rape lasted so that the fear could have been contained. No drawn-out fear. But women at sex hazarded birth and hence lifetimes. The fear did not stop but permeated everywhere. She told the man, "I think I'm pregnant." He organized the raid against her.

On nights when my mother and father talked about their life back home, sometimes they mentioned an "outcast table" whose business they still seemed to be settling, their voices tight. In a commensal tradition, where food is precious, the powerful older people made wrongdoers eat alone.

Instead of letting them start separate new lives like the Japanese, who could become samurais and geishas, the Chinese family, faces averted but eyes glowering sideways, hung on to the offenders and fed them leftovers. My aunt must have lived in the same house as my parents and eaten at an outcast table. My mother spoke about the raid as if she had seen it, when she and my aunt, a daughter-in-law to a different household, should not have been living together at all. Daughters-in-law lived with their husbands' parents, not their own; a synonym for marriage in Chinese is "taking a daughter-in-law." Her husband's parents could have sold her, mortgaged her, stoned her. But they had sent her back to her own mother and father, a mysterious act hinting at disgraces not told me. Perhaps they had thrown her out to deflect the avengers.

20   She was the only daughter; her four brothers went with her father, husband, and uncles "out on the road" and for some years became western men. When the goods were divided among the family, three of the brothers took land, and the youngest, my father, chose an education. After my grandparents gave their daughter away to her husband's family, they had dispensed all the adventure and all the property. They expected her alone to keep the traditional ways, which her brothers, now among the barbarians, could fumble without detection. The heavy, deep-rooted women were to maintain the past against the flood, safe for returning. But the rare urge west had fixed upon our family, and so my aunt crossed boundaries not delineated in space.

The work of preservation demands that the feelings playing about in one's guts not be turned into action. Just watch their passing like cherry blossoms. But perhaps my aunt, my forerunner, caught in a slow life, let dreams grow and fade and after some months or years went toward what persisted. Fear at the enormities of the forbidden kept her desires delicate, wire and bone. She looked at a man because she liked the way the hair was tucked behind his ears, or she liked the question-mark line of a long torso curving at the shoulder and straight at the hip. For warm eyes or a soft voice or a slow walk—that's all—a few hairs, a line, a brightness, a sound, a pace, she gave up family. She offered us up for a charm that vanished with tiredness, a pigtail that didn't toss when the wind died. Why, the wrong lighting could erase the dearest thing about him.

It could very well have been, however, that my aunt did not take subtle enjoyment of her friend, but, a wild woman, kept rollicking company. Imagining her tree with sex doesn't fit, though. I don't know any woman like that, or men either. Unless I see her life branching into mine, she gives me no ancestral help.

To sustain her being in love, she often worked at herself in the mirror, guessing at the colors and shapes that would interest him, changing them frequently in order to hit on the right combination. She wanted him to look back.

On a farm near the sea, a woman who tended her appearance reaped a reputation for eccentricity. All the married women blunt-cut their hair in flaps about their ears or pulled it back in tight bulls. No nonsense. Neither style blew easily into heart-catching tangles. And at their weddings they displayed themselves in their long hair for the last time. "It brushed the backs of my knees," my mother tells us. "It was braided, and even so, it brushed the backs of my knees."

25   At the mirror my aunt combed individuality into her bob. A bun could have been contrived to escape into black streamers blowing in the wind or in quiet wisps about her face, but only the older women in our picture album wear buns. She brushed her hair back from her forehead, tucking the flaps behind her ears. She looped a piece of thread, knotted into a circle between her index fingers and thumbs, and ran the double strand across her forehead. When she closed her fingers as if she were making a pair of shadow geese bite, the string twisted together catching the little hairs. Then she pulled the thread away from her skull, ripping the hairs out neatly, her eyes watering from the needles of pain. Opening her fingers, she cleaned the thread, then rolled it along her hairline and the tops of her eyebrows. My mother did the same to me and my sisters and herself. I used to believe that the expression "caught by the short hairs" meant a captive held with a depilatory string. It especially hurt at the temples, but my mother said we were lucky we didn't have to have our feet bound when we were seven. Sisters used to sit on their beds and cry together, she said, as their mothers or their slaves removed the bandages for a few minutes each night and let the blood gush back into their veins. I hope that the man my aunt loved appreciated a smooth brow, that he wasn't just a tits-and-ass man.

Once my aunt found a freckle on her chin, at a spot that the almanac said predestined her unhappiness. She dug it out with a hot needle and washed the wound with peroxide.

More attention to her looks than these pullings of hairs and pickings at spots would have caused gossip among the villagers. They owned work clothes and good clothes, and they wore good clothes for feasting the new seasons. But since a woman combing her hair hexes beginnings, my aunt rarely found an occasion to look her best. Women looked like great sea snails—the corded wood, babies, and laundry they carried were the whorls on their backs. The Chinese did not admire a bent back; goddesses and warriors stood straight. Still there must have been a marvelous freeing of beauty when a worker laid down her burden and stretched and arched.

Such commonplace loveliness, however, was not enough for my aunt. She dreamed of a lover for the fifteen days of New Year's, the time for families to exchange visits, money, and food. She plied her secret comb. And sure enough she cursed the year, the family, the village, and herself.

Even as her hair lured her imminent lover, many other men looked at her. Uncles, cousins, nephews, brothers would have looked, too, had they been home between journeys. Perhaps they had already been restraining their curiosity, and they left, fearful that their glances, like a field of nesting birds, might be startled and caught. Poverty hurt, and that was their first reason for leaving. But another, final reason for leaving the crowded house was the never-said.

30   She may have been unusually beloved, the precious only daughter, spoiled and mirror gazing because of the affection the family lavished on her. When her husband left, they welcomed the chance to take her back from the in-laws; she could live like the little daughter for just a while longer. There are stories that my grandfather was different from other people, "crazy ever since the little Jap bayoneted him in the head." He used to put his naked penis on the dinner table, laughing. And one day he brought home a baby girl, wrapped up inside his brown western-style greatcoat. He had traded one of his sons, probably my father, the youngest, for her. My grandmother made him trade back. When he finally got a daughter of his own, he doted on her. They must have all loved her, except perhaps my father, the only brother who never went back to China, having once been traded for a girl.

Brothers and sisters, newly men and women, had to efface their sexual color and present plain miens. Disturbing hair and eyes, a smile like no other threatened the ideal of five generations living under one roof. To focus blurs, people shouted face to face and yelled from room to room. The immigrants I know have loud voices, unmodulated to American tones even after years away from the village where they called their friendships out across the fields. I have not been able to stop my mother's screams in public libraries or over telephones. Walking erect (knees straight, toes pointed forward, not pigeon-toed, which is Chinese-feminine) and speaking in an inaudible voice, I have tried to turn myself American-feminine. Chinese communication was loud, public. Only sick people had to whisper. But at the dinner table, where the family members came nearest one another, no one could talk, not the outcasts nor any eaters. Every word that falls from the mouth is a coin lost. Silently they gave and accepted food with both hands. A preoccupied child who took his bowl with one hand got a sideways glance. A complete moment of total attention is due everyone alike. Children and lovers have no singularity here, but my aunt used a secret voice, a separate attentiveness.

She kept the man's name to herself throughout her labor and dying; she did not accuse him that he be punished with her. To save her inseminator's name she gave silent birth.

He may have been somebody in her own household, but intercourse with a man outside the family would have been no less abhorrent. All the village were kinsmen, and the titles shouted in loud country voices never let kinship be forgotten. Any man within visiting distance would have been neutralized as a lover—"brother," "younger brother," "older brother"—one hundred and fifteen relationship titles. Parents researched birth charts probably not so much to assure good fortune as to circumvent incest in a population that has but one hundred surnames. Everybody has eight million relatives. How useless then sexual mannerisms, how dangerous.

As it came from an atavism deeper than fear, I used to add "brother" silently to boys' names. It hexed the boys, who would or would not ask me to dance, and made them less scary and as familiar and deserving of benevolence as girls.

35   But, of course, I hexed myself also—no dates. I should have stood up, both arms waving, and shouted out across libraries, "Hey, you! Love me back." I had no idea, though, how to make attraction selective, how to control its direction and magnitude. If I made myself American-pretty so that the five or six Chinese boys in the class fell in love with me, everyone else—the Caucasian, Negro, and Japanese boys—would too. Sisterliness, dignified and honorable, made much more sense.

Attraction eludes control so stubbornly that whole societies designed to organize relationships among people cannot keep order, not even when they bind people to one another from childhood and raise them together. Among the very poor and the wealthy, brothers married their adopted sisters, like doves. Our family allowed some romance, paying adult brides' prices and providing dowries so that their sons and daughters could marry strangers. Marriage promises to turn strangers into friendly relatives—a nation of siblings.

In the village structure, spirits shimmered among the live creatures, balanced and held in equilibrium by time and land. But one human being flaring up into violence could open up a black hole, a maelstrom that pulled in the sky. The frightened villagers, who depended on one another to maintain the real, went to my aunt to show her a personal, physical representation of the break she had made in the "roundness." Misallying couples snapped off the future, which was to be embodied in true offspring. The villagers punished her for acting as if she could have a private life, secret and apart from them.

If my aunt had betrayed the family at a time of large grain yields and peace, when many boys were born, and wings were being built on many houses, perhaps she might have escaped such severe punishment. But the men—hungry, greedy, tired of planting in dry soil, cuckolded—had been forced to leave the village in order to send food-money home. There were ghost plagues, bandit plagues, wars with the Japanese, floods. My Chinese brother and sister had died of an unknown sickness. Adultery, perhaps only a mistake during good times, became a crime when the village needed food.

The round moon cakes and round doorways, the round tables of graduated size that fit one roundness inside another, round windows and rice bowls—these talismans had lost their power to warn this family of the law: a family must be whole, faithfully keeping the descent line by having sons to feed the old and the dead, who in turn look after the family. The villagers came to show my aunt and her lover-in-hiding a broken house. The villagers were speeding up the circling of events because she was too short sighted to see that her infidelity had already harmed the village, that waves of consequences would return unpredictably, sometimes in disguise, as now, to hurt her. This roundness had to be made coin sized so that she would see its circumference: punish her at the birth of her baby. Awaken her to the inexorable. People who refused fatalism because they could invent small resources insisted on culpability. Deny accidents and wrest fault from the stars.

40   After the villagers left, their lanterns now scattering in various directions toward home, the family broke their silence and cursed her. "Aiaa, we're going to die. Death is coming. Death is coming. Look what you've done. You've killed us. Ghost! Dead ghost! Ghost! You've never been born." She ran out into the fields, far enough from the house so that she could no longer hear their voices, and pressed herself against the earth, her own land no more. When she felt the birth coming, she thought that she had been hurt. Her body seized together. "They've hurt me too much," she thought. "This is gall, and it will kill me." Her forehead and knees against the earth, her body convulsed and then released her onto her back. The black well of sky and stars went out and out and out forever; her body and her complexity seemed to disappear. She was one of the stars, a bright dot in blackness, without home, without a companion, in eternal cold and silence. An agoraphobia rose in her, speeding higher and higher, bigger and bigger; she would not be able to contain it; there would be no end to fear.

Flayed, unprotected against space, she felt pain return, focusing her body. This pain chilled her—a cold, steady kind of surface pain. Inside, spasmodically, the other pain, the pain of the child, heated her. For hours she lay on the ground, alternately body and space. Sometimes a vision of normal comfort obliterated reality: she saw the family in the evening gambling at the dinner table, the young people massaging their elders' backs. She saw them congratulating one another, high joy on the mornings the rice shoots came up. When these pictures burst, the stars drew yet further apart. Black space opened.

She got to her feet to fight better and remembered that old-fashioned women gave birth in their pigsties to fool the jealous, pain-dealing gods, who do not snatch piglets. Before the next spasms could stop her, she ran to the pigsty, each step a rushing out into emptiness. She climbed over the fence and knelt in the dirt. It was good to have a fence enclosing her, a tribal person alone.

Laboring, this woman who had carried her child as a foreign growth that sickened her every day, expelled it at last. She reached down to touch the hot, wet, moving mass, surely smaller than anything human, and could feel that it was human after all—fingers, toes, nails, nose. She pulled it up on to her belly, and it lay curled there, butt in the air, feet precisely tucked one under the other. She opened her loose shirt and buttoned the child inside. After resting, it squirmed and thrashed and she pushed it up to her breast. It turned its head this way and that until it found her nipple. There, it made little snuffling noises. She clenched her teeth at its preciousness, lovely as a young calf, a piglet, a little dog.

She may have gone to the pigsty as a last act of responsibility: she would protect this child as she had protected its father. It would look after her soul, leaving supplies on her grave. But how would this tiny child without family find her grave when there would be no marker for her anywhere, neither in the earth nor the family hall? No one would give her a family hall name. She had taken the child with her into the wastes. At its birth the two of them had felt the same raw pain of separation, a wound that only the family pressing tight could close. A child with no descent line would not soften her life but only trail after her, ghostlike, begging her to give it purpose. At dawn the villagers on their way to the fields would stand around the fence and look.

45   Full of milk, the little ghost slept. When it awoke, she hardened her breasts against the milk that crying loosens. Toward morning she picked up the baby and walked to the well.

Carrying the baby to the well shows loving. Otherwise abandon it. Turn its face into the mud. Mothers who love their children take them along. It was probably a girl; there is some hope of forgiveness for boys.

"Don't tell anyone you had an aunt. Your father does not want to hear her name. She has never been born." I have believed that sex was unspeakable and words so strong and fathers so frail that "aunt" would do my father mysterious harm. I have thought that my family, having settled among immigrants who had also been their neighbors in the ancestral land, needed to clean their name, and a wrong word would incite the kinspeople even here. But there is more to this silence: they want me to participate in her punishment. And I have.

In the twenty years since I heard this story I have not asked for details nor said my aunt's name; I do not know it. People who can comfort the dead can also chase after them to hurt them further—a reverse ancestor worship. The real punishment was not the raid swiftly inflicted by the villagers, but the family's deliberately forgetting her. Her betrayal so maddened them, they saw to it that she would suffer forever, even after death. Always hungry, always needing, she would have to beg food from other ghosts, snatch and steal it from those whose living descendants give them gifts. She would have to fight the ghosts massed at cross roads for the buns a few thoughtful citizens leave to decoy her away from village and home so that the ancestral spirits could feast unharassed. At peace, they could act like gods, not ghosts, their descent lines providing them with paper suits and dresses, spirit money, paper houses, paper automobiles, chicken, meat, and rice into eternity—essences delivered up in smoke and flames, steam and incense rising from each rice bowl. In an attempt to make the Chinese care for people outside the family, Chairman Mao encourages us now to give our paper replicas to the spirits of outstanding soldiers and workers, no matter whose ancestors they may be. My aunt remains forever hungry. Goods are not distributed evenly among the dead.

My aunt haunts me—her ghost drawn to me because now, after fifty years of neglect, I alone devote pages of paper to her, though not origamied into houses and clothes. I do not think she always means me well. I am telling on her, and she was a spite suicide, drowning herself in the drinking water.

The Chinese are always very frightened of the drowned one, whose weeping ghost, wet hair hanging and skin bloated, waits silently by the water to pull down a substitute.

Writing Log/Journal Assignment

In your opinion, how might the act of drowning herself and her illegitimate child in the family well represent an attempt by Kingston's aunt to protect her identity and maintain some type of dignity? Does she challenge any family or social values?

Individual and Collaborative Considerations

1. Kingston's narrative deals with cultural identity, relating it to traditional Chinese values and Chinese American values. How does Kingston relate to the values of her Chinese ancestors?
2. Why does Kingston's mother tell her the story of her aunt "without a name"? What impression does her mother make on her? Do they share the same attitude towards her aunt? Why? Why not?
3. In what way might the fate of Kingston's aunt be a product of the constraints imposed by the social values and traditional roles of women in China? What "unspeakable" act did Kingston's aunt commit?
4. What was the "real punishment"—the lasting punishment inflicted on Kingston's aunt? How did her punishment deprive her of an "identity"?
5. Why does Kingston's aunt now "haunt" her? How might this suggest that Kingston's personal identity has been enriched by values, beliefs, and superstitions of two societies?

Writing Activities

1. Construct an informative narrative you might use someday (or could have used) to explain family mysteries and family relationships. You might begin your essay by prewriting about "skeletons" or "ghosts" in your family closet. What did they do or not do? Why do you and family members prefer to disassociate yourselves with these "skeletons" or "ghosts"? How might other family members learn valuable lessons from their living kin or ancestors?
2. Write an essay in which you analyze how the pressure to conform to a set of social values affects the development of individuality and a personal identity. Generate supporting material from readings, personal observations, and experience.

❋

Axolotl

Julio Cortázar

Born in 1914 to Argentinean parents living in Brussels, Julio Cortázar moved to Argentina four years later and grew up there. He studied at the university for a while and taught school, but a clash with the Peronist government caused him to resign his position. (He would later get involved in political causes from the Cuban Revolution to Nicaraguan conflict, donating royalties from his writings to the Sandinista cause.) In 1952, he moved to Paris, France, where he lived working as a translator for UNESCO until he died in February 1984. Cortázar was a man of multiple talents; he was a poet, an author, an amateur jazz musician, and a translator. As a young writer he was influenced by Jorge Luis Borges who published his first short story in 1946. Ten of Cortázar's works have been translated and published in this country, including his first collection of short stories, *Bestiary* (1952), as well as *The Winners* (1960), *Hopscotch* (1963), *The End of the Game and Other Stories* (1965), *62: A Model Kit* (1968), and *We Love Glenda So Much* (1980). Two of his stories have been the basis for movies: *Blow-up* (Michelangelo Antonioni, director) and *Week End* (Jean-Luc Goderd, director). By providing a surrealist—if not fantastic—quality to the normal or mundane occurrences in life, Cortázar's characters frequently observe "cracks in reality." Such is the case with "Axolotl"; in fact, in Cortázar's short stories, encounters with "unreality" and search for meaning in life sometimes strike us as comical, but their implication might suggest something quite tragic.

There was a time when I thought a great deal about the axolotls. I went to see them in the aquarium at the Jardin des Plantes and stayed for hours watching them, observing their immobility, their faint movements. Now I am an axolotl.

I got to them by chance one spring morning when Paris was spreading its peacock tail after a wintry Lent. I was heading down the boulevard Port-Royal, then I took Saint-Marcel and L'Hôpital and saw green among all that grey and remembered the lions. I was friend of the lions and panthers, but had never gone into the dark, humid building that was the aquarium. I left my bike against the gratings and went to look at the tulips. The lions were sad and ugly and my panther was asleep. I decided on the aquarium, looked obliquely at banal fish until, unexpectedly, I hit it off with the axolotls. I stayed watching them for an hour and left, unable to think of anything else.

In the library at Sainte-Geneviève, I consulted a dictionary and learned that axolotls are the larval stage (provided with gills) of a species of salamander of the genus Ambystoma. That they were Mexican I knew already by looking at them and their little pink Aztec faces and the placard at the top of the tank. I read that specimens of them had been found in Africa capable of living on dry land during the periods of drought, and continuing their life under water when the rainy season came. I found their Spanish name, *ajolote*, and the mention that they were edible, and that their oil was used (no longer used, it said) like cod-liver oil.

I didn't care to look up any of the specialized works, but the next day I went back to the Jardin des Plantes. I began to go every morning, morning and afternoon some days. The aquarium guard smiled perplexedly taking my ticket. I would lean up against the iron bar in front of the tanks and set to watching them. There's nothing strange in this, because after the first minute I knew that we were linked, that something infinitely lost and distant kept pulling us together. It had been enough to detain me that first morning in front of the sheet of glass where some bubbles rose through the water. The axolotls huddled on the wretched narrow (only I can know how narrow and wretched) floor of moss and stone in the tank. There were nine specimens, and the majority pressed their heads against the glass, looking with their eyes of gold at whoever came near them. Disconcerted, almost ashamed, I felt it a lewdness to be peering at these silent and immobile figures heaped at the bottom of the tank. Mentally I isolated one, situated on the right and somewhat apart from the others, to study it better. I saw a rosy little body, translucent (I thought of those Chinese figurines of milky glass), looking like a small lizard about six inches long, ending in a fish's tail of extraordinary delicacy, the most sensitive part of our body. Along the back ran a transparent fin which joined with the tail, but what obsessed me was the feet, of the slenderest nicety, ending in tiny fingers with minutely human nails. And then I discovered its eyes, its face. Inexpressive features, with no other trait save the eyes, two orifices, like brooches, wholly of transparent gold, lacking any life but looking, letting themselves be penetrated by my look, which seemed to travel past the golden level and lose itself in a diaphanous interior mystery. A very slender black halo ringed the eye and etched it onto the pink flesh, onto the rosy stone of the head, vaguely triangular, but with curved and irregular sides which gave it a total likeness to a statuette corroded by time. The mouth was masked by the triangular plane of the face, its considerable size would be guessed only in profile; in front a delicate crevice barely slit the lifeless stone. On both sides of the head where the ears should have been, there grew three tiny sprigs red as coral, a vegetal outgrowth, the gills, I suppose. And they were the only thing quick about it; every ten or fifteen seconds the sprigs pricked up stiffly and again subsided. Once in a while a foot would barely move, I saw the diminutive toes poise mildly on the moss. It's that we don't enjoy moving a lot, and the tank is so cramped—we barely move in any direction and we're hitting one of the others with our tail or our head—difficulties arise, fights, tiredness. The time feels like it's less if we stay quietly.

5   It was their quietness that made me lean toward them fascinated the first time I saw the axolotls. Obscurely I seemed to understand their secret will, to abolish space and time with an indifferent immobility. I knew better later; the gill contraction, the tentative reckoning of the delicate feet on the stones, the abrupt swimming (some of them swim with a simple undulation of the body) proved to me that they were capable of escaping that mineral lethargy in which they spent whole hours. Above all else, their eyes obsessed me. In the standing tanks on either side of them, different fishes showed me the simple stupidity of their handsome eyes so similar to our own. The eyes of the axolotls spoke to me of the presence of a different life, of another way of seeing. Glueing my face to the glass (the guard would cough fussily once in a while), I tried to see better those diminutive golden points, that entrance to the infinitely slow and remote world of these rosy creatures. It was useless to tap with one finger on the glass directly in front of their faces; they never gave the least reaction. The golden eyes continued burning with their soft, terrible light; they continued looking at me from an unfathomable depth which made me dizzy.

And nevertheless they were close. I knew it before this, before being an axolotl. I learned it the day I came near them for the first time. The anthropomorphic features of a monkey reveal the reverse of what most people believe, the distance that is traveled from them to us. The absolute lack of similarity between axolotls and human beings proved to me that my recognition was valid, that I was not propping myself up with easy analogies. Only the little hands . . . But an eft, the common newt, has such hands also, and we are not at all alike. I think it was the axolotls' heads, that triangular pink shape with the tiny eyes of gold. That looked and knew. That laid the claim. They were not *animals.*

It would seem easy, almost obvious, to fall into mythology. I began seeing in the axolotls a metamorphosis which did not succeed in revoking a mysterious humanity. I imagined them aware, slaves of their bodies, condemned infinitely to the silence of the abyss, to a hopeless meditation. Their blind gaze, the diminutive gold disc without expression and nonetheless terribly shining, went through me like a message: "Save us, save us." I caught myself mumbling words of advice, conveying childish hopes. They continued to look at me, immobile; from time to time the rosy branches of the gills stiffened. In that instant I felt a muted pain; perhaps they were seeing me, attracting my strength to penetrate into the impenetrable thing of their lives. They were not human beings, but I had found in no animal such a profound relation with myself. The axolotls were like witnesses of something, and at times like horrible judges. I felt ignoble in front of them; there was such a terrifying purity in those transparent eyes. They were larvas, but larva means disguise and also phantom. Behind those Aztec faces, without expression but of an implacable cruelty, what semblance was awaiting its hour?

I was afraid of them. I think that had it not been for feeling the proximity of other visitors and the guard, I would not have been bold enough to remain alone with them. "You eat them alive with your eyes, hey," the guard said, laughing; he likely thought I was a little cracked. What he didn't notice was that it was they devouring me slowly with their eyes, in a cannibalism of gold. At any distance from the aquarium, I had only to think of them, it was as though I were being affected from a distance. It got to the point that I was going every day, and at night I thought of them immobile in the darkness, slowly putting a hand out which immediately encountered another. Perhaps their eyes could see in the dead of night, and for them the day continued indefinitely. The eyes of axolotls have no lids.

I know now that there was nothing strange, that that had to occur. Leaning over in front of the tank each morning, the recognition was greater. They were suffering, every fiber of my body reached toward that stifled pain, that stiff torment at the bottom of the tank. They were lying in wait for something, a remote dominion destroyed, an age of liberty when the world had been that of the axolotls. Not possible that such a terrible expression which was attaining the overthrow of that forced blankness on their stone faces should carry any message other than one of pain, proof of that eternal sentence, of that liquid hell they were undergoing. Hopelessly, I wanted to prove to myself that my own sensibility was projecting a nonexistent consciousness upon the axolotls. They and I knew. So there was nothing strange in what happened. My face was pressed against the glass of the aquarium, my eyes were attempting once more to penetrate the mystery of those eyes of gold without iris, without pupil. I saw from very close up the face of an axolotl immobile next to the glass. No transition and no surprise, I saw my face against the glass, I saw it on the outside of the tank, I saw it on the other side of the glass. Then my face drew back and I understood.

10   Only one thing was strange: to go on thinking as usual, to know. To realize that was, for the first moment, like the horror of a man buried alive awaking to his fate. Outside, my face came close to the glass again, I saw my mouth, the lips compressed with the effort of understanding the axolotls. I was an axolotl and now I knew instantly that no understanding was possible. He was outside the aquarium, his thinking was a thinking outside the tank. Recognizing him, being him himself, I was an axolotl and in my world. The horror began—I learned in the same moment—of believing myself prisoner in the body of an axolotl, metamorphosed into him with my human mind intact, buried alive in an axolotl, condemned to move lucidly among unconscious creatures. But that stopped when a foot just grazed my face, when I moved just a little to one side and saw an axolotl next to me who was looking at me, and understood that he knew also, no communication possible, but very clearly. Or I was also in him, or all of us were thinking humanlike, incapable of expression, limited to the golden splendor of our eyes looking at the face of the man pressed against the aquarium.

He returned many times, but he comes less often now. Weeks pass without his showing up. I saw him yesterday, he looked at me for a long time and left briskly. It seemed to me that he was not so much interested in us any more, that he was coming out of habit. Since the only thing I do is think, I could think about him a lot. It occurs to me that at the beginning we continued to communicate, that he felt more than ever one with the mystery which was claiming him. But the bridges were broken between him and me, because what was his obsession is now an axolotl, alien to his human life. I think that at the beginning I was capable of returning to him in a certain way—ah, only in a certain way—and of keeping awake his desire to know us better. I am an axolotl for good now, and if I think like a man it's only because every axolotl thinks like a man inside his rosy stone semblance. I believe that all this succeeded in communicating something to him in those first days, when I was still he. And in this final solitude to which he no longer comes, I console myself by thinking that perhaps he is going to write a story about us, that, believing he's making up a story, he's going to write all this about axolotls.

Writing Log/Journal Assignment

Relate an incident when you visited a zoo, an aquarium, or an aviary and studied its inhabitants, *or* describe a pet or farm animal you knew well. Regardless of the journal assignment you select, did you ever feel you made "contact" with the nonhuman creature? (Did you ever read your dog's or cat's thoughts?)

Individual and Collaborative Considerations

1. What is an axolotl? Describe its characteristics.
2. The aquarium holding the axolotls mesmerizes the narrator; why? When does the narrator begin to ape the actions of the axolotl? What does he do?
3. Locate the different points of view in paragraph 4. What is beginning to happen here? Does one point of view dominate the essay? Explain.
4. Why was the narrator initially afraid of the axolotls? Were his fears justified?
5. Who is the speaker in the final paragraph? In what way is this significant? How does the final speaker pull together the rest of the story? What, if anything, did the narrator who began the story "come to understand" about human nature?

Writing Activities

1. Which is more important to character development: the ability to think and reason, or the power to move and "do"? Construct an essay stating

your opinion, justifying it with examples drawn from personal observations and readings.

2. Many times the act of metamorphosis seems quite logical, if not appropriate in dreams. Analyze Cortázar's essay and explain how and why presenting at least part of his story in a "dreamlike" or "surreal" state contributes to or detracts from its ultimate effect. (Do you find yourself drawn into the narrator's world or repulsed by it?)

❋

Queen Victoria and Me

Leonard Cohen

Canadian-born poet, novelist, musician Leonard Cohen was educated in New York and took up residence on a small Greek island during the 1960s. A year after earning a degree at McGill University in 1955, Cohen published his first novel, *The Favorite Game*. Subsequent novels include *Beautiful Losers*. In the late 1960s, Cohen began to set some of his lyrics to music. His volumes of poetry include *Let Us Compare Mythologies* (1956), *Spice-Box of the Earth* (1961), and *Selected Poems 1956–1968* (1968). Many of Cohen's early works depict a wandering, searching figure—full of youth, desiring love—much like the speaker in the following poem who relates to Queen Victoria of England. Just as he laments the loss of his lover, Queen Victoria mourns the death of Prince Albert. (After Prince Albert died, Queen Victoria was not seen in public for three years; altogether, she mourned the death of her husband for forty years—until she died!) The commonalties between the poem's speaker and Queen Victoria fuse them in an "incomparable sense of loss."

Queen Victoria
my father and all his tobacco loved you
I love you too in all your forms
the slim unlovely virgin anyone would lay
5 the mean governess of the huge pink maps
the solitary mourner of a prince
Queen Victoria
I am cold and rainy
I am dirty as a glass roof in a train station
10 I feel like an empty cast iron exhibition
I want ornaments on everything
because my love she gone with other boys

Queen Victoria
do you have a punishment under the white lace
will you be short with her
make her read little Bibles
will you spank her with a mechanical corset
I want her pure as power
I want her skin slightly musty with petticoats
will you wash the easy bidets out of her head
Queen Victoria
I'm not much nourished by modern love
Will you come into my life
with your sorrow and your black carriages
and your perfect memory
Queen Victoria
The 20th century belongs to you and me
Let us be two severe giants
(not less lonely for our partnership)
who discolor test tubes in the halls of science
who turn up unwelcome at every World's Fair
heavy with proverb and correction
confusing the star-dazed tourists
with our incomparable sense of loss

Writing Log/Journal Assignment

Look up Queen Victoria of England in an encyclopedia. What impressed you (positively or negatively) most about her?

Individual and Collaborative Considerations

1. Effective writing often consists of the selection and arrangement of words. Jot down a few you find powerful or memorable (e.g., "perfect memory").
2. Why do you imagine Cohen uses the constant invocation to Queen Victoria? What do his questions ask? What is the effect of the repetition of her name?
3. What does the speaker mean when he says "not much nourished by modern love"? How might looking to Queen Victoria as a mentor in his life be appropriate? Do they share anything in common in their lives (figuratively or literally)?
4. Considering the information you researched on Queen Victoria, why might she or what she represents be "unwelcome at every World's Fair"? What typically happens at a World's Fair?
5. What is the tone of Cohen's poem? How is it appropriate to his subject matter?

Writing Activities

1. Write an essay appealing to a public figure for guidance in a situation. What constitutes the person's qualifications to mentor you? As opposed to a formal essay, this paper will take the form of a letter. The important thing here is to distinguish between sincere and patronizing diction.

2. How is a person's sense of identity sometimes defined by a relationship to another person? Cohen writes about his feeling of emptiness following the termination of a love affair, and Queen Victoria is a symbol of perpetual mourning. Place Cohen's theme into a personal context and write an essay prescribing how to come to terms with a love affair or special relationship that has come to an end.

✳

Ego Tripping
(there may be a reason why)

Nikki Giovanni

Nikki Giovanni, who currently teaches at Virginia Polytechnic and State University, is not only a fine essayist but also a prolific poet. Her works include *Black Talk, Black Feeling* (1967), *Black Judgment* (1968), *Spin a Soft Black Song: Poems for Children* (1971), *My House: Poems* (1972), *Cotton Candy on a Rainy Day* (1978), *Those Who Ride in the Night Winds* (1983), and *Sacred Cows . . . and Other Edibles* (1988). An early influence on her works was her maternal grandmother, Louvenia Terrell Watson, with whom she lived for two years during high school. She instilled Giovanni with a sense of African American consciousness that would become a guiding force in Giovanni's poetry during the 1960s and 1970s. Experiences had always helped shape Giovanni's works, and by the time "Ego Tripping" appeared in *The Women and the Men* (1983), her work had moved from Black nationalism to a more humanist worldview, partially due to her international travels.

> I was born in the congo
> I walked to the fertile crescent and built
>   the sphinx
> I designed a pyramid so tough that a star
>   that only glows every one hundred years falls
>   into the center giving divine perfect light
> I am bad

5

I sat on the throne
    drinking nectar with allah
I got hot and sent an ice age to europe
    to cool my thirst
My oldest daughter is nefertiti
    the tears from my birth pains
    created the nile
I am a beautiful woman

I gazed on the forest and burned
    out the sahara desert
    with a packet of goat's meat
    and a change of clothes
I crossed it in two hours
I am a gazelle so swift
    so swift you can't catch me

    For a birthday present when he was three
I gave my son hannibal an elephant
    He gave me rome for mother's day
My strength flows ever on

My son noah built new / ark and
I stood proudly at the helm
    as we sailed on a soft summer day
I turned myself into myself and was
    jesus
    men intone my loving name
    All praises, All praises
I am the one who would save

I sowed diamonds in my back yard
My bowels deliver uranium
    the filings from my fingernails are
    semi-precious jewels
    On a trip north
I caught a cold and blew
My nose giving oil to the arab world
I am so hip even my errors are correct
I sailed west to reach east and had to round off
    the earth as I went
    The hair from my head thinned and gold was laid
    across three continents

I am so perfect so divine so ethereal so surreal
I cannot be comprehended
    except by permission

I mean . . . I . . . can fly
    like a bird in the sky.

Writing Log/Journal Assignment

Write a few lines of verse or prose explaining in your own words how you interpret the concept of "ego tripping."

Individual and Collaborative Considerations

1. Who is the speaker in this poem? Does the first-person pronoun "I" really indicate that the poet, Giovanni, and the speaker are one and the same? Explain your answer.
2. What is the effect of starting 21 of 51 lines with "I"? What does the repetition reinforce or suggest?
3. With how many of the historical or biblical figures Giovanni alludes to are you familiar? In what way does your familiarity with these people enrich your understanding of the poem? (How is the speaker "ego tripping," anyway?)
4. What is the relationship between *hubris* (pride), ego, and identity? Can people find meaningful identities in excess or conceit?
5. Giovanni's poem carries a parenthetical subtitle: *(there may be a reason why)*. Explain what you think she is referring to here.

Writing Activities

1. In an argumentative paper, persuade your readers that in order to get in touch with their cultural roots, they should examine themselves in light of their ancestors, using metaphor, simile, and hyperbole (exaggeration for the point of emphasis).
2. Write a paper that answers the question "Who am I?" Using standard essay structure, begin your essay by stating your thesis (the big picture) followed by supporting paragraphs outlining who and what you are in particular. Conclude by placing your supporting paragraphs into proper perspective with your thesis.

ADDITIONAL TOPICS AND ISSUES FOR WRITING AND RESEARCH

1. Compare and contrast how two communities you (or someone you know) belonged to developed self-esteem, promoted personal growth, and nurtured individual development. What were the benefits of belonging to each community? Did the communities create dependencies? Explain.
2. Much has been said about the great "super highway" which will link all parts of America in a giant information transmission (output) and

retrieval system. Write an essay explaining how such a system might change our present methods of social interaction. Balance your discussions of the benefits of the "super highway" with potential problems in social identification. For instance, will the disadvantaged and low-income citizens in the United States find themselves further stratified from economic opportunities? After you refocus your supporting material in the concluding paragraph, you might make a prediction about the emerging "super highway" and American society.

3. Do "clothes" make the person? How often have you criticized people merely because you felt their clothes were "tacky" or "unstylish"? Write an essay arguing how becoming a "fashion statement" might be a substitute for or the source of character development and personality.

4. In modern society, is developing culture a matter of becoming a master at video games or reading both ancient and modern masterpieces of literature, visiting museums, and attending the opera and ballet? Present your point of view in a sharply defined thesis, supported with several representative examples for each discussion point.

5. First names (*given names* as opposed to *family names*—last names) are a definite means of identity. Survey a wide group of parents from diverse social, economic, and ethnic backgrounds, asking them how and why they selected the name(s) for their child (children). How often did their children assume a nickname? Were there years when some names seemed particularly popular? Why? After you assess your findings, write a short position paper on the topic of "naming children." What conclusions can you reach on the basis of your survey?

6. Workaholics have been criticized as people who seek a sense of purpose and meaning in life through compulsive attention to work. Do a bit of research and interview some workaholics you know—or people who *seem* to be workaholics. What motivates them? What do they do in their free time (or do they have free time?)? Why do they seem to derive such satisfaction from work? Ultimately, based on your interviews and research, write a paper either dispelling or supporting the notion that "workaholics" are helplessly addicted to work.

7. Why do people place so much importance on getting an "A" or a "B" in a class? Does the "C" student really know less than the "A" student? To what extent do some people lose sight of the educational process (what they are learning) in the quest for a high grade-point average? In a fully developed composition, examine and analyze the way people often use letter grades to define themselves as individuals.

8. Write an essay explaining the role your cultural identity plays in your life. How, for instance, does your cultural identity play a part in determining the clothes you wear, the food you eat, or the language you prefer to speak?

9. Is it possible for anyone to be totally original in thought and action? Why? Why not? How plausible is it to "be" someone else? Bearing these questions in mind, critique the role modern advertising agencies,

television programs, and the film industry play in influencing behavior and creating attitudes.

10. Write a narrative essay about a place where you feel uniquely yourself—unintimidated by other people and their opinion. What makes your "place" unique? Why do you feel free to "be yourself" rather than to play a role encouraged by your peers? How often do you get to go to your special "place"? Has it always been where it is now? Will it last into the future?

Starting Points for Research

Identity

- Alternate lifestyles
- Anthropology
- Collective unconscious
- Commercial products
- Community identity
- Computers and the electronic highway
- Cults
- Cultural identity/subculture identity
- Depersonalization
- DNA
- Dreams
- Electronic equipment and identification
- Ethnic identity
- Family and home
- Fashion (clothes, jewelry, body enhancements, tattoos)
- Gangs and youth groups
- Gender
- Group identity
- Handwriting analysis
- Identity and motion pictures
- Identity disorders
- Individuality and homogeneity
- Lifestyles
- Loss of and search for identity
- Medical jurisprudence
  Fingerprints and footprints
  Forensic anthropology
  Voice prints
- Ontology
- Personality
- Plastic surgery and "makeovers"
- Political parties (affiliations)
- Psychology
- Religious and spiritual groups
- Scholastic grades and personal identity
- Self-realization
- Social identities
- Social psychology
- Television/commercials
- Theory of knowledge

6

Relationships: Friends, Family, and Lovers

Backward I gaze;
one whom I chanced to meet
is lost in haze.
SHIKI

Essays

Judith Viorst   Friends, Good Friends—and Such Good Friends

•

E. B. White   Once More to the Lake

•

Alice Walker   Brothers and Sisters

•

Fiction

Kay Boyle   Astronomer's Wife

•

D. H. Lawrence   The Horse Dealer's Daughter

•

Isabel Allende   Our Secret

•

Poetry

Rita Dove   Daystar

•

H. D. (Hilda Doolittle)   Circe

In order to establish meaningful relationships with others, people usually need to have some sense of personal identity. Whereas the question in an identity search might be "who am I?" for an individual, it becomes "who are we?" or "what are we?" when entering a relationship. Both traditional and nontraditional relationships can be further categorized as friends, acquaintances, family members, and lovers. In "Friends, Good Friends—and Such Good Friends," Judith Viorst directs many questions at the first category of relationships, friends. What is a friend? How might definitions of friendship differ between cultures or gender? Do various age groups use the same criteria for judging friends, or should friends ever be judged at all? She discovers, however, that there is no single definition for a friend—only approximations.

There are many aspects of family relationships. E. B. White, for instance, observes the theme of family unity in his essay "Once More to the Lake." There the narrator emphasizes the fact that more than simple blood lines bond father and son together. He views the two of them as one person in spirit until a change occurs giving him insight into his own mortality.

Children present family relationships with a new set of dynamics. Apart from the challenge they present their parents, they are constantly testing each other. Sibling rivalries are common between brothers and sisters. It is easy to understand how and why one sibling might desire the material goods or parental affection received by another. Alice Walker looks at siblings from a different perspective in "Brothers and Sisters," however. The males—brothers—in Walker's family shared privileged information and were given sexual liberties and encouragement denied to the women.

Rita Dove's poem "Daystar" illustrates a different point of view towards family members. Although the speaker accepts responsibility for family relationships by acknowledging her commitment to others, she by no means excludes a right to time or space for herself. At night the speaker spends time just thinking about "the place that was hers / for an hour."

Sometimes the line between friends and lovers is not neatly defined, and many relationships are products of "chance" not "design"; such is the case of the plumber and Mrs. Ames from Kay Boyle's "Astronomer's Wife." Mrs. Ames takes a definite interest in the plumber; he spoke so directly, answered so reasonably, seemed so "down to earth." The plumber reciprocated with an interest in her. His appearance awakens an apparent emotional deadness in Mrs. Ames—a void that may have developed between Mrs. Ames and her husband, the astronomer, a man forever with his head in the clouds.

The bonds in relationships take many forms. Friends enjoy each other's companionship and often share common interests, secrets, hobbies, or occupations. In other relationships, the concept of love plays a pivotal role. What exactly is love? Poets and musicians from Ovid to H. D. (Hilda Doolittle) have wrestled with the concept of love, arriving at approximations of behavior, discussing the ineffable through metaphor and figurative language. Virgil once wrote "love conquers all" (Eclogues X, I. 69), attesting to the power and force of love. The notion of "love is blind" was presented by the old Italian knight named January from "The Miller's Tale" in Geoffrey Chaucer's *Canterbury Tales*, and Shakespeare said "love is an ever-fixed mark." Modern literature also is filled with testimonies of and dedications to love. As with the classical writers, there is no authoritative agreement on the precise meaning of the word; it simply seems to grow in its application to daily activities ("I love my Mitsubishi television").

People love for different reasons: physical gratification, mental stimulation, and emotional support. "Our Secret" by Isabel Allende presents two lovers united one day for no particular reason. Unlike in encounters with others, their pasts have a common thread, and they are able to share more than pleasures of the flesh; they can tell each other their most hidden secrets. The discovery of love—something that had been waiting to surface—brings life and future prospects to Mabel and Fergusson in D. H. Lawrence's "The Horse Dealer's Daughter."

H. D.'s poetry makes allusions to other people, places, and things, adding a special dimension to the points she wants to convey. In H. D.'s poem, "Circe," *unrequited love* is expressed through an allusion to Circe, an enchantress from Greek mythology. She fell in love with Odysseus as he was returning home after the Trojan War, but for all her magic, Circe could not make him love her (moly, an herb, protected Odysseus from her charms). Similarly, the speaker in the poem cannot make the one man she loves return her affections.

Glancing back over Shiki's haiku poem, you can see how it could apply equally well to lovers and friends: Once either has been left behind, looking back and attempting to recapture a special relationship is usually quite difficult. The special friend or loved one seems to "get lost in a haze." Will love survive in the twenty-first century? Already, the public has been inundated with computerized dating services and shows like *The Dating Game* and *The Love Connection*, undoubtedly adding to society's confusion—not to mention lack of consensus—about the meaning of love and purpose of relationships.

From acquaintances and platonic friends to soul mates and lovers, relationships in general continue to grow and develop or fizzle and die. In the following essays, stories, and poems, note in particular how relationships evolve. You might want to jot down types of friendships or relationships brought to mind as a result of readings; such insights may provide you with fresh, interesting ideas for writing about relationships between friends, family, and lovers.

RHETORIC AT WORK

How often have you let a symbol or other figurative language express what you felt unable to say in words? The quality of a relationship might best be expressed through figurative language or emotionally charged words. On the other hand, love might be associated with specific symbols (hearts), plants (roses), and sweets (candy). As you read and write about friends, family, and lovers, the language you use will be most important in expressing your information. Practice your own ability to describe people, places, and things figuratively as you read through the literary works in this chapter. After reading Rita Dove's "Daystar," for instance, turn to your journal, and write an entry in the same spirit as you perceive the poem—either in verse or prose. Your creativity may actually help you to develop *style* and *voice* which will distinguish your future writings. How you say you love someone can make all the difference between conveying deceit and sincerity (and therefore credibility).

A Checklist for Writing about *Relationships: Friends, Family, and Lovers*

1. Did I limit my topic sufficiently? What do I want to say about *relationships?* Is my thesis carefully focused?
2. Did I organize my material clearly so that readers unfamiliar with my topic won't have to guess at my references?
3. Do my sentences flow into each other? Have I used enough sentence variety to maintain reader interest?
4. When I revised my draft, did I consider how a word's denotation or connotation could strengthen my theme or make a desired connection between people or things?
5. How might definition provide an ideal rhetorical strategy for developing my thesis about different types of human relationships?
6. Does my diction reflect my attitude towards my thesis about lovers or friends?
7. In an essay analyzing some aspect of sibling relationships, did I pay particular attention to the cultural values, especially ones that motivated actions?
8. Do my examples specifically illustrate my thesis? Do I provide several examples to support each supporting point?
9. Am I approaching the topic "human relationships" reverentially, cynically, or sentimentally? How does the mood of my essay complement my intent?

---***---

Friends, Good Friends—and Such Good Friends

Judith Viorst

Judith Viorst has established herself as a well-known journalist and essay-ist with works appearing in many popular magazines and journals throughout the United States. Her works include *How Did I Get to Be Forty and Other Atrocities* (1976) and *If I Were in Charge of the World and Other Worries* (1981). Viorst has also written several children's books such as *My Mama Says There Aren't Any Zombies, Ghosts, Vampires, Creatures, Demons, Monsters, Fiends, Goblins, or Things* (1973), and she has been the recipient of many writing awards, including an Emmy for her poems that were used on *The Anne Bancroft Show* (1970). The following essay in which she divides and classifies different types of friendships originally appeared in *Redbook*. Prior to reading Viorst's essay, brainstorm your own meaning of "friendship." What sorts of questions do you believe must be addressed in order to achieve an inclusive, satisfactory definition of the word?

1   Women are friends, I once would have said, when they totally love and support and trust each other, and bare to each other the secrets of their souls, and run—no questions asked—to help each other, and tell their harsh truths to each other (no, you can't wear that dress, unless you lose ten pounds first) when truths must be told.

2   Women are friends, I once would have said, when they share the same affection for Ingmar Bergman, plus train rides, cats, warm rain, charades, Camus, and hate with equal ardor Newark and Brussels sprouts and Law-rence Welk and camping.

3   In other words, I once would have said that a friend is a friend all the way, but now I believe that's a narrow point of view. For the friendships I have and the friendships I see are conducted at many levels of intensity, serve many different functions, meet different needs and range from those as all-the-way as the friendship of the soul sisters mentioned above to that of the most nonchalant and casual playmates.

4   Consider these varieties of friendship:

5   1. Convenience friends. These are the women with whom, if our paths weren't crossing all the time, we'd have no particular reason to be friends: a next-door neighbor, a woman in our car pool, the mother of one of our children's closest friends or maybe some mommy with whom we serve juice and cookies each week at the Glenwood Co-op Nursery.

6   Convenience friends are convenient indeed. They'll lend us their cups and silverware for a party. They'll drive our kids to soccer when we're sick.

They'll take us to pick up our car when we need a lift to the garage. They'll even take our cats when we go on vacation. As we will for them.

7 But we don't, with convenience friends, ever come too close or tell too much; we maintain our public face and emotional distance. "Which means," says Elaine, "that I'll talk about being overweight but not about being depressed. Which means I'll admit being mad but not blind with rage. Which means I might say that we're pinched this month but never that I'm worried sick over money."

8 But which doesn't mean that there isn't sufficient value to be found in these friendships of mutual aid, in convenience friends.

9 2. Special-interest friends. These friendships aren't intimate, and they needn't involve kids or silverware or cats. Their value lies in some interest jointly shared. And so we may have an office friend or a yoga friend or a tennis friend or a friend from the Women's Democratic Club.

10 "I've got one woman friend," says Joyce, "who likes, as I do, to take psychology courses. Which makes it nice for me—and nice for her. It's fun to go with someone you know and it's fun to discuss what you've learned, driving back from the classes." And for the most part, she says, that's all they discuss.

11 "I'd say that what we're doing is *doing* together, not being together," Suzanne says of her Tuesday-doubles friends. "It's mainly a tennis relationship, but we play together well. And I guess we all need to have a couple of playmates."

12 I agree.

13 *My* playmate is a shopping friend, a woman of marvelous taste, a woman who knows exactly *where* to buy *what*, and furthermore is a woman who always knows beyond a doubt what one ought to be buying. I don't have the time to keep up with what's new in eyeshadow, hemlines and shoes and whether the smock look is in or finished already. But since (oh, shame!) I care a lot about eyeshadow, hemlines and shoes, and since I don't *want* to wear smocks if the smock look is finished, I'm very glad to have a shopping friend.

14 3. Historical friends. We all have a friend who knew us when . . . maybe way back in Miss Meltzer's second grade, when our family lived in that three-room flat in Brooklyn, when our dad was out of work for seven months, when our brother Allie got in that fight where they had to call the police, when our sister married the endodontist from Yonkers and when, the morning after we lost our virginity, she was the first, the only, friend we told.

15 The years have gone by and we've gone separate ways and we've little in common now, but we're still an intimate part of each other's past. And so whenever we go to Detroit we always go to visit this friend of our girlhood. Who knows how we looked before our teeth were straightened. Who knows how we talked before our voice got unBrooklyned. Who knows what we ate before we learned about artichokes. And who, by her presence, puts

us in touch with an earlier part of ourself, a part of ourself it's important never to lose.

16   "What this friend means to me and what I mean to her," says Grace, "is having a sister without sibling rivalry. We know the texture of each other's lives. She remembers my grandmother's cabbage soup. I remember the way her uncle played the piano. There's simply no other friend who remembers those things."

17   4. Crossroads friends. Like historical friends, our crossroads friends are important for *what was*—for the friendship we shared at a crucial, now past, time of life. A time, perhaps, when we roomed in college together; or worked as eager young singles in the Big City together; or went together, as my friend Elizabeth and I did through pregnancy, birth and that scary first year of new motherhood.

18   Crossroads friends forge powerful links, links strong enough to endure with not much more contact than once-a-year letters at Christmas. And out of respect for those crossroads years, for those dramas and dreams we once shared, we will always be friends.

19   5. Cross-generational friends. Historical friends and crossroads friends seem to maintain a special kind of intimacy—dormant but always ready to be revived—and though we may rarely meet, whenever we do connect, it's personal and intense. Another kind of intimacy exists in the friendships that form across generations in what one woman calls her daughter-mother and her mother-daughter relationships.

20   Evelyn's friend is her mother's age—"but I share so much more than I ever could with my mother"—a woman she talks to of music, of books and of life. "What I get from her is the benefit of her experience. What she gets—and enjoys—from me is a youthful perspective. It's a pleasure for both of us."

21   I have in my own life a precious friend, a woman of sixty-five who has lived very hard, who is wise, who listens well; who has been where I am and can help me understand it; and who represents not only an ultimate ideal mother to me but also the person I'd like to be when I grow up.

22   In our daughter role we tend to do more than our share of self-revelation; in our mother role we tend to receive what's revealed. It's another kind of pleasure—playing wise mother to a questing younger person. It's another very lovely kind of friendship.

23   6. Part-of-a-couple friends. Some of the women we call our friends we never see alone—we see them as part of a couple at couples' parties. And though we share interests in many things and respect each other's views, we aren't moved to deepen the relationship. Whatever the reason, a lack of time or—and this is more likely—a lack of chemistry, our friendship remains in the context of a group. But the fact that our feeling on seeing each other is always, "I'm *so* glad she's here" and the fact that we spend half the evening talking together says that this too, in its own way, counts as a friendship.

24   (Other part-of-a-couple friends are the friends that came with the marriage, and some of these are friends we could live without. But sometimes, alas, she married our husband's best friend; and sometimes, alas, she *is* our husband's best friend. And so we find ourself dealing with her, somewhat against our will, in a spirit of what I'll call *reluctant* friendship.)

25   7. Men who are friends. I wanted to write just of women friends, but the women I've talked to won't let me—they say I must mention man-woman friendships too. For these friendships can be just as close and as dear as those that we form with women. Listen to Lucy's description of one such friendship:

26   "We've found we have things to talk about that are different from what he talks about with my husband and different from what I talk about with his wife. So sometimes we call on the phone or meet for lunch. There are similar intellectual interests—we always pass on to each other the books that we love—but there's also something tender and caring too."

27   In a couple of crises, Lucy says, "he offered himself, for talking and for helping. And when someone died in his family he wanted me there. The sexual, flirty part of our friendship is very small, but *some*—just enough to make it fun and different." She thinks—and I agree—that the sexual part, though small is always *some*, is always there when a man and a woman are friends.

28   It's only in the past few years that I've made friends with men, in the sense of a friendship that's *mine,* not just part of two couples. And achieving with them the ease and the trust I've found with women friends has value indeed. Under the dryer at home last week, putting on mascara and rouge, I comfortably sat and talked with a fellow named Peter. Peter, I finally decided, could handle the shock of me minus mascara under the dryer. Because we care for each other. Because we're friends.

29   8. There are medium friends, and pretty good friends, and very good friends indeed, and these friendships are defined by their level of intimacy. And what we'll reveal at each of these levels of intimacy is calibrated with care. We might tell a medium friend, for example, that yesterday we had a fight with our husband. And we might tell a pretty good friend that this fight with our husband made us so mad that we slept on the couch. And we might tell a very good friend that the reason we got so mad in that fight that we slept on the couch had something to do with that girl who works in his office. But it's only to our very best friends that we're willing to tell all, to tell what's going on with that girl in his office.

30   The best of friends, I still believe, totally love and support and trust each other, and bare to each other the secrets of their souls, and run—no questions asked—to help each other, and tell harsh truths to each other when they must be told.

31   But we needn't agree about everything (only twelve-year-old girl friends agree about *everything*) to tolerate each other's point of view. To accept without judgment. To give and to take without ever keeping score. And to be

there, as I am for them and as they are for me, to comfort our sorrows, to celebrate our joys.

Writing Log/Journal Assignment

What is a *best friend* anyway? Explain your philosophy in a journal entry. Identify the person's traits and qualities to illustrate why he or she is a "special person."

Individual and Collaborative Considerations

1. How does Viorst categorize varieties of friends?
2. Which category does Viorst value highly and why?
3. In what way does Viorst develop your understanding of each category of friend she presents?
4. After presenting each category of friend, Viorst further defines the word *friend*, stating that "There are medium friends, and pretty good friends, and very good friends indeed. . . ." How does she distinguish these three friendships?
5. Who is the intended audience in this essay? Has anyone been excluded? Defend your position.

Writing Activities

1. Brainstorm the words *friends* and *friendship*. Who or what do you associate with each word? Write an essay in which you divide and classify your own, original categories of friendship. Like Viorst, use a variety of concrete examples to illustrate and develop your categories.
2. Develop a thesis and write an essay expressing how and why your significant other, lover, spouse, fiancée, or companion could also be your best friend. Does "the sexual, flirty part" of such a relationship ever get in the way? Does it make you vulnerable?

✳

Once More to the Lake

E. B. White

Elwyn Brooks White (1899–1985) was a well-known essayist and contributing editor for *The New Yorker*, and his essays frequently appeared in magazines, including *The New Yorker* and *Harper's*. In collaboration with author James Thurber, White wrote the satire *Is Sex Necessary?* (1929). White's other works include *The Lady Is Cold, Stuart Little* (1945), *Charlotte's Web* (1952), *The Trumpet of the Swan* (1970), and *The Essays of E. B. White* (1977). White also revised William Strunk's *The Elements of Style*, a classic guide. "Once More to the Lake" originally appeared in *One Man's Meat*, and it offers White's childhood recollection of summer visits to a lake—a lake he has finally returned to with his own son. The lake itself seemed frozen in time; it seemed as though "there had been no years" since his last visit, and he and his son were one and the same person.

1   One summer, along about 1904, my father rented a camp on a lake in Maine and took us all there for the month of August. We all got ring worm from some kittens and had to rub Pond's Extract on our arms and legs night and morning, and my father rolled over in a canoe with all his clothes on; but outside of that the vacation was a success and from then on none of us ever thought there was any place in the world like that lake in Maine. We returned summer after summer—always on August 1 for one month. I have since become a salt-water man, but sometimes in summer there are days when the restlessness of the tides and the fearful cold of the sea water and the incessant wind that blows across the afternoon and into the evening make me wish for the placidity of a lake in the woods. A few weeks ago this feeling got so strong I bought myself a couple of bass hooks and a spinner and returned to the lake where we used to go, for a week's fishing and to revisit old haunts.

2   I took along my son, who had never had any fresh water up his nose and who had seen lily pads only from train windows. On the journey over to the lake I began to wonder what it would be like. I wondered how time would have marred this unique, this holy spot—the coves and streams, the hills that the sun set behind, the camps and the paths behind the camps. I was sure that the tarred road would have found it out, and I wondered in what other ways it would be desolated. It is strange how much you can remember about places like that once you allow your mind to return into the grooves that lead back. You remember one thing, and that suddenly reminds you of another thing. I guess I remembered clearest of all the early mornings, when the lake was cool and motionless, remembered how the bedroom smelled of the lumber it was made of and of the wet woods whose scent entered through the screen. The partitions in the camp were thin and did not extend clear to the top of the rooms, and as I was always the first up I would dress softly so as not to wake the others, and sneak out into the sweet outdoors and start out in the canoe, keeping close along the shore in the long shadows of the pines. I remembered being very careful never to rub my paddle against the gunwale for fear of disturbing the stillness of the cathedral.

3   The lake had never been what you would call a wild lake. There were cottages sprinkled around the shores, and it was in farming country although the shores of the lake were quite heavily wooded. Some of the cottages were

owned by nearby farmers, and you would live at the shore and eat your meals at the farmhouse. That's what our family did. But although it wasn't wild, it was a fairly large and undisturbed lake and there were places in it that, to a child at least, seemed infinitely remote and primeval.

4   I was right about the tar: it led to within half a mile of the shore. But when I got back there, with my boy, and we settled into a camp near a farmhouse and into the kind of summertime I had known, I could tell that it was going to be pretty much the same as it had been before—I knew it, lying in bed the first morning, smelling the bedroom and hearing the boy sneak quietly out and go off along the shore in a boat. I began to sustain the illusion that he was I, and therefore, by simple transposition, that I was my father. This sensation persisted, kept cropping up all the time we were there. It was not an entirely new feeling, but in this setting it grew much stronger. I seemed to be living a dual existence. I would be in the middle of some simple act, I would be picking up a bait box or laying down a table fork, or I would be saying something, and suddenly it would be not I but my father who was saying the words or making the gesture. It gave me a creepy sensation.

5   We went fishing the first morning. I felt the same damp moss covering the worms in the bait can, and saw the dragonfly alight on the tip of my rod as it hovered a few inches from the surface of the water. It was the arrival of this fly that convinced me beyond any doubt that everything was as it always had been, that the years were a mirage and that there had been no years. The small waves were the same, chucking the rowboat under the chin as we fished at anchor, and the boat was the same boat, the same color green and the ribs broken in the same places, and under the floorboards the same fresh-water leavings and debris—the dead helgramite, the wisps of moss, the rusty discarded fishhook, the dried blood from yesterday's catch. We stared silently at the tips of our rods, at the dragonflies that came and went. I lowered the tip of mine into the water, tentatively, pensively dislodging the fly, which darted two feet away, poised, darted two feet back, and came to rest again a little farther up the rod. There had been no years between the ducking of this dragonfly and the other one—the one that was part of memory. I looked at the boy, who was silently watching his fly, and it was my hands that held his rod, my eyes watching. I felt dizzy and didn't know which rod I was at the end of.

6   We caught two bass, hauling them in briskly as though they were mackerel, pulling them over the side of the boat in a businesslike manner without any landing net, and stunning them with a blow on the back of the head. When we got back for a swim before lunch, the lake was exactly where we had left it, the same number of inches from the dock, and there was only the merest suggestion of a breeze. This seemed an utterly enchanted sea, this lake you could leave to its own devices for a few hours and come back to, and find that it had not stirred, this constant and trustworthy body of water. In the shallows, the dark, water-soaked sticks and twigs, smooth and old, were undulating in clusters on the bottom against the clean ribbed sand, and the track of the mussel was plain. A school of minnows swam by, each

minnow with its small individual shadow, doubling the attendance, so clear and sharp in the sunlight. Some of the other campers were in swimming, along the shore, one of them with a cake of soap, and the water felt thin and clear and unsubstantial. Over the years there had been this person with the cake of soap, this cultist, and here he was. There had been no years.

7   Up to the farmhouse to dinner through the teeming, dusty field, the road under our sneakers was only a two-track road. The middle track was missing, the one with the marks of the hooves and the splotches of dried, flaky manure. There had always been three tracks to choose from in choosing which track to walk in; now the choice was narrowed down to two. For a moment I missed terribly the middle alternative. But the way led past the tennis court, and something about the way it lay there in the sun reassured me; the tape had loosened along the backline, the alleys were green with plantains and other weeds, and the net (installed in June and removed in September) sagged in the dry noon, and the whole place steamed with midday heat and hunger and emptiness. There was a choice of pie for dessert, and one was blueberry and one was apple, and the waitresses were the same country girls, there having been no passage of time, only the illusion of it as in a dropped curtain—the waitresses were still fifteen; their hair had been washed, that was the only difference—they had been to the movies and seen the pretty girls with the clean hair.

8   Summertime, oh, summertime, pattern of life indelible, the fade proof lake, the woods unshatterable, the pasture with the sweetfern and the juniper forever and ever, summer without end; this was the background, and the life along the shore was the design, the cottagers with their innocent and tranquil design, their tiny docks with the flagpole and the American flag floating against the white clouds in the blue sky, the little paths over the roots of the trees leading from camp to camp and the paths leading back to the outhouses and the can of lime for sprinkling, and at the souvenir counters at the store the miniature birch-bark canoes and the postcards that showed things looking a little better than they looked. This was the American family at play, escaping the city heat, wondering whether the newcomers in the camp at the head of the cove were "common" or "nice," wondering whether it was true that the people who drove up for Sunday dinner at the farmhouse were turned away because there wasn't enough chicken.

9   It seemed to me, as I kept remembering all this, that those times and those summers had been infinitely precious and worth saving. There had been jollity and peace and goodness. The arriving (at the beginning of August) had been so big a business in itself, at the railway station the farm wagon drawn up, the first smell of the pine-laden air, the first glimpse of the smiling farmer, and the great importance of the trunks and your father's enormous authority in such matters, and the feel of the wagon under you for the long ten-mile haul, and at the top of the last long hill catching the first view of the lake after eleven months of not seeing this cherished body of water. The shouts and cries of the other campers when they saw you, and the trunks to be unpacked, to give up their rich burden. (Arriving was less exciting now-

adays, when you sneaked up in your car and parked it under a tree near the camp and took out the bags and in five minutes it was all over, no fuss, no loud wonderful fuss about trunks.)

10   Peace and goodness and jollity. The only thing that was wrong now, really, was the sound of the place, an unfamiliar nervous sound of the outboard motors. This was the note that jarred, the one thing that would sometimes break the illusion and set the years moving. In those other summertimes all motors were inboard; and when they were at a little distance, the noise they made was a sedative, an ingredient of summer sleep. They were one-cylinder and two-cylinder engines, and some were make-and-break and some were jump-spark, but they all made a sleepy sound across the lake. The one-lungers throbbed and fluttered, and the twin-cylinder ones purred and purred, and that was a quiet sound, too. But now the campers all had outboards. In the day time, in the hot mornings, these motors made a petulant, irritable sound; at night, in the still evening when the afterglow lit the water, they whined about one's ears like mosquitoes. My boy loved our rented outboard, and his great desire was to achieve single-handed mastery over it, and authority, and he soon learned the trick of choking it a little (but not too much), and the adjustment of the needle valve. Watching him I would remember the things you could do with the old one-cylinder engine with the heavy flywheel, how you could have it eating out of your hand if you got really close to it spiritually. Motor boats in those days didn't have clutches, and you would make a landing by shutting off the motor at the proper time and coasting in with a dead rudder. But there was a way of reversing them, if you learned the trick, by cutting the switch and putting it on again exactly on the final dying revolution of the flywheel, so that it would kick back against compression and begin reversing. Approaching a dock in a strong following breeze, it was difficult to slow up sufficiently by the ordinary coasting method, and if a boy felt he had complete mastery over his motor, he was tempted to keep it running beyond its time and then reverse it a few feet from the dock. It took a cool nerve, because if you threw the switch a twentieth of a second too soon you would catch the flywheel when it still had speed enough to go up past center, and the boat would leap ahead, charging bull-fashion at the dock.

11   We had a good week at the camp. The bass were biting well and the sun shone endlessly, day after day. We would be tired at night and lie down in the accumulated heat of the little bedrooms after the long hot day and the breeze would stir almost imperceptibly outside and the smell of the swamp drift in through the rusty screens. Sleep would come easily and in the morning the red squirrel would be on the roof, tapping out his gay routine. I kept remembering everything, lying in bed in the mornings—the small steamboat that had a long rounded stern like the lip of a Ubangi, and how quietly she ran on the moon light sails, when the older boys played their mandolins and the girls sang and we ate doughnuts dipped in sugar, and how sweet the music was on the water in the shining night, and what it had felt like to think about girls then. After breakfast we would go up to the store and the

things were in the same place—the minnows in a bottle, the plugs and spinners disarranged and pawed over by the youngsters from the boys' camp, the Fig Newtons and the Beeman's gum. Outside, the road was tarred and cars stood in front of the store. Inside, all was just as it had always been, except there was more Coca-Cola and not so much Moxie and root beer and birch beer and sarsaparilla. We would walk out with the bottle of pop apiece and sometimes the pop would backfire up our noses and hurt. We explored the streams, quietly, where the turtles slid off the sunny logs and dug their way into the soft bottom; and we lay on the town wharf and fed worms to the tame bass. Everywhere we went I had trouble making out which was I, the one walking at my side, the one walking in my pants.

12   One afternoon while we were there at that lake a thunderstorm came up. It was like the revival of an old melodrama that I had seen long ago with childish awe. The second-act climax of the drama of the electrical disturbance over a lake in America had not changed in any important respect. This was the big scene, still the big scene. The whole thing was so familiar, the first feeling of oppression and heat and a general air around camp of not wanting to go very far away. In midafternoon (it was all the same) a curious darkening of the sky, and a lull in everything that had made life tick; and then the way the boats suddenly swung the other way at their moorings with the coming of a breeze out of the new quarter, and the premonitory rumble. Then the kettle drum, then the snare, then the bass drum and cymbals, then crackling light against the dark, and the gods grinning and licking their chops in the hills. Afterward the calm, the rain steadily rustling in the calm lake, the return of light and hope and spirits, and the campers running out in joy and relief to go swimming in the rain, their bright cries perpetuating the deathless joke about how they were getting simply drenched, and the children screaming with delight at the new sensation of bathing in the rain, and the joke about getting drenched linking the generations in a strong indestructible chain. And the comedian who waded in carrying an umbrella.

13   When the others went swimming, my son said he was going in, too. He pulled his dripping trunks from the line where they had hung all through the shower and wrung them out. Languidly, and with no thought of going in, I watched him, his hard little body, skinny and bare, saw him wince slightly as he pulled up around his vitals the small, soggy, icy garment. As he buckled the swollen belt, suddenly my groin felt the chill of death.

Writing Log/Journal Assignment

Write a journal entry in which you try to recapture a particularly special moment in time in your life with your family (a memory).

Individual and Collaborative Considerations

1. In what ways is the lake White returned to with his son like the lake he used to visit every summer with his family?

2. Describe the dominant tone of White's essay. What enables him to (1) create and (2) sustain his tone or mood? Does anything seem to disrupt his frame of mind?
3. What do you find effective or interesting about White's narrative techniques? How might you want to use similar techniques in your own writings?
4. How does White foreshadow the conclusion of his essay? What subtle clues does he drop to show the lake has changed and is not "frozen in time"?
5. Demonstrate how White uses specific, concrete words and active verbs to successfully convey specific details, especially those enabling you to visualize, hear, and smell the *special environment.*

Writing Activities

1. At the lake with his son, White comments, "I began to sustain the illusion that he was I, and therefore, by simple transposition, that I was my father." Write a narrative essay illustrating a situation where, like White, you sustained an illusion that you were another person.
2. Write about a shocking moment of revelation; maybe you realized you are growing old or drifting apart from old, seemingly inseparable relationships. Perhaps you became aware of the lack of power you have over your friends, relatives, or employees.

Brothers and Sisters

Alice Walker

Alice Walker was born in Eatonton, Georgia, in 1944—the eighth child of African American sharecroppers. Her works include *The Third Life of Grange Copeland* (1970), *Revolutionary Petunias* (1973), *Meridian* (1976), *You Can't Keep a Good Woman Down* (1981), and *The Color Purple*, for which she won the Pulitzer Prize and National Book Award for fiction (1983), *In Search of Our Mother's Gardens* (1984), *Horses Make a Landscape Look More Beautiful* (1984), *Temple of My Familiar* (1989), and *Possessing the Secret of Joy* (1992). In addition to her own work, Walker writes and lectures on African American authors like Zora Neal Hurston, Jean Toomer, and Langston Hughes—individuals who provided some of the models and inspiration for her own writing. Walker, who has always considered herself a "womanist," became a spokesperson for problems in African American families—especially those dealing with gender inequities. In "Brothers and

Sisters," for instance, she illustrates the double standard her parents set for the boys and girls in her family.

1   We lived on a farm in the South in the fifties, and my brothers, the four of them I knew (the fifth had left home when I was three years old), were allowed to watch animals being mated. This was not unusual; nor was it considered unusual that my older sister and I were frowned upon if we even asked, innocently, what was going on. One of my brothers explained the mating one day, using words my father had given him: "The bull is getting a little something on his stick," he said. And he laughed. "What stick?" I wanted to know. "Where did he get it? How did he pick it up? Where did he put it?" All my brothers laughed.

2   I believe my mother's theory about raising a large family of five boys and three girls was that the father should teach the boys and the mother teach the girls the facts, as one says, of life. So my father went around talking about bulls getting something on their sticks and she went around saying girls did not need to know about such things. They were "womanish" (a very bad way to be in those days) if they asked.

3   The thing was, watching the matings filled my brothers with an aimless sort of lust, as dangerous as it was unintentional. They knew enough to know that cows, months after mating, produced calves, but they were not bright enough to make the same connection between women and their offspring.

4   Sometimes, when I think of my childhood, it seems to me a particularly hard one. But in reality, everything awful that happened to me didn't seem to happen to *me* at all, but to my older sister. Through some incredible power to negate my presence around people I did not like, which produced invisibility (as well as an ability to appear mentally vacant when I was nothing of the kind), I was spared the humiliation she was subjected to, though at the same time, I felt every bit of it. It was as if she suffered for my benefit, and I vowed early in my life that none of the things that made emergence so miserable for her would happen to me.

5   The fact that she was not allowed at official matings did not mean she never saw any. While my brothers followed my father to the mating pens on the other side of the road near the barn, she stationed herself near the pigpen, or followed our many dogs until they were in a mating mood, or, failing to witness something there, she watched the chickens. On a farm it is impossible *not* to be conscious of sex, to wonder about it, to dream . . . but to whom was she to speak of her feelings? Not to my father, who thought all young women perverse. Not to my mother, who pretended all her children grew out of stumps she magically found in the forest. Not to me, who never found anything wrong with this lie.

6   When my sister menstruated she wore a thick packet of clean rags between her legs. It stuck out in front like a penis. The boys laughed at her as she served them at the table. Not knowing any better, and because our par-

ents did not dream of actually *discussing* what was going on, she would giggle nervously at herself. I hated her for giggling, and it was at those times I would think of her as dim-witted. She never complained, but she began to have strange fainting fits whenever she had her period. Her head felt as if it were splitting, she said, and everything she ate came up again. And her cramps were so severe she could not stand. She was forced to spend several days of each month in bed.

7   My father expected all of his sons to have sex with women. "Like bulls," he said, "a man *needs* to get a little something on his stick." And so, on Saturday nights, into town they went, chasing the girls. My sister was rarely allowed into town alone, and if the dress she wore fit too snugly at the waist, or if her cleavage dipped too far below her collarbone, she was made to stay home.

8   "But why can't I go too," she would cry, her face screwed up with the effort not to wail.

9   "They're boys, your brothers, *that's* why they can go."

10   Naturally, when she got the chance, she responded eagerly to boys. But when this was discovered she was whipped and locked up in her room.

11   I would go in to visit her.

12   "Straight Pine," she would say, "you don't know what it *feels* like to want to be loved by a man."

13   "And if this is what you get for feeling like it I never will," I said, with—I hoped—the right combination of sympathy and disgust.

14   "Men smell so good," she would whisper ecstatically. "And when they look into your eyes, you just melt."

15   Since they were so hard to catch, naturally she thought almost any of them terrific.

16   "Oh, that Alfred!" she would moon over some mediocre, square-headed boy, "he's so *sweet!*" And she would take his ugly picture out of her bosom and kiss it.

17   My father was always warning her not to come home if she ever found herself pregnant. My mother constantly reminded her that abortion was a sin. Later, although she never became pregnant, her period would not come for months at a time. The painful symptoms, however, never varied or ceased. She fell for the first man who loved her enough to beat her for looking at someone else, and when I was still in high school, she married him.

18   My fifth brother, the one I never knew, was said to be different from the rest. He had not liked matings. He would not watch them. He thought the cows should be given a choice. My father had disliked him because he was soft. My mother took up for him. "Jason is just tender-hearted," she would say in a way that made me know he was her favorite; "he takes after me." It was true that my mother cried about almost anything.

19   Who was this oldest brother? I wondered.

20   "Well," said my mother, "he was someone who always loved you. Of course he was a great big boy when you were born and out working on his own. He worked on a road gang building roads. Every morning before he

left he would come in the room where you were and pick you up and give you the biggest kisses. He used to look at you and just smile. It's a pity you don't remember him."

21   I agreed.

22   At my father's funeral I finally "met" my oldest brother. He is tall and black with thick gray hair above a young-looking face. I watched my sister cry over my father until she blacked out from grief. I saw my brothers sobbing, reminding each other of what a great father he had been. My oldest brother and I did not shed a tear between us. When I left my father's grave he came up and introduced himself. "You don't ever have to walk alone," he said, and put his arms around me.

23   One out of five ain't *too* bad, I thought, snuggling up.

24   But I didn't discover until recently his true uniqueness: He is the only one of my brothers who assumes responsibility for all his children. The other four all fathered children during those Saturday-night chases of twenty years ago. Children—my nieces and nephews whom I will probably never know— they neither acknowledge as their own, provide for, or even see.

25   It was not until I became a student of women's liberation ideology that I could understand and forgive my father. I needed an ideology that would define his behavior in context. The black movement had given me an ideology that helped explain his colorism (he *did* fall in love with my mother partly because she was so light; he never denied it). Feminism helped explain his sexism. I was relieved to know his sexist behavior was not something uniquely his own, but rather, an imitation of the behavior of the society around us.

26   All partisan movements add to the fullness of our understanding of society as a whole. They never detract; or, in any case, one must not allow them to do so. Experience adds to experience. "The more things the better," as O'Connor and Welty both have said, speaking, one of marriage, the other of Catholicism.

27   I desperately needed my father and brothers to give me male models I could respect, because white men (for example; being particularly handy in this sort of comparison)—whether in films or in person—offered man as dominator, as killer, and always as hypocrite.

28   My father failed because he copied the hypocrisy. And my brothers— except for one—never understood they must represent half the world to me, as I must represent the other half to them.*

Writing Log/Journal Assignment

Write a journal about privileges boys often enjoy which are not available to girls. Your journal may include anything from specific information to activities.

---

*Since this essay was written, my brothers have offered their name, acknowledgment, and some support to all their children. [Walker's note]

Individual and Collaborative Considerations

1. Why was Walker's sister "not allowed at official matings" of farm animals? How effective was this restriction?
2. In what way does Walker's father encourage and approve of his sons being promiscuous? How does Walker's father establish a double standard for conduct—especially on Saturday nights—between his sons and daughters? To what extent do you think Walker's father is like many fathers in the United States today?
3. How was Walker's fifth brother, Jason, different from his other brothers? What was his "true uniqueness"?
4. Why do you imagine Alice and Jason were the only two not to cry at their father's funeral? How did the other family members carry on? What sort of things did they say about him?
5. What finally enabled Walker to "forgive" her father? How? Why?

Writing Activities

1. Construct an argumentative thesis about the hypocrisy or double standards parents use when raising their children. Next, develop your essay using as many examples as you can find through research, interviews (of both parents and children), and personal experience.
2. Who should be responsible for informing children about "the facts of life"? Is an observation of mating animals or a command to abstain from any sexual activity, including a kiss, any substitute for an informed discussion about the potential consequences of sex? Take a position on the topic "Parental Responsibility and Sex Education," defending it in view of the world today (the population explosion, AIDS).

Astronomer's Wife

Kay Boyle

Born in Minnesota in 1903, Kay Boyle became an expatriate in France for many years of her life, returning to the United States in 1941. Her stories are published in *Wedding Day* (1930), *First Lover* (1933), *The White Horses of Vienna* (1936), *The Crazy Hunter* (1940), *Thirty Stories* (1946), *The Smoking Mountain* (1951), *Nothing Ever Breaks Except the Heart* (1966), and *Fifty Stories* (1980). Boyle was also the author of several novels, including *Plagued by the Nightingale* (1931), *Year Before Lust* (1932), *Gentlemen, I Address You Privately* (1933), *My Next Bride* (1934), *Death of a Man* (1936), *Monday Night*

(1938), *The Youngest Camel* (1939), *Primer for Combat* (1942), *Avalanche* (1943), *A Frenchman Must Die* (1946), *His Human Majesty* (1949), *Generation without Farewell* (1959), and *The Underground Woman* (1975). Boyle also wrote several volumes of poetry, including *Glad Day* (1938), *American Citizen* (1944), and *Testament to My Students* (1970). Her collection of essays on social issues is entitled *The Long Walk at San Francisco State* (1970). In "Astronomer's Wife," the speaker must choose for a moment between a relationship with a man (the plumber) firmly rooted in the "real world" and a relationship with a scholar (her husband) who is always peering out of it. Regardless of what the plumber's eyes conveyed, his appearance awakens an emotional deadness—a void between Mrs. Ames and her husband, the astronomer, forever with his head in the clouds.

There is an evil moment on awakening when all things seem to pause. But for women, they only falter and may be set in action by a single move: a lifted hand and the pendulum will swing, or the voice raised and through every room the pulse takes up its beating. The astronomer's wife felt the interval gaping and at once filled it to the brim. She fetched up her gentle voice and sent it warily down the stairs for coffee, swung her feet out upon the oval mat, and hailed the morning with her bare arms' quivering flesh drawn taut in rhythmic exercise: left, left, left my wife and fourteen children, right, right, right in the middle of the dusty road.

The day would proceed from this, beat by beat, without reflection, like every other day. The astronomer was still asleep, or feigning it, and she, once out of bed, had come into her own possession. Although scarcely ever out of sight of the impenetrable silence of his brow, she would be absent from him all the day in being clean, busy, kind. He was a man of other things, a dreamer. At times he lay still for hours, at others he sat upon the roof behind his telescope, or wandered down the pathway to the road and out across the mountains. This day, like any other, would go on from the removal of the spot left there from dinner on the astronomer's vest to the severe thrashing of the mayonnaise for lunch. That man might be each time the new arching wave, and woman the undertow that sucked him back, were things she had been told by his silence were so.

In spite of the earliness of the hour, the girl had heard her mistress's voice and was coming up the stairs. At the threshold of the bedroom she paused, and said: "Madame, the plumber is here."

The astronomer's wife put on her white and scarlet smock very quickly and buttoned it at the neck. Then she stepped carefully around the motionless spread of water in the hall.

5   "Tell him to come right up," she said. She laid her hands on the bannisters and stood looking down the wooden stairway. "Ah, I am Mrs. Ames," she said softly as she saw him mounting. "I am Mrs. Ames," she said softly, softly down the flight of stairs. "I am Mrs. Ames," spoken soft as a willow weeping. "The professor is still sleeping. Just step this way."

The plumber himself looked up and saw Mrs. Ames with her voice hushed, speaking to him. She was a youngish woman, but this she had forgotten. The mystery and silence of her husband's mind lay like a chiding finger on her lips. Her eyes were gray, for the light had been extinguished in them. The strange dim halo of her yellow hair was still uncombed and sideways on her head.

For all of his heavy boots, the plumber quieted the sound of his feet, and together they went down the hall, picking their way around the still lake of water that spread as far as the landing and lay docile there. The plumber was a tough, hardy man; but he took off his hat when he spoke to her and looked her fully, almost insolently in the eye.

"Does it come from the wash-basin," he said, "or from the other . . . ?"

"Oh, from the other," said Mrs. Ames without hesitation.

10   In this place the villas were scattered out few and primitive, and although beauty lay without there was no reflection of her face within. Here all was awkward and unfit; a sense of wrestling with uncouth forces gave everything an austere countenance. Even the plumber, dealing as does a woman with matters under hand, was grave and stately. The mountains round about seemed to have cast them into the shadow of great dignity.

Mrs. Ames began speaking of their arrival that summer in the little villa, mourning each event as it followed on the other.

"Then, just before going to bed last night," she said, "I noticed something was unusual."

The plumber cast down a folded square of sack-cloth on the brimming floor and laid his leather apron on it. Then he stepped boldly onto the heart of the island it shaped and looked long into the overflowing bowl.

"The water should be stopped from the meter in the garden," he said at last.

15   "Oh, I did that," said Mrs. Ames, "the very first thing last night. I turned it off at once, in my nightgown, as soon as I saw what was happening. But all this had already run in."

The plumber looked for a moment at her red kid slippers. She was standing just at the edge of the clear, pure-seeming tide.

"It's no doubt the soil lines," he said severely. "It may be that something has stopped them, but my opinion is that the water seals aren't working. That's the trouble often enough in such cases. If you had a valve you wouldn't be caught like this."

Mrs. Ames did not know how to meet this rebuke. She stood, swaying a little, looking into the plumber's blue relentless eye.

"I'm sorry—I'm sorry that my husband," she said, "is still—resting and cannot go into this with you. I'm sure it must be very interesting. . . ."

20   "You'll probably have to have the traps sealed," said the plumber grimly, and at the sound of this Mrs. Ames' hand flew in dismay to the side of her face. The plumber made no move, but the set of his mouth as he looked at her seemed to soften. "Anyway, I'll have a look from the garden end," he said.

"Oh, do," said the astronomer's wife in relief. Here was a man who spoke of action and object as simply as women did! But however hushed her voice had been, it carried clearly to Professor Ames who lay, dreaming and solitary, upon his bed. He heard their footsteps come down the hall, pause, and skip across the pool of overflow.

"Katherine!" said the astronomer in a ringing tone. "There's a problem worthy of your mettle!"

Mrs. Ames did not turn her head, but led the plumber swiftly down the stairs. When the sun in the garden struck her face, he saw there was a wave of color in it, but this may have been anything but shame.

"You see how it is," said the plumber, as if leading her mind away. "The drains run from these houses right down the hill, big enough for a man to stand upright in them, and clean as a whistle too." There they stood in the garden with the vegetation flowering in disorder all about. The plumber looked at the astronomer's wife. "They come out at the torrent on the other side of the forest beyond there," he said.

25   But the words the astronomer had spoken still sounded in her in despair. The mind of man, she knew, made steep and sprightly flights, pursued illusion, took foothold in the nameless things that cannot pass between the thumb and finger. But whenever the astronomer gave voice to the thoughts that soared within him, she returned in gratitude to the long expanses of his silence. Desert-like they stretched behind and before the articulation of his scorn.

Life, life is an open sea, she sought to explain it in sorrow, and to survive women cling to the floating debris on the tide. But the plumber had suddenly fallen upon his knees in the grass and had crooked his fingers through the ring of the drains' trap-door. When she looked down she saw that he was looking up into her face, and she saw too that his hair was as light as gold.

"Perhaps Mr. Ames," he said rather bitterly, "would like to come down with me and have a look around?"

"Down?" said Mrs. Ames in wonder.

"Into the drains," said the plumber brutally. "They're a study for a man who likes to know what's what."

30   "Oh, Mr. Ames," said Mrs. Ames in confusion. "He's still—still in bed, you see."

The plumber lifted his strong, weathered face and looked curiously at her. Surely it seemed to him strange for a man to linger in bed, with the sun pouring yellow as wine all over the place. The astronomer's wife saw his lean cheeks, his high, rugged bones, and the deep seams in his brow. His flesh was as firm and clean as wood, stained richly tan with the climate's rigor. His fingers were blunt, but comprehensible to her, gripped in the ring and holding the iron door wide. The backs of his hands were bound round and round with ripe blue veins of blood.

"At any rate," said the astronomer's wife, and the thought of it moved her lips to smile a little, "Mr. Ames would never go down there alive. He likes going up," she said. And she, in her turn, pointed, but impudently, towards the heavens. "On the roof. Or on the mountains. He's been up on the tops of them many times."

"It's a matter of habit," said the plumber, and suddenly he went down the trap. Mrs. Ames saw a bright little piece of his hair still shining, like a star, long after the rest of him had gone. Out of the depths, his voice, hollow and dark with foreboding, returned to her. "I think something has stopped the elbow," was what he said.

This was speech that touched her flesh and bone and made her wonder. When her husband spoke of height, having no sense of it, she could not picture it nor hear. Depth or magic passed her by unless a name were given. But madness in a daily shape, as elbow stopped, she saw clearly and well. She sat down on the grasses, bewildered that it should be a man who had spoken to her so.

35 She saw the weeds springing up, and she did not move to tear them up from life. She sat powerless, her senses veiled, with no action taking shape beneath her hands. In this way some men sat for hours on end, she knew, tracking a single thought back to its origin. The mind of man could balance and divide, weed out, destroy. She sat on the full, burdened grasses, seeking to think, and dimly waiting for the plumber to return.

Whereas her husband had always gone up, as the dead go, she knew now that there were others who went down, like the corporeal being of the dead. That men were then divided into two bodies now seemed clear to Mrs. Ames. This knowledge stunned her with its simplicity and took the uneasy motion from her limbs. She could not stir, but sat facing the mountains' rocky flanks, and harking in silence to lucidity. Her husband was the mind, this other man the meat, of all mankind.

After a little, the plumber emerged from the earth: first the light top of his head, then the burnt brow, and then the blue eyes fringed with whitest lash. He braced his thick hands flat on the pavings of the garden-path and swung himself completely from the pit.

"It's the soil lines," he said pleasantly. "The gases," he said as he looked down upon her lifted face, "are backing up the drains."

"What in the world are we going to do?" said the astronomer's wife softly. There was a young and strange delight in putting questions to which true answers would be given. Everything the astronomer had ever said to her was a continuous query to which there could be no response.

40 "Ah, come, now," said the plumber, looking down and smiling. "There's a remedy for every ill, you know. Sometimes it may be that," he said as if speaking to a child, "or sometimes the other thing. But there's always a help for everything amiss."

Things come out of herbs and make you young again, he might have been saying to her; or the first good rain will quench any drought; or time of itself will put a broken bone together.

"I'm going to follow the ground pipe out right to the torrent," the plumber was saying. "The trouble's between here and there and I'll find it on the way. There's nothing at all that can't be done over for the caring," he was saying, and his eyes were fastened on her face in insolence, or gentleness, or love.

The astronomer's wife stood up, fixed a pin in her hair, and turned around towards the kitchen. Even while she was calling the servant's name, the plumber began speaking again.

"I once had a cow that lost her cud," the plumber was saying. The girl came out on the kitchen-step and Mrs. Ames stood smiling at her in the sun.

45 "The trouble is very serious, very serious," she said across the garden. "When Mr. Ames gets up, please tell him I've gone down."

She pointed briefly to the open door in the pathway, and the plumber hoisted his kit on his arm and put out his hand to help her down.

"But I made her another in no time," he was saying, "out of flowers and things and what-not."

"Oh," said the astronomer's wife in wonder as she stepped into the heart of the earth. She took his arm, knowing that what he said was true.

Writing Log/Journal Assignment

Create an imaginary dialogue between the plumber and the astronomer. You might have them discuss anything from politics, poetry, and practical sense to starry-eyed and earth-bound visions. Somewhere in this assignment, bring up the subject of love, and possibly, the astronomer's wife.

Individual and Collaborative Considerations

1. Explain the associations you make with the occupation of a plumber and vocation of an astronomer. Which is more practical—if either?
2. In what way does Mrs. Ames seem to be locked in a loveless marriage? What type of person does Mr. Ames, the astronomer, seem to be? What do the few words he speaks in the story reveal about him?
3. Why do you imagine Mrs. Ames takes such delight in asking questions that have answers and watching a man present solutions to problems?
4. Is this a story of love, a story of friendship, or both? With his eyes "fastened on her face in insolence, or gentleness, or love," what might the plumber be insinuating when he says, "There's nothing at all that can't be done over for the caring"?
5. Analyze the final paragraph in Boyle's story: " 'Oh,' said the astronomer's wife in wonder as she stepped into the heart of the earth. She took his arm, knowing that what he said was true."

Writing Activities

1. Similar to D. H. Lawrence's "The Horse Dealer's Daughter," Boyle's story deals with an awakening of repressed emotions. Write an essay explain-

ing and analyzing the process you went through to awaken emotions that you repressed for social, cultural, or personal reasons. What friendships became possible for you? How did you become receptive to others?

2. Write an essay in which you examine the symbolism associated with a particular type of relationship: physical, spiritual, and so forth. What you have to say about such symbolism will serve as your thesis.

The Horse Dealer's Daughter

D. H. Lawrence

D. H. Lawrence grew up in a household amidst poverty and turmoil, and by the time he was fifteen years old, he had to leave school and work part time as a clerk. He later became a teacher, at which time *The White Peacock* (1911), followed by *The Trespasser* (1912), appeared. Subsequent novels include *Sons and Lovers* (1913), *The Rainbow* (1915), *Women in Love* (1916—although he did not find a publisher until 1920), *The Lost Girl* (1920), *Aaron's Rod* (1922), *Kangaroo* (1923), *The Plumed Serpent* (1926), and *Lady Chatterly's Lover* (1928). Highly renowned for his short stories, Lawrence assembled several collections such as *The Prussian Officer* (1914), *England, My England* (1922), and *The Woman Who Rode Away* (1928). Lawrence was also a fine poet and published several volumes of verse: *Love Poems* (1913), *Look! We Have Come Through!* (1917), *Birds, Beasts and Flowers* (1923), *Pansies* (1929), and *Complete Poems* (3 vols., 1957). Among his nonfiction works are *Movements in European History* (1921), *Psychoanalysis and the Unconscious* (1921), *Fantasia of the Unconscious* (1922), *Studies in Classic American Literature* (1923), *Apocalypse* (1931), and *The Letters of D. H. Lawrence* (1932). Despite Lawrence's prolific literary output, his works were frequently censored due to their explicit sexual content and disregard for "conventional moral attitudes." As can be seen in "The Horse Dealer's Daughter," his writing style is harshly realistic and highly controlled. He believed one of the most important functions of fiction was to provide an emotional experience although "no emotion is supreme or exclusively worth living for. All emotions go to the achieving of a living relationship between a human being and the other human being or creature or thing he becomes purely related to."

"Well, Mabel, and what are you going to do with yourself?" asked Joe, with foolish flippancy. He felt quite safe himself. Without listening for an answer, he turned aside, worked a grain of tobacco to the tip of his tongue and spat it out. He did not care about anything, since he felt safe himself.

The three brothers and the sister sat round the desolate breakfast table, attempting some sort of desultory consultation. The morning's post had given the final tap to the family fortune, and all was over. The dreary dining room itself, with its heavy mahogany furniture, looked as if it were waiting to be done away with.

But the consultation amounted to nothing. There was a strange air of ineffectuality about the three men, as they sprawled at table, smoking and reflecting vaguely on their own condition. The girl was alone, a rather short, sullen-looking young woman of twenty-seven. She did not share the same life as her brothers. She would have been goodlooking, save for the impassive fixity of her face, "bull-dog," as her brothers called it.

There was a confused tramping of horses' feet outside. The three men all sprawled round in their chairs to watch. Beyond the dark holly bushes that separated the strip of lawn from the highroad, they could see a cavalcade of shire horses swinging out of their own yard, being taken for exercise. This was the last time. These were the last horses that would go through their hands. The young men watched with critical, callous look. They were all frightened at the collapse of their lives, and the sense of disaster in which they were involved left them no inner freedom.

5   Yet they were three fine, well-set fellows enough. Joe, the eldest, was a man of thirty-three, broad and handsome in a hot, flushed way. His face was red, he twisted his black moustache over a thick finger, his eyes were shallow and restless. He had a sensual way of uncovering his teeth when he laughed, and his bearing was stupid. Now he watched the horses with a glazed look of helplessness in his eyes, a certain stupor of downfall.

The great draught-horses swung past. They were tied head to tail, four of them, and they heaved along to where a lane branched off from the highroad, planting their great hoofs floutingly in the fine black mud, swinging their great rounded haunches sumptuously, and trotting a few sudden steps as they were led into the lane, round the corner. Every movement showed a massive, slumbrous strength, and a stupidity which held them in subjection. The groom at the head looked back, jerking the leading rope. And the cavalcade moved out of sight up the lane, the tail of the last horse, bobbed up tight and stiff, held out taut from the swinging great haunches as they rocked behind the hedges in a motion-like sleep.

Joe watched with glazed hopeless eyes. The horses were almost like his own body to him. He felt he was done for now. Luckily he was engaged to a woman as old as himself, and therefore her father, who was steward of a neighboring estate, would provide him with a job. He would marry and go into harness. His life was over, he would be a subject animal now.

He turned uneasily aside, the retreating steps of the horses echoing in his ears. Then, with foolish restlessness, he reached for the scraps of bacon rind from the plates, and making a faint whistling sound, flung them to the terrier that lay against the fender. He watched the dog swallow them, and waited till the creature looked into his eyes. Then a faint grin came on his face, and in a high, foolish voice he said:

"You won't get much more bacon, shall you, you little bitch?"

10 The dog faintly and dismally wagged its tail, then lowered its haunches, circled round, and lay down again.

There was another helpless silence at the table. Joe sprawled uneasily in his seat, not willing to go till the family conclave was dissolved. Fred Henry, the second brother, was erect, clean-limbed, alert. He had watched the passing of the horses with more sang-froid. If he was an animal, like Joe, he was an animal which controls, not one which is controlled. He was master of any horse, and he carried himself with a well-tempered air of mastery. But he was not master of the situations of life. He pushed his coarse brown moustache upwards, off his lip, and glanced irritably at his sister, who sat impassive and inscrutable.

"You'll go and stop with Lucy for a bit, shan't you?" he asked. The girl did not answer.

"I don't see what else you can do," persisted Fred Henry.

"Go as a skivvy," Joe interpolated laconically.

15 The girl did not move a muscle.

"If I was her, I should go in for training for a nurse," said Malcolm, the youngest of them all. He was the baby of the family, a young man of twenty-two, with a fresh, jaunty *museau*.

But Mabel did not take any notice of him. They had talked at her and round her for so many years, that she hardly heard them at all.

The marble clock on the mantelpiece softly chimed the half-hour, the dog rose uneasily from the hearthrug and looked at the party at the breakfast table. But still they sat on in ineffectual conclave.

"Oh, all right," said Joe suddenly, apropos of nothing. "I'll get a move on."

20 He pushed back his chair, straddled his knees with a downward jerk, to get them free, in horsey fashion, and went to the fire. Still he did not go out of the room; he was curious to know what the others would do or say. He began to charge his pipe, looking down at the dog and saying, in a high, affected voice:

"Going wi' me? Going wi' me are ter? Tha'rt goin' further tha that counts on just now, dost hear?"

The dog faintly wagged its tail, the man stuck out his jaw and covered his pipe with his hands, and puffed intently, losing himself in the tobacco, looking down all the while at the dog with an absent brown eye. The dog looked at him in mournful distrust. Joe stood with his knees stuck out, in real horsey fashion.

"Have you had a letter from Lucy?" Fred Henry asked of his sister.

"Last week," came the neutral reply.

25 "And what does she say?"

There was no answer.

"Does she *ask* you to go and stop there?" persisted Fred Henry.

"She says I can if I like."

"Well, then, you'd better. Tell her you'll come on Monday."

30   This was received in silence.

"That's what you'll do then, is it?" said Fred Henry, in some exasperation.

But she made no answer. There was a silence of futility and irritation in the room. Malcolm grinned fatuously.

"You'll have to make up your mind between now and next Wednesday," said Joe loudly, "or else find yourself lodgings on the curbstone."

The face of the young woman darkened, but she sat on immutable.

35   "Here's Jack Fergusson!" exclaimed Malcolm, who was looking aimlessly out of the window.

"Where?" exclaimed Joe, loudly.

"Just gone past."

"Coming in?"

Malcolm craned his neck to see the gate.

40   "Yes," he said.

There was a silence. Mabel sat on like one condemned, at the head of the table. Then a whistle was heard from the kitchen. The dog got up and barked sharply. Joe opened the door and shouted:

"Come on."

After a moment a young man entered. He was muffled up in overcoat and a purple woolen scarf, and his tweed cap, which he did not remove, was pulled down on his head. He was of medium height, his face was rather long and pale, his eyes looked tired.

"Hello, Jack! Well, Jack!" exclaimed Malcolm and Joe. Fred Henry merely said, "Jack."

45   "What's doing?" asked the newcomer, evidently addressing Fred Henry.

"Same. We've got to be out by Wednesday. Got a cold?"

"I have—got it bad, too."

"Why don't you stop in?"

"*Me* stop in? When I can't stand on my legs, perhaps I shall have a chance." The young man spoke huskily. He had a slight Scotch accent.

50   "It's a knock-out, isn't it," said Joe, boisterously, "if a doctor goes round croaking with a cold. Looks bad for the patients, doesn't it?"

The young doctor looked at him slowly.

"Anything the matter with *you*, then?" he asked sarcastically.

"Not as I know of. Damn your eyes, I hope not. Why?"

"I thought you were very concerned about the patients, wondered if you might be one yourself."

55   "Damn it, no, I've never been patient to no flaming doctor, and hope I never shall be," returned Joe.

At this point Mabel rose from the table, and they all seemed to become aware of her existence. She began putting the dishes together. The young doctor looked at her, but did not address her. He had not greeted her. She went out of the room with the tray, her face impassive and unchanged.

"When are you off then, all of you?" asked the doctor.

"I'm catching the eleven-forty," replied Malcolm. "Are you goin' down wi' th' trap, Joe?"

"Yes, I've told you I'm going down wi' th' trap, haven't I?"

60 "We'd better be getting her in then. So long, Jack, if I don't see you before I go," said Malcolm, shaking hands.

He went out, followed by Joe, who seemed to have his tail between his legs.

"Well, this is the devil's own," exclaimed the doctor, when he was left alone with Fred Henry. "Going before Wednesday, are you?"

"That's the orders," replied the other.

"Where, to Northampton?"

65 "That's it."

"The devil!" exclaimed Fergusson, with quiet chagrin.

And there was silence between the two.

"All settled up, are you?" asked Fergusson.

"About."

70 There was another pause.

"Well, I shall miss yer, Freddy, boy," said the young doctor.

"And I shall miss thee, Jack," returned the other.

"Miss you like hell," mused the doctor.

Fred Henry turned aside. There was nothing to say. Mabel came in again, to finish clearing the table.

75 "What are *you* going to do, then, Miss Pervin?" asked Fergusson. "Going to your sister's, are you?"

Mabel looked at him with her steady, dangerous eyes, that always made him uncomfortable, unsettling his superficial ease.

"No," she said.

"Well, what in the name of fortune *are* you going to do? Say what you mean to do," cried Fred Henry, with futile intensity.

But she only averted her head, and continued her work. She folded the white table-cloth, and put on the chenille cloth.

80 "The sulkiest bitch that ever trod!" muttered her brother.

But she finished her task with perfectly impassive face, the young doctor watching her interestedly all the while. Then she went out.

Fred Henry stared after her, clenching his lips, his blue eyes fixing in sharp antagonism, as he made a grimace of sour exasperation.

"You could bray her into bits, and that's all you'd get out of her," he said in a small, narrowed tone.

The doctor smiled faintly.

85 "What's she *going* to do, then?" he asked.

"Strike me if *I* know!" returned the other.

There was a pause. Then the doctor stirred.

"I'll be seeing you to-night, shall I?" he said to his friend.

"Ay—where's it to be? Are we going over to Jessdale?"

90 "I don't know. I've got such a cold on me. I'll come round to the Moon and Stars, anyway."

"Let Lizzie and May miss their night for once, eh?"

"That's it—if I feel as I do now."

"All's one—"

The two young men went through the passage and down to the back door together. The house was large, but it was servantless now, and desolate. At the back was a small bricked house-yard, and beyond that a big square, graveled fine and red, and having stables on two sides. Sloping, dank, winter-dark fields stretched away on the open sides.

95 But the stables were empty. Joseph Pervin, the father of the family, had been a man of no education, who had become a fairly large horse dealer. The stables had been full of horses, there was a great turmoil and come-and-go of horses and of dealers and grooms. Then the kitchen was full of servants. But of late things had declined. The old man had married a second time, to retrieve his fortunes. Now he was dead and everything was gone to the dogs, there was nothing but debt and threatening.

For months, Mabel had been servantless in the big house, keeping the home together in penury for her ineffectual brothers. She had kept house for ten years. But previously it was with unstinted means. Then, however brutal and coarse everything was, the sense of money had kept her proud, confident. The men might be foul-mouthed, the women in the kitchen might have bad reputations, her brothers might have illegitimate children. But so long as there was money, the girl felt herself established, and brutally proud, reserved.

No company came to the house, save dealers and coarse men. Mabel had no associates of her own sex, after her sister went away. But she did not mind. She went regularly to church, she attended to her father. And she lived in the memory of her mother, who had died when she was fourteen, and whom she had loved. She had loved her father, too, in a different way, depending upon him, and feeling secure in him, until at the age of fifty-four he married again. And then she had set hard against him. Now he had died and left them all hopelessly in debt.

She had suffered badly during the period of poverty. Nothing, however, could shake the curious sullen, animal pride that dominated each member of the family. Now, for Mabel, the end had come. Still she would not cast about her. She would follow her own way just the same. She would always hold the keys of her own situation. Mindless and persistent, she endured from day to day. Why should she think? Why should she answer anybody? It was enough that this was the end, and there was no way out. She need not pass any more darkly along the main street of the small town, avoiding every eye. She need not demean herself any more, going into the shops and buying the cheapest food. This was at an end. She thought of nobody, not even of herself. Mindless and persistent, she seemed in a sort of ecstasy to be coming nearer to her fulfillment, her own glorification, approaching her dead mother, who was glorified.

In the afternoon she took a little bag, with shears and sponge and a small scrubbing brush, and went out. It was a gray, wintry day, with saddened, dark green fields and an atmosphere blackened by the smoke of foundries not far off. She went quickly, darkly along the causeway, heeding nobody, through the town to the churchyard.

100   There she always felt secure, as if no one could see her, although as a matter of fact she was exposed to the stare of every one who passed along under the churchyard wall. Nevertheless, once under the shadow of the great looming church, among the graves, she felt immune from the world, re-served within the thick churchyard wall as in another country.

Carefully she clipped the grass from the grave, and arranged the pinky white, small chrysanthemums in the tin cross. When this was done, she took an empty jar from a neighboring grave, brought water, and carefully, most scrupulously sponged the marble headstone and the coping-stone.

It gave her sincere satisfaction to do this. She felt in immediate contact with the world of her mother. She took minute pains, went through the park in a state bordering on pure happiness, as if in performing this task she came into a subtle, intimate connection with her mother. For the life she followed here in the world was far less real than the world of death she inherited from her mother.

The doctor's house was just by the church. Fergusson, being a mere hired assistant, was slave to the countryside. As he hurried now to attend to the outpatients in the surgery, glancing across the graveyard with his quick eyes, he saw the girl at her task at the grave. She seemed so intent and remote, it was like looking into another world. Some mystical element was touched in him. He slowed down as he walked, watching her as if spellbound.

She lifted her eyes, feeling him looking. Their eyes met. And each looked away again at once, each feeling, in some way, found out by the other. He lifted his cap and passed on down the road. There remained distinct in his consciousness, like a vision, the memory of her face, lifted from the tomb-stone in the churchyard, and looking at him with slow, large, portentous eyes. It *was* portentous, her face. It seemed to mesmerize him. There was a heavy power in her eyes which laid hold of his whole being, as if he had drunk some powerful drug. He had been feeling weak and done before. Now the life came back into him, he felt delivered from his own fretted, daily self.

105   He finished his duties at the surgery as quickly as might be, hastily filling up the bottle of the waiting people with cheap drugs. Then, in perpetual haste, he set off again to visit several cases in another part of his round, before teatime. At all times he preferred to walk if he could, but particularly when he was not well. He fancied the motion restored him.

The afternoon was falling. It was gray, deadened, and wintry, with a slow, moist, heavy coldness sinking in and deadening all the faculties. But why should he think or notice? He hastily climbed the hill and turned across the dark green fields, following the black cindertrack. In the distance, across a shallow dip in the country, the small town was clustered like smouldering ash, a tower, a spire, a heap of low, raw, extinct houses. And on the nearest fringe of the town, sloping into the dip, was Oldmeadow, the Pervins' house. He could see the stables and the outbuildings distinctly, as they lay towards him on the slope. Well, he would not go there many more times! Another resource would be lost to him, another place gone: the only company he cared for in the alien, ugly little town he was losing. Nothing but work, drudgery, constant hastening from dwelling to dwelling among the colliers and the iron-workers. It wore him out, but at the same time he had a craving for it. It was a stimulant to him to be in the homes of the working people, moving as it were through the innermost body of their life. His nerves were excited and gratified. He could come so near, into the very lives of the rough, inarticulate, powerfully emotional men and women. He grumbled, he said he hated the hellish hole. But as a matter of fact it excited him, the contact with the rough, strongly-feeling people was a stimulant applied direct to his nerves.

Below Oldmeadow, in the green, shallow, soddened hollow of fields, lay a square, deep pond. Roving across the landscape, the doctor's quick eye detected a figure in black passing through the gate of the field, down towards the pond. He looked again. It would be Mabel Pervin. His mind suddenly became alive and attentive.

Why was she going down there? He pulled up on the path on the slope above, and stood staring. He could just make sure of the small black figure moving in the hollow of the failing day. He seemed to see her in the midst of such obscurity, that he was like a clairvoyant, seeing rather with the mind's eye than with ordinary sight. Yet he could see her positively enough, while he kept his eye attentive. He felt, if he looked away from her, in the thick, ugly falling dusk, he would lose her altogether.

He followed her minutely as she moved, direct and intent, like something transmitted rather than stirring in voluntary activity, straight down the field towards the pond. There she stood on the bank for a moment. She never raised her head. Then she waded slowly into the water.

110   He stood motionless as the small black figure walked slowly and deliberately towards the center of the pond, very slowly, gradually moving deeper into the motionless water, and still moving forward as the water got up to her breast. Then he could see her no more in the dusk of the dead afternoon.

"There!" he exclaimed. "Would you believe it?"

And he hastened straight down, running over the wet, soddened fields, pushing through the hedges, down into the depression of callous wintry obscurity. It took him several minutes to come to the pond. He stood on the bank, breathing heavily. He could see nothing. His eyes seemed to penetrate the dead water. Yes, perhaps that was the dark shadow of her black clothing beneath the surface of the water.

He slowly ventured into the pond. The bottom was deep, soft clay, he sank in, and the water clasped dead cold round his legs. As he stirred he could smell the cold, rotten clay that fouled up into the water. It was objectionable in his lungs. Still, repelled and yet not heeding, he moved deeper into the pond. The cold water rose over his thighs, over his loins, upon his abdomen. The lower part of his body was all sunk in the hideous cold element. And the bottom was so deeply soft and uncertain he was afraid of pitching with his mouth underneath. He could not swim, and was afraid.

He crouched a little, spreading his hands under the water and moving them round, trying to feel for her. The dead cold pond swayed upon his chest. He moved again, a little deeper, and again, with his hands underneath, he felt all around under the water. And he touched her clothing. But it evaded his fingers. He made a desperate effort to grasp it.

115 And so doing he lost his balance and went under, horribly, suffocating in the foul earthy water, struggling madly for a few moments. At last, after what seemed an eternity, he got his footing, rose again into the air and looked around. He gasped, and knew he was in the world. Then he looked at the water. She had risen near him. He grasped her clothing, and drawing her nearer, turned to take his way to land again.

He went very slowly, carefully, absorbed in the slow progress. He rose higher, climbing out of the pond. The water was now only about his legs; he was thankful, full of relief to be out of the clutches of the pond. He lifted her and staggered on to the bank, out of the horror of wet, gray clay.

He laid her down on the bank. She was quite unconscious and running with water. He made the water come from her mouth, he worked to restore her. He did not have to work very long before he could feel the breathing begin again in her; she was breathing naturally. He worked a little longer. He could feel her live beneath his hands; she was coming back. He wiped her face, wrapped her in his overcoat, looked round into the dim, dark gray world, then lifted her and staggered down the bank and across the fields.

It seemed an unthinkably long way, and his burden so heavy he felt he would never get to the house. But at last he was in the stableyard, and then in the house-yard. He opened the door and went into the house. In the kitchen he laid her down on the hearthrug, and called. The house was empty. But the fire was burning in the grate.

Then again he kneeled to attend to her. She was breathing regularly, her eyes were wide open and as if conscious, but there seemed something missing in her look. She was conscious in herself, but unconscious of her surroundings.

120 He ran upstairs, took blankets from a bed, and put them before the fire to warm. Then he removed her saturated, earthy-smelling clothing, rubbed her dry with a towel, and wrapped her naked in the blankets. Then he went into the dining-room, to look for spirits. There was a little whisky. He drank a gulp himself, and put some into her mouth.

The effect was instantaneous. She looked full into his face, as if she had been seeing him for some time, and yet had only just become conscious of him.

"Dr. Fergusson?" she said.

"What?" he answered.

He was divesting himself of his coat, intending to find some dry clothing upstairs. He could not bear the smell of the dead, clayey water, and he was mortally afraid of his own health.

125 "What did I do?" she asked.

"Walked into the pond," he replied. He had begun to shudder like one sick, and could hardly attend to her. Her eyes remained full on him, he seemed to be going dark in his mind, looking back at her helplessly. The shuddering became quieter in him, his life came back in him, dark and unknowing, but strong again.

"Was I out of my mind?" she asked, while her eyes were fixed on him all the time.

"Maybe, for the moment," he replied. He felt quiet, because his strength came back. The strange fretful strain had left him.

"Am I out of my mind now?" she asked.

130 "Are you?" he reflected a moment. "No," he answered truthfully. "I don't see that you are." He turned his face aside. He was afraid now, because he felt dazed, and felt dimly that her power was stronger than his, in this issue. And she continued to look at him fixedly all the time. "Can you tell me where I shall find some dry things to put on?" he asked.

"Did you dive into the pond for me?" she asked.

"No," he answered. "I walked in. But I went in overhead as well."

There was silence for a moment. He hesitated. He very much wanted to go upstairs to get into dry clothing. But there was another desire in him. And she seemed to hold him. His will seemed to have gone to sleep, and left him, standing there slack before her. But he felt warm inside himself. He did not shudder at all, though his clothes were sodden on him.

"Why did you?" she asked.

135 "Because I didn't want you to do such a foolish thing," he said.

"It wasn't foolish," she said, still gazing at him as she lay on the floor, with a sofa cushion under her head. "It was the right thing to do. _I_ knew best, then."

"I'll go and shift these wet things," he said. But still he had not the power to move out of her presence, until she sent him. It was as if she had the life of his body in her hands, and he could not extricate himself. Or perhaps he did not want to.

Suddenly she sat up. Then she became aware of her own immediate condition. She felt the blankets about her, she knew her own limbs. For a moment it seemed as if her reason were going. She looked round, with wild eye, as if seeking something. He stood still with fear. She saw her clothing lying scattered.

"Who undressed me?" she asked, her eyes resting full and inevitable on his face.

140 "I did," he replied, "to bring you round."

For some moments she sat and gazed at him awfully, her lips parted.

"Do you love me, then?" she asked.

He only stood and stared at her, fascinated. His soul seemed to melt.

She shuffled forward on her knees, and put her arms round him, round his legs, as he stood there, pressing her breasts against his knees and thighs, clutching him with strange, convulsive certainty, pressing his thighs against her, drawing him to her face, her throat, as she looked up at him with flaring, humble eyes of transfiguration, triumphant in first possession.

145 "You love me," she murmured, in strange transport, yearning and triumphant and confident. "You love me. I know you love me, I know."

And she was passionately kissing his knees, through the wet clothing, passionately and indiscriminately kissing his knees, his legs, as if unaware of everything.

He looked down at the tangled wet hair, the wild, bare, animal shoulders. He was amazed, bewildered, and afraid. He had never thought of loving her. He had never wanted to love her. When he rescued her and restored her, he was a doctor, and she was a patient. He had had no single personal thought of her. Nay, this introduction of the personal element was very distasteful to him, a violation of his professional honor. It was horrible to have her there embracing his knees. It was horrible. He revolted from it, violently. And yet—and yet—he had not the power to break away.

She looked at him again, with the same supplication of powerful love, and that same transcendent, frightening light of triumph. In view of the delicate flame which seemed to come from her face like a light, he was powerless. And yet he had never intended to love her. He had never intended. And something stubborn in him could not give way.

"You love me," she repeated, in a murmur of deep, rhapsodic assurance. "You love me."

150 Her hands were drawing him, drawing him down to her. He was afraid, even a little horrified. For he had, really, no intention of loving her. Yet her hands were drawing him towards her. He put out his hand quickly to steady himself, and grasped her bare shoulder. A flame seemed to burn the hand that grasped her soft shoulder. He had no intention of loving her: his whole will was against his yielding. It was horrible. And yet wonderful was the touch of her shoulders, beautiful the shining of her face. Was she perhaps mad? He had a horror of yielding to her. Yet something in him ached also.

He had been staring away at the door, away from her. But his hand remained on her shoulder. She had gone suddenly very still. He looked down at her. Her eyes were now wide with fear, with doubt, the light was dying from her face, a shadow of terrible grayness was returning. He could not bear the touch of her eyes' question upon him, and the look of death behind the question.

With an inward groan he gave way, and let his heart yield towards her. A sudden gentle smile came on his face. And her eyes, which never left his face, slowly, slowly filled with tears. He watched the strange water rise in her eyes, like some slow fountain coming up. And his heart seemed to burn and melt away in his breast.

He could not bear to look at her any more. He dropped on his knees and caught her head with his arms and pressed her face against his throat. She was very still. His heart, which seemed to have broken, was burning with a kind of agony in his breast. And he felt her slow, hot tears wetting his throat. But he could not move.

He felt the hot tears wet his neck and the hollows of his neck, and he remained motionless, suspended through one of man's eternities. Only now it had become indispensable to him to have her face pressed close to him; he could never let her go again. He could never let her head go away from the close clutch of his arm. He wanted to remain like that forever, with his heart hurting him in a pain that was also life to him. Without knowing, he was looking down on her damp, soft brown hair.

155 Then, as it were suddenly, he smelt the horrid stagnant smell of that water. And at the same moment she drew away from him and looked at him. Her eyes were wistful and unfathomable. He was afraid of them, and he fell to kissing her, not knowing what he was doing. He wanted her eyes not to have that terrible, wistful, unfathomable look.

When she turned her face to him again, a faint delicate flush was glowing, and there was again dawning that terrible shining of joy in her eyes, which really terrified him, and yet which he now wanted to see, because he feared the look of doubt still more.

"You love me?" she said, rather faltering.

"Yes." The word cost him a painful effort. Not because it wasn't true. But because it was too newly true, the *saying* seemed to tear open again his newly torn heart. And he hardly wanted it to be true, even now.

She lifted her face to him, and he bent forward and kissed her on the mouth, gently, with the one kiss that is an eternal pledge. And as he kissed her his heart strained again in his breast. He never intended to love her. But now it was over. He had crossed over the gulf to her, and all that he had left behind had shriveled and become void.

160 After the kiss, her eyes again slowly filled with tears. She sat still, away from him, with her face drooped aside, and her hands folded in her lap. The tears fell very slowly. There was complete silence. He too sat there motionless and silent on the hearthrug. The strange pain of his heart that was broken seemed to consume him. That he should love her? That this was love! That he should be ripped open in this way! Him, a doctor! How they would all jeer if they knew! It was agony to him to think they might know.

In the curious naked pain of the thought he looked again to her. She was sitting there drooped into a muse. He saw a tear fall, and his heart flared hot. He saw for the first time that one of her shoulders was quite uncovered, one arm bare, he could see one of her small breasts; dimly, because it had become almost dark in the room.

"Why are you crying?" he asked, in an altered voice.

She looked up at him, and behind her tears the consciousness of her situation for the first time brought a dark look of shame to her eyes.

"I'm not crying, really," she said, watching him half frightened.

165   He reached his hand, and softly closed it on her bare arm.

"I love you! I love you!" he said in a soft, low vibrating voice, unlike himself.

She shrank, and dropped her head. The soft, penetrating grip of his hand on her arm distressed her. She looked up at him.

"I want to go," she said. "I want to go and get you some dry things."

"Why?" he said. "I'm all right."

170   "But I want to go," she said. "And I want you to change your things."

He released her arm, and she wrapped herself in the blanket, looking at him rather frightened. And still she did not rise.

"Kiss me," she said wistfully.

He kissed her, but briefly, half in anger.

Then, after a second, she rose nervously, all mixed up in the blanket. He watched her in her confusion, as she tried to extricate herself and wrap herself up so that she could walk. He watched her relentlessly, as she knew. And as she went, the blanket trailing, and as he saw a glimpse of her feet and her white leg, he tried to remember her as she was when he had wrapped her in the blanket. But then he didn't want to remember, because she had been nothing to him then, and his nature revolted from remembering her as she was when she was nothing to him.

175   A tumbling, muffled noise from within the dark house startled him. Then he heard her voice—"There are clothes." He rose and went to the foot of the stairs, and gathered up the garments she had thrown down. Then he came back to the fire, to rub himself down and dress. He grinned at his own appearance when he had finished.

The fire was sinking, so he put on coal. The house was now quite dark, save for the light of a street-lamp that shone in faintly from beyond the holly trees. He lit the gas with matches he found on the mantelpiece. Then he emptied the pockets of his own clothes, and threw all his wet things in a heap into the scullery. After which he gathered up her sodden clothes, gently, and put them in a separate heap on the copper-top in the scullery.

It was six o'clock on the clock. His own watch had stopped. He ought to go back to the surgery. He waited, and still she did not come down. So he went to the foot of the stairs and called:

"I shall have to go."

Almost immediately he heard her coming down. She had on her best dress of black voile, and her hair was tidy, but still damp. She looked at him—and in spite of herself, smiled.

180   "I don't like you in those clothes," she said.

"Do I look a sight?" he answered.

They were shy of one another.

"I'll make you some tea," she said.

"No, I must go."

185 "Must you?" And she looked at him again with the wide, strained, doubtful eyes. And again, from the pain of his breast, he knew how he loved her. He went and bent to kiss her, gently, passionately, with his heart's painful kiss.

"And my hair smells so horrible," she murmured in distraction. "And I'm so awful, I'm so awful! Oh, no, I'm too awful." And she broke into bitter, heart-broken sobbing. "You can't want to love me, I'm horrible."

"Don't be silly, don't be silly," he said, trying to comfort her, kissing her, holding her in his arms. "I want you, I want to marry you, we're going to be married, quickly, quickly—tomorrow if I can."

But she only sobbed terribly, and cried:

"I feel awful. I feel awful. I feel I'm horrible to you."

190 "No, I want you, I want you," was all he answered, blindly, with that terrible intonation which frightened her almost more than her horror lest he should *not* want her.

Writing Log/Journal Assignment

Do you believe in love at first sight? Why? Why not? Discuss your position in a brief journal entry.

Individual and Collaborative Considerations

1. In what way does Lawrence's story explore the theme of *awakening?* Exactly who *awakes* from what and when?
2. Lawrence was interested in myths and folklore, and this was often reflected in his creative works. What motifs (recurring themes) from specific fairy tales or myths are apparent in "The Horse Dealer's Daughter"?
3. What sorts of words characterize Mabel's brothers? How do they contribute to the story?
4. How might you symbolically interpret *the horse, the dog, the cemetery, the pond,* and *the kiss* in Lawrence's story?
5. Is "The Horse Dealer's Daughter" an appropriate or a misleading story title? Explain your answer.

Writing Activities

1. Have you ever misunderstood a situation completely and yet found a new direction in your life because of it? Have you ever experienced an unexpected encounter with another person that changed the rest of your

life? Where? How? Why? Write an essay blending exposition and narration to explain how the event evolved.

2. Compare and contrast Mabel and one of her brothers or Fergusson and one (or more) of Mabel's brothers. How do their value systems distinguish their depth of character and sensitivity towards others?

❋

Our Secret

Isabel Allende

Born in Peru, Chilean writer Isabel Allende was a journalist in Chile for years and also had her own television program. Following the assassination of Dr. Salvador Allende Gossens, her father's first cousin (and Chile's first elected Marxist–Leninist president), Allende fled with her family to Venezuela before she started to write fiction in 1981. Allende has written several novels: *The House of Spirits* (1982), *Of Love and Shadows* (1986), *Eva Luna* (1988), and *Paula* (1995). Other works include *The Stories of Eva Luna* (1991), the source of "Our Secret." Allende currently lives in San Rafael, California, where she continues to write and lecture.

She let herself be caressed, drops of sweat in the small of her back, her body exuding the scent of burnt sugar, silent, as if she divined that a single sound could nudge its way into memory and destroy everything, reducing to dust this instant in which he was a person like any other, a casual lover she had met that morning, another man without a past attracted to her wheat-colored hair, her freckled skin, the jangle of her Gypsy bracelets, just a man who had spoken to her in the street and begun to walk with her, aimlessly, commenting on the weather and the traffic, watching the crowd, with the slightly forced confidence of her countrymen in this foreign land, a man without sorrow or anger, without guilt, pure as ice, who merely wanted to spend the day with her, wandering through bookstores and parks, drinking coffee, celebrating the chance of having met, talking of old nostalgias, of how life had been when both were growing up in the same city, in the same barrio, when they were fourteen, you remember, winters of shoes soggy from frost, and paraffin stoves, summers of peach trees, there in the now forbidden country. Perhaps she was feeling a little lonely, or this seemed an opportunity to make love without complications, but, for whatever reason, at the end of the day, when they had run out of pretexts to walk any longer, she had taken his hand and led him to her house. She shared with other exiles a sordid apartment in a yellow building at the end of an alley filled with garbage cans. Her room was tiny: a mattress on the floor covered with a striped blanket, bookshelves improvised from boards stacked on two rows of bricks, books, posters, clothing on a chair, a suitcase in the corner. She had removed her clothes without preamble, with the attitude of a little girl eager to please. He tried to make love to her. He stroked her body patiently, slipping over her hills and valleys, discovering her secret routes, kneading her, soft clay upon the sheets, until she yielded, and opened to him. Then he retreated, mute, reserved. She gathered herself, and sought him, her head on his belly, her face hidden, as if constrained by modesty, as she fondled him, licked him, spurred him. He tried to lose himself; he closed his eyes and for a while let her do as she was doing, until he was defeated by sadness, or shame, and pushed her away. They lighted another cigarette. There was no complicity now; the urgent anticipation that had united them during the day was lost, and all that was left were two vulnerable people lying on a mattress, without memory, floating in the terrible vacuum of unspoken words. When they had met that morning they had had no extraordinary expectations, they had had no particular plan, only companionship, and a little pleasure, that was all, but at the hour of their coming together they had been engulfed by melancholy. We're tired, she smiled, seeking excuses for the desolation that had settled over them. In a last attempt to buy time, he took her face in his hands and kissed her eyelids. They lay down side by side, holding hands, and talked about their lives in this country where they had met by chance, a green and generous land in which, nevertheless, they would forever be foreigners. He thought of putting on his clothes and saying goodbye, before the tarantula of his nightmares poisoned the air, but she looked so young and defenseless, and he wanted to be her friend. Her friend, he thought, not her lover; her friend, to share quiet moments, without demands or commitments; her friend, someone to be with, to help ward off fear. He did not leave, or let go her hand. A warm, tender feeling, an enormous compassion for himself and for her, made his eyes sting. The curtain puffed out like a sail, and she got up to close the window, thinking that darkness would help them recapture their desire to be together, to make love. But darkness was not good; he needed the rectangle of light from the street, because without it he felt trapped again in the abyss of the timeless ninety centimeters of his cell, fermenting in his own excrement, delirious. Leave the curtain open, I want to look at you, he lied, because he did not dare confide his night terrors to her, the wracking thirst, the bandage pressing upon his head like a crown of nails, the visions of caverns, the assault of so many ghosts. He could not talk to her about that, because one thing leads to another, and he would end up saying things that had never been spoken. She returned to the mattress, stroked him absently, ran her fingers over the small lines, exploring them. Don't worry, it's nothing contagious, they're just scars, he laughed, almost with a sob. The girl perceived his anguish and stopped, the gesture suspended, alert. At that moment he should have told her that this was not the beginning of a new love, not even of a passing affair; it was merely an instant of truce, a brief moment of innocence, and soon, when she fell asleep, he would go; he should have told her that there was no future for them, no secret gestures, that they would not stroll hand in hand through the streets again, nor share lovers' games, but he could not speak, his voice was buried somewhere in his gut, like a claw. He knew he was sinking. He tried to cling to the reality that was slipping away from him, to anchor his mind on anything, on the jumble of clothing on the chair, on the books piled on the floor, on the poster of Chile on the wall, on the coolness of this Caribbean night, on the distant street noises; he tried to concentrate on this body that had been offered him, think only of the girl's luxuriant hair, the caramel scent of her skin. He begged her voicelessly to help him save those seconds, while she observed him from the far edge of the bed, sitting cross-legged like a fakir, her pale breasts and the eye of her navel also observing him, registering his trembling, the chattering of his teeth, his moan. He thought he could hear the silence growing within him; he knew that he was coming apart, as he had so often before and he gave up the struggle, releasing his last hold on the present, letting himself plunge down the endless precipice. He felt the crusted straps on his ankles and wrists, the brutal charge, the torn tendons, the insulting voices demanding names, the unforgettable screams of Ana, tortured beside him, and of the others, hanging by their arms in the courtyard.

What's the matter? For God's sake, what's wrong? Ana's voice was asking from far away. No, Ana was still bogged in the quicksands to the south. He thought he could make out a naked girl, shaking him and calling his name, but he could not get free of the shadows with their snaking whips and rippling flags. Hunched over, he tried to control the nausea. He began to weep for Ana and for all the others. What is it, what's the matter? Again the girl, calling him from somewhere. Nothing! Hold me! he begged, and she moved toward him timidly, and took him in her arms, lulled him like a baby, kissed his forehead, said, Go ahead, cry, cry all you want; she laid him flat on his back on the mattress and then, crucified, stretched out upon him.

For a thousand years they lay like that, together, until slowly the hallucinations faded and he returned to the room to find himself alive in spite of everything, breathing, pulsing, the girl's weight on his body, her head resting on his chest, her arms and legs atop his: two frightened orphans. And at that moment, as if she knew everything, she said to him, Fear is stronger than desire, than love or hatred or guilt or rage, stronger than loyalty. Fear is all-consuming . . . , and he felt her tears rolling down his neck. Everything stopped: she had touched his most deeply hidden wound. He had a presentiment that she was not just a girl willing to make love for the sake of pity but that she knew the thing that crouched beyond the silence, beyond absolute solitude, beyond the sealed box where he had hidden from the Colonel and his own treachery, beyond the memory of Ana Diaz and the other betrayed *compañeros* being led in one by one with their eyes blindfolded. How could she know all that?

She sat up. As she groped for the switch, her slender arm was silhouetted against the pale haze of the window. She turned on the light and, one by one, removed her metal bracelets, dropping them noiselessly on the mattress. Her hair was half covering her face when she held out her hands to him. White scars circled her wrists, too. For a timeless instant he stared at them, unmoving, until he understood everything, love, and saw her strapped to the electric grid, and then they could embrace, and weep, hungry for pacts and confidences, for forbidden words, for promises of tomorrow, shared, finally, the most hidden secret.

Writing Log/Journal Assignment

Freewrite about what you consider or would consider your own "tarantula of nightmares." Carefully consider the associations made with a tarantula.

Individual and Collaborative Considerations

1. How does Allende's descriptive language enable you to visualize the scenes she describes?
2. Why do you imagine Allende has such an extremely long first paragraph followed by several shorter, more standard paragraphs? What information are you initially presented with? How does the story conclude? What effect might Allende be trying to achieve through this structure?
3. Explain the significance of the scars beneath the Gypsy bracelets.
4. What secret do the two lovers share? When do they become aware of their common tragedy?
5. When the woman says, "Fear is stronger than desire, than love or hatred or guilt or rage, stronger than loyalty," why do you think she touches his most "deeply hidden wound"? (Who was Ana?)

Writing Activities

1. Write an essay about a secret you kept hidden until a particular incident or a special individual enabled you to talk about it. In your paper, you might include your own philosophy explaining what can make a person "open up" and speak to another about hidden secrets.
2. Do you agree or disagree that love is stronger than fear or vice versa? Take a position on the claim, construct a thesis, and argue your position using examples drawn from contemporary society, personal experience, and readings.

Daystar

Rita Dove

A former poet laureate of the United States, Rita Dove was born in Akron and studied at Miami University in Ohio. She earned her Master of Fine Arts in Creative Writing from the University of Iowa. Currently, she is a Professor of English at the University of Virginia and serves as associate editor of *Calloo*, a journal dedicated to African and African American arts. Her works include *The Yellow House in the Corner* (1980), *Museum* (1983), *Thomas and Beulah* (1986)—for which she was awarded the 1987 Pulitzer Prize in poetry—and *Grace Notes* (1989). Dove's insightful poems were often based on stories she heard from her grandparents or, as in the case of "Daystar," they dealt with aspects of human relationships and individual needs.

She wanted a little room for thinking;
but she saw diapers steaming on the line,
a doll slumped behind the door.
So she lugged a chair behind the garage
5   to sit out the children's naps.

Sometimes there were things to watch—
the pinched armor of a vanished cricket,
a floating maple leaf. Other days
she stared until she was assured
10 when she closed her eyes
she'd see only her own vivid blood.

She had an hour, at best, before Lisa appeared
pouting from the top of the stairs.
And just *what* was mother doing
15 out back with the field mice? Why,

building a palace. Later
that night when Thomas rolled over and
lurched into her, she would open her eyes
and think of the place that was hers
20 for an hour—where
she was nothing,
pure nothing, in the middle of the day.

Writing Log/Journal Assignment

Freewrite about anything that relates to solitude. You might want to explore such things as how spiritual growth and personal fulfillment can best be achieved.

Individual and Collaborative Considerations

1. From what point of view is the poem written? Who are Thomas and Lisa? Why did Dove decide not to name the woman who is the actual subject of the poem?
2. What does the woman in the poem want? Do you think what she desires is unreasonable? Why? Why not?
3. Explain the lines "when she closed her eyes / she'd see only her own vivid blood." Why do you think she picked the phrase "vivid blood" to express her point? What images are suggested by the phrase?
4. Would you describe the woman in the poem as happy, depressed, resigned, or content with her situation? Why?
5. Why did Dove entitle her poem "Daystar"? What do you associate with a star? How would its appearance during daylight hours be a positive symbol?

Writing Activities

1. Write a brief narrative about a place that is totally yours—even if only for a few minutes during the day. What are its characteristics? How do you respond to your environment?
2. Construct an essay arguing the merits and rewards of being a homemaker versus being a career individual.

Circe

H. D. (Hilda Doolittle)

Born in Pennsylvania (1886–1961), Hilda Doolittle, known by her initials H. D., was an early member in the imagist school, demonstrating many of its principles in her first volume of poetry *Sea Garden* (1916). Future works would include *Hymen* (1921), *Heliodora and Other Poems* (1924), *Collected Poems* (1925), *Hippolytus Temporizes* (1927), *The Walls Do Not Fall* (1944),

Tribute to Angels (1945), *Flowering of the Rod* (1946), *By Avon River* (1949), *Helen in Egypt* (1961), and *Collected Poems 1912–1944* (1983). In addition to poetry, H. D. wrote prose fiction, published as *Palimpsest* (1926), *Hedylus* (1928), *The Hedgehog* (1936), and *Bid Me to Live* (1960). Her later works also included a memoir to Ezra Pound called *End of Torment* (1958). H. D.'s early poetry has been likened to "magic spells," and the poet herself often appears in her verse in the role of a high priestess who has come to celebrate a natural event. Even though she distrusts her ability to recreate the world around her, she takes some comfort in knowing that the secrets of the gods are stored in "man's very speech."

It was easy enough
to bend them to my wish,
it was easy enough
to alter them with a touch,
5   but you
adrift on the great sea,
how shall I call you back?
Cedar and white ash,
rock-cedar and sand plants
10   and tamarisk
red cedar and white cedar
and black cedar from the inmost forest,
fragrance upon fragrance
and all of my sea-magic is for nought.

15   It was easy enough—
a thought called them
from the sharp edges of the earth;
they prayed for a touch,
they cried for the sight of my face,
20   they entreated me
till in pity
I turned each to his own self.

Panther and panther,
then a black leopard
25   follows close—
black panther and red
and a great hound,
a god-like beast,
cut the sand in a clear ring
30   and shut me from the earth,
and cover the sea-sound
with their throats,
and the sea-roar with their own barks

35   and bellowing and snarls,
    and the sea-stars
    and the swirl of the sand,
    and the rock-tamarisk
    and the wind resonance—
    but not your voice.

40   It is easy enough to call men
    from the edges of the earth.
    It is easy enough to summon them to my feet
    with a thought—
    it is beautiful to see the tall panther
45   and the sleek deer-hounds
    circle in the dark.
    It is easy enough
    to make cedar and white ash fumes
    into palaces
50   and to cover the sea-caves
    with ivory and onyx.

    But I would give up
    rock-fringes of coral
    and the inmost chamber
55   of my island palace
    and my own gifts
    and the whole region
    of my power and magic
    for your glance.

Writing Log/Journal Assignment

Circe was an enchantress, and in *The Odyssey*, she transformed all of Odysseus' men into swine; he, himself, was protected from her charms and magic. H. D. alludes to Odysseus in this poem as the one man she could not dominate through her magic nor win with her love. In your journal, write your own concept of *love*—possibly the love you can never have (do not worry about following any formal poetic structure), using allusions to your culture's heroes or heroines.

Individual and Collaborative Considerations

1. What are the most striking images in "Circe"? Why do you suppose so many images are nature oriented?
2. How is H. D.'s verse a love poem? What is taking place?
3. Why does H. D. use a wide variety of colors in her poem? How does it affect her presentation of imagery?

4. Several images and lines such as "It was easy enough" are repeated several times throughout the poem. Explain how they function as unifying devices.
5. What is the tone of H. D.'s poem? How does it reinforce her attitude towards the loved one she cannot have? Which lines emphasize her longing and frustration?

Writing Activities

1. Write an essay about the desire to control a loved one and what it can lead to. What happens when a would-be lover refuses to be dominated? Why would one person want to control another person in the first place?
2. Compare and contrast the advantages and disadvantages of acquiring love (physical or spiritual) from someone who gives it to you freely to obtaining the same love through deception or magic.

ADDITIONAL TOPICS AND ISSUES FOR WRITING AND RESEARCH

1. Examine the concept of friendship and human relationships within groups and on a one-to-one basis. Are relationships with the same gender any different between women and men? If so, how? What does friendship provide?
2. Single-parent families, latch-key children, economic hardships, and health problems are just a few of the trials facing a large part of America's population. Isolate one of those areas, devise an original thesis, and construct a well-supported essay defending your viewpoint.
3. Describe your relationship with your spouse, lover, siblings, or significant other. On what foundation is it built? What are its most distinctive qualities?
4. Write an essay expanding on or disproving the notion that love can be explained in scientific terms as a blend of adrenaline and dopamine.
5. Write an argumentative essay demonstrating how and why you should or should not lend a friend a large sum of money, go with a friend on an extended trip where you are confined to close quarters, or buy an expensive item with a friend.
6. Research and write an essay about arranged marriages and cross-cultural marriages. Consider social, cultural, religious, political, and economic situations that may encourage or discourage them.
7. In a carefully reasoned essay, argue that the love you bear for a friend is different from the love you have for a spouse, companion, or significant other. To what extent might having sex with a friend change the relationship? Why?

8. Compare and contrast the sort of conflicts that arise between brothers, between sisters, and between sisters and brothers. What are the short-term and long-term effects of sibling rivalries in philosophical and psychological terms?

9. Many people say they prefer to have pets instead of children because pets do not need baby-sitters or inhibit a lifestyle. Both, however, require commitment and a sense of responsibility. In a comparative essay, show how the dependency of a dog on its owner and a child on his or her parents is similar.

10. In what way does sibling rivalry prepare children for a world full of competition and aggression? What could be its negative results? Do you think the "me" generation of the 1980s and 1990s reflect the values of a competitive child or a sensitive, responsible adult? Write an essay explaining your views and developing your analogies.

Starting Points for Research

Lovers, Love, and Marriage

- First loves
- Intimacy (psychology)
- Attachment behavior
- Courtly love
- Unrequited love
- Courtship
- Heterosexual relationships
- Homosexual relationships
- Bisexuality
- Maternal love
- Paternal love
- Platonic love
- Love in art
- Love in literature
- Sex in art
- Sex in literature
- Sexual ethics
- Sexual fantasies
- Sexual abuse
- Role-playing
- Senses and sensation
- Sex in dreams (psychology)
- Love in music
- Love potions/aphrodisiacs
- Lovemaking

Friends and Family

- Female
- Male
- Childhood friends
- Interpersonal relations
- Fraternal/maternal societies
- Friendly fire
- Pen pals
- Benefit societies
- Labor and laboring classes
- Friendship in art
- Friendship in music
- Friendship in literature
- Childhood friendship
- Friendly visiting
- Friends of the library
- Friendship quilts
- Among peers
- Among elders
- Platonic friendships
- Political relationships
- Friends and money
- Partnerships
- Professional relationships
- Friends as family
- Friendship letters

Starting Points for Research (*continued*)

Lovers, Love, and Marriage

- Sex surrogates (therapy)
- Cultural customs
- Marriage laws
- Weddings
- Marital property
- Divorce
- Gay/lesbian weddings
- Separation
- Polygamy
- Monogamy
- Paternity suits
- Common law (spouse)
- Wills
- Famous married performers
- Stereotypes
- Astrology and marriage
- Beast marriage
- Bigamy
- Bisexuality in marriage
- Concubine
- Endogamy and exogamy
- Free love
- Honeymoons (practices)
- Teen-age marriages
- Customs and rites
- Marriage of the mentally handicapped
- Marriage proposal
- Marriages of royalty and nobility
- Mail-order spouses (brides in particular)
- Dowries
- Posthumous marriage
- Employment and marriage
- Marriage counseling
- Commuter marriages
- Dispensations
- Annulment of marriage
- Sex in marriage
- Mixed marriages
- Mate selection
- Fortune hunters/gold diggers

Friends and Family

- Siblings
- Abused children
- Inheritance and succession
- Blood relatives
- Relatives by marriage
- Childbirth
- Child support
- Mother-in-law jokes
- Father-in-law jokes
- Twin children
- Adoption
- Illegitimate children
- Vacations
- Movies
- Television programs
- Familial behavior (in animals)
- Aunts
- Uncles
- Surrogate families
- Birth order
- Broken homes
- Only child
- Communication in the home
- Heads of household
- Family size
- Dual-career families
- Host family—foreign students
- Parenthood
- Presidents—families
- Tribes
- Widows
- Widowers
- Health and hygiene
- Family reunions
- Religious life
- Family violence
- Family in mass media
- Day care for families
- Family farms
- Family trees

7

Dreams and Disillusionment

*I take my leave
in my dream there stretches a streak—
the river of heaven.*
NATSUME SOSEKI

Essays

Ursula Le Guin   Fantasy

•

Dick Gregory   Shame

Fiction

Kurt Vonnegut, Jr.   Harrison Bergeron

•

Woody Allen   The Kugelmass Episode

•

Bernard Malamud   The Magic Barrel

•

Poetry

Leslie Marmon Silko   Love Poem

•

William Butler Yeats   The Second Coming

•

Robinson Jeffers   To the Stone-cutters

What is a dream? On the one hand, it may be an ideal, a hope, a goal, or an objective. Martin Luther King, Jr., had a dream of social equality and opportunity for all people—a vision for humanity—and it has been a source of inspiration and encouragement for people from all social, economic, and ethnic backgrounds. A dream may be a vision dealing with the dignity, health, and welfare of the human race, or it could be a personal goal or ambition (becoming a well-known film director). On the other hand, a dream may be a concept grounded in further extensions of the *fantastic*. A good example of this would be Kurt Vonnegut's story "Harrison Bergeron," which begins "The year was 2081, and everybody was finally equal." Such a dream can easily become a nightmare, hounding and haunting you even during daylight hours, however, when the *perfect* nature of society becomes oppressive and anti-Utopian. Kugelmass, the protagonist in Woody Allen's short story "The Kugelmass Episode," also has just such a dream when his fantasy to become Madame Bovary's lover is realized, and she returns to New York with him through *Persky's Magic Box*.

The flip side of a dream would be disillusionment, just as the antithesis of a fantasy would be reality. Disillusionment is a natural response to a situation or a person when you discover your expectations were unreal or your faith in something was unmerited. If you go to a motion picture expecting to watch the best movie you have ever seen, and it turns out to be average or unexceptional, disappointment results. Often the momentum of expectations makes your disillusionment with reality not only understandable but also justified. As Dick Gregory points out in "Shame," he placed so much importance on impressing Helene Tucker that he became more than simply disillusioned when his teacher denied him the opportunity to contribute to a classroom fund-raising activity; he experienced *shame*.

In "The Second Coming," William Butler Yeats observed the human race slouching "towards Bethlehem to be reborn" and had no illusions about the inherent goodness of others. His hopes and dreams for the human race lay in the future because he believed in regenerative cycles of history. Rather than looking at dreams and disillusionment of particular people or society, Yeats addresses residents of the world with his mystical vision.

Dreams and disillusionment, fantasy and reality can be explored and appreciated from several perspectives. Ursula Le Guin's essay "Fantasy" introduces readers to a literary genre; Robinson Jeffers' poem "To the Stone-cutters" elicits images carved in rock, a testament to another's dream or vision in the past; and Bernard Malamud's story "The Magic Barrel" presents a poignant look at appearance versus reality—availability versus worthiness. Other works such as Leslie Marmon Silko's "Love Poem" look back to the last chapter: "Relationships: Friends, Family, and Lovers" with one notable difference. Silko not only addresses her lover whose memory haunts her but also the sights, sounds, and smells of nature. Such sensory imagery provide Silko with recollections—the only thing remaining of her hopes and dreams.

RHETORIC AT WORK

How are words used when referring to cherished dreams? Usually, usage will depend on the nature of the dream itself; is it grounded in the fantastic or in our understanding of the real world? The attainable dream may be described using precise diction, reflecting the exact nature of your goal. Meanwhile, words conveying shadowy images and surreal associations may mirror fantastic dreams which, no matter how hard we try, we just cannot achieve without the use of figurative language. As you work through this chapter, review the various types of figurative language discussed in part 1 of *Thresholds* from time to time. Also, note how each author uses the different forms of figurative language in the following essays, short stories, and poems.

A Checklist for Writing about *Dreams and Disillusionment*

1. What is the nature of my dream? What point am I trying to make about it?
2. Is my dream attainable? How can I make it a reality? What is the distinction between a vision or a dream and a fantasy?
3. Do I organize my material coherently? Will my reader understand my intended relationship between dreams and disillusionment?
4. What controlling idea helps to unify my essay?
5. In what way has my diction reflected the real or surreal nature of my topic? Do I use figurative language to help express abstract aspects of dreams and visions?
6. Have I considered and used the stylistic advantages of one method of punctuation over another?
7. Do I replace trite, worn-out clichés with fresh, original expressions?
8. How does my final paragraph draw my essay to a natural, satisfying conclusion?

Fantasy

Ursula Le Guin

A native of Berkeley, California, Ursula Le Guin, has been the author of over thirty books. She received her Bachelors of Arts from Radcliff and her Masters of Arts from Columbia University; then she moved on to Paris, France (on a Fulbright scholarship), where she met and married her future husband, Charles Le Guin, a historian. After publishing *Rocannon's World* (1964), Le Guin wrote a succession of books for all age groups. She became particularly well known for her science-fiction and fantasy stories. Some of her science-fiction novels include *Planet of Exile* (1966), *City of Illusions* (1967), *The Left Hand of Darkness* (1969), *The Dispossessed* (1974), *Very Far from Anywhere Else* (1976), and *The Water Is Wide*. Her works of fantasy include *A Wizard of Earthsea* (1968), *The Tombs of Atuan* (1972), *The Farthest Shore* (1972), *Malafrena* (1979), *The Beginning Place* (1980), and *Always Coming Home* (1985). Le Guin further wrote three volumes of short fiction: *The Wind's Twelve Quarters* (1975), *Orsinian Tales* (1976), and *The Compass Rose* (1982). *The Language of the Night: Essays on Fantasy and Science Fiction* (1979) and *Dancing on the Edge of the World: Thoughts on Words, Women, and Places* (1989) represent her two collections of essays. Le Guin's following essay was written as an introduction to *The Book of Fantasy*, edited by Jorge Luis Borges.

1   There are two books which I look upon as esteemed and cherished great-aunts or grandmothers, wise and mild though sometimes rather dark of counsel, to be turned to when the judgment hesitates for want of material to form itself upon. One of these books provides facts, of a peculiar sort. The other does not. The *I Ching* or Book of Changes is the visionary elder who has outlived fact, the Ancestor so old she speaks a different tongue. Her counsel is sometimes appallingly clear, sometimes very obscure indeed. 'The little fox crossing the river wets its tail,' she says, smiling faintly, or, 'A dragon appears in the field,' or, 'Biting upon dried gristly meat . . .' One retires to ponder long upon such advice. The other Auntie is younger, and speaks English—indeed, she speaks more English than anybody else. She offers fewer dragons and much more dried gristly meat. And yet the *Oxford English Dictionary*, or *A New English Dictionary on Historical Principles*, is also a Book of Changes. Most wonderful in its transmutations, it is not a Book of Sand, yet is inexhaustible; not an Aleph, yet all we can ever say is there, if we can but find it.

2   'Auntie!' I say (magnifying glass in hand, because my edition, the Compact Auntie, is compressed into two volumes of terrifyingly small print)—

'Auntie! please tell me about *fantasy*, because I want to talk about *The Book of Fantasy*, but I am not sure what I am talking about.'

3   'Fantasy, or Phantasy,' replies Auntie, clearing her throat, 'is from the Greek φαντασια, lit. "a making visible." ' She explains that φαντασια, is related to φαντάζειν, 'to make visible,' or in Late Greek, 'to imagine, have visions,' and to φαντειν, 'to show.' And she summarizes the older uses of the word in English: an appearance, a phantom, the mental process of sensuous perception, the faculty of imagination, a false notion, caprice, or whim. Then, though she eschews the casting of yarrow stalks or coins polished with sweet oil, being after all an Englishwoman, she begins to tell the Changes: the mutations of a word moving through the minds of people moving through the centuries. She shows how a word that to the Schoolmen of the late Middle Ages meant 'the mental apprehension of an object of perception,' that is, the mind's very act of linking itself to the phenomenal world, came in time to signify just the reverse—an hallucination, or a phantasm, or the habit of deluding oneself. After which, doubling back on its tracks like a hare, the word *fantasy* was used to mean the imagination, 'the process, the faculty, or the result of forming mental representations of things not actually present.' This definition seems very close to the Scholastic sense of *fantasy*, but leads, of course, in quite the opposite direction—going so far in that direction, these days, as often to imply that the representation is extravagant, or visionary, or merely fanciful. (*Fancy* is *fantasy's* own daughter, via elision of the penult; while *fantastic* is a sister-word with a family of her own.)

4   So *fantasy* remains ambiguous; it stands between the false, the foolish, the delusory, the shallows of the mind, and the mind's deep connection with the real. On this threshold sometimes it faces one way, masked and beribboned, frivolous, an escapist; then it turns, and we glimpse as it turns the face of an angel, bright truthful messenger, arisen Urizen.

5   Since the *Oxford English Dictionary* was compiled, the tracks of the word *fantasy* have been complicated still further by the comings and goings of psychologists. The technical uses in psychology of *fantasy* and *phantasy* have deeply influenced our sense and use of the word; and they have also given us the handy verb *to fantasize*. But Auntie does not acknowledge the existence of that word. Into the Supplement, through the back door, she admits only *fantasist*; and she defines the newcomer, politely but with, I think, a faint curl of the lip, as 'one who "weaves" fantasies.' One might think that a fantasist was one who fantasizes, but it is not so. Currently, one who fantasizes is understood either to be daydreaming, or to be using the imagination therapeutically as a means of discovering reasons Reason does not know, discovering oneself to oneself. A fantasist is one who writes a fantasy for others. But the element of discovery is there, too.

6   Auntie's use of 'weave' may be taken as either patronizing or quaint, for writers don't often say nowadays that they 'weave' their works, but bluntly that they write them. Fantasists earlier in the century, in the days of victorious Realism, were often apologetic about what they did, offering it as something less than 'real' fiction—mere fancywork, bobble-fringing to literature.

More fantasists are rightly less modest now that what they do is generally recognized as literature, or at least as a genre of literature, or at least as a genre of subliterature, or at least as a commercial product. For *fantasies* are rife and many-colored on the bookstalls. The head of the fabled Unicorn is laid upon the lap of Mammon, and the offering is acceptable to Mammon. Fantasy, in fact, has become quite a business.

7   But when one night in Buenos Aires in 1937 three friends sat talking together about fantastic literature, it was not yet a business. Nor was it even known as fantastic literature, when one night in a villa in Geneva in 1818 three friends sat talking together, telling one another ghost stories. They were Mary Shelley, her husband Percy, and Lord Byron—and Claire Clairmont was probably with them, and the strange young Dr. Polidori—and they told awful tales, and Mary Shelley was frightened. 'We will each,' cried Byron, 'write a ghost story!' So Mary went away and thought about it, fruitlessly, until a few nights later she dreamed a nightmare in which a 'pale student' used strange arts and machineries to arouse from unlife the 'hideous phantasm of a man.' And so, alone of the friends, she wrote her ghost story, *Frankenstein: or, A Modern Prometheus*, which I think is the first great modern fantasy. There are no ghosts in it; but fantasy, as the Dictionary showed us, is often seen as ghoulie-mongering. Because ghosts inhabit, or haunt, one part of the vast domain of fantastic literature, both oral and written, people familiar with that corner of it call the whole thing Ghost Stories, or Horror Tales; just as others call it Fairyland after the part of it they know or love best, and others call it Science Fiction, and others call it Stuff and Nonsense. But the nameless being given life by Dr. Frankenstein's, or Mary Shelley's, arts and machineries is neither ghost nor fairy, and science-fictional only in intent; stuff and nonsense he is not. He is a creature of fantasy, archetypal, deathless. Once raised he will not sleep again, for his pain will not let him sleep, the unanswered moral questions that woke with him will not let him rest in peace. When there began to be money in the fantasy business, plenty of money was made out of him in Hollywood, but even that did not kill him. If his story were not too long for this anthology, it might well be here; very likely it was mentioned on that night in 1937 in Buenos Aires, when Jorge Luis Borges, Adolfo Bioy Casares, and Silvina Ocampo fell to talking—so Casares tells us—'about fantastic literature . . . discussing the stories which seemed best to us. One of us suggested that if we put together the fragments of the same type we had listed in our notebooks, we would have a good book. As a result we drew up this book . . . simply a compilation of stories from fantastic literature which seemed to us to be the best.'

8   So that, charmingly, is how *The Book of Fantasy* came to be, fifty years ago. Three friends talking. No plans, no definitions, no business, except the intention of 'having a good book.' Of course, in the making of such a book by such makers, certain definitions were implied by inclusion, and by exclusion other definitions were ignored; so one will find, perhaps for the first time, horror and ghosts and fairy and science-fiction stories all together within the

covers of *The Book of Fantasy;* while any bigot wishing to certify himself as such by dismissing it as all stuff and nonsense is tacitly permitted to do so. The four lines in the book by Chuang Tzu should suffice to make him think twice, permanently.

9   It is an idiosyncratic selection, and completely eclectic. Some of the stories will be familiar to anyone who reads, others are exotic discoveries. A very well-known piece such as 'The Cask of Amontillado' seems less predictable, set among works and fragments from the Orient and South America and distant centuries, by Kafka, Swedenborg, Cortázar, Agutagawa, Niu Chiao; its own essential strangeness is restored to it. There is some weighting towards writers, especially English writers, of the late nineteenth and early twentieth centuries, which reflects, I imagine, the taste of the anthologizers and perhaps particularly that of Borges, who was himself a member and direct inheritor of the international tradition of fantasy which included Kipling and Chesterton.

10   Perhaps I should not say 'tradition,' since it has no name as such and little recognition in critical circles, and is distinguished in college English departments mainly by being ignored; but I believe that there is a company of fantasists that Borges belonged to even as he transcended it, and which he honored even as he transformed it. As he included these older writers in *The Book of Fantasy,* it may be read truly as his 'notebook' of sources and affiliations and elective affinities. Some chosen, such as Bloy or Andreyev, may seem rather heavyhanded now, but others are treasurable. The Dunsany story, for instance, is not only very beautiful, as the early poetry of Yeats is beautiful, but is also, fascinatingly, a kind of miniature or concave-mirror of the anthology itself. The book is full of such reflections and interconnections. Beerbohm's familiar tale of 'Enoch Soames,' read here, seems to involve and concern other writings and writers in the book; so that I now believe that when people gather in the Reading Room of the British Library on June 3rd, 1997, to wait for poor Enoch's phantom and watch him discover his *Fungoids,* still ignored by critics and professors and the heartless public, still buried ignominious in the Catalogue,—I believe that among those watching there will be other phantoms; and among those, perhaps, Borges. For he will see then, not as through a glass, darkly.

11   If in the 1890s fantasy appeared to be a kind of literary fungus-growth, if in the 1920s it was still perceived as secondary, if in the 1980s it has been degraded by commercial exploitation, it may well seem quite safe and proper to the critics to ignore it. And yet I think that our narrative fiction has been going slowly and vaguely and massively, not in the wash and slap of fad and fashion but as a deep current, for years, in one direction, and that that direction is the way of fantasy.

12   An American fiction writer now may yearn toward the pure veracity of Sarah Orne Jewett or Dreiser's *Sister Carrie,* as an English writer, such as Margaret Drabble, may look back with longing to the fine solidities of Bennett; but the limited and rationally perceived societies in which those books were written, and their shared language, are lost. Our society—global, mul-

tilingual, enormously irrational—can perhaps describe itself only in the global, intuitional language of fantasy.

13   So it may be that the central ethical dilemma of our age, the use or non-use of annihilating power, was posed most cogently in fictional terms by the purest of fantasists. Tolkien began *The Lord of the Rings* in 1937 and finished it about ten years later. During those years, Frodo withheld his hand from the Ring of Power, but the nations did not.

14   So it is that Italo Calvino's *Invisible Cities* serves many of us as a better guidebook to our world than any Michelin or Fodor's.

15   So it is that the most revealing and accurate descriptions of our daily life in contemporary fiction may be shot through with strangeness, or displaced in time, or set upon imaginary planets, or dissolved into the phantasmagoria of drugs or of psychosis, or may rise from the mundane suddenly into the visionary and as simply descend from it again.

16   So it is that the 'magical realists' of South America are read for their entire truthfulness to the way things are, and have lent their name as perhaps the most fitting to the kind of fiction most characteristic of our times.

17   And so it is that Jorge Luis Borges's own poems and stories, his reflections, his libraries, labyrinths, forking paths, and amphisbaenae, his books of tigers, of rivers, of sand, of mysteries, of changes, have been and will be honored by so many readers for so long: because they are beautiful, because they are nourishing, because they do supremely well what poems and stories do, fulfilling the most ancient, urgent function of words, just as the *I Ching* and the *Dictionary* do: to form for us 'mental representations of things not actually present,' so that we can form a judgment of what world we live in and where we might be going in it.

Writing Log/Journal Assignment

If someone asked what you considered two of the best books ever written, what would your response be and why?

Individual and Collaborative Considerations

1. Le Guin "looks to" two books; what are they? Explain the distinctive characteristics of each.
2. Where does the word *fantasy* or *phantasy* originate? What does it mean?
3. In what way is *fantasy* ambiguous?
4. Why does Le Guin relate the circumstances under which *Frankenstein: or, A Modern Prometheus* was written? What is the link between it and *The Book of Fantasy*, edited by Jorge Luis Borges, Adolfo Bioy Casares, and Silvina Ocampo?
5. To what extent do you agree with Le Guin when she writes: "Our society—global, multilingual, enormously irrational—can perhaps describe itself only in the global, intuitional language of fantasy"?

Writing Activities

1. Le Guin notes that in many minds, "fantasy appeared to be a kind of literary fungus-growth" considered second-rate writing in the 1920s and "degraded by commercial exploitation" in the 1980s. Select two or three science-fiction novels and write a persuasive essay arguing that they deserve artistic recognition equivalent to other great works of world literature. Make sure you offer concrete examples of what you consider "traditionally accepted masterpieces" for comparative purposes.

2. Define your own concept of *the fantastic*. Illustrate its prominence in art, literature, dance, film, and music. Where does the fantastic lead readers? What can it fulfill?

✳

Shame

Dick Gregory

In his time, Dick Gregory—born in 1932—has suffered hardships as a slum-kid, enjoyed promise as an outstanding athlete, and worked night clubs as a comedian—shaping his act initially in sympathy with the civil rights movement and later with the antiwar sentiment in the United States. In 1968, Gregory ran for president of the United States as a candidate of the Peace and Freedom Party, and he remains politically active. Gregory has received several accommodations in recognition for his work, such as the Ebony-Topaz Heritage and Freedom Award (1978). His books include *From the Back of the Bus* (1962), *No More Lies: The Myth and Reality of American History* (1971), *Dick Gregory's Political Primer* (1972), and *Up from Nigger* (1976). "Shame," a selection from his autobiographical novel *Nigger* (1964), details the depths of his disillusionment when he learned the meaning of shame at school and why Helene Tucker's face followed him around for twenty-two years because of his humiliating experience.

1 **I** never learned hate at home, or shame. I had to go to school for that. I was about seven years old when I got my first big lesson. I was in love with a little girl named Helene Tucker, a light-complected little girl with pigtails and nice manners. She was always clean and she was smart in school. I think I went to school then mostly to look at her. I brushed my hair and even got me a little old handkerchief: It was a lady's handkerchief, but I didn't want Helene to see me wipe my nose on my hand. The pipes were frozen again, there was no water in the house, but I washed my socks and shirt every

night. I'd get a pot, and go over to Mister Ben's grocery store, and stick my pot down into his soda machine. Scoop out some chopped ice. By evening the ice melted to water for washing. I got sick a lot that winter because the fire would go out at night before the clothes were dry. In the morning I'd put them on, wet or dry, because they were the only clothes I had.

2 Everybody's got a Helene Tucker, a symbol of everything you want. I loved her for her goodness, her cleanness, her popularity. She'd walk down my street and my brothers and sisters would yell, "Here comes Helene," and I'd rub my tennis sneakers on the back of my pants and wish my hair wasn't so nappy and the white folks' shirt fit me better. I'd run out on the street. If I knew my place and didn't come too close, she'd wink at me and say hello. That was a good feeling. Sometimes I'd follow her all the way home, and shovel the snow off her walk and try to make friends with her Momma and her aunts. I'd drop money on her stoop late at night on my way back from shining shoes in the taverns. And she had a Daddy, and he had a good job. He was a paper hanger.

3 I guess I would have gotten over Helene by summertime, but something happened in that classroom that made her face hang in front of me for the next twenty-two years. When I played the drums in high school it was for Helene and when I broke track records in college it was for Helene and when I started standing behind microphones and heard applause I wished Helene could hear it, too. It wasn't until I was twenty-nine years old and married and making money that I finally got her out of my system. Helene was sitting in that classroom when I learned to be ashamed of myself.

4 It was on a Thursday. I was sitting in the back of the room, in a seat with a chalk circle drawn around it. The idiot's seat, the troublemaker's seat.

5 The teacher thought I was stupid. Couldn't spell, couldn't read, couldn't do arithmetic. Just stupid. Teachers were never interested in finding out that you couldn't concentrate because you were so hungry, because you hadn't had any breakfast. All you could think about was noontime, would it ever come? Maybe you could sneak into the cloakroom and steal a bite of some kid's lunch out of a coat pocket. A bite of something. Paste. You can't really make a meal of paste, or put it on bread for a sandwich, but sometimes I'd scoop a few spoonfuls out of the paste jar in the back of the room. Pregnant people get strange tastes. I was pregnant with poverty. Pregnant with dirt and pregnant with smells that made people turn away, pregnant with cold and pregnant with shoes that were never bought for me, pregnant with five other people in my bed and no Daddy in the next room, and pregnant with hunger. Paste doesn't taste too bad when you're hungry.

6 The teacher thought I was a troublemaker. All she saw from the front of the room was a little black boy who squirmed in his idiot's seat and made noises and poked the kids around him. I guess she couldn't see a kid who made noises because he wanted someone to know he was there.

7 It was on a Thursday, the day before the Negro payday. The eagle always flew on Friday. The teacher was asking each student how much his father would give to the Community Chest. On Friday night, each kid would get

the money from his father, and on Monday he would bring it to the school. I decided I was going to buy me a Daddy right then. I had money in my pocket from shining shoes and selling papers, and whatever Helene Tucker pledged for her Daddy I was going to top it. And I'd hand the money right in. I wasn't going to wait until Monday to buy me a Daddy.

8   I was shaking, scared to death. The teacher opened her book and started calling out our names alphabetically.

9   "Helene Tucker?"

10   "My Daddy said he'd give two dollars and fifty cents."

11   "That's very nice, Helene. Very nice indeed."

12   That made me feel pretty good. It wouldn't take too much to top that. I had almost three dollars in dimes and quarters in my pocket. I stuck my hand in my pocket and held onto the money, waiting for her to call my name. But the teacher closed her book after she called everybody else in the class.

13   I stood up and raised my hand.

14   "What is it now?"

15   "You forgot me."

16   She turned toward the blackboard. "I don't have time to be playing with you, Richard."

17   "My Daddy said he'd . . ."

18   "Sit down, Richard, you're disturbing the class."

19   "My Daddy said he'd give . . . fifteen dollars."

20   She turned around and looked mad.

21   "We are collecting this money for you and your kind, Richard Gregory. If your Daddy can give fifteen dollars you have no business being on relief."

22   "I got it right now, I got it right now, my Daddy gave it to me to turn in today, my Daddy said . . ."

23   "And furthermore," she said, looking right at me, her nostrils getting big and her lips getting thin and her eyes opening wide, "we know you don't have a Daddy."

24   Helene Tucker turned around, her eyes full of tears. She felt sorry for me. Then I couldn't see her too well because I was crying, too.

25   "Sit down, Richard."

26   And I always thought the teacher kind of liked me. She always picked me to wash the blackboard on Friday, after school. That was a big thrill, it made me feel important. If I didn't wash it, come Monday the school might not function right.

27   "Where are you going, Richard?"

28   I walked out of school that day, and for a long time I didn't go back very often. There was shame there.

29   Now there was shame everywhere. It seemed like the whole world had been inside that classroom, everyone had heard what the teacher had said, everyone had turned around and felt sorry for me. There was shame in going to the Worthy Boys Annual Christmas Dinner for you and your kind, be-

cause everybody knew what a worthy boy was. Why couldn't they just call it the Boys Annual Dinner, why'd they have to give it a name? There was shame in wearing the brown and orange and white plaid mackinaw the welfare gave to three thousand boys. Why'd it have to be the same for everybody so when you walked down the street the people could see you were on relief? It was a nice warm mackinaw and it had a hood, and my Momma beat me and called me a little rat when she found out I stuffed it in the bottom of a pail full of garbage way over on Cottage Street. There was shame in running over to Mister Ben's at the end of the day and asking for his rotten peaches, there was shame in asking Mrs. Simmons for a spoonful of sugar, there was shame in running out to meet the relief truck. I hated that truck, full of food for you and your kind. I ran into the house and hid when it came. And then I started to sneak through alleys, to take the long way home so the people going into White's Eat Shop wouldn't see me. Yeah, the whole world heard the teacher that day, we all know you don't have a Daddy.

Writing Log/Journal Assignment

In paragraph 2, Gregory states: "Everybody's got a Helene Tucker, a symbol of everything you want." Write a brief journal entry about the symbolic Helene Tucker in your life.

Individual and Collaborative Considerations

1. Where did Dick Gregory have to go to experience shame? How long did it last?
2. While Gregory's piece seems to deal with identity on the one hand, it points to the need for some sort of ideal or dream on the other. Discuss both in context.
3. Gregory wrote *Nigger*, his autobiography, more than thirty years ago. In what way are his language and references dated? Does he assume anything in particular on the part of his audience? Support your viewpoint.
4. Why do you think Gregory puts himself through so much pain and humiliation? Besides an overt attempt to impress Helene Tucker, what *dream* does he seem to be following? What is the effect of his disillusionment?
5. In the final paragraph, Gregory states: "Now there was shame everywhere." Why does he say that? What examples illustrate his point?

Writing Activities

1. Write a personal narrative exploring the importance of individual "dignity." Use specific examples—either an extended narrative like Gregory

or a group of narratives—to illustrate the controlling idea of your essay. You may want to draw some conclusions regarding the steps taken to achieve "dignity" and the concept of "dignity" itself.

2. Take a concept like shame, fear, love, hate, or embarrassment and write a definition essay, graphically illustrating the real meaning of the word. Your thesis should state something specific about the concept you define (e.g., love is just a four-letter word); then, devote the body of your essay to arguing, illustrating, and defining your concept in relation to your thesis.

✳

Harrison Bergeron

Kurt Vonnegut, Jr.

Kurt Vonnegut, Jr., was born in Indianapolis in 1922 and prior to being drafted in World War II, he studied biochemistry at Cornell. During the war, Vonnegut was captured by the Germans and held prisoner in an underground slaughterhouse in Dresden. He would later draw on his Dresden experience when he wrote the surrealistic dark comedy *Slaughterhouse Five* (1969). Vonnegut's works frequently blend science-fiction concepts and satire to comment on the human race and the tyrannies of automation. His numerous novels include *Player Piano* (1952), *The Sirens of Titan* (1959), *Mother Night* (1961), *Cat's Cradle* (1963), *God Bless You, Mr. Rosewater* (1965), *Breakfast of Champions* (1973), *Slapstick* (1976), *Jailbird* (1979), and *Deadeye Dick* (1982). Vonnegut's collections of short stories and essays include *Welcome to the Monkey House* (1968), *Wampeters, Foma, and Granfallons* (1974), and *Palm Sunday* (1981). He has also written a play, *Happy Birthday Wanda June* (1970), as well as television scripts. The following reading, Vonnegut's anti-Utopian story, "Harrison Bergeron," takes a satirical look at a futuristic society where people are handicapped to ensure equality.

The year was 2081, and everybody was finally equal. They weren't only equal before God and the law. They were equal every which way. Nobody was smarter than anybody else. Nobody was better looking than anybody else. Nobody was stronger or quicker than anybody else. All this equality was due to the 211th, 212th, and 213th Amendments to the Constitution, and to the unceasing vigilance of agents of the United States Handicapper General.

Some things about living still weren't quite right, though. April, for instance, still drove people crazy by not being springtime. And it was in that clammy month that the H-G men took George and Hazel Bergeron's fourteen-year-old son, Harrison, away.

It was tragic, all right, but George and Hazel couldn't think about it very hard. Hazel had a perfectly average intelligence, which meant she couldn't think about anything except in short bursts. And George, while his intelligence was way above normal, had a little mental handicap radio in his ear. He was required by law to wear it at all times. It was tuned to a government transmitter. Every twenty seconds or so, the transmitter would send out some sharp noise to keep people like George from taking unfair advantage of their brains.

George and Hazel were watching television. There were tears on Hazel's cheeks, but she'd forgotten for the moment what they were about.

5   On the television screen were ballerinas.

A buzzer sounded in George's head. His thoughts fled in panic, like bandits from a burglar alarm.

"That was a real pretty dance, that dance they just did," said Hazel.

"Huh?" said George.

"That dance—it was nice," said Hazel.

10   "Yup," said George. He tried to think a little about the ballerinas. They weren't really very good—no better than anybody else would have been, anyway. They were burdened with sashweights and bags of birdshot, and their faces were masked, so that no one, seeing a free and graceful gesture or a pretty face, would feel like something the cat drug in. George was toying with the vague notion that maybe dancers shouldn't be handicapped. But he didn't get very far with it before another noise in his ear radio scattered his thoughts.

George winced. So did two out of the eight ballerinas.

Hazel saw him wince. Having no mental handicap herself, she had to ask George what the latest sound had been.

"Sounded like somebody hitting a milk bottle with a ball peen hammer," said George.

"I'd think it would be real interesting, hearing all the different sounds," said Hazel, a little envious. "All the things they think up."

15   "Um," said George.

"Only, if I was Handicapper General, you know what I would do?" said Hazel. Hazel, as a matter of fact, bore a strong resemblance to the Handicapper General, a woman named Diana Moon Glampers. "If I was Diana Moon Glampers," said Hazel, "I'd have chimes on Sunday—just chimes. Kind of in honor of religion."

"I could think, if it was just chimes," said George.

"Well—maybe make 'em real loud," said Hazel. "I think I'd make a good Handicapper General."

"Good as anybody else," said George.

20   "Who knows better'n I do what normal is?" said Hazel.

"Right," said George. He began to think glimmeringly about his abnormal son who was now in jail, about Harrison, but a twenty-one-gun salute in his head stopped that.

"Boy!" said Hazel, "that was a doozy, wasn't it?"

It was such a doozy that George was white and trembling, and tears stood on the rims of his red eyes. Two of the eight ballerinas had collapsed to the studio floor, were holding their temples.

"All of a sudden you look so tired," said Hazel. "Why don't you stretch out on the sofa, so's you can rest your handicap bag on the pillows, honey-bunch." She was referring to the forty-seven pounds of birdshot in a canvas bag, which was padlocked around George's neck. "Go on and rest the bag for a little while," she said. "I don't care if you're not equal to me for a while."

25　George weighed the bag with his hands. "I don't mind it," he said. "I don't notice it any more. It's just a part of me."

"You been so tired lately—kind of wore out," said Hazel. "If there was just some way we could make a little hole in the bottom of the bag, and just take out a few of them lead balls. Just a few."

"Two years in prison and two thousand dollars fine for every ball I took out," said George. "I don't call that a bargain."

"If you could just take a few out when you came home from work," said Hazel. "I mean—you don't compete with anybody around here. You just set around."

"If I tried to get away with it," said George, "then other people'd get away with it—and pretty soon we'd be right back to the dark ages again, with everybody competing against everybody else. You wouldn't like that, would you?"

30　"I'd hate it," said Hazel.

"There you are," said George. "The minute people start cheating on laws, what do you think happens to society?"

If Hazel hadn't been able to come up with an answer to this question, George couldn't have supplied one. A siren was going off in his head.

"Reckon it'd fall all apart," said Hazel.

"What would?" said George blankly.

35　"Society," said Hazel uncertainly. "Wasn't that what you just said?"

"Who knows?" said George.

The television program was suddenly interrupted for a news bulletin. It wasn't clear at first as to what the bulletin was about, since the announcer, like all announcers, had a serious speech impediment. For about half a minute, and in a state of high excitement, the announcer tried to say, "Ladies and gentlemen—"

He finally gave up, handed the bulletin to a ballerina to read.

"That's all right—" Hazel said of the announcer, "he tried. That's the big thing. He tried to do the best he could with what God gave him. He should get a nice raise for trying so hard."

40   "Ladies and gentlemen—" said the ballerina, reading the bulletin. She must have been extraordinarily beautiful, because the mask she wore was hideous. And it was easy to see that she was the strongest and most graceful of all the dancers, for her handicap bags were as big as those worn by two-hundred-pound men.

And she had to apologize at once for her voice, which was a very unfair voice for a woman to use. Her voice was a warm, luminous, timeless melody. "Excuse me—" she said, and she began again, making her voice absolutely uncompetitive.

"Harrison Bergeron, age fourteen," she said in a grackle squawk, "has just escaped from jail, where he was held on suspicion of plotting to overthrow the government. He is a genius and an athlete, is under-handicapped, and should be regarded as extremely dangerous."

A police photograph of Harrison Bergeron was flashed on the screen upside down, then sideways, upside down again, then right side up. The picture showed the full length of Harrison against a background calibrated in feet and inches. He was exactly seven feet tall.

The rest of Harrison's appearance was Halloween and hardware. Nobody had ever borne heavier handicaps. He had outgrown hindrances faster than the H-G men could think them up. Instead of a little ear radio for a mental handicap, he wore a tremendous pair of earphones, and spectacles with thick wavy lenses. The spectacles were intended to make him not only half blind, but to give him whanging headaches besides.

45   Scrap metal was hung all over him. Ordinarily, there was a certain symmetry, a military neatness to the handicaps issued to strong people, but Harrison looked like a walking junkyard. In the race of life, Harrison carried three hundred pounds.

And to offset his good looks, the H-G men required that he wear at all times a red rubber ball for a nose, keep his eyebrows shaved off, and cover his even white teeth with black caps at snaggle-tooth random.

"If you see this boy," said the ballerina, "do not—I repeat, do not—try to reason with him."

There was the shriek of a door being torn from its hinges.

Screams and barking cries of consternation came from the television set. The photograph of Harrison Bergeron on the screen jumped again and again, as though dancing to the tune of an earthquake.

50   George Bergeron correctly identified the earthquake, and well he might have—for many was the time his own home had danced to the same crashing tune. "My God—" said George, "that must be Harrison!"

The realization was blasted from his mind instantly by the sound of an automobile collision in his head.

When George could open his eyes again, the photograph of Harrison was gone. A living, breathing Harrison filled the screen.

Clanking, clownish, and huge, Harrison stood in the center of the studio. The knob of the uprooted studio door was still in his hand. Ballerinas, technicians, musicians, and announcers cowered on their knees before him, expecting to die.

"I am the Emperor!" cried Harrison. "Do you hear? I am the Emperor! Everybody must do what I say at once!" He stamped his foot and the studio shook.

55 "Even as I stand here—" he bellowed, "crippled, hobbled, sickened—I am a greater ruler than any man who ever lived! Now watch me become what I can become!"

Harrison tore the straps of his handicap harness like wet tissue paper, tore straps guaranteed to support five thousand pounds.

Harrison's scrap-iron handicaps crashed to the floor.

Harrison thrust his thumbs under the bar of the padlock that secured his head harness. The bar snapped like celery. Harrison smashed his head-phones and spectacles against the wall.

He flung away his rubber-ball nose, revealed a man that would have awed Thor, the god of thunder.

60 "I shall now select my Empress!" he said, looking down on the cowering people. "Let the first woman who dares rise to her feet claim her mate and her throne!"

A moment passed, and then a ballerina arose, swaying like a willow.

Harrison plucked the mental handicap from her ear, snapped off her physical handicaps with marvelous delicacy. Last of all, he removed her mask.

She was blindingly beautiful.

"Now—" said Harrison, taking her hand, "shall we show the people the meaning of the word dance? Music!" he commanded.

65 The musicians scrambled back into their chairs, and Harrison stripped them of their handicaps, too. "Play your best," he told them, "and I'll make you barons and dukes and earls."

The music began. It was normal at first—cheap, silly, false. But Harrison snatched two musicians from their chairs, waved them like batons as he sang the music as he wanted it played. He slammed them back into their chairs.

The music began again and was much improved.

Harrison and his Empress merely listened to the music for a while—lis-tened gravely, as though synchronizing their heartbeats with it.

They shifted their weights to their toes.

70 Harrison placed his big hands on the girl's tiny waist, letting her sense the weightlessness that would soon be hers.

And then, in an explosion of joy and grace, into the air they sprang!

Not only were the laws of the land abandoned, but the law of gravity and the laws of motion as well.

They reeled, whirled, swiveled, flounced, capered, gamboled, and spun.

They leaped like deer on the moon.

75 The studio ceiling was thirty feet high, but each leap brought the dancers nearer to it.

It became their obvious intention to kiss the ceiling.

They kissed it.

And then, neutralizing gravity with love and pure will, they remained suspended in air inches below the ceiling, and they kissed each other for a long, long time.

It was then that Diana Moon Glampers, the Handicapper General, came into the studio with a double-barreled ten-gauge shotgun. She fired twice, and the Emperor and the Empress were dead before they hit the floor.

80 Diana Moon Glampers loaded the gun again. She aimed it at the musicians and told them they had ten seconds to get their handicaps back on.

It was then that the Bergerons' television tube burned out.

Hazel turned to comment about the blackout to George. But George had gone out into the kitchen for a can of beer.

George came back in with the beer, paused while a handicap signal shook him up. And then he sat down again. "You been crying?" he said to Hazel.

"Yup," she said.

85 "What about?" he said.

"I forget," she said. "Something real sad on television."

"What was it?" he said.

"It's all kind of mixed up in my mind," said Hazel.

"Forget sad things," said George.

90 "I always do," said Hazel.

"That's my girl," said George. He winced. There was the sound of a riveting gun in his head.

"Gee—I could tell that one was a doozy," said Hazel.

"You can say that again," said George.

"Gee—" said Hazel, "I could tell that one was a doozy."

Writing Log/Journal Assignment

Write a brief character sketch of George and Hazel. What details were most memorable about them? Which were most disturbing?

Individual and Collaborative Considerations

1. How does the setting established at the start of the story provide a framework for the rest of it?
2. What attempt has been made to make society ideal or "utopian"?
3. When do we first hear of Harrison Bergeron? Where is he? Why?
4. What sort of handicaps does Bergeron have? What did he look like?
5. What did Harrison and the ballerina (his Empress) do, and what was the consequence of their actions? What role did Diana Moon Glampers play in this story?

Writing Activities

1. Construct an analytical paper wherein you define and illustrate the perfect utopian society. What social system would suit the diverse demands and needs of individuals from different social, economic, and political backgrounds? In a Utopian society, how is gender or racial inequity addressed? How is peace maintained? How is good will perpetuated?
2. What happens to individuals who disrupt the status quo? Construct a thesis that answers this question and demonstrate its validity by examining what happened to figures in recent history who have attempted to enact progressive social change.

※

The Kugelmass Episode

Woody Allen

Woody Allen, a comedian, actor, screenwriter, and essayist, was born in Brooklyn, New York, in 1935 and began writing jokes when he was a high school student. Early in his career he wrote for several television programs, including *The Tonight Show*. Among the many films Allen has written and directed are *Bananas* (1970), *Play It Again Sam* (1972), the Academy Award–winning *Annie Hall* (1975), and *Manhattan* (1979). His books and collections of essays include *Getting Even* (1971), *Without Feathers* (1975), and *Side Effects* (1980). Allen's films and short fiction tend to be humorous, cynical, and yet romantic. His characters, like Kugelmass, are often neurotic and face "emotionally desperate circumstances." The following short story, "The Kugelmass Episode," was initially published in *The New Yorker* and won the O. Henry Award as one of the best short stories of 1978.

Kugelmass, a professor of humanities at City College, was unhappily married for the second time. Daphne Kugelmass was an oaf. He also had two dull sons by his first wife, Flo, and was up to his neck in alimony and child support.

"Did I know it would turn out so badly?" Kugelmass whined to his analyst one day. "Daphne had promise. Who suspected she'd let herself go and swell up like a beach ball? Plus she had a few bucks, which is not in itself a healthy reason to marry a person, but it doesn't hurt, with the kind of operating nut I have. You see my point?"

Kugelmass was bald and as hairy as a bear, but he had soul.

"I need to meet a new woman," he went on. "I need to have an affair. I may not look the part, but I'm a man who needs romance. I need softness, I need flirtation. I'm not getting younger, so before it's too late I want to make love in Venice, trade quips at '21,' and exchange coy glances over red wine and candlelight. You see what I'm saying?"

5   Dr. Mandel shifted in his chair and said, "An affair will solve nothing. You're so unrealistic. Your problems run much deeper."

"And also this affair must be discreet," Kugelmass continued. "I can't afford a second divorce. Daphne would really sock it to me."

"Mr. Kugelmass—"

"But it can't be anyone at City College, because Daphne also works there. Not that anyone on the faculty at C.C.N.Y. is any great shakes, but some of those coeds . . ."

"Mr. Kugelmass—"

10   "Help me. I had a dream last night. I was skipping through a meadow holding a picnic basket and the basket was marked 'Options.' And then I saw there was a hole in the basket."

"Mr. Kugelmass, the worst thing you could do is act out. You must simply express your feelings here, and together we'll analyze them. You have been in treatment long enough to know there is no overnight cure. After all, I'm an analyst, not a magician."

"Then perhaps what I need is a magician," Kugelmass said, rising from his chair. And with that he terminated his therapy.

A couple of weeks later, while Kugelmass and Daphne were moping around in their apartment one night like two pieces of old furniture, the phone rang.

"I'll get it," Kugelmass said. "Hello."

15   "Kugelmass?" a voice said. "Kugelmass, this is Persky."

"Who?"

"Persky. Or should I say The Great Persky?"

"Pardon me?"

"I hear you're looking all over town for a magician to bring a little exotica into your life? Yes or no?"

20   "Sh-h-h," Kugelmass whispered. "Don't hang up. Where are you calling from, Persky?"

Early the following afternoon, Kugelmass climbed three flights of stairs in a broken-down apartment house in the Bushwick section of Brooklyn. Peering through the darkness of the hall, he found the door he was looking for and pressed the bell. I'm going to regret this, he thought to himself.

Seconds later, he was greeted by a short, thin, waxy-looking man.

"*You're* Persky the Great?" Kugelmass said.

"The Great Persky. You want a tea?"

25   "No, I want romance. I want music. I want love and beauty."

"But not tea, eh? Amazing. O.K., sit down."

Persky went to the back room, and Kugelmass heard the sounds of boxes and furniture being moved around. Persky reappeared, pushing before him a large object on squeaky roller-skate wheels. He removed some old silk handkerchiefs that were lying on its top and blew away a bit of dust. It was a cheap-looking Chinese cabinet, badly lacquered.

"Persky," Kugelmass said, "what's your scam?"

"Pay attention," Persky said. "This is some beautiful effect. I developed it for a Knights of Pythias date last year, but the booking fell through. Get into the cabinet."

30 "Why, so you can stick it full of swords or something?"

"You see any swords?"

Kugelmass made a face and, grunting, climbed into the cabinet. He couldn't help noticing a couple of ugly rhinestones glued onto the raw plywood just in front of his face. "If this is a joke," he said.

"Some joke. Now, here's the point. If I throw any novel into this cabinet with you, shut the doors, and tap it three times, you will find yourself projected into that book."

Kugelmass made a grimace of disbelief.

35 "It's the emess," Persky said. "My hand to God. Not just a novel, either. A short story, a play, a poem. You can meet any of the women created by the world's best writers. Whoever you dreamed of. You could carry on all you like with a real winner. Then when you've had enough you give a yell, and I'll see you're back here in a split second."

"Persky, are you some kind of outpatient?"

"I'm telling you it's on the level," Persky said.

Kugelmass remained skeptical. "What are you telling me—that this cheesy home-made box can take me on a ride like you're describing?"

"For a double sawbuck."

40 Kugelmass reached for his wallet. "I'll believe this when I see it," he said.

Persky tucked the bills in his pants pocket and turned toward his bookcase. "So who do you want to meet? Sister Carrie? Hester Prynne? Ophelia? Maybe someone by Saul Bellow? Hey, what about Temple Drake? Although for a man your age she'd be a workout."

"French. I want to have an affair with a French lover."

"Nana?"

"I don't want to have to pay for it."

45 "What about Natasha in 'War and Peace'?"

"I said French. I know! What about Emma Bovary? That sounds to me perfect."

"You got it, Kugelmass. Give me a holler when you've had enough." Persky tossed in a paperback copy of Flaubert's novel.

"You sure this is safe?" Kugelmass asked as Persky began shutting the cabinet doors.

"Safe. Is anything safe in this crazy world?" Persky rapped three times on the cabinet and then flung open the doors.

50 Kugelmass was gone. At the same moment, he appeared in the bedroom of Charles and Emma Bovary's house at Yonville. Before him was a beautiful

woman, standing alone with her back turned to him as she folded some linen. I can't believe this, thought Kugelmass, staring at the doctor's ravishing wife. This is uncanny. I'm here. It's her.

Emma turned in surprise. "Goodness, you startled me," she said.

"Who are you?" She spoke in the same fine English translation as the paperback.

It's simply devastating, he thought. Then, realizing that it was he whom she had addressed, he said, "Excuse me. I'm Sidney Kugelmass. I'm from City College. A professor of humanities. C.C.N.Y.? Uptown. I— oh, boy!"

Emma Bovary smiled flirtatiously and said, "Would you like a drink? A glass of wine, perhaps?"

55   She is beautiful, Kugelmass thought. What a contrast with the troglodyte who shared his bed! He felt a sudden impulse to take this vision into his arms and tell her she was the kind of woman he had dreamed of all his life.

"Yes, some wine," he said hoarsely. "White. No, red. No, white. Make it white."

"Charles is out for the day," Emma said, her voice full of playful implication.

After the wine, they went for a stroll in the lovely French countryside. "I've always dreamed that some mysterious stranger would appear and rescue me from the monotony of this crass rural existence," Emma said, clasping his hand. They passed a small church. "I love what you have on," she murmured. "I've never seen anything like it around here. It's so . . . so modern."

"It's called a leisure suit," he said romantically. "It was marked down." Suddenly he kissed her. For the next hour they reclined under a tree and whispered together and told each other deeply meaningful things with their eyes. Then Kugelmass sat up. He had just remembered he had to meet Daphne at Bloomingdale's. "I must go," he told her. "But don't worry, I'll be back."

60   "I hope so," Emma said.

He embraced her passionately, and the two walked back to the house. He held Emma's face cupped in his palms, kissed her again, and yelled, "O.K., Persky! I got to be at Bloomingdale's by three-thirty."

There was an audible pop, and Kugelmass was back in Brooklyn.

"So? Did I lie?" Persky asked triumphantly.

"Look, Persky, I'm right now late to meet the ball and chain at Lexington Avenue, but when can I go again? Tomorrow?"

65   "My pleasure. Just bring a twenty. And don't mention this to anybody."

"Yeah. I'm going to call Rupert Murdoch."

Kugelmass hailed a cab and sped off to the city. His heart danced on point. I am in love, he thought, I am the possessor of a wonderful secret. What he didn't realize was that at this very moment students in various classrooms across the country were saying to their teachers, "Who is this character on page 100? A bald Jew is kissing Madame Bovary?" A teacher in Sioux Falls, South Dakota, sighed and thought, Jesus, these kids, with their pot and acid. What goes through their minds!

Daphne Kugelmass was in the bathroom-accessories department at Bloomingdale's when Kugelmass arrived breathlessly. "Where've you been?" she snapped. "It's four-thirty."

"I got held up in traffic," Kugelmass said.

70   Kugelmass visited Persky the next day, and in a few minutes was again passed magically to Yonville. Emma couldn't hide her excitement at seeing him. The two spent hours together, laughing and talking about their different backgrounds. Before Kugelmass left, they made love. "My God, I'm doing it with Madame Bovary!" Kugelmass whispered to himself. "Me, who failed freshman English."

As the months passed, Kugelmass saw Persky many times and developed a close and passionate relationship with Emma Bovary. "Make sure and always get me into the book before page 120," Kugelmass said to the magician one day. "I always have to meet her before she hooks up with this Rodolphe character."

"Why?" Persky said. "You can't beat his time?"

"Beat his time. He's landed gentry. Those guys have nothing better to do than flirt and ride horses. To me, he's one of those faces you see in the pages of *Women's Wear Daily*. With the Helmut Berger hairdo. But to her he's hot stuff."

"And her husband suspects nothing?"

75   "He's out of his depth. He's a lackluster little paramedic who's thrown in his lot with a jitterbug. He's ready to go to sleep by ten, and she's putting on her dancing shoes. Oh, well . . . See you later."

And once again Kugelmass entered the cabinet and passed instantly to the Bovary estate at Yonville. "How you doing, cupcake?" he said to Emma.

"Oh, Kugelmass," Emma sighed. "What I have to put up with. Last night at dinner, Mr. Personality dropped off to sleep in the middle of the dessert course. I'm pouring my heart out about Maxim's and the ballet, and out of the blue I hear snoring."

"It's O.K., darling. I'm here now," Kugelmass said, embracing her. I've earned this, he thought, smelling Emma's French perfume and burying his nose in her hair. I've suffered enough. I've paid enough analysts. I've searched till I'm weary. She's young and nubile, and I'm here a few pages after Leon and just before Rodolphe. By showing up during the correct chapters, I've got the situation knocked.

Emma, to be sure, was just as happy as Kugelmass. She had been starved for excitement, and his tales of Broadway night life, of fast cars and Hollywood and TV stars, enthralled the young French beauty.

80   "Tell me again about O. J. Simpson," she implored that evening, as she and Kugelmass strolled past Abbé Bournisien's church.

"What can I say? The man is great. He sets all kinds of rushing records. Such moves. They can't touch him."

"And the Academy Awards?" Emma said wistfully. "I'd give anything to win one."

"First you've got to be nominated."

"I know. You explained it. But I'm convinced I can act. Of course, I'd want to take a class or two. With Strasberg maybe. Then, if I had the right agent—"

85 "We'll see, we'll see. I'll speak to Persky."

That night, safely returned to Persky's flat, Kugelmass brought up the idea of having Emma visit him in the big city.

"Let me think about it," Persky said. "Maybe I could work it. Stranger things have happened." Of course, neither of them could think of one.

"Where the hell do you go all the time?" Daphne Kugelmass barked at her husband as he returned home late that evening. "You got a chippie stashed somewhere?"

"Yeah, sure, I'm just the type," Kugelmass said wearily. "I was with Leonard Popkin. We were discussing Socialist agriculture in Poland. You know Popkin. He's a freak on the subject."

90 "Well, you've been very odd lately," Daphne said. "Distant. Just don't forget about my father's birthday. On Saturday?"

"Oh, sure, sure," Kugelmass said, heading for the bathroom.

"My whole family will be there. We can see the twins. And Cousin Hamish. You should be more polite to Cousin Hamish—he likes you."

"Right, the twins," Kugelmass said, closing the bathroom door and shutting out the sound of his wife's voice. He leaned against it and took a deep breath. In a few hours, he told himself, he would be back in Yonville again, back with his beloved. And this time, if all went well, he would bring Emma back with him.

At three-fifteen the following afternoon, Persky worked his wizardry again. Kugelmass appeared before Emma, smiling and eager. The two spent a few hours at Yonville with Binet and then remounted the Bovary carriage. Following Persky's instructions, they held each other tightly, closed their eyes, and counted to ten. When they opened them, the carriage was just drawing up at the side door of the Plaza Hotel, where Kugelmass had optimistically reserved a suite earlier in the day.

95 "I love it! It's everything I dreamed it would be," Emma said as she swirled joyously around the bedroom, surveying the city from their window. "There's F.A.O. Schwarz. And there's Central Park, and the Sherry is which one? Oh, there—I see. It's too divine."

On the bed there were boxes from Halston and Saint Laurent. Emma unwrapped a package and held up a pair of black velvet pants against her perfect body.

"The slacks suit is by Ralph Lauren," Kugelmass said. "You'll look like a million bucks in it. Come on, sugar, give us a kiss."

"I've never been so happy!" Emma squealed as she stood before the mirror. "Let's go out on the town. I want to see 'Chorus Line' and the Guggenheim and this Jack Nicholson character you always talk about. Are any of his flicks showing?"

"I cannot get my mind around this," a Stanford professor said. "First a strange character named Kugelmass, and now she's gone from the book. Well, I guess the mark of a classic is that you can reread it a thousand times and always find something new."

100   The lovers passed a blissful weekend. Kugelmass had told Daphne he would be away at a symposium in Boston and would return Monday. Savoring each moment, he and Emma went to the movies, had dinner in Chinatown, passed two hours at a discothèque, and went to bed with a TV movie. They slept till noon on Sunday, visited SoHo, and ogled celebrities at Elaine's. They had caviar and champagne in their suite on Sunday night and talked until dawn. That morning, in the cab taking them to Persky's apartment, Kugelmass thought, It was hectic, but worth it. I can't bring her here too often, but now and then it will be a charming contrast with Yonville.

At Persky's, Emma climbed into the cabinet, arranged her new boxes of clothes neatly around her, and kissed Kugelmass fondly. "My place next time," she said with a wink. Persky rapped three times on the cabinet. Nothing happened.

"Hmm," Persky said, scratching his head. He rapped again, but still no magic. "Something must be wrong," he mumbled.

"Persky, you're joking!" Kugelmass cried. "How can it not work?"

"Relax, relax. Are you still in the box, Emma?"

105   "Yes."

Persky rapped again—harder this time.

"I'm still here, Persky."

"I know, darling. Sit tight."

"Persky, we *have* to get her back," Kugelmass whispered. "I'm a married man, and I have a class in three hours. I'm not prepared for anything more than a cautious affair at this point."

110   "I can't understand it," Persky muttered. "It's such a reliable little trick."

But he could do nothing. "It's going to take a little while," he said to Kugelmass. "I'm going to have to strip it down. I'll call you later."

Kugelmass bundled Emma into a cab and took her back to the Plaza. He barely made it to his class on time. He was on the phone all day, to Persky and to his mistress. The magician told him it might be several days before he got to the bottom of the trouble.

"How was the symposium?" Daphne asked him that night.

"Fine, fine," he said, lighting the filter end of a cigarette.

115   "What's wrong? You're as tense as a cat."

"Me? Ha, that's a laugh. I'm as calm as a summer night. I'm just going to take a walk." He eased out the door, hailed a cab, and flew to the Plaza.

"This is no good," Emma said. "Charles will miss me."

"Bear with me, sugar," Kugelmass said. He was pale and sweaty. He kissed her again, raced to the elevators, yelled at Persky over a pay phone in the Plaza lobby, and just made it home before midnight.

"According to Popkin, barley prices in Kraków have not been this stable since 1971," he said to Daphne, and smiled wanly as he climbed into bed.

120   The whole week went by like that. On Friday night, Kugelmass told Daphne there was another symposium he had to catch, this one in Syracuse. He hurried back to the Plaza, but the second weekend there was nothing like the first." "Get me back into the novel or marry me," Emma told Kugelmass. "Meanwhile, I want to get a job or go to class, because watching TV all day is the pits."

"Fine. We can use the money," Kugelmass said. "You consume twice your weight in room service."

"I met an Off Broadway producer in Central Park yesterday, and he said I might be right for a project he's doing," Emma said.

"Who is this clown?" Kugelmass asked.

"He's not a clown. He's sensitive and kind and cute. His name's Jeff Something-or-Other, and he's up for a Tony."

125   Later that afternoon, Kugelmass showed up at Persky's drunk.

"Relax," Persky told him. "You'll get a coronary."

"Relax. The man says relax. I've got a fictional character stashed in a hotel room, and I think my wife is having me tailed by a private shamus."

"O.K., O.K. We know there's a problem." Persky crawled under the cabinet and started banging on something with a large wrench.

"I'm like a wild animal," Kugelmass went on. "I'm sneaking around town, and Emma and I have had it up to here with each other. Not to mention a hotel tab that reads like the defense budget."

130   "So what should I do? This is the world of magic," Persky said. "It's all nuance."

"Nuance, my foot. I'm pouring Dom Pérignon and black eggs into this little mouse, plus her wardrobe, plus she's enrolled at the Neighborhood Playhouse and suddenly needs professional photos. Also, Persky, Professor Fivish Kopkind, who teaches Comp Lit and who has always been jealous of me, has identified me as the sporadically appearing character in the Flaubert book. He's threatened to go to Daphne. I see ruin and alimony; jail. For adultery with Madame Bovary, my wife will reduce me to beggary."

"What do you want me to say? I'm working on it night and day. As far as your personal anxiety goes, that I can't help you with. I'm a magician, not an analyst."

By Sunday afternoon, Emma had locked herself in the bathroom and refused to respond to Kugelmass's entreaties. Kugelmass stared out the window at the Wollman Rink and contemplated suicide. Too bad this is a low floor, he thought, or I'd do it right now. Maybe if I ran away to Europe and started life over . . . Maybe I could sell the *International Herald Tribune*, like those young girls used to.

The phone rang. Kugelmass lifted it to his ear mechanically.

135   "Bring her over," Persky said. "I think I got the bugs out of it."

Kugelmass's heart leaped. "You're serious?" he said. "You got it licked?"

"It was something in the transmission. Go figure."

"Persky, you're a genius. We'll be there in a minute. Less than a minute."

Again the lovers hurried to the magician's apartment, and again Emma Bovary climbed into the cabinet with her boxes. This time there was no kiss. Persky shut the doors, took a deep breath, and tapped the box three times. There was the reassuring popping noise, and when Persky peered inside, the box was empty. Madame Bovary was back in her novel. Kugelmass heaved a great sigh of relief and pumped the magician's hand.

140 "It's over," he said. "I learned my lesson. I'll never cheat again, I swear it." He pumped Persky's hand again and made a mental note to send him a necktie.

Three weeks later, at the end of a beautiful spring afternoon, Persky answered his doorbell. It was Kugelmass, with a sheepish expression on his face.

"O.K., Kugelmass," the magician said. "Where to this time?"

"It's just this once," Kugelmass said. "The weather is so lovely, and I'm not getting any younger. Listen, you've read 'Portnoy's Complaint'? Remember The Monkey?"

"The price is now twenty-five dollars, because the cost of living is up, but I'll start you off with one freebie, due to all the trouble I caused you."

145 "You're good people," Kugelmass said, combing his few remaining hairs as he climbed into the cabinet again. "This'll work all right?"

"I hope. But I haven't tried it much since all that unpleasantness."

"Sex and romance," Kugelmass said from inside the box. "What we go through for a pretty face."

Persky tossed in a copy of "Portnoy's Complaint" and rapped three times on the box. This time, instead of a popping noise there was a dull explosion, followed by a series of crackling noises and a shower of sparks. Persky leaped back, was seized by a heart attack, and dropped dead. The cabinet burst into flames, and eventually the entire house burned down.

Kugelmass, unaware of this catastrophe, had his own problems. He had not been thrust into "Portnoy's Complaint," or into any other novel, for that matter. He had been projected into an old textbook, "Remedial Spanish," and was running for his life over a barren, rocky terrain as the word *"tener"* ("to have")—a large and hairy irregular verb—raced after him on its spindly legs.

Writing Log/Journal Assignment

Write a paragraph or so explaining the various ways you have "escaped" boring periods in your life. (Do you daydream? If you do, exactly what do you daydream about and why?)

Individual and Collaborative Considerations

1. What is the initial conflict in this short story? Why does Persky seem to have the answers to all his problems?

2. How does Allen describe Kugelmass? How does he measure up to what you consider the picture of good health and male virility? Why then do you think Allen characterized him in such a manner?
3. Cite some specific instances in the story where Allen satirizes the academic profession. In what way is satire a key element in Allen's humor?
4. Why does Kugelmass begin to get weary of Madame Bovary?
5. In what way is Allen's ironic conclusion (thrusting Kugelmass into a remedial Spanish textbook where he is chased by *tener*, a "large and hairy irregular verb" meaning "to have," rather than into *Portnoy's Complaint*) almost poetic justice?

Writing Activities

1. Have you ever desired an illicit relationship with a fictional character or perhaps an encounter with an historical figure? If so, who? If not, think for a moment about which fictional or historical figure you would want to meet and why. Then write an essay stating your preference as well as how you arrived at your conclusion.
2. Construct a thesis around the notion that "escapism" into books, films, the past (nostalgia), or the future is an essential part of a healthy life. Begin your essay by defining precisely what you mean by "escapism" and go on to defend your thesis with a wide variety of representative examples (people who indulge in some form of escapism).

The Magic Barrel

Bernard Malamud

Born in Brooklyn in 1914, Bernard Malamud was the son of Russian immigrant parents. He frequently blended sharp wit and satire as he addressed the human condition in novels and stories ranging from mythic baseball players to unhappy experiences of Jews. His first novel was *The Natural* (1953), followed by *The Assistant* (1957) and *A New Life* (1961). Later novels included *The Fixer* (1967)—which won the Pulitzer Prize and the National Book Award—*Pictures of a Fiddleman* (1969), *The Tenants* (1971), *Dublin's Lives* (1979), and *God's Grace* (1982). In addition to his novels, Malamud wrote several short story collections, including *The Magic Barrel*, winner of the National Book Award (1958), *Idiots First* (1963), *Rembrandt's Hat* (1973), and *Stories* (1983). Although Malamud's stories often reflected his interest in minority groups and social situations, he said he used Jewish material in many of his works "because I know it." In a lecture he gave in Israel, Malamud also remarked that "personally, I handle the Jew as a symbol of the tragic experience of man existentially."

Not long ago there lived in uptown New York, in a small, almost meager room, though crowded with books, Leo Finkle, a rabbinical student in the Yeshivah University. Finkle, after six years of study, was to be ordained in June and had been advised by an acquaintance that he might find it easier to win himself a congregation if he were married. Since he had no present prospects of marriage, after two tormented days of turning it over in his mind, he called in Pinye Salzman, a marriage broker whose two-line advertisement he had read in the *Forward*.

The matchmaker appeared one night out of the dark fourth-floor hallway of the graystone rooming house where Finkle lived, grasping a black, strapped portfolio that had been worn thin with use. Salzman, who had been long in the business, was of slight but dignified build, wearing an old hat, and an overcoat too short and tight for him. He smelled frankly of fish, which he loved to eat, and although he was missing a few teeth, his presence was not displeasing, because of an amiable manner curiously contrasted with mournful eyes. His voice, his lips, his wisp of beard, his bony fingers were animated, but gave him a moment of repose and his mild blue eyes revealed a depth of sadness, a characteristic that put Leo a little at ease although the situation, for him, was inherently tense.

He at once informed Salzman why he had asked him to come, explaining that his home was in Cleveland, and that but for his parents, who had married comparatively late in life, he was alone in the world. He had for six years devoted himself almost entirely to his studies, as a result of which, understandably, he had found himself without time for a social life and the company of young women. Therefore he thought it the better part of trial and error—of embarrassing fumbling—to call in an experienced person to advise him on these matters. He remarked in passing that the function of the marriage broker was ancient and honorable, highly approved in the Jewish community, because it made practical the necessary without hindering joy. Moreover, his own parents had been brought together by a matchmaker. They had made, if not a financially profitable marriage—since neither had possessed any worldly goods to speak of—at least a successful one in the sense of their everlasting devotion to each other. Salzman listened in embarrassed surprise, sensing a sort of apology. Later, however, he experienced a glow of pride in his work, an emotion that had left him years ago, and he heartily approved of Finkle.

The two went to their business. Leo had led Salzman to the only clear place in the room, a table near a window that overlooked the lamp-lit city. He seated himself at the matchmaker's side but facing him, attempting by an act of will to suppress the unpleasant tickle in his throat. Salzman eagerly unstrapped his portfolio and removed a loose rubber band from a thin packet of much-handled cards. As he flipped through them, a gesture and sound that physically hurt Leo, the student pretended not to see and gazed steadfastly out the window. Although it was still February, winter was on its last legs, signs of which he had for the first time in years begun to notice. He now observed the round white moon, moving high in the sky through a cloud menagerie, and watched with half-open mouth as it penetrated a huge hen, and dropped out of her like an egg laying itself. Salzman, though pretending through eyeglasses he had just slipped on to be engaged in scanning the writing on the cards, stole occasional glances at the young man's distinguished face, noting with pleasure the long, severe scholar's nose, brown eyes heavy with learning, sensitive yet ascetic lips, and a certain, almost hollow quality of the dark cheeks. He gazed around at shelves upon shelves of books and let out a soft, contented sigh.

5   When Leo's eyes fell upon the cards, he counted six spread out in Salzman's hand.

"So few?" he asked in disappointment.

"You wouldn't believe me how much cards I got in my office," Salzman replied. "The drawers are already filled to the top, so I keep them now in a barrel, but is every girl good for a new rabbi?"

Leo blushed at this, regretting all he had revealed of himself in a curriculum vitae he had sent to Salzman. He had thought it best to acquaint him with his strict standards and specifications, but in having done so, felt he had told the marriage broker more than was absolutely necessary.

He hesitantly inquired, "Do you keep photographs of your clients on file?"

10   "First comes family, amount of dowry, also what kind promises," Salzman replied, unbuttoning his tight coat and settling himself in the chair. "After comes pictures, rabbi."

"Call me Mr. Finkle. I'm not yet a rabbi."

Salzman said he would, but instead called him doctor, which he changed to rabbi when Leo was not listening too attentively.

Salzman adjusted his horn-rimmed spectacles, gently cleared his throat and read in an eager voice the contents of the top card:

"Sophie P. Twenty-four year. Widow one year. No children. Educated high school and two years college. Father promises eight thousand dollars. Has wonderful wholesale business. Also real estate. On the mother's side comes teachers, also one actor. Well known on Second Avenue."

15   Leo gazed up in surprise. "Did you say a widow?"

"A widow don't mean spoiled, rabbi. She lived with her husband maybe four months. He was a sick boy she made a mistake to marry him."

"Marrying a widow has never entered my mind."

"This is because you have no experience. A widow, especially if she is young and healthy like this girl, is a wonderful person to marry. She will be thankful to you the rest of her life. Believe me, if I was looking now for a bride, I would marry a widow."

Leo reflected, then shook his head.

20   Salzman hunched his shoulders in an almost imperceptible gesture of disappointment. He placed the card down on the wooden table and began to read another:

"Lily H. High school teacher. Regular. Not a substitute. Has savings and new Dodge car. Lived in Paris one year. Father is successful dentist thirty-five years. Interested in professional man. Well Americanized family. Wonderful opportunity.

"I knew her personally," said Salzman. "I wish you could see this girl. She is a doll. Also very intelligent. All day you could talk to her about books and theyater and what not. She also knows current events."

"I don't believe you mentioned her age?"

"Her age?" Salzman said, raising his brows. "Her age is thirty-two years."

25   Leo said after a while, "I'm afraid that seems a little too old."

Salzman let out a laugh. "So how old are you, rabbi?"

"Twenty-seven."

"So what is the difference, tell me, between twenty-seven and thirty-two? My own wife is seven years older than me. So what did I suffer?—Nothing. If Rothschild's daughter wants to marry you, would you say on account her age, no?"

"Yes," Leo said dryly.

30   Salzman shook off the no in the yes. "Five years don't mean a thing. I give you my word that when you will live with her for one week you will forget her age. What does it mean five years—that she lived more and knows more than somebody who is younger? On this girl, God bless her, years are not wasted. Each one that it comes makes better the bargain."

"What subject does she teach in high school?"

"Languages. If you heard the way she speaks French, you will think it is music. I am in the business twenty-five years, and I recommend her with my whole heart. Believe me, I know what I'm talking, rabbi."

"What's on the next card?" Leo said abruptly.

Salzman reluctantly turned up the third card:

35   "Ruth K. Nineteen years. Honor student. Father offers thirteen thousand cash to the right bridegroom. He is a medical doctor. Stomach specialist with marvelous practice. Brother in law owns own garment business. Particular people."

Salzman looked as if he had read his trump card.

"Did you say nineteen?" Leo asked with interest.

"On the dot."

"Is she attractive?" He blushed. "Pretty?"

40   Salzman kissed his finger tips. "A little doll. On this I give you my word. Let me call the father tonight and you will see what means pretty."

But Leo was troubled. "You're sure she's that young?"

"This I am positive. The father will show you the birth certificate."

"Are you positive there isn't something wrong with her?" Leo insisted.

"Who says there is wrong?"

45   "I don't understand why an American girl her age should go to a marriage
broker."

A smile spread over Salzman's face.

"So for the same reason you went, she comes."

Leo flushed. "I am pressed for time."

Salzman, realizing he had been tactless, quickly explained. "The father
came, not her. He wants she should have the best, so he looks around himself. When we will locate the right boy he will introduce him and encourage.
This makes a better marriage than if a young girl without experience takes
for herself. I don't have to tell you this."

50   "But don't you think this young girl believes in love?"

Leo spoke uneasily.

Salzman was about to guffaw but caught himself and said soberly, "Love
comes with the right person, not before."

Leo parted dry lips but did not speak. Noticing that Salzman had snatched
a glance at the next card, he cleverly asked, "How is her health?"

"Perfect," Salzman said, breathing with difficulty. "Of course, she is a
little lame on her right foot from an auto accident that it happened to her
when she was twelve years, but nobody notices on account she is so brilliant
and also beautiful."

55   Leo got up heavily and went to the window. He felt curiously bitter and
upbraided himself for having called in the marriage broker. Finally, he shook
his head.

"Why not?" Salzman persisted, the pitch of his voice rising.

"Because I detest stomach specialists."

"So what do you care what is his business? After you marry her do you
need him? Who says he must come every Friday night in your house?"

Ashamed of the way the talk was going, Leo dismissed Salzman, who
went home with heavy, melancholy eyes.

60   Though he had felt only relief at the marriage broker's departure, Leo was
in low spirits the next day. He explained it as arising from Salzman's failure
to produce a suitable bride for him. He did not care for his type of clientele.
But when Leo found himself hesitating whether to seek out another matchmaker, one more polished than Pinye, he wondered if it could be—his prot-
estations to the contrary, and although he honored his father and mother—
that he did not, in essence, care for the matchmaking institution? This
thought he quickly put out of mind yet found himself still upset. All day he
ran around in the woods—missed an important appointment, forgot to give
out his laundry, walked out of a Broadway cafeteria without paying and had
to run back with the ticket in his hand; had even not recognized his landlady
in the street when she passed with a friend and courteously called out, "A
good evening to you, Doctor Finkle." By nightfall, however, he had regained
sufficient calm to sink his nose into a book and there found peace from his
thoughts.

Almost at once there came a knock on the door. Before Leo could say
enter, Salzman, commercial cupid, was standing in the room. His face was

gray and meager, his expression hungry, and he looked as if he would expire on his feet. Yet the marriage broker managed, by some trick of the muscles, to display a broad smile.

"So good evening. I am invited?"

Leo nodded, disturbed to see him again, yet unwilling to ask the man to leave.

Beaming still, Salzman laid his portfolio on the table. "Rabbi, I got for you tonight good news."

65 "I've asked you not to call me rabbi. I'm still a student."

"Your worries are finished. I have for you a first-class bride."

"Leave me in peace concerning this subject." Leo pretended lack of interest.

"The world will dance at your wedding."

"Please, Mr. Salzman, no more."

70 "But first must come back my strength," Salzman said weakly. He fumbled with the portfolio straps and took out of the leather case an oily paper bag, from which he extracted a hard, seeded roll and a small, smoked white fish. With a quick motion of his hand he stripped the fish out of its skin and began ravenously to chew. "All day in a rush," he muttered.

Leo watched him eat.

"A sliced tomato you have maybe?" Salzman hesitantly inquired.

"No."

The marriage broker shut his eyes and ate. When he had finished he carefully cleaned up the crumbs and rolled up the remains of the fish, in the paper bag. His spectacled eyes roamed the room until he discovered, amid some piles of books, a one-burner gas stove. Lifting his hat he humbly asked, "A glass tea you got, rabbi?"

75 Conscience-stricken, Leo rose and brewed the tea. He served it with a chunk of lemon and two cubes of lump sugar, delighting Salzman.

After he had drunk his tea, Salzman's strength and good spirits were restored.

"So tell me, rabbi," he said amiably, "you considered some more the three clients I mentioned yesterday?"

"There was no need to consider."

"Why not?"

80 "None of them suits me."

"What then suits you?"

Leo let it pass because he could give only a confused answer.

Without waiting for a reply, Salzman asked, "You remember this girl I talked to you—the high school teacher?"

"Age thirty-two?"

85 But, surprisingly, Salzman's face lit in a smile. "Age twenty-nine."

Leo shot him a look. "Reduced from thirty-two?"

"A mistake," Salzman avowed. "I talked today with the dentist. He took me to his safety deposit box and showed me the birth certificate. She was twenty-nine years last August. They made her a party in the mountains where she went for her vacation. When her father spoke to me the first time I forgot to write the age and I told you thirty-two, but now I remember this was a different client, a widow.''

''The same one you told me about? I thought she was twenty-four?''

''A different. Am I responsible that the world is filled with widows?''

90 ''No, but I'm not interested in them, nor for that matter, in school teachers.''

Salzman pulled his clasped hands to his breast. Looking at the ceiling he devoutly exclaimed, ''Yiddishe kinder, what can I say to somebody that he is not interested in high school teachers? So what then you are interested?''

Leo flushed but controlled himself.

''In what else will you be interested,'' Salzman went on, ''if you not interested in this fine girl that she speaks four languages and has personally in the bank ten thousand dollars? Also her father guarantees further twelve thousand. Also she has a new car, wonderful clothes, talks on all subjects, and she will give you a first-class home and children. How near do we come in our life to paradise?''

''If she's so wonderful, why wasn't she married ten years ago?''

95 ''Why?'' said Salzman with a heavy laugh. ''—Why? Because she is *partikiler.* This is why. She wants the best.''

Leo was silent, amused at how he had entangled himself. But Salzman had aroused his interest in Lily H., and he began seriously to consider calling on her. When the marriage broker observed how intently Leo's mind was at work on the facts he had supplied, he felt certain they would soon come to an agreement.

Late Saturday afternoon, conscious of Salzman, Leo Finkle walked with Lily Hirschorn along Riverside Drive. He walked briskly and erectly, wearing with distinction the black fedora he had that morning taken with trepidation out of the dusty hat box on his closet shelf, and the heavy black Saturday coat he had thoroughly whisked clean. Leo also owned a walking stick, a present from a distant relative, but quickly put temptation aside and did not use it. Lily, petite and not unpretty, had on something signifying the approach of spring. She was au courant, animatedly, with all sorts of subjects, and he weighed her words and found her surprisingly sound—score another for Salzman, whom he uneasily sensed to be somewhere around, hiding perhaps high in a tree along the street, flashing the lady signals with a pocket mirror; or perhaps a cloven-hoofed Pan, piping nuptial ditties as he danced his invisible way before them, strewing wild buds on the walk and purple grapes in their path, symbolizing fruit of a union, though there was of course still none.

Lily startled Leo by remarking, ''I was thinking of Mr. Salzman, a curious figure, wouldn't you say?''

Not certain what to answer, he nodded.

100 She bravely went on, blushing. ''I for one am grateful for his introducing us. Aren't you?''

He courteously replied, "I am."

"I mean," she said with a little laugh—and it was all in good taste, or at least gave the effect of being not in bad—"do you mind that we came together so?"

He was not displeased with her honesty, recognizing that she meant to set the relationship aright, and understanding that it took a certain amount of experience in life, and courage, to want to do it quite that way. One had to have some sort of past to make that kind of beginning.

He said that he did not mind. Salzman's function was traditional and honorable—valuable for what it might achieve, which, he pointed out, was frequently nothing.

105   Lily agreed with a sigh. They walked on for a while and she said after a long silence, again with a nervous laugh, "Would you mind if I asked you something a little bit personal? Frankly, I find the subject fascinating." Although Leo shrugged, she went on half embarrassedly, "How was it that you came to your calling? I mean was it a sudden passionate inspiration?"

Leo, after a time, slowly replied, "I was always interested in the Law."

"You saw revealed in it the presence of the Highest?"

He nodded and changed the subject. "I understand that you spent a little time in Paris, Miss Hirschorn?"

"Oh, did Mr. Salzman tell you, Rabbi Finkle?" Leo winced but she went on, "It was ages ago and almost forgotten. I remember I had to return for my sister's wedding."

110   And Lily would not be put off. "When," she asked in a trembly voice, "did you become enamored of God?"

He stared at her. Then it came to him that she was talking not about Leo Finkle, but of a total stranger, some mystical figure, perhaps even passionate prophet that Salzman had dreamed up for her—no relation to the living or dead. Leo trembled with rage and weakness. The trickster had obviously sold her a bill of goods, just as he had him, who'd expected to become acquainted with a young lady of twenty-nine, only to behold, the moment he laid eyes upon her strained and anxious face, a woman past thirty-five and aging rapidly. Only his self control had kept him this long in her presence.

"I am not," he said gravely, "a talented religious person," and in seeking words to go on, found himself possessed by shame and fear. "I think," he said in a strained manner, "that I came to God not because I loved Him, but because I did not."

This confession he spoke harshly because its unexpectedness shook him.

Lily wilted. Leo saw a profusion of loaves of bread go flying like ducks high over his head, not unlike the winged loaves by which he had counted himself to sleep last night. Mercifully, then, it snowed, which he would not put past Salzman's machinations.

115   He was infuriated with the marriage broker and swore he would throw him out of the room the minute he reappeared. But Salzman did not come that night, and when Leo's anger had subsided, an unaccountable despair grew in its place. At first he thought this was caused by his disappointment

in Lily, but before long it became evident that he had involved himself with Salzman without a true knowledge of his own intent. He gradually realized—with an emptiness that seized him with six hands—that he had called in the broker to find him a bride because he was incapable of doing it himself. This terrifying insight he had derived as a result of his meeting and conversation with Lily Hirschorn. Her probing questions had somehow irritated him into revealing—to himself more than her—the true nature of his relationship to God, and from that it had come upon him, with shocking force, that apart from his parents, he had never loved anyone. Or perhaps it went the other way, that he did not love God so well as he might, because he had not loved man. It seemed to Leo that his whole life stood starkly revealed and he saw himself for the first time as he truly was—unloved and loveless. This bitter but somehow not fully unexpected revelation brought him to a point of panic, controlled only by extraordinary effort. He covered his face with his hands and cried.

The week that followed was the worst of his life. He did not eat and lost weight. His beard darkened and grew ragged. He stopped attending seminars and almost never opened a book. He seriously considered leaving the Yeshivah, although he was deeply troubled at the thought of the loss of all his years of study—saw them like pages torn from a book, strewn over the city—and at the devastating effect of this decision upon his parents. But he had lived without knowledge of himself, and never in the Five Books and all the Commentaries—mea culpa—had the truth been revealed to him. He did not know where to turn, and in all this desolating loneliness there was no *to whom*, although he often thought of Lily but not once could bring himself to go downstairs and make the call. He became touchy and irritable, especially with his landlady, who asked him all manner of personal questions; on the other hand, sensing his own disagreeableness, he waylaid her on the stairs and apologized abjectly, until mortified, she ran from him. Out of this, however, he drew the consolation that he was a Jew and that a Jew suffered. But gradually, as the long and terrible week drew to a close, he regained his composure and some idea of purpose in life: to go on as planned. Although he was imperfect, the ideal was not. As for his quest of a bride, the thought of continuing afflicted him with anxiety and heartburn, yet perhaps with this new knowledge of himself he would be more successful than in the past. Perhaps love would now come to him and a bride to that love. And for this sanctified seeking who needed a Salzman?

The marriage broker, a skeleton with haunted eyes, returned that very night. He looked, withal, the picture of frustrated expectancy—as if he had steadfastly waited the week at Miss Lily Hirschorn's side for a telephone call that never came.

Casually coughing, Salzman came immediately to the point: "So how did you like her?"

Leo's anger rose and he could not refrain from chiding the matchmaker: "Why did you lie to me, Salzman?"

Salzman's pale face went dead white, the world had snowed on him.

"Did you not state that she was twenty-nine?" Leo insisted.

120

"I give you my word—"

"She was thirty-five, if a day. *At least* thirty-five."

"Of this don't be too sure. Her father told me—"

125   "Never mind. The worst of it was that you lied to her."

"How did I lie to her, tell me?"

"You told her things about me that weren't true. You made me out to be more, consequently less than I am. She had in mind a totally different person, a sort of semi-mystical Wonder Rabbi."

"All I said, you was a religious man."

"I can imagine."

130   Salzman sighed. "This is my weakness that I have," he confessed. "My wife says to me I shouldn't be a salesman, but when I have two fine people that they would be wonderful to be married, I am so happy that I talk too much." He smiled wanly. "This is why Salzman is a poor man."

Leo's anger left him. "Well, Salzman, I'm afraid that's all."

The marriage broker fastened hungry eyes on him.

"You don't want any more a bride?"

"I do," said Leo, "but I have decided to seek her in a different way. I am no longer interested in an arranged marriage. To be frank, I now admit the necessity of premarital love. That is, I want to be in love with the one I marry."

135   "Love?" said Salzman, astounded. After a moment he remarked, "For us, our love is our life, not for the ladies. In the ghetto they—"

"I know, I know," said Leo. "I've thought of it often. Love, I have said to myself, should be a by-product of living and worship rather than its own end. Yet for myself I find it necessary to establish the level of my need and fulfill it."

Salzman shrugged but answered, "Listen, rabbi, if you want love, this I can find for you also. I have such beautiful clients that you will love them the minute your eyes see them."

Leo smiled unhappily. "I'm afraid you don't understand."

But Salzman hastily unstrapped his portfolio and withdrew a manila packet from it.

140   "Pictures," he said, quickly laying the envelope on the table.

Leo called after him to take the pictures away, but as if on the wings of the wind, Salzman had disappeared.

March came. Leo had returned to his regular routine. Although he felt not quite himself yet—lacked energy—he was making plans for a more active social life. Of course it would cost something, but he was an expert in cutting corners; and when there were no corners left he would make circles rounder. All the while Salzman's pictures had lain on the table, gathering dust. Occasionally as Leo sat studying, or enjoying a cup of tea, his eyes fell on the manila envelope, but he never opened it.

The days went by and no social life to speak of developed with a member of the opposite sex—it was difficult, given the circumstances of his situation. One morning Leo toiled up the stairs to his room and stared out the window at the city. Although the day was bright his view of it was dark. For some time he watched the people in the street below hurrying along and then turned with a heavy heart to his little room. On the table was the packet. With a sudden relentless gesture he tore it open. For a half-hour he stood by the table in a state of excitement, examining the photographs of the ladies Salzman had included. Finally, with a deep sigh he put them down. There were six, of varying degrees of attractiveness, but look at them long enough and they all became Lily Hirschorn: all past their prime, all starved behind bright smiles, not a true personality in the lot. Life, despite their frantic yoo-hooings, had passed them by; they were pictures in a briefcase that stank of fish. After a while, however, as Leo attempted to return the photographs into the envelope, he found in it another, a snapshot of the type taken by a machine for a quarter. He gazed at it a moment and let out a cry.

Her face deeply moved him. Why, he could at first not say. It gave him the impression of youth—spring flowers, yet age—a sense of having been used to the bone, wasted; this came from the eyes, which were hauntingly familiar, yet absolutely strange. He had a vivid impression that he had met her before, but try as he might he could not place her although he could almost recall her name, as if he had read it in her own handwriting. No, this couldn't be; he would have remembered her. It was not, he affirmed, that she had an extraordinary beauty—no, though her face was attractive enough; it was that *something* about her moved him. Feature for feature, even some of the ladies of the photographs could do better; but she leaped forth to his heart—had *lived*, or wanted to—more than just wanted, perhaps regretted how she had lived—had somehow deeply suffered: it could be seen in the depths of those reluctant eyes, and from the way the light enclosed and shone from her, and within her, opening realms of possibility: this was her own. Her he desired. His head ached and eyes narrowed with the intensity of his gazing, then as if an obscure fog had blown up in the mind, he experienced fear of her and was aware that he had received an impression, somehow, of evil. He shuddered, saying softly, it is thus with us all. Leo brewed some tea in a small pot and sat sipping it without sugar, to calm himself. But before he had finished drinking, again with excitement he examined the face and found it good: good for Leo Finkle. Only such a one could understand him and help him seek whatever he was seeking. She might, perhaps, love him. How she had happened to be among the discards in Salzman's barrel he could never guess, but he knew he must urgently go find her.

145   Leo rushed downstairs, grabbed up the Bronx telephone book, and searched for Salzman's home address. He was not listed, nor was his office. Neither was he in the Manhattan book. But Leo remembered having written down the address on a slip of paper after he had read Salzman's advertisement in the "personals" column of the *Forward*. He ran up to his room and tore through his papers, without luck. It was exasperating. Just when he needed the matchmaker he was nowhere to be found. Fortunately Leo remembered to look in his wallet. There on a card he found his name written and a Bronx address. No phone number was listed, the reason—Leo now recalled—he had originally communicated with Salzman by letter. He got

on his coat, put a hat on over his skull cap and hurried to the subway station. All the way to the far end of the Bronx he sat on the edge of his seat. He was more than once tempted to take out the picture and see if the girl's face was as he remembered it, but he refrained, allowing the snapshot to remain in his inside coat pocket, content to have her so close. When the train pulled into the station he was waiting at the door and bolted out. He quickly located the street Salzman had advertised.

The building he sought was less than a block from the subway, but it was not an office building, nor even a loft, nor a store in which one could rent office space. It was a very old tenement house. Leo found Salzman's name in pencil on a soiled tag under the bell and climbed three dark flights to his apartment. When he knocked, the door was opened by a thin, asthmatic, gray-haired woman, in felt slippers.

"Yes?" she said, expecting nothing. She listened without listening. He could have sworn he had seen her, too, before but knew it was an illusion.

"Salzman—does he live here? Pinye Salzman," he said, "the matchmaker?"

She stared at him a long minute. "Of course."

150   He felt embarrassed. "Is he in?"

"No." Her mouth, though left open, offered nothing more.

"The matter is urgent. Can you tell me where his office is?"

"In the air." She pointed upward.

"You mean he has no office?" Leo asked.

155   "In his socks."

He peered into the apartment. It was sunless and dingy, one large room divided by a half-open curtain, beyond which he could see a sagging metal bed. The near side of the room was crowded with rickety chairs, old bureaus, a three-legged table, racks of cooking utensils, and all the apparatus of a kitchen. But there was no sign of Salzman or his magic barrel, probably also a figment of the imagination. An odor of frying fish made Leo weak to the knees.

"Where is he?" he insisted. "I've got to see your husband."

At length she answered, "So who knows where he is? Every time he thinks a new thought he runs to a different place. Go home, he will find you."

"Tell him Leo Finkle."

160   She gave no sign she had heard.

He walked downstairs, depressed.

But Salzman, breathless, stood waiting at his door.

Leo was astounded and overjoyed. "How did you get here before me?"

"I rushed."

165   "Come inside."

They entered. Leo fixed tea, and a sardine sandwich for Salzman. As they were drinking he reached behind him for the packet of pictures and handed them to the marriage broker.

Salzman put down his glass and said expectantly, "You found somebody you like?"

"Not among these."

The marriage broker turned away.

170 "Here is the one I want." Leo held forth the snapshot.

Salzman slipped on his glasses and took the picture into his trembling hand. He turned ghastly and let out a groan.

"What's the matter?" cried Leo.

"Excuse me. Was an accident this picture. She isn't for you."

Salzman frantically shoved the manila packet into his portfolio. He thrust the snapshot into his pocket and fled down the stairs.

175 Leo, after momentary paralysis, gave chase and cornered the marriage broker in the vestibule. The landlady made hysterical outcries but neither of them listened.

"Give me back the picture, Salzman."

"No." The pain in his eyes was terrible.

"Tell me who she is then."

"This I can't tell you. Excuse me."

180 He made to depart, but Leo, forgetting himself, seized the matchmaker by his tight coat and shook him frenziedly.

"Please," sighed Salzman. *"Please."*

Leo ashamedly let him go. "Tell me who she is," he begged. "It's very important for me to know."

"She is not for you. She is a wild one—wild, without shame. This is not a bride for a rabbi."

"What do you mean wild?"

185 "Like an animal. Like a dog. For her to be poor was a sin. This is why to me she is dead now."

"In God's name, what do you mean?"

"Her I can't introduce to you," Salzman cried.

"Why are you so excited?"

"Why, he asks," Salzman said, bursting into tears. "This is my baby, my Stella, she should burn in hell."

190 Leo hurried up to bed and hid under the covers. Under the covers he thought his life through. Although he soon fell asleep he could not sleep her out of his mind. He woke, beating his breast. Though he prayed to be rid of her, his prayers went unanswered. Through days of torment he endlessly struggled not to love her; fearing success, he escaped it. He then concluded to convert her to goodness, himself to God. The idea alternately nauseated and exalted him.

He perhaps did not know that he had come to a final decision until he encountered Salzman in a Broadway cafeteria. He was sitting alone at a rear table, sucking the bony remains of a fish. The marriage broker appeared haggard, and transparent to the point of vanishing.

Salzman looked up at first without recognizing him. Leo had grown a pointed beard and his eyes were weighted with wisdom.

"Salzman," he said, "love has at last come to my heart."

"Who can love from a picture?" mocked the marriage broker.

195 "It is not impossible."

"If you can love her, then you can love anybody. Let me show you some new clients that they just sent me their photographs. One is a little doll."

"Just her I want," Leo murmured.

"Don't be a fool, doctor. Don't bother with her."

"Put me in touch with her, Salzman," Leo said humbly. "Perhaps I can be of service."

200 Salzman had stopped eating and Leo understood with emotion that it was now arranged.

Leaving the cafeteria, he was, however, afflicted by a tormenting suspicion that Salzman had planned it all to happen this way.

Leo was informed by letter that she would meet him on a certain corner, and she was there one spring night, waiting under a street lamp. He appeared, carrying a small bouquet of violets and rosebuds. Stella stood by the lamp post, smoking. She wore white with red shoes, which fitted his expectations, although in a troubled moment he had imagined the dress red, and only the shoes white. She waited uneasily and shyly. From afar he saw that her eyes—clearly her father's—were filled with desperate innocence. He pictured, in her, his own redemption. Violins and lit candles revolved in the sky. Leo ran forward with flowers outthrust.

Around the corner, Salzman, leaning against a wall, chanted prayers for the dead.

Writing Log/Journal Assignment

What is the most important thing in a marriage? Write a journal entry responding to Salzman's comment that "Love comes with the right person, not before."

Individual and Collaborative Considerations

1. Describe the matchmaker. What seems to motivate his actions throughout the story?
2. How does Malamud use word order to capture a distinct speech pattern or dialect when Salzman speaks (e.g., "I am invited?" instead of "Am I invited?"). Cite several similar instances of Salzman's speech patterns.
3. What shocking revelation does Finkle have as a result of his conversation with Lily? In what way might you say it changed his life considerably?
4. Who is Stella? Why does Salzman refuse to introduce Stella to Finkle? Don't you find it odd that Finkle balked at women Salzman presented as desirable and was awestruck by "a sinner" of the world? What might explain his attraction to the latter?
5. Why do you imagine Salzman is around the corner from the place Stella meets Finkle, "leaning against a wall" and chanting "prayers for the dead"?

Writing Activities

1. Analyze what you have learned about life, love, and yourself through your relationships with other people. How did some people validate your dreams while others just caused disillusionment? As often as possible, explain how—although your situation was different than Finkle's—you had experiences similar to his.
2. Finkle pictures "his own redemption" in Salzman's daughter, suggesting that he must suffer in order to atone for something (perhaps his realization he had never truly loved anyone). Write an essay arguing that people like Leo Finkle frequently enter into relationships for the wrong reasons. In addition to making reference to "The Magic Barrel," support your discussion points with examples from the media, personal experience, and library research.

❋

Love Poem

Leslie Marmon Silko

Born in Albuquerque, New Mexico, in 1930, Leslie Marmon Silko received her Bachelor of Arts in English from the University of New Mexico and set out to become a lawyer. Her interest in law, however, yielded to her gifts as a teacher and an author. Silko is a writer of both fiction and verse; her novels include *Ceremony* (1977) and *Almanac of the Dead* (1991). *Laguna Woman* (1974) represents a collection of her poems and short stories, as does *Storyteller* (1981). In the following poem, Silko evokes the "dream state" she feels—through the use of poignant sensory images of nature— "when the rain comes with the wind" and reminds her of the man she loved.

Rain smell comes with the wind
                              out of the southwest
Smell of the sand dunes
                    tall grass glistening
5   in the rain.
Warm raindrops that fall easy
                              (this woman)
The summer is born.
Smell of her breathing new life
10   small gray toads on damp sand.

(this woman)
>>> whispering to dark wide leaves
>>> white moon blossoms dripping

>>>>>> tracks in the sand.
15   Rain smell
>>> I am full of hunger
>>> deep and longing to touch
wet tall grass, green and strong beneath.
This woman loved a man
20   and she breathed to him
>>> her damp earth song.
I am haunted by this story
I remember it in cottonwood leaves

>>>>> their fragrance in the shade.
25   I remember it in the wide blue sky
when the rain smell comes with the wind.

Writing Log/Journal Assignment

Describe what the wind smells like after it rains. What does rain symbolize to you?

Individual and Collaborative Considerations

1. How does Silko's diction (word choice) appeal to the senses: touch, taste, smell, sound, and sight? What is her relationship with nature?
2. What does the author assert by the repeated references to rain and "the rain smell"?
3. Why do you imagine the speaker is "haunted" by the story of a woman who loved a man?
4. Where is the setting for Silko's poem? What time of year is it?
5. Silko's poem is full of nature imagery. What does it add to her verse?

Writing Activities

1. In a descriptive narrative, write about the time of year you closely associate with romance and why. What dreams did you foster? What became of them? Were your dreams realistic or fantastic? Supply your readers with details and reasoning, so that they can fully appreciate the logical, concrete nature of your argument.
2. Analyze some aspect of nature (moon positions, astrology, snow, hurricanes). A starting point for this essay could be a review of the nature imagery in Silko's poem. Does any of it interest you? If so, use your favorite prewriting method to achieve a focus for your material and then write your paper.

The Second Coming

William Butler Yeats

William Butler Yeats was born in Dublin, Ireland, in 1865. Of Anglo-Irish parents, he was in continual movement between Ireland and England throughout his life. His father and brother were both painters, and he too considered painting for a career but turned to poetry instead. His early poems were influenced by painters like the Pre-Raphaelites. As a young man, he fell in love with Maude Gonne and became obsessed with her. Although he never married her, women such as Lady Augusta Gregory, an Irish aristocrat, played an important part in his life. She, along with others, helped Yeats create an Irish national theater. Yeats later married Georgie Hyde-Lees, who, in order to keep her husband's attention, engaged in automatic writing, supposedly communicating with the spirit world. As a result of these writings, Yeats produced *A Vision* (1925), his mystical view of history. Subsequently, Georgie confessed she had faked the automatic writings, but his fascination with the occult continued. In his maturity, Yeats developed a style of poetry that is symbolic, mystical, and deeply concerned with cycles of history and the future of the human race. In 1923, Yeats won the Nobel Prize for literature.

Turning and turning in the widening gyre
The falcon cannot hear the falconer;
Things fall apart; the centre cannot hold;
Mere anarchy is loosed upon the world,
5   The blood-dimmed tide is loosed, and everywhere
The ceremony of innocence is drowned;
The best lack all conviction, while the worst
Are full of passionate intensity.
Surely some revelation is at hand;
10   Surely the Second Coming is at hand.
The Second Coming! Hardly are those words out
When a vast image out of *Spiritus Mundi*
Troubles my sight: somewhere in sands of the desert
A shape with lion body and the head of a man,
15   A gaze blank and pitiless as the sun,
Is moving its slow thighs, while all about it
Reel shadows of the indignant desert birds.
The darkness drops again; but now I know
That twenty centuries of stony sleep
20   Were vexed to nightmare by a rocking cradle,
And what rough beast, its hour come round at last,
Slouches towards Bethlehem to be reborn?

Writing Log/Journal Assignment

Words and word groups often influence or guide readers. Jot down the title of Yeats' poem, "The Second Coming," and write about anything it brings to mind.

Individual and Collaborative Considerations

1. What is a "gyre"?
2. In the first eight lines of the poem, which words create the feeling of disintegration or destruction?
3. *Spiritus Mundi* refers to the "spirit or state of the universe" or collective unconscious. Why does "a vast image out of *Spiritus Mundi*" trouble the speaker's sight?
4. What sorts of images pervade Yeats' poem? How and why are they appropriate to his subject matter? After reading this poem, do any particular images remain with you? Which ones?
5. How does the line "Slouches towards Bethlehem to be reborn" relate to the title of Yeats' poem?

Writing Activities

1. Note that this poem ends in a question: "And what rough beast, its hour come round at last / Slouches towards Bethlehem to be reborn?" Write a persuasive essay hypothesizing and detailing your answer to the question.
2. Yeats believed that history was cyclical and that every two thousand years there is a "rebirth." In a thoroughly illustrated essay, define your own view of history.

To the Stone-cutters

Robinson Jeffers

Robinson Jeffers was born in Pittsburgh, and his family traveled widely prior to settling in California when he was sixteen. As an adult he lived in Carmel, California, and it became the site for much of his poetry. Jeffers' works include *Flagon and Apples* (1912), *Californians* (1916), *Tamar and Other Poems* (1924), *The Women at Big Sur* (1927), *Cawdor, and Other Poems* (1928), *Dear Judas, and Other Poems* (1929), *Descent to the Dead* (1931), *Thur-*

so's Landing, and Other Poems (1932), *Your Heart to the Hawks, and Other Poems* (1933), *Solstice, and Other Poems* (1935), *Such Counsels You Gave to Me, and Other Poems* (1937), *Selected Poetry of Robinson Jeffers* (1938), and *Hungerfield and Other Poems* (1945). His later books include *The Beginning and the End* (1963), a posthumous collection, and *What Odd Experiments* (1981), a collection of unpublished poems. Rocks often appear in Jeffers' poems, like "To the Stone-cutters," as "principles of dynamism and revered inertness." The *Norton Introduction to Modern Poetry* notes that "strength is the quality that Robinson Jeffers admires and that he seeks in his own poetry."

Stone-cutters fighting time with marble, you foredefeated
Challengers of oblivion
Eat cynical earnings, knowing rock splits, records fall down,
The square-limbed Roman letters
5   Scale in the thaws, wear in the rain. The poet as well
Builds his monument mockingly;
For man will be blotted out, the blithe earth die, the brave sun
Die blind, his heart blackening;
Yet stones have stood a thousand years, and pained thoughts found
10   The honey peace in old poems.

Writing Log/Journal Assignment

What does the title "To the Stone-cutters" suggest to you? What images came to your mind? Jot down your responses in your journal or writing log.

Individual and Collaborative Considerations

1. Why might the efforts of poets be considered similar to the work of stone-cutters?
2. Explain the lines "The poet as well/Builds his monument mockingly;/For man will be blotted out, the blithe earth will die. . . ."
3. How does this poem lean towards being a commentary on the dreams of generations as personified through poetry and architecture? Explain your answer.
4. Discuss the tone in Jeffers' poem. How does it create a definite mood?
5. What does Jeffers imply about both ancient stones and old poems?

Writing Activities

1. The Romans "fought time with marble." With what do you challenge the "ravages of time"? What possession of yours do you imagine will still be around two thousand years from now? How is it like a stone monument?

Write an essay explaining how you would build your own "monument mockingly."

2. Using tone to reflect your attitude towards your subject, write an essay about how people seek to immortalize themselves while they are living and provide the reasons they fear death.

ADDITIONAL TOPICS AND ISSUES FOR WRITING AND RESEARCH

1. Write an essay comparing and contrasting Kurt Vonnegut's "Harrison Bergeron" to Woody Allen's "The Kugelmass Episode." How do both authors use irony to highlight the anti-utopian nature of situations in particular and society in general?

2. Have you ever worked hard at a task only to have others claim your work as theirs? Have you ever applied for a job (in-house or otherwise) for which you have thoroughly prepared yourself, only to lose the opportunity to a less qualified person? Write an essay analyzing the excitement and anticipation awaiting you at the completion of your task or acquisition of a job. Follow your analysis explaining your disillusionment in not being able to complete or receive credit for what you had begun.

3. Compromising a position in order to achieve some sort of agreement often leaves all parties concerned dissatisfied—especially in the political arena. Select several local, state, or federal political figures and write an essay illustrating how and why voters feel righteously betrayed when elected officials make concessions on issues (e.g., allowing some assault rifles to further a vision or activate a dream). Are there instances where compromising is unforgivable? If so, which ones?

4. "Too many parents attempt to live out their own fantasies and dreams through their children." Build a thesis around this observation and support it with several detailed examples taken from your immediate experiences and those of the lives around you. (You may include sports stars and celebrities.)

5. Write an essay in which you compare and contrast your "waking dreams" to your "sleeping dreams" for a specific purpose (e.g., to show that one type of dream is more visionary than another). If you wish, divide and classify the nature of each type of dream for easy comparison and contrast.

6. Do you ever discuss your dreams with others? What has been the strangest dream you can recall? If all of your dreams, including your nightmares, reveal something about your personality, what has been your most insightful dream to date? After introducing your subject matter and establishing a focus in your essay, briefly retell your dream. Then,

follow your dream with an analysis, suggesting its possible meanings or implications.

7. Take a situation where you pretended to be someone else, either to impress friends or to act out a fantasy, only to get caught in your "little lie." In a narrative essay, describe your fantasy or façade, why you thought it was necessary or important to project, how you executed the façade, and what ultimately happened to you (possibly, how you acted out your alter ego). In your concluding paragraph, you might offer some illuminating remarks about the broader implications of being someone other than yourself.

8. Explain the causes and the effects of disillusionment by demonstrating your thesis with detailed examples and illustrations derived from personal experience, observations, and readings.

9. Write an essay explaining how and why dreams are essential to healthy development and how disillusionment often follows the unsuccessful pursuit of a dream. Use vivid words and examples to convey the intensity of disillusionment.

10. Using several representative examples to validate each discussion point, explain the causes and the effects of too much daydreaming. Do you daydream? What happens?

Starting Points for Research

Dreams

- Visions
- Fantasy
- Sleep
- Somnambulism
- Children's dreams
- Women's dreams
- Men's dreams
- Dreams in literature
- Dreams in art
- Religious dreams
- Dreams in politics
- Utopian society
- Shangri-la
- Treasures
- Magic realism
- Social change
- Career dreams
- World domination
- Professional respect
- Romanticism

Disillusionment

- Nightmares (figurative/literal)
- Censorship
- Repression
- Epiphanies
- Reprisals
- Reality
- Setbacks and restraints
- Fears
- Disappointment and the psyche
- Deviant behavior and let downs
- Lack of professionalism
- Hope and helplessness
- Image betrayal
- Façades
- Movie stars
- Vain revolutions
- Money talks
- Creativity and its control
- Image versus reality
- Unrealized dreams

8

Sacrifice and Fulfillment

*A child arranges
rice cakes in a row,
Each time saying
"This one is mine."*

ISSA

Essays

In its simplest sense, a sacrifice might be explained as the conscious act of giving up something precious and meaningful for the sake of someone or something you consider of greater significance or value. As Robert Hayden observes in his poem "Those Winter Sundays," the selfless sacrifice is often taken for granted, and only through hindsight does he appreciate how his father sought neither acclaim nor recognition for getting up early on Sunday—his day off—to make a fire so that others in the house were comfortable when they awoke.

People have made sacrifices to deities—gods and goddesses—for thousands of years in order to appease their wrath or receive their good graces. When people planted crops, they would sacrifice something dear to them—perhaps their best sheep or prized bull—and hope that in exchange, they would receive a bountiful harvest. When a natural disaster like a volcanic eruption occurred, often a person was sacrificed to quench the thirst of the fire god or goddess in the mountain. The answer to a drought in Grace Ogot's "The Rain Came" also was the sacrifice of one human—Oganda, the chief's only daughter—for the well-being of the entire tribe.

People who make sacrifices in their lives do more than ritually slay animals—even human beings—to receive something of greater importance in return. When standards, ideals, or value systems are compromised for the well-being of others, one is infinitely involved in a sacrifice. The protagonist, Gimpel, in Isaac Bashevis Singer's short story "Gimpel the Fool," sacrifices his dignity and happiness when he marries because his wife sleeps with just about everyone but himself. Eager to please, and anxious to believe only positive things, Gimpel provides his wife's children with a positive role model. His fulfillment comes when he casts off the bonds of his material wealth and ends his days a vagabond.

Day-to-day sacrifices may seem trivial when compared to devoting one's entire life towards making a relationship work. Kate Chopin's "The Story of an Hour," a classic tale of marriage, sacrifice, self-discovery, and freedom, exposes the repressive yet unspoken nature of many marriage relationships. After she briefly grieves upon hearing a report about her husband's death, Mrs. Mallard has a chance to reconsider her relationship to the world around her and realizes she is "Free, free, free!" Now Mrs. Mallard thinks she will find a new level of fulfillment in her life.

Sometimes a genuine sacrifice becomes blurred when people insist on being martyrs. A self-proclaimed martyr actually receives personal fulfillment in sacrifices; therefore, in the strictest sense, such a person *acquires* rather than *gives*. People who hate large crowds yet are always throwing parties are definitely self-proclaimed martyrs. That is not to say that the father in Robert Hayden's "Those Winter Sundays" is a self-proclaimed martyr. After all, a martyr usually does not initiate actions but is the unwilling receptor of them.

There are also many ways to look at fulfillment. Relationships, education, food, music, and entertainment can all be fulfilling. Fulfillment—like sacrifices—can be physical, intellectual, emotional, or spiritual in nature. In a selection taken from *The Autobiography of Malcolm X* entitled "Homemade Education," Malcolm X found fulfillment in expanding his ability to read and write. He said he never felt so free—unlimited—as when he could use the power of words.

Pleasure is another form of fulfillment. Enjoying accomplishments, reveling in the company of friends and family can be most rewarding. Pastimes or behavior some would criticize can be most pleasurable: building or remodeling homes, digging in the garden, sailing paper boats down gutters, making mud pies, singing in the shower, or dancing in a mirror are just some of the small things in life which deserve to be appreciated. Denise Levertov is most appreciative and aware of "small things," particularly things that are concealed within "something of another nature," as she writes in her poem "Pleasures." Other people receive a twisted sense of fulfillment from hating other people, places, and things. As Suzanne Britt points out in "Love and Hate," poets and musicians may enjoy singing about love, but they still spend most of their time talking about hate or at least love–hate relationships. The public's taste for negative news broadcasts merely affirms the idea that pleasure and fulfillment may be achieved through hatred and negativity.

RHETORIC AT WORK

As you read and reflect on the poems, stories, and essays in "Sacrifice and Fulfillment," you might once again focus on the denotative and connotative

---

A Checklist for Writing about *Sacrifice and Fulfillment*

1. Does my essay appeal to my readers' ethics (*ethos*), emotions (*pathos*), or logic (*logos*)? How do I enable them to understand and appreciate my thesis?
2. What structures do I use to show my readers the cause–effect relationships that lead to sacrifice or fulfillment?
3. Can my readers follow the progression of my essay? Do I organize material in clear, coherent fashion?
4. How do I indicate the desired relationship between words, clauses, and entire paragraphs? Are my linking devices clear?
5. To what extent do I use metaphors, similes, and other figurative language to express instances of sacrifice and fulfillment?
6. Does the tone of my essay reflect my attitude towards my topic?
7. Do I take advantage of the denotative and connotative meanings of words to subtly convey themes of sacrifice or fulfillment?

qualities of words. Which—if any—of the individuals in the forthcoming readings are self-proclaimed martyrs or exemplify selfless sacrifice? How does diction enable the authors to subtly or blatantly reveal attributes of the people in question?

※

Love and Hate

Suzanne Britt

A journalist and essayist, Suzanne Britt has written articles appearing in a wide range of news magazines, journals, and papers: the *Dickens Dispatch,* *Newsweek,* the Des Moines *Register* and *Tribune,* the *Baltimore Sun, Newsday,* and *The New York Times.* Her books include *Skinny People Are Dull and Crunchy Like Carrots* (1982), *Show and Tell* (1983), and *A Writer's Rhetoric* (1988). Britt often develops her satirical essays by using some form of comparison and contrast. She particularly enjoys exposing the follies of human behavior and the absurdity of stereotypes. In "Love and Hate," Britt highlights the ironical fact that many individuals love to "hate"; in fact, they receive some sort of perverse fulfillment by hating.

1   I used to want everybody to like me. Now I'm satisfied if nobody hates me. Indifference works just as well as hate and isn't half as messy. Hate stirs the acids in the stomach and contorts the face.

2   A woman once told me she was sorry we had lost the knack for full-blown hating, in the best, feuding, Hatfield versus McCoy sense. She said she'd rather really hate one person than be condemned to a lifetime of insipid niceness. I see her point, but disagree. Having recently seen the face of hate, I can say, unequivocally, that I hate hate.

3   I have gone to the source of all wisdom, *John Bartlett's Familiar Quotations,* to find the answers to my questions about love and hate. I counted 833 listings under "love," not counting "loved," "lover," "loves," "loveth," "loving," and "loving-kindness." "Hate" scored only 75, not counting "hated," "hateful," "hater," "hates," "hating," and "hatred." Some people might cite the score as evidence of love's victory. I'm not cynical, but I don't. Direct experience shows that love is losing in the real world, the world not according to *Bartlett's.* We write about love, but we act out hate.

4   Few of our written words have to do with hate. We don't sing hate songs, write hate sonnets, send hate greetings, or create Harlequin hate novels. The poison-pen note and the assassin's wild missive represent isolated flare-ups of hate. These hate words are off the charts, the obvious work, we say, of

society's misfits. Love, however, pours from the pen onto the page, not into life.

5 Many times we write effusive declarations of love, but then we won't lift a finger or risk a reputation for the beloved. In contrast, we daily see hate in action, and not only in child abuse, murder, and rape. Hate functions in our daily lives, without words, silent and deadly: the killing glances of spouses over the morning newspaper; the sworn social enemies who exit through the back door while the object of their hate enters through the front door; the adolescent fist pushed through the wall or door; the blood-curdling scream reverberating through the suburban neighborhood.

6 Hate is so much a part of life, we scarcely try to hide it. Mothers bark ferociously at little children nipping at their heels. Obscenities fly across the ball field. The switchblade gleams in the school corridor, between history and poetry class.

7 Hate is vigorous. It seems justified. The excellent reasons for hating line up like crisply attired soldiers in a dress parade: she's so bossy, I can't stand her; he thinks he's so smart, the idiot; when she gets that look on her face, I could smack her; she's not "our kind of people." Hate rattles the world: the plate sails through the kitchen; doors slam; feet stomp; the fist goes in the stomach; the blow falls well below the belt.

8 Love is another, secret matter. Love operates underground, in hidden acts of tenderness and sympathy: hands grasp under the table; eyes seek eyes; small generosities and charities go unheralded, unnoticed. Love is speechless, blushing.

9 Love does not make the world go round. It makes the world uncomfortable. If you have ever loved someone, you will note that forces join to combat or crush it. All is hateful sabotage. We chalk up altruism to a neurotic need for glory. When mothers love sons, we whisper of sexual disorientation. When fathers love daughters, we imagine hidden lust. When love binds people, we look for ways to break the connection, sternly advising the lovers to keep their feet on the ground, their heads out of the clouds.

10 Love has a hard time loving. Asked why we love someone, we can scarcely name the reasons. No one is more tongue-tied than a lover stating the attributes of the beloved. But all the reasons for hating come out in measured, logical, well-rehearsed speeches. The hater seems sensible. He has good cause, we say, for striking people from his list, as if people were groceries, charts, categories in books. If we want to be entirely justified in hating, all we have to do is come up with a suitable label, and the hated object flutters and dies on the impeccably scientific field of justification and classification.

11 We resist love's flowing motion. Hate holds off the changes and adjustments we so much fear. Hate fossilizes. If we can stay in our deep rut of hating, we won't be vulnerable. We can petrify the world. We can hold on to the person we hate the way a dog guards an old bone.

12 Let one person speak of love, however, and all the no-nonsense folks will gather, prepared to shoot down every case for loving with the small stones of their objections: be careful; you might get hurt; save your love for heaven; plant your feet in hell for now.

13   Put my arguments for hate to any earthly test, and you will find me painfully right. If you take the risk of loving, you will not go far along the green mountaintop of bliss before you encounter the granite face of hate.

14   You begin to suspect that hate is more often based not on something you *did* but on something the hater *is*. Nothing will appease a full-fledged hater. His brooding calculations work against the lover. The hater has stayed awake all through the black night, marshalling his defenses, planning his meticulous strategies. While love works its wonders in the lives of those who choose it, the hater pursues his dark work, alone.

15   If I could have one wish, I would choose love big enough to take in all kinds and degrees of loving. I would let words of love be replaced by sunny, open acts of loving. I would rather, in the end, *be* in love than *write* about it. So, no doubt, would all the poets, saints, and sages.

Writing Log/Journal Assignment

In a journal, jot down what you love and hate about people, places, and things, justifying—if you can—your love or hate for the respective person, place, or thing.

Individual and Collaborative Considerations

1. In comparing the virtues of love to hate, which does Britt seem to prefer and why? Where does she first express her attitude? Do you think her real attitude differs from her verbal (written) attitude?
2. The concepts of love and hate are rather abstract. What does Britt do to make them concrete for her readers?
3. To what extent does Britt use figurative language to help explain material? Why might figurative language be more successful than literal language in this sort of expository essay?
4. According to Britt, "Love has a hard time loving." Explain what she means by this, referring to specific examples from her essay.
5. What does Britt suggest in the final paragraph? Do you believe her when she says, "I would rather, in the end, *be* in love than *write* about it"?

Writing Activities

1. Write an essay explaining how either *love* or *hate* fulfills your life and the lives of those around you. What human need does love or hate fulfill? When? Where? Why?
2. Construct a thesis built around the theme of love and its relationship to self-sacrifice. You might begin your introductory paragraph by defining love, leading to a specific thesis about love and self-sacrifice. Offer as many detailed, concrete examples supporting your thesis as possible in order to make what you claim seem representative of people in general.

❋

Homemade Education

Malcolm X

Born in Omaha, Nebraska, in 1925, Malcolm X, the son of a Black separatist preacher, spent his early childhood in middle America. When his father died, Malcolm X became involved with life on the streets, which ultimately led to his imprisonment for burglary. Denouncing his Christian name—his slave name—he took the name "X" and became devoted to the Black Muslim movement, which was headed by the honorable Elijah Muhammad. Malcolm X began to correspond with Elijah Muhammad while still in prison, and Malcolm X's desire to further his writing skills was directly responsible for the "Homemade Education" discussed in the following essay, an excerpt from *The Autobiography of Malcolm X*. Malcolm X's relationship to Elijah led him to become a militant leader of the Black Revolution. Ironically, he was preaching the brotherhood of man when assassinated in 1965.

1   It was because of my letters that I happened to stumble upon starting to acquire some kind of homemade education.

2   I became increasingly frustrated at not being able to express what I wanted to convey in letters that I wrote, especially those to Mr. Elijah Muhammad. In the street, I had been the most articulate hustler out there—I had commanded attention when I said something. But now, trying to write simple English, I not only wasn't articulate, I wasn't even functional. How would I sound writing in slang, the way I would *say* it, something such as, "Look, daddy, let me pull your coat about a cat, Elijah Muhammad—"

3   Many who today hear me somewhere in person, or on television, or those who read something I've said, will think I went to school far beyond the eighth grade. This impression is due entirely to my prison studies.

4   It had really begun back in Charlestown Prison, when Bimbi first made me feel envy of his stock of knowledge. Bimbi had always taken charge of any conversation he was in, and I had tried to emulate him. But every book I picked up had few sentences which didn't contain anywhere from one to nearly all of the words that might as well have been in Chinese. When I just skipped those words, of course, I really ended up with little idea of what the book said. So I had come to the Norfolk Prison Colony still going through only book-reading motions. Pretty soon, I would have quit even these motions unless I had received the motivation that I did.

5   I saw that the best thing I could do was get hold of a dictionary—to study to learn some words. I was lucky enough to reason also that I should try to

improve my penmanship. It was sad. I couldn't even write in a straight line. It was both ideas together that moved me to request a dictionary along with some tablets and pencils from the Norfolk Prison Colony school.

6   I spent two days just riffling uncertainly through the dictionary's pages. I'd never realized so many words existed! I didn't know *which* words I needed to learn. Finally, just to start some kind of action, I began copying.

7   In my slow, painstaking, ragged handwriting, I copied into my tablet everything printed on that first page, down to the punctuation marks.

8   I believe it took me a day. Then, aloud, I read back, to myself, everything I'd written on the tablet. Over and over, aloud, to myself, I read my own handwriting.

9   I woke up the next morning, thinking about those words—immensely proud to realize that not only had I written so much at one time, but I'd written words that I never knew were in the world. Moreover, with a little effort, I also could remember what many of these words meant. I reviewed the words whose meanings I didn't remember. Funny thing, from the dictionary first page right now, that "aardvark" springs to my mind. The dictionary had a picture of it, a long-tailed, long-eared, burrowing African mammal, which lives off termites caught by sticking out its tongue as an anteater does for ants.

10   I was so fascinated that I went on—I copied the dictionary's next page. And the same experience came when I studied that. With every succeeding page, I also learned of people and places and events from history. Actually the dictionary is like a miniature encyclopedia. Finally the dictionary's A section had filled a whole tablet—and I went on into the B's. That was the way I started copying what eventually became the entire dictionary. It went a lot faster after so much practice helped me to pick up handwriting speed. Between what I wrote in my tablet, and writing letters, during the rest of my time in prison I would guess I wrote a million words.

11   I suppose it was inevitable that as my word-base broadened, I could for the first time pick up a book and read and now begin to understand what the book was saying. Anyone who has read a great deal can imagine the new world that opened. Let me tell you something: from then until I left that prison, in every free moment I had, if I was not reading in the library, I was reading on my bunk. You couldn't have gotten me out of books with a wedge. Between Mr. Muhammad's teachings, my correspondence, my visitors—usually Ella and Reginald—and my reading of books, months passed without my even thinking about being imprisoned. In fact, up to then, I had never been so truly free in my life.

Writing Log/Journal Assignment

To fully appreciate Malcolm X's method of broadening his vocabulary, write a journal entry where you copy a few definitions from the dictionary—exactly as written—into your notebook. Then reflect on the fact that Malcolm

X copied the entire dictionary by hand. Conclude the entry with your opinion of "homemade education."

Individual and Collaborative Considerations

1. Who or what motivated Malcolm X to increase his word base? Why? How?
2. Describe the overall tone of "Homemade Education." How does the tone reinforce the purpose of the essay?
3. In what way might process analysis be the most appropriate rhetorical strategy for developing Malcolm X's essay?
4. What do the final two sentences in this essay suggest about the real power of words and the actual meaning of freedom?
5. What do you believe is the best method or combined methods for increasing your own word base? How would your word acquisition strategies be different from yet similar to the strategies Malcolm X used?

Writing Activities

1. Brainstorm the following words: education, relaxation, occupation, and investigation. Who or what did you associate with each word? Review the lists you brainstormed asking yourself the question "how" and jot down your responses. Ultimately, devise a thesis and write a process essay explaining how *one* of the words you brainstormed is accomplished (e.g., how to learn, how to relax, how to select an occupation, how to conduct an investigation).
2. Rather than explaining how to do something, write an essay explaining how something was done: how a bridge was built, how a coalition was formed, how a social movement began, how a movie was made, and so on. Pay particular attention to chronology and the accuracy of any cause–effect relationships you mention in your paper. Both may play a part in supporting or undermining the validity of your thesis and your essay in general.

The Story of an Hour

Kate Chopin

Kate Chopin, French Creole on her mother's side of the family, was born in Missouri in 1851. She began her literary career by submitting stories to magazines like the *Atlantic Monthly* and the *Saturday Evening Post*. Several stories about Creole life later appeared in *Bayou Folk* (1874) and *A Night in Arcadie*. Her novels include *At Fault* (1890) and *The Awakening* (1899). Chopin modeled many of her stories after Guy de Maupassant and used Louisiana dialects to add local color and authenticity to her work. However, it was not easy being a Southern female author in the United States one hundred years ago. Many of her readers in the 1890s were not ready to accept her frank discussion of sexuality and woman's emotions—particularly when they challenged dominant folkways and mores in society. As a result, magazine editors constantly rejected submissions like "The Story of an Hour" that questioned popular social behavior.

Knowing that Mrs. Mallard was afflicted with a heart trouble, great care was taken to break to her as gently as possible the news of her husband's death.

It was her sister Josephine who told her, in broken sentences; veiled hints that revealed in half concealing. Her husband's friend Richards was there, too, near her. It was he who had been in the newspaper office when intelligence of the railroad disaster was received, with Brently Mallard's name leading the list of "killed." He had only taken the time to assure himself of its truth by a second telegram, and had hastened to forestall any less careful, less tender friend in bearing the sad message.

She did not hear the story as many women have heard the same, with a paralyzed inability to accept its significance. She wept at once, with sudden, wild abandonment, in her sister's arms. When the storm of grief had spent itself she went away to her room alone. She would have no one follow her.

There stood, facing the open window, a comfortable, roomy armchair. Into this she sank, pressed down by a physical exhaustion that haunted her body and seemed to reach into her soul.

5   She could see in the open square before her house the tops of trees that were all aquiver with the new spring life. The delicious breath of rain was in the air. In the street below a peddler was crying his wares. The notes of a distant song which some one was singing reached her faintly, and countless sparrows were twittering in the eaves.

There were patches of blue sky showing here and there through the clouds that had met and piled one above the other in the west facing her window.

She sat with her head thrown back upon the cushion of the chair, quite motionless, except when a sob came up into her throat and shook her, as a child who has cried itself to sleep continues to sob in its dreams.

She was young, with a fair, calm face, whose lines bespoke repression and even a certain strength. But now there was a dull stare in her eyes, whose gaze was fixed away off yonder on one of those patches of blue sky. It was not a glance of reflection, but rather indicated a suspension of intelligent thought.

There was something coming to her and she was waiting for it, fearfully. What was it? She did not know; it was too subtle and elusive to name. But she felt it creeping out of the sky, reaching toward her through the sounds, the scents, the color that filled the air.

10   Now her bosom rose and fell tumultuously. She was beginning to recognize this thing that was approaching to possess her, and she was striving to beat it back with her will—as powerless as her two white slender hands would have been.

When she abandoned herself a little whispered word escaped her slightly parted lips. She said it over and over under her breath: "Free, free, free!" The vacant stare and the look of terror that had followed it went from her eyes. They stayed keen and bright. Her pulses beat fast, and the coursing blood warmed and relaxed every inch of her body.

She did not stop to ask if it were not a monstrous joy that held her. A clear and exalted perception enabled her to dismiss the suggestion as trivial.

She knew that she would weep again when she saw the kind, tender hands folded in death; the face that had never looked save with love upon her, fixed and gray and dead. But she saw beyond that bitter moment a long procession of years to come that would belong to her absolutely. And she opened and spread her arms out to them in welcome.

There would be no one to live for during those coming years, she would live for herself. There would be no powerful will bending her in that blind persistence with which men and women believe they have a right to impose a private will upon a fellow creature. A kind intention or a cruel intention made the act seem no less a crime as she looked upon it in that brief moment of illumination.

15   And yet she had loved him—sometimes. Often she had not. What did it matter! What could love, the unsolved mystery, count for in face of this possession of self-assertion which she suddenly recognized as the strongest impulse of her being.

"Free! Body and soul free!" she kept whispering.

Josephine was kneeling before the closed door with her lips to the keyhole, imploring for admission. "Louise, open the door! I beg; open the door—you will make yourself ill. What are you doing, Louise? For heaven's sake open the door."

"Go away. I am not making myself ill." No; she was drinking in a very elixir of life through that open window.

Her fancy was running riot along those days ahead of her. Spring days, and summer days, and all sorts of days that would be her own. She breathed a quick prayer that life might be long. It was only yesterday she had thought with a shudder that life might be long.

20   She arose at length and opened the door to her sister's importunities. There was a feverish triumph in her eyes, and she carried herself unwittingly like a goddess of Victory. She clasped her sister's waist, and together they descended the stairs. Richards stood waiting for them at the bottom.

Someone was opening the front door with a latchkey. It was Brently Mallard who entered, a little travel-stained, composedly carrying his gripsack and umbrella. He had been far from the scene of the accident, and did not even know there had been one. He stood amazed at Josephine's piercing cry; at Richards' quick motion to screen him from the view of his wife.

But Richards was too late.

When the doctors came they said she had died of heart disease—of joy that kills.

Writing Log/Journal Assignment

Relate how you felt when you learned about a shocking incident. What was your immediate reaction? How did you feel when you had time to put everything into perspective?

Individual and Collaborative Considerations

1. Describe what Mrs. Mallard looks like; how does she feel as the story opens?
2. How do the few sentences of dialogue in the story actually accentuate important points? What might have been lost without the sparse dialogue?
3. Why does Mrs. Mallard keep whispering, "Free! Body and soul free!" What sort of relationship do you imagine she had with her husband? How much information does Chopin give her readers? What sacrifices do you think she has made?
4. What sort of imagery does Chopin use in the scene where Mrs. Mallard recognizes her new freedom resulting from her husband's death?
5. Why is the doctor's diagnosis of the cause of Mrs. Mallard's death so ironic?

Writing Activities

1. Brainstorm on the life and death imagery in the "The Story of an Hour." Then consider the possibilities for an essay topic (e.g., from death comes life). Use references to Chopin's "The Story of an Hour" and other resources to illustrate your thesis.
2. Compare and contrast Mrs. Ames' quest for freedom and independence from her husband in "Astronomer's Wife" to that of Mrs. Mallard in "The Story of an Hour."

---　※　---

Gimpel the Fool

Isaac Bashevis Singer

Polish-born author Isaac Bashevis Singer immigrated to the United States in 1935, following his brother to New York City, where he established himself as a journalist. He wrote in Yiddish for the *Jewish Daily Forward;* there he also published most of his fiction. Among his many collections of short stories are *Gimpel the Fool* (1957), *The Spinoza of Market Street* (1961), *Short Friday* (1964), *Zlateh the Goat* (1966), *The Séance* (1968), *A Friend of Kafka* (1970), *A Crown of Feathers* (1973), *Passions* (1978), and *Collected Stories* (1982). His novels include *Satan in Goray* (1935 Yiddish, 1955 English), *The Family Moskat* (1950), *The Magician of Lublin* (1960), *The Slave* (1962), *The Manor* (1967), *The Estate* (1969), *Enemies* (1970), *Shosha* (1978), and *The Penitent* (1983). Singer was also the author of children's books such as *When Shlemihl Went to Warsaw* (1968) and *A Day of Pleasure* (1970). Additionally, Singer published several memoirs, including *In My Father's Court* (1966) and *Love and Exile* (1984). Singer explores the past and present traditions of Jewish life in his writings. He said he likes writing about individuals who are "obsessed by some mania or fixed idea, and everything turns around this idea." In "Gimpel the Fool," for instance, he looks at the mental and spiritual levels of human existence. Singer was awarded a Nobel Prize in 1978.

I

I am Gimpel the fool. I don't think myself a fool. On the contrary. But that's what folks call me. They gave me the name while I was still in school. I had seven names in all: imbecile, donkey, flax-head, dope, glump, ninny, and fool. The last name stuck. What did my foolishness consist of? I was easy to take in. They said, "Gimpel, you know the rabbi's wife has been brought to childbed?" So I skipped school. Well, it turned out to be a lie. How was I supposed to know? She hadn't had a big belly. But I never looked at her belly. Was that really so foolish? The gang laughed and hee hawed, stomped and danced and chanted a good-night prayer. And instead of the raisins they give when a woman's lying in, they stuffed my hand full of goat turds. I was no weakling. If I slapped someone he'd see all the way to Cracow. But I'm really not a slugger by nature. I think to myself: Let it pass. So they take advantage of me.

I was coming home from school and heard a dog barking. I'm not afraid of dogs, but of course I never want to start up with them. One of them may be mad, and if he bites there's not a Tartar in the world who can help you. So I made tracks. Then I looked around and saw the whole market place wild with laughter. It was no dog at all but Wolf-Leib the thief. How was I supposed to know it was he? It sounded like a howling bitch.

When the pranksters and leg-pullers found that I was easy to fool, every one of them tried his luck with me. "Gimpel, the Czar is coming to Frampol; Gimpel, the moon fell down in Turbeen; Gimpel, little Hodel Furpiece found a treasure behind the bathhouse." And I like a *golem* believed everyone. In the first place, everything is possible, as it is written in *The Wisdom of the Fathers*, I've forgotten just how. Second, I had to believe when the whole town came down on me! If I ever dared to say, "Ah, you're kidding!" there was trouble. People got angry. "What do you mean! You want to call everyone a liar?" What was I to do? I believed them, and I hope at least that did them some good.

I was an orphan. My grandfather who brought me up was already bent toward the grave. So they turned me over to a baker, and what a time they gave me there! Every woman or girl who came to bake a batch of noodles had to fool me at least once. "Gimpel, there's a fair in Heaven; Gimpel, the rabbi gave birth to a calf in the seventh month; Gimpel, a cow flew over the roof and laid brass eggs." A student from the *yeshiva* came once to buy a roll, and he said, "You, Gimpel, while you stand here scraping with your baker's shovel the Messiah has come. The dead have arisen." "What do you mean?" I said. "I heard no one blowing the ram's horn!" He said, "Are you deaf?" And all began to cry, "We heard it, we heard!" Then in came Rietze the candle-dipper and called out in her hoarse voice, "Gimpel, your father and mother have stood up from the grave. They're looking for you."

5   To tell the truth, I knew very well that nothing of the sort had happened, but all the same, as folks were talking, I threw on my wool vest and went out. Maybe something had happened. What did I stand to lose by looking? Well, what a cat music went up! And then I took a vow to believe nothing more. But that was no go either. They confused me so that I didn't know the big end from the small.

I went to the rabbi to get some advice. He said, "It is written, better to be a fool all your days than for one hour to be evil. You are not a fool. They are the fools. For he who causes his neighbor to feel shame loses Paradise himself." Nevertheless, the rabbi's daughter took me in. As I left the rabbinical court she said, "Have you kissed the wall yet?" I said, "No, what for?" She answered, "It's the law; you've got to do it after every visit." Well, there didn't seem to be any harm in it. And she burst out laughing. It was a fine trick. She put one over on me, all right.

I wanted to go off to another town, but then everyone got busy matchmaking, and they were after me so they nearly tore my coat tails off. They talked at me and talked until I got water on the ear. She was no chaste maiden, but they told me she was virgin pure. She had a limp, and they said it was deliberate, from coyness. She had a bastard, and they told me the child was her little brother. I cried, "You're wasting your time. I'll never marry that whore." But they said indignantly, "What a way to talk! Aren't you ashamed of yourself? We can take you to the rabbi and have you fined for giving her a bad name." I saw then that I wouldn't escape them so easily and I thought: They're set on making me their butt. But when you're married the husband's the master, and if that's all right with her it's agreeable to me too. Besides, you can't pass through life unscathed, nor expect to.

I went to her clay house, which was built on the sand, and the whole gang, hollering and chorusing, came after me. They acted like bear-baiters. When we came to the well they stopped all the same. They were afraid to start anything with Elka. Her mouth would open as if it were on a hinge, and she had a fierce tongue. I entered the house. Lines were strung from wall to wall and clothes were drying. Barefoot she stood by the tub, doing the wash. She was dressed in a worn hand-me-down gown of plush. She had her hair put up in braids and pinned across her head. It took my breath away, almost, the reek of it all.

Evidently she knew who I was. She took a look at me and said, "Look who's here! He's come, the drip. Grab a seat."

10   I told her all; I denied nothing. "Tell me the truth," I said, "are you really a virgin, and is that mischievous Yechiel actually your little brother? Don't be deceitful with me, for I'm an orphan."

"I'm an orphan myself," she answered, "and whoever tries to twist you up, may the end of his nose take a twist. But don't let them think they can take advantage of me. I want a dowry of fifty guilders, and let them take up a collection besides. Otherwise they can kiss my you-know-what." She was very plainspoken. I said, "It's the bride and not the groom who gives a dowry." Then she said, "Don't bargain with me. Either a flat yes or a flat no. Go back where you came from."

I thought: No bread will ever be baked from *this* dough. But ours is not a poor town. They consented to everything and proceeded with the wedding. It so happened that there was a dysentery epidemic at the time. The ceremony was held at the cemetery gates, near the little corpse-washing hut. The fellows got drunk. While the marriage contract was being drawn up I heard the most pious high rabbi ask, "Is the bride a widow or a divorced woman?" And the sexton's wife answered for her, "Both a widow and divorced." It was a black moment for me. But what was I to do, run away from under the marriage canopy?

There was singing and dancing. An old granny danced opposite me, hugging a braided white *chalah*. The master of revels made a "God 'a mercy" in memory of the bride's parents. The schoolboys threw burrs, as on *Tishe b'Av* fast day. There were a lot of gifts after the sermon: a noodle board, a kneading trough, a bucket, brooms, ladles, household articles galore. Then I took a look and saw two strapping young men carrying a crib. "What do we need this for?" I asked. So they said, "Don't rack your brains about it. It's all right, it'll come in handy." I realized I was going to be rooked. Take it another way though, what did I stand to lose? I reflected: I'll see what comes of it. A whole town can't go altogether crazy.

II

At night I came where my wife lay, but she wouldn't let me in. "Say, look here, is this what they married us for?" I said. And she said, "My monthly has come." "But yesterday they took you to the ritual bath, and that's afterwards, isn't it supposed to be?" "Today isn't yesterday," said she, "and yesterday's not today. You can beat it if you don't like it." In short, I waited.

15   Not four months later, she was in childbed. The townsfolk hid their laughter with their knuckles. But what could I do? She suffered intolerable pains and clawed at the walls. "Gimpel," she cried, "I'm going. Forgive me!" The house filled with women. They were boiling pans of water. The screams rose to the welkin.

The thing to do was to go to the house of prayer to repeat psalms, and that was what I did.

The townsfolk liked that, all right. I stood in a corner saying psalms and prayers, and they shook their heads at me. "Pray, pray!" they told me. "Prayer never made any woman pregnant." One of the congregation put a straw to my mouth and said, "Hay for the cows." There was something to that too, by God!

She gave birth to a boy. Friday at the synagogue the sexton stood up before the Ark, pounded on the reading table, and announced, "The wealthy Reb Gimpel invites the congregation to a feast in honor of the birth of a son." The whole house of prayer rang with laughter. My face was flaming. But there was nothing I could do. After all, I *was* the one responsible for the circumcision honors and rituals.

Half the town came running. You couldn't wedge another soul in. Women brought peppered chick-peas, and there was a keg of beer from the tavern. I ate and drank as much as anyone, and they all congratulated me. Then there was a circumcision, and I named the boy after my father, may he rest in peace. When all were gone and I was left with my wife alone, she thrust her head through the bed-curtain and called me to her.

20   "Gimpel," said she, "why are you silent? Has your ship gone and sunk?"

"What shall I say," I answered. "A fine thing you've done to me! If my mother had known of it she'd have died a second time."

She said, "Are you crazy, or what?"

"How can you make such a fool," I said, "of one who should be the lord and master?"

"What's the matter with you?" she said. "What have you taken it into your head to imagine?"

25   I saw that I must speak bluntly and openly. "Do you think this is the way to use an orphan?" I said. "You have borne a bastard."

She answered, "Drive this foolishness out of your head. The child is yours."

"How can he be mine?" I argued. "He was born seventeen weeks after the wedding."

She told me then that he was premature. I said, "Isn't he a little too premature?" She said, she had had a grandmother who carried just as short a time and she resembled this grandmother of hers as one drop of water does another. She swore to it with such oaths that you would have believed a peasant at the fair if he had used them. To tell the plain truth, I didn't believe her; but when I talked it over next day with the schoolmaster, he told me that the very same thing had happened to Adam and Eve. Two they went up to bed, and four they descended.

"There isn't a woman in the world who is not the granddaughter of Eve," he said.

30   That was how it was; they argued me dumb. But then, who really knows how such things happen?

I began to forget my sorrow. I loved the child madly, and he loved me too. As soon as he saw me he'd wave his little hands and want me to pick him up, and when he was colicky I was the only one who could pacify him. I bought him a little bone teething ring and a little gilded cap. He was forever catching the evil eye from someone, and then I had to run to get one of those abracadabras for him that would get him out of it. I worked like an ox. You know how expenses go up when there's an infant in the house. I don't want to lie about it; I didn't dislike Elka either, for that matter. She swore at me and cursed, and I couldn't get enough of her. What strength she had! One of her looks could rob you of the power of speech. And her orations! Pitch and sulphur, that's what they were full of, and yet somehow also full of charm. I adored her every word. She gave me bloody wounds though.

In the evening I brought her a white loaf as well as a dark one, and also poppyseed rolls I baked myself. I thieved because of her and swiped everything I could lay hands on: macaroons, raisins, almonds, cakes. I hope I may be forgiven for stealing from the Saturday pots the women left to warm in the baker's oven. I would take out scraps of meat, a chunk of pudding, a chicken leg or head, a piece of tripe, whatever I could nip quickly. She ate and became fat and handsome.

I had to sleep away from home all during the week, at the bakery. On Friday nights when I got home she always made an excuse of some sort. Either she had heartburn, or a stitch in the side, or hiccups, or headaches. You know what women's excuses are. I had a bitter time of it. It was rough. To add to it, this little brother of hers, the bastard, was growing bigger. He'd put lumps on me, and when I wanted to hit back she'd open her mouth and curse so powerfully I saw a green haze floating before my eyes. Ten times a day she threatened to divorce me. Another man in my place would have taken French leave and disappeared. But I'm the type that bears it and says nothing. What's one to do? Shoulders are from God, and burdens too.

One night there was a calamity in the bakery; the oven burst, and we almost had a fire. There was nothing to do but go home, so I went home. Let me, I thought, also taste the joy of sleeping in bed in midweek. I didn't want to wake the sleeping mite and tiptoed into the house. Coming in, it seemed to me that I heard not the snoring of one but, as it were, a double snore, one a thin enough snore and the other like the snoring of a slaughtered ox. Oh, I didn't like that! I didn't like it at all. I went up to the bed, and things suddenly turned black. Next to Elka lay a man's form. Another in my place would have made an uproar, and enough noise to rouse the whole town, but the thought occurred to me that I might wake the child. A little thing like that—why frighten a little swallow, I thought. All right then, I went back to the bakery and stretched out on a sack of flour and till morning I never shut an eye. I shivered as if I had had malaria. "Enough of being a donkey," I said to myself. "Gimpel isn't going to be a sucker all his life. There's a limit even to the foolishness of a fool like Gimpel."

35   In the morning I went to the rabbi to get advice, and it made a great commotion in the town. They sent the beadle for Elka right away. She came, carrying the child. And what do you think she did? She denied it denied everything, bone and stone! "He's out of his head," she said, "I know nothing of dreams or divinations." They yelled at her, warned her, hammered on the table, but she stuck to her guns: it was a false accusation, she said.

The butchers and the horse-traders took her part. One of the lads from the slaughterhouse came by and said to me, "We've got our eye on you, you're a marked man." Meanwhile, the child started to bear down and soiled itself. In the rabbinical court there was an Ark of the Covenant and they couldn't allow that, so they sent Elka away.

I said to the rabbi, "What shall I do?"

"You must divorce her at once," said he.

"And what if she refuses?" I asked.

40   He said, "You must serve the divorce. That's all you'll have to do."

I said, "Well, all right, rabbi. Let me think about it."

"There's nothing to think about," said he. "You mustn't remain under the same roof with her."

"And if I want to see the child?" I asked.

"Let her go, the harlot," said he, "and her brood of bastards with her."

45   The verdict he gave was that I mustn't even cross her threshold—never again, as long as I should live.

During the day it didn't bother me so much. I thought: It was bound to happen, the abscess had to burst. But at night when I stretched out upon the sacks I felt it all very bitterly. A longing took me, for her and for the child. I wanted to be angry, but that's my misfortune exactly, I don't have it in me to be really angry. In the first place—this was how my thoughts went— there's bound to be a slip sometimes. You can't live without errors. Probably that lad who was with her led her on and gave her presents and what not, and women are often long on hair and short on sense, and so he got around her. And then since she denies it so, maybe I was only seeing things? Hallucinations do happen. You see a figure or a mannikin or something, but when you come up closer it's nothing, there's not a thing there. And if that's so, I'm doing her an injustice. And when I got so far in my thoughts I started to weep. I sobbed so that I wet the flour where I lay. In the morning I went to the rabbi and told him that I had made a mistake. The rabbi wrote on with his quill, and he said that if that were so he would have to reconsider the whole case. Until he had finished I wasn't to go near my wife, but I might send her bread and money by messenger.

III

Nine months passed before all the rabbis could come to an agreement. Letters went back and forth. I hadn't realized that there could be so much erudition about a matter like this.

Meanwhile, Elka gave birth to still another child, a girl this time. On the Sabbath I went to the synagogue and invoked a blessing on her. They called me up to the Torah, and I named the child for my mother-in-law—may she rest in peace. The louts and loudmouths of the town who came into the bakery gave me a going over. All Frampol refreshed its spirits because of my trouble and grief. However, I resolved that I would always believe what I was told. What's the good of *not* believing? Today it's your wife you don't believe; tomorrow it's God Himself you won't take stock in.

By an apprentice who was her neighbor I sent her daily a corn or a wheat loaf, or a piece of pastry, rolls or bagels, or, when I got the chance, a slab of pudding, a slice of honeycake, or wedding strudel—whatever came my way. The apprentice was a goodhearted lad, and more than once he added something on his own. He had formerly annoyed me a lot, plucking my nose and digging me in the ribs, but when he started to be a visitor to my house he became kind and friendly. "Hey, you, Gimpel," he said to me, "You have a very decent little wife and two fine kids. You don't deserve them."

50 "But the things people say about her," I said.

"Well, they have long tongues," he said, "and nothing to do with them but babble. Ignore it as you ignore the cold of last winter."

One day the rabbi sent for me and said, "Are you certain, Gimpel, that you were wrong about your wife?"

I said, "I'm certain."

"Why, but look here! You yourself saw it."

55 "It must have been a shadow," I said.

"The shadow of what?"

"Just of one of the beams, I think."

"You can go home then. You owe things to the Yanover rabbi. He found an obscure reference in Maimonides that favored you."

I seized the rabbi's hand and kissed it.

60 I wanted to run home immediately. It's no small thing to be separated for so long a time from wife and child.

Then I reflected: I'd better go back to work now, and go home in the evening. I said nothing to anyone, although as far as my heart was concerned it was like one of the Holy Days. The women teased and twitted me as they did every day, but my thought was: Go on, with your loose talk. The truth is out, like the oil upon the water. Maimonides says it's right, and therefore it is right!

At night, when I covered the dough to let it rise, I took my share of bread and a little sack of flour and started homeward. The moon was full and the stars were glistening, something to terrify the soul. I hurried onward, and before me darted a long shadow. It was winter, and a fresh snow had fallen. I had a mind to sing, but it was growing late and I didn't want to wake the householders. Then I felt like whistling, but I remembered that you don't whistle at night because it brings the demons out. So I was silent and walked as fast as I could.

Dogs in the Christian yards barked at me when I passed, but I thought: Bark your teeth out! What are you but mere dogs? Whereas I am a man, the husband of a fine wife, the father of promising children.

As I approached the house my heart started to pound as though it were the heart of a criminal. I felt no fear, but my heart went thump! thump! Well, no drawing back. I quietly lifted the latch and went in. Elka was asleep. I looked at the infant's cradle. The shutter was closed, but the moon forced its way through the cracks. I saw the newborn child's face and loved it as soon as I saw it—immediately—each tiny bone.

65 Then I came nearer to the bed. And what did I see but the apprentice lying there beside Elka. The moon went out all at once. It was utterly black, and I trembled. My teeth chattered. The bread fell from my hands, and my wife waked and said, "Who is that, ah?"

I muttered, "It's me."

"Gimpel?" she asked. "How come you're here? I thought it was forbidden."

"The rabbi said," I answered and shook as with a fever.

"Listen to me, Gimpel," she said, "go out to the shed and see if the goat's all right. It seems she's been sick," I have forgotten to say that we had a goat. When I heard she was unwell I went into the yard. The nannygoat was a good little creature. I had a nearly human feeling for her.

70 With hesitant steps I went up to the shed and opened the door. The goat stood there on her four feet. I felt her everywhere, drew her by the horns, examined her udders, and found nothing wrong. She had probably eaten too much bark. "Good night, little goat," I said. "Keep well." And the little beast answered with a "Maa" as though to thank me for the good will.

I went back. The apprentice had vanished.

"Where," I asked, "is the lad?"

"What lad?" my wife answered.

"What do you mean?" I said. "The apprentice. You were sleeping with him."

75 "The things I have dreamed this night and the night before," she said, "may they come true and lay you low, body and soul! An evil spirit has taken root in you and dazzles your sight." She screamed out, "You hateful creature! You moon calf! You spook! You uncouth man! Get out, or I'll scream all Frampol out of bed!"

Before I could move, her brother sprang out from behind the oven and struck me a blow on the back of the head. I thought he had broken my neck. I felt that something about me was deeply wrong, and I said, "Don't make a scandal. All that's needed now is that people should accuse me of raising spooks and *dybbuks.*" For that was what she had meant. "No one will touch bread of my baking."

In short, I somehow calmed her.

"Well," she said, "that's enough. Lie down and be shattered by wheels."

Next morning I called the apprentice aside. "Listen here, brother!" I said. And so on and so forth. "What do you say?" He stared at me as though I had dropped from the roof or something.

80   "I swear," he said, "you'd better go to an herb doctor or some healer. I'm afraid you have a screw loose, but I'll hush it up for you." And that's how the thing stood.

To make a long story short, I lived twenty years with my wife. She bore me six children, four daughters and two sons. All kinds of things happened, but I neither saw nor heard. I believed, and that's all. The rabbi recently said to me, "Belief in itself is beneficial. It is written that a good man lives by faith."

Suddenly my wife took sick. It began with a trifle, a little growth upon the breast. But she evidently was not destined to live long; she had no years. I spent a fortune on her. I have forgotten to say that by this time I had a bakery of my own and in Frampol was considered to be something of a rich man. Daily the healer came, and every witch doctor in the neighborhood was brought. They decided to use leeches, and after that to try cupping. They even called a doctor from Lublin, but it was too late. Before she died she called me to her bed and said, "Forgive me, Gimpel."

I said, "what is there to forgive? You have been a good and faithful wife."

"Woe, Gimpel!" she said. "It was ugly how I deceived you all these years. I want to go clean to my Maker, and so I have to tell you that the children are not yours."

85   If I had been clouted on the head with a piece of wood it couldn't have bewildered me more.

"Whose are they?" I asked.

"I don't know," she said, "there were a lot. . . . But they are not yours." And as she spoke she tossed her head to the side, her eyes turned glassy, and it was all up with Elka. On her whitened lips there remained a smile.

I imagined that, dead as she was, she was saying, "I deceived Gimpel. That was the meaning of my brief life."

IV

One night, when the period of mourning was done, as I lay dreaming on the flour sacks, there came the Spirit of Evil himself and said to me, "Gimpel, why do you sleep?"

90   I said, "What should I be doing? Eating *kreplech?*"

"The whole world deceives you," he said, "and you ought to deceive the world in your turn."

"How can I deceive all the world?" I asked him.

He answered, "You might accumulate a bucket of urine every day and at night pour it into the dough. Let the sages of Frampol eat filth."

"What about judgment in the world to come?" I said.

95 "There is no world to come," he said.

"They've sold you a bill of goods and talked you into believing you carried a cat in your belly. What nonsense!"

"Well then," I said, "and is there a God?"

He answered, "There is no God either."

"What," I said, "*is* there, then?"

100 "A thick mire."

He stood before my eyes with a goatish beard and horn, long-toothed, and with a tail. Hearing such words, I wanted to snatch him by the tail, but I tumbled from the flour sacks and nearly broke a rib. Then it happened that I had to answer the call of nature, and, passing, I saw the risen dough, which seemed to say to me, "Do it!" In brief, I let myself be persuaded.

At dawn the apprentice came. We kneaded the bread, scattered caraway seeds on it, and set it to bake. Then the apprentice went away, and I was left sitting in the little trench by the oven, on a pile of rags. Well, Gimpel, I thought, you've revenged yourself on them for all the shame they've put on you. Outside the frost glittered, but it was warm beside the oven. The flames heated my face. I bent my head and fell into a doze.

I saw in a dream, at once, Elka in her shroud. She called to me, "What have you done, Gimpel?"

I said to her, "It's all your fault," and started to cry.

105 "You fool!" she said. "You fool! Because I was false is everything false too? I never deceived anyone but myself. I'm paying for it all, Gimpel. They spare you nothing here."

I looked at her face. It was black; I was startled and waked, and remained sitting dumb. I sense that everything hung in the balance. A false step now and I'd lose eternal life. But God gave me His help. I seized the long shovel and took out the loaves, carried them into the yard, and started to dig a hole in the frozen earth.

My apprentice came back as I was doing it. "What are you doing boss?" he said, and grew pale as a corpse.

"I know what I'm doing," I said, and I buried it all before his very eyes.

Then I went home, took my hoard from its hiding place, and divided it among the children. "I saw your mother tonight," I said. "She's turning black, poor thing."

110 They were so astonished they couldn't speak a word.

"Be, well," I said, "and forget that such a one as Gimpel ever existed." I put on my short coat, a pair of boots, took the bag that held my prayer shawl in one hand, my stock in the other, and kissed the mezuzah. When people saw me in the street they were greatly surprised.

"Where are you going?" they said.

I answered, "Into the world." And so I departed from Frampol.

I wandered over the land, and good people did not neglect me. After many years I became old and white; I heard a great deal, many lies and falsehoods, but the longer I lived the more I understood that there were really no lies. Whatever doesn't really happen is dreamed at night. It happens to one if it doesn't happen to another, tomorrow if not today, or a century hence if not next year. What difference can it make? Often I heard tales of which I said, "Now this is a thing that cannot happen." But before a year had elapsed I heard that it actually had come to pass somewhere.

115 Going from place to place, eating at strange tables, it often happens that I spin yarns—improbable things that could never have happened—about devils, magicians, windmills, and the like. The children run after me, calling, "Grandfather, tell us a story." Sometimes they ask for particular stories, and I try to please them. A fat young boy once said to me, "Grandfather, it's the same story you told us before." The little rogue, he was right.

So it is with dreams too. It is many years since I left Frampol, but as soon as I shut my eyes I am there again. And whom do you think I see? Elka. She is standing by the washtub, as at our first encounter, but her face is shining and her eyes are as radiant as the eyes of a saint, and she speaks outlandish words to me, strange things. When I wake I have forgotten it all. But while the dream lasts I am comforted. She answers all my queries, and what comes out is that all is right. I weep and implore, "Let me be with you." And she consoles me and tells me to be patient. The time is nearer than it is far. Sometimes she strokes and kisses me and weeps upon my face. When I awaken I feel her lips and taste the salt of her tears.

No doubt the world is entirely an imaginary world, but it is only once removed from the true world. At the door of the hovel where I lie, there stands the plank on which the dead are taken away. The gravedigger Jew has his spade ready. The grave waits and the worms are hungry; the shrouds are prepared—I carry them in my beggar's sack. Another *shnorrer* is waiting to inherit my bed of straw. When the time comes I will go joyfully. Whatever may be there, it will be real, without complication, without ridicule, without deception. God be praised: there even Gimpel cannot be deceived.

Writing Log/Journal Assignment

Freewrite about a particularly fulfilling event in your life or a time when making sacrifices to ensure the safety, comfort, or happiness of others was more important to you than anything else.

Individual and Collaborative Considerations

1. Why do people refer to Gimpel as a fool? In what way is Gimpel actually very wise?
2. Describe Gimpel's first encounter with Elka, his unfaithful wife to be. How does their meeting foreshadow their dismal relationship? What happens once they get married?

3. When did Gimpel imagine Elka saying, "I deceived Gimpel. That was the meaning of my brief life?" What occurred?
4. Who entices Gimpel to seek revenge for the wrongs he has suffered? What does he do to get even with the townspeople who heaped shame on him for years? Ironically, who keeps him from being untrue to his character?
5. How did Gimpel end his days? Would you say he was basically the same person at the end of the story as in the beginning—albeit a few years older? Defend your position.

Writing Activities

1. Write an essay demonstrating how and why *trust and belief* in other people is better than *suspicion and doubt*. Depending on your point of view, it may be effective to adopt a humorous tone for your composition.
2. Though Gimpel could have gotten even with the townspeople through his physical act of urinating in the dough of the bread they would buy and eat, he would have suffered spiritually for his maliciousness. Write an essay explaining how, like Gimpel, you devised the perfect way to avenge yourself on others who had deceived you, only to abandon it at the last moment.

※

The Rain Came

Grace Ogot

Born in 1930, Grace Ogot, an African writer from Kenya, has published one novel, *The Promised Land,* and a volume of short stories, *Land without Thunder,* in addition to children's stories. She lived in London for a number of years and moved on to Uganda where she worked as a public relations director. In her stories like "The Rain Came," Ogot deals with traditional ways of life—in this case of the Luo people—prior to the introduction of European folkways and mores.

The chief was still far from the gate when his daughter Oganda saw him. She ran to meet him. Breathlessly she asked her father, "What is the news, great Chief? Everyone in the village is anxiously waiting to hear when it will rain." Labong'o held out his hands for his daughter but he did not say a word. Puzzled by her father's cold attitude Oganda ran back to the village to warn the others that the chief was back.

The atmosphere in the village was tense and confused. Everyone moved aimlessly and fussed in the yard without actually doing any work. A young woman whispered to her co-wife, "If they have not solved this rain business today, the chief will crack." They had watched him getting thinner and thinner as the people kept on pestering him. "Our cattle lie dying in the fields," they reported. "Soon it will be our children and then ourselves. Tell us what to do to save our lives, oh great Chief." So the chief had daily pleaded with the Almighty through the ancestors to deliver them from their great distress.

Instead of calling the family together and giving them the news immediately, Labong'o went to his own hut, a sign that he was not to be disturbed. Having replaced the shutter, he sat in the dimly-lit hut to contemplate.

It was no longer a question of being the chief of hunger-stricken people that weighed Labong'o's heart. It was the life of his only daughter that was at stake. At the time when Oganda came to meet him, he saw the glittering chain shining around her waist. The prophecy was complete. "It is Oganda, Oganda, my only daughter, who must die so young." Labong'o burst into tears before finishing the sentence. The chief must not weep. Society had declared him the bravest of men. But Labong'o did not care any more. He assumed the position of a simple father and wept bitterly. He loved his people, the Luo, but what were the Luo for him without Oganda? Her life had brought a new life in Labong'o's world and he ruled better than he could remember. How would the spirit of the village survive his beautiful daughter? "There are so many homes and so many parents who have daughters. Why choose this one? She is all I have." Labong'o spoke as if the ancestors were there in the hut and he could see them face to face. Perhaps they were there, warning him to remember his promise on the day he was enthroned when he said aloud, before the elders, "I will lay down my life, if necessary, and the life of my household, to save this tribe from the hands of the enemy." "Deny! Deny!" he could hear the voice of his forefathers mocking him.

5 When Labong'o was made chief he was only a young man. Unlike his father he ruled for many years with only one wife. But people mocked him secretly because his only wife did not bear him a daughter. He married a second, a third and a fourth wife. But they all gave birth to male children. When Labong'o married a fifth wife, she bore him a daughter. They called her Oganda, meaning "beans," because her skin was very smooth. Out of Labong'o's twenty children, Oganda was the only girl. Though she was the chief's favorite, her mother's co-wives swallowed their jealous feelings and showered her with love. After all, they said, Oganda was a girl whose days in the royal family were numbered. She would soon marry at a tender age and leave the enviable position to someone else.

Never in his life had he been faced with such an impossible decision. Refusing to yield to the rain-maker's request would mean sacrificing the whole tribe, putting the interests of the individual above those of the society. More than that. It would mean disobeying the ancestors, and most probably wiping the Luo people from the surface of the earth. On the other hand, to let Oganda die as a ransom for the people would permanently cripple Labong'o spiritually. He knew he would never be the same chief again.

The words of Nditi, the medicine-man, still echoed in his ears. "Podho, the ancestor of the Luo, appeared to me in a dream last night and he asked me to speak to the chief and the people," Nditi had said to the gathering of tribesmen. "A young woman who has not known a man must die so that the country may have rain. While Podho was still talking to me, I saw a young woman standing at the lakeside, her hands raised above her head. Her skin was as a tender young deer's. Her tall slender figure stood like a lonely reed at the river bank. Her sleepy eyes wore a sad look like that of a bereaved mother. She wore a gold ring on her left ear and a glittering brass chain around her waist. As I still marvelled at the beauty of this young woman, Podho told me, 'Out of all the women in this land, we have chosen this one. Let her offer herself a sacrifice to the lake monster! And on that day, the rain will come down in torrents. Let everyone stay at home on that day, lest he be carried away by the floods.'"

Outside, there was a strange stillness, except for the thirsty birds that sang lazily on the dying trees. The blinding midday heat had forced the people into their huts. Not far away from the chief's hut two guards were snoring away quietly. Labong'o removed his crown and the large eagle-head that hung loosely on his shoulders. He left the hut and, instead of asking Nyabogo the messenger to beat the drum, he went straight and beat it himself. In no time the whole household had assembled under the *siala* tree where he usually addressed them. He told Oganda to wait a while in her grandmother's hut.

When Labong'o stood to address his household his voice was hoarse and tears choked him. He started to speak but words refused to leave his lips. His wives and sons knew there was danger, perhaps their enemies had declared war on them. Labong'o's eyes were red and they could see he had been weeping. At last he told them, "One whom we love and treasure will be taken away from us. Oganda is to die." Labong'o's voice was so faint that he could not hear it himself. But he continued, "The ancestors have chosen her to be offered as a sacrifice to the lake monster in order that we may have rain."

10   For a moment there was dead silence among the people. They were completely stunned; and as some confused murmur broke out Oganda's mother fainted and was carried off to her own hut. But the other people rejoiced. They danced around singing and chanting, "Oganda is the lucky one to die for the people; if it is to save the people, let Oganda go."

In her grandmother's hut Oganda wondered what the whole family was discussing about her that she could not hear. Her grandmother's hut was well away from the chief's court and much as she strained her ears, she could not hear what they were saying. "It must be marriage," she concluded. It was an accepted custom for the family to discuss their daughter's future marriage behind her back. A faint smile played on Oganda's lips as she thought of the several young men who swallowed saliva at the mere mention of her name.

There was Kech, the son of an elder in a neighbouring clan. Kech was very handsome. He had sweet, meek eyes and a roaring laughter. He could make a wonderful father, Oganda thought. But they would not be a good match. Kech was a bit too short to be her husband. It would humiliate her to have to look down at Kech each time she spoke to him. Then she thought of Dimo, the tall young man who had already distinguished himself as a brave warrior and an outstanding wrestler. Dimo loved Oganda, but Oganda thought he would make a cruel husband, always quarrelling and ready to fight. No, she did not like him. Oganda fingered the glittering chain on her waist as she thought of Osinda. A long time ago when she was quite young Osinda had given her that chain and, instead of wearing it around her neck several times, she wore it round her waist where it could permanently stay. She heard her heart pounding so loudly as she thought of him. She whispered, "Let it be you they are discussing, Osinda the lovely one. Come now and take me away. . . ."

The lean figure in the doorway startled Oganda who was rapt in thought about the man she loved. "You have frightened me, Grandma," said Oganda laughing. "Tell me, is it my marriage you were discussing? You can take it from me that I won't marry any of them." A smile played on her lips again. She was coaxing her grandma to tell her quickly, to tell her they were pleased with Osinda.

In the open space outside the excited relatives were dancing and singing. They were coming to the hut now, each carrying a gift to put at Oganda's feet. As their singing got nearer Oganda was able to hear what they were saying: "If it is to save the people, if it is to give us rain, let Oganda go. Let Oganda die for her people and for her ancestors." Was she mad to think that they were singing about her? How could she die? She found the lean figure of her grandmother barring the door. She could not get out. The look on her grandmother's face warned her that there was danger around the corner. "Mother, it is not marriage then?" Oganda asked urgently. She suddenly felt panicky, like a mouse cornered by a hungry cat. Forgetting that there was only one door in the hut, Oganda fought desperately to find another exit. She must fight for her life. But there was none.

15   She closed her eyes, leapt like a wild tiger through the door, knocking her grandmother flat to the ground. There outside in mourning garments Labong'o stood motionless, his hands folded at the back. He held his daughter's hand and led her away from the excited crowd to the little red-painted hut where her mother was resting. Here he broke the news officially to his daughter.

For a long time the three souls who loved one another dearly sat in darkness. It was no good speaking. And even if they tried, the words could not have come out. In the past they had been like three cooking-stones, sharing their burdens. Taking Oganda away from them would leave two useless stones which would not hold a cooking-pot.

News that the beautiful daughter of the chief was to be sacrificed to give the people rain spread across the country like wind. And at sunset the chief's village was full of relatives and friends who had come to congratulate Oganda. Many more were on their way, coming, carrying their gifts. They would dance till morning to keep her company. And in the morning they would prepare her a big farewell feast. All these relatives thought it a great honour to be selected by the spirits to die in order that the society might live. "Oganda's name will always remain a living name among us," they boasted.

Of course it was an honour, a great honour, for a woman's daughter to be chosen to die for the country. But what could the mother gain once her only daughter was blown away by the wind? There were so many other women in the land, why choose her daughter, her only child? Had human life any meaning at all?—other women had houses full of children while Oganda's mother had to lose her only child!

In the cloudless sky the moon shone brightly and the numerous stars glittered. The dancers of all age groups assembled to dance before Oganda, who sat close to her mother sobbing quietly. All these years she had been with her people she thought she understood them. But now she discovered that she was a stranger among them. If they really loved her as they had always professed, why were they not sympathetic? Why were they not making any attempt to save her? Did her people really understand what it felt like to die young? Unable to restrain her emotions any longer, she sobbed loudly as her age-group got up to dance. They were young and beautiful and very soon they would marry and have their own children. They would have husbands to love and little huts for themselves. They would have reached maturity. Oganda touched the chain around her waist as she thought of Osinda. She wished Osinda were there too, among her friends. "Perhaps he is ill," she thought gravely. The chain comforted Oganda—she would die with it around her waist and wear it in the underground world.

20 In the morning a big feast of many different dishes was prepared for Oganda so that she could pick and choose. "People don't eat after death," they said. The food looked delicious but Oganda touched none of it. Let the happy people eat. She contented herself with sips of water from a little calabash.

The time for her departure was drawing near and each minute was precious. It was a day's journey to the lake. She was to walk all night, passing through the great forest. But nothing could touch her, not even the denizens of the forest. She was already anointed with sacred oil. From the time Oganda received the sad news she had expected Osinda to appear any moment. But he was not there. A relative told her that Osinda was away on a private visit. Oganda realized that she would never see her dear one again.

In the afternoon the whole village stood at the gate to say good-bye and to see her for the last time. Her mother wept on her neck for a long time. The great chief in a mourning skin came to the gate barefooted and mingled with the people—a simple father in grief. He took off his wrist bracelet and put it on his daughter's wrist, saying, "You will always live among us. The spirit of our forefathers is with you."

Tongue-tied and unbelieving Oganda stood there before the people. She had nothing to say. She looked at her home once more. She could hear her heart beating so painfully within her. All her childhood plans were coming to an end. She felt like a flower nipped in the bud never to enjoy the morning dew again. She looked at her weeping mother and whispered, "Whenever you want to see me, always look at the sunset. I will be there."

Oganda turned southwards to start her trek to the lake. Her parents, relatives, friends and admirers stood at the gate and watched her go. Her beautiful, slender figure grew smaller and smaller till she mingled with the thin dry trees in the forest.

25   As Oganda walked the lonely path that wound its way in the wilderness, she sang a song and her own voice kept her company.

> The ancestors have said Oganda must die;
> The daughter of the chief must be sacrificed.
> When the lake monster feeds on my flesh,
> The people will have rain;
> Yes, the rain will come down in torrents.
> The wind will blow, the thunder will roar.
> And the floods will wash away the sandy beaches
> When the daughter of the chief dies in the lake.
> My age-group has consented,
> My parents have consented,
> So have my friends and relatives;
> Let Oganda die to give us rain.
> My age group are young and ripe,
> Ripe for womanhood and motherhood;
> But Oganda must die young,
> Oganda must sleep with the ancestors.
> Yes, rain will come down in torrents.

The red rays of the setting sun embraced Oganda and she looked like a burning candle in the wilderness.

The people who came to hear her sad song were touched by her beauty. But they all said the same thing: "If it is to save the people, if it is to give us rain, then be not afraid. Your name will forever live among us."

At midnight Oganda was tired and weary. She could walk no more. She sat under a big tree and, having sipped water from her calabash, she rested her head on the tree trunk and slept. When she woke up in the morning the sun was high in the sky. After walking for many hours she reached the *tong*, a strip of land that separated the inhabited part of the country from the sacred place—*kar lamo*. No lay man could enter this place and come out alive—only those who had direct contact with the spirits and the Almighty were allowed to enter his holy of holies. But Oganda had to pass through this sacred land on her way to the lake, which she had to reach at sunset.

A large crowd gathered to see her for the last time. Her voice was now hoarse and painful but there was no need to worry any more. Soon she would not have to sing. The crowd looked at Oganda sympathetically, mumbling words she could not hear. But none of them pleaded for her life. As Oganda opened the gate a child, a young child, broke loose from the crowd and ran toward her. The child took a small ear-ring from her sweaty hands and gave it to Oganda, saying, "When you reach the world of the dead, give this ear-ring to my sister. She died last week. She forgot the ring." Oganda, taken aback by this strange request, took the little ring and handed her precious water and food to the child. She did not need them now. Oganda did not know whether to laugh or cry. She had heard mourners sending their love to their sweethearts, long dead, but this idea of sending gifts was new to her.

30 Oganda held her breath as she crossed the barrier to enter the sacred land. She looked appealingly at the crowd but there was no response. Their minds were too preoccupied with their own survival. Rain was the precious medicine they were longing for and the sooner Oganda could get to her destination the better.

A strange feeling possessed the princess as she picked her way in the sacred land. There were strange noises that often startled her and her first reaction was to take to her heels. But she remembered that she had to fulfill the wish of her people. She was exhausted, but the path was still winding. Then suddenly the path ended on sandy land. The water had retreated miles away from the shore, leaving a wide stretch of sand. Beyond this was the vast expanse of water.

Oganda felt afraid. She wanted to picture the size and shape of the monster, but fear would not let her. The people did not talk about it, nor did the crying children who were silenced at the mention of its name. The sun was still up but it was no longer hot. For a long time Oganda walked ankle-deep in the sand. She was exhausted and longed desperately for her calabash of water. As she moved on she had a strange feeling that something was following her. Was it the monster? Her hair stood erect and a cold paralysing feeling ran along her spine. She looked behind, sideways and in front but there was nothing except a cloud of dust.

Oganda began to hurry but the feeling did not leave her and her whole body seemed to be bathing in its perspiration. The sun was going down fast and the lake shore seemed to move along with it. Oganda started to run. She must be at the lake before sunset. As she ran she heard a noise coming from behind. She looked back sharply and something resembling a moving bush was frantically running after her. It was about to catch up with her.

Oganda ran with all her strength. She was now determined to throw herself into the water even before sunset. She did not look back but the creature was upon her. She made an effort to cry out, as in a nightmare, but she could not hear her own voice. The creature caught up with Oganda. A strong hand grabbed her. But she fell flat on the sand and fainted.

35   When the lake breeze brought her back to consciousness a man was bending over her. "O . . . !" Oganda opened her mouth to speak, but she had lost her voice. She swallowed a mouthful of water poured into her mouth by the stranger.

"Osinda, Osinda! Please let me die. Let me run, the sun is going down. Let me die. Let them have rain."

Osinda fondled the glittering chain around Oganda's waist and wiped tears from her face. "We must escape quickly to an unknown land," Osinda said urgently. "We must run away from the wrath of the ancestors and the retaliation of the monster."

"But the curse is upon me, Osinda, I am no good for you any more. And moreover the eyes of the ancestors will follow us everywhere and bad luck will befall us. Nor can we escape from the monster."

Oganda broke loose, afraid to escape, but Osinda grabbed her hands again. "Listen to me, Oganda! Listen! Here are two coats!" He then covered the whole of Oganda's body, except her eyes, with a leafy attire made from the twigs of bwombwe. "These will protect us from the eyes of the ancestors and the wrath of the monster. Now let us run out of here." He held Oganda's hand and they ran from the sacred land, avoiding the path that Oganda had followed.

40   The bush was thick and the long grass entangled their feet as they ran. Half-way through the sacred land they stopped and looked back. The sun was almost touching the surface of the water. They were frightened. They continued to run, now faster, to avoid the sinking sun.

"Have faith, Oganda—that thing will not reach us."

When they reached the barrier and looked behind them, trembling, only a tip of the sun could be seen above the water's surface.

"It is gone! It is gone!" Oganda wept, hiding her face in her hands.

"Weep not, the daughter of the chief. Let us run, let us escape."

45   There was a lightning flash in the distance. They looked up, frightened. That night it rained in torrents as it had not done for a long, long time.

Writing Log/Journal Assignment

Relate an incident wherein you made a major personal sacrifice in the interest of others. Did you act freely or out of a sense of duty? How did those you assisted through your sacrifice acknowledge your deed?

Individual and Collaborative Considerations

1. What type of sacrifice must the Chief make for the good of his people? How does he feel about it?
2. In what way was Oganda chosen to be sacrificed to the lake monster?
3. What would be the implications of disobeying the rain-maker's request to (a) the tribe and (b) their ancestors?
4. How did most of the tribe respond when Labong'o informed them of the decision to sacrifice Oganda? How did they view her fate?
5. In your opinion, is there really any curse on Oganda? Why did she and Osinda conceal themselves in coats and cover themselves "with a leafy attire made from the twigs of bwombwe"?

Writing Activities

1. Often family vacations are a matter of compromise not consensus, and the individual who feels he or she has made the largest sacrifice frequently reminds everyone else of it. Write a narrative account of just such a trip. You may want to take a particular angle on the "sacrifice" in question. For instance, your introductory paragraph could lead to the fact that your brother seized the moment of self-sacrifice less for the common good of all than for the opportunity to play "the martyr." If you have never had such a vacation, use your imagination to write a creative response to the writing prompt.
2. What motivates a person to set aside personal desires to further the goals of a larger community? Explore this issue by classifying and defining the different forms a sacrifice may take. You may want to consider the benefits and disadvantages associated with each sacrifice.

✳

Those Winter Sundays

Robert Hayden

Poet and editor Robert Hayden was born in Detroit, educated at Wayne State University, and taught at Fisk University in Tennessee from 1946 to 1969 and the University of Michigan from 1969 to 1980. In addition to his editorial work for *Baha'i World Faith Magazine,* he edited an anthology titled *Kaleidoscope: Poems by American Negro Poets* (1967). Hayden's collections of verse include *Heart-Shape in the Dust* (1940), *The Lion and the Archer* (1948), *A Ballad of Remembrance* (1962), *Selected Poems* (1966), *Angle of Ascent: New and Collected Poems* (1979), and *Robert Hayden: Selected Poems* (1985).

Sundays too my father got up early
and put his clothes on in the blueblack cold,
then with cracked hands that ached
from labor in the weekday weather made
5   banked fires blaze. No one ever thanked him.

I'd wake and hear the cold splintering, breaking.
When the rooms were warm, he'd call,
and slowly I would rise and dress,
fearing the chronic angers of that house.

10   Speaking indifferently to him,
who had driven out the cold
and polished my good shoes as well.
What did I know, what did I know
of love's austere and lonely offices?

Writing Log/Journal Assignment

Write a reflective journal entry about a task performed by one of your parents, relatives, or guardians in your youth that you simply took for granted.

Individual and Collaborative Considerations

1. How would you describe the tone or mood of this poem?
2. In what way does the poet appeal to the reader's sense of sound, sight, touch?
3. Explain how the opening line "Sundays too my father got up early" sets the tone for Hayden's poem.
4. How does Hayden build intensity in his poem—intensity leading to the final two lines: "What did I know, what did I know / of love's austere and lonely offices?"
5. What does the speaker regret?

Writing Activities

1. Write an essay explaining a moment in your life when you realized something very important (e.g., your father or mother performed various tasks out of love—not out of duty). Your thesis will probably be your epiphany or understanding of a situation. In the body of your paper, you can

analyze and explain what you formerly took for granted. Your conclusion should place all information into perspective with your thesis. (Suggestion: It might help to review your response to the journal exercise before you begin prewriting.)

2. Write an essay devoted to explaining the real meaning and reason for *regret*. Since there is not one reason for *regret*, the possible number of thesis statements is likewise very broad. To convincingly argue your thesis paragraph, you will want to make sure you have answered the questions "how" and "why."

✳

Pleasures

Denise Levertov

Of Russian and Welsh ancestry, Denise Levertov came to the United States after marrying an American in 1948. Prior to her move, she published a collection of her verse titled *The Double Image* (1946). Levertov's creative output has been considerable since her arrival in the United States: *Here and Now* (1957), *Five Poems* (1958), *Overland to the Islands* (1958), *With Eyes at the Back of Our Heads* (1959), *The Jacob's Ladder* (1961), *O Taste and See* (1964), *The Sorrow Dance* (1967), *Relearning the Alphabet* (1970), *To Stay Alive* (1971), *Footprints* (1975), and *Candles in Babylon* (1982). In 1973 she also published *The Poet of the World*, a collection of essays on the Vietnam War—a war that greatly affected her poetry (she wrote many poems sympathizing with mistreated people—the real victims of war). Overall, however, most of her early and late poetry is not political. Levertov proudly identifies with mystics of the past. As she explains in the following poem, she gains pleasure and fulfillment from "small things," especially "things of another nature."

> I like to find
> what's not found
> at once, but lies
>
> within something of another nature,
> in repose, distinct.
> Gull feathers of glass, hidden
> in white pulp: the bones of squid
> which I pull out and lay
> blade by blade on the draining board—

5

10   tapered as if for swiftness, to pierce
                           the heart, but fragile, substance
                           belying design.   Or a fruit, *mamey,*

                           cased in tough brown peel, the flesh
                           rose-amber, and the seed:
15   the seed a stone of wood, carved and

                           polished, walnut-colored, formed
                           like a brazilnut, but large,
                           large enough to fill
                           the hungry palm of a hand.

20   I like the juicy stem of grass that grows
                           within the coarser leaf folded round,
                           and the butteryellow glow

                           in the narrow flute from which the morning-glory
                           opens blue and cool on a hot afternoon.

Writing Log/Journal Assignment

Freewrite about the sort of things that give you pleasure—no matter how trite or how profound, how silly, or how intellectual.

Individual and Collaborative Considerations

1. What does Levertov like to find? Where?
2. Individually or in a group, write a list containing the things you like to find. Attempt to visually convey the items on your list in the same manner Levertov used in her poem. Share your list with others and discuss the importance of diction.
3. How does Levertov establish the tone or mood in "Pleasures"?
4. Which words or word groups convey the most powerful sensory images to you? Explain your answer.
5. Why do you imagine finding things "within something of another nature" gives Levertov so much pleasure?

Writing Activities

1. How do simple pleasures lead to personal fulfillment? Write an essay explaining how the seemingly small things in life—simple pleasures—are often more important than elaborate events.
2. Compare and contrast the speaker's sense of fulfillment in Levertov's "Pleasures" to the tailor's sense of fulfillment through pain in the follow-

ing poem, "Inside the Jacket," by Juan Felipe Herrera. What conclusions can you reach about the "relative" merits of each?

✳

Inside the Jacket

Juan Felipe Herrera

In addition to *Facegames* (1987), the source of the following poem, Juan Felipe Herrera has authored several books, including *Rebozos of Love* (1974), *Exiles of Desire* (1983), and *Night in Tunisia* (1985). Herrera's following poem, a combination of narration and description, evolves from simple, straightforward language in the first six stanzas in which he introduces his reader to his memory and explains who the "mexicano working in a sweat shop" was and what he did for a living. The figurative language that comes into play in the final two stanzas describes the tailor at work— a scene Herrera finds quite marvelous, something unsuited for description using ordinary words.

I remember, many years ago,
a mexicano working in a sweat shop
on E Street by the library

I could see him through the windows;
5   a tailor by trade.

I thought about asking him.
to make me a suit for graduation.

His fingers were so thin, so dark.

Usually, he labored on a sport coat.
10   I could tell the owner had granted him
privacy.

He seemed happy and at ease.
One evening, I passed by and looked
at his finery; his project:

15   venom lacing
a serpent feverishly winding out of the earth
wrapping around the furniture, into the ceiling,

20
a gold lacing, swelling
pouring out into the night,
an iridescent skin, leaping
out of his scarred hands,
spreading across the city.

Writing Log/Journal Entry

The tailor in the poem is "happy and at ease"; how does this compare or contrast with your image of a tailor?

Individual and Collaborative Considerations

1. What is the speaker in the poem doing?
2. Who or what might the "serpent" represent in his poem? What subtle clues lead you to your conclusion?
3. Why has the poet titled his poem "Inside the Jacket"?
4. What kind of language is used at the beginning of the poem? What images does this language bring to mind? How does Herrera's initial use of language change by the end of the poem? What pictures come to mind when you read the last two stanzas?
5. Does the tailor enjoy his work? Is it a "labor of love" or "hate"? Explain whatever side you take on this question.

Writing Assignments

1. Write a short narrative wherein you describe an incident in which you watched someone like a pizza maker or a baker performing his or her job. Describe this person as poetically as you can.
2. Simplistic words or language bring universal images to mind. For instance, when the word "cat" is mentioned, the readers will always visualize a four-legged animal with whiskers. When symbolic words are employed, however, different images pop into our minds, and every reader will have a different mental image. Write a paragraph or two in which you describe something in simple, straightforward language. Repeat the description in another paragraph and treat the same subject abstractly or symbolically—using figurative language.

ADDITIONAL TOPICS AND ISSUES FOR WRITING AND RESEARCH

1. How is nostalgia a powerful source of fulfillment and an instrument of persuasion? Take a look at the advertising market and fashion design. In what way does the past—and our associations with it—sell itself?

2. Write an essay comparing and contrasting "self-sacrifice" and "personal fulfillment." In what way do they share similar yet very different qualities? How is a sacrifice sometimes fulfilling?

3. Write an essay arguing that the depletion of our natural resources and the extinction of nature's creatures are sacrifices society cannot afford to make. To narrow your thesis, you may want to limit your focus to *animals* like tigers, elephants, or coyotes; *birds* like condors, bald eagles, or whooping cranes; *fish* like some species of sharks, salmon, or blowfish; or *aquatic mammals* like some species of dolphins, otters, or whales.

4. What supreme sacrifice have you as a student, parent, or responsible adult made for the good of those around you? What was the nature of your sacrifice and how did others benefit from it? Were they aware of your "selfless" act? If you had known nobody would recognize your personal sacrifice, would you still have made it? Why? Why not? These are just some of the questions you might ask yourself as you prewrite and develop a thesis on the true nature of sacrifice.

5. Demonstrate how and why a blue-collar job is more difficult than a white-collar job. Consider several representative examples of both blue- and white-collar jobs as you develop and argue your thesis.

6. Research and write a persuasive essay arguing that involvement in politics at the local, state, and national level presents individuals with fulfilling opportunities for careers in government.

7. Research a particular philosophy like existentialism, feminism, or Confucianism. What are its basic principles? Using a particular philosophy as your point of view, analyze any topic or issue as presented in an essay, short story, or poem from this chapter.

8. In the past, the call for jury duty was taken from a list of registered voters. As a result, many Americans did not register to vote. Have you ever served on a jury? How much of your time do you owe the government? Write an essay arguing that serving on a jury is either more of a *privilege* than a *sacrifice* or more of a *sacrifice* than a *privilege*.

9. Write an essay arguing that a sense of "guilt" often ruins financial or material gains when you acquire them through dishonesty or deception (selling a car in bad shape to a trusting, unsuspecting person).

10. Describe the most memorable concert, ballet, public reading, or drama you ever attended. What made it particularly special? How did you feel when the performance concluded? Why and how was it personally fulfilling?

Starting Points for Research

Sacrifice	Fulfillment
• Personal possessions	• Capitalism
• Religious sacrifice	• Fortunes
• Social sacrifice	• Spiritualism
• Gender sacrifices	• Religions
• Scapegoats	• Employment
• Worship	• Aesthetics
• Taurobolium	• Ethics
• Votive offerings	• Self-realization
• Libations	• Self-help books
• Human sacrifice	• Building self-confidence
• Sacrifice of virgins	• Individuality
• Self-sacrifice	• Self-perception
• Dignity and sacrifice	• Self-satisfaction
• Ideals	• Self-realization in art
• Selflessness	• Self-realization in literature
• Martyrs	• Self-service
• Temperance and ego	• Self-love (psychology)
• Diets	• Self-culture
• Habit breaking	• Self-government
• Self-denial	• Altruism
• Family, duty, and sacrifice	• Narcissism
• Control	• Self-help groups
• Sovereignty	• Reflexive knowledge

9

Sounds and Sights: Music, Movies, and Human Dramas

*For a baby who
keeps crying, she lights a lamp
evening in autumn.*
KAWAHIGASHI HEKIGODO

Essays

Gary Soto   The Concert

•

Susan Allen Toth   Cinematypes

•

Bill Swanson   Screwball Noir

Fiction

Nathanael West   Hollywood Locusts

•

Toni Cade Bambara   Blues Ain't No Mockin Bird

•

Poetry

Reginald Lockett   When They Came to Take Him

•

Rose Anna Higashi   Thoughts of a Gambler's Lover

•

Theodore Roethke   Child on Top of a Greenhouse

The sounds and sights of *popular culture* play a big part in our lives, for they embrace all forms of visual and audio theater. Sounds and sights surround us from the instant we awake in the morning until we drift off to sleep at night, creating a sensory overload of intriguing and distracting stimuli; this overload will continue to inundate us as we move towards the twenty-first century. From the congested streets and traffic jams of big cities to the single-lane gravel roads of rural America, something is always happening; something is always changing; something is always beginning anew. Since we experience and appreciate many of the events we confront daily through the five senses—sight, sound, touch, taste, and smell—dramas continue to unfold in familiar yet novel ways. Yet what we need to learn is how to deal with this *sensory overload.*

In the following pages, we will consider many sounds and sights presented by such authors as Gary Soto, who describes a concert he and his wife attended in Oaxaca, Mexico; poet Rose Anna Higashi, whose dramatic monologue creates a persona and closely inspects her immediate environment; Theodore Roethke, who looks at a child who is in the midst of grown-ups—yet in a place he should not be (on top of a greenhouse); and Nathanael West's Tod Hackett, a Hollywood set designer and would-be artist, who finds himself caught in an apocalyptic riot in Los Angeles.

Many human dramas are all the more poignant—if not tragic—because individuals fall victim to a society full of prejudice, robbing them of dignity and respect. Reginald Lockett's "When They Came to Take Him" vividly exemplifies just such a situation, for a man—regardless of his obvious refinement and taste—is "blown away" because all the police "saw was that he was black / believed armed and dangerous." Susan Allen Toth examines various cinematypes, the art film, the movie with socially redeeming qualities, the entertaining (feel-good) film, and old musicals as well as the sorts of people who watch them, in her essay titled "Cinematypes." Therein she shows the multilayered nature of responses to sights and sounds.

In popular culture, sounds and sights operate on many levels to reflect on the experiences of everyday life. Toni Cade Bambara's "Blues Ain't No Mockin Bird" explains what motivated the low-income family of Grand-daddy Cain to react as it did when confronted by forerunners of tabloid news specializing in human misery. Bill Swanson's essay "Screwball Noir," in contrast, probes not only the visual experience of watching a motion picture but also its appeal to the serious, the humorous, the bleak, and the startling sides of our nature. "Screwball Noir" creates its own vocabulary for depicting human dramas, its language being based on caricature, genre, and allusion.

RHETORIC AT WORK

The following essays, short stories, and poems invite a close inspection of *diction* (word use). In particular, we have many instances in essays like

"Cinematypes" and "Screwball Noir" where *word choice* helps to classify and define the author's topic. Other pieces of literature like "When They Came to Take Him," "Thoughts of a Gambler's Lover," and "Child on Top of a Greenhouse" find the respective authors and poets making use of vibrant diction to "paint a picture" with words.

Make two lists of words in your writing log/journal, one being a list of your personal vocabulary and the other being a collection of concrete nouns and active verbs. Place all the (1) "new" vocabulary words you encounter and (2) words that help define something in the forthcoming readings under the first title heading. Under the second title heading, list "striking" examples of *concrete nouns* and *active verbs* that were strategically used by the authors and poets. Save this list for class discussion as well as a resource for an individual writing assignment or a collaborative activity. (Suggestion: Maintain your two-part list for class readings for the remainder of the course.)

A Checklist for Writing about *Sounds and Sights: Music, Movies, and Human Dramas*

1. Did I appeal to my reader's five senses: touch, taste, sound, sight, and smell? How did appeals to the "senses" further enhance the objective of my essay?
2. Did I use individual words to establish the "tone" and convey meaning in my essay? How? When? Where?
3. In what way did I employ *concrete nouns* to make abstract or general thoughts tangible and memorable?
4. Did I remember to use *active verbs* to bring the action in an essay, short story, or poem to life?
5. What rhetorical strategies assisted me in organizing and developing my essay? Should I have added more "definition" to clarify major terms? Would classifying items in my composition improve reader comprehension?
6. Did my overall efforts work to *show* rather than simply *tell* my reader what I think, feel, and "sense"?
7. Did I remember to provide sufficient time transitions so that my reader could follow any chronology of events I present in my "human drama"?
8. How did I effectively develop my essay? What sort of examples or evidence did I offer my reader to defend my thesis?

---- ☀ ----

The Concert

Gary Soto

Gary Soto is the author of several poetry collections, including *The Elements of San Joaquin* (1977), *Black Hair* (1985), *Living Up the Street* (1985), and *Who Will Know Us?* (1990). His prose works include *Home Course in Religion* (1991). Besides writing poetry and prose, Soto has edited such popular anthologies as *California Childhood* (1988) and has directed a film, *The Bicycle*. He received the Before Columbus 1985 American Book Award and the Academy of American Poets Prize, as well as fellowships from the Guggenheim Foundation and the National Endowment for the Arts. Once an instructor at UC Berkeley, Soto is now concentrating his time on writing and speaking. In the following narrative from *Small Faces* (1986), Soto illustrates how music of the National Symphony cut across all barriers of social class and elitism, and Soto watched in fascination as "the poor sat on the fifth tier on painted boxes, bodies leaning in the direction of the music that couldn't arrive fast enough to meet their lives."

1   **O**nce in Mexico City and tired of its noise and rushed people, my wife and I flew to Oaxaca, a city known for its pottery, weavings, and the nearby ruins of Monte Alban and Mitla. We stayed in a hotel whose courtyard was sheltered by a huge skylight that let in a hazy, almost silver light. For two days we took buses to the ruins, bought Mexican toys, and walked from one end of the town to the other in search of out-of-the-way shops.

2   On our last night we went to hear the National Symphony. I bought low-priced tickets but when we tried to sit on the ground floor, a portly usher pointed us to the stairwell. We climbed to the next landing where another usher told us to keep climbing by rolling his eyes toward *el paraiso*—the gallery of cheap seats. We climbed two more flights, laughing that we were going to end up on the roof with the pigeons. An unsmiling usher handed us programs as we stepped to the door. We looked around, amazed at the gray, well-painted boxes that were our seats. There were no crushed velvet chairs with ornate wooden arms, no elegant men and women with perfect teeth. Most were Indians and campesinos, and a few university students holding hands, heads pressed together in love.

3   I led Carolyn to the boxes in the front row against the rail and together we looked far down where the others sat. Their rumblings rose like heat. They fanned themselves and smiled wide enough for us to see their teeth. We watched them until an old man touched my shoulder, said *con permiso* and took small steps to get past me to the box on our left. When he sat down

I smiled at him as I wanted to be friendly. But he didn't look at me. He took out a pair of glasses from his breast pocket. They were broken, taped together at the bridge. I looked away, embarrassed to see that he was poor, but stole a glance when the program began: I saw his coat, slack and full from wear, and his pants with oily spots. His shoes were rope sandals. His tie was short, like a withered arm. I watched his face in profile that showed a knot of tape protruding from his glasses; a profile that went unchanged as it looked down at the symphony.

4   I listened but felt little as the violins tugged and pulled and scratched through an hour of performance. When the music stopped and the conductor turned around, moon faced and trying to hide his happiness by holding back a grin, I craned my neck over the rail and watched the *elegantes* applaud and smile at one another. We applauded, too, and looked around, smiling. We were busy with an excitement that lit our eyes. But while the *elegantes* got up to take drinks and stand in the foyer under torches, those around us leaned against the wall to smoke and talk in whispers. A group of young men played cards and, in a sudden win, laughed so hard that the usher came over to quiet them down.

5   We stayed for the second half—something by Haydn—but no matter how hard I tried to study the movements of musicians and conductor on his carpeted box, I couldn't help but look around the room at the Indians and campesinos whose faces, turned in profile in the half-lit shadows, held an instinctive awareness of the music. They would scratch a cheek or an elbow, speak quietly to one another, and sometimes squirm on the boxes. But most were attentive. It amazed me. I had never known the poor to appreciate such music, and I had lived among the poor since I was a child. These field laborers and rug weavers listened to music that was not part of their lives, music written to titillate the aristocrats who wanted so much to rise above the dirty faces of the poor. The poor sat on the fifth tier on painted boxes, bodies leaning in the direction of the music that couldn't arrive fast enough to meet their lives.

6   When the concert ended, the old man next to me stood up and asked for permission to pass. I pinched my knees together and Carolyn stood up. She sat back down and together, heads touching like lovers, we looked down to the first floor where the *elegantes* chatted with drinks and fluttery fans, and shook each other's hands as if celebrating their wealth.

7   After awhile we got up and, with campesinos who were talking about a recently read book, descended the four flights to the ground.

Writing Log/Journal Assignment

Write an account of a concert or play you have attended. What do you recall about the diversity of the audience, their attire, and their particular behavior? What do you recollect about the concert or the play as a whole? How did you feel you "fit in" with those around you? Explain.

Individual and Collaborative Considerations

1. Who or what fascinated Soto the most when he went to a classical concert in Oaxaca, Mexico?
2. Who are the *elegantes?* How do they contrast with other members of the audience?
3. What do the people sitting around Soto do during the intermission at the concert? How do the *elegantes* spend their intermission?
4. Explain the inherent irony in Soto's comment that "These field laborers and rug weavers listened to music that was not part of their lives."
5. Soto himself is well aware of the social stratification at the concert. How does he relate it in his narrative essay?

Writing Activities

1. Construct an essay that demonstrates how and why music can or cannot successfully cross barriers imposed by a social class. As you formulate your thesis, you might want to bear in mind the active role sound (music) plays in many "human dramas," and that people tend to thrive on drama.
2. Just as Soto compared and contrasted two social classes in attendance at the National Symphony in Oaxaca, Mexico, compare and contrast two of Susan Allen Toth's "Cinematypes" (pp. 270–273) or two members from different social classes who watch the same movie, and ultimately reach some conclusions about the power of visual communication, the cinema, to bridge (or widen, as the case may be) the gap and the barriers between individuals.

Cinematypes

Susan Allen Toth

Born in Iowa, Susan Allen Toth attended Smith College, Berkeley, and the University of Minnesota, where she received her Ph.D. in 1969. Presently, she is an English professor at Macalester College in St. Paul, where she teaches and does research in American regionalist fiction, women's studies, and geography in literature. She is the author of *Blooming: A Small-Town Girlhood* (1981), *Ivy Days: Making My Way Out East* (1984), and *How to Prepare for Your High School Reunion* (1990). "Cinematypes," which uses the rhetorical mode of classification in its development, was initially printed in the May 1980 issue of *Harpers Magazine* with the subtitle, "Going to the Movies."

1 **A**aron takes me only to art films. That's what I call them, anyway: strange movies with vague poetic images I don't always understand, long dreamy movies about a distant Technicolor past, even longer black-and-white movies about the general meaninglessness of life. We do not go unless at least one reputable critic has found the cinematography superb. We went to *The Devil's Eye*,[1] and Aaron turned to me in the middle and said, "My God, this is *funny*." I do not think he was pleased.

2 When Aaron and I go to the movies, we drive our cars separately and meet by the box office. Inside the theater he sits tentatively in his seat, ready to move if he can't see well, poised to leave if the film is disappointing. He leans away from me, careful not to touch the bare flesh of his arm against the bare flesh of mine. Sometimes he leans so far I am afraid he may be touching the woman on his other side. If the movie is very good, he leans forward, too, peering between the heads of the couple in front of us. The light from the screen bounces off his glasses; he gleams with intensity, sitting there on the edge of his seat, watching the screen. Once I tapped him on the arm so I could whisper a comment in his ear. He jumped.

3 After *Belle de Jour*[2] Aaron said he wanted to ask me if he could stay overnight. "But I can't," he shook his head mournfully before I had a chance to answer, "because I know I never sleep well in strange beds." Then he apologized for asking. "It's just that after a film like that," he said, "I feel the need to assert myself."

4 Pete takes me only to movies that he thinks have redeeming social value. He doesn't call them "films." They tend to be about poverty, war, injustice, political corruption, struggling unions in the 1930s, and the military-industrial complex. Pete doesn't like propaganda movies, though, and he doesn't like to be too depressed, either. We stayed away from the *Sorrow and the Pity*; it would be, he said, just too much. Besides, he assured me, things are never that hopeless. So most of the movies we see are made in Hollywood. Because they are always topical, these movies offer what Pete calls "food for thought." When we saw *Coming Home*,[3] Pete's jaw set so firmly with the first half-hour that I knew we would end up at Poppin' Fresh Pies afterward.

5 When Pete and I go to the movies, we take turns driving so no one owes anyone else anything. We leave the car far from the theater so we don't have to pay for a parking space. If it's raining or snowing, Pete offers to let me off at the door, but I can tell he'll feel better if I go with him while he finds a spot, so we share the walk too. Inside the theater Pete will hold my hand when I get scared if I ask him. He puts my hand firmly on his knee and covers it completely with his own hand. His knee never twitches. After a

---

[1]Swedish director Ingmar Bergman—best known for the starkness and seriousness of his works—directed this 1960 satiric comedy.

[2]Catherine Deneuve plays the role of a prostitute in this sensual 1967 movie by Spanish film director Luis Buñuel.

[3]*The Sorrow and the Pity* was a 1972 documentary by Marcel Ophuls about France during the Nazi occupation. *Coming Home* was a film starring Jon Voight about Vietnam Veterans and his returning home.

while, when the scary part is past, he loosens his hand slightly and I know that is a signal to take mine away. He sits companionably close, letting his jacket just touch my sweater, but he does not infringe. He thinks I ought to know he is there if I need him.

6   One night, after *The China Syndrome*,[4] I asked Pete if he wouldn't like to stay for a second drink, even though it was past midnight. He thought a while about that, considering my offer from all possible angles, but finally he said no. Relationships today, he said, have a tendency to move too quickly.

7   Sam likes movies that are entertaining. By that he means movies that Will Jones in the *Minneapolis Tribune* loved and either *Time* or *Newsweek* rather liked; also movies that do not have sappy love stories, are not musicals, do not have subtitles, and will not force him to think. He does not go to movies to think. He, liked *California Suite* and *The Seduction of Joe Tynan*,[5] though the plots, he said, could have been zippier. He saw it all coming too far in advance, and that took the fun out. He doesn't like to know what is going to happen. "I just want my brain to be tickled," he says. It is very hard for me to pick out movies for Sam.

8   When Sam takes me to the movies, he pays for everything. He thinks that's what a man ought to do. But I buy my own popcorn, because he doesn't approve of it; the grease might smear his flannel slacks. Inside the theater, Sam makes himself comfortable. He takes off his jacket, puts one arm around me, and all during the movie he plays with my hand, stroking my palm, beating a small tattoo on my wrist. Although he watches the movie intently, his body operates on instinct. Once I inclined my head and kissed him lightly just behind his ear. He beat a faster tattoo on my wrist, quick and musical, but he didn't look away from the screen.

9   When Sam takes me home from the movies, he stands outside my door and kisses me long and hard. He would like to come in, he says regretfully, but his steady girlfriend in Duluth wouldn't like it. When the *Tribune* gives a movie four stars, he has to save it to see with her. Otherwise her feelings might be hurt.

10   I go to some movies by myself. On rainy Sunday afternoons I often sneak into a revival house or a college auditorium for old Technicolor musicals. *Kiss Me Kate, Seven Brides for Seven Brothers, Calamity Jane,* and even once, *The Sound of Music.* Wearing saggy jeans so I can prop my feet on the seat in front, I sit toward the rear where no one can see me. I eat large handfuls of popcorn with double butter. Once the movie starts, I feel completely at home. Howard Keel and I are old friends; I grin back at him on the screen. I know the sound tracks by heart. Sometimes when I get really carried away I hum along with Kathryn Grayson, remembering how I once thought I would fill out a formal like that. I am rather glad now I never did. Skirts whirl, feet tap, acrobatic young men perform impossible feats, and then the camera

---

[4]This 1979 movie warned against the dangers of nuclear power plants.
[5]Alan Alda starred in these popular 1979 comedies.

dissolves into a dream sequence I know I can comfortably follow. It is not, thank God, Bergman.

11   If I can't find an old musical, I settle for Hepburn and Tracy, vintage Grant or Gable, on adventurous days Claudette Colbert or James Stewart. Before I buy my ticket I make sure it will all end happily. If necessary, I ask the girl at the box office. I have never seen *Stella Dallas* or *Intermezzo*.[6] Over the years I have developed other peccadilloes: I will, for example, see anything that is redeemed by Thelma Ritter. At the end of *Daddy Long Legs* I wait happily for the scene when Fred Clark, no longer angry, at last pours Thelma a convivial drink. They smile at each other, I smile at them, I feel they are smiling at me. In the movies I go to by myself, the men and women always like each other.

Writing Log/Journal Assignment

Consider the sort of films that you have seen throughout your life; how did those who accompanied you to the movies determine what sort of film you watched? Did it make any difference if you went with a group of friends, your family, or a love interest? Why? Why not?

Individual and Collaborative Considerations

1. Discuss the basic "cinematypes" the author identifies in her essay. What relationship do you see between Toth's various escorts and the films they like to watch?
2. What effect does the author's reference to specific movies have on her readers?
3. How does Toth use classification and description to develop this essay? In what way does this rhetorical strategy help her to organize her material?
4. What is the basic tone of Toth's composition, and how does it suit the overall objective of her essay?
5. When is Toth "completely at home" at the cinema?

Writing Activities

1. Compose an essay wherein you group or classify people and movie "types" based on personal experience and observation. A starting point for this assignment might be your initial response to the theme of "cinematypes" from the Writing Log/Journal Assignment.
2. How is popular culture portrayed in different types of modern movies? Select at least two recent movies that represent different "types" of film

---

[6]Two tearjerkers made in the 1930s.

and write a comparative essay in which you analyze the relationship between the movie "type" and its treatment of popular culture. Before you begin, you may want to focus yourself a bit by clearly defining what you mean by "popular culture" (e.g., media, music, fashion, fads).

❋

Screwball Noir

Bill Swanson

Bill Swanson, among other subjects, teaches film classes at South Puget Sound Community College in Olympia, Washington, where he is also adviser of the international students. He has coedited two books with Michael Nagler, *Wives and Husbands: Twenty Short Stories about Marriage* and *Stolen Moments: Twenty Stories about Desire,* and is currently coauthoring a college reader focusing on cultural literacy. He has always wanted to write an article with the word "screwball" in the title and finally seized the opportunity.

1   **M**artin Scorsese's *After Hours* and Jonathan Demme's *Something Wild* represent a new style of filmmaking that emerged in the 1980's. The aesthetics of these films—and some forty others directed in this decade by David Lynch, Susan Seidelman, Alan Rudolph, Alex Cox, Bill Forsyth, Albert Brooks, Jim Jarmusch, among others—are based upon post-modern pastiche, a self-conscious genre mixing that brings together black humor, screwball dialogue, and cinematic parody, mixed together with a cool irony that combines Brechtian alienation, counter-cultural satire and the deadpan put-on of the Theater of the Absurd. These films are a reflection of the era that produced them—the era when young white professionals with MBA's and a gleam of larceny in their eyes ruled the land (or, at least, wanted to). These films—like their often maladroit central characters—are simultaneously sophisticated and innocent; they are also technologically advanced, aesthetically eclectic, ethically confused and politically ambiguous. They capture the *zeitgeist* of yuppie zealotry, Reaganomic nihilism and baby-boomer anxiety. I will outline the characteristics of this genre, discuss these two films in some detail and suggest some possible implications on the direction of film in the nineties.

2   When the Iran-Contra scandal broke into the news in 1986, *Something Wild,* a film directed by Jonathan Demme, had just arrived in theatres. Ronald Reagan and the whole cast of characters involved in the arms-for-hostages

scandal were caught up in a plot that might have been pitched to a producer by an ambitious agent as *"Mr. Smith Goes to Washington* meets *The Big Sleep"* or *"All the President's Men* meets *Chinatown."* On the witness stand at John Poindexter's trial, the president, trying to recall the events of the early eighties was as tortured as Gregory Peck had been in *Spellbound,* trying to recall whether or not he had murdered his brother. In short, Demme's film had to compete against news events that were as implausible as a badly written film. *Something Wild* and *After Hours,* like many other films of the eighties, met this challenge by taking on a new style of story-telling, a new way of creating filmic reality—a style labeled by film historian Jack Ellis as **Screwball Noir.** These films represent a fresh departure from the more predictable methods employed in commercial blockbusters, a new sensibility finding its own style of expression in the genres of the past.

3   This genre is related to the larger discourse of post-modern theories of culture and criticism that proliferates both within and outside the academic world, and is well illustrated by *After Hours* and *Something Wild.* Postmodernism is a word that appears in so many areas of discourse that it now appears nearly impossible to define it in any concise way. In the general area of aesthetics and cultural criticism *it seems to represent a growing consensus that there no longer is a cultural consensus.* The explosion of information and forms in electronic communication, the nearly unlimited access to all form of cultural expression from the past, the de-centering effect of academic specialization and proliferation of forms of criticism, the commodification of every tangible and intangible aspect of public and private life, the endless demand of all forms of media for new product, the fragmentation of cultural transmission into millions of commercials, sound bites, re-reruns, paperbacks, radio stations, CD's, newspapers, computer networks, comic books, trade journals, Sony walkmen, headsets for jogging, academic publications, tabloids, magazines, talk-radio, TV news, political ads, cable and satellite television, school teachers, professors, evangelists, salesmen, spin doctors, and annual conferences that all compete for our attention simultaneously twenty-four hours a day, combine to create a cultural condition that—like Yaweh of the Old Testament—can't be named. So instead, the word "postmodernism,"—a thirteen-letter tetragrammaton—has been devised to refer to an on-going phenomenon that we have all experienced but are too confused or overwhelmed to describe.

4   Jean-François Lyotard, author of *The Post-Modern Condition,* for example, suggests that narratives are the adhesive that hold a culture together. This was true especially for primitive cultures who could pass on their collective knowledge to each generation through the oral tradition. In the post-modern world there is no unifying narrative—except for the development and methods of science which eradicate all other narratives. So a post-modern film shows us characters who are caught up in the world of multiple narratives and in the case of these two films the audience experiences the anxiety of the loss of narrative by trying to follow the illogic of the plot itself. The plot becomes just a mix of various kinds of stories.

5   The mix of techniques is part of the pastiche effect so typical of post-modern works. The films replicate the disorientation that is created by the random mixture of cultures and media. Our everyday life consists of improbable and bizarre juxtapositions. The ordinary sequence of narrative cause and effect now seems too contrived and orderly. The world is now experienced as not so much chaotic as layered by multiple forms of order. For example, when I was in college, my friends and I would sometimes have the TV on with the sound off during parties. The music from the stereo and the pictures on the TV screen and the conversations at the party would overlap, creating unforeseen effects that were simultaneously humorous, strange and banal. It's like watching a music video now. The images, sounds and words pass by so quickly you don't have time to think about what they mean. You stand back, agog at the speed of it all.

6   Screwball Noir began in the late seventies / early eighties with films like *Eraserhead* (David Lynch, 1978), *Melvin and Howard* (Jonathan Demme, 1980), *Modern Romance* (Albert Brooks, 1981), *Smithereens* (Susan Seidelman, 1982), *The King of Comedy* (Martin Scorsese, 1983), *Local Hero* (Bill Forsyth, 1983), and *Valley Girl* (Martha Coolidge, 1983). These films represent a post-modern consciousness that looks upon film history as a warehouse of images that can be brought up at any time and utilized in new narrative frameworks. By now so many films of all types—westerns, horror, sci-fi, romantic comedy, detective—have been made that the genres seemed to have reached an endpoint of creative exhaustion. Even realism has been stylized in so many ways that when filmmakers such as Martin Scorsese, Woody Allen and Steven Spielberg make films in black and white (*Raging Bull, Manhattan*, and *Schindler's List*), the films come across as more arty than realistic. Their very need to appear authentic makes them seem even more artificial. The post-modern filmmaker now relies on reference to other films as a way to make statements about actual social reality that we experience outside the theatre. The Screwball Noir label is a shorthand way to refer to this method that puts together a film as a *pastiche* of earlier styles, methods, images and techniques; the shadowy and morally ambiguous world of Film Noir has been spliced together with the giddy, sophisticated humor of the Screwball Comedy. The two styles are an unlikely combination since they represent antithetical moods, themes and artistic intentions.

ORIGINS: THE DETECTIVE STORY AND FILM NOIR

Down these mean streets a man must
go who is not himself mean, who is
neither tarnished nor afraid.

RAYMOND CHANDLER, "THE SIMPLE ART
OF MURDER"

7   The detective story was invented by Edgar Allan Poe in the 1840's. His first stories in this genre—"Murders of the Rue Morgue," "The Purloined Let-

ter," and "The Gold Bug"—established the basic conventions of the genre: a high-minded and cerebral detective uses his powers of observation and ratiocination (Poe's term) to solve crimes that have baffled the police. The detective sees and understands things that elude ordinary police officers and (by implication) ordinary readers. Detectives are ingenious crusaders against crime and injustice that employ the rational methods of science and logic in order to understand the chain of cause and effect that leads to crime.

8   The detective story combines two elements of American culture that have made it continuously popular. It is consistent with our Puritan tradition, which suggests that evil exists even in the most banal of circumstances and that, especially where you least expect it, duplicitous satanic forces are loose in the world, and strenuous efforts must be made to eradicate them. The detective is often not a police officer (a paid functionary of the state) but a lone wolf, a self-reliant hero, who sees the true nature of crime and is willing to *do something about it*. Detectives are shrewd in the ways of the world; they are incorruptible; they are not easily deceived. They work for little money or no money at all because, after all, virtue is its own reward. Like those seventeenth-century divines who sailed for the New World (and contemporary television evangelists) they are ready to do battle with Satan anywhere in the world. Detectives, however, rarely display any overtly religious attitudes. Part of the implicit irony of detective stories derives from our knowledge that detectives do not *appear* virtuous.

9   Sam Spade (*The Maltese Falcon*, 1940) and Philip Marlowe (*Murder My Sweet*, 1944; *The Big Sleep*, 1946) are archetypal Film Noir detectives. They don't live on inherited wealth but in cheap apartments on the seedy side of town. Spade, like one of Dashiell Hammett's other detectives, Nick Charles, plies his trade in San Francisco. Nick Charles, though, represents the whimsical lifestyle of a Nob Hill dilettante, who dabbles in crime solving for a hobby. He is in the British tradition of Sherlock Holmes, Lord Peter Whimsey and Miss Marple—a clever and perspicacious observer who uses reasoning to deduce who the wrong-doer is. These detectives represent the triumph of mind over brawn. Sam Spade, on the other hand, is a denizen of the Tenderloin, a former gumshoe who has had to always work for a living. He represents the power of will over circumstance. He's a stoic, not a dandy. Philip Marlowe, similarly, inhabits the side of Los Angeles that is a million miles from Hollywood. When he goes into a bar for a drink, he runs into floozies and stevedores and grifters. This is the City of Angels, but the angels are watching over the junkyard of the American Dream. Marlowe isn't just up against crime; he's up against tinsel town fakery, charlatans, and wealthy drug addicts who can get by on their inheritance. Marlowe resembles Spade except for Marlowe's gift for gab. Spade's use of language is strictly functional; Marlowe enjoys the rough banter of the barroom and the taxicab. He's a wiseguy who let's you know he's not going to be taken in by anyone.

10   Both these private eyes are loners who would be disinclined to stick their noses into other people's business except that they need the cash; it's just their job. They don't really want to save the world—you'd have to be a *sap* to believe that was possible—they just want to pay their rent and have

enough left over to afford a bottle of good whiskey. This ironic image of the reluctant hero who seems to refuse the call to heroism allows a detective story to conceal its moralistic intentions which if they were overtly expressed would come across as preachy and didactic.

11   These detectives are methodical, scientific and practical. They are doers, not thinkers. In *The Maltese Falcon*, Spade shows his disdain for pseudo-intellectuals (Gutman), arty-types (Joel Cairo) and punks (Wilmer). Spade and Marlowe are pragmatic and down-to-earth. They perceive a problem (a crime has been committed); they a make accurate observations (they identify the clues); they propose an hypothesis; they carry out an experiment; they reach a conclusion based on objective facts. Thus the detective combines those two elements of American culture that are often seen in opposition: the moral fervor to make right the wrongs of this world and the hard-headed practical knowledge to make it happen. The detective hero thus represents a reconciliation of religion and science in a popular art form. The audience experiences the vicarious thrills of watching criminal acts performed and then sees justice done—or at least violence. In the early tales, say those by Poe and Doyle, it was sufficient for the criminal to be *detected* and presumably put on trial, but in the detective stories since the late 1920's the hero has also come to play the role of judge, jury and executioner. In *The Big Sleep* Marlowe is expected to kill the hit-man Canino and not bring him in for trial. These films seem to provide a catharsis for audiences who want to see justice administered by swift means without any fancy talk about rights, presumed innocence or civil liberties. These guys live in a tough world, and they know it. Like Philip Marlowe says, "So many guns around and so few brains."

12   Film Noir emerged in the 1940's in such films as *The Maltese Falcon* (John Huston, 1940), *Murder My Sweet* (Edward Dmytryck, 1944), *The Big Sleep* (Howard Hawks, 1946), and *Out of the Past* (Jacques Tourneur, 1947) and represents a dark, urban world of crime, murder and betrayal. These films captured the disillusionment, the moral anguish that followed in the wake of World War II. They reveal, in stark black and white contrast, the existential dread and uncertainty of a world forced to contemplate the Holocaust, the Cold War and the threat of nuclear war. Not that any of these specific issues are dealt with in the films, but they reflect the feeling of moral ambiguity and the threat of sudden violence that hung as a backdrop to the whole era.

13   The style had its roots in the German Expressionist films of the 1920's, and were, in fact, made by emigrés who had come to Hollywood to escape from the Nazi regime. Directors like Robert Siodmack (*The Killers*, 1944; *Criss Cross*, 1949), Billy Wilder (*Double Indemnity*, 1944; *Sunset Boulevard*, 1950), Otto Preminger (*Laura*, 1944; *Fallen Angel*, 1946) and Fritz Lang (*Scarlet Street*, 1945; *The Big Heat*, 1953) had their start in German film; there were, as well, many technicians who brought the art direction, lighting and editing methods to Hollywood from their experience in German studios. German Expressionist film used the physical objects photographed on the screen to capture subjective and nightmarish experiences that suggested the power of irrational and powerful states of mind. In the American Film Noir period of

the forties this meant that the urban landscape—New York especially—became not merely a large city but a dark, rainswept dreamscape in which flashing neon lights competed with headlights and police sirens as lonely and frightened individuals looked for escape from a steel and cement labyrinth of unfriendly streets. In *Scarlet Street,* for example, Edward G. Robinson—as Chris Cross—portrays a small-time embezzler who sees a woman getting beat up on the street at night and rushes to her aid. The woman, called "Lazylegs,"—played by Joan Bennet—plays upon his feelings and sexual frustrations until by the end of the film she has fleeced him of his money and made him into a muttering and guilt-ridden madman. The plot is melodramatic; the conflict between good and evil exaggerated; but the film is a masterpiece of cinematic style. The imagery draws us into a strange, high-contrast world in which the weird angles of the skyscrapers cast gloomy shadows over hidden alleys that conceal hidden crimes and hidden motives.

14   Filmmakers in the eighties looked back to this stylized universe of black and white images and drew upon it in order to reflect upon the moral ambiguities of the decade that brought us white-collar crime—the S & L debacle, Michael Milken, Ivan Boesky, The Keating Five—and high-tech clandestine operations that involved the CIA, off-the-shelf-Bahamian-corporations, Manuel Noriega, the Sultan of Brunei, numbered Swiss bank accounts, Special Prosecutors, Congressional investigations, and innumerable resignations and denials. It was the era of the Yuppie, those curiously amoral young men and women in expensive suits who went to the Big City to make their first million before they were forty. Their aspirations and behavior created the situations that made raw material for many of the best films of the decade. The Yuppie, for whatever his or her moral failings, never cast quite as sinister a shadow, as, say, the Gangster or the Outlaw. There was, in fact, something distinctly comic about the combination of outsized ambition and feckless naiveté in these new filmic types. This partly explains why Screwball Comedy also became an influence.

THE LIGHTER SIDE OF CHAOS: SCREWBALL COMEDY

15   In 1934, Franklin Delano Roosevelt was in his second year of office, Scott Fitzgerald published *Tender Is the Night,* Cole Porter wrote "Anything Goes," Luigi Pirandello won the Nobel Prize for Literature, Hitler and Mussolini met for the first time in Venice and two new comedies appeared from Hollywood, *The Thin Man* (W. S. Van Dyke) and *It Happened One Night* (Frank Capra), establishing a new style later dubbed Screwball Comedy. These films made use of the newly developed microphone to bring verbal wit and repartée to the screen. The dialogue between Nick and Nora Charles (William Powell and Myrna Loy) in *The Thin Man* is subtly provocative, quick and smart. No matter what is going on around them—a police interrogation, a party, gunfire—they maintain a bright sense of detachment; they seem

primarily concerned with each other's response to what is going on rather than getting caught up in the events themselves. They don't take anything very seriously, least of all themselves. Nick's avocation as a private eye is treated as an amusing hobby more than a serious confrontation with evil-doers. Myrna Loy represents the epitome of the female leads in these films: elegant but unflappable, sophisticated but not haughty, witty but not frivolous. Other actresses in these films include Claudette Colbert, Katharine Hepburn, Jean Arthur, Carol Lombard, Ginger Rogers and Irene Dunne. The label "screwball" creates a slightly distorted image of the female characters since it suggests a certain degree of dim-wittedness, but that is far from the predominant source of the humor. Even when the characters are slightly wacky—as those portrayed by Carol Lombard in *My Man Godfrey* or Katharine Hepburn in *Bringing Up Baby,* the playful disregard for conventions and impudent irresponsibility give the characters a sense of high-spir-ited fun that makes mere intelligence seem quite dull by comparison. In *Bringing Up Baby,* Katharine Hepburn plays an accident-prone woman who uses her improbable bad luck to undermine the arid fastidiousness of Cary Grant, who plays the role of a bespectacled paleontologist who is more interested in dinosaur bones than in women. In the end lunacy triumphs over academia, and the film makes us delighted to see the professor finally wise up.

16   The women in Screwball Comedies represent a subversive sense of humor that disarms the world by not taking it seriously. In *It Happened One Night,* Claudette Colbert plays a spoiled debutante on the run from her father and marriage. When Clark Gable, a tough-talking reporter who has found her out, attempts to show her how to hitch-hike and fails to get a single car to stop, she blithely steps to the side of the road and pretends to adjust the snaps on the garter belt to her nylons. The first passing farmer in a Model T slams on his brake in order to offer a ride. It's a comic moment of ingenu-ity and gentle oneupsmanship. She knows more about the world than he thinks she knows; she's not as "screwball" as she seems. This sense of self-possession behind a feminine mask is one of the things that makes these kinds of characters seem ahead of their times. These women know what the roles and the rules are, but they find a way to do as they please. In *Sylvia Scarlet* (George Cukor, 1936), Katharine Hepburn plays the daughter of a circus performer wanted by the law and disguises herself as a boy in order to aid in their escape. Even in her disguise she manages to seduce Cary Grant, who gives a sly performance as a sexually ambiguous acrobat. This film was a little too much of a gender-bender for its own time and flopped at the box office, but in recent years it has had a revival because of its play-fulness regarding sexual roles. In *The Awful Truth* (Leo McCarey, 1937), Irene Dunne plays a woman who divorces her husband (again, Cary Grant) so that he will have to woo her back again; in *His Girl Friday* (Howard Hawks, 1940), Rosalind Russell plays the redoubtable newspaper reporter Hildy Johnson who almost chooses a cozy domestic life as the wife-to-be of an insurance salesman (Ralph Bellamy) but through the manipulations of her

ex-husband (Cary Grant) she sees that her life is her work and manages to solve a murder case and expose the mayor's political corruption in the process; in *The Philadelphia Story* (George Cukor, 1940), Katharine Hepburn plays an upper-class Philadelphian named Tracy Lord who manages to spend the eve of her high-society wedding getting drunk, offending her husband-to-be, and falling in love with a newspaper reporter (James Stewart), and in the morning she re-marries her first husband, C. K. Dexter Haven—played by the ubiquitous Cary Grant. In Screwball Comedies the men are like puppeteers who suddenly discover that their own hands are attached to strings and that those strings are in the hands of a woman. And in these films the woman is a shrewd and canny competitor who is full of playful irony, unconventional attitudes and liberating wit. These are the very qualities that found resurgence in the Screwball Noir films of the Eighties. The Yuppie met his foil in the unpredictable alliances with women who took a somewhat different path through the social jungle.

SCREWBALL NOIR: TWO EXAMPLES

17   Two films, *Something Wild* (Jonathan Demme, 1986) and *After Hours* (Martin Scorsese, 1985), represent the defining characteristics of Screwball Noir. In *Something Wild*, Charley Driggs (Jeff Daniels), a newly promoted regional manager for an investment firm, skips out on his check at lunch and is spotted by a young woman in a black wig who calls herself Lulu (Melanie Griffith). She threatens to turn him in and then offers him a ride in her car; disarmed, amused and confused, Charley accepts. This opening scene reveals some of Demme's film technique. When we first see Lulu, she is reading a biography of Frida Kahlo, the Mexican surrealist painter who was married to Diego Rivera and had a love affair with Leon Trotsky. This allusion suggests Lulu's connection to the artistic and political underground. The name Lulu and her black, helmet-style wig are an allusion to the Lulu portrayed by Louise Brooks in *Pandora's Box* (G. W. Pabst, 1929), one of the key works of German Expressionism. Lulu in the silent film seduces a married and prosperous German businessman and brings about his downfall. Melanie Griffith's Lulu is also like Lola in the *Blue Angel* (Josef von Sternberg, 1929)—out to bring down a bourgeois male by making him her sexual pawn and by exposing his hypocrisy. In *Something Wild*, when Lulu sees Charley walk out without paying she chides him for it. She enjoys making him see his own dark side since he seems so determined to deny it. Lulu is the repressed feminine, a Jungian shadow figure, a trickster—call her what you will—but she has a zany irresponsibility that both mirrors Charley's darker impulses and contains the possibility of his transformation into something a little more human.

18   These films might as well be dubbed "American Surrealism," or as Jean Baudrillard, the French social theorist, might say, *hyperrealism*; that is a form of simulated reality that draws upon and uses other forms of simulated

reality. Luis Buñuel, the Spanish surrealist, provides the spirit of this movement. He also mixed the serious and the comic, acts of cruelty and moments of humor in films like *Viridiana* (1961), *The Exterminating Angel* (1962), *Tristana* (1970), *The Discreet Charm of the Bourgeoisie* (1972), *Phantom of Liberty* (1974) and *That Obscure Object of Desire* (1977). The mixture of the fantastic and the real suggests the surrealist's eye for the marvelous, the weird intermixture of the artificial and the actual. Buñuel slits a woman's eyeball at the beginning of *Le Chien Andalou* (1924); Kyle McLachlan finds an ear in *Blue Velvet* (1986); Griffin Dunne as Paul in *After Hours* leafs through Marcy's (Rosanna Arquette) book on burn therapy and, later, scans her body for scars after she has committed suicide, and thereby gets the audience to join him in a combination of voyeurism and necrophilia. In Screwball Noir characters often find themselves in situations without knowing what the rules are. Paul has come to see Marcy because he is attracted to her, presumably wants to go to bed with her. (She noticed him reading Henry Miller's *Tropic of Cancer* in a coffee shop in the same way Charley noticed Lulu reading Frida Kahlo's biography in *Something Wild*.) When he thinks she may be badly scarred from a burn accident his lusty feelings make him uneasy. What should he do? Continue to pursue her? Let on that he knows about her burns? But he doesn't know for sure that she is burned. Forget the whole thing and leave? He is forced to think about why he is there in the first place. Does he want sex, conversation, a social date? A few hours later after she had committed suicide, he has to decide whether or not to lift the blanket and look at her body to see if she really does have bad burn scars. This would seem to be a prurient bit of curiosity, yet an understandable one given the tension created by the earlier scene. The interesting thing is *the film makes the audience want him to lift the blanket.* Furthermore, when she is shown to have no scars, the question then seems trivial, and a shallow and vain consideration since the woman has now taken her life for other reasons which no one will ever know. The woman remains a complete mystery. He doesn't know who she was, how she felt or why she did what she did. How could he explain all this to the police? He does the minimum thing required: he calls the police and leaves a sign which says, "Dead Body" with an arrow pointing in the direction of the bedroom. The effect is tragic, unsettling, perplexing and comic. It is the absurdist humor of Luis Buñuel, Samuel Beckett and Harold Pinter translated into the breezy social environment of the Reaganesque Eighties where morality and personal responsibility are apparently nothing more than memories from the cultural past.

19   In *Something Wild*, when Charley hops in the convertible with Lulu, he confides to her, "I'm a rebel. In '81, I went for long-term muni's." Moments later his beeper goes off, and she throws it out the window. Before the day is through Charley has failed to return to work, run out on another restaurant tab, helped rob a liquor store, spent the afternoon having sex in a motel room and gotten himself handcuffed. The following day, Charley and Lulu bribe a car salesman with stolen money and buy Charley a blue leisure suit at a

second-hand store. Lulu sheds her black wig and informs Charley that her real name is Audrey Henkel, and she picked him up so he could accompany her to her high school reunion. When they stop to visit Lulu's mom Peaches, Charley pretends to be Lulu's new husband. The movie up to this point has had the comic feeling of a Screwball Comedy, but at the high school reunion Lulu meets her first husband Ray Sinclair (Ray Liotta) who has just gotten out of prison. He's jealous, violent and psychopathic; he's a character right out of Film Noir who in the forties would have been played by Jack Palance or Richard Widmark or Dan Duryea. He's not bad looking, but, as we soon see, remains a thug at heart.

20   From then on the film takes a much more sinister turn. Ray beats up Charley and takes Lulu with him. Charley manages to get Lulu back when he follows them to a restaurant, then simply asks her to leave with him after he notices police officers sitting in a booth nearby. Ray is stymied and gets stuck with the check. The rest of the film is mostly chase and culminates in a vicious fight scene in which Charley kills Ray. This is more than a surprise ending. It is entirely inconsistent with the tone and structure of the first half of the film. In an earlier era this might have been ascribed to inept screen-writing, but this film is too full of knowing cues to have arrived at this structure by accident. The film ends where it began—at the cafe where Charley walked out on his bill. Audrey, who disappeared following the encounter with Ray, magically re-appears dressed in a smart checkered dress and hat, looking happy, and glad to see Charley. The film returns to the traditional comedic ending—reconciliation, love and, from the look of things, marriage. Both Charley and Audrey have come full circle from the beginning of the film. He has abandoned his artificial business self, a fabricated corporate image which made it easier for him to fit in at work but alienated him from himself. She has escaped from the prison of her own past. She is no longer the bad girl from the high school in Pennsylvania, or Ray's wife. She has shed her negative identity and become a person of her own making in a black-and-white outfit. Lulu had black hair and black dress; Audrey had blonde hair and white dress. Her final outfit is a black-and-white ensemble that makes her look like a *Vogue* model; the new colors announce her new sense of balance and composure.

21   In *After Hours* a diffident young word processor named Paul tries to pick up a young woman reading *Tropic of Cancer* in a Manhattan coffee shop. This opening, like that in *Something Wild*, signals the beginning of a descent to the underworld. This young woman, Marco, like Lulu is a post-modern Persephone who will take young Paul to the Soho netherworld where he will find himself lost among the shades of a night world he has hardly imagined. Paul is just trying to pick up a girl; he gets her number and later that evening, a little bored from channel surfing and being alone, he calls her up and she invites him to come down to her place. En route, his money flies out the window of the cab. Arriving at Marcy's flat he finds her roommate Kiki, clad in a leather skirt and black bra working on a paper maché sculpture that

resembles Edvard Munch's "The Scream." The name Kiki connects her with the American surrealist painter and photographer Man Ray who had a lover name Kiki and used her as a subject in many of his photographs.

22   This film, like *Something Wild,* has many allusions to the art world and makes ironic references to the contrast between the Modernist high culture of the early twentieth century and the Post-modernist pop culture of the present. The very first scene in *After Hours* has Paul showing one of his young co-workers how to use a computer. The young man tells Paul his goal is to start his own literary magazine and publish it himself. He's talking like a young Ezra Pound, but Paul makes no acknowledgment of his words; he's blandly oblivious to such thoughts.

23   The plot of *After Hours* nearly defies synopsis. Paul's adventure in Lower Manhattan is as confusing and frenetic as Leopold Bloom's visit to Night-town in *Ulysses.* He encounters several women and men who fail to help him in his quest to get back home. First, there is Marcy who seems to be interested in him but—inexplicably—commits suicide, Kiki who invites him to a sado-masochistic rock club, Julie with a bee-hive hair-do who thinks and dresses like a go-go dancer from the sixties, Gail who drives a Mr. Frosty truck and offers him a ride home, only to turn on him in the street and accuse him of burglary, the gay guy who brings Paul to his apartment but can't understand Paul's story and finally Joan, the Peggy Lee fan, who saves him from the mob by covering him with paper maché and turning him into a statue. Paul, like Odysseus, seems to have a spell cast upon him and no matter what he does the uncaring fates prevent him from breaking away from this nightmarish urban landscape. The women he meets are certainly as offbeat as any in Screwball Comedy, but they are not as carefree. They seem disconnected and estranged; their impulses are not derived from a sense of play but from desperation and fear. Paul goes from one frustrating encounter to another until finally his life is threatened. He somehow becomes like so many of Hitchcock's heroes a wrongly accused man, alone and in flight in a strange world he cannot understand.

24   Coincidence is a conventional feature of fictional narrative. Rather than avoid such plot contrivances as some realist films do, *After Hours* makes use of many implausible coincidences. Paul loses twenty dollars, then sees twenty dollars stuck to the statue; the subway fares change the very night Paul has no money; Marcy is Tom-the-bartender's girlfriend; Julie has one of Kiki's bagel paperweights; a news article describing a man in exactly Paul's situation is found stuck to Paul's arm; the cash register in the Terminal Bar breaks down just as the bartender offers to loan Paul money; the barten-der's apartment is in one of the apartment buildings that has been vandal-ized; Neil and Pepé, the burglars, are also friend's of Kiki's and decide to buy her sculpture; Julie is an artist who can make a wanted poster of Paul, and she works in a copy center; Paul runs into another sculptor, Joan, in the Club Berlin and she does exactly the same kind of sculpture that Kiki does; she hides Paul in a screaming figure just like Kiki's; Neil and Pepé steal Paul and thus save him from the mob; Paul falls out of their van just as they reach

the front door of his company. These coincidences call attention to the artificiality of the story. They would normally add coherence and the sense of cause and effect in a storyline. In this film though coincidence seems to rage out of control; synchronicity falls upon Paul like a curse so that his every action seems to reverberate back on him. He is like a billiard ball on a very small table: he keeps getting hit over and over by the same balls. The irony here is that coincidence serves to de-structure the plot so that the inner logic of events seems to have a perverse logic of its own; Paul seems caught up in something much larger than himself, a pattern of events that serve no other purpose but to frustrate his efforts to get home. He tries to explain this to the gay guy who picks him up. He tries to make sense out of the evening's events by narrating them to another person, but the gay guy is not interested and sees Paul's whole monologue as some unexplainable digression. Paul's explanation gets him neither help nor sympathy. His narrative can't make sense out of his experience, not even to himself.

25   Both *After Hours* and *Something Wild* are about the mixture of naiveté and fear that make white upwardly mobile young professionals vulnerable in the amoral, essentially nihilistic, social climate that makes their laissez-faire economic world possible. When Charley says he is a rebel because he invested in "muni's" in 1981, he's revealing the distance between his abstract world of numbers and computations, the world in which quantitative analysis is the only source of value, and the actual world on the street where Lulu takes real risks acting out her fantasies.

26   In *After Hours,* Paul finds himself in the unreal world in which all the private lives have become encompassed by media images; he can't seem to locate any baseline reality, any norms of communication that would make it possible for him to figure out what's going on. He's like a man who has entered the world we see on television or in movies. Life itself has become a fabrication, an imitation of life. When he finally escapes, he is encapsulated in a statue, a work of art. He has spent the whole night trying to understand the world around him but he has been defeated by the sheer proliferation of coded rituals and behaviors. The film ends with Paul's return to his desk, shabby, dust-covered and exhausted. He's come full circle, but he hasn't really gone anywhere. The camera circles him and seems to spin round and round out of control as the credits roll. For all the comedy and absurd moments in this film, we come away with that noirish sense of fatigue and moral ennui.

27   On the other hand, in *Something Wild* Charley experiences a displacement of self, a transformation of identity, that comes about as a result of Lulu's efforts to initiate him into her unconventional world. Lulu puts Charley in situations that force him to betray his values; her purpose is to make him see that he never believed in those values to begin with. She sees that Charley was only pretending to be the Regional Manager for a large corporation, and a responsible, goal-oriented middle-class college graduate with his eye on the future. Lulu is a trickster who gets him to shed his old identity with the same aplomb that she convinces him to wear handcuffs in bed and escape

from a bill in a restaurant by taking a running leap into the back of a convertible. Lulu frees him from the tyranny of unconscious conformity; her screwball antics have a liberatory effect. They let loose the repression that makes Charley finally come to a definition of himself that allows him to assert some identity, to make real choices.

28   Films construct realities by using and referring to the conventions of films from the past. This helps to make films popular and familiar for audiences. It is also a source of irony for filmmakers who play with audience expectations in order to make satiric criticism of actuality and to call attention to the artificiality of the films themselves. Films of this type continue the Modernist concern with art that reflects on the nature of art. They also reflect the post-modernist concern with the vast effects created by mass media and popular culture. This style could be interpreted as a way for filmmakers to work with the economic constraints of the film business and still produce works that are critical and transgressive in relation to mainstream consumer culture; or they could be interpreted as just another "new and improved" form of a commodity that must continue to defamiliarize itself in order to get audience attention in an increasingly media-dense and cynical environment.

Writing Log/Journal Assignments

1. Make a list of movies, television shows, and works of fiction that have had a significant impact on you and put them into categories. Try to describe how the categories affected you differently.
2. Reflect on what you can learn from viewing films from the past. What can they tell us about the era in which they were produced? Of what value is this knowledge to us now?

Individual and Collaborative Considerations

1. Why do some people get pleasure from reading or viewing certain types of stories over and over again? Think of genres like romance novels, horror movies, science fiction, and detective stories.
2. After reading Swanson's essay, what would you say "post-modernism" is?
3. Think of some recent films that did not seem realistic at all but still seemed to connect with you or audiences in general. Try to explain how the film managed to communicate its ideas.
4. Make your own personal list of "The Best Five Films Ever Made" and compare it with someone else's. Determine what criteria you have in common for selecting films. Define the differences in your tastes.
5. Think of a movie that reminds you of other movies that you have seen and explain the connections.

Writing Activities

1. Write a short review of a recent film that includes a discussion of other films by the same director or that include some of the actors.
2. Write an essay in which you decide whether or not films are really "escapist entertainment" or the most influential art form ever invented.

Hollywood Locusts

Nathanael West

Nathanael West was a pseudonym of Nathan Wallenstein Weinstein, an author from New York whose work did not attract too much acclaim during his lifetime, yet met with critical recognition soon after his death. His works, often satiric, tend to dwell on the frailties of the human condition. West's books include *The Dream Life of Balso Snell* (1931), *Miss Lonelyhearts* (1933), and *A Cool Million* (1934). Like many of his contemporaries, West did some script writing in Hollywood. This experience provided him with the insights and grotesque descriptions of the film business—and those associated with it—which would be the basis for his most famous novel, *The Day of the Locust* (1939).

When Tod reached the street, he saw a dozen great violet shafts of light moving across the evening sky in wide crazy sweeps. Whenever one of the fiery columns reached the lowest point of its arc, it lit for a moment the rose-colored domes and delicate minarets of Kahn's Persian Palace Theatre. The purpose of this display was to signal the world premiere of a new picture.

Turning his back on the searchlights, he started in the opposite direction, toward Homer's place. Before he had gone very far, he saw a clock that read a quarter past six and changed his mind about going back just yet. He might as well let the poor fellow sleep for another hour and kill some time by looking at the crowds.

When still a block from the theatre, he saw an enormous electric sign that hung over the middle of the street. In letters ten feet high he read that—

MR. KAHN A PLEASURE DOME DECREED

Although it was still several hours before the celebrities would arrive, thousands of people had already gathered. They stood facing the theatre with their backs toward the gutter in a thick line hundreds of feet long. A big squad of policemen was trying to keep a lane open between the front rank of the crowd and the façade of the theatre.

5   Tod entered the lane while the policeman guarding it was busy with a woman whose parcel had torn open, dropping oranges all over the place. Another policeman shouted for him to get the hell across the street, but he took a chance and kept going. They had enough to do without chasing him. He noticed how worried they looked and how careful they tried to be. If they had to arrest someone, they joked good-naturedly with the culprit, making light of it until they got him around the corner, then they whaled him with their clubs. Only so long as the man was actually part of the crowd did they have to be gentle.

Tod had walked only a short distance along the narrow lane when he began to get frightened. People shouted, commenting on his hat, his carriage, and his clothing. There was a continuous roar of catcalls, laughter and yells, pierced occasionally by a scream. The scream was usually followed by a sudden movement in the dense mass and part of it would surge forward wherever the police line was weakest. As soon as that part was rammed back, the bulge would pop out somewhere else.

The police force would have to be doubled when the stars started to arrive. At the sight of their heroes and heroines, the crowd would turn demoniac. Some little gesture, either too pleasing or too offensive, would start it moving and then nothing but machine guns would stop it. Individually the purpose of its members might simply be to get a souvenir, but collectively it would grab and rend.

A young man with a portable microphone was describing the scene. His rapid, hysterical voice was like that of a revivalist preacher whipping his congregation toward the ecstasy of fits.

"What a crowd, folks! What a crowd! There must be ten thousand excited, screaming fans outside Kahn's Persian tonight. The police can't hold them. Here, listen to them roar."

10   He held the microphone out and those near it obligingly roared for him.

"Did you hear it? It's a bedlam, folks. A veritable bedlam! What excitement! Of all the premieres I've attended, this is the most . . . the most . . . stupendous, folks. Can the police hold them? Can they? It doesn't look so, folks. . . ."

Another squad of police came charging up. The sergeant pleaded with the announcer to stand further back so the people couldn't hear him. His men threw themselves at the crowd. It allowed itself to be hustled and shoved out of habit and because it lacked an objective. It tolerated the police, just as a bull elephant does when he allows a small boy to drive him with a light stick.

Tod could see very few people who looked tough, nor could he see any working men. The crowd was made up of the lower middle classes, every other person one of his torchbearers.

Just as he came near the end of the lane, it closed in front of him with a heave, and he had to fight his way through. Someone knocked his hat off and when he stooped to pick it up, someone kicked him. He whirled around angrily and found himself surrounded by people who were laughing at him. He knew enough to laugh with them. The crowd became sympathetic. A stout woman slapped him on the back, while a man handed him his hat, first brushing it carefully with his sleeve. Still another man shouted for a way to be cleared.

15   By a great deal of pushing and squirming, always trying to look as though he were enjoying himself, Tod finally managed to break into the open. After rearranging his clothes, he went over to a parking lot and sat down on the low retaining wall that ran along the front of it. New groups, whole families, kept arriving. He could see a change come over them as soon as they had become part of the crowd. Until they reached the line, they looked diffident, almost furtive, but the moment they had become part of it, they turned arrogant and pugnacious. It was a mistake to think them harmless curiosity seekers. They were savage and bitter, especially the middle-aged and the old, and had been made so by boredom and disappointment.

All their lives they had slaved at some kind of dull, heavy labor behind desks and counters, in the fields and at tedious machines of all sorts, saving their pennies and dreaming of the leisure that would be theirs when they had enough. Finally that day came. They could draw a weekly income of ten or fifteen dollars. Where else should they go but California, the land of sunshine and oranges?

Once there, they discover that sunshine isn't enough. They get tired of oranges, even of avocado pears and passion fruit. Nothing happens. They don't know what to do with their time. They haven't the mental equipment for leisure, the money nor the physical equipment for pleasure. Did they slave so long just to go to an occasional Iowa picnic? What else is there? They watch the waves come in at Venice. There wasn't any ocean where most of them came from, but after you've seen one wave, you've seen them all. The same is true of the airplanes at Glendale. If only a plane would crash once in a while so that they could watch the passengers being consumed in a "holocaust of flame," as the newspapers put it. But the planes never crash.

Their boredom becomes more and more terrible. They realize that they've been tricked and burn with resentment. Every day of their lives they read the newspapers and went to the movies. Both fed them on lynchings, murder, sex crimes, explosions, wrecks, love nests, fires, miracles, revolutions, wars. This daily diet made sophisticates of them. The sun is a joke. Oranges can't titillate their jaded palates. Nothing can ever be violent enough to make taut their slack minds and bodies. They have been cheated and betrayed. They have slaved and saved for nothing.

Tod stood up. During the ten minutes he had been sitting on the wall, the crowd had grown thirty feet and he was afraid that his escape might be cut off if he loitered much longer. He crossed to the other side of the street and started back.

20   He was trying to figure what to do if he were unable to wake Homer when, suddenly, he saw his head bobbing above the crowd. He hurried

toward him. From his appearance, it was evident that there was something definitely wrong.

Homer walked more than ever like a badly made automaton and his features were set in a rigid, mechanical grin. He had his trousers on over his nightgown and part of it hung out of his open fly. In both of his hands were suitcases. With each step, he lurched to one side then the other, using the suitcases for balance weights.

Tod stopped directly in front of him, blocking his way. "Where're you going?"

"Wayneville," he replied, using an extraordinary amount of jaw movement to get out this single word.

"That's fine. But you can't walk to the station from here. It's in Los Angeles."

25   Homer tried to get around him, but he caught his arm.

"We'll get a taxi. I'll go with you."

The cabs were all being routed around the block because of the preview. He explained this to Homer and tried to get him to walk to the corner.

"Come on, we're sure to get one on the next street."

Once Tod got him into a cab, he intended to tell the driver to go to the nearest hospital. But Homer wouldn't budge, no matter how hard he yanked and pleaded. People stopped to watch them, others turned their heads curiously. He decided to leave him and get a cab.

30   "I'll come right back," he said.

He couldn't tell from either Homer's eyes or expression whether he heard, for they both were empty of everything, even annoyance. At the corner he looked around and saw that Homer had started to cross the street, moving blindly. Brakes screeched and twice he was almost run over, but he didn't swerve or hurry. He moved in a straight diagonal. When he reached the other curb, he tried to get on the sidewalk at a point where the crowd was very thick and was shoved violently back. He made another attempt and this time a policeman grabbed him by the back of the neck and hustled him to the end of the line. When the policeman let go of him, he kept on walking as though nothing had happened.

Tod tried to get over to him, but was unable to cross until the traffic lights changed. When he reached the other side, he found Homer sitting on a bench, fifty or sixty feet from the outskirts of the crowd.

He put his arm around Homer's shoulder and suggested that they walk a few blocks further. When Homer didn't answer, he reached over to pick up one of the valises. Homer held on to it.

"I'll carry it for you," he said, tugging gently.

35   "Thief!"

Before Homer could repeat the shout, he jumped away. It would be extremely embarrassing if Homer shouted thief in front of a cop. He thought of phoning for an ambulance. But then, after all, how could he be sure that Homer was crazy? He was sitting quietly on the bench, minding his own business.

Tod decided to wait, then try again to get him into a cab. The crowd was growing in size all the time, but it would be at least half an hour before it over-ran the bench. Before that happened, he would think of some plan. He moved a short distance away and stood with his back to a store window so that he could watch Homer without attracting attention.

About ten feet from where Homer was sitting grew a large eucalyptus tree and behind the trunk of the tree was a little boy. Tod saw him peer around it with great caution, then suddenly jerk his head back. A minute later he repeated the maneuver. At first Tod thought he was playing hide and seek, then noticed that he had a string in his hand which was attached to an old purse that lay in front of Homer's bench. Every once in a while the child would jerk the string, making the purse hop like a sluggish toad. Its torn lining hung from its iron mouth like a furry tongue and a few uncertain flies hovered over it.

Tod knew the game the child was playing. He used to play it himself when he was small. If Homer reached to pick up the purse, thinking there was money in it, he would yank it away and scream with laughter.

40   When Tod went over to the tree, he was surprised to discover that it was Adore Loomis, the kid who lived across the street from Homer. Tod tried to chase him, but he dodged around the tree, thumbing his nose. He gave up and went back to his original position. The moment he left, Adore got busy with his purse again. Homer wasn't paying any attention to the child, so Tod decided to let him alone.

Mrs. Loomis must be somewhere in the crowd, he thought. Tonight when she found Adore, she would give him a hiding. He had torn the pocket of his jacket and his Buster Brown collar was smeared with grease.

Adore had a nasty temper. The completeness with which Homer ignored both him and his pocketbook made him frantic. He gave up dancing it at the end of the string and approached the bench on tiptoes, making ferocious faces, yet ready to run at Homer's first move. He stopped when about four feet away and stuck his tongue out. Homer ignored him. He took another step forward and ran through a series of insulting gestures.

If Tod had known that the boy held a stone in his hand, he would have interfered. But he felt sure that Homer wouldn't hurt the child and was waiting to see if he wouldn't move because of his pestering. When Adore raised his arm, it was too late. The stone hit Homer in the face. The boy turned to flee, but tripped and fell. Before he could scramble away, Homer landed on his back with both feet, then jumped again.

Tod yelled for him to stop and tried to yank him away. He shoved Tod and went on using his heels. Tod hit him as hard as he could, first in the belly, then in the face. He ignored the blows and continued to stamp on the boy. Tod hit him again and again, then threw both arms around him and tried to pull him off. He couldn't budge him. He was like a stone column.

45   The next thing Tod knew, he was torn loose from Homer and sent to his knees by a blow in the back of the head that spun him sideways. The crowd in front of the theatre had charged. He was surrounded by churning legs

and feet. He pulled himself erect by grabbing a man's coat, then let himself be carried along backwards in a long, curving swoop. He saw Homer rise above the mass for a moment, shoved against the sky, his jaw hanging as though he wanted to scream but couldn't. A hand reached up and caught him by his open mouth and pulled him forward and down.

There was another dizzy rush. Tod closed his eyes and fought to keep upright. He was jostled about in a hacking cross surf of shoulders and backs, carried rapidly in one direction and then in the opposite. He kept pushing and hitting out at the people around him, trying to face in the direction he was going. Being carried backwards terrified him.

Using the eucalyptus tree as a landmark, he tried to work toward it by slipping sideways against the tide, pushing hard when carried away from it and riding the current when it moved toward his objective. He was within only a few feet of the tree when a sudden, driving rush carried him far past it. He struggled desperately for a moment, then gave up and let himself be swept along. He was the spearhead of a flying wedge when it collided with a mass going in the opposite direction. The impact turned him around. As the two forces ground against each other, he was turned again and again, like a grain between millstones. This didn't stop until he became part of the opposing force. The pressure continued to increase until he thought he must collapse. He was slowly pushed into the air. Although relief for his cracking ribs could be gotten by continuing to rise, he fought to keep his feet on the ground. Not being able to touch was an even more dreadful sensation than being carried backwards.

There was another rush, shorter this time, and he found himself in a dead spot where the pressure was less and equal. He became conscious of a terrible pain in his left leg, just above the ankle, and tried to work it into a more comfortable position. He couldn't turn his body, but managed to get his head around. A very skinny boy, wearing a Western Union cap, had his back wedged against his shoulder. The pain continued to grow and his whole leg as high as the groin throbbed. He finally got his left arm free and took the back of the boy's neck in his fingers. He twisted as hard as he could. The boy began to jump up and down in his clothes. He managed to straighten his elbow, by pushing at the back of the boy's head, and so turn half way around and free his leg. The pain didn't grow less.

There was another wild surge forward that ended in another dead spot. He now faced a young girl who was sobbing steadily. Her silk print dress had been torn down the front and her tiny brassiere hung from one strap. He tried by pressing back to give her room, but she moved with him every time he moved. Now and then, she would jerk violently and he wondered if she was going to have a fit. One of her thighs was between his legs. He struggled to get free of her, but she clung to him, moving with him and pressing against him.

50   She turned her head and said, "Stop, stop," to someone behind her.

He saw what the trouble was. An old man, wearing a Panama hat and horn-rimmed glasses, was hugging her. He had one of his hands inside her dress and was biting her neck.

Tod freed his right arm with a heave, reached over the girl and brought his fist down on the man's head. He couldn't hit very hard but managed to knock the man's hat off, also his glasses. The man tried to bury his face in the girl's shoulder, but Tod grabbed one of his ears and yanked. They started to move again. Tod held on to the ear as long as he could, hoping that it would come away in his hand. The girl managed to twist under his arm. A piece of her dress tore, but she was free of her attacker.

Another spasm passed through the mob and he was carried toward the curb. He fought toward a lamp-post, but he was swept by before he could grasp it. He saw another man catch the girl with the torn dress. She screamed for help. He tried to get to her, but was carried in the opposite direction. This rush also ended in a dead spot. Here his neighbors were all shorter than he was. He turned his head upward toward the sky and tried to pull some fresh air into his aching lungs, but it was all heavily tainted with sweat.

In this part of the mob no one was hysterical. In fact, most of the people seemed to be enjoying themselves. Near him was a stout woman with a man pressing hard against her from in front. His chin was on her shoulder, and his arms were around her. She paid no attention to him and went on talking to the woman at her side.

55   "The first thing I knew," Tod heard her say, "there was a rush and I was in the middle."

"Yeah. Somebody hollered, 'Here comes Gary Cooper,' and then wham!"

"That ain't it," said a little man wearing a cloth cap and pull over sweater. "This is a riot you're in."

"Yeah," said a third woman, whose snaky gray hair was hanging over her face and shoulders. "A pervert attacked a child."

"He ought to be lynched."

60   Everybody agreed vehemently.

"I come from St. Louis," announced the stout woman, "and we had one of them pervert fellers in our neighborhood once. He ripped up a girl with a pair of scissors."

"He must have been crazy," said the man in the cap. "What kind of fun is that?"

Everybody laughed. The stout woman spoke to the man who was hugging her.

"Hey, you," she said. "I ain't no pillow."

65   The man smiled beatifically but didn't move. She laughed, making no effort to get out of his embrace.

"A fresh guy," she said.

The other woman laughed.

"Yeah," she said, "this is a regular free-for-all."

The man in the cap and sweater thought there was another laugh in his comment about the pervert.

70   "Ripping up a girl with scissors. That's the wrong tool."

He was right. They laughed even louder than the first time.

"You'd a done it different, eh, kid?" said a young man with a kidney-shaped head and waxed mustaches.

The two women laughed. This encouraged the man in the cap and he reached over and pinched the stout woman's friend. She squealed.

"Lay off that," she said good-naturedly.

75 "I was shoved," he said.

An ambulance siren screamed in the street. Its wailing moan started the crowd moving again and Tod was carried along in a slow, steady push. He closed his eyes and tried to protect his throbbing leg. This time, when the movement ended, he found himself with his back to the theatre wall. He kept his eyes closed and stood on his good leg. After what seemed like hours, the pack began to loosen and move again with a churning motion. It gathered momentum and rushed. He rode it until he was slammed against the base of an iron rail which fenced the driveway of the theatre from the street. He had the wind knocked out of him by the impact, but managed to cling to the rail. He held on desperately, fighting to keep from being sucked back. A woman caught him around the waist and tried to hang on. She was sobbing rhythmically. Tod felt his fingers slipping from the rail and kicked backwards as hard as he could. The woman let go.

Despite the agony in his leg, he was able to think clearly about his picture, "The Burning of Los Angeles." After his quarrel with Faye, he had worked on it continually to escape tormenting himself, and the way to it in his mind had become almost automatic.

As he stood on his good leg, clinging desperately to the iron rail, he could see all the rough charcoal strokes with which he had blocked it out on the big canvas. Across the top, parallel with the frame, he had drawn the burning city, a great bonfire of architectural styles, ranging from Egyptian to Cape Cod colonial. Through the center, winding from left to right, was a long hill street and down it, spilling into the middle foreground, came the mob carrying baseball bats and torches. For the faces of its members, he was using the innumerable sketches he had made of the people who come to California to die; the cultists of all sorts, economic as well as religious, the wave, airplane, funeral and preview watchers—all those poor devils who can only be stirred by the promise of miracles and then only to violence. A super "Dr. Know-All Pierce-All" had made the necessary promise and they were marching behind his banner in a great united front of screwballs and screwboxes to purify the land. No longer bored, they sang and danced joyously in the red light of the flames.

In the lower foreground, men and women fled wildly before the vanguard of the crusading mob. Among them were Faye, Harry, Homer, Claude and himself. Faye ran proudly, throwing her knees high. Harry stumbled along behind her, holding on to his beloved derby hat with both hands. Homer seemed to be falling out of the canvas, his face half-asleep, his big hands clawing the air in anguished pantomime. Claude turned his head as he ran to thumb his nose at his pursuers. Tod himself picked up a small stone to throw before continuing his flight.

80 He had almost forgotten both his leg and his predicament, and to make his escape still more complete he stood on a chair and worked at the flames

in an upper corner of the canvas, modeling the tongues of fire so that they licked even more avidly at a corinthian column that held up the palmleaf roof of a nutburger stand.

He had finished one flame and was starting on another when he was brought back by someone shouting in his ear. He opened his eyes and saw a policeman trying to reach him from behind the rail to which he was clinging. He let go with his left hand and raised his arm. The policeman caught him by the wrist, but couldn't lift him. Tod was afraid to let go until another man came to aid the policeman and caught him by the back of his jacket. He let go of the rail and they hauled him up and over it.

When they saw that he couldn't stand, they let him down easily to the ground. He was in the theatre driveway. On the curb next to him sat a woman crying into her skirt. Along the wall were groups of other disheveled people. At the end of the driveway was an ambulance. A policeman asked him if he wanted to go to the hospital. He shook his head no. He then offered him a lift home. Tod had the presence of mind to give Claude's address.

He was carried through the exit to the back street and lifted into a police car. The siren began to scream and at first he thought he was making the noise himself. He felt his lips with his hands. They were clamped tight. He knew then it was the siren. For some reason this made him laugh and he began to imitate the siren as loud as he could.

Writing Log/Journal Assignment

Explain your conception of the "American Dream." What does the dream include? What does it seem to promise? How can it be achieved? How much of the "American Dream" has been realized thus far in your life?

Individual and Collaborative Considerations

1. Why do the people in this story feel "cheated" and "betrayed"? In what way might their frustrations be explained as disillusionment with the American Dream?
2. What is the setting of this apocalyptic story? In what way might this be significant? How does Homer Simpson become the catalyst for the riot at the movie premiere?
3. West asserts that many of the inhabitants of Los Angeles have waited all their lives to start "living the good life." What harsh reality do they face in Hollywood, the microcosm of the American Dream?
4. In what way are the thousands of fans *waiting* to capture a glimpse of their film icons at the movie premiere representative of individuals *waiting* to begin living in Hollywood?
5. Tod, the set designer, was a would-be artist, just as many of the other people he observed were "want-to-be" grotesques, high on hope and low on talent. What does Tod recognize about himself during the riot? What

insight does he gain into his unfinished painting titled "The Burning of Los Angeles"?

Writing Activities

1. Describe an incident you have observed, heard about, or participated in where people engaged in senseless violence—not unlike the swarming of locusts—possibly as the result of being "cheated" of something or "betrayed" by someone. Then, analyze the cause or causes that led up to the incident, as well as what set an impending event into motion. Relate your experience to "Hollywood Locusts" whenever possible.

2. The glamour of Hollywood, movie capital of the world when this story was written, had a great deal to do with its attractive lure. However, many who came to Hollywood expecting one thing found another, and often, what people did find invariably led to disappointment and disillusionment. Write an essay in which you compare and contrast the inhabitants of Hollywood—and Los Angeles in general—today, to the people West mentions in "Hollywood Locusts." How are those who live in Los Angeles in the 1990s similar to yet different from those who lived in Los Angeles in 1939 when *The Day of the Locust*, the source of this story, was published?

✳

Blues Ain't No Mockin Bird

Toni Cade Bambara

An author, teacher, and civil rights activist, Toni Cade Bambara was born in New York and grew up in Harlem. Bambara's talents are many; she has been an editor, critic, writer, and a dancer. Her works include *The Sea Birds Are Still Alive* (1977), *The Salt Eaters* (1980), and *If Blessing Comes* (1987). In addition, she has edited two anthologies of African American literature. The following story, an excerpt from *Gorilla, My Love* (1972), traces the Cain family's reaction to filmmakers who believe a movie itself is always more important than the people in it.

The puddle had frozen over, and me and Cathy went stompin in it. The twins from next door, Tyrone and Terry, were swingin so high out of sight we forgot we were waitin our turn on the tire. Cathy jumped up and came

down hard on her heels and started tap-dancin. And the frozen patch splin-
terin every which way underneath kinda spooky. "Looks like a plastic spider
web," she said. "A sort of weird spider, I guess, with many mental problems." But really it looked like the crystal paperweight Granny kept in the
parlor. She was on the back porch, Granny was, making the cakes drunk.
The old ladle dripping rum into the Christmas tins, like it used to drip maple
syrup into the pails when we lived in the Judsons' woods, like it poured
cider into the vats when we were on the Cooper place, like it used to scoop
buttermilk and soft cheese when we lived at the dairy. "Go tell that man we
ain't a bunch of trees."

"Ma'am?"

"I said to tell that man to get away from here with that camera." Me and
Cathy look over toward the meadow where the men with the station wagon'd been roamin around all mornin. The tall man with a huge camera
lassoed to his shoulder was buzzin our way.

"They're makin movie pictures," yelled Tyrone, stiffenin his legs and
twistin so the tire'd come down slow so they could see.

5   "They're makin movie pictures," sang out Terry.

"That boy don't never have anything original to say," say Cathy
grown-up.

By the time the man with the camera had cut across our neighbor's yard,
the twins were out of the trees swingin low and Granny was onto the steps,
the screen door bammin soft and scratchy against her palms. "We thought
we'd get a shot or two of the house and everything and then—"

"Good mornin," Granny cut him off. And smiled that smile.

"Good mornin," he said, head all down the way Bingo does when you
yell at him about the bones on the kitchen floor. "Nice place you got here,
Aunty. We thought we'd take a—"

10   "Did you?" said Granny with her eyebrows. Cathy pulled up her socks
and giggled.

"Nice things here," said the man, buzzin his camera over the yard. The
pecan barrels, the sled, me and Cathy, the flowers, the printed stones along
the drive way, the trees, the twins, the toolshed.

"I don't know about the thing, the it, and the stuff," said Granny, still
talkin with her eyebrows. "Just people here is what I tend to consider."

Camera man stopped buzzin. Cathy giggled into her collar.

"Mornin, ladies," a new man said. He had come up behind us when we
weren't lookin. "And gents," discoverin the twins givin him a nasty look.
"We're filmin for the county," he said with a smile. "Mind if we shoot a bit
around here?"

15   "I do indeed," said Granny with no smile. Smilin man was smiling up a
storm. So was Cathy. But he didn't seem to have another word to say, so he
and the camera man backed on out of the yard, but you could hear the
camera buzzin still.

"Suppose you just shut that machine off," said Granny real low through
her teeth, and took a step down off the porch and then another.

"Now, Aunty," Camera said, pointin the thing straight at her.

"Your mama and I are not related."

Smilin man got his notebook out and a chewed-up pencil. "Listen," he said movin back into our yard, "we'd like to have a statement from you . . . for the film. We're filmin for the county, see. Part of the food-stamp campaign. You know about the food stamps?"

20   Granny said nuthin.

"Maybe there's somethin you want to say for the film. I see you grow your own vegetables," he smiled real nice. "If more folks did that, see, there'd be no need—" Granny wasn't sayin nuthin. So they backed on out, buzzin at our clothesline and the twins' bicycles, then back on down to the meadow. The twins were danglin in the tire, lookin at Granny. Me and Cathy were waitin, too, cause Granny always got somethin to say. She teaches steady with no letup. "I was on this bridge one time," she started off. "Was a crowd cause this man was goin to jump, you understand. And a minister was there and the police and some other folks. His woman was there, too."

"What was they doin?" asked Tyrone.

"Tryin to talk him out of it was what they was doin. The minister talkin about how it was a mortal sin, suicide. His woman takin bites out of her own hand and not even knowin it, so nervous and cryin and talkin fast."

"So what happened?" asked Tyrone.

25   "So here comes . . . this person . . . with a camera, takin pictures of the man and the minister and the woman. Takin pictures of the man in his misery about to jump, cause life so bad and people been messin with him so bad. This person takin up the whole roll of film practically. But savin a few, of course."

"Of course," said Cathy, hatin the person. Me standin there wonderin how Cathy knew it was "of course" when I didn't and it was my grandmother.

After a while Tyrone say, "Did he jump?"

"Yeh, did he jump?" say Terry all eager.

And Granny just stared at the twins till their faces swallow up the eager and they don't even care anymore about the man jumpin. Then she goes back onto the porch and lets the screen door go for itself. I'm lookin to Cathy to finish the story cause she knows Granny's whole story before me even. Like she knew how come we move so much and Cathy ain't but a third cousin we picked up on the way last Thanksgivin visitin. But she knew it was on account of people drivin Granny crazy till she'd get up in the night and start packin. Mumblin and packin and wakin everybody up sayin, "Let's get away from here before I kill me somebody." Like people wouldn't pay her for things like they said they would. Or Mr. Judson bringin us boxes of old clothes and raggedy magazines. Or Mrs. Cooper comin in our kitchen and touchin everything and sayin how clean it all was. Granny goin crazy, and Granddaddy Cain pullin her off the people, sayin, "Now, now, Cora." But next day loadin up the truck, with rocks all in his jaw, madder than Granny in the first place.

30   "I read a story once," said Cathy soundin like Granny teacher. "About this lady Goldilocks who barged into a house that wasn't even hers. And not invited, you understand. Messed over the people's groceries and broke up the people's furniture. Had the nerve to sleep in the folks' bed."

"Then what happened?" asked Tyrone. "What they do, the folks, when they come in to all this mess?"

"Did they make her pay for it?" asked Terry, makin a fist. "I'd've made her pay me."

I didn't even ask. I could see Cathy actress was very likely to just walk away and leave us in mystery about this story which I heard was about some bears.

"Did they throw her out?" asked Tyrone, like his father sounds when he's bein extra nasty-plus to the washin-machine man.

35   "Woulda," said Terry. "I woulda gone upside her head with my fist and—"

"You woulda done whatcha always do—go cry to Mama, you big baby," said Tyrone. So naturally Terry starts hittin on Tyrone, and next thing you know they tumblin out the tire and rollin on the ground. But Granny didn't say a thing or send the twins home or step out on the steps to tell us about how we can't afford to be fightin amongst ourselves. She didn't say nuthin. So I get into the tire to take my turn. And I could see her leanin up against the pantry table, starin at the cakes she was puttin up for the Christmas sale, mumblin real low and grumpy and holdin her forehead like it wanted to fall off and mess up the rum cakes.

Behind me I hear before I can see Granddaddy Cain comin through the woods in his field boots. Then I twist around to see the shiny black oilskin cuttin through what little left there was of yellows, red, and oranges. His great white head not quite round cause of this bloody thing high on his shoulder, like he was wearin a cap on sideways. He takes the shortcut through the pecan grove, and the sound of twigs snapping overhead and underfoot travels clear and cold all the way up to us. And here comes Smilin and Camera up behind him like they was going to do somethin. Folks like to go for him sometimes. Cathy say it's because he's so tall and quiet and like a king. And people just can't stand it. But Smilin and Camera don't hit him on the head or nuthin. They just buzz on him as he stalks by with the chicken hawk slung over his shoulder, squawkin, drippin red down the back of the oilskin. He passes the porch and stops a second for Granny to see he's caught the hawk at last, but she's just starin and mumblin, and not at the hawk. So he nails the bird to the toolshed door, the hammerin crackin through the eardrums. And the bird flappin himself to death and droolin down the door to paint the gravel on the driveway red, then brown, then black. And the two men movin up on tiptoe like they was invisible or we were blind, one. "Get them persons out of my flower bed, Mister Cain," say Granny moanin real low like at a funeral.

"How come your grandmother calls her husband 'Mister Cain' all the time?" Tyrone whispers all loud and noisy and from the city and don't know no better. Like his mama, Miss Myrtle, tell us never mind the formality as if we had no better breeding than to call her Myrtle, plain. And then this awful thing—a giant hawk—come wailin up over the meadow, flyin low and tilted and screamin, zig zaggin through the pecan grove, breakin branches and hollerin, snappin past the clothesline, flyin even which way, flyin into things reckless with crazy.

"He's come to claim his mate," say Cathy fast, and ducks down. We all fall quick and flat into the gravel driveway, stones scrapin my face. I squinch my eyes open again at the hawk on the door, tryin to fly up out of her death like it was just a sack flown into by mistake. Her body holdin her there on that nail, though. The mate beatin the air overhead and clutchin for hair, for heads, for landin space.

40   The camera man duckin and bendin and runnin and fallin, jigglin the camera and scared. And Smilin jumpin up and down swipin at the huge bird, tryin to bring the hawk down with just his raggedy ole cap. Granddaddy Cain straight up and silent, watchin the circles of the hawk, then aimin the hammer off his wrist. The giant bird fallin, silent and slow. Then here comes Camera and Smilin all big and bad now that the awful screechin thing is on its back and broken, here they come. And Granddaddy Cain looks up at them like it was the first time noticin, but not payin them too much mind cause he's listenin, we all listenin, to that low groanin music comin from the porch. And we figure any minute, somethin in my back tells me any minute now, Granny gonna bust through that screen with somethin in her hand and murder on her mind. So Granddaddy say above the buzzin, but quiet, "Good day, gentlemen." Just like that. Like he'd invited them in to play cards and they'd stayed too long and all the sandwiches were gone and Reverend Webb was droppin by and it *was time to go.*

They didn't know what to do. But like Cathy say, folks can't stand Granddaddy tall and silent and like a king. They can't neither. The smile the men smilin is pullin the mouth back and showin the teeth. Lookin like the wolf man, both of them. Then Grandaddy holds his hand out—this huge hand I used to sit in when I was a baby and he'd carry me through the house to my mother like I was a gift on a tray. Like he used to on the trains. They called the other men just waiters. But they spoke of Granddaddy separate and said, The Waiter. And said he had engines in his feet and motors in his hands and couldn't no train throw him off and couldn't nobody turn him round. They were big enough for motors, his hands were. He held that one hand out all still and it gettin to be not at all a hand but a person in itself.

"He wants you to hand him the camera," Smilin whispers to Camera, tiltin his head to talk secret like they was in the jungle or somethin and come upon a native that don't speak the language. The men start untyin the straps, and they put the camera into that great hand speckled with the hawk's blood all black and crackly now. And the hand don't even drop with the weight, just the fingers move, curl up around the machine. But Granddaddy lookin straight at the men. They lookin at each other and everywhere but at Grand-daddy's face.

"We filmin for the county, see," say Smilin. "We puttin together a movie for the foodstamp program . . . filmin all around these parts. Uhh, filmin for the county."

"Can I have my camera back?" say the tall man with no machine on his shoulder, but still keepin it high like the camera was still there or needed to be. "Please, sir." Then Granddaddy's other hand flies up like a sudden and gentle bird, slaps down fast on top of the camera and lifts off half like it was a calabash cut for sharing.

45   "Hey," Camera jumps forward. He gathers up the parts into his chest and everything unrollin and fallin all over. "Whatcha tryin to do? You'll ruin the film." He looks down into his chest of metal reels and things like he's pro-tectin a kitten from the cold.

"You standin in the misses' flower beds," say Granddaddy. "This is our own place."

The two men look at him, then at each other, then back at the mess in the cameraman's chest, and they just back off. One sayin over and over all the way down to the meadow, "Watch it, Bruno. Keep ya fingers off the film." Then Granddaddy picks up the hammer and jams it into the oilskin pocket, scrapes his boots, and goes into the house. And you can hear the squish of his boots headin through the house. And you can see the funny shadow he throws from the parlor window onto the ground by the string-bean patch. The hammer draggin the pocket of the oilskin out so Granddaddy looked even wider. Granny was hummin now—high, not low and grumbly. And she was doin the cakes again, you could smell the molasses from the rum.

"There's this story I'm goin to write one day," say Cathy dreamer. "About the proper use of the hammer."

"Can I be in it?" Tyrone say with his hand up like it was a matter of first come, first served.

50   "Perhaps," say Cathy, climbin onto the tire to pump us up. "If you there and ready."

Writing Log/Journal Assignment

How do the media exploit human discomfort and misery? Write a journal entry exploring this topic in detail, citing examples of it drawn from your personal experience or the lives of those around you—including the lives you observe on television.

Individual and Collaborative Considerations

1. Explain your interpretation of the plot of the story in relationship to its title: "Blues Ain't No Mockin Bird." (You may find it useful to consider

the sort of bird that actually appears in the story as well as what a mocking bird does.)

2. Bambara uses colloquial language throughout her story. What is the ultimate effect of such language?
3. Why does Granny dislike the cameramen so much? Does she like being photographed? How does she feel about media people in general?
4. Discuss Bambara's point of view in this essay.
5. Describe Granddaddy; what sort of person does he seem to be, based on his actions and his demeanor?

Writing Activities

1. Write an essay about an incident where a person—or group of people—retaliated against the news media in general or its representatives in particular in one way or another. In writing this essay, you will want to consider: (1) the rationale behind their actions, (2) the actions themselves, and (3) the results of their actions.
2. Construct a narrative essay that includes a good deal of dialogue—a colloquial dialect you are comfortable with and well versed in—to create a mood of authenticity of setting and characterization. Since there are many forms of English outside of the "standard English" used in schools and businesses, this paper will provide you with an opportunity to communicate in your chosen dialect in order to examine its rhetorical effectiveness on your audience.

✳

When They Came to Take Him

Reginald Lockett

Reginald Lockett is a prolific writer whose poetry, literary reviews, critiques, and prose have appeared in more than thirty-seven anthologies. His collected works of poetry include *Good Time and No Bread* (1978) and *Where the Birds Sing Bass* (1995). Following the publication of *Good Times and No Bread,* poet Al Young commented that "like a jubilant Saturday night deejay, Lockett spins out one celebration of life after another in a yea-saying street idiom guaranteed to keep listeners turned to his spot on the dial." Sounds and sights are not always positive, however, and in "When They Came to Take Him," Lockett presents the tragic effects of human prejudices—an incident justifying lamentation rather than celebration. Currently, Lockett teaches at San Jose City College and lives in Oakland, California.

When they came for him,
it wasn't the gentility of his
tastefully painted, neat single-level
victorian house tucked away
in a decent neighborhood
that they saw.
when they came to take him,
it wasn't the meticulously
restored vintage jaguar in the garage
or the shiny MG parked
in the driveway that they
took note of.
when they had come
to subdue him, it wasn't
the aesthetic choice of furniture,
original paintings, carvings,
and prints
they looked on in awe at.
when they entered his space,
uninvited, to force on him
their lopsided wills, it
wasn't the impressive collection of books
that covered one whole wall or the
careful
selection of jazz classics they came
to train their cold, insensitive gazes on.
when they had come to
confront him, it wasn't the
conservative tweed, chic tie and handmade shoes
he wore they came all dressed in blue
to out flaunt.
when they had come to exercise the powers
vested in them to uproot him
from his own being, it wasn't the master of arts
degree, secure job with a bank,
and superb fiction and criticism
he wrote that
they took into consideration that morning
on the last day in may.
when they came to capture his spirit
and erase his vision,
it wasn't the intelligence in his eyes,
the ready pride in his face, and the gentleness
in his voice that they wanted to see.
no.
all they saw was that he was black,

> believed armed and dangerous,
> and resisting arrest when they fired a 12 gauge
> riot pump, point-blank,
> 50   dead off in his chest.

Writing Log/Journal Assignment

Jot down your immediate impression of the "victim" and the people referred to as "they" in Lockett's poem. Do you think you could single out either one in a crowd of people? Why or why not? How might the inability to distinguish true character give way to prejudice in "judgment calls"?

Individual and Collaborative Considerations

1. Who is Lockett most likely referring to as "they" in "When They Came to Take Him"? Why do you imagine he chose to use a third-person plural pronoun to refer to "them"? How might this point of view suit the point of his poem?
2. In what way does Lockett build "tension" in this poem?
3. How is the issue of racial prejudice demonstrated?
4. There is a good deal of irony—tragic irony—in Lockett's poem. What exactly are the things "they" never bother to notice once "they" believe the owner of the house is Black, armed, and dangerous?
5. Would "they" have responded any differently to a man who was suspected of being armed and dangerous if his racial heritage was other than African American? Justify your point of view.

Writing Activities

1. Man's injustice to another man based on programmed notions—prejudices—tends to be the theme of Lockett's poem. Granted, there is no way of knowing whether the "victim" was "likely" to have been armed or not; still, the fact that he was Black quite possibly increased the probability of the unknown in "their" eyes, despite evidence that suggested the contrary. Write an essay comparing your own "human drama" involving racism or prejudice to Lockett's poem. How were your experiences alike? How were they similar? Bring your comparative paper to a close by drawing some conclusions based on observations and readings discussed in your essay.
2. Go through a recent newspaper or magazine like *Time*, *Newsweek*, or *U.S. News and World Report* and locate articles on recent tragic shootings. Next, select one article in particular and do some more research on the incident to get the maximum amount of information as you can on it. Finally,

based on the facts and statistics you have collected, write up your own account of the event. Make sure to qualify claims and details if you cannot corroborate them with your source materials.

✳

Thoughts of a Gambler's Lover

Rose Anna Higashi

Rose Anna Higashi is a professor of English, specializing in Japanese literature, English literature, and composition. Her poems appear in numerous magazines and journals, and her recent personal journal and poetry collection titled *Blue Wings* was published by Paulist Press in 1995. Recently, Higashi completed *Finding the Poet*, a poetry textbook. She has also written a novel, *Waiting for Rain*. Many people, places, and things have played a part in shaping Higashi's prose and poetry over the years: her hometown, Joplin, Missouri; authors Matsuo Basho, Gerard Manley Hopkins, and Robert Browning; mysticism and spirituality. In "Thoughts of a Gambler's Lover," Higashi employs vivid imagery coupled with sensory descriptions to capture the essence of human dramas in a casino.

It's Halloween, shortly after five, and the evening feeling
Has already started to settle in. Here in Las Vegas,
From the balcony of our room at the Stardust, my gaze darts
Down at an odd rooftop—heat vents, air conditioning units,
5   Mottled asphalt, a carelessly thrown away broom—
Who could have left it there? From the floor below mine,
The smell of cigar smoke wafts upwards.
I remember the hotel in Monte Carlo; the balcony there
Came out and over the sea, the waves lapped all night,
10   And the evenings were long and warm.
We ate croissants in the morning air,
And he won at every game he played.
He is even here. But the cab driver who brought us back
From Caesar's was giving his riders Mars Bars
15   For trick or treat, just as I had been craving
Something sweet.

The sky has darkened a little now. There's a crescent moon,
Just above the horizon, and a strange glow

	Covers the foothills. The signs at the Silver Slipper
20	And the Frontier flash on and on, and even the Greyhound
	Bus sign looked like a casino, with its blue outlined dog
	Revolving forever. A real dog barks somewhere in the desert.
	Some early partiers are already out on the street;
	One woman is dressed as a spider with eight arms.
25	If I could choose a costume, I'd be the Magician,
	And wand myself away from this place.

Writing Log/Journal Assignment

What did the references to dressing up in costumes or Halloween in general bring to mind? Freewrite on the topics of "costumes," "disguises," and "role-playing," noting the sorts of people and occasions you associate with each.

Individual and Collaborative Considerations

1. Trace the thought progression of "the gambler's lover" from the beginning to the end of the poem.
2. What sort of words does Higashi use to appeal to her reader's sense of sight, smell, taste, touch, and hearing?
3. How does the poet contrast Monte Carlo to Las Vegas? Do you think she really likes either place? Explain.
4. Critically assess how Higashi's vivid imagery captures the essence of a gambling establishment. Base your knowledge of gambling establishments on examples drawn from your personal experience, observations (television and in movies), and readings as you analyze Higashi's poem.
5. Apart from the obvious fact that it is Halloween eve, why might Las Vegas be a logical place to come and observe people in "costumes," assuming roles?

Writing Activities

1. If you, like Higashi, could be a magician, what situation or place in your life would you want to "wand away"? What conflicts confront you in your present situation or place? How might distancing yourself from a situation or place truly resolve the problem? (Or would it?)
2. Write an analysis commenting on the settings where various kinds of human dramas would be likely to take place; in Higashi's poem for instance, we have a poem set in Las Vegas, a city of bright lights, gambling, and entertainment. In such a setting one might expect "excitement" after winning money or "depression" after losing one's life savings at the slot machines or gambling tables in the casinos.

❋

Child on Top of a Greenhouse

Theodore Roethke

A poet and an English professor, Theodore Roethke was a native of Michigan. His first book of poetry was titled *Open House* and was distinguished by his intense use of plant imagery—often denoting growth and decay—imagery which would pervade much of his later poetry. Roethke's subsequent works of poetry included *The Lost Son* (1948), *Praise to the End* (1951), *The Waking*—for which he won the Pulitzer Prize (1953), *Words for the Wind* (1958), *I Am! Says the Land* (1961), and *The Far Field* (1964), a posthumous gathering of his work. *On the Poet and His Craft*, a collection of Roethke's lectures and essays, appeared in 1965 and publication of his selected letters appeared in 1968.

The wind billowing out the seat of my britches,
My feet crackling splinters of glass and dried putty,
The half-grown chrysanthemums staring up like accusers,
Up through the streaked glass, flashing with sunlight,
5   A few white clouds all rushing eastward,
A line of elms plunging and tossing like horses,
And everyone, everyone pointing up and shouting!

Writing Log/Journal Assignment

Write about an instance in your life when you were caught in a situation doing something considered taboo—an instance where everyone and everything around you seemed to express disapproval.

Individual and Collaborative Considerations

1. What are the major images in Roethke's poem?
2. A human drama can occur in almost any setting. How does Roethke let the reader know what the weather is like while the child walks precariously on the greenhouse roof? How does knowledge of the weather increase the dramatic tension?
3. Identify the poet's use of personification in the poem and discuss its overall effect in the poem. What would have been lost without the use of personification?
4. How would you characterize the "mood" of "Child on Top of a Greenhouse"?

5. Explain how Roethke's use of concrete nouns helps make actions in his poem vivid and memorable.

Writing Activities

1. Revise your Writing Log/Journal Assignment, relating your experience using personification (providing plants, animals, and elements with human characteristics) and other figurative language.
2. Interview one of your friends or acquaintances regarding memorable childhood experiences, situations where they were caught doing things they were not supposed to be doing. Then, after analyzing your information, write a character profile of the person you interviewed, providing vivid details about his or her "transgressions" to clearly justify your conclusions.

ADDITIONAL TOPICS AND ISSUES FOR WRITING AND RESEARCH

1. Write an essay in which you prove or disprove the phrase "a picture is worth a thousand words." Substantiate your argument with an analysis of several representative photographs or pictures drawn from popular magazines or art books.
2. Television and the media have often been accused of influencing and shaping attitudes towards topics and issues—viewpoints that might tend to be biased or limited in scope. For instance, in 1993 there were a couple of articles regarding American oil companies—and their interests—in Somalia. These articles, and the information thereof, quickly slipped out of the public's eye. What do you imagine happened? Write a brief composition in which you examine potential causes and effects of media "massage" or "message."
3. Critique a play, a television show, a concert, a speech, or any other presentation you choose. Note the strong points as well as the weak, *showing* rather than *telling* your readers what occurred by appealing to their senses: sound, sight, touch, taste, and smell. (The selective use of concrete nouns and active verbs will greatly assist you in such an exposition.)
4. After rereading "Thoughts of a Gambler's Lover" and "When They Came to Take Him," write an essay wherein you discuss the importance of establishing an appropriate tone in a piece of literature (exemplified in detail by specific references to these two poems). When you revise your paper, address the issue of the appropriateness of tone in your own writing—in this case, a critical analysis.

5. Using Swanson's definition of film types as your authoritative frame of reference, analyze a recent movie you have seen which seems to embody the elements of *film noir* or *screwball noir*. Show how your movie selection clearly fits the genre you ascribe to it by offering a detailed examination of plot, characterization, and setting.

6. Compare and contrast at least two "tabloid news" shows such as *Inside Edition, A Current Affair,* and *Hard Copy.* What is the objective of "tabloid news" shows? How much of the information is really "news"? How much seems to be hearsay? Ultimately, draw some conclusions about "tabloid news" television shows based on your analysis.

7. Study a cross-selection of films by a particular movie director, identifying his or her "style" or "signature" through cinematographic techniques and treatment of themes and motifs. Some highly visible directors with an array of films to research include Cecil B. DeMille, David Lean, Robert Altman, Martin Scorsese, Igmar Bergman (Swedish), Akira Kurosawa (Japanese), Francis Ford Coppola, Penny Marshall, Woody Allen, Stanley Kubrick, John Ford, Luis Buñuel, Rob Reiner, Lina Werthmuller, Spike Lee, Dorothy Arzner, Alfred Hitchcock, Billy Wilder, Satyajit Ray (Indian), and Thomas Alaea (Cuban).

8. Contact *Arts and Entertainment,* a cable television channel, and get information pertaining to the restoration of classic films. You might also write the UCLA Film Arts School. With the assistance of your library research, authoritative evidence, and personal background, write your own argument that old films—including silent pictures—should be preserved at all costs. Make sure you present several fresh points in your argument—points that may be obvious to you but as yet not considered or written about by others.

9. Research the history and growth of a particular musician, recording artist, or musical group. What can you deduce were the multiple causes that ultimately led to the individual's or group's success and recognition in the music field?

10. Music presents many topics of research and evaluation simply because of the diverse histories and genres of music one can examine and appreciate. Select a particular genre of music such as jazz, folk, classical, rock 'n roll, soul, bluegrass, country and western, hip-hop, or any country's indigenous music. (Be mindful that all of these genres contain subcategories.) Freewrite on the genre of your choice. What pattern tends to evolve as you write? Which themes or motifs reappear? Perhaps if you were writing about jazz, you continued to return to jazz musicians. If so, perhaps the focus—the thesis—of your paper would have something specific to say about jazz musicians. You will use facts, examples, and expert testimony (information and quotes gleaned from your research), just as you would in any other essay, to backup your thesis.

Starting Points for Research

Movies and Human Dramas

- Minorities and motion pictures
- Motion picture production
- Monster movies
- Motion pictures and literature
- Disaster films
- Sex exploitation in films
- 3-D films
- Westerns
- Documentary films
- Police films
- Racism in motion pictures
- War films
- The Academy Awards
- Nature movies and television shows
- Rites and ceremonies in motion pictures
- Science fiction films
- Misogyny in movies
- Erotic films
- Politics and modern movies
- Existentialism in films
- Animated movies
- Underground movements in motion pictures
- Motion pictures and the arts

Music

- Composers
- Ethnic instruments
- Jazz forms (cool, hot)
- Folk music
- National music
- Symphony orchestras
- Improvisations
- Street music
- Radio music
- Movie sound tracks
- Realism in music
- Rock and roll
- Singing/voice
- Electronic music
- Television and music
- Ethnic music
- Computer music
- Environmental music
- Elevator music
- Music theory
- Musicians
- Music awards
- Recording studios

10

Competition, Betrayal, and Treachery

In the village
Where I was born
Even the flies
bite deep
ISSA

Essays

George Lakoff   Metaphor and War

•

Umberto Eco   The Suicides of the Temple

•

Fiction

Amy Tan   Rules of the Game

•

Luisa Valenzuela   The Censors

•

Shirley Jackson   The Lottery

•

Poetry

Gary Snyder   Mother Earth: Her Whales

•

Judith Wright   Naked Girl and Mirror

•

A. E. Housman   To an Athlete Dying Young

The past and present have much in common, particularly when you consider human motivations and priorities. There is a basic need for competition, especially as it relates to self-preservation. Competition pits people, places, and things against another for an ultimate purpose: to win a game, to outbid a rival investor, and so forth. In most competitions, regardless of the number of people involved, there is only one winner. Additionally, no matter how many times a person emerges victorious in a competition, defeat is ever present, ever possible, and ever threatening. A. E. Housman considers this inevitability when he writes about a former sports competitor in his poem "To an Athlete Dying Young." The athlete in his poem is more fortunate than others, according to Housman, because he will never have to see the day when his records are broken; he died a champion.

Certainly, competition is not restricted to sports or business rivals. Amy Tan explains how Waverly Jong learned "the art of invisible strength" from her mother, Lindo, a quality she applied to her way of doing and thinking about things in "Rules of the Game." Later, Waverly applied her "invisible strength" to chess matches and became a champion. If anything, her life was not unlike a game itself, for she was always planning her next move—especially against her mother.

Yet another instance of competition (and treachery, considering what has happened to the environment and its creatures) occurs in Gary Snyder's "Mother Earth: Her Whales." Competition and treachery here are at the most basic level possible: struggles between nature trying to survive and the destructive ways of humans attempting to dominate the planet—regardless of the cost.

Betrayal and treachery may be cases of competition taken to the extreme. Betrayal usually involves forfeiting some element of trust—possibly privileged information—or unquestioned allegiance in return for personal gain. Treachery, on the other hand, is an enlarged form of betrayal, without any element of trust or allegiance to begin with. Whereas it is possible to exercise caution when dealing with treacherous people whose reputations precede them, it is difficult to identify a lack of sincerity among those you trust. Most people would like to be able to confide in others, comfortable with the belief that their inner secrets and deepest feelings will remain confidential. Unfortunately, once people open up their lives and share their hopes, dreams, fears, and joys with others, they also become quite vulnerable. As illustrated in Umberto Eco's "The Suicides of the Temple," placing trust and faith in a person like Jim Jones empowered him to dictate his "flock's" moves, for they replaced their reasoning abilities with faith.

Judith Wright has a different problem in "Naked Girl and Mirror," for she is quite aware of what is going on around her; she has not been betrayed by another person. The speaker, her own betrayer, reproaches the changes taking place in her own body, caught up in a state of denial. The matter of acceptance or *buy in* constitutes the major conflict in Wright's "Naked Girl and Mirror"; her betrayal is more of a personal than a social decision.

The theme of treachery and betrayal takes a twist in Luisa Valenzuela's "The Censors," where the protagonist takes a job at the *Censor Secret Com-*

mand to locate a letter he sent to his beloved, only to end up a part of the very system he had been trying to outsmart. The system itself is treacherous and deceitful, but it is little or nothing without people who *buy into* it and its values. Similarly, Shirley Jackson's "The Lottery" exemplifies the irony behind the *buy in* to an annual civic activity whose very nature is ominous. Treachery involved in a ritual practice—which Tessie willingly would have inflicted on another—ends up being Tessie's own nemesis.

RHETORIC AT WORK

An element of irony is often an integral part of betrayal since what one expects and what one receives can differ drastically. Keep track of situational irony, verbal irony, and dramatic irony in the following literary works by leaving notations in the margins whenever a form of irony appears. Then ask yourself how that particular form of irony contributed to the meaning of an essay, a short story, or a poem.

A Checklist for Writing about *Competition, Betrayal, and Treachery*

1. What is the nature of my topic? Am I talking about competition, betrayal, treachery, or all three? What do I want to achieve in my paper?
2. Would blending rhetorical modes assist me in developing my material best? If the nature of my essay is descriptive, how might explaining the causes or effects of betrayal, treachery, or competition complement my development of material?
3. How does my organization of supporting material fit the purpose of my essay? Is my topic argumentative? Do I build in emphasis, offering my weakest evidence first, leaving my strongest argument until last?
4. Do I use concrete details in place of abstract thoughts? How do I demonstrate treacherous acts or competitive situations?
5. Do I arrive at a conclusion logically derived from the evidence in my essay?
6. How does my use of denotation and connotation further my writing objectives?
7. What figurative language do I use for emphasis? Would understatement ever be appropriate? Where? When?
8. Did I proofread to locate and correct careless punctuation and grammatical errors that could have othewise obscured meaning?

———————————————— ✳ ————————————————

Metaphor and War

George Lakoff

George Lakoff was born in 1941, educated at Massachusetts Institute of Technology and Indiana University, and presently teaches linguistics at the University of California at Berkeley. He is particularly interested in the relationship between metaphors and human perception. He has coauthored several books with Mark Johnson, *Metaphors We Live By* (1980), and Mark Turner, *More Than Cool Reason: The Power of Poetic Metaphor* (forthcoming). Lakoff's other works include *Women, Fire, and Dangerous Things: What Categories Reveal about the Mind* (1987).

1 **M**etaphors can kill. Secretary of State Baker sees Saddam as "sitting on our economic lifeline." President Bush sees him as having a "stranglehold" on our economy. General Schwartzkopf characterizes the occupation of Kuwait as a "rape." The President says that the U.S. is in the Gulf to "protect freedom, protect our future, and protect the innocent," and that we must "push Saddam Hussein back." Saddam is seen as Hitler. It is vital, literally vital, to understand just what role metaphorical thought is playing in this war.

2 Metaphorical thought is commonplace and inescapable; in itself, it is neither good nor bad. Abstractions and enormously complex situations are routinely understood via metaphor, so it is not surprising that we use extensive, and mostly unconscious, systems of metaphor to understand the complexities and abstractions of international relations and war. The use of a metaphor, however, becomes pernicious when it hides realities in a harmful way.

3 It is important to distinguish what is metaphorical from what is not. Pain, dismemberment, death, starvation, and the death and injury of loved ones are not metaphorical. They are real, and in this war they are afflicting hundreds, perhaps thousands, of real human beings.

4 The Gulf war has been accompanied by systems of metaphor which have been used by military and foreign policy experts and by the public at large. It is important to look at these metaphor systems in order to see the realities they may be obscuring.

THE STATE-AS-PERSON SYSTEM

5 In international politics, a state is usually conceptualized as a person, engaging in social relations within a world community. Its land-mass is its home. It lives in a neighborhood, and has neighbors, friends, and enemies.

States are seen as having inherent dispositions: they can be peaceful or aggressive, responsible or irresponsible, industrious or lazy.

6   Well-being is wealth. The general well-being of a state is understood in economic terms: its economic health. A serious threat to economic health can thus be seen as a death threat. To the extent that a nation's economy depends on foreign oil, that oil supply becomes a "lifeline" (reinforced by the image of an oil pipeline).

7   Strength for a state is military strength.

8   Maturity for the person-state is industrialization. Unindustrialized nations are "underdeveloped," with industrialization as a natural state to be reached. Third World nations are thus immature children, to be taught how to develop properly or disciplined if they get out of line. Nations that fail to industrialize at a rate considered normal are seen as akin to retarded children and judged as "backward" nations.

9   Morality is a matter of accounting, of keeping the moral books balanced. A wrongdoer incurs a debt, and he must be made to pay. The moral books can be balanced by a return to the situation prior to the wrongdoing, by giving back what has been taken, by recompense, or by punishment. Justice is the balancing of the moral books.

10   War in this metaphor is a fight between two people, a form of hand-to-hand combat. Thus, the U.S. seeks to "push Iraq back out of Kuwait" or "deal the enemy a heavy blow," or "deliver a knockout punch." A just war is thus a form of combat for the purpose of settling moral accounts.

11   The most common discourse form in the West where there is combat to settle moral accounts is the classic fairy tale in which people are replaced by states.

THE FAIRY TALE OF THE JUST WAR

12   Cast of characters: a villain, a victim, and a hero. The victim and the hero may be the same person.

13   The scenario: A crime is committed by the villain against an innocent victim (typically an assault, theft, or kidnapping). The offense occurs due to an imbalance of power and creates a moral imbalance. The hero either gathers helpers or decides to go it alone. The hero makes sacrifices; he undergoes difficulties, typically making an arduous heroic journey to a treacherous terrain. The villain is inherently evil, perhaps even a monster, and thus reasoning with him is out of the question. The hero is left with no choice but to engage the villain in battle. The hero defeats the villain and rescues the victim. The moral balance is restored. Victory is achieved. The hero, who always acts honorably, has proved his manhood and achieved glory. The sacrifice was worthwhile. The hero receives acclaim, along with the gratitude of the victim and the community.

14   Experts in international relations have an additional system of metaphors. The principal one is Clausewitz's metaphor:

WAR IS POLITICS PURSUED BY OTHER MEANS

15 Karl von Clausewitz was a Prussian general who perceived war in terms of political cost-benefit analysis. Each nation-state has political objectives, and war may best serve those objectives. The political "gains" are to be weighed against acceptable "costs." When the costs of war exceed the political gains, the war should cease.

16 In Clausewitzian terms, war is justified when there is more to be gained by going to war than by not going to war. Morality is absent from the Clausewitzian equation, except when there is a political cost to acting immorally or a political gain from acting morally.

17 Clausewitz's metaphor only allows war to be justified on pragmatic, not moral, and pragmatic grounds, the Fairy Tale of the Just War and Clausewitz's metaphor must mesh: The "worthwhile sacrifices" of the fairy tale must equal the Clausewitzian "costs" and the "victory" in the fairy tale must equal the Clausewitzian "gains."

18 Clausewitz's metaphor is the perfect expert's metaphor, since it requires specialists in political cost-benefit mathematics of economics, probability theory, decision theory, and game theory in the name of making foreign policy rational and scientific.

19 Clausewitz's metaphor is commonly seen as literally true, but it is, in fact, metaphorical. It uses the State-As-Person metaphor. It turns qualitative effects on human beings into quantifiable costs and gains, thus seeing political action as economics, and it sees war in terms of only one dimension of war, that of political expediency.

20 To bear in mind what is hidden by Clausewitz's metaphor, we should consider an alternative metaphor that is *not* used by professional strategists or by the general public to understand war as we engage in it:

WAR IS VIOLENT CRIME: MURDER, ASSAULT, KIDNAPPING, ARSON, RAPE, AND THEFT

21 Here, war is understood only in terms of its moral dimension, and not, say, its political or economic dimension. The metaphor highlights those aspects of war that would otherwise be seen as major crimes.

22 There is an Us-Them asymmetry in the public use of the War-As-Crime metaphor. The Iraqi invasion of Kuwait is reported in terms of murder, theft, and rape. The American air war or potential ground attack is never discussed in terms of murder, assault, and arson. Allied conduct of the war is seen, in Clausewitzian terms, as rational calculation, while the Iraqi invasion is discussed not as a rational move by Saddam but as the work of a madman. We see Us as rational, moral, and courageous and Them as criminal and insane.

WAR AS A COMPETITIVE GAME

23   It has long been noted that we understand war as a competitive game, like chess, or as a sport, like football or boxing. It is a metaphor in which there is a clear winner and loser, and a clear end to the game. The metaphor highlights strategic thinking, teamwork, preparedness, the spectators in the world arena, the glory of winning and the shame of defeat.

24   This metaphor is taken very seriously. There is a long tradition in the West of training military officers in team sports and chess. The military is trained to win. This can lead to a metaphor conflict, as it did in Vietnam, since Clausewitz's metaphor seeks to maximize geopolitical gains, which may or may not be consistent with absolute military victory.

25   The situation at present is that the public has accepted the rescue scenario of the just war fairy tale as providing moral justification. The President, for internal political reasons, has accepted the competitive game metaphor as taking precedence over Clausewitz's metaphor: If he must choose, he will go for the military win over maximizing geopolitical gains.

26   Throughout the congressional debate leading up to the war, and in all the expert opinion that has occupied our attention since the war began, the metaphors determining our understanding of the conflict have not been questioned.

IS SADDAM IRRATIONAL?

27   The villain in the Fairy Tale of the Just War may be cunning, but he cannot be rational. You just do not reason with a demon, nor do you enter into negotiations with him. The logic of the metaphor demands that Saddam be irrational. But is he?

28   Administration policy is confused on the issue. Clausewitz's metaphor, as used by military strategists, assumes that the enemy is rational: He too is maximizing gains and minimizing costs. Our strategy from the outset has been to "increase the cost" to Saddam. That assumes he is rational and is maximizing his self-interest.

29   At the same time, he is being called irrational. Our fear of Iraq's possession of nuclear weapons depends on it. If Saddam is rational, he should follow the logic of deterrence. We have thousands of hydrogen bombs in warheads. Israel is estimated to have between one hundred and two hundred deliverable atomic bombs. The argument that Saddam and the Iraqi military would not be deterred by our nuclear arsenal and by Israel's assumes irrationality.

30   Saddam is certainly immoral, ruthless, and brutal, but there is no evidence that he is anything but rational. Everything he has done, from assassinating political opponents, to using poison gas against his political enemies, the Kurds, to invading Kuwait, can be seen as furthering his own self-interest.

Is Kuwait an Innocent Victim?

31   The classical victim is innocent. To the Iraqis, Kuwait was anything but an innocent ingenue. The war with Iran virtually bankrupted Iraq. Kuwait had agreed to help finance the war, but after the war, the Kuwaitis insisted on repayment of the "loan." Kuwaitis had invested hundreds of billions in Europe, America, and Japan, but would not invest in Iraq after the war to help it rebuild. On the contrary, Kuwait began what amounted to economic warfare against Iraq by overproducing its oil quota to hold oil prices down.

32   In addition, Kuwait had drilled laterally into Iraqi territory in the Rumaiah oil field and had extracted oil from Iraqi territory. Kuwait further took advantage of Iraq by buying its currency at extremely low exchange rates. Subsequently, wealthy Kuwaitis used that Iraqi currency on trips to Iraq, where they bought Iraqi goods at bargain rates. Among the things they bought most flamboyantly were liquor and prostititues—widows and orphans of men killed in the war, who, because of the state of the economy, had no other means of support. All this did not endear Kuwaitis to Iraqis, who were suffering from over seventy percent inflation.

33   Moreover, Kuwaitis had long been resented for good reason by Iraqis and Muslims from other nations. Capital rich but labor poor, Kuwait imported cheap labor from other Muslim countries to do its least pleasant work. At the time of the invasion, there were 400,000 Kuwaiti citizens living in Kuwait next to 2.2 million foreign laborers who were denied rights of citizenry and treated by the Kuwaitis as lesser beings. In short, to the Iraqis and to other labor-exporting Arab countries, Kuwait is badly miscast as a purely innocent victim.

34   This does not in any way justify the horrors perpetrated on the Kuwaitis by the Iraqi army. But it is part of what is hidden when Kuwait is cast as an innocent victim. The "legitimate government" that we seek to reinstall is an oppressive monarchy.

Is "Victory" Possible?

35   In a fairy tale or a game, victory is well-defined. Once it is achieved, the story or game is over. Neither is likely to be the case in the Gulf war, since history continues.

36   What will constitute "victory" in this war? The President's stated objectives are total Iraqi withdrawal and restoration of the Kuwaiti monarchy. But no one believes the matter will end there, since Saddam would still be in power with a significant part of his forces intact. If, on the other hand, we conquer Iraq, wiping out its military capability, how will Iraq be governed? No puppet government that we could set up will govern effectively since it will be hated by the entire populace. Since Saddam has wiped out all op-

position, the only remaining effective government for the country would be his Ba'ath party. Will it count as a victory if Saddam's friends wind up in power? If not, what other choice is there? And if Iraq has no remaining military force, how will it defend itself against Syria and Iran? It will certainly not be a "victory" for us if either of them takes over Iraq.

37   In all the talk about victory over Iraq, there has been little clarification about what victory would be. And if "victory" cannot be defined, neither can "worthwhile sacrifice."

38   The metaphors used in the West to conceptualize the Gulf crisis disregard the most powerful political ideas in the Arab world: Arab nationalism and Islamic fundamentalism. The first seeks to form a racially based all-Arab nation, the second, a theocratic all-Islamic state. Though bitterly opposed to one another, they share a great deal. Both are conceptualized in family terms, an Arab brotherhood and an Islamic brotherhood. Both see brotherhoods as more legitimate than existing states. Both are at odds with the State-As-Person metaphor, in which currently existing states are distinct entities with a right to exist in perpetuity.

39   Also hidden by our metaphors is perhaps the most important daily concern throughout the Arab world: Arab dignity.

40   Weakness is a major theme in the Arab world, and is often conceptualized in sexual terms, even more than in the West. American officials, in speaking of the "rape" of Kuwait, are conceptualizing a weak, defenseless country as female and a strong militarily powerful country as male. Similarly, it is common for Arabs to conceptualize the colonization and subsequent domination of the Arab world by the West, especially the U.S., as emasculation.

41   An Arab proverb that was reported to be popular in Iraq in the days before the war was that "It is better to be a cock for a day than a chicken for a year." The message is clear: It is better to be male, that is, strong and dominant, for a short period of time than to be female, that is, weak and defenseless, for a long time. Much of the popular support for Saddam among Arabs is due to the fact that he is seen as standing up to the U.S., even if only for a while and that there is a dignity in this. If upholding dignity is an essential part of what defines Saddam's "rational self-interest," it is vitally important for our government to know this, since he may be willing to continue the war to "be a cock for a day."

42   The U.S. does not have anything like a proper understanding of the issue of Arab dignity. Take the question of whether Iraq will come out of this with part of the Rumailah oil fields and two islands that would give it a port on the Gulf. From Iraq's point of view these are seen as economic necessities if Iraq is to rebuild. President Bush has spoken of this as "rewarding aggression," using a "Third-World-Countries-As-Children" metaphor, where the great powers are grown-ups who have the obligation to reward or punish children so as to make them behave properly. This is exactly the attitude that grates on Arabs, who want to be treated with dignity. Instead of seeing Iraq as a sovereign nation that has taken military action for economic

purposes, the President treats Iraq as if it were a child gone bad, who has become the neighborhood bully and should be properly disciplined by the grown-ups.

43 The issue of the Rumailah oil fields and the two islands has alternatively been discussed in the media in terms of "saving face." Saving face is a very different concept than upholding Arab dignity and insisting on being treated as an equal, not an inferior.

44 Our insistence on using a State-As-Person metaphor, meanwhile, obscures the real and diverse costs of the war. The State-As-Person metaphor highlights the ways in which states act as units, and hides the internal structure of the state. Class structure is hidden by this metaphor, as are ethnic composition, religious rivalry, political parties, the ecology, the influence of the military and of corporations (especially multinational corporations).

45 Consider the question of our "national interest." It is in a person's interest to be healthy and strong. The State-As-Person metaphor translates this into a "national interest" of economic health and military strength. But what is in the "national interest" may or may not be in the interest of many ordinary citizens, groups, or institutions, who may become poorer as the GNP rises and weaker as the military gets stronger.

46 The "national interest" is a metaphorical concept, and it is defined in America by politicians and policymakers. For the most part, they are influenced more by the rich than the poor, more by large corporations than small businesses, and more by developers than ecological activists.

47 When President Bush argues that the war is "serving our vital national interests," he is using a metaphor that hides exactly whose interests are being served and whose are not. For example, poor people, especially blacks and Hispanics, are represented in the military in disproportionately large numbers, and in an extended ground war, they will suffer proportionally more casualties. Thus the war is less in the interest of ethnic minorities and the poor than the white upper classes.

48 Also hidden are the interests of the military itself, which are served when war is justified. Hopes that, after the Cold War, the military might play a smaller role have been dashed by the President's decision to go to war.

49 The State-As-Person metaphor has also allowed for a particularly ghoulish cost-benefit analysis about the continuing air war. There is a lot of talk about American deaths in a potential ground war as potential "costs," while Iraqi soldiers killed by the air war count as gains. The cost-benefit accounting leads us to devalue the lives of Iraqis, even when most of those actually killed are not villains at all but simply innocent draftees or reservists or civilians.

50 The classic fairy tale defines what constitutes a hero: it is a person who rescues an innocent victim and who defeats and punishes a guilty and inherently evil villain, and who does so for moral rather than venal reasons. But in this war, is America functioning as a hero?

51 It doesn't fit the profile very well.

52   America appears as classic hero only if you don't look carefully at how the metaphor is applied to the current situation. It is here that the State-As-Person metaphor functions in a way that continues to hide vital truths. The State-As-Person metaphor hides the internal structure of states and allows us to think of Kuwait as a unitary entity, the defenseless maiden to be rescued in the fairy tale. The metaphor hides the monarchical character of Kuwait, and the way Kuwaitis treat women and the vast majority of the people who live in their country. The State-As-Person metaphor also hides the internal structures of Iraq, and thus hides the actual people who are being killed, maimed, or otherwise harmed in this war. The same metaphor also hides the internal structure of the U.S., and therefore hides the fact that it is the poor and minorities who will make the most sacrifices while not getting any significant benefit from this war. And it hides the main ideas that drive Middle Eastern politics.

53   Metaphors can kill, and sometimes the first victim is truth.

Writing Log/Journal Assignment

Jot down several metaphors regarding war or armed combat and then compare your list to your classmates'. After that, jot down and briefly discuss the metaphors you commonly (though probably unconsciously) use to discuss bad dreams, great experiences, and new revelations.

Individual and Collaborative Considerations

1. Why are metaphors dangerous? What do they often conceal?
2. In Clausewitzian terms, when is war justifiable? When is it time to end a war? What is missing from Clausewitz's metaphor?
3. Explain what is meant by the "Us-Them" asymmetry.
4. What would be the moral dimension of war? Does it too have limitations? What was ironic about the American air war in Iraq?
5. Do you think the media have used Clausewitz's or the State-As-Person metaphor? What has been lost or gained in the process?

Writing Activities

1. Analyze a recent military conflict in any part of the world from the perspective of the Clausewitzian "justifiable war."
2. Write an essay persuading your readers that the metaphors used to cloak the brutishness of war reveal that the human race still relies on the military muscle of primitive civilizations rather than the intelligent minds in modern society to reach consensus on topics and issues.

———————————————— ✳ ————————————————

The Suicides of the Temple

Umberto Eco

Umberto Eco is an acclaimed novelist whose works include *The Name of the Rose* and *The Open Work*. The following essay, "The Suicides of the Temple," has been taken from one of Eco's more recent books, *Travels in Hyperreality*. Although "The Suicides of the Temple" overtly examines how people allow themselves to be placed in situations where their lives are placed in peril, it also touches on the fact that the mass suicides ordered by Jim Jones, leader of the People's Temple, are not as disturbing as the sheer hypocrisy of "normal people" who "try desperately to repress a reality that has been before their eyes for at least two thousand years." Atrocities like those at the People's Temple are nothing new.

1   The strangest thing about the story of the People's Temple suicides is the media reaction, both in America and in Europe. Their reaction is: "Inconceivable, an inconceivable event." In other words, it seems inconceivable that a person long considered respectable, like Jim Jones (all those who knew him over these past years, who contributed to his charitable activities or exploited him for garnering votes, have unanimously defined him as an altruistic preacher, a fascinating personality, a convinced integrationist, a good democrat, or as we Italians would say, an "antifascist"), could then go mad, turn into a bloodthirsty autocrat, a kind of Bokassa who stole the savings of his faithful followers, used drugs, indulged in the most promiscuous sex, hetero and homo, and commended the slaughter of those who attempted to escape his rule. It seems incredible that so many nice people followed him blindly, and to the point of suicide. It seems incredible that a neo-Christian sect, gentle, mystical-communist in its inspiration, should end up transformed into a gang of killers, driving its escapees to seek police protection against the menace of murder. It seems incredible that respectable pensioners, students, blacks eager for social integration, should abandon beautiful, pleasant California, all green lawns and spring breezes, to go and bury themselves in the equatorial jungle, teeming with piranhas and poisonous snakes. It is incredible that the families of the brainwashed young could not make the government intervene strongly, and that only at the end poor Congressman Ryan started an inquiry, which cost him his life. All, all incredible, in other words, unheard of, what's the world coming to, what next?

2   We remain stunned not by Jim Jones but by the unconscious hypocrisy of "normal" people. Normal people try desperately to repress a reality that has

been before their eyes for at least two thousand years. For the story of the People's Temple is old, a matter of flux and reflex, of eternal returns. Refusal to remember these things leads us then to see in terrorist phenomena the hand of the CIA or the Czechs. If only evil really did come always from across the border. The trouble is that it comes not from horizontal distances but from vertical. Certain answers, that is, must be sought from Freud and Lacuna, not from the secret services.

3   What's more, American politicians and journalists didn't even have to go and read the sacred texts on the history of millenarian sects or the classics of psychoanalysis. The story of the People's Temple is told in one of the latest books of that sly operator Harold Robins (sly because he always concocts his novels with bits of reality, whether it's the story of Heftier or Porphyry Rubrics or some Arab magnate). The book in question is *Dreams Die First*. There is the Reverend Sam (who happens to bear a very close resemblance to the Reverend Sun Moon), who has founded a laboratory to which the young initiates bring all their money; he then invests it in shrewd financial speculations. Sam preaches peace and harmony, introduces his young people to the most complete sexual promiscuity, sets up a mystical retreat in the jungle, where he imposes rigid discipline, initiation through drugs, with torture and persecution for those attempting escape, until finally the borderlines between worship, criminality, and rites à la Manson family become very faint. This is the Robins novel. But Robins invents nothing, not even at the level of fictional translation of real-life events.

4   Some decades ahead of him, in *The Diane Curse,* the great Dashed Hamlet portrays a Holy Grail cult, naturally set in California—where else?—which begins by enrolling rich members and taking their money. The cult is not at all violent, even if the initiations (here, too) involve drugs and sleight of hand (among other things, the staging recalls that of the mysteries). The prophet, according to Hamlet, was an impressive man: When he looked at you, you felt all confused. Then he went crazy and believed he could do and achieve anything. . . . He dreamed of convincing the whole world of his divinity. . . . He was a madman who would see no limit to his power.

5   You can almost think you are hearing the interviews published during the past few days in the *New York Times*. He was a wonderfully sweet and kind person, a magnetic personality, he made you feel you belonged to a community. And the lawyer Mark Lane tries to clarify how Jones was seized with paranoia, by thirst for absolute power. And if we now reread the book, *The Family,* that Ed Sanders wrote about Charles Manson's California cult and its degeneration, we find everything already there.

6   So why do these things happen, and why in California? The second half of the question is fairly ingenuous. There are certain reasons why California is specially fertile in producing cults, but the basic scenario is far older. In brief, Jones's cult, the People's Temple, had all the characteristics of the millenarian movements throughout Western history from the first centuries of Christianity down to the present. (And I speak only of these because there would be no room to talk about Jewish millenarianism or analogous cults in

the Orient, or various corybantisms in the classical age, or similar manifestations on the African continent, found, unchanged, today in Brazil.)

7   The Christian series probably begins in the third century A.D. with the extreme wing of the Donatists, the Circoncellions, who went around armed with clubs, attacking the imperial troops, assassinating their sworn enemies, those loyal to the Church of Rome. They blinded their theological adversaries with mixtures of lime and vinegar; thirsting for martyrdom, they would stop wayfarers and threaten death if they refused to martyr them; they organized sumptuous funeral banquets and then killed themselves by jumping off cliffs. In the wake of the various interpretations of the Apocalypse, tense with expectation of the millennium, the various medieval movements arose, the fraticelli and the apostolics of Gherardo Segarelli, from which was born the revolt of Fra Dolcino, the brothers of the free spirit, the swindlers suspected of satanism, the various Catharist groups who sometimes committed suicide by starving themselves (the *endura*). In the twelfth century, Tanchelm, endowed with impressive charisma, had his followers give him all their wealth and he scoured Flanders; Eudes de l'Etoile dragged his followers through the forests of Brittany until they all ended on the pyre; during the Crusades the bands of Tafurs, all hairy and dirty, took to sacking, cannibalism, the massacre of the Jews; insuperable in battle, these Tafurs were feared by the Saracens; later the sixteenth-century Revolutionary of the Upper Rhine fiercely pursued the massacre of ecclesiastics; in the thirteenth century flagellant movements spread (the Crucifers, Brothers of the Cross, the secret Flagellants of Thuringia), moving from one village to another, lashing themselves until they bled. The Reformation period witnessed the mystical communism of the city of Munster, where followers of Thomas Munzer, under John of Leyden, set up a theocratic state, sustained by violence and persecution. Believers had to renounce all worldly goods, were forced into sexual promiscuity, while the leader increasingly assumed divine and imperial attributes, and any recalcitrants were locked in the church for days and days until they were all prostrate, bowing before the will of the prophet; then finally everything was purified in an immense massacre in which all the faithful lost their lives.

8   It could be observed that suicide is not the rule in all these movements, but violent death—bloodbath, destruction on the pyre—certainly is. And it is easy to understand why the theme of suicide (for that matter present among the Circoncellions) seems to become popular only today; the reason is that for those past movements the desire for martyrdom, death, and purification was satisfied by the authorities in power. You have only to read a masterpiece of our Italian medieval literature, the story of Fra Michele the Minorite, to see how the promise of the stake had a sure, uplifting fascination for the martyr, who could moreover hold others responsible for that death which he nevertheless so ardently desired. Naturally in today's California, where even a mass murderer like Manson lives quietly in prison and applies for parole, where, in other words, authority refuses to administer death, the desire for martyrdom must take on more active forms: *Do it yourself*, in short.

9   The historical parallels are endless (the eighteenth century *camisards*, for example, the Cevenne prophets in the seventeenth, the Convulsionarians of San Medardo, down to the various Shakers, Pentecostals, and Glossolalics now invading Italy and in many places absorbed into the Catholic Church). But if you simply compare the characteristics of the Jim Jones cult with a synthetic model of the various millenarian cults (overlooking the various differences) you will find some constant elements. The cult is born in a moment of crisis (spiritual, social, economic), attracting on the one hand the truly poor and on the other some "rich" with a self-punishing syndrome; it announces the end of the world and the coming of the Antichrist (Jones expected a fascist coup d'état and nuclear holocaust). It starts with a program of common ownership of property and convinces the initiates that they are the elect. As such they become more at home with their bodies, and after a strict phase they progress to practices of extreme sexual freedom. The leader, endowed with charisma, subjects everyone to his own psychological power and, for the common good, exploits both the material donations and the willingness of the faithful to be mystically possessed. Not infrequently drugs or forms of self-hypnosis are employed to create a psychological cohesion for the group. The leader proceeds through successive stages of divinization. The group goes from self-flagellation to violence against the unfaithful and then to violence against themselves, in their desire for martyrdom. On the one hand, a persecution delirium rages, and on the other the group's oddness actually unleashes genuine persecution, which accuses the group of crimes it hasn't even committed.

10   In Jones's case, the liberal attitude of American society drove him to invent a plot (the congressman coming to desroy them) and then the self-destructive occasion. Obviously, the theme of the flight through the forest is also present. In other words, the church of the People's Temple is only one of many examples of a revival of the millenarian cults in which at the end (after a start justified by situations of social crisis, pauperism, injustice, protest against authority and the immorality of the times), the elect are overwhelmed by the temptation, gnostic in origin, which asserts that to free themselves from the rule of the angels, lords of the cosmos, they have to pass through all the forms of perversion and cross the swamp of evil.

11   So then, why today? Why in the United States to such an extent, why in California? If millenarianism is born out of social insecurity and explodes in moments of historical crisis, in other countries it can take on socially positive forms (revolution, conquest, struggle against the tyrant, even nonviolent pursuit of martyrdom, as for the early Christians; and in all these cases it is supported by solid theory, which allows the social justification of one's own sacrifice); or it can imitate the historically positive forms, while rejecting social justification (as happens with the Red Brigades). In America, where there is now no central object against which to join battle as there was during the war in Vietnam, where the society allows even aliens to receive unemployment compensation, but where loneliness and the mechanization of life drive people to drugs or to talking to themselves in the street, the search for

the alternative cult becomes frantic. California is a paradise cut off from the world, where all is allowed and all is inspired by an obligatory model of "happiness" (there isn't even the filth of New York or Detroit; you are condemned to be happy). Any promise of community life, of a "new deal," of regeneration is therefore good. It can come through jogging, satanic cults, new Christianities. The threat of the "fault" which will one day tear California from the mainland and cast her adrift exerts a mythical pressure on minds made unstable by all the artificiality. Why not Jones and the good death he promises?

12   The truth is that, in this sense, there is no difference between the destructive madness of the Khmers, who wipe out the populations of cities and create a mystical republic of revolutionaries dedicated to death, and the destructive madness of someone who contributes a hundred thousand dollars to the prophet. America takes a negative view of Chinese austerity, of the sense of permanent campaign among the Cubans, the sinister madness of the Cambodians. But then when it finds itself facing the appearance of the same desire for millenarian renewal, and sees it distorted in the asocial form of mass suicide, it cannot understand that the promise to reach Saturn one day is not enough. And so it says something "inconceivable" has happened.

Writing Log/Journal Assignment

Prior to reading this article, what *acts* by economical, political, or religious groups did you consider outrageous, asocial, and "inconceivable"? Why? What value system did you use to "judge" the normalcy of others and yourself?

Individual and Collaborative Considerations

1. What is millenarianism? How does it evolve?
2. How does Eco develop, explain, and support the notion that "we remain stunned not by Jim Jones but by the unconscious hypocrisy of 'normal' people"?
3. Explain Eco's attitude towards incredulous—if not self-righteous—Americans, specifically in terms of the People's Temple mass suicide and generally in terms of the "destructive madness" in the world around us.
4. As Eco points out, in moments of crisis, certain extreme actions such as "revolution, conquest, struggle against the tyrant, even nonviolent pursuit of martyrdom" are "supported by solid theory" allowing "the social justification of one's own sacrifice." In your lifetime, how many "moments of crisis" do you recall that *polarized* people, inspiring them to act in common accord?
5. How and why do cults like the People's Temple come to exist? What historical precedents does Eco offer and why?

Writing Activities

1. Jim Jones, like the more contemporary David Koresh, has been called the anti-Christ. What is an anti-Christ? Write an essay persuading your readers of the newest anti-Christ (recently, one religious group identified and accused Barney—the dinosaur host of a children's show—of being the anti-Christ!). You may take either a serious or humorous approach to the topic.
2. Using personal experience, observation, research, and readings to support your position, write an essay supporting or disproving Eco's contention that "California is a paradise cut off from the world, where all is allowed and all is inspired by an obligatory model of *happiness.*"

Rules of the Game

Amy Tan

Born in Oakland, California, Amy Tan was a graduate of San Jose State University and a freelance writer before publishing her prize-winning book *The Joy Luck Club* (1989). Tan's stories have been published in numerous popular magazines, including *The Atlantic, Grand Street, Lear's,* and *McCall's.* Her second novel, *The Kitchen God's Wife* (1992), was followed by two children's books illustrated by Gretchen Schield: *The Moon Lady* (1992) and *The Chinese Siamese Cat* (1994); Tan recently completed her third novel, *The Hundred Secret Senses* (1995). She lives in San Francisco. In addition to writing, Tan sings for *The Rock Bottom Remainders,* a rock group including such popular writers as Dave Berry and Stephen King (their motto is "We play music as well as Metallica writes novels"). In "Rules of the Game," Waverly is literally competitive—the chess champion—but at some point, she takes her "invisible strength" and its source for granted. As a result, hubris betrays Waverly, and figuratively and literally, the rules she ignored affect her competitive skills.

I was six when my mother taught me the art of invisible strength. It was a strategy for winning arguments, respect from others, and eventually, though neither of us knew it at the time, chess games.

"Bite back your tongue," scolded my mother when I cried loudly, yanking her hand toward the store that sold bags of salted plums. At home, she said, "Wise guy, he not go against wind. In Chinese we say, Come from South, blow with wind—poom!—North will follow. Strongest wind cannot be seen."

The next week I bit back my tongue as we entered the store with the forbidden candies. When my mother finished her shopping, she quietly plucked a small bag of plums from the rack and put it on the counter with the rest of the items.

My mother imparted her daily truths so she could help my older brothers and me rise above our circumstances. We lived in San Francisco's China-town. Like most of the other Chinese children who played in the back alleys of restaurants and curio shops, I didn't think we were poor. My bowl was always full, three five-course meals every day, beginning with a soup full of mysterious things I didn't want to know the names of.

5   We lived on Waverly Place, in a warm, clean, two-bedroom flat that sat above a small Chinese bakery specializing in steamed pastries and dim sum. In the early morning, when the alley was still quiet, I could smell fragrant red beans as they were cooked down to a pasty sweetness. By daybreak, our flat was heavy with the odor of fired sesame balls and sweet curried chicken crescents. From my bed, I would listen as my father got ready for work, then locked the door behind him, one-two-three clicks.

At the end of our two-block alley was a small sandlot playground with swings and slides well-shined down the middle with use. The play area was bordered by wood-slat benches where old-country people sat cracking roasted watermelon seeds with their golden teeth and scattering the husks to an impatient gathering of gurgling pigeons. The best playground, how-ever, was the dark alley itself. It was crammed with daily mysteries and adventures. My brothers and I would peer into the medicinal herb shop, watching old Li dole out onto a stiff sheet of white paper the right amount of insect shells, saffron-colored seeds, and pungent leaves for his ailing cus-tomers. It was said that he once cured a woman dying of an ancestral curse that had eluded the best of American doctors. Next to the pharmacy was a printer who specialized in gold-embossed wedding invitations and festive red banners.

Farther down the street was Ping Yuen Fish Market. The front window displayed a tank crowded with doomed fish and turtles struggling to gain footing on the slimy green-tiled sides. A hand-written sign informed tourists, "Within this store, is all for food, not for pet." Inside, the butchers with their bloodstained white smocks deftly gutted the fish while customers cried out their orders and shouted, "Give me your freshest," to which the butchers always protested, "All are freshest." On less crowded market days, we would inspect the crates of live frogs and crabs which we were warned not to poke, boxes of dried cuttlefish, and row upon row of iced prawns, squid, and slippery fish. The sanddabs made me shiver each time; their eyes lay on one flattened side and reminded me of my mother's story of a careless girl who ran into a crowded street and was crushed by a cab. "Was smash flat," reported my mother.

At the corner of the alley was Hong Sing's, a four-table café with a re-cessed stairwell in front that led to a door marked "Tradesmen." My brothers and I believed the bad people emerged from this door at night. Tourists never went to Hong Sing's, since the menu was printed only in Chinese. A Caucasian man with a big camera once posed me and my playmates in front of the restaurant. He had us move to the side of the picture window so the photo would capture the roasted duck with its head dangling from a juice-covered rope. After he took the picture, I told him he should go into Hong Sing's and eat dinner. When he smiled and asked me what they served, I shouted, "Guts and duck's feet and octopus gizzards!" Then I ran off with my friends, shrieking with laughter as we scampered across the alley and hid in the entryway grotto of the China Gem Company, my heart pounding with hope that he would chase us.

My mother named me after the street that we lived on: Waverly Place Jong, my official name for important American documents. But my family called me Meimei, "Little Sister." I was the youngest, the only daughter. Each morning before school, my mother would twist and yank on my thick black hair until she had formed two tightly wound pigtails. One day, as she struggled to weave a hard-toothed comb through my disobedient hair, I had a sly thought.

10 I asked her, "Ma, what is Chinese torture?" My mother shook her head. A bobby pin was wedged between her lips. She wetted her palm and smoothed the hair above my ear, then pushed the pin in so that it nicked sharply against my scalp.

"Who say this word?" she asked without a trace of knowing how wicked I was being. I shrugged my shoulders and said, "Some boy in my class said Chinese people do Chinese torture."

"Chinese people do many things," she said simply. "Chinese people do business, do medicine, do painting. Not lazy like American people. We do torture. Best torture."

My older brother Vincent was the one who actually got the chess set. We had gone to the annual Christmas party held at the First Chinese Baptist Church at the end of the alley. The missionary ladies had put together a Santa bag of gifts donated by members of another church. None of the gifts had names on them. There were separate stacks for boys and girls of differ-ent ages.

One of the Chinese parishioners had donned a Santa Claus costume and a stiff paper beard with cotton balls glued to it. I think the only children who thought he was the real thing were too young to know that Santa Claus was not Chinese. When my turn came up, the Santa man asked me how old I was. I thought it was a trick question; I was seven according to the American formula and eight by the Chinese calendar. I said I was born on March 17, 1951. That seemed to satisfy him. He then solemnly asked if I had been a very, very good girl this year and did I believe in Jesus Christ and obey my parents. I knew the only answer to that. I nodded back with equal solemnity.

15   Having watched the other children opening their gifts, I already knew that the big gifts were not necessarily the nicest ones. One girl my age got a large coloring book of biblical characters, while a less greedy girl who selected a smaller box received a glass vial of lavender toilet water. The sound of the box was also important. A ten-year-old boy had chosen a box that jangled when he shook it. It was a tin globe of the world with a slit for inserting money. He must have thought it was full of dimes and nickels, because when he saw that it had just ten pennies, his face fell with such undisguised disappointment that his mother slapped the side of his head and led him out of the church hall, apologizing to the crowd for her son who had such bad manners he couldn't appreciate such a fine gift.

As I peered into the sack, I quickly fingered the remaining presents, testing their weight, imagining what they contained. I chose a heavy, compact one that was wrapped in shiny silver foil and a red satin ribbin. It was a twelve-pack of Life Safers and I spent the rest of the party arranging and rearranging the candy tubes in the order of my favorites. My brother Winston chose wisely as well. His present turned out to be a box of intricate plastic parts; the instructions on the box proclaimed that when they were properly assembled he would have an authentic miniature replica of a World War II submarine.

Vincent got the chess set, which would have been a very decent present to get at a church Christmas party, except it was obviously used and, as we discovered later, it was missing a black pawn and a white knight. My mother graciously thanked the unknown benefactor, saying, "Too good. Cost too much." At which point, an old lady with fine white, wispy hair nodded toward our family and said with a whistling whisper, "Merry, merry Christmas."

When we got home, my mother told Vincent to throw the chess set away. "She not want it. We not want it," she said, tossing her head stiffly to the side with a tight, proud smile. My brothers had deaf ears. They were already lining up the chess pieces and reading from the dog-eared instruction book.

I watched Vincent and Winston play during Christmas week. The chess board seemed to hold elaborate secrets waiting to be untangled. The chessmen were more powerful than Old Li's magic herbs that cured ancestral curses. And my brothers wore such serious faces that I was sure something was at stake that was greater than avoiding the tradesmen's door to Hong Sing's.

20   "Let me! Let me!" I begged between games when one brother or the other would sit back with a deep sigh of relief and victory, the other annoyed, unable to let go of the outcome. Vincent at first refused to let me play, but when I offered my Life Savers as replacements for the buttons that filled in for the missing pieces, he relented. He chose the flavors: wild cherry for the black pawn and peppermint for the white knight. Winner could eat both.

As our mother sprinkled flour and rolled out small doughy circles for the steamed dumplings that would be our dinner that night, Vincent explained the rules, pointing to each piece. "You have sixteen pieces and so do I. One king and queen, two bishops, two knights, two castles, and eight pawns. The pawns can only move forward one step, except on the first move. Then they can move two. But they can only take men by moving crossways like this, except in the beginning, when you can move ahead and take another pawn."

"Why?" I asked as I moved my pawn. "Why can't they move more steps?"

"Because they're pawns," he said.

"But why do they go crossways to take other men. Why aren't there any women and children?"

25   "Why is the sky blue? Why must you always ask stupid questions?" asked Vincent. "This is a game. These are the rules. I didn't make them up. See. Here. In the book." He jabbed a page with a pawn in his hand. "Pawn. P-A-W-N. Pawn. Read it yourself."

My mother patted the flour off her hands. "Let me see book," she said quietly. She scanned the pages quickly, not reading the foreign English symbols, seeming to search deliberately for nothing in particular.

"This American rules," she concluded at last. "Every time people come out from foreign country, must know rules. You not know, judge say Too bad, go back. They not telling you why so you can use their way go forward. They say, Don't know why, you find out yourself. But they knowing all the time. Better you take it, find out why yourself." She tossed her head back with a satisfied smile.

I found out about all the whys later. I read the rules and looked up all the big words in a dictionary. I borrowed books from the Chinatown library. I studied each chess piece, trying to absorb the power each contained.

I learned about opening moves and why it's important to control the center early on; the shortest distance between two points is straight down the middle. I learned about the middle game and why tactics between two adversaries are like clashing ideas; the one who plays better has the clearest plans for both attacking and getting out of traps. I learned why it is essential in the endgame to have foresight, a mathematical understanding of all possible moves, and patience; all weaknesses and advantages become evident to a strong adversary and are obscured to a tiring opponent. I discovered that for the whole game one must gather invisible strengths and see the endgame before the game begins.

30   I also found out why I should never reveal "why" to others. A little knowledge withheld is a great advantage one should store for future use. That is the power of chess. It is a game of secrets in which one must show and never tell.

I loved the secrets I found within the sixty-four black and white squares. I carefully drew a handmade chessboard and pinned it to the wall next to my bed, where at night I would stare for hours at imaginary battles. Soon I no longer lost any games or Life Savers, but I lost my adversaries. Winston and Vincent decided they were more interested in roaming the streets after school in their Hopalong Cassidy cowboy hats.

On a cold spring afternoon, while walking home from school, I detoured through the playground at the end of our alley. I saw a group of old men, two seated across a folding table playing a game of chess, others smoking pipes, eating peanuts, and watching. I ran home and grabbed Vincent's chess set, which was bound in a cardboard box with rubber bands. I also carefully selected two prized rolls of Life Savers. I came back to the park and approached a man who was observing the game.

"Want to play?" I asked him. His face widened with surprise and he grinned as he looked at the box under my arm.

"Little sister, been a long time since I play with dolls," he said, smiling benevolently. I quickly put the box down next to him on the bench and displayed my retort.

35   Lau Po, as he allowed me to call him, turned out to be a much better player than my brothers. I lost many games and many Life Savers. But over the weeks, with each diminishing roll of candies, I added new secrets. Lau Po gave me the names. The Double Attack from the East and West Shores. Throwing Stones on the Drowning Man. The Sudden Meeting of the Clan. The Surprise from the Sleeping Guard. The Humble Servant Who Kills the King. Sand in the Eyes of Advancing Forces. A Double Killing Without Blood.

There were also the fine points of chess etiquette. Keep captured men in neat rows, as well-tended prisoners. Never announce "Check" with vanity, lest someone with an unseen sword slit your throat. Never hurl pieces into the sandbox after you have lost a game, because then you must find them again, by yourself, after apologizing to all around you. By the end of the summer, Lau Po had taught me all he knew, and I had become a better chess player.

A small weekend crowd of Chinese people and tourists would gather as I played and defeated my opponents one by one. My mother would join the crowds during these outdoor exhibition games. She sat proudly on the bench, telling my admirers with proper Chinese humility, "Is luck."

A man who watched me play in the park suggested that my mother allow me to play in local chess tournaments. My mother smiled graciously, an answer that meant nothing. I desperately wanted to go, but I bit back my tongue. I knew she would not let me play among strangers. So as we walked home I said in a small voice that I didn't want to play in the local tournament. They would have American rules. If I lost, I would bring shame on my family.

"Is shame you fall down nobody push you," said my mother.

40   During my first tournament, my mother sat with me in the front row as I waited for my turn. I frequently bounced my legs to unstick them from the cold metal seat of the folding chair. When my name was called, I leapt up.

My mother unwrapped something in her lap. It was her *chang*, a small tablet of red jade which held the sun's fire. "Is luck," she whispered, and tucked it into my dress pocket. I turned to my opponent, a fifteen-year-old boy from Oakland. He looked at me, wrinkling his nose.

As I began to play, the boy disappeared, the color ran out of the room, and I saw only my white pieces and his black ones waiting on the other side. A light wind began blowing past my ears. It whispered secrets only I could hear.

"Blow from the South," it murmured. "The wind leaves no trail." I saw a clear path, the traps to avoid. The crowd rustled. "Shhh! Shhh!" said the corners of the room. The wind blew stronger. "Throw sand from the East to distract him." The knight came forward ready for the sacrifice. The wind hissed, louder and louder. "Blow, blow, blow. He cannot see. He is blind now. Make him lean away from the wind so he is easier to knock down."

"Check," I said, as the wind roared with laughter. The wind died down to little puffs, my own breath.

My mother placed my first trophy next to a new plastic chess set that the neighborhood Tao society had given to me. As she wiped each piece with a soft cloth, she said, "Next time win more, lose less."

45 "Ma, it's not how many pieces you lose," I said. "Sometimes you need to lose pieces to get ahead."

"Better to lose less, see if you really need."

At the next tournament, I won again, but it was my mother who wore the triumphant grin.

"Lost eight piece this time. Last time was eleven. What I tell you? Better off lose less!" I was annoyed, but I couldn't say anything.

I attended more tournaments, each one farther away from home. I won all games, in all divisions. The Chinese bakery downstairs from our flat displayed my growing collection of trophies in its window, amidst the dust-covered cakes that were never picked up. The day after I won an important regional tournament, the window encased a fresh sheet cake with whipped-cream frosting and red script saying, "Congratulations, Waverly Jong, Chinatown Chess Champion." Soon after that, a flower shop, headstone engraver, and funeral parlor offered to sponsor me in national tournaments. That's when my mother decided I no longer had to do the dishes. Winston and Vincent had to do my chores.

50 "Why does she get to play and we do all the work," complained Vincent.

"Is new American rules," said my mother. "Meimei play, squeeze all her brains out for win chess. You play, worth squeeze towel."

By my ninth birthday, I was a national chess champion. I was still some 429 points away from grand-master status, but I was touted as the Great American Hope, a child prodigy and a girl to boot. They ran a photo of me in *Life* magazine next to a quote in which Bobby Fischer said, "There will never be a woman grand master." "Your move, Bobby," said the caption.

The day they took the magazine picture I wore neatly plaited braids clipped with plastic barrettes trimmed with rhinestones. I was playing in a large high school auditorium that echoed with phlegmy coughs and the squeaky rubber knobs of chair legs sliding across freshly waxed wooden floors. Seated across from me was an American man, about the same age as Lau Po, maybe fifty. I remember that his sweaty brow seemed to weep at my every move. He wore a dark, malodorous suit. One of his pockets was stuffed with a great white kerchief on which he wiped his palm before sweeping his hand over the chosen chess piece with great flourish.

In my crisp pink-and-white dress with scratchy lace at the neck, one of two my mother had sewn for these special occasions, I would clasp my hands under my chin, the delicate points of my elbows poised lightly on the table in the manner my mother had shown me for posing for the press. I would swing my patent leather shoes back and forth like an impatient child riding on a school bus. Then I would pause, suck in my lips, twirl my chosen piece in midair as if undecided, and then firmly plant it in its new threatening place, with a triumphant smile thrown back at my opponent for good measure.

55   I no longer played in the alley of Waverly Place. I never visited the playground where the pigeons and old men gathered. I went to school, then directly home to learn new chess secrets, cleverly concealed advantages, more escape routes.

But I found it difficult to concentrate at home. My mother had a habit of standing over me while I plotted out my games. I think she thought of herself as my protective ally. Her lips would be sealed tight, and after each move I made, a soft "Hmmmmph" would escape from her nose.

"Ma, I can't practice when you stand there like that," I said one day. She retreated to the kitchen and made loud noises with the pots and pans. When the crashing stopped, I could see out of the corner of my eye that she was standing in the doorway. "Hmmmmph!" Only this one came out of her tight throat.

My parents made many concessions to allow me to practice. One time I complained that the bedroom I shared was so noisy that I couldn't think. Thereafter, my brothers slept in a bed in the living room facing the street. I said I couldn't finish my rice; my head didn't work right when my stomach was too full. I left the table with half-finished bowls and nobody complained. But there was one duty I couldn't avoid. I had to accompany my mother on Saturday market days when I had no tournament to play. My mother would proudly walk with me, visiting many shops, buying very little. "This is my daughter Wave-ly Jong," she said to whoever looked her way.

One day, after we left a shop I said under my breath, "I wish you wouldn't do that, telling everybody I'm your daughter." My mother stopped walking. Crowds of people with heavy bags pushed past us on the sidewalk, bumping into first one shoulder, then another.

60   "Aiii-ya. So shame be with mother?" She grasped my hand even tighter as she glared at me.

   I looked down. "It's not that, it's just so obvious. It's just so embarrassing."

   "Embarrass you be my daughter?" Her voice was cracking with anger.

   "That's not what I meant. That's not what I said."

   "What you say?"

65   I knew it was a mistake to say anything more, but I heard my voice speaking. "Why do you have to use me to show off? If you want to show off, then why don't you learn to play chess."

   My mother's eyes turned into dangerous black slits. She had no words for me, just sharp silence.

   I felt the wind rushing around my hot ears. I jerked my hand out of my mother's tight grasp and spun around, knocking into an old woman. Her bag of groceries spilled to the ground.

   "Aii-ya! Stupid girl!" my mother and the woman cried. Oranges and tin cans careened down the sidewalk. As my mother stooped to help the old woman pick up the escaping food, I took off.

   I raced down the street, dashing between people, not looking back as my mother screamed shrilly, "Meimei! Meimei!" I fled down an alley, past dark curtained shops and merchants washing the grime off their windows. I sped into the sunlight, into a large street crowded with tourists examining trinkets and souvenirs. I ducked into another dark alley, down another street, up another alley. I ran until it hurt and I realized I had nowhere to go, that I was not running from anything. The alleys contained no escape routes.

70   My breath came out like angry smoke. It was cold. I sat down on an upturned plastic pail next to a stack of empty boxes, cupping my chin with my hands, thinking hard. I imagined my mother, first walking briskly down one street or another looking for me, then giving up and returning home to await my arrival. After two hours, I stood up on creaking legs and slowly walked home.

   The alley was quiet and I could see the yellow lights shining from our flat like two tiger's eyes in the night. I climbed the sixteen steps to the door, advancing quietly up each so as not to make any warning sounds. I turned the knob; the door was locked. I heard a chair moving, quick steps, the locks turning—click! click! click!—and then the door opened.

   "About time you got home," said Vincent. "Boy, are you in trouble."

   He slid back to the dinner table. On a platter were the remains of a large fish, its fleshy head still connected to bones swimming upstream in vain escape. Standing there waiting for my punishment, I heard my mother speak in a dry voice.

   "We not concerning this girl. This girl not have concerning for us."

75   Nobody looked at me. Bone chopsticks clinked against the insides of bowls being emptied into hungry mouths.

   I walked into my room, closed the door, and lay down on my bed. The room was dark, the ceiling filled with shadows from the dinnertime lights of neighboring flats.

In my head, I saw a chessboard with sixty-four black and white squares. Opposite me was my opponent, two angry black slits. She wore a triumphant smile. "Strongest wind cannot be seen," she said.

Her black men advanced across the plane, slowly marching to each successive level as a single unit. My white pieces screamed as they scurried and fell off the board one by one. As her men drew closer to my edge, I felt myself growing light. I rose up into the air and flew out the window. Higher and higher, above the alley, over the tops of tiled roofs, where I was gathered up by the wind and pushed up toward the night sky until everything below me disappeared and I was alone.

I closed my eyes and pondered my next move.

Writing Log/Journal Assignment

How do you or someone you know act when you have won some sort of competition?

Individual and Collaborative Considerations

1. What is the "art of invisible strength"?
2. Where does Waverly get her competitive spirit? Does she credit her source? How?
3. Waverly faces many chess opponents, but she ultimately defeats most of them. What event marks the decline of her success as a chess player?
4. With whom must Waverly figuratively ponder her next chess move at the end of the story? Explain.
5. Characterize Waverly's attitude. How does she view her mother and the other people around her? Are her opinions of others justified?

Writing Activities

1. What is the source of the rise and decline of one's competitive spirit? Write an essay examining the issue in detail, drawing on several representative examples of fiercely competitive individuals who for some reason or another lost their competitive edge.
2. Analyze the *art of invisible strength* in your own life, as well as your *competitive spirit*. To what extent do both play an important role in how you interact with others? Are there special situations wherein you call on your *art of invisible strength*? If so, when? Where?

The Censors

Luisa Valenzuela

Argentinean novelist Luisa Valenzuela was born in Buenos Aires and
graduated from the University of Buenos Aires. She now resides in New
York City, a fellow of the New York Institute for Humanities. Before she
fled Argentina following the death of Juan Perón in 1974, she published
Clara: Thirteen Short Stories and a Novel (1966). Her other works include
Strange Things Happen Here (1979), *Other Weapons* (1986), *The Lizard's Tale*
(1983), which she claimed was "a mythicized and damning view of recent
Argentine history" and would have never been published in Argentina,
and *Open Door* (1988), a collection of stories she dedicated to her mother,
Luisa Mercedes Levinson—an author in her own right. After the publication of *The Lizard's Tale*, Valenzuela's literary style changed from the magical realism of Jorge Luis Borges and Gabriel García Márquez to more
conventional realism as in "The Censors." She once stated that "magical
realism was a beautiful resting place, but the thing to do is go forward."
Valenzuela's most recent works include *Black Novel* (1992) and *Simetrias*
(1994), a collection of short stories published in Spanish by Editorial Sud-
americana, Buenos Aires.

P oor Juan! One day they caught him with his guard down before he could
even realize that what he had taken as a stroke of luck was really one of
fate's dirty tricks. These things happen the minute you're careless and you
let down your guard, as one often does. Juancito let happiness—a feeling
you can't trust—get the better of him when he received from a confidential
source Mariana's new address in Paris and he knew that she hadn't forgotten
him. Without thinking twice, he sat down at his table and wrote her a letter.
The letter that keeps his mind off his job during the day and won't let him
sleep at night (what had he scrawled, what had he put on that sheet of paper
he sent to Mariana?).

Juan knows there won't be a problem with the letter's contents, that it's
irreproachable, harmless. But what about the rest? He knows that they examine, sniff, feel, and read between the lines of each and every letter, and
check its tiniest comma and most accidental stain. He knows that all letters
pass from hand to hand and go through all sorts of tests in the huge censorship offices and that, in the end, very few continue on their way. Usually
it takes months, even years, if there aren't any snags; all this time the freedom, maybe even the life, of both sender and receiver is in jeopardy. And
that's why Juan's so down in the dumps: thinking that something might

happen to Mariana because of his letters. Of all people, Mariana, who must finally feel safe there where she always dreamed she'd live. But he knows that the *Censor's Secret Command* operates all over the world and cashes in on the discount in air rates; there's nothing to stop them from going as far as that hidden Paris neighborhood, kidnapping Mariana, and returning to their cozy homes, certain of having fulfilled their noble mission.

Well, you've got to beat them to the punch, do what everyone tries to do: sabotage the machinery, throw sand in its gears, get to the bottom of the problem so as to stop it.

This was Juan's sound plan when he, like many others, applied for a censor's job—not because he had a calling or needed a job: no, he applied simply to intercept his own letter, a consoling but unoriginal idea. He was hired immediately, for each day more and more censors are needed and no one would bother to check on his references.

5   Ulterior motives couldn't be overlooked by the *Censorship Division*, but they needn't be too strict with those who applied. They knew how hard it would be for those poor guys to find the letter they wanted and even if they did, what's a letter or two when the new censor would snap up so many others? That's how Juan managed to join the *Post Office's Censorship Division*, with a certain goal in mind.

The building had a festive air on the outside which contrasted with its inner staidness. Little by little, Juan was absorbed by his job and he felt at peace since he was doing everything he could to get his letter for Mariana. He didn't even worry when, in his first month, he was sent to *Section K* where envelopes are very carefully screened for explosives.

It's true that on the third day, a fellow worker had his right hand blown off by a letter, but the division chief claimed it was sheer negligence on the victim's part. Juan and the other employees were allowed to go back to their work, albeit feeling less secure. After work, one of them tried to organize a strike to demand higher wages for unhealthy work, but Juan didn't join in; after thinking it over, he reported him to his superiors and thus got promoted.

You don't form a habit by doing something once, he told himself as he left his boss's office. And when he was transferred to *Section F*, where letters are carefully checked for poison dust, he felt he had climbed a rung in the ladder.

By working hard, he quickly reached *Section E* where the work was more interesting, for he could now read and analyze the letters' contents. Here he could even hope to get hold of his letter which, judging by the time that had elapsed, had gone through the other sections and was probably floating around in this one.

10   Soon his work became so absorbing that his noble mission blurred in his mind. Day after day he crossed out whole paragraphs in red ink, pitilessly chucking many letters into the censored basket. These were horrible days when he was shocked by the subtle and conniving ways employed by people to pass on subversive messages; his instincts were so sharp that he found

behind a simple "the weather's unsettled" or "prices continue to soar" the wavering hand of someone secretly scheming to overthrow the Government.

His zeal brought him swift promotion. We don't know if this made him happy. Very few letters reached him in *Section B*—only a handful passed the other hurdles—so he read them over and over again, passed them under a magnifying glass, searched for microprint with an electronic microscope, and tuned his sense of smell so that he was beat by the time he made it home. He'd barely manage to warm up his soup, eat some fruit, and fall into bed, satisfied with having done his duty. Only his darling mother worried, but she couldn't get him back on the right road. She'd say, though it wasn't always true: Lola called, she's at the bar with the girls, they miss you, they're waiting for you. Or else she'd leave a bottle of red wine on the table. But Juan wouldn't overdo it: any distraction could make him lose his edge and the perfect censor had to be alert, keen, attentive, and sharp to nab cheats. He had a truly patriotic task, both self-denying and uplifting.

His basket for censored letters became the best fed as well as the most cunning basket in the whole *Censorship Division.* He was about to congratulate himself for having finally discovered his true mission, when his letter to Mariana reached his hands. Naturally, he censored it without regret. And just as naturally, he couldn't stop them from executing him the following morning, another victim of his devotion to his work.

Writing Log/Journal Assignment

In an extended journal entry, explain the one thing in life you would like to censor and how you would go about doing so.

Individual and Collaborative Considerations

1. Why does Juan take a job at the *Censorship Division* known as the *Censor's Secret Command?* What motivates him?
2. Compare the inside to the outside of the *Censorship Division* building. How did Juan content himself working there?
3. In order to gain promotions within the *Censorship Division,* what sort of thing does Juan do? What patterns of behavior does he establish, and where do they lead him?
4. How does Juan lose his original sense of identity and purpose? What obscures his original focus in the story?
5. Why is the conclusion particularly ironic? Were you anticipating a twist in the plot?

Writing Activities

1. Write an essay arguing that censorhip plays an important role in maintaining social stability and acceptable morality in civilized cultures.

Illustrate your thesis by making references to several representative cultures where censorship serves a positive function.

2. In a well-reasoned essay, argue that censorship in any form—verbal, written, or in the arts—is wrong and unacceptable in the United States, which guarantees freedom of expression in the Bill of Rights.

✳

The Lottery

Shirley Jackson

A native of California and graduate of Syracuse University, Shirley Jackson is probably best known for her stories and novels exploring the dimensions of the human psyche, motivation, and social behavior. Blending suspense with Gothic motifs, horror, and the macabre, Jackson wrote such works as *The Road through the Wall* (1948), *The Lottery* (1949), *The Bird's Nest* (1954), *The Haunting of Hill House* (1959), *We Have Always Lived in the Castle* (1962), and *Come Along with Me* (1968). Humorous accounts of her life with her children include *Life Among the Savages* (1953) and *Raising Demons* (1957). Jackson also wrote several works for children: *The Witchcraft of Salem Village* (1959), *The Bad Children*—a play—(1959), and *Nine Magic Wishes* (1963). Jackson regarded "The Lottery" as a moral allegory that revealed the potential for evil in all human beings. When "The Lottery" was first published in *The New Yorker* on June 28, 1948, it engendered more letters than any other piece of fiction ever published by the magazine. Ironically, as Jackson pointed out in a college lecture in 1960, "people at first were not so much concerned with what the story meant; what they wanted to know was where these lotteries were held, and whether they could watch."

The morning of June 27th was clear and sunny, with the fresh warmth of a full-summer day; the flowers were blossoming profusely and the grass was richly green. The people of the village began to gather in the square, between the post office and the bank, around ten o'clock; in some towns there were so many people that the lottery took two days and had to be started on June 26th, but in this village, where there were only about three hundred people, the whole lottery took less than two hours, so it could begin at ten o'clock in the morning and still be through in time to allow the villagers to get home for noon dinner.

The children assembled first, of course. School was recently over for the summer, and the feeling of liberty sat uneasily on most of them; they tended to gather together quietly for a while before they broke into boisterous play, and their talk was still of the classroom and the teacher, of books and reprimands. Bobby Martin had already stuffed his pockets full of stones, and the other boys soon followed his example, selecting the smoothest and roundest stones; Bobby and Harry Jones and Dickie Delacroix—the villagers pronounced this name "Dellacroy"—eventually made a great pile of stones in one corner of the square and guarded it against the raids of the other boys. The girls stood aside, talking among themselves, looking over their shoulders at the boys, and the very small children rolled in the dust or clung to the hands of their older brothers or sisters.

Soon the men began to gather, surveying their own children, speaking of planting and rain, tractors and taxes. They stood together, away from the pile of stones in the corner, and their jokes were quiet and they smiled rather than laughed. The women, wearing faded house dresses and sweaters, came shortly after their menfolk. They greeted one another and exchanged bits of gossip as they went to join their husbands. Soon the women, standing by their husbands, began to call to their children, and the children came reluctantly, having to be called four or five times. Bobby Martin ducked under his mother's grasping hand and ran, laughing, back to the pile of stones. His father spoke up sharply, and Bobby came quickly and took his place between his father and his oldest brother.

The lottery was conducted—as were the square dances, the teenage club, the Halloween program—by Mr. Summers, who had time and energy to devote to civic activities. He was a round-faced, jovial man and he ran the coal business, and people were sorry for him, because he had no children and his wife was a scold. When he arrived in the square, carrying the black wooden box, there was a murmur of conversation among the villagers, and he waved and called, "Little late today, folks." The postmaster, Mr. Graves, followed him, carrying a three-legged stool, and the stool was put in the center of the square and Mr. Summers set the black box down on it. The villagers kept their distance, leaving a space between themselves and the stool, and when Mr. Summers said, "Some of you fellows want to give me a hand?" there was a hesitation before two men, Mr. Martin and his oldest son, Baxter, came forward to hold the box steady on the stool while Mr. Summers stirred up the papers inside it.

5   The original paraphernalia for the lottery had been lost long ago, and the black box now resting on the stool had been put into use even before Old Man Warner, the oldest man in town, was born. Mr. Summers spoke frequently to the villagers about making a new box, but no one liked to upset even as much tradition as was represented by the black box. There was a story that the present box had been made with some pieces of the box that had preceded it, the one that had been constructed when the first people settled down to make a village here. Every year, after the lottery, Mr. Summers began talking again about a new box, but every year the subject was allowed to fade off without anything's being done. The black box grew shabbier each year; by now it was no longer completely black but splintered badly

along one side to show the original wood color, and in some places faded or stained.

Mr. Martin and his oldest son, Baxter, held the black box securely on the stool until Mr. Summers had stirred the papers thoroughly with his hand. Because so much of the ritual had been forgotten or discarded, Mr. Summers had been successful in having slips of paper substituted for the chips of wood that had been used for generations. Chips of wood, Mr. Summers had argued, had been all very well when the village was tiny, but now that the population was more than three hundred and likely to keep on growing, it was necessary to use something that would fit more easily into the black box. The night before the lottery, Mr. Summers and Mr. Graves made up the slips of paper and put them in the box, and it was then taken to the safe of Mr. Summers' coal company and locked up until Mr. Summers was ready to take it to the square next morning. The rest of the year, the box was put away, sometimes one place, sometimes another; it had spent one year in Mr. Graves's barn and another year underfoot in the post office, and sometimes it was set on a shelf in the Martin grocery and left there.

There was a great deal of fussing to be done before Mr. Summers declared the lottery open. There were the lists to make up—of heads of families, heads of households in each family, members of each household in each family. There was the proper swearing-in of Mr. Summers by the postmaster, as the official of the lottery; at one time, some people remembered, there had been a recital of some sort, performed by the official of the lottery, a perfunctory, tuneless chant that had been rattled off duly each year; some people believed that the official of the lottery used to stand just so when he said or sang it, others believed that he was supposed to walk among the people, but years and years ago this part of the ritual had been allowed to lapse. There had been, also, a ritual salute, which the official of the lottery had had to use in addressing each person who came up to draw from the box, but this also had changed with time, until now it was felt necessary only for the official to speak to each person approaching. Mr. Summers was very good at all this; in his clean white shirt and blue jeans, with one hand resting carelessly on the black box, he seemed very proper and important as he talked interminably to Mr. Graves and the Martins.

Just as Mr. Summers finally left off talking and turned to the assembled villagers, Mrs. Hutchinson came hurriedly along the path to the square, her sweater thrown over her shoulders, and slid into place in the back of the crowd. "Clean forgot what day it was," she said to Mrs. Delacroix, who stood next to her, and they both laughed softly. "Thought my old man was out back stacking wood," Mrs. Hutchinson went on, "and then I looked out the window and the kids was gone, and then I remembered it was the twenty-seventh and came a-running." She dried her hands on her apron, and Mrs. Delacroix said, "You're in time, though. They're still talking away up there."

Mrs. Hutchinson craned her neck to see through the crowd and found her husband and children standing near the front. She tapped Mrs. Delacroix on the arm as a farewell and began to make her way through the crowd. The people separated good-humoredly to let her through; two or three people said, in voices just loud enough to be heard across the crowd, "Here comes your Missus, Hutchinson," and "Bill, she made it after all." Mrs. Hutchinson reached her husband, and Mr. Summers, who had been waiting, said cheerfully, "Thought we were going to have to get on without you, Tessie." Mrs. Hutchinson said, grinning, "Wouldn't have me leave m'dishes in the sink, now, would you, Joe?" and soft laughter ran through the crowd as the people stirred back into position after Mrs. Hutchinson's arrival.

10   "Well, now," Mr. Summers said soberly, "guess we better get started, get this over with, so's we can go back to work. Anybody ain't here?"

"Dunbar," several people said. "Dunbar, Dunbar."

Mr. Summers consulted his list. "Clyde Dunbar," he said. "That's right. He's broke his leg, hasn't he? Who's drawing for him?"

"Me, I guess," a woman said, and Mr. Summers turned to look at her. "Wife draws for her husband," Mr. Summers said. "Don't you have a grown boy to do it for you, Janey?" Although Mr. Summers and everyone else in the village knew the answer perfectly well, it was the business of the official of the lottery to ask such questions formally. Mr. Summers waited with an expression of polite interest while Mrs. Dunbar answered.

"Horace's not but sixteen yet," Mrs. Dunbar said regretfully. "Guess I gotta fill in for the old man this year."

15   "Right," Mr. Summers said. He made a note on the list he was holding. Then he asked, "Watson boy drawing this year?"

A tall boy in the crowd raised his hand. "Here," he said. "I'm drawing for m'mother and me." He blinked his eyes nervously and ducked his head as several voices in the crowd said things like "Good fellow, Jack," and "Glad to see your mother's got a man to do it."

"Well," Mr. Summers said, "I guess that's everyone. Old Man Warner make it?"

"Here," a voice said, and Mr. Summers nodded.

A sudden hush fell on the crowd as Mr. Summers cleared his throat and looked at the list. "All ready?" he called. "Now, I'll read the names—heads of families first—and the men come up and take a paper out of the box. Keep the paper folded in your hand without looking at it until everyone has had a turn. Everything clear?"

20   The people had done it so many times that they only half listened to the directions; most of them were quiet, wetting their lips, not looking around. Then Mr. Summers raised one hand high and said "Adams." A man disengaged himself from the crowd and came forward. "Hi, Steve," Mr. Summers said, and Mr. Adams said, "Hi, Joe." They grinned at one another humorlessly and nervously. Then Mr. Adams reached into the black box and took out a folded paper. He held it firmly by one corner as he turned and went hastily back to his place in the crowd, where he stood a little apart from his family, not looking down at his hand.

"Allen," Mr. Summers said. "Anderson. . . . Bentham."

"Seems like there's no time at all between lotteries any more," Mrs. Delacroix said to Mrs. Graves in the back row. "Seems like we got through with the last one only last week."

"Time sure goes fast," Mrs. Graves said.

"Clark. . . . Delacroix."

25   "There goes my old man," Mrs. Delacroix said. She held her breath while her husband went forward.

"Dunbar," Mr. Summers said, and Mrs. Dunbar went steadily to the box while one of the women said, "Go on, Janey," and another said, "There she goes."

"We're next," Mrs. Graves said. She watched while Mr. Graves came around from the side of the box, greeted Mr. Summers gravely, and selected a slip of paper from the box. By now, all through the crowd there were men holding the small folded papers in their large hands, turning them over and over nervously. Mrs. Dunbar and her two sons stood together, Mrs. Dunbar holding the slip of paper.

"Harburt. . . . Hutchinson."

"Get up there, Bill," Mrs. Hutchinson said, and the people near her laughed.

30   "Jones."

"They do say," Mr. Adams said to Old Man Warner, who stood next to him, "that over in the north village they're talking of giving up the lottery."

Old Man Warner snorted. "Pack of crazy fools," he said. "Listening to the young folks, nothing's good enough for *them*. Next thing you know, they'll be wanting to go back to living in caves, nobody work any more, live *that* way for a while. Used to be a saying about 'Lottery in June, corn be heavy soon.' First thing you know, we'd all be eating stewed chickweed and acorns. There's *always* been a lottery," he added petulantly. "Bad enough to see young Joe Summers up there joking with everybody."

"Some places have already quit lotteries," Mrs. Adams said.

"Nothing but trouble in *that*," Old Man Warner said stoutly. "Pack of young fools."

35   "Martin." And Bobby Martin watched his father go forward. "Over-dyke. . . . Percy."

"I wish they'd hurry," Mrs. Dunbar said to her older son. "I wish they'd hurry."

"They're almost through," her son said.

"You get ready to run tell Dad," Mrs. Dunbar said.

Mr. Summers called his own name and then stepped foward precisely and selected a slip from the box. Then he called, "Warner."

40   "Seventy-seventh year I been in the lottery," Old Man Warner said as he went through the crowd. "Seventy-seventh time."

"Watson." The tall boy came awkwardly through the crowd. Someone said, "Don't be nervous, Jack," and Mr. Summers said, "Take your time, son."

"Zanini."

After that, there was a long pause, a breathless pause, until Mr. Summers, holding his slip of paper in the air, said, "All right, fellows." For a minute, no one moved, and then all the slips of paper were opened. Suddenly, all the women began to speak at once, saying, "Who is it?" "Who's got it?" "Is it the Dunbars?" "Is it the Watsons?" Then the voices began to say, "It's Hutchinson. It's Bill." "Bill Hutchinson's got it."

"Go tell your father," Mrs. Dunbar said to her older son.

45   People began to look around to see the Hutchinsons. Bill Hutchinson was standing quiet staring down at the paper in his hand. Suddenly, Tessie Hutchinson shouted to Mr. Summers, "You didn't give him time enough to take any paper he wanted. I saw you. It wasn't fair."

"Be a good sport, Tessie," Mrs. Delacroix called, and Mrs. Graves said, "All of us took the same chance."

"Shut up, Tessie," Bill Hutchinson said.

"Well, everyone," Mr. Summers said, "that was done pretty fast, and now we've got to be hurrying a little more to get done in time." He consulted his next list. "Bill," he said, "You draw for the Hutchinson family. You got any other households in the Hutchinsons?"

"There's Don and Eva," Mrs. Hutchinson yelled. "Make *them* take their chance!"

50   "Daughters draw with their husbands' families, Tessie," Mr. Summers said gently. "You know that as well as anyone else."

"It wasn't *fair*," Tessie said.

"I guess not, Joe," Bill Hutchinson said regretfully. "My daughter draws with her husband's family, that's only fair. And I've got no other family except the kids."

"Then, as far as drawing for families is concerned, it's you," Mr. Summers said in explanation, "and as far as drawing for households is concerned, that's you, too. Right?"

"Right," Bill Hutchinson said.

55   "How many kids, Bill?" Mr. Summers asked formally.

"Three," Bill Hutchinson said. "There's Bill, Jr., and Nancy, and little Dave, and Tessie and me."

"All right, then," Mr. Summers said. "Harry, you got their tickets back?"

Mr. Graves nodded and held up the slips of paper. "Put them in the box, then," Mr. Summers directed. "Take Bill's and put it in."

"I think we ought to start over," Mrs. Hutchinson said, as quietly as she could. "I tell you it wasn't *fair*. You didn't give him time enough to choose. *Every*body saw that."

60   Mr. Graves had selected the five slips and put them in the box, and dropped all the papers but those onto the ground, where the breeze caught them and lifted them off.

"Listen, everybody," Mrs. Hutchinson was saying to the people around her."

"Ready, Bill?" Mr. Summers asked, and Bill Hutchinson, with one quick glance around at his wife and children, nodded.

"Remember," Mr. Summers said, "take the slips and keep them folded until each person has taken one. Harry, you help little Dave." Mr. Graves took the hand of the little boy, who came willingly with him up to the box.

"Take a paper out of the box, Davy," Mr. Summers said. Davy put his hand into the box and laughed. "Take just *one* paper," Mr. Summers said. "Harry, you hold it for him." Mr. Graves took the child's hand and removed the folded paper from the tight fist and held it while little Dave stood next to him and looked up at him wonderingly.

"Nancy next," Mr. Summers said. Nancy was twelve, and her school friends breathed heavily as she went forward, switching her skirt, and took a slip daintily from the box. "Bill, Jr.," Mr. Summers said, and Billy, his face red and his feet over-large, nearly knocked the box over as he got a paper out. "Tessie," Mr. Summers said. She hesitated for a minute, looking around defiantly, and then set her lips and went up to the box. She snatched a paper out and held it behind her.

65   "Bill," Mr. Summers said, and Bill Hutchinson reached into the box and felt around, bringing his hand out at last with the slip of paper in it.

The crowd was quiet. A girl whispered, "I hope it's not Nancy," and the sound of the whisper reached the edges of the crowd.

"It's not the way it used to be," Old Man Warner said clearly. "People ain't the way they used to be."

"All right," Mr. Summers said. "Open the papers. Harry, you open little Dave's."

Mr. Graves opened the slip of paper and there was a general sigh through the crowd as he held it up and everyone could see that it was blank. Nancy and Bill, Jr., opened theirs at the same time, and both beamed and laughed, turning around to the crowd and holding their slips of paper above their heads.

70   "Tessie," Mr. Summers said. There was a pause, and then Mr. Summers looked at Bill Hutchinson, and Bill unfolded his paper and showed it. It was blank.

"It's Tessie," Mr. Summers said, and his voice was hushed. "Show us her paper, Bill."

Bill Hutchinson went over to his wife and forced the slip of paper out of her hand. It had a black spot on it, the black spot Mr. Summers had made the night before with the heavy pencil in the coal-company office. Bill Hutchinson held it up, and there was a stir in the crowd.

"All right, folks," Mr. Summers said. "Let's finish quickly."

Although the villagers had forgotten the ritual and lost the original black box, they still remembered to use stones. The pile of stones the boys had made earlier was ready; there were stones on the ground with the blowing scraps of paper that had come out of the box. Mrs. Delacroix selected a stone so large she had to pick it up with both hands and turned to Mrs. Dunbar. "Come on," she said. "Hurry up."

75   Mrs. Dunbar had small stones in both hands, and she said, gasping for breath, "I can't run at all. You'll have to go ahead and I'll catch up with you."

The children had stones already, and someone gave little Davy Hutchinson a few pebbles.

Tessie Hutchinson was in the center of a cleared space by now, and she held her hands out desperately as the villagers moved in on her. "It isn't fair," she said. A stone hit her on the side of the head.

Old Man Warner was saying, "Come on, come on, everyone." Steve Adams was in the front of the crowd of villagers, with Mrs. Graves beside him.

"It isn't fair, it isn't right," Mrs. Hutchinson screamed, and then they were upon her.

Writing Log/Journal Assignment

Freewrite about the things you have always associated with a lottery. Have you ever entered a lottery yourself? What did you anticipate? What actually occurred?

Individual and Collaborative Considerations

1. When Jackson's story opens, what are people doing? In what way do their actions build anticipation or curiosity in what follows?
2. Who or what are some of the symbols of tradition in "The Lottery"?
3. Why is there a yearly lottery in this town to begin with? What function does it serve? What rituals are associated with it?
4. Tess arrives at the lottery scene just minutes before the yearly ritual begins and jokes: "Clean forgot what day this was." Based on the dialogue and descriptions in the story, what sort of person do you think Tessie is? Why is or why is she not a fitting "winner" of the lottery?
5. How does irony play an important role in Jackson's story? What does it add to the tale? Jot down some representative examples of verbal and situational irony.

Writing Activities

1. Explore the topic of traditional ritual practices through your favorite method of prewriting. How is tradition perpetuated through ritual—or is it? Would traditional practices cease in the absence of ritual? In a well-reasoned essay, take a stance on this issue and argue your position using a variety of supporting examples.
2. In the simplest sense, Tessie's fortune illustrates the irony of an eager *victimizer* who becomes the *victim*. Brainstorm the words *victimizer* and *victim*. With whom do you associate the two words? Write an essay about contemporary examples of *victimizers* who became *victims*. Begin your introductory paragraph with an allusion to or quotation from Jackson's "The Lottery"; conclude the paragraph with your thesis, focusing on the "real life" people your paper will analyze.

Mother Earth: Her Whales

Gary Snyder

Pulitzer Prize–winning author Gary Snyder was a prominent figure of the Beat movement—a bohemian movement rallying against the folkways and mores of established society—as well as a naturalist. He studied for three years with a Zen master in Japan, studies which guided him in his search for the wordless "world of human nature." His works include *A Range of Poems* (1966), *The Back Country* (1968), *Regarding Wave* (1970), *Manzanita* (1972), *Turtle Island* (1974 Pulitzer Prize winner), and *Axe and Handles;* his essay collections include *Earth House Hold* (1969), *The Old Ways* (1977), and *The Real Work* (1982). Snyder now lives in a northern California forest and continues to write for environmental and wildlife magazines.

> An owl winks in the shadows
> A lizard lifts on tiptoe, breathing hard
> Young male sparrow stretches up his neck,
>   big head, watching—
>
> 5   The grasses are working in the sun. Turn it green.
> Turn it sweet. That we may eat.
> Grow our meat.
>
> Brazil says "sovereign use of Natural Resources"
> Thirty thousand kinds of unknown plants.
> 10   The living actual people of the jungle
>   sold and tortured—
> And a robot in a suit who peddles a delusion called "Brazil"
>   can speak for *them?*
>
> The whales turn and glisten, plunge
> 15   and sound and rise again,
>   Hanging over subtly darkening deeps
> Flowing like breathing planets
>   in the sparkling whorls of
>   the living light—
>
> 20   And Japan quibbles for words on
>   what kinds of whales they can kill?
> A once-great Buddhist nation
>   dribbles methyl mercury
>   like gonorrhea
> 25   in the sea

Pére David's Deer, the Elaphure,
Lived in the tule marshes of the Yellow River
Two thousand years ago—and lost its home to rice—
The forests of Lo-yang were logged and all the silt &
30   Sand flowed down, and gone, by 1200 AD—

Wild Geese hatched out in Siberia
    head south over basins of the Yang, the Huang,
    what we call "China"
On flyways they have used a million years
35   Ah China, where are the tigers, the wild boars,
    the monkeys
       like the snows of yesteryear
Gone in a mist, a flash, and the dry hard ground
Is parking space for fifty thousand trucks.
40   IS man most precious of all things?
—then let us love him, and his brothers, all those
Fading living beings—
North American, Turtle Island, taken by invaders
    who wage war around the world
45   May ants, may abalone, otters, wolves, and elk
Rise! and pull away their giving
    from the robot nations.

Solidarity. The people.
Standing Tree People!
50   Flying Bird People!
Swimming Sea People!
Four-legged, two-legged, people!

How can the head-heavy power-hungry politic scientist
Government   two-world   Capitalist-Imperialist
55   Third-world   Communist   paper-shuffling male
    non-farmer   jet-set   bureaucrats
Speak for the green of the leaf? Speak for the soil.
(Ah Margaret Mead . . . do you sometimes dream of Samoa?)

The robots argue how to parcel out our Mother Earth
To last a little longer
    like vultures flapping
Belching, gurgling,
    near a dying Doe.

"In yonder field a slain knight lies—
We'll fly to him and eat his eyes
    with a down
   derry derry derry down down."

An Owl winks in the shadow
A lizard lifts on tiptoe
70   breathing hard
The whales turn and glisten
            plunge and
Sound, and rise again
Flowing like breathing planets

75   In the sparkling whorls

Of living light.

Writing Log/Journal Assignment

Write a journal entry about anything that the word *ecology* brings to your mind.

Individual and Collaborative Considerations

1. In what way does Snyder's poem address the theme of sacrifice? Does it contain a more dominant theme? If so, what is it?
2. What do the whales in this poem literally and figuratively represent?
3. Explain the role of nature imagery in Snyder's poem. Would anything have been lost without it? If so, what would have been lost? Justify your answer.
4. How would you characterize the tone of Snyder's poem?
5. The speaker in the poem calls for solidarity; to whom is he appealing?

Writing Activities

1. You have no doubt heard from someone that what sets the human race apart from other animals is the ability to think, feel, and reason. The speaker, however, questions, "IS man most precious of all things?" Take a defensible position on this question. What must the human race cease to do if it is to exist harmoniously?
2. Write a prose reply to Snyder's poem calling for solidarity from the point of view of *Mother Earth*. Present your readers with a "modest proposal" for addressing the long-term needs (and sacrifices involved) of nature which also satisfy the short-term desires (personal fulfillment) of society. (This essay assignment would be an ideal opportunity to use humor and satire to develop your material.)

Naked Girl and Mirror

Judith Wright

Australian poet Judith Wright was educated at the University of Sydney
and has been politically active in such things as the antiwar movement in
the 1960s and Australia's conservationist movement. In fact, she was the
cofounder and former president of the Wildlife Preservation Society of
Queensland, and she presently lives on a wildlife preserve. Her poems
tend to approach subject matter from a female perspective. She has written over a dozen volumes of poetry and many children's books, as well as
collections of essays. Her works include *Woman to Man* (1949), *New Language: An Anthology of Australian Verse* (1957), *Charles Harpur* (1963), *Preoc-
cupations in Australian Poetry* (1965), and *Collected Poems* (1971).

This is not I. I had no body once—
only what served my need to laugh and run
and stare at stars and tentatively dance
on the fringe of foam and wave and sand and sun.
5 Eyes loved, hands reached for me, but I was gone
on my own currents, quicksilver, thistle down.
Can I be trapped at last in that soft face?

I stare at you in fear, dark brimming eyes.
Why do you watch me with that immoderate plea—
10 "Look under these curled lashes, recognize
that you were always here; know me—be me."
Smooth one-hermaphrodite shoulders, too tenderly
your long slope runs, above those sudden shy
curves furred with light that spring below your space.

15 No, I have been betrayed. If I had known
that this girl waited between a year and a year,
I'd not have chosen her bough to dance upon.
Betrayed, by that little darkness here, and here
this swelling softness and that frightened stare
20 from eyes I will not answer; shut out here
from my own self, by its new body grace—

for I am betrayed by someone lovely. Yes,
I see you are lovely, hateful naked girl.
Your lips in the mirror tremble as I refuse
25 to know or claim you. Let me go—let me be gone.

You are half of some other who may never come.
Why should I tend you? You are not my own;
you seek that other—he will be your home.

Yet I pity your eyes in the mirror, misted with tears;
30   I lean to your kiss. I must serve you; I will obey.
Some day we may love. I may miss your going, some day,
though I shall always resent your dumb and fruitful years.
Your lovers shall learn better, and bitterly too,
if their arrogance dares to think I am part of you.

Writing Log/Journal Assignment

Symbols and figurative language help to convey the poet's intensity and emotional trauma as she comes to her awareness of who she is. Rewrite her poem in your own words, using a first-person narrative.

Individual and Collaborative Considerations

1. How has the poet's body betrayed her?
2. What does a mirror do? What does it reflect? What does the speaker resent?
3. Who is the "half of some other who may never come"?
4. Identify the poem's tone. How does it lend itself to the theme of self-realization?
5. What do you think the poet meant with the final two lines: "Your lovers shall learn better, and bitterly too / if their arrogance dares to think I am part of you"?

Writing Activities

1. Spinning off the idea that one's mind does not always correspond with changes in the physical makeup of the body, write an essay arguing for equity in the decision-making process before one's body goes through a change (e.g., I want input before my body decides to develop a spare tire). Feel free to use techniques of humor as you develop your paper.
2. Compare and contrast two personalities you have noticed in another person that seem to compete for overall dominance of character. Perhaps the person you write about likes to take photographs of wildlife and has warm regard for house pets but also enjoys killing animals for sport. Your conclusion will be speculative; which personality will most likely emerge as the dominant trait? Why?

✳

To an Athlete Dying Young

A. E. Housman

English author A. E. Housman was educated at St. John's College, Oxford, and wrote and published three volumes of verse: *A Shropshire Lad* (1898), *Last Poems* (1922), and the posthumous *More Poems* (1936). In 1939, these three volumes were brought together in *Collected Poems*. Housman worked as a clerk for the Patent Office in London for many years before securing his post as Latin Professor at Cambridge. *Praefanda* (1931) was a collection of obscene and bawdy passages from Latin authors. *Selected Prose* (1961), edited by John Carter, contains some of the more notorious prefaces. As illustrated in the following poem, "To an Athlete Dying Young," one of Housman's favorite themes revolves around doomed youth, forced to ac-cept the brevity of life, and the enjoyment of what pleasure and beauty one can while one can.

> The time you won your town the race
> We chaired you through the marketplace;
> Man and boy stood cheering by,
> And home we brought you shoulder-high.
>
> Today, the road all runners come,
> Shoulder-high we bring you home,
> And set you at your threshold down,
> Townsman of a stiller town.
>
> Smart lad, to slip betimes away
> From fields where glory does not stay,
> And early though the laurel grows
> It withers quicker than the rose.
>
> Eyes the shady night has shut
> Cannot see the record cut,
> And silence sounds no worse than cheers
> After earth has stopped the ears:
>
> Now you will not swell the rout
> Of lads that wore their honors out,
> Runners whom renown outran
> And the name died before the man.

5

10

15

20

So set, before its echoes fade,
The fleet foot on the sill of shade,
And hold to the low lintel up
The still-defended challenge cup.

25   And round that early-laureled head
Will flock to gaze the strengthless dead,
And find unwithered on its curls
The garland briefer than a girls.

Writing Log/Journal Assignment

Brainstorm the "athletic comeback." Which individuals from contemporary society literally "retired" in full glory from their respective sport, only to tarnish their image with an embarrassing "comeback"?

Individual and Collaborative Considerations

1. Who is the speaker in "To an Athlete Dying Young"?
2. How does the speaker respond to the young athlete's death?
3. What is the effect of rhyme in this poem? That is, what function does rhyme seem to serve? How well do you think this poem would have worked if written without rhyme? Explain your opinion.
4. Discuss the mood of Housman's poem with your classmates.
5. Why do you think Housman uses so much symbolic and figurative language in his poem? What does he seem to accomplish in doing so?

Writing Activities

1. To what extent do you agree with Housman's premise that it is better to die young—with all one's fame, glory, and records in place—than to become a forgotten name? In a persuasive essay, argue either for or against Housman's position, using verifiable examples to support your major discussion points.
2. Write an essay in which you argue that something usually considered in a negative light is actually preferable to any alternative. In Housman's poem, this theme would be "death is preferable to an ignominious life for an athlete." Other angles on this topic include poverty may be preferable to riches, fasting may be more desirable than feasting, and walking may be more ideal than driving. Make sure you establish a sharp argumentative edge in your thesis paragraph to "set up" the rest of your paper.

ADDITIONAL TOPICS AND ISSUES
FOR WRITING AND RESEARCH

1. Compromising a position in order to achieve some sort of agreement often leaves all parties concerned dissatisfied—especially in the political arena. Select several local, state, or federal political figures and write an essay illustrating how and why voters feel righteously *betrayed* when elected officials make concessions on issues (e.g., the politician who campaigns as a pacifist and then—once elected—champions a bill allowing citizens to purchase assault rifles). Are there instances where compromising is unforgivable? If so, which ones?

2. Explain your relationship with another person in terms of a competitive game. Such an essay encourages the use of similes to establish parallel characteristics and actions.

3. What behavior could be considered to be an act of betrayal? How might you justify betrayal? After taking a stance on this issue, develop and support it in a paper using specific examples drawn from observations and readings.

4. Examine the current political arena. What degree of competition exists among public officials? How do they show respect for each other—if at all? Write an essay demonstrating how the nature of competition among politicians affects citizens positively or negatively.

5. Compare and contrast two recent motion pictures dealing with the themes of treachery and betrayal or competition. You may determine the nature or ultimate purpose (thesis) for comparing and contrasting them. When selecting films to analyze, you will probably want to make sure that there are enough similarities between them to establish meaningful comparisons.

6. Justify telling lies—a type of betrayal or dishonesty. Whom do you lie to and why? Do lying and deceit have any socially redeemable qualities? Explain your point of view in a thoroughly developed argumentative essay.

7. Describe an incident wherein you betrayed someone else's trust or someone betrayed yours. What did you do? How did you react?

8. Write an essay arguing that *trickery* is akin to *treachery*. Begin by freewriting about the word *trickery*. Who or what do you associate with the word? Do you know someone who is always attempting to trick people into believing or doing something? Sharpen your focus; what do you specifically have to say about your topic? Finally, back up your thesis with a wide range of supporting material.

9. Cheating on a test or at a competitive game may help you get a good grade or win a game, but can you ever take much pride in your accomplishment? Will you feel fulfilled by a grade you did not earn? How much satisfaction can you have in being unfair? Construct an

argumentative essay defending cheating. Allow the tone of your paper to inform your reader of your real attitude towards the topic.

10. How is change in public figures a kind of betrayal? Do movie stars, musicians, politicians, artists, and others owe it to their appreciative fans or supporters to maintain a consistent public image? Should actors restrict themselves to particular roles and character types? Should musicians stick with a single style of music or change? Should politicians either always vote liberal or always vote conservative? Must artists use the same painting techniques throughout their career? Take a stand on this issue; then, write a clearly defined, well-reasoned argumentative paper developing your thesis.

Starting Points for Research

Competition

- Competing risks
- Big business
- Business ethics
- Economics
- Conglomerate corporations
- Laissez-faire
- Monopolies
- Cartels
- Duopolies
- Government competition
- Oligopolies
- Social Darwinism
- Premeditated crimes
- International competition
- Unfair competition
- Trade secrets
- Biotic competition
- Ecological competition
- Species competition
- Competitive fishing
- Competition among twins
- Competitive psychology
- Sibling rivalry
- Contests
- Sports competitions
- Competitive examinations

Betrayal and Treachery

- Commercial blacklists
- Business espionage
- Commercial dumping
- Commercial crimes
- Unfair trade policies
- Elections—corrupt practices
- Forgery
- False testimony
- Fraud
- Fixed lotteries
- Treason
- Set-ups/framing people
- Struggle
- Kidnapping
- Lies
- Misrepresentation
- Character assassination
- Struggle for survival
- Physical
- Mental
- Trust and deceit
- Premeditated crimes
- Insincerity
- Conspiracy
- Competitive antagonists
- Disloyalty
- Fixed fights, races, contests
- Blackmail

11

Conflict and Resolution

After weeks of watching the roof leak
I fixed it tonight
by moving a single board
GARY SNYDER

Essays

George Orwell   Shooting an Elephant

•

Albert Camus   The Myth of Sisyphus

•

Fiction

Gabriel García Márquez   A Very Old Man with Enormous Wings

•

Jack London   To Build a Fire

•

Charlotte Perkins Gilman   The Yellow Wall-Paper

•

Poetry

Emily Dickinson   Because I Could Not Stop for Death

•

Amiri Baraka   Ka 'Ba

•

The Lu   Nightmare

Chapter 11, Conflict and Resolution, broadens the approach to topics and issues presented in chapter 10, Competition, Betrayal, and Treachery. Whether you ponder fact and fiction in the magical realism of Gabriel García Márquez's "A Very Old Man with Enormous Wings" or delve into the existential quandary of Sisyphus futilely pushing a rock up a hill—knowing it will roll back down—in Albert Camus' "The Myth of Sisyphus," you are confronting conflicts.

Conflict occurs between friends, colleagues, spouses, parents and children, people and their government, people and their churches, people and animals, people and machines, people and technology, and also between nations. Regardless of the situation, when faced with a conflict people naturally seek some sort of resolution. If a nation is at war, the natural resolve is peace. Should a person be wronged, the first inclination might be to exact some sort of "fitting" revenge. Another option would be to "turn the other cheek" and forgive the transgressor. Still other individuals, like the protagonist in Jack London's "To Build a Fire," face conflicts where they have no say over the outcome of the situation. The story's conflict centers around a man whose objective is survival in icy weather—seventy-five degrees below zero (a formidable antagonist). Conflicts may be caused by prejudices, misunderstandings, contradictions of fact, or oppression. It would be difficult to find an essay, story, or poem void of conflict, yet the types of conflicts readers encounter are quite varied. In "Shooting an Elephant," George Orwell focuses readers on his inner conflict between what he knew was correct and ethical and what he realized was expected of him (kill the elephant) since he was a symbol of imperialism and White man's rule in the East. Amiri Baraka considers the conflict of a culture in "Ka 'Ba," and The Lu muses on the inescapable inhumanity and horrors of war in "Nightmare."

The counterproductive cure the doctor/husband prescribes for his wife in Charlotte Perkins Gilman's short story "The Yellow Wall-Paper" presents still another set of dynamics. Gilman looks at the extent a person might have to go and the price he or she may have to pay in order to move beyond oppressing (conflicting) forces. In contrast, although the speaker comes to terms with death (after the fact) in Emily Dickinson's poem "Because I Could Not Stop for Death," it (death) was not anything she sought or welcomed. Thus, the fact that "death" did not have to "stop" for her clarifies the initial conflict, whereas the rest of the poem describes the civility of death and her acquiescence to it.

RHETORIC AT WORK

Conflict invites a close scrutiny of dialectics, the process where contradictions are disclosed and resolved, in argumentation. Resolution or acceptance of a situation can often be reflected in writing by the changing mood or transformation of attitude towards a subject reflected by diction. Make a list consisting of four columns. In your first column place the title of the literary work you read. Next, in column two, jot down words about people, places, and things that initiate some sort of conflict in the selection. List the opposite of each word (or phrase) in column two in the third column. In your fourth column, look back at your initial word in column two and then write down the narrator's or speaker's attitude towards it at the end of the literary piece. For example:

"Shooting an Elephant"	kill	create	regret
"To Build a Fire"	cold	warm	acceptance/comfort
"A Very Old Man with Enormous Wings"	angel	devil	villager disinterest

By all means be creative. Building your rhetorical effectiveness through word associations is the real focus here. You may want to provide headings for each column to clearly delineate each.

A Checklist for Writing about *Conflict and Resolution*

1. What is the objective or purpose of my composition? What sort of conflict am I writing about? How might some methods of problem solving serve the purpose of my paper better than others?
2. When and where did the conflict I am analyzing originate? Did I offer my readers a brief overview of it?
3. How did I bring the conflict presented in my essay to some sort of resolution?
4. What dialectic did I explore in my essay?
5. What steps did I take to "connect" with my intended audience?
6. Does my diction create tension and remind my readers of the issue under analysis? How?
7. How did I project my attitude towards my topic?

✳

Shooting an Elephant

George Orwell

Born in Bengal, India, and educated in England, George Orwell (1903–
1950) went back to work in the Middle East, serving with the Indian Imperial Police from 1922 to 1927. His experiences inspired his first novel,
Burmese Days (1934), and gave him a new understanding of the meaning
of British rule and imperialism. Subsequent works include *Down and Out
in Paris and London* (1933), *Keep the Aspidistra Flying* (1936), *The Road to
Wigan Pier* (1937), *Homage to Catalonia* (1938), and *Coming Up for Air* (1939).
His political satires *Animal Farm* (1945) and *1984* (1949) remain among his
most popular works. Orwell also assembled several collections of essays:
Inside the Whale (1940), *Critical Essays* (1946), and *Shooting an Elephant*
(1950). Orwell's *Collected Essays, Journalism, and Letters* (four volumes,
1968) appeared eighteen years after his death. In his essay "Shooting an
Elephant," Orwell argues that "when the white man turns tyrant it is his
own freedom that he destroys," and he demonstrates his point by referring to an incident in Burma where, contrary to his better judgment, he
committed an unnecessary act merely to avoid looking like a fool.

1 **I**n Moulmein, in Lower Burma, I was hated by large numbers of people—
the only time in my life that I have been important enough for this to happen
to me. I was sub-divisional police officer of the town, and in an aimless, petty
kind of way anti-European feeling was very bitter. No one had the guts to
raise a riot, but if a European woman went through the bazaars alone somebody would probably spit betel juice over her dress. As a police officer I was
an obvious target and was baited whenever it seemed safe to do so. When
a nimble Burman tripped me up on the football field and the referee (another
Burman) looked the other way, the crowd yelled with hideous laughter. This
happened more than once. In the end the sneering yellow faces of young
men that met me everywhere, the insults hooted after me when I was at a
safe distance, got badly on my nerves. The young Buddhist priests were the
worst of all. There were several thousands of them in the town and none of
them seemed to have anything to do except stand on street corners and jeer
at Europeans.

2   All this was perplexing and upsetting. For at that time I had already made
up my mind that imperialism was an evil thing and the sooner I chucked
up my job and got out of it the better. Theoretically—and secretly, of
course—I was all for the Burmese and all against their oppressors, the British. As for the job I was doing, I hated it more bitterly than I can perhaps

make clear. In a job like that you see the dirty work of Empire at close quarters. The wretched prisoners huddling in the stinking cages of the lock-ups, the grey, cowed faces of the long-term convicts, the scarred buttocks of the men who had been flogged with bamboos—all these oppressed me with an intolerable sense of guilt. But I could get nothing into perspective. I was young and ill-educated and I had had to think out my problems in the utter silence that is imposed on every English man in the East. I did not even know that the British Empire is dying, still less did I know that it is a great deal better than the younger empires that are going to supplant it. All I knew was that I was stuck between my hatred of the empire I served and my rage against the evil-spirited little beasts who tried to make my job impossible. With one part of my mind I thought of the British Raj as an unbreakable tyranny, as something clamped down, in *saecula saeculorum*, upon the will of prostrate peoples; with another part I thought that the greatest joy in the world would be to drive a bayonet into a Buddhists priest's guts. Feelings like these are the normal byproducts of imperialism; ask any Anglo-Indian official, if you can catch him off duty.

3   One day something happened which in a roundabout way was enlightening. It was a tiny incident in itself, but it gave me a better glimpse than I had had before of the real nature of imperialism—the real motives for which despotic governments act. Early one morning the sub-inspector at a police station at the other end of the town rang me up on the phone and said that an elephant was ravaging the bazaar. Would I please come and do something about it? I did not know what I could do, but I wanted to see what was happening and I got on to a pony and started out. I took my rifle, an old .44 Winchester and much too small to kill an elephant, but I thought the noise might be useful *in terrorem*. Various Burmans stopped me on the way and told me about the elephant's doings. It was not, of course, a wild elephant, but a tame one which had gone "must." It had been chained up, as tame elephants always are when their attack of "must" is due, but on the previous night it had broken its chain and escaped. Its mahout, the only person who could manage it when it was in that state, had set out in pursuit, but had taken the wrong direction and was now twelve hours' journey away, and in the morning the elephant had suddenly reappeared in the town. The Burmese population had no weapons and were quite helpless against it. It had already destroyed somebody's bamboo hut, killed a cow and raided some fruit-stalls and devoured the stock; also it had met the municipal rubbish van and, when the driver jumped out and took to his heels, had turned the van over and inflicted violences upon it.

4   The Burmese sub-inspector and some Indian constables were waiting for me in the quarter where the elephant had been seen. It was a very poor quarter, a labyrinth of squalid bamboo huts, thatched with palm-leaf, winding all over a steep hillside. I remember that it was a cloudy, stuffy morning at the beginning of the rains. We began questioning people as to where the elephant had gone, and, as usual, failed to get any definite information. That is invariably the case in the East; a story always sounds clear enough at a

distance, but the nearer you get to the scene of events the vaguer it becomes. Some of the people said that the elephant had gone in one direction, some said that he had gone in another, some professed not even to have heard of an elephant. I had almost made up my mind that the whole story was a pack of lies, when we heard yells a little distance away. There was a loud, scandalized cry of "Go away, child! Go away this instant!" and an old woman with a switch in her hand came round the corner of a hut, violently shooing away a crowd of naked children. Some more women followed, clicking their tongues and exclaiming; evidently there was something that the children ought not to have seen. I rounded the hut and saw a man's dead body sprawling in the mud. He was an Indian, a black Dravidian coolie, almost naked, and he could not have been dead many minutes. The people said that the elephant had come suddenly upon him round the corner of the hut, caught him with its trunk, put its foot on his back and ground him into the earth. This was the rainy season and the ground was soft, and his face had scored a trench a foot deep and a couple of yards long. He was lying on his belly with arms crucified and head sharply twisted to one side. His face was coated with mud, the eyes wide open, the teeth bared and grinning with an expression of unendurable agony. (Never tell me, by the way, that the dead look peaceful. Most of the corpses I have seen looked devilish.) The friction of the great beast's foot had stripped the skin from his back as neatly as one skins a rabbit. As soon as I saw the dead man I sent an orderly to a friend's house nearby to borrow an elephant rifle. I had already sent back the pony, not wanting it to go mad with fright and throw me if it smelled the elephant.

5   The orderly came back in a few minutes with a rifle and five cartridges, and meanwhile some Burmans had arrived and told us that the elephant was in the paddy fields below, only a few hundred yards away. As I started forward practically the whole population of the quarter flocked out of the houses and followed me. They had seen the rifle and were all shouting excitedly that I was going to shoot the elephant. They had not shown much interest in the elephant when he was merely ravaging their homes, but it was different now that he was going to be shot. It was a bit of fun to them, as it would be to an English crowd; besides they wanted the meat. It made me vaguely uneasy. I had no intention of shooting the elephant—I had merely sent for the rifle to defend myself if necessary—and it is always unnerving to have a crowd following you. I marched down the hill, looking and feeling a fool, with the rifle over my shoulder and an ever-growing army of people jostling at my heels. At the bottom, when you got away from the huts, there was a metalled road and beyond that a miry waste of paddy fields a thousand yards across, not yet ploughed but soggy from the first rains and dotted with coarse grass. The elephant was standing eight yards from the road, his life side towards us. He took not the slightest notice of the crowd's approach. He was tearing up bunches of grass, beating them against his knees to clean them and stuffing them into his mouth.

6   I had halted on the road. As soon as I saw the elephant I knew with perfect certainty that I ought not to shoot him. It is a serious matter to shoot a

working elephant—it is comparable to destroying a huge and costly piece of machinery—and obviously one ought not to do it if it can possibly be avoided. And at that distance, peacefully eating, the elephant looked no more dangerous than a cow. I thought then and I think now that his attack of "must" was already passing off; in which case he would merely wander harmlessly about until the mahout came back and caught him. Moreover, I did not in the least want to shoot him. I decided that I would watch him for a little while to make sure that he did not turn savage again, and then go home.

7   But at that moment I glanced round at the crowd that had followed me. It was an immense crowd, two thousand at the least and growing every minute. It blocked the road for a long distance on either side. I looked at the sea of yellow faces above the garish clothes—faces all happy and excited over this bit of fun, all certain that the elephant was going to be shot. They were watching me as they would watch a conjurer about to perform a trick. They did not like me, but with the magical rifle in my hands I was momentarily worth watching. And suddenly I realized that I should have to shoot the elephant after all. The people expected it of me and I had got to do it; I could feel their two thousand wills pressing me forward, irresistibly. And it was at this moment, as I stood there with the rifle in my hands, that I first grasped the hollowness, the futility of the white man's dominion in the East. Here was I, the white man with his gun, standing in front of the unarmed native crowd—seemingly the leading actor of the piece; but in reality I was only an absurd puppet pushed to and fro by the will of those yellow faces behind. I perceived in this moment that when the white man turns tyrant it is his own freedom that he destroys. He becomes a sort of hollow, posing dummy, the conventionalized figure of a sahib. For it is the condition of his rule that he shall spend his life in trying to impress the "natives," and so in every crisis he has got to do what the "natives" expect of him. He wears a mask, and his face grows to fit it. I had got to shoot the elephant. I had committed myself to doing it when I sent for the rifle. A sahib has got to act like a sahib; he has got to appear resolute, to know his own mind and do definite things. To come all that way, rifle in hand, with two thousand people marching at my heels, and then to trail feebly away, having done nothing— no, that was impossible. The crowd would laugh at me. And my whole life, every white man's life in the East, was one long struggle not to be laughed at.

8   But I did not want to shoot the elephant. I watched him beating his bunch of grass against his knees, with the preoccupied grandmotherly air that elephants have. It seemed to me that it would be murder to shoot him. At that age I was not squeamish about killing animals, but I had never shot an elephant and never wanted to. (Somehow it always seems worse to kill a *large* animal.) Besides, there was the beast's owner to be considered. Alive, the elephant was worth at least a hundred pounds; dead, he would only be worth the value of his tusks, five pounds, possibly. But I had got to act quickly. I turned to some experienced-looking Burmans who had been there

when we arrived, and asked them how the elephant had been behaving. They all said the same thing: he took no notice of you if you left him alone, but he might charge if you went too close to him.

9   It was perfectly clear to me what I ought to do. I ought to walk up to within, say, twenty-five yards of the elephant and test his behavior. If he charged I could shoot, if he took no notice of me it would be safe to leave him until the mahout came back. But also I knew that I was going to do no such thing. I was a poor shot with a rifle and the ground was soft mud into which one would sink at every step. If the elephant charged and I missed him, I should have about as much chance as a toad under a steam-roller. But even then I was not thinking particularly of my own skin, only of the watchful yellow faces behind. For at that moment, with the crowd watching me, I was not afraid in the ordinary sense, as I would have been if I had been alone. A white man mustn't be frightened in front of "natives"; and so, in general, he isn't frightened. The sole thought in my mind was that if anything went wrong those two thousand Burmans would see me pursued, caught, trampled on and reduced to a grinning corpse like that Indian up the hill. And if that happened it was quite probable that some of them would laugh. That would never do. There was only one alternative. I shoved the cartridges into the magazine and lay down on the road to get a better aim.

10   The crowd grew very still, and a deep, low, happy sigh, as of people who see the theatre curtain go up at last, breathed from innumerable throats. They were going to have their bit of fun after all. The rifle was a beautiful German thing with cross-hair sights. I did not then know that in shooting an elephant one would shoot to cut an imaginary bar running from ear-hole to ear-hole. I ought, therefore, as the elephant was sideways on, to have aimed straight at his ear-hole; actually I aimed several inches in front of this, thinking the brain would be further forward.

11   When I pulled the trigger I did not hear the bang or feel the kick—one never does when a shot goes home—but I heard the devilish roar of glee that went up from the crowd. In that instant, in too short a time, one would have thought, even for the bullet to get there, a mysterious, terrible change had come over the elephant. He neither stirred nor fell, but every line on his body had altered. He looked suddenly stricken, shrunken, immensely old, as though the frightful impact of the bullet had paralyzed him without knocking him down. At last, after what seemed a long time—it might have been five seconds, I dare say—he sagged flabbily to his knees. His mouth slobbered. An enormous senility seemed to have settled upon him. One could have imagined him thousands of years old. I fired again into the same spot. At the second shot he did not collapse but climbed with desperate slowness to his feet and stood weakly upright, with legs sagging and head drooping. I fired a third time. That was the shot that did [it] for him. You could see the agony of it jolt his whole body and knock the last remnant of strength from his legs. But in falling he seemed for a moment to rise, for as his hind legs collapsed beneath him he seemed to tower upwards like a huge rock toppling, his trunk reaching skywards like a tree. He trumpeted, for the

first and only time. And then down he came, his belly towards me, with a crash that seemed to shake the ground even where I lay.

12   I got up. The Burmans were already racing past me across the mud. It was obvious that the elephant would never rise again, but he was not dead. He was breathing very rhythmically with long rattling gasps, his great mound of a side painfully rising and falling. His mouth was wide open—I could see far down into the caverns of pale pink throat. I waited a long time for him to die, but his breathing did not weaken. Finally I fired my two remaining shots into the spot where I thought his heart must be. The thick blood welled out of him like red velvet, but still he did not die. His body did not even jerk when the shots hit him, the tortured breathing continued without a pause. He was dying, very slowly and in great agony, but in some world remote from me where not even a bullet could damage him further. I felt that I had got to put an end to that dreadful noise. It seemed dreadful to see the great beast lying there, powerless to move and yet powerless to die, and not even to be able to finish him. I sent back for my small rifle and poured shot after shot into his heart and down his throat. They seemed to make no impression. The tortured gasps continued as steadily as the ticking of a clock.

13   In the end I could not stand it any longer and went away. I heard later that it took him half an hour to die. Burmans were bringing dahs and baskets even before I left, and I was told they had stripped his body almost to the bones by the afternoon.

14   Afterwards, of course, there were endless discussions about the shooting of the elephant. The owner was furious, but he was only an Indian and could do nothing. Besides, legally I had done the right thing, for a mad elephant has to be killed, like a mad dog, if its owner fails to control it. Among the Europeans opinion was divided. The older men said I was right, the younger men said it was a damn shame to shoot an elephant for killing a coolie, because an elephant was worth more than any damn Coringhee coolie. And afterwards I was very glad that the coolie had been killed; it put me legally in the right and it gave me a sufficient pretext for shooting the elephant. I often wondered whether any of the others grasped that I had done it solely to avoid looking a fool.

Writing Log/Journal Assignment

What does the ability to *act freely* mean to you? Write a short journal entry detailing what it would be like to lose the ability to act as you like. You might illustrate your point with a hypothetical or verifiable example.

Individual and Collaborative Considerations

1. What is the narrator's attitude towards the Burmese? What is their attitude towards him? Why?

2. How does Orwell build tension in his narrative? What is the major conflict? Is it ever resolved? How?
3. What does the elephant literally represent? What might the elephant figuratively represent? How? Why?
4. Referring to specific words and phrases, show how Orwell's vivid descriptions helped to achieve the purpose of his narrative.
5. Why did Orwell really kill the elephant? In retrospect, how does he feel about the event?

Writing Activities

1. In "Shooting an Elephant," George Orwell shapes his narrative around the controlling idea, "When the white man turns tyrant it is his own freedom that he destroys." His essay is an argument—a narrative used to justify his actions. Write an original extended narrative (in the same spirit as Orwell's essay) that argues and illustrates a thesis.
2. Write an essay explaining and analyzing what motivated you to do something (shoot an elephant—figuratively speaking) contrary to your better judgment—perhaps to avoid feeling foolish, cowardly, or "uncool."

✳

The Myth of Sisyphus

Albert Camus

Born in 1913, Albert Camus' deaf, illiterate mother raised and nurtured him with the values of love and caring for other individuals, as well as an intolerance for cruelty and injustice. Following the German occupation of France in 1941, Camus became one of the main intellectual leaders of the Resistance, and he wrote editorials for *Combat*, a French underground paper which he openly published in 1946. Camus' life experiences helped forge the attitudes and beliefs that found their way into his writings. His first novel attracting wide recognition was *The Stranger* (1942), and though it remains his best-known novel, he is also widely admired for *The Plague* (1947) and *The Fall* (1956). In 1957, Camus received the Nobel Prize for literature and was honored in particular for his relentless pursuit of "the problems of the human conscience in our time." Camus' writings often are associated with "the absurd" and "existentialism," a philosophy assuming "that existence precedes essence, that the significant fact is that we and things in general exist, but that these things have no meaning for us except as we through acting upon them can create meaning." In "The

Myth of Sisyphus," taken from Camus' collection of essays by the same name, Sisyphus knows his task is hopeless, yet because a person "is as much through his passions as his torture," Sisyphus' labors might be perceived as a heroic affirmation of life.

1   The gods had condemned Sisyphus to ceaselessly rolling a rock to the top of a mountain, whence the stone would fall back of its own weight. They had thought with some reason that there is no more dreadful punishment than futile and hopeless labor.

2   If one believes Homer, Sisyphus was the wisest and most prudent of mortals. According to another tradition, however, he was disposed to practice the profession of highwayman. I see no contradiction in this. Opinions differ as to the reasons why he became the futile laborer of the underworld. To begin with, he is accused of a certain levity in regard to the gods. He stole their secrets. Aegina, the daughter of Aesopus, was carried off by Jupiter. The father was shocked by that disappearance and complained to Sisyphus. He, who knew of the abduction, offered to tell about it on condition that Aesopus would give water to the citadel of Corinth. To the celestial thunderbolts he preferred the benediction of water. He was punished for this in the underworld. Homer tell us also that Sisyphus had put Death in chains. Pluto could not endure the sight of his deserted, silent empire. He dispatched the god of war, who liberated Death from the hands of her conqueror.

3   It is said also that Sisyphus, being near to death, rashly wanted to test his wife's love. He ordered her to cast his unburied body into the middle of the public square. Sisyphus woke up in the underworld. And there, annoyed by an obedience so contrary to human love, he obtained from Pluto permission to return to earth in order to chastise his wife. But when he had seen again the face of this world, enjoyed water and sun, warm stones and the sea, he no longer wanted to go back to the infernal darkness. Recalls, signs of anger, warnings were of no avail. Many years more he lived facing the curve of the gulf, the sparkling sea, and the smiles of earth. A decree of the gods was necessary. Mercury came and seized the impudent man by the collar and, snatching him from his joys, led him forcibly back to the underworld, where his rock was ready for him.

4   You have already grasped that Sisyphus is the absurd hero. He is, as much through his passions as through his torture. His scorn of the gods, his hatred of death, and his passion for life won him that unspeakable penalty in which the whole being is exerted toward accomplishing nothing. This is the price that must be paid for the passions of this earth. Nothing is told us about Sisyphus in the underworld. Myths are made for the imagination to breathe life into them. As for this myth, one sees merely the whole effort of a body straining to raise the huge stone, to roll it and push it up a slope a hundred times over; one sees the face screwed up, the cheek tight against the stone,

the shoulder bracing the clay-covered mass, the foot wedging it, the fresh start with arms outstretched, the wholly human security of two earth-clotted hands. At the very end of his long effort measured by skyless space and time without depth, the purpose is achieved. Then Sisyphus watches the stone rush down in a few moments toward that lower world whence he will have to push it up again toward the summit. He goes back down to the plain.

5   It is during that return, that pause, that Sisyphus interests me. A face that toils so close to stones is already stone itself! I see that man going back down with a heavy yet measured step toward the torment of which he will never know the end. That hour like a breathing-space which returns as surely as his suffering, that is the hour of consciousness. At each of those moments when he leaves the heights and gradually sinks toward the lairs of the gods, he is superior to his fate. He is stronger than his rock.

6   If this myth is tragic, that is because its hero is conscious. Where would his torture be, indeed, if at every step the hope of succeeding upheld him? The workman of today works every day in his life at the same tasks, and this fate is no less absurd. But it is tragic only at the rare moments when it becomes conscious. Sisyphus, proletarian of the gods, powerless and rebellious, knows the whole extent of his wretched condition: it is what he thinks of during his descent. The lucidity that was to constitute his torture at the same time crowns his victory. There is no fate that cannot be surmounted by scorn.

7   If the descent is thus sometimes performed in sorrow, it can also take place in joy. This word is not too much. Again I fancy Sisyphus returning toward his rock, and the sorrow was in the beginning. When the images of earth cling too tightly to memory, when the call of happiness becomes too insistent, it happens that melancholy rises in man's heart: this is the rock's victory, this is the rock itself. The boundless grief is too heavy to bear. These are our nights of Gethsemane. But crushing truths perish from being acknowledged. Thus, Oedipus at the outset obeys fate without knowing it. But from the moment he knows, his tragedy begins. Yet at the same moment, blind and desperate, he realizes that the only bond linking him to the world is the cool hand of a girl. Then a tremendous remark rings out: "Despite so many ordeals, my advanced age and the nobility of my soul make me conclude that all is well." Sophocles' Oedipus, like Dostoyevsky's Kirilov, thus gives the recipe for the absurd victory. Ancient wisdom confirms modern heroism.

8   One does not discover the absurd without being tempted to write a manual of happiness. "What! by such narrow ways?" There is but one world, however. Happiness and the absurd are two sons of the same earth. They are inseparable. It would be a mistake to say that happiness necessarily springs from the absurd discovery. It happens as well that the feeling of the absurd springs from happiness. "I conclude that all is well," says Oedipus, and that remark is sacred. It echoes in the wild and limited universe of man. It teaches that all is not, has not been, exhausted. It drives out of this world

a god who had come into it with dissatisfaction and a preference for futile sufferings. It makes of fate a human matter, which must be settled among men.

9 All Sisyphus' silent joy is contained therein. His fate belongs to him. His rock is his thing. Likewise, the absurd man, when he contemplates his torment, silences all the idols. In the universe suddenly restored to its silence, the myriad wondering little voices of the earth rise up. Unconscious, secret calls, invitations from all the faces, they are the necessary reverse and price of victory. There is no sun without shadow, and it is essential to know the night. The absurd man says yes and his effort will henceforth be unceasing. If there is a personal fate, there is no higher destiny, or at least there is but one which he concludes is inevitable and despicable. For the rest, he knows himself to be the master of his days. At that subtle moment when man glances backward over his life, Sisyphus returning toward his rock, in that slight pivoting he contemplates that series of unrelated actions which becomes his fate, created by him, combined under his memory's eye and soon sealed by his death. Thus, convinced of the wholly human origin of all that is human, a blind man eager to see who knows that the night has no end, he is still on the go. The rock is still rolling.

10 I leave Sisyphus at the foot of the mountain! One always finds one's burden again. But Sisyphus teaches the higher fidelity that negates the gods and raises rocks. He too concludes that all is well. This universe henceforth without a master seems to him neither sterile nor futile. Each atom of that stone, each mineral flake of that night-filled mountain, in itself forms a world. The struggle itself toward the heights is enough to fill a man's heart. One must imagine Sisyphus happy.

Writing Log/Journal Assignment

What is your understanding of "existentialism"? If you have never heard of it before, ask around the classroom and get a sense of it from a classmate. Otherwise, consult your librarian or a dictionary for a brief definition. For a journal entry, paraphrase your definition.

Individual and Collaborative Considerations

1. Why did the gods condemn Sisyphus to endlessly push a rock up a hill only to have it roll back down when he reached the top?
2. Why is Sisyphus an "absurd" hero?
3. In what way is Sisyphus' plight "existential"?
4. How does Camus structure his essay?
5. In modern society, what analogies or parallels can you make with Sisyphus? Who are some individuals in the public eye who seem to be "ceaselessly rolling a rock to the top of a mountain"?

Writing Activities

1. Construct an essay arguing that "one does not discover the absurd without being tempted to write a manual of happiness" or vice versa. While allusions to Camus' essay would be great, support the bulk of your paper by defending your own argument with fresh examples.
2. Look back at your definition of existentialism. Then argue a topic or issue from an existential point of view.

✳

A Very Old Man with Enormous Wings

Gabriel García Márquez

Gabriel García Márquez was born in 1928 in Arcataca, a small town off the coast of Colombia. In the early 1960s, after working as a journalist and foreign correspondent, he moved to Mexico City, where he continues to live. In 1982 he was awarded the Nobel Prize for literature, celebrating his short stories and novels, which tend to blend the fantastic (or magical) with realism—the incredible with the believable. One of his better known works, *One Hundred Years of Solitude* (1967), holds the distinction of being the first Latin American book to land on the international best-seller list! His first novel, *The Leaf Storm*, was published in 1955. His subsequent novels and collections of short stories include *No One Writes to the Colonel and Other Stories* (1968), *Leaf Storm and Other Stories* (1972), *Innocent Eréndira and Other Stories* (1978), *Chronicle of a Death Foretold* (1981), *Collected Stories* (1984), *Love in the Time of Cholera* (1985), and *The General in His Labyrinth*—his fictional autobiography (1989). Márquez always credits his grandmother's knowledge of Caribbean folklore as his source of inspiration and information for "magical realism." Márquez says his stories like "A Very Old Man with Enormous Wings" originate with an image, "not an idea or concept. This image grows until the whole story takes its shape as it might in real life." He further states that "it always amuses me that the biggest praise for my work comes for the imagination while the truth is that there's not a single line in all my work that does not have a basis in reality. The problem is that Caribbean reality resembles the wildest imagination."

On the third day of rain they had killed so many crabs inside the house that Pelayo had to cross his drenched courtyard and throw them into the sea, because the newborn child had a temperature all night and they thought it was due to the stench. The world had been sad since Tuesday. Sea and sky were a single ash-gray thing and the sands of the beach, which on March nights glimmered like powdered light, had become a stew of mud and rotten shellfish. The light was so weak at noon that when Pelayo was coming back to the house after throwing away the crabs, it was hard for him to see what it was that was moving and groaning in the rear of the courtyard. He had to go very close to see that it was an old man, a very old man, lying face down in the mud, who, in spite of his tremendous efforts, couldn't get up, impeded by his enormous wings.

Frightened by that nightmare, Pelayo ran to get Elisenda, his wife, who was putting compresses on the sick child, and he took her to the rear of the courtyard. They both looked at the fallen body with mute stupor. He was dressed like a ragpicker. There were only a few faded hairs left on his bald skull and very few teeth in his mouth, and his pitiful condition of a drenched great-grandfather had taken away any sense of grandeur he might have had. His huge buzzard wings, dirty and half-plucked, were forever entangled in the mud. They looked at him so long and so closely that Pelayo and Elisenda very soon overcame their surprise and in the end found him familiar. Then they dared speak to him, and he answered in an incomprehensible dialect with a strong sailor's voice. That was how they skipped over the inconvenience of the wings and quite intelligently concluded that he was a lonely castaway from some foreign ship wrecked by the storm. And yet, they called in a neighbor woman who knew everything about life and death to see him, and all she needed was one look to show them their mistake.

"He's an angel," she told them. "He must have been coming for the child, but the poor fellow is so old that the rain knocked him down."

On the following day everyone knew that a flesh-and-blood angel was held captive in Pelayo's house. Against the judgment of the wise neighbor woman, for whom angels in those times were the fugitive survivors of a celestial conspiracy, they did not have the heart to club him to death. Pelayo watched over him all afternoon from the kitchen, armed with his bailiff's club, and before going to bed he dragged him out of the mud and locked him up with the hens in the wire chicken coop. In the middle of the night, when the rain stopped, Pelayo and Elisenda were still killing crabs. A short time afterward the child woke up without a fever and with a desire to eat. Then they felt magnanimous and decided to put the angel on a raft with fresh water and provisions for three days and leave him to his fate on the high seas. But when they went out into the courtyard with the first light of dawn, they found the whole neighborhood in front of the chicken coop having fun with the angel, without the slightest reverence, tossing him things to eat through the openings in the wire as if he weren't a supernatural creature but a circus animal.

5   Father Gonzaga arrived before seven o'clock, alarmed at the strange news. By that time onlookers less frivolous than those at dawn had already arrived and they were making all kinds of conjectures concerning the captive's future. The simplest among them thought that he should be named mayor of

the world. Others of sterner mind felt that he should be promoted to the rank of five-star general in order to win all wars. Some visionaries hoped that he could be put to stud in order to implant on earth a race of winged wise men who could take charge of the universe. But Father Gonzaga, before becoming a priest, had been a robust woodcutter. Standing by the wire, he reviewed his catechism in an instant and asked them to open the door so that he could take a close look at that pitiful man who looked more like a huge decrepit hen among the fascinated chickens. He was lying in a corner drying his open wings in the sunlight among the fruit peels and breakfast left overs that the early risers had thrown him. Alien to the impertinences of the world, he only lifted his antiquarian eyes and murmured something in his dialect when Father Gonzaga went into the chicken coop and said good morning to him in Latin. The parish priest had his first suspicion of an imposter when he saw that he did not understand the language of God or know how to greet His ministers. Then he noticed that seen close up he was much too human: he had an unbearable smell of the outdoors, the back side of his wings was strewn with parasites and his main feathers had been mistreated by terrestrial winds, and nothing about him measured up to the proud dignity of angels. Then he came out of the chicken coop and in a brief sermon warned the curious against the risks of being ingenuous. He reminded them that the devil had the bad habit of making use of carnival tricks in order to confuse the unwary. He argued that if wings were not the essential element in determining the difference between a hawk and an airplane, they were even less so in the recognition of angels. Nevertheless, he promised to write a letter to his bishop so that the latter would write to his primate so that the latter would write to the Supreme Pontiff in order to get the final verdict from the highest courts.

His prudence fell on sterile hearts. The news of the captive angel spread with such rapidity that after a few hours the courtyard had the bustle of a marketplace and they had to call in troops with fixed bayonets to disperse the mob that was about to knock the house down. Elisenda, her spine all twisted from sweeping up so much marketplace trash, then got the idea of fencing in the yard and charging five cents admission to see the angel.

The curious came from far away. A traveling carnival arrived with a flying acrobat who buzzed over the crowd several times, but no one paid any attention to him because his wings were not those of an angel but, rather, those of a sidereal bat. The most unfortunate invalids on earth came in search of health: a poor woman who since childhood had been counting her heartbeats and had run out of numbers; a Portuguese man who couldn't sleep because the noise of the stars disturbed him; a sleepwalker who got up at night to undo the things he had done while awake; and many others with less serious ailments. In the midst of that shipwreck disorder that made the earth tremble, Pelayo and Elisenda were happy with fatigue, for in less than a week they had crammed their rooms with money and the line of pilgrims waiting their turn to enter still reached beyond the horizon.

The angel was the only one who took no part in his own act. He spent his time trying to get comfortable in his borrowed nest, befuddled by the hellish heat of the oil lamps and sacramental candles that had been placed along the wire. At first they tried to make him eat some mothballs, which, according to the wisdom of the wise neighbor woman, were the food prescribed for angels. But he turned them down, just as he turned down the papal lunches that the penitents brought him, and they never found out whether it was because he was an angel or because he was an old man that in the end he ate nothing but eggplant mush. His only supernatural virtue seemed to be patience. Especially during the first days, when the hens pecked at him, searching for the stellar parasites that proliferated in his wings, and the cripples pulled out feathers to touch their defective parts with, and even the most merciful threw stones at him, trying to get him to rise so they could see him standing. The only time they succeeded in arousing him was when they burned his side with an iron for branding steers, for he had been motionless for so many hours that they thought he was dead. He awoke with a start, ranting in his hermetic language and with tears in his eyes, and he flapped his wings a couple of times, which brought on a whirlwind of chicken dung and lunar dust and a gale of panic that did not seem to be of this world. Although many thought that his reaction had been one not of rage but of pain, from then on they were careful not to annoy him, because the majority understood that his passivity was not that of a hero taking his ease but that of a cataclysm in repose.

Father Gonzaga held back the crowd's frivolity with formulas of maidservant inspiration while awaiting the arrival of a final judgment on the nature of the captive. But the mail from Rome showed no sense of urgency. They spent their time finding out if the prisoner had a navel, if his dialect had any connection with Aramaic, how many times he could fit on the head of a pin, or whether he wasn't just a Norwegian with wings. Those meager letters might have come and gone until the end of time if a providential event had not put an end to the priest's tribulations.

10   It so happened that during those days, among so many other carnival attractions, there arrived in town the traveling show of the woman who had been changed into a spider for having disobeyed her parents. The admission to see her was not only less than the admission to see the angel, but people were permitted to ask her all manner of questions about her absurd state and to examine her up and down so that no one would ever doubt the truth of her horror. She was a frightful tarantula the size of a ram and with the head of a sad maiden. What was most heartrending, however, was not her outlandish shape but the sincere affliction with which she recounted the details of her misfortune. While still practically a child she had sneaked out of her parents' house to go to a dance, and while she was coming back through the woods after having danced all night without permission, a fearful thunderclap rent the sky in two and through the crack came the lightning bolt of brimstone that changed her into a spider. Her only nourishment came

from the meatballs that charitable souls chose to toss into her mouth. A spectacle like that, full of so much human truth and with such a fearful lesson, was bound to defeat without even trying that of a haughty angel who scarcely deigned to look at mortals. Besides, the few miracles attributed to the angel showed a certain mental disorder, like the blind man who didn't recover his sight but grew three new teeth, or the paralytic who didn't get to walk but almost won the lottery, and the leper whose sores sprouted sunflowers. Those consolation miracles, which were more like mocking fun, had already ruined the angel's reputation when the woman who had been changed into a spider finally crushed him completely. That was how Father Gonzaga was cured forever of his insomnia and Pelayo's courtyard went back to being as empty as during the time it had rained for three days and crabs walked through the bedrooms.

The owners of the house had no reason to lament. With the money they saved they built a two-story mansion with balconies and gardens and high netting so that crabs wouldn't get in during the winter, and with iron bars on the windows so that angels wouldn't get in. Pelayo also set up a rabbit warren close to town and gave up his job as bailiff for good, and Elisenda bought some satin pumps with high heels and many dresses of iridescent silk, the kind worn on Sunday by the most desirable women in those times. The chicken coop was the only thing that didn't receive any attention. If they washed it down with creolin and burned tears of myrrh inside it every so often, it was not in homage to the angel but to drive away the dungheap stench that still hung everywhere like a ghost and was turning the new house into an old one. At first, when the child learned to walk, they were careful that he not get too close to the chicken coop. But then they began to lose their fears and got used to the smell, and before the child got his second teeth he'd gone inside the chicken coop to play, where the wires were falling apart. The angel was no less standoffish with him than with other mortals, but he tolerated the most ingenious infamies with the patience of a dog who had no illusions. They both came down with chicken pox at the same time. The doctor who took care of the child couldn't resist the temptation to listen to the angel's heart, and he found so much whistling in the heart and so many sounds in his kidneys that it seemed impossible for him to be alive. What surprised him most, however, was the logic of his wings. They seemed so natural on that completely human organism that he couldn't understand why other men didn't have them too.

When the child began school it had been some time since the sun and rain had caused the collapse of the chicken coop. The angel went dragging himself about here and there like a stray dying man. They would drive him out of the bedroom with a broom and a moment later find him in the kitchen. He seemed to be in so many places at the same time that they grew to think that he'd been duplicated, that he was reproducing himself all through the house, and the exasperated and unhinged Elisenda shouted that it was awful living in that hell full of angels. He could scarcely eat and his antiquarian eyes had also become so foggy that he went about bumping into posts. All he had left were the bare cannulae of his last feathers. Pelayo threw a blanket over him and extended him the charity of letting him sleep in the shed, and only then did they notice that he had a temperature at night, and was delirious with the tongue twisters of an old Norwegian. That was one of the few times they became alarmed, for they thought he was going to die and not even the wise neighbor woman had been able to tell them what to do with dead angels.

And yet he not only survived his worst winter, but seemed improved with the first sunny days. He remained motionless for several days in the farthest corner of the courtyard, where no one would see him, and at the beginning of December some large, stiff feathers began to grow on his wings, the feathers of a scarecrow, which looked more like another misfortune of decrepitude. But he must have known the reason for those changes, for he was quite careful that no one should notice them, that no one should hear the sea chanteys that he sometimes sang under the stars. One morning Elisenda was cutting some bunches of onions for lunch when a wind that seemed to come from the high seas blew into the kitchen. Then she went to the window and caught the angel in his first attempts at flight. They were so clumsy that his fingernails opened a furrow in the vegetable patch and he was on the point of knocking the shed down with the ungainly flapping that slipped on the light and couldn't get a grip on the air. But he did manage to gain altitude. Elisenda let out a sigh of relief, for herself and for him, when she saw him pass over the last houses, holding himself up in some way with the risky flapping of a senile vulture. She kept watching him even when she was through cutting the onions and she kept on watching until it was no longer possible for her to see him, because then he was no longer an annoyance in her life but an imaginary dot on the horizon of the sea.

Writing Log/Journal Assignment

Márquez's stories have often been classified as *magical realism*. In a paragraph or so, explore the possible meanings of the phrase.

Individual and Collaborative Considerations

1. What is a miracle? Do miracles occur in this story?
2. Describe the state of affairs at Pelayo and Elisenda's home prior to the arrival of *the very old man with enormous wings.*
3. When does Pelayo discover the stranger? How does he respond to the old man? What does Elisenda declare *the very old man with enormous wings* is?
4. Human expectations often conflict with reality in Márquez's tale. Why? To what extent do expectations impose limitations on a person?
5. How many instances of decay and renewal can you find in this story? Describe them.

Writing Activities

1. Compare and contrast your conception of an angel to the one presented in Márquez's story. What makes your idea of an angel more real or spiritual than the one Márquez offers? Why do you prefer one angel over another?
2. Write an essay demonstrating how people in the past and present seem to appreciate *exceptional* people or situations most when they are no longer around. Make frequent allusions to "The Very Old Man with Enormous Wings" to clarify or lead off your discussion points.

❈

To Build a Fire

Jack London

Jack London was an adventurer, a reporter, and a novelist. He was a participant in the Klondike Gold Rush as well as a common sailor, and his memories frequently provided the narrative framework for his short stories and novels. His first collection of short stories, *Son of the Wolf* (1900), was followed by several novels, often about the sea and the Yukon—usually picturing man as a "super brute": *The Call of the Wild* (1903), *The People of the Abyss* (1903), *White Fang* (1906), *Martin Eden* (1909), *South Sea Tales* (1911), and *John Barleycorn* (1913). In "To Build a Fire," the protagonist wants to survive in the harsh wilderness (an antagonist of sorts). Nature, however, does not make bargains with anyone, so he cannot count on diplomacy ending his conflict.

Day had broken cold and gray, exceedingly cold and gray, when the man turned aside from the main Yukon trail and climbed the high earth-bank, where a dim and little-travelled trail led eastward through the fat spruce timberland. It was a steep bank, and he paused for breath at the top, excusing the act to himself by looking at his watch. It was nine o'clock. There was no sun nor hint of sun, though there was not a cloud in the sky. It was a clear day, and yet there seemed an intangible pall over the face of things, a subtle gloom that made the day dark, and that was due to the absence of sun. This fact did not worry the man. He was used to the lack of sun. It had been days since he had seen the sun, and he knew that a few more days must pass before that cheerful orb, due south, would just peep above the sky line and dip immediately from view.

The man flung a look back along the way he had come. The Yukon lay a mile wide and hidden under three feet of ice. On top of this ice were as many feet of snow. It was all pure white, rolling in gentle undulations where the ice jams of the freeze-up had formed. North and south, as far as the eye could see, it was unbroken white, save for a dark hairline that curved and twisted from around the spruce-covered island to the south, and that curved and twisted away into the north, where it disappeared behind another spruce-covered island. This dark hairline was the trail—the main trail—that led south five hundred miles to the Chilcoot Pass, Dyea, and salt water; and that led north seventy miles to Dawson, and still on to the north a thousand miles to Nulato, and finally to St. Michael, on Bering Sea, a thousand miles and half a thousand more.

But all this—the mysterious, far-reaching hairline trail, the absence of sun from the sky, the tremendous cold, and the strangeness and weirdness of it all—made no impression on the man. It was not because he was long used to it. He was a newcomer in the land, a *chechaquo*, and this was his first winter. The trouble with him was that he was without imagination. He was quick and alert in the things of life, but only in the things, and not in the significances. Fifty degrees below zero meant eighty-odd degrees of frost. Such fact impressed him as being cold and uncomfortable, and that was all. It did not lead him to meditate upon his frailty as a creature of temperature, and upon man's frailty in general, able only to live within certain narrow limits of heat and cold; and from there on it did not lead him to the conjectural field of immortality and man's place in the universe. Fifty degrees below zero stood for a bite of frost that hurt and that must be guarded against by the use of mittens, ear flaps, warm moccasins, and thick socks. Fifty degrees below zero was to him just precisely fifty degrees below zero. That there should be anything more to it than that was a thought that never entered his head.

As he turned to go on, he spat speculatively. There was a sharp, explosive crackle that startled him. He spat again. And again, in the air, before it could fall to the snow, the spittle crackled. He knew that at fifty below spittle crackled on the snow, but this spittle had crackled in the air. Undoubtedly it was colder than fifty below—how much colder he did not know. But the temperature did not matter. He was bound for the old claim on the left fork of Henderson Creek, where the boys were already. They had come over across the divide from the Indian Creek country, while he had come the roundabout way to take a look at the possibilities of getting out logs in the spring from the islands in the Yukon. He would be in to camp by six o'clock; a bit after dark, it was true, but the boys would be there, a fire would be going, and a hot supper would be ready. As for lunch, he pressed his hand against the protruding bundle under his jacket. It was also under his shirt, wrapped up in a handkerchief and lying against the naked skin. It was the only way to keep the biscuits from freezing. He smiled agreeably to himself as he thought of those biscuits, each cut open and sopped in bacon grease, and each enclosing a generous slice of fried bacon.

5   He plunged in among the big spruce trees. The trail was faint. A foot of snow had fallen since the last sled had passed over, and he was glad he was without a sled, travelling light. In fact, he carried nothing but the lunch wrapped in the handkerchief. He was surprised, however, at the cold. It certainly was cold, he concluded, as he rubbed his numb nose and cheekbones with his mittened hand. He was a warm-whiskered man, but the hair on his face did not protect the high cheekbones and the eager nose that thrust itself aggressively into the frosty air.

At the man's heels trotted a dog, a big native husky, the proper wolf dog, gray-coated and without any visible or temperamental difference from its brother, the wild wolf. The animal was depressed by the tremendous cold. It knew that it was no time for travelling. Its instinct told it a truer tale than was told to the man by the man's judgment. In reality, it was not merely colder than fifty below zero; it was colder than sixty below, than seventy below. It was seventy-five below zero. Since the freezing point is thirty-two above zero, it meant that one hundred and seven degrees of frost obtained. The dog did not know anything about thermometers. Possibly in its brain there was no sharp consciousness of a condition of very cold such as was in the man's brain. But the brute had its instinct. It experienced a vague but menacing apprehension that subdued it and made it slink along at the man's heels, and that made it question eagerly every unwonted movement of the man as if expecting him to go into camp or to seek shelter somewhere and build a fire. The dog had learned fire, and it wanted fire, or else to burrow under the snow and cuddle its warmth away from the air.

The frozen moisture of its breathing had settled on its fur in a fine powder of frost, and especially were its jowls, muzzle, and eyelashes whitened by its crystalled breath. The man's red beard and mustache were likewise frosted, but more solidly, the deposit taking the form of ice and increasing with every warm, moist breath he exhaled. Also, the man was chewing tobacco, and the muzzle of ice held his lips so rigidly that he was unable to clear his chin when he expelled the juice. The result was that a crystal beard of the color and solidity of amber was increasing its length on his chin. If he fell down it would shatter itself, like glass, into brittle fragments. But he did not mind the appendage. It was the penalty all tobacco chewers paid in that country, and he had been out before in two cold snaps. They had not been so cold as this, he knew, but by the spirit thermometer at Sixty Mile he knew they had been registered at fifty below and at fifty-five.

He held on through the level stretch of woods for several miles, crossed a wide flat, and dropped down a bank to the frozen bed of a small stream. This was Henderson Creek, and he knew he was ten miles from the forks. He looked at his watch. It was ten o'clock. He was making four miles an hour, and he calculated that he would arrive at the forks at half-past twelve. He decided to celebrate that event by eating his lunch there.

The dog dropped in again at his heels, with a tail drooping discouragement, as the man swung along the creek bed. The furrow of the old sled trail was plainly visible, but a dozen inches of snow covered the marks of the last runners. In a month no man had come up or down that silent creek. The man held steadily on. He was not much given to thinking, and just then particularly he had nothing to think about save that he would eat lunch at the forks and that at six o'clock he would be in camp with the boys. There was nobody to talk to; and, had there been, speech would have been impossible because of the ice muzzle on his mouth. So he continued monotonously to chew tobacco and to increase the length of his amber beard.

10   Once in a while the thought reiterated itself that it was very cold and that he had never experienced such cold. As he walked along he rubbed his cheekbones and nose with the back of his mittened hand. He did this automatically, now and again changing hands. But, rub as he would, the instant he stopped his cheekbones were numb, and the following instant the end of his nose went numb. He was sure to frost his cheeks; he knew that, and experienced a pang of regret that he had not devised a nose strap of the sort Bud wore in cold snaps. Such a strap passed across the cheeks, as well, and saved them. But it didn't matter much, after all. What were frosted cheeks? A bit painful, that was all; they were never serious.

Empty as the man's mind was of thoughts, he was keenly observant, and he noticed the changes in the creek, the curves and bends and timber jams, and always he sharply noted where he placed his feet. Once, coming around a bend, he shied abruptly, like a startled horse, curved away from the place where he had been walking, and retreated several paces back along the trail. The creek he knew was frozen clear to the bottom—no creek could contain water in that arctic winter—but he knew also that there were springs that bubbled out from the hillsides and ran along under the snow and on top the ice of the creek. He knew that the coldest snaps never froze these springs, and he knew likewise their danger. They were traps. They hid pools of water under the snow that might be three inches deep, or three feet. Sometimes a skin of ice half an inch thick covered them, and in turn was covered by the snow. Sometimes there were alternate layers of water and ice skin, so that when one broke through he kept on breaking through for a while, sometimes wetting himself to the waist.

That was why he had shied in such panic. He had felt the give under his feet and heard the crackle of a snow-hidden ice skin. And to get his feet wet in such a temperature meant trouble and danger. At the very least it meant delay, for he would be forced to stop and build a fire, and under its protection to bare his feet while he dried his socks and moccasins. He stood and studied the creek bed and its banks, and decided that the flow of water came from the right. He reflected awhile, rubbing his nose and cheeks, then skirted to the left, stepping gingerly and testing the footing for each step. Once clear of the danger, he took a fresh chew of tobacco and swung along at his four-mile gait.

In the course of the next two hours he came upon several similar traps. Usually the snow above the hidden pools had a sunken, candied appearance that advertised the danger. Once again, however, he had a close call; and once, suspecting danger, he compelled the dog to go on in front. The dog did not want to go. It hung back until the man shoved it forward, and then it went quickly across the white, unbroken surface. Suddenly it broke through, floundered to one side, and got away to firmer footing. It had wet its forefeet and legs, and almost immediately the water that clung to it turned to ice. It made quick efforts to lick the ice off its legs, then dropped down in the snow and began to bite out the ice that had formed between the toes. This was a matter of instinct. To permit the ice to remain would mean sore feet. It did not know this. It merely obeyed the mysterious prompting that arose from the deep crypts of its being. But the man knew, having achieved a judgment on the subject, and he removed the mitten from his right hand and helped tear out the ice particles. He did not expose his fingers more than a minute, and was astonished at the swift numbness that smote them. It certainly was cold. He pulled on the mitten hastily, and beat the hand savagely across his chest.

At twelve o'clock the day was at its brightest. Yet the sun was too far south on its winter journey to clear the horizon. The bulge of the earth intervened between it and Henderson Creek, where the men walked under a clear sky at noon and cast no shadow. At half-past twelve, to the minute, he arrived at the forks of the creek. He was pleased at the speed he had made. If he kept it up, he would certainly be with the boys by six. He unbuttoned his jacket and shirt and drew forth his lunch. The action consumed no more than a quarter of a minute, yet in that brief moment the numbness laid hold of the exposed fingers. He did not put the mitten on, but, instead, struck the fingers a dozen sharp smashes against his leg. Then he sat down on a snow-covered log to eat. The sting that followed upon the striking of his fingers against his leg ceased so quickly that he was startled. He had had no chance to take a bite of biscuit. He struck the fingers repeatedly and returned them to the mitten, baring the other hand for the purpose of eating. He tried to take a mouthful, but the ice muzzle prevented. He had forgotten to build a fire and thaw out. He chuckled at his foolishness, and as he chuckled he noted the numbness creeping into the exposed fingers. Also, he noted that the stinging which had first come to his toes when he sat down was already passing away. He wondered whether the toes were warm or numb. He moved them inside the moccasins and decided that they were numb.

15   He pulled the mitten on hurriedly and stood up. He was a bit frightened. He stamped up and down until the stinging returned into the feet. It certainly was cold, was his thought. That man from Sulphur Creek had spoken the truth when telling how cold it sometimes got in the country. And he had laughed at him at the time! That showed one must not be too sure of things. There was no mistake about it, it *was* cold. He strode up and down, stamping his feet and threshing his arms, until reassured by the returning warmth. Then he got out matches and proceeded to make a fire. From the undergrowth, where high water of the previous spring had lodged a supply of seasoned twigs, he got his firewood. Working carefully from a small beginning, he soon had a roaring fire, over which he thawed the ice from his face and in the protection of which he ate his biscuits. For the moment the cold

of space was outwitted. The dog took satisfaction in the fire, stretching out close enough for warmth and far enough away to escape being singed.

When the man had finished, he filled his pipe and took his comfortable time over a smoke. Then he pulled on his mittens, settled the ear flaps of his cap firmly about his ears, and took the creek trail up the left fork. The dog was disappointed and yearned back toward the fire. This man did not know cold. Possibly all the generations of his ancestry had been ignorant of cold, of real cold, of cold one hundred and seven degrees below freezing point. But the dog knew; all its ancestry knew, and it had inherited the knowledge. And it knew that it was not good to walk abroad in such fearful cold. It was the time to lie snug in a hole in the snow and wait for a curtain of cloud to be drawn across the face of outer space whence this cold came. On the other hand, there was no keen intimacy between the dog and the man. The one was the toil slave of the other, and the only caresses it had ever received were the caresses of the whip lash and of harsh and menacing throat sounds that threatened the whip lash. So the dog made no effort to communicate its apprehension to the man. It was not concerned in the welfare of the man; it was for its own sake that it yearned back toward the fire. But the man whistled, and spoke to it with the sound of whip lashes, and the dog swung in at the man's heels and followed after.

The man took a chew of tobacco and proceeded to start a new amber beard. Also, his moist breath quickly powdered with white his mustache, eyebrows, and lashes. There did not seem to be so many springs on the left fork of the Henderson, and for half an hour the man saw no signs of any. And then it happened. At a place where there were no signs, where the soft, unbroken snow seemed to advertise solidity beneath, the man broke through. It was not deep. He wet himself halfway to the knees before he floundered out to the firm crust.

He was angry, and cursed his luck aloud. He had hoped to get into camp with the boys at six o'clock, and this would delay him an hour, for he would have to build a fire and dry out his footgear. This was imperative at that low temperature—he knew that much; and he turned aside to the bank, which he climbed. On top, tangled in the underbrush about the trunks of several small spruce trees, was a high-water deposit of dry firewood—sticks and twigs, principally, but also larger portions of seasoned branches and fine, dry, last year's grasses. He threw down several large pieces on top of the snow. This served for a foundation and prevented the young flame from drowning itself in the snow it otherwise would melt. The flame he got by touching a match to a small shred of birch bark that he took from his pocket. This burned even more readily than paper. Placing it on the foundation, he fed the young flame with wisps of dry grass and with the tiniest dry twigs.

He worked slowly and carefully, keenly aware of his danger. Gradually, as the flame grew stronger, he increased the size of the twigs with which he fed it. He squatted in the snow, pulling the twigs out from their entanglement in the brush and feeding directly to the flame. He knew there must be no failure. When it is seventy-five below zero, a man must not fail in his first attempt to build a fire—that is, if his feet are wet. If his feet are dry, and he fails, he can run along the trail for half a mile and restore his circulation. But the circulation of wet and freezing feet cannot be restored by running when it is seventy-five below. No matter how fast he runs, the wet feet will freeze the harder.

20   All this the man knew. The old-timer on Sulphur Creek had told him about it the previous fall, and now he was appreciating the advice. Already all sensation had gone out of his feet. To build the fire he had been forced to remove his mittens, and the fingers had quickly gone numb. His pace of four miles an hour had kept his heart pumping blood to the surface of his body and to all the extremities. But the instant he stopped, the action of the pump eased down. The cold of space smote the unprotected tip of the planet, and he, being on that unprotected tip, received the full force of the blow. The blood of his body recoiled before it. The blood was alive, like the dog, and like the dog it wanted to hide away and cover itself up from the fearful cold. So long as he walked four miles an hour, he pumped that blood, willy-nilly, to the surface; but now it ebbed away and sank down into the recesses of his body. The extremities were the first to feel its absence. His wet feet froze the faster, and his exposed fingers numbed the faster, though they had not yet begun to freeze. Nose and cheeks were already freezing, while the skin of all his body chilled as it lost its blood.

But he was safe. Toes and nose and cheeks would be only touched by the frost, for the fire was beginning to burn with strength. He was feeding it with twigs the size of his finger. In another minute he would be able to feed it with branches the size of his wrist, and then he could remove his wet footgear, and, while it dried, he could keep his naked feet warm by the fire, rubbing them at first, of course, with snow. The fire was a success. He was safe. He remembered the advice of the old-timer on Sulphur Creek, and smiled. The old-timer had been very serious in laying down the law that no man must travel alone in the Klondike after fifty below. Well, here he was; he had had the accident; he was alone; and he had saved himself. Those old-timers were rather womanish, some of them, he thought. All a man had to do was to keep his head, and he was all right. Any man who was a man could travel alone. But it was surprising, the rapidity with which his cheeks and nose were freezing. And he had not thought his fingers could go lifeless in so short a time. Lifeless they were, for he could scarcely make them move together to grip a twig, and they seemed remote from his body and from him. When he touched a twig, he had to look and see whether or not he had hold of it. The wires were pretty well down between him and his finger ends.

All of which counted for little. There was the fire, snapping and crackling and promising life with every dancing flame. He started to untie his moccasins. They were coated with ice; the thick German socks were like sheaths of iron half-way to the knees; and the moccasin strings were like rods of steel all twisted and knotted as by some conflagration. For a moment he tugged with his numb fingers, then, realizing the folly of it, he drew his sheath knife.

But before he could cut the strings, it happened. It was his own fault or, rather, his mistake. He should not have built the fire under the spruce tree. He should have built it in the open. But it had been easier to pull the twigs from the brush and drop them directly on the fire. Now the tree under which he had done this carried a weight of snow on its boughs. No wind had blown for weeks, and each bough was fully freighted. Each time he had pulled a twig he had communicated a slight agitation to the tree—an imperceptible agitation, so far as he was concerned, but an agitation sufficient to bring about the disaster. High up in the tree one bough capsized its load of snow. This fell on the boughs beneath, capsizing them. This process continued, spreading out and involving the whole tree. It grew like an avalanche, and it descended without warning upon the man and the fire, and the fire was blotted out! Where it had burned was a mantle of fresh and disordered snow.

The man was shocked. It was as though he had just heard his own sentence of death. For a moment, he sat and stared at the spot where the fire had been. Then he grew very calm. Perhaps the old-timer on Sulphur Creek was right. If he had only had a trail mate he would have been in no danger now. The trail mate could have built the fire. Well, it was up to him to build the fire over again, and this second time there must be no failure. Even if he succeeded, he would most likely lose some toes. His feet must be badly frozen by now, and there would be some time before the second fire was ready.

25   Such were his thoughts, but he did not sit and think them. He was busy all the time they were passing through his mind. He made a new foundation for a fire, this time in the open, where no treacherous tree could blot it out. Next he gathered dry grasses and tiny twigs from the high-water flotsam. He could not bring his fingers together to pull them out, but he was able to gather them by the handful. In this way he got many rotten twigs and bits of green moss that were undesirable, but it was the best he could do. He worked methodically, even collecting an armful of the larger branches to be used later when the fire gathered strength. And all the while the dog sat and watched him, a certain yearning wistfulness in its eye, for it looked upon him as the fire provider, and the fire was slow in coming.

When all was ready, the man reached in his pocket for a second piece of birch bark. He knew the bark was there, and, though he could not feel it with his fingers, he could hear its crisp rustling as he fumbled for it. Try as he would, he could not clutch hold of it. And all the time, in his consciousness, was the knowledge that each instant his feet were freezing. This thought tended to put him in a panic, but he fought against it and kept calm. He pulled on his mittens with his teeth, and threshed his arms back and forth, beating his hands with all his might against his sides. He did this sitting down, and he stood up to do it; and all the while the dog sat in the snow, its wolf brush of a tail curled around warmly over its forefeet, its sharp wolf ears pricked forward intently as it watched the man. And the man, as he beat and threshed with his arms and hands, felt a great surge of envy as he regarded the creature that was warm and secure in its natural covering.

After a time he was aware of the first faraway signals of sensation in his beaten fingers. The faint tingling grew stronger till it evolved into a stinging ache that was excruciating, but which the man hailed with satisfaction. He stripped the mitten from his right hand and fetched forth the birch bark. The exposed fingers were quickly going numb again. Next he brought out his bunch of sulphur matches. But the tremendous cold had already driven the life out of his fingers. In his effort to separate one match from the others, the whole bunch fell in the snow. He tried to pick it out of the snow, but failed. The dead fingers could neither touch nor clutch. He was very careful. He drove the thought of his freezing feet, and nose, and cheeks, out of his mind, devoting his whole soul to the matches. He watched, using the sense of vision in place of that of touch, and when he saw his fingers on each side the bunch, he closed them—that is, he willed to close them, for the wires were down, and the fingers did not obey. He pulled the mitten on the right hand, and beat it fiercely against his knee. Then, with both mittened hands, he scooped the bunch of matches, along with much snow, into his lap. Yet he was no better off.

After some manipulation he managed to get the bunch between the heels of his mittened hands. In this fashion he carried it to his mouth. The ice crackled and snapped when by a violent effort he opened his mouth. He drew the lower jaw in, curled the upper lip out of the way, and scraped the bunch with his upper teeth in order to separate a match. He succeeded in getting one, which he dropped on his lap. He was no better off. He could not pick it up. Then he devised a way. He picked it up in his teeth and scratched it on his leg. Twenty times he scratched before he succeeded in lighting it. As it flamed he held it with his teeth to the birch bark. But the burning brimstone went up his nostrils and into his lungs, causing him to cough spasmodically. The match fell into the snow and went out.

The old-timer on Sulphur Creek was right, he thought in the moment of controlled despair that ensued: after fifty below, a man should travel with a partner. He beat his hands, but failed in exciting any sensation. Suddenly he bared both hands, removing the mittens with his teeth. He caught the whole bunch between the heels of his hands. His arm muscles not being frozen enabled him to press the hand heels tightly against the matches. Then he scratched the bunch along his leg. It flared into flame, seventy sulphur matches at once! There was no wind to blow them out. He kept his head to one side to escape the strangling fumes, and held the blazing bunch to the birch bark. As he so held it, he became aware of sensation in his hand. His flesh was burning. He could smell it. Deep down below the surface he could feel it. The sensation developed into pain that grew acute. And still he endured it, holding the flame of the matches clumsily to the bark that would not light readily because his own burning hands were in the way, absorbing most of the flame.

30   At last, when he could endure no more, he jerked his hands apart. The blazing matches fell sizzling into the snow, but the birch bark was alight. He

began laying dry grasses and the tiniest twigs on the flame. He could not pick and choose, for he had to lift the fuel between the heels of his hands. Small pieces of rotten wood and green moss clung to the twigs, and he bit them off as well as he could with his teeth. He cherished the flame carefully and awkwardly. It meant life, and it must not perish. The withdrawal of blood from the surface of his body now made him begin to shiver, and he grew more awkward. A large piece of green moss fell squarely on the little fire. He tried to poke it out with his fingers, but his shivering frame made him poke too far, and he disrupted the nucleus of the little fire, the burning grasses and tiny twigs separating and scattering. He tried to poke them together again, but in spite of the tenseness of the effort, his shivering got away from him, and the twigs were hopelessly scattered. Each twig gushed a puff of smoke and went out. The fire provider had failed. As he looked apathetically about him, his eyes chanced on the dog, sitting across the ruins of the fire from him, in the snow, making restless, hunching movements, slightly lifting one forefoot and then the other, shifting its weight back and forth on them with wistful eagerness.

The sight of the dog put a wild idea into his head. He remembered the tale of the man, caught in the blizzard, who killed a steer and crawled inside the carcass, and so was saved. He would kill the dog and bury his hands in the warm body until the numbness went out of them. Then he could build another fire. He spoke to the dog, calling it to him; but in his voice was a strange note of fear that frightened the animal, who had never known the man to speak in such a way before. Something was the matter, and its suspicious nature sensed danger—it knew not what danger, but somewhere, somehow, in its brain arose an apprehension of the man. It flattened its ears down at the sound of the man's voice, and its restless, hunching movements and the liftings and shiftings of its forefeet became more pronounced; but it would not come to the man. He got on his hands and knees and crawled toward the dog. This unusual posture again excited suspicion, and the animal sidled mincingly away.

The man sat up in the snow for a moment and struggled for calmness. Then he pulled on his mittens, by means of his teeth, and got upon his feet. He glanced down at first in order to assure himself that he was really standing up, for the absence of sensation in his feet left him unrelated to the earth. His erect position in itself started to drive the webs of suspicion from the dog's mind; and when he spoke peremptorily, with the sound of whip lashes in his voice, the dog rendered its customary allegiance and came to him. As it came within reaching distance, the man lost his control. His arms flashed out to the dog, and he experienced genuine surprise when he discovered that his hands could not clutch, that there was neither bend nor feeling in the fingers. He had forgotten for the moment that they were frozen and that they were freezing more and more. All this happened quickly, and before the animal could get away, he encircled its body with his arms. He sat down in the snow, and in this fashion held the dog, while it snarled and whined and struggled.

But it was all he could do, hold its body encircled in his arms and sit there. He realized that he could not kill the dog. There was no way to do it. With his helpless hands he could neither draw nor hold his sheath knife nor throttle the animal. He released it, and it plunged wildly away, with tail between its legs, and still snarling. It halted forty feet away and surveyed him curiously, with ears sharply pricked forward.

The man looked down at his hands in order to locate them, and found them hanging on the ends of his arms. It struck him as curious that one should have to use his eyes in order to find out where his hands were. He began threshing his arms back and forth, beating the mittened hands against his sides. He did this for five minutes, violently, and his heart pumped enough blood up to the surface to put a stop to his shivering. But no sensation was aroused in the hands. He had an impression that they hung like weights on the ends of his arms, but when he tried to run the impression down, he could not find it.

35   A certain fear of death, dull and oppressive, came to him. This fear quickly became poignant as he realized that it was no longer a mere matter of freezing his fingers and toes, or of losing his hands and feet, but that it was a matter of life and death with the chances against him. This threw him into a panic, and he turned and ran up the creek bed along the old, dim trail. The dog joined in behind and kept up with him. He ran blindly, without intention, in fear such as he had never known in his life. Slowly, as he plowed and floundered through the snow, he began to see things again—the banks of the creek, the old timber jams, the leafless aspens, and the sky. The running made him feel better. He did not shiver. Maybe, if he ran on, his feet would thaw out; and anyway, if he ran far enough, he would reach camp and the boys. Without doubt he would lose some fingers and toes and some of his face; but the boys would take care of him, and save the rest of him when he got there. And at the same time there was another thought in his mind that said he would never get to the camp and the boys; that it was too many miles away, that the freezing had too great a start on him, and that he would soon be stiff and dead. This thought he kept in the background and refused to consider. Sometimes it pushed itself forward and demanded to be heard, but he thrust it back and strove to think of other things.

It struck him as curious that he could run at all on feet so frozen that he could not feel them when they struck the earth and took the weight of his body. He seemed to himself to skim along above the surface, and to have no connection with the earth. Somewhere he had once seen a winged Mercury, and he wondered if Mercury felt as he felt when skimming over the earth.

His theory of running until he reached the camp and the boys had one flaw in it: he lacked the endurance. Several times he stumbled, and finally he tottered, crumpled up, and fell. When he tried to rise, he failed. He must sit and rest, he decided, and next time he would merely walk and keep on going. As he sat and regained his breath, he noted that he was feeling quite warm and comfortable. He was not shivering, and it even seemed that a warm glow had come to his chest and trunk. And yet, when he touched his nose and cheeks, there was no sensation. Running would not thaw them out. Nor would it thaw out his hands and feet. Then the thought came to him that the frozen portions of his body must be extending. He tried to keep this thought down, to forget it, to think of something else; he was aware of the panicky feeling that it caused, and he was afraid of the panic. But the thought asserted itself, and persisted, until it produced a vision of his body totally frozen. This was too much, and he made another wild run along the trail. Once he slowed down to a walk, but the thought of the freezing extending itself made him run again.

And all the time the dog ran with him, at his heels. When he fell down a second time, it curled its tail over its forefeet and sat in front of him, facing him, curiously eager and intent. The warmth and security of the animal angered him, and he cursed it till it flattened down its ears appeasingly. This time the shivering came more quickly upon the man. He was losing in his battle with the frost. It was creeping into his body from all sides. The thought of it drove him on, but he ran no more than a hundred feet, when he staggered and pitched headlong. It was his last panic. When he had recovered his breath and control, he sat up and entertained in his mind the conception of meeting death with dignity. However, the conception did not come to him in such terms. His idea of it was that he had been making a fool of himself, running around like a chicken with its head cut off—such was the simile that occurred to him. Well, he was bound to freeze anyway, and he might as well take it decently. With this new-found peace of mind came the first glimmerings of drowsiness. A good idea, he thought, to sleep off to death. It was like taking an anesthetic. Freezing was not so bad as people thought. There were lots worse ways to die.

He pictured the boys finding his body next day. Suddenly he found himself with them, coming along the trail and looking for himself. And, still with them, he came around a turn in the trail and found himself lying in the snow. He did not belong with himself any more, for even then he was out of himself, standing with the boys and looking at himself in the snow. It certainly was cold, was his thought. When he got back to the States he could tell the folks what real cold was. He drifted on from this to a vision of the old-timer on Sulphur Creek. He could see him quite clearly, warm and comfortable, and smoking a pipe.

40 "You were right, old hoss; you were right," the man mumbled to the old-timer of Sulphur Creek.

Then the man drowsed off into what seemed to him the most comfortable and satisfying sleep he had ever known. The dog sat facing him and waiting. The brief day drew to a close in a long, slow twilight. There were no signs of a fire to be made, and, besides, never in the dog's experience had it known a man to sit like that in the snow and make no fire. As the twilight drew on, its eager yearning for the fire mastered it, and with a great lifting and shifting of forefeet, it whined softly, then flattened its ears down in anticipation of being chidden by the man. But the man remained silent. Later the dog whined loudly. And still later it crept close to the man and caught the scent of death. This made the animal bristle and back away. A little longer it de-layed, howling under the stars that leaped and danced and shone brightly in the cold sky. Then it turned and trotted up the trail in the direction of the camp it knew, where were the other food providers and fire providers.

Writing Log/Journal Assignment

Write a journal entry focusing on the coldest day—or part of a day—you have ever experienced. What did you do to keep warm? Was your chill due to nature (snow) or human progress (an air conditioner)?

Individual and Collaborative Considerations

1. How does London illustrate the severity of the weather? How do details appeal to the senses? Give some examples.
2. Throughout the story, the man chews and spits tobacco. Since chewing tobacco dehydrates a person, why is this a rather ironic practice?
3. Explain the relationship between the man and his dog. How might he use his dog as a possible means of warming his numb hands?
4. If we view this story as man against nature, what steps does the man take to defeat the cruel weather? How does nature ultimately triumph over the man?
5. As stated in the annotation in the table of contents, the man in the Yukon not only fights for his life, but he also reasons that there are worse ways of dying. What might these be? (Include your own insights drawn from outside the story.)

Writing Activities

1. Write an essay epitomizing the struggle between human beings (and their *civilized achievements*) and nature. The conflict you select will function as the thesis of your essay. Your analysis may blend any number of rhetor-ical modes of development (e.g., comparison/contrast, definition).
2. Compose an essay demonstrating the many ways of coming to terms with death, possibly offering an insight as to how acceptance of mortality is the ultimate resolution between life and death. One way to begin this writing prompt would be to review Individual and Collaborative Con-siderations question 5.

✳

The Yellow Wall-Paper

Charlotte Perkins Gilman

Born in Hartford, Connecticut, Charlotte Perkins Gilman—like her great-aunt Harriet Beecher Stowe—concerned herself at a very early age with social injustices, especially those affecting women. During the 1890s, she gained quite a reputation as a lecturer, and she also became known for her many feminist tracts. Her works include *Women and Economics* (1898), *Children* (1900), *The Home* (1904), *Human Work* (1904), *Moving the Mountain* (1911), *Herland* (1915; unpublished until 1978), and *With Her in Ourland* (1916). Gilman also published her own journal called *The Forerunner* between 1909 and 1917. Gilman drew from her own experiences—the extreme depression following her daughter's birth—mixing it with fiction when she wrote "The Yellow Wall-Paper." Like the speaker in the story, Gilman was forbidden by her doctor, S. Weir Mitchell, to engage in any sort of strenuous activity—particularly writing (the one thing she wanted to do more than anything else).

It is very seldom that mere ordinary people like John and myself secure ancestral halls for the summer.

A colonial mansion, a hereditary estate, I would say a haunted house, and reach the height of romantic felicity—but that would be asking too much of fate!

Still I will proudly declare that there is something queer about it.

Else, why should it be let so cheaply? And why have stood so long untenanted?

5   John laughs at me, of course, but one expects that in marriage.

John is practical in the extreme. He has no patience with faith, an intense horror of superstitition, and he scoffs openly at any talk of things not to be felt and seen and put down in figures.

John is a physician, and *perhaps*—(I would not say it to a living soul, of course, but this is dead paper and a great relief to my mind—) *perhaps* that is one reason I do not get well faster.

You see he does not believe I am sick!

And what can one do?

10   If a physician of high standing, and one's own husband, assures friends and relatives that there is really nothing the matter with one but temporary nervous depression—a slight hysterical tendency—what is one to do?

My brother is also a physician, and also of high standing, and he says the same thing.

So I take phosphates or phosphites[1]—whichever it is, and tonics, and journeys, and air, and exercise, and am absolutely forbidden to "work" until I am well again.

Personally, I disagree with their ideas.

Personally, I believe that congenial work, with excitement and change, would do me good.

15   But what is one to do?

I did write for a while in spite of them; but it *does* exhaust me a good deal—having to be so sly about it, or else meet with heavy opposition.

I sometimes fancy that in my condition if I had less opposition and more society and stimulus—but John says the very worst thing I can do is to think about my condition, and I confess it always makes me feel bad.

So I will let it alone and talk about the house.

The most beautiful place! It is quite alone, standing well back from the road, quite three miles from the village. It makes me think of English places that you read about, for there are hedges and walls and gates that lock, and lots of separate little houses for the gardeners and people.

20   There is a *delicious* garden! I never saw such a garden—large and shady, full of box-bordered paths, and lined with long grape-covered arbors with seats under them.

There were greenhouses, too, but they are all broken now.

There was some legal trouble, I believe, something about the heirs and co-heirs; anyhow, the place has been empty for years.

That spoils my ghostliness, I am afraid, but I don't care—there is something strange about the house—I can feel it.

I even said so to John one moonlight evening, but he said what I felt was a *draught*, and shut the window.

25   I get unreasonably angry with John sometimes. I'm sure I never used to be so sensitive. I think it is due to this nervous condition.

But John says if I feel so, I shall neglect proper self-control; so I take pains to control myself—before him, at least, and that makes me very tired.

I don't like our room a bit. I wanted one downstairs that opened on the piazza and had roses all over the window, and such pretty old-fashioned chintz hangings! But John would not hear of it.

He said there was only one window and not room for two beds, and no near room for him if he took another.

He is very careful and loving, and hardly lets me stir without special direction.

30   I have a schedule prescription for each hour in the day; he takes all care from me, and so I feel basely ungrateful not to value it more.

He said we came here solely on my account, that I was to have perfect rest and all the air I could get. "Your exercise depends on your strength, my

---

[1]Both terms refer to salts of phosphorous acid. The narrator, however, means "phosphate," a carbonated beverage of water, flavoring, and a small amount of phosphoric acid.

dear," said he, "and your food somewhat on your appetite; but air you can absorb all the time." So we took the nursery at the top of the house.

It is a big, airy room, the whole floor nearly, with windows that look all ways, and air and sunshine galore. It was nursery first and then play-room and gymnasium, I should judge; for the windows are barred for little children, and there are rings and things in the walls.

The paint and paper look as if a boys' school had used it. It is stripped off—the paper—in great patches all around the head of my bed, about as far as I can reach, and in a great place on the other side of the room low down. I never saw a worse paper in my life.

One of those sprawling flamboyant patterns committing every artistic sin.

35   It is dull enough to confuse the eye in following, pronounced enough to constantly irritate and provoke study, and when you follow the lame uncertain curves for a little distance they suddenly commit suicide—plunge off at outrageous angles, destroy themselves in unheard of contradictions.

The color is repellent, almost revolting; a smouldering unclean yellow, strangely faded by the slow-turning sunlight.

It is a dull yet lurid orange in some places, a sickly sulphur tint in others.

No wonder the children hated it! I should hate it myself if I had to live in this room long.

There comes John, and I must put this away—he hates to have me write a word.

40   We have been here two weeks, and I haven't felt like writing before, since that first day.

I am sitting by the window now, up in this atrocious nursery, and there is nothing to hinder my writing as much as I please, save lack of strength.

John is away all day, and even some nights when his cases are serious.

I am glad my case is not serious!

But these nervous troubles are dreadfully depressing.

45   John does not know how much I really suffer. He knows there is no *reason* to suffer, and that satisfies him.

Of course it is only nervousness. It does weigh on me so not to do my duty in any way!

I meant to be such a help to John, such a real rest and comfort, and here I am a comparative burden already!

Nobody would believe what an effort it is to do what little I am able—to dress and entertain, and order things.

It is fortunate Mary is so good with the baby. Such a dear baby!

50   And yet I *cannot* be with him, it makes me so nervous.

I suppose John never was nervous in his life. He laughs at me so about this wall-paper!

At first he meant to repaper the room, but afterwards he said that I was letting it get the better of me, and that nothing was worse for a nervous patient than to give way to such fancies.

He said that after the wall-paper was changed it would be the heavy bedstead, and then the barred windows, and then that gate at the head of the stairs, and so on.

"You know the place is doing you good," he said, "and really, dear, I don't care to renovate the house just for a three month's rental."

55   "Then do let us go downstairs," I said, "there are such pretty rooms there."

Then he took me in his arms and called me a blessed little goose, and said he would go down cellar, if I wished, and have it whitewashed into the bargain.

But he is right enough about the beds and windows and things.

It is an airy and comfortable room as any one need wish, and, of course, I would not be so silly as to make him uncomfortable just for a whim.

I'm really getting quite fond of the big room, all but that horrid paper.

60   Out of one window I can see the garden, those mysterious deep-shaded arbors, the riotous old-fashioned flowers, and bushes and gnarly trees.

Out of another I get a lovely view of the bay and a little private wharf belonging to the estate. There is a beautiful shaded lane that runs down there from the house. I always fancy I see people walking in these numerous paths and arbors, but John has cautioned me not to give way to fancy in the least. He says that with my imaginative power and habit of story-making, a nervous weakness like mine is sure to lead to all manner of excited fancies, and that I ought to use my will and good sense to check the tendency. So I try.

I think sometimes that if I were only well enough to write a little it would relieve the press of ideas and rest me.

But I find I get pretty tired when I try.

It is so discouraging not to have any advice and companionship about my work. When I get really well, John says we will ask Cousin Henry and Julia down for a long visit; but he says he would as soon put fireworks in my pillow-case as to let me have those stimulating people about now.

65   I wish I could get well faster.

But I must not think about that. This paper looks to me as if it *knew* what a vicious influence it had!

There is a recurrent spot where the pattern lolls like a broken neck and two bulbous eyes stare at you upside down.

I get positively angry with the impertinence of it and the everlastingness. Up and down and sideways they crawl, and those absurd, unblinking eyes are everywhere. There is one place where two breadths didn't match, and the eyes go all up and down the line, one a little higher than the other.

I never saw so much expression in an inanimate thing before, and we all know how much expression they have! I used to lie awake as a child and get more entertainment and terror out of blank walls and plain furniture than most children could find in a toy-store.

70   I remember what a kindly wink the knobs of our big, old bureau used to have, and there was one chair that always seemed like a strong friend.

I used to feel that if any of the other things looked too fierce I could always hop into that chair and be safe.

The furniture in this room is no worse than inharmonious, however, for we had to bring it all from downstairs. I suppose when this was used as a playroom they had to take the nursery things out, and no wonder! I never saw such ravages as the children have made here.

The wall-paper, as I said before, is torn off in spots, and it sticketh closer than a brother—they must have had perseverance as well as hatred.

Then the floor is scratched and gouged and splintered, the plaster itself is dug out here and there, and this great heavy bed which is all we found in the room, looks as if it had been through the wars.

75   But I don't mind it a bit—only the paper.

There comes John's sister. Such a dear girl as she is, and so careful of me! I must not let her find me writing.

She is a perfect and enthusiastic housekeeper, and hopes for no better profession. I verily believe she thinks it is the writing which made me sick!

But I can write when she is out, and see her a long way off from these windows.

There is one that commands the road, a lovely shaded winding road, and one that just looks off over the country. A lovely country, too, full of great elms and velvet meadows.

80   This wall-paper has a kind of sub-pattern in a different shade, a particularly irritating one, for you can only see it in certain lights, and not clearly then.

But in the places where it isn't faded and where the sun is just so—I can see a strange, provoking, formless sort of figure, that seems to skulk about behind that silly and conspicuous front design.

There's sister on the stairs!

Well, the Fourth of July is over! The people are all gone and I am tired out. John thought it might do me good to see a little company, so we just had mother and Nellie and the children down for a week.

Of course I didn't do a thing. Jennie sees to everything now.

85   But it tired me all the same.

John says if I don't pick up faster he shall send me to Weir Mitchell[2] in the fall.

But I don't want to go there at all. I had a friend who was in his hands once, and she says he is just like John and my brother, only more so!

Besides, it is such an undertaking to go so far.

I don't feel as if it was worth while to turn my hand over for anything, and I'm getting dreadfully fretful and querulous.

90   I cry at nothing, and cry most of the time.

[2]Silas Weir Mitchell (1829–1914)—a Philadelphia neurologist-psychologist who introduced the "rest cure" for nervous diseases.

Of course I don't when John is here, or anybody else, but when I am alone.

And I am alone a good deal just now. John is kept in town very often by serious cases, and Jennie is good and lets me alone when I want her to.

So I walk a little in the garden or down that lovely lane, sit on the porch under the roses, and lie down up here a good deal.

I'm getting really fond of the room in spite of the wall-paper. Perhaps *because* of the wall-paper.

95   It dwells in my mind so!

I lie here on this great immovable bed—it is nailed down, I believe—and follow that pattern about by the hour. It is as good as gymnastics, I assure you. I start, we'll say, at the bottom, down in the corner over there where it has not been touched, and I determine for the thousandth time that I *will* follow that pointless pattern to some sort of a conclusion.

I know a little of the principle of design, and I know this thing was not arranged on any laws of radiation, or alternation, or repetition, or symmetry, or anything else that I ever heard of.

It is repeated, of course, by the breadths, but not otherwise.

Looked at in one way each breadth stands alone, the bloated curves and flourishes—a kind of "debased Romanesque" with *delirium tremens*[3] go waddling up and down in isolated columns of fatuity.

100   But, on the other hand, they connect diagonally, and the sprawling outlines run off in great slanting waves of optic horror, like a lot of wallowing seaweeds in full chase.

The whole thing goes horizontally, too, at least it seems so, and I exhaust myself in trying to distinguish the order of its going in that direction.

They have used a horizontal breadth for a frieze, and that adds wonderfully to the confusion.

There is one end of the room where it is almost intact, and there, when the crosslights fade and the low sun shines directly upon it, I can almost fancy radiation after all,—the interminable grotesques seems to form around a common center and rush off in headlong plunges of equal distraction.

It makes me tired to follow it. I will take a nap I guess.

105 I don't know why I should write this.

I don't want to.

I don't feel able.

And I know John would think it absurd. But I *must* say what I feel and think in some way—it is such a relief!

But the effort is getting to be greater than the relief.

110   Half the time now I am awfully lazy, and lie down ever so much.

John says I mustn't lose my strength, and has me take cod liver oil and lots of tonics and things, to say nothing of ale and wine and rare meat.

---

[3]Mental confusion caused by alcohol poisoning and characterized by physical tremors and hallucinations.

Dear John! He loves me very dearly, and hates to have me sick. I tried to have a real earnest reasonable talk with him the other day, and tell him how I wish he would let me go and make a visit to Cousin Henry and Julia.

But he said I wasn't able to go, nor able to stand it after I got there; and I did not make out a very good case for myself, for I was crying before I had finished.

It is getting to be a great effort for me to think straight. Just this nervous weakness I suppose.

115 And dear John gathered me up in his arms, and just carried me upstairs and laid me on the bed, and sat by me and read to me till it tired my head.

He said I was his darling and his comfort and all he had, and that I must take care of myself for his sake, and keep well.

He says no one but myself can help me out of it, that I must use my will and self-control and not let any silly fancies run away with me.

There's one comfort, the baby is well and happy, and does not have to occupy this nursery with the horrid wall-paper.

If we had not used it, that blessed child would have! What a fortunate escape! Why, I wouldn't have a child of mine, an impressionable little thing, live in such a room for worlds.

120 I never thought of it before, but it is lucky that John kept me here after all, I can stand it so much easier than a baby, you see.

Of course I never mention it to them any more—I am too wise,—but I keep watch of it all the same.

There are things in that paper that nobody knows but me, or ever will.

Behind that outside pattern the dim shapes get clearer every day.

It is always the same shape, only very numerous.

125 And it is like a woman stooping down and creeping about behind that pattern. I don't like it a bit. I wonder—I begin to think—I wish John would take me away from here!

It is so hard to talk with John about my case, because he is so wise, and because he loves me so.

But I tried it last night.

It was moonlight. The moon shines in all around just as the sun does.

I hate to see it sometimes, it creeps so slowly, and always comes in by one window or another.

130 John was asleep and I hated to waken him, so I kept still and watched the moonlight on that undulating wall-paper till I felt creepy.

The faint figure behind seemed to shake the pattern, just as if she wanted to get out.

I got up softly and went to feel and see if the paper *did* move, and when I came back John was awake.

"What is it, little girl?" he said. "Don't go walking about like that—you'll get cold."

I thought it was a good time to talk, so I told him that I really was not gaining here, and that I wished he would take me away.

135   "Why, darling!" said he, "our lease will be up in three weeks, and I can't see how to leave before.

"The repairs are not done at home, and I cannot possibly leave town just now. Of course if you were in any danger, I could and would, but you really are better, dear, whether you can see it or not. I am a doctor, dear, and I know. You are gaining flesh and color, your appetite is better, I feel really much easier about you."

"I don't weigh a bit more," said I, "nor as much; and my appetite may be better in the evening when you are here, but it is worse in the morning when you are away!"

"Bless her little heart!" said he with a big hug, "she shall be as sick as she pleases! But now let's improve the shining hours by going to sleep, and talk about it in the morning!"

"And you won't go away?" I asked gloomily.

140   "Why, how can I, dear? It is only three weeks more and then we will take a nice little trip of a few days while Jennie is getting the house ready. Really dear you are better!"

"Better in body perhaps—" I began, and stopped short, for he sat up straight and looked at me with such a stern, reproachful look that I could not say another word.

"My darling," said he, "I beg of you, for my sake and for our child's sake, as well as for your own, that you will never for one instant let that idea enter your mind! There is nothing so dangerous, so fascinating, to a temperament like yours. It is a false and foolish fancy. Can you not trust me as a physician when I tell you so?"

So of course I said no more on that score, and we went to sleep before long. He thought I was asleep first, but I wasn't, and lay there for hours trying to decide whether that front pattern and the back pattern really did move together or separately.

On a pattern like this, by daylight, there is a lack of sequence, a defiance of law, that is a constant irritant to a normal mind.

145   The color is hideous enough, and unreliable enough, and infuriating enough, but the pattern is torturing.

You think you have mastered it, but just as you get well underway in following, it turns back-somersault and there you are. It slaps you in the face, knocks you down, and tramples upon you. It is like a bad dream.

The outside pattern is a florid arabesque, reminding one of a fungus. If you can imagine a toadstool in joints, an interminable string of toadstools, budding and sprouting in endless convolutions—why, that is something like it.

That is, sometimes!

There is one marked peculiarity about this paper, a thing nobody seems to notice but myself, and that is that it changes as the light changes.

150   When the sun shoots in through the east window—I always watch for that first long, straight ray—it changes so quickly that I never can quite believe it.

That is why I watch it always.

By moonlight—the moon shines in all night when there is a moon—I wouldn't know it was the same paper.

At night in any kind of light, in twilight, candlelight, lamplight, and worst of all by moonlight, it becomes bars! The outside pattern I mean, and the woman behind it is as plain as can be.

I didn't realize for a long time what the thing was that showed behind, that dim sub-pattern, but now I am quite sure it is a woman.

155 By daylight she is subdued, quiet. I fancy it is the pattern that keeps her so still. It is so puzzling. It keeps me quiet by the hour.

I lie down ever so much now. John says it is good for me, and to sleep all I can.

Indeed he started the habit of making me lie down for an hour after each meal.

It is a very bad habit I am convinced, for you see I don't sleep.

And that cultivates deceit, for I don't tell them I'm awake—O no!

160 The fact is I am getting a little afraid of John.

He seems very queer sometimes, and even Jennie has an inexplicable look.

It strikes me occasionally, just as a scientific hypothesis,—that perhaps it is the paper!

I have watched John when he did not know I was looking, and come into the room suddenly on the most innocent excuses, and I've caught him several times *looking at the paper!* And Jennie too. I caught Jennie with her hand on it once.

She didn't know I was in the room, and when I asked her in a quiet, a very quiet voice, with the most restrained manner possible, what she was doing with the paper—she turned around as if she had been caught stealing, and looked quite angry—asked me why I should frighten her so!

165 Then she said that the paper stained everything it touched, that she had found yellow smooches on all my clothes and John's, and she wished we would be more careful!

Did not that sound innocent? But I know she was studying that pattern, and I am determined that nobody shall find it out but myself!

Life is very much more exciting now than it used to be. You see I have something more to expect, to look forward to, to watch. I really do eat better, and am more quiet than I was.

John is so pleased to see me improve! He laughed a little the other day, and said I seemed to be flourishing in spite of my wall-paper.

I turned it off with a laugh. I had no intention of telling him it was *because* of the wall-paper—he would make fun of me. He might even want to take me away.

170 I don't want to leave now until I have found it out. There is a week more, and I think that will be enough.

I'm feeling ever so much better! I don't sleep much at night, for it is so interesting to watch developments; but I sleep a good deal in the daytime.

In the daytime it is tiresome and perplexing.

There are always new shoots on the fungus, and new shades of yellow all over it. I cannot keep count of them, though I have tried conscientiously.

It is the strangest yellow, that wall-paper! It makes me think of all the yellow things I ever saw—not beautiful ones like buttercups, but old foul, bad yellow things.

175   But there is something else about that paper—the smell! I noticed it the moment we came into the room, but with so much air and sun it was not bad. Now we have had a week of fog and rain, and whether the windows are open or not, the smell is here.

It creeps all over the house.

I find it hovering in the dining-room, skulking in the parlor, hiding in the hall, lying in wait for me on the stairs.

It gets into my hair.

Even when I go to ride, if I turn my head suddenly and surprise it—there is that smell!

180   Such a peculiar odor, too! I have spent hours in trying to analyze it, to find what it smelled like.

It is not bad—at first, and very gentle, but quite the subtlest, most enduring odor I ever met.

In this damp weather it is awful, I wake up in the night and find it hanging over me.

It used to disturb me at first. I thought seriously of burning the house— to reach the smell.

But now I am used to it. The only thing I can think of that it is like is the *color* of the paper! A yellow smell.

185   There is a very funny mark on this wall, low down, near the mopboard. A streak that runs round the room. It goes behind every piece of furniture, except the bed, a long, straight, even *smooch*, as if it had been rubbed over and over.

I wonder how it was done and who did it, and what they did it for. Round and round and round—round and round and round!—it makes me dizzy!

I really have discovered something at last.

Through watching so much at night, when it changes so, I have finally found out.

The front pattern *does* move—and no wonder! The woman behind shakes it!

190   Sometimes I think there are a great many women behind, and sometimes only one, and she crawls around fast, and her crawling shakes it all over.

Then in the very bright spots she keeps still, and in the very shady spots she just takes hold of the bars and shakes them hard.

And she is all the time trying to climb through. But nobody could climb through that pattern—it strangles so; I think that is why it has so many heads.

They get through, and then the pattern strangles them off and turns them upside down, and makes their eyes white!

If those heads were covered or taken off it would not be half so bad.

195 I think that woman gets out in the daytime!

And I'll tell you why—privately—I've seen her!

I can see her out of every one of my windows!

It is the same woman, I know, for she is always creeping, and most women do not creep by daylight.

I see her in that long shaded lane, creeping up and down. I see her in those dark grape arbors, creeping all around the garden.

200 I see her on that long road under the trees, creeping along, and when a carriage comes she hides under the blackberry vines.

I don't blame her a bit. It must be very humiliating to be caught creeping by daylight!

I always lock the door when I creep by daylight. I can't do it at night, for I know John would suspect something at once.

And John is so queer now, that I don't want to irritate him. I wish he would take another room! Besides, I don't want anybody to get that woman out at night but myself.

I often wonder if I could see her out of all the windows at once.

205 But, turn as fast as I can, I can only see out of one at one time.

And though I always see her, she *may* be able to creep faster than I can turn!

I have watched her sometimes away off in the open country, creeping as fast as a cloud shadow in a high wind.

If only that top pattern could be gotten off from the under one! I mean to try it, little by little.

I have found out another funny thing, but I shan't tell it this time! It does not do to trust people too much.

210 There are only two more days to get this paper off, and I believe John is beginning to notice. I don't like the look in his eyes.

And I heard him ask Jennie a lot of professional questions about me. She had a very good report to give.

She said I slept a good deal in the daytime.

John knows I don't sleep very well at night, for all I'm so quiet!

He asked me all sorts of questions, too, and pretended to be very loving and kind.

215 As if I couldn't see through him!

Still, I don't wonder he acts so, sleeping under this paper for three months.

It only interests me, but I feel sure John and Jennie are secretly affected by it.

Hurrah! This is the last day, but it is enough. John to stay in town over night, and won't be out until this evening.

Jennie wanted to sleep with me—the sly thing! But I told her I should undoubtedly rest better for a night all alone.

220　That was clever, for really I wasn't alone a bit! As soon as it was moonlight and that poor thing began to crawl and shake the pattern, I got up and ran to help her.

I pulled and she shook, I shook and she pulled, and before morning we had peeled off yards of that paper.

A strip about as high as my head and half around the room.

And then when the sun came and that awful pattern began to laugh at me, I declared I would finish it to-day!

We got away to-morrow, and they are moving all my furniture down again to leave things as they were before.

225　Jennie looked at the wall in amazement, but I told her merrily that I did it out of pure spite at the vicious thing.

She laughed and said she wouldn't mind doing it herself, but I must not get tired.

How she betrayed herself that time!

But I am here, and no person touches this paper but me—not *alive!*

She tried to get me out of the room—it was too patent! But I said it was so quiet and empty and clean now that I believed I would lie down again and sleep all I could; and not to wake me even for dinner—I would call when I woke.

230　So now she is gone, and the servants are gone, and the things are gone, and there is nothing left but that great bedstead nailed down, with the canvas mattress we found on it.

We shall sleep downstairs to-night, and take the boat home to-morrow.

I quite enjoy the room, now it is bare again.

How those children did tear about here!

This bedstead is fairly gnawed!

235　But I must get to work.

I have locked the door and thrown the key down into the front path.

I don't want to go out, and I don't want to have anybody come in, till John comes.

I want to astonish him.

I've got a rope up here that even Jennie did not find. If that woman does get out, and tries to get away, I can tie her!

240　But I forgot I could not reach far without anything to stand on!

This bed will *not* move!

I tried to lift and push it until I was lame, and then I got so angry I bit off a little piece at one corner—but it hurt my teeth.

Then I peeled off all the paper I could reach standing on the floor. It sticks horribly and the pattern just enjoys it! All those strangled heads and bulbous eyes and waddling fungus growths just shriek with derision!

I am getting angry enough to do something desperate. To jump out of the window would be admirable exercise, but the bars are too strong even to try.

245　Besides I wouldn't do it. Of course not. I know well enough that a step like that is improper and might be misconstrued.

I don't like to *look* out of the windows even—there are so many of those creeping women, and they creep so fast.

I wonder if they all come out of that wall-paper as I did?

But I am securely fastened now by my well-hidden rope—you don't get *me* out in the road there!

I suppose I shall have to get back behind the pattern when it comes night, and that is hard!

250 It is so pleasant to be out in this great room and creep around as I please!

I don't want to go outside. I won't, even if Jennie asks me to.

For outside you have to creep on the ground, and everything is green instead of yellow.

But here I can creep smoothly on the floor, and my shoulder just fits in that long smooch around the wall, so I cannot lose my way.

Why there's John at the door!

255 It is no use, young man, you can't open it!

How he does call and pound!

Now he's crying for an axe.

It would be a shame to break down that beautiful door!

"John dear!" said I in the gentlest voice, "the key is down by the front steps, under a plaintain leaf!"

260 That silenced him for a few moments.

Then he said—very quietly indeed, "Open the door, my darling!"

"I can't," said I. "The key is down by the front door under a plaintain leaf!"

And then I said it again, several times, very gently and slowly, and said it so often that he had to go and see, and he got it of course, and came in. He stopped short by the door.

"What is the matter?" he cried. "For God's sake, what are you doing!"

265 I kept on creeping just the same, but I looked at him over my shoulder.

"I've got out at last," said I, "in spite of you and Jane? And I've pulled off most of the paper, so you can't put me back!"

Now why should that man have fainted? But he did, and right across my path by the wall, so that I had to creep over him every time!

Writing Log/Journal Assignment

Select a wallpapered room in your own home or somewhere else and stare at it for about ten to fifteen minutes. Then, immediately write down your observations in your journal. Did designs in the wallpaper move and come to life? Explain.

Individual and Collaborative Considerations

1. Compare the monologue at the beginning of "The Yellow Wall-Paper" to that at the end of the story. In what way have the narrator's observations, descriptions, likes, and dislikes changed?

2. What do you perceive as the overall conflict in Gilman's story? Who or what seems antagonistic towards the narrator?
3. The narrator initially has an outlet to release some of her anxieties; what happens?
4. Why do you imagine the narrator is never identified by name? How would you describe her self-esteem? How does she perceive her "self"?
5. How does the narrator resolve her conflict? What symbolic act informs you that she has overcome her anxieties?

Writing Activities

1. Construct an essay arguing that loyalty to people or respect for their profession should or should not take precedence over duty to one's self (what is best for you). Use details and examples drawn from contemporary American society to demonstrate the validity of your argument.
2. Compare and contrast the theme of escape from commitment and its restraints in "The Yellow Wall-Paper" by Gilman and "The Story of an Hour" (chapter 8) by Kate Chopin.

❋

Because I Could Not Stop for Death

Emily Dickinson

Emily Dickinson (1830–1886) lived a secluded life, and although she never married, she did cultivate several "intellectual" relationships with men she referred to as "tutors." Dickinson was encouraged to develop her poetic talents by Reverend Charles Wadsworth, a man she regarded as her "dearest earthly friend," modeling her image of "the lover" (known only to her imagination) in her verse after him. Publication had never been important to Dickinson; she never gave her consent to publish the few poems printed during her life, and her manuscripts were chaotic and disorganized. Editors, including Mabel L. Todd and Martha Dickinson Bianchi, did assemble some volumes of her work: *Poems* (1890), *Poems: Second Series* (1891), *Poems: Third Series* (1896) *The Single Hound* (1914), *Further Poems* (1923), *Poems: Centenary Edition* (1930), *Unpublished Poems* (1936), and *Bolts of Melody* (1945). A scholarly edition of *The Poems of Emily Dickinson* (1955) and Dickinson's *Letters* (1958) both were published in three volumes. *The Manuscript Books of Emily Dickinson* (1982) offered readers a look at her canon of 1147 poems in facsimile. The title of Dickinson's following poem, "Because I Could Not Stop for Death," identifies her conflict with life, death, and rebirth, and she develops her verse with a rich variety of concrete images and figurative language.

Because I could not stop for Death—
He kindly stopped for me—
The Carriage held but just Ourselves—
And Immortality.

5 We slowly drove—He knew no haste
And I had put away
My labor and my leisure too,
For His Civility—

We passed the School, where Children strove
10 At recess—in the Ring—
We passed the Fields of Gazing Grain—
We passed the Setting Sun—

Or rather—He passed Us—
The Dews drew quivering and chill—
15 For only Gossamer, my Gown—My
Tippet—only tulle—

We paused before a House that seemed
A Swelling of the Ground—
The Roof was scarcely visible—
20 The Cornice—in the Ground—

Since then—'tis Centuries—and yet
Feels shorter than the Day
I first surmised the Horses' Heads
Were toward Eternity—

Writing Log/Journal Assignment

What incidents or symbols do you associate with the different stages of life?
Jot down a few of them in your journal.

Individual and Collaborative Considerations

1. How does Dickinson characterize *death?*
2. To what extent does Dickinson's use of rhyme help to unify groups of thoughts?
3. Discuss how and why the images in stanza 3 represent stages in life.
4. Describe the speaker's attitude towards her *journey.* In what way does it help establish the dominant tone of the piece?
5. The first line of the poem, "Because I could not stop for Death—," suggests that the speaker was too preoccupied with life to die. What change seems to have taken place between the first and the last stanza?

Writing Activities

1. The theme of expectation versus reality (expectation and reality of death) runs strong in Dickinson's poem. Write an essay explaining how the reality of a situation did not live up to your expectation of an event.
2. Return to your journal entry and reexamine your thoughts on symbols representing stages in life. How might you update your symbols? Write an essay tracing your own life and development, using the symbols you have developed. (The essay should begin in the past, continue in the present, and conclude in the future tense.)

Ka 'Ba

Amiri Baraka (LeRoi Jones)

An essayist, poet, novelist, and playwright, Imamu Amiri Baraka is well known as a leader of the Black Arts Movement during the 1960s and for his plays such as *The Dutchman, The Slave, The Toilet* (1964), and *Four Black Revolutionary Plays* (1969). Other works include *Preface to a Twenty Volume Suicide Note* (1961), *The System of Dante's Hell* (1965), *Black Magic: Poetry 1961–1967* (1967), *Selected Poetry of Imamu Amiri Baraka/LeRoi Jones* (1979), *Reggae or Not* (1982), and *The Music: Reflections on Jazz* (1982). Baraka rejected traditional poetic forms and also the dominant White culture. He denounced his Christian name, LeRoi Jones, and adopted his Muslim name, Imamu Amiri Baraka, which he later shorted to Amiri Baraka. His work—especially the early poems—reflects a Black Nationalist's stance.

A closed window looks down
on a dirty courtyard, and black people
call across or scream across or walk across
defying physics in the stream of their will

5   Our world is full of sound
Our world is more lovely than anyone's
tho we suffer, and kill each other
and sometimes fail to walk the air

We are beautiful people
10   with african imaginations
full of masks and dances and swelling chants
with african eyes, and noses, and arms,
though we sprawl in gray chains in a place
full of winters, when what we want is sun.

15 We have been captured,
brothers. And we labor
to make our getaway, into
the ancient image, into a new

correspondence with ourselves
20 and our black family. We need magic
now we need the spells, to raise up
return, destroy, and create. What will be

the sacred words?

Writing Log/Journal Assignment

Write a journal entry about your cultural heritage. If you feel removed from it, explore subconscious connections and associations to your heritage through your favorite prewriting method.

Individual and Collaborative Considerations

1. Explain what Baraka celebrates in his poem.
2. What is the "getaway" Baraka refers to?
3. Despite suffering, what does Baraka claim as his heritage, a heritage shared by Black people worldwide?
4. How does Baraka build tension in "Ka 'Ba"?
5. What do you imagine are the "magic words" that destroy and create?

Writing Activities

1. Write an essay in which you argue that revolution is the only sure means of social and economic change in society. Select representative examples drawn from recent history to illustrate and support your thesis.
2. If you wanted to draw people together and unify them under a common cause, what would it be? What obstacles would you face, and how would your proceed despite adversity? Write an essay defining your cause, explaining how you would move from conflict to satisfactory resolution.

---·米·---

Nightmare

The Lu

As noted in the chapter introduction, dreams can be literal or figurative manifestations of hopes, visions, and aspirations during our waking and sleeping hours. Disillusionment results when the true nature of idealism or faith in concepts, people, places, politics, and philosophies becomes known to a person. The title of The Lu's poem, "Nightmare," suggests the horrific potential of unrealized dreams. When nothing satisfies one's expectations, or images reflect the disturbing and distasteful qualities of a subject, we perceive the desirable through a new lens—a lens quite probably rooted in harsh reality rather than the fantastic. Before you read Lu's poem, jot down if or how you believe an ideal society can evolve as the result of war.

> I dreamed I lay in a puddle of blood,
> propped on one elbow, howling souls all around,
> sunset colors cracking, and everything
> plunged in a screaming red.
> 5   Suddenly I realized this was life,
> no beauty or pleasure, no escape
> in gentle dreams, no laughter
> that wouldn't turn into sobs.
> Malevolent fate knew what she wanted
> 10   from me: She'd pin me down to struggle
> on the earth's surface like an ant
> or mosquito. She'd bind my limbs,
> release, pursue, and bind again.
> If only this petty body would dissolve!
> 15   If only I could sleep in peace!
> But she shakes my soul, pries open my eyes,
> while, from the brink of an abyss, a severed hand
> forces me to look at the enormity of the world
> where men are drinking hot blood,
> 20   swallowing some, spitting the rest at each other.

Writing Log/Journal Assignment

What does the word "nighmare" immediately bring to mind? Describe what you consider a figurative *nightmare* (e.g., a horrifying encounter with another person, place, or thing) during the daylight hours. Also, write as much as you can about a literal *nightmare* you have had.

Individual and Collaborative Considerations

1. What is the "nightmare" in this poem? What does the speaker realize?
2. How well do you think Bich, the translator of Lu's poem, carefully selected words to convey the sense of the original poem? In what way is the diction vivid and visual?
3. Go through the poem and find as many instances of figurative language as you can, particularly metaphors, similes, and personification.
4. What does the speaker wish could happen? What occurs?
5. How might Lu effectively convey the same information from her poem in an essay?

Writing Activities

1. Brainstorm a list of *nightmares* and select one you would like to consider in detail. Then, write an essay arguing or explaining how the *nightmare* could be resolved. (Your journal entry might be a good place for brainstorming *nightmares*.)
2. Write an essay about the many methods of problem solving. What makes one method more effective or more lasting than another? How might one method of problem solving be more of a *Band-Aid* than a solution?

ADDITIONAL TOPICS AND ISSUES FOR WRITING AND RESEARCH

1. Write an essay wherein you identify the most important conflict (problem) the human race must universally recognize and immediately address as this century comes to a close. What method would you prescribe for dealing with your urgent topic of concern to all? How will you enable citizens of the world to give input to your plan? Most importantly, how will you be certain that everyone "buys in" and continues to support your proposal for the duration of the project?
2. Tradition and change often create friction and conflict between people and within ourselves. Take a situation like the presence of Moslem women on college campuses thirty years ago and compare your findings to what is common place today. In these changing times, argue how and why the pressures of economic and cultural forces play a large role in the upheaval of social norms. Your conclusion might speculate about the future of tradition.
3. How do members of your academic community feel about offering English as a Second Language classes? Survey students, faculty, and

administrators at your college. Next, create a thesis arguing for the importance of understanding and appreciating cultural plurality. Use the responses you received in your survey to emphasize the need for your thesis or to indicate the support it already has.

4. Ecology became an international concern by 1972, but since the industrial countries caused most of the pollution problems, poor countries did not feel they should share equal blame or burden for cleaning up the environment. Which side do you agree with? Considering the many forms of pollution throughout the world, does everyone contribute to the problem? Take a position on this issue and write an essay defending your point of view.

5. Solutions are usually a lot more difficult to devise than problems are to locate. Brainstorm, cluster, or prewrite about the problem or problems encountered in a dysfunctional family. Then, in a carefully reasoned essay, offer a plan of action or solution to the problem.

6. Write an essay explaining the causes of jealousy, rage, anger, or frustration. Conclude your essay with a plan of action, one that explains how to deal with power of emotions.

7. Domestic violence has been receiving more exposure recently than ever before. Some say it is on the rise while others contend it has always been with us—just ignored. Write an essay explaining a realistic way of curbing domestic violence in America. Consider methods of your own design rather than solutions like hiring more police.

8. Construct an essay speculating how some people tend to work hard towards excluding others from opportunities. What could be the rationale behind depriving fellow human beings of the chance to advance their learning, to rise on a corporate ladder, or to exercise the right to speak?

9. Write a proposal suggesting a solution to the worldwide population explosion. Be realistic; many people are not willing to use contraceptives for religious reasons, and abortion is not a particularly attractive alternative.

10. In an argumentative essay, discuss why many people accept military conflict as a means of solving problems. Are problems ever really resolved through an act of force or coercion? When? Where? For how long? Use as many examples of warfare drawn from recent history as you can to support your thesis.

Starting Points for Research

Conflict	Resolution
• Social	• Problem solving
• Ethnic	• Crisis management
• Generation gap	• Mediation
• Interpersonal	• Negotiation
• Humans and nature	• Arbitration and award
• Psychological conflicts	• Conflict management
• Conflict in cultures	• Stress and suicide
• Conflict of interests	• Diplomacy
• Sexual identity	• Attitude adjustments
• Religious (crisis in faith)	• Dispute settlements
• Church versus state	• Lawsuits
• Gender inequality	• Government loopholes (IRA)
• Segregation	• Power of attorney
• Terrorism	• Revolution
• Counterculture	• Equality
• Police violence	• Cultural pluralism
• Probate law and practice	• Indifference
• Environmental laws and practice	• Grass-roots activism
• Automobile safety regulations	• Compliance with regulations
• Neighborhood quarrels	• Consensus building
• Feuds	• Shared governance
• Altercations	• Treaties
• Battles / wars	• The United Nations
• Parent and child	• Contracts
• Employee and employer	• Peacekeepers (military)
• Labor laws	• Jails / prisons
• Rape	• Vigilante justice
• Battery and assault	• Work farms
• Murder	• Rehabilitation centers

12

Initiations and Rituals

Child as he is
He bows his head
To the sacred offerings
of the New Year.
ISSA

Essays

Joseph Campbell   The Call to Adventure

•

Letty Cottin Pogrebin   Superstitious Minds

•

Paula Gunn Allen   Spirit Woman

•

Fiction

Hernando Téllez   Just Lather, That's All

•

James Joyce   Araby

•

Poetry

Sylvia Plath   Morning Song

•

Lawrence Ferlinghetti   Constantly Risking Absurdity

•

Katharine Harer   Rockaway

When was the last time you were aware of participating in a ritual? Do you have a particular manner for dressing in the morning (socks first, underpants, shirt or blouse?) Does consciousness of a ritual action make it any less important to you? Rituals come in many forms among most people for diverse purposes and occasions. From a handshake to a kiss, a victory dance (in sports) to a marching pattern, a senate procedure to a church service, rituals refer to a body of ceremonies or habitual actions. The surfers in Katharine Harer's poem "Rockaway," for instance, are locked in ritual behavior from the moment they step out of their cars until they return from the ocean with a "salty wet glaze on their skin." Ceremonies or rituals, of course, need not always be pleasant, as witnessed in Sylvia Plath's somewhat disturbing picture of motherhood in "Morning Song."

An initiation usually takes a person from a known world of experiences into the unknown. It might be a "rites of passage," celebrating the movement of a child into adolescence, or an adolescent into adulthood. In other instances, a person is initiated through mysteries into a fraternity, sorority, social club, or professional association. In your daily life, you are constantly being introduced to new fads, styles, ideas, and lifestyles, so in reality, the process of initiation does not necessarily conclude with an elaborate ceremony. Throughout this chapter, you will take a look at many different ritual practices as well as the diverse ways you can look at initiations. "Just Lather, That's All" by Hernando Téllez could be considered both in terms of initiation and ritual. On the one hand, the barber has been thrust into a position where with a razor, a tool of his trade, and an occasion—when Captain Torres comes in for a shave—he has been initiated into a world of strange power over life and death. On the other hand, there is a particular ritual associated with shaving, from lathering the face to slicing off whiskers.

The theme of initiation can be found in all literary genres. Joseph Campbell deals with it in his nonfiction piece "The Call to Adventure." There, an initiation into a world of unknown experiences is coupled with trials and explained as part of the heroic journey. Similarly, Letty Cottin Pogrebin's mother initiates her daughter to the importance of superstitions, and, in turn, Pogrebin passes on the insights to her own son in "Superstitious Minds." In Paula Gunn Allen's "Spirit Woman," the narrator experiences initiation rites into the world of the double women "born of the same mind, the same spirit." "Araby," James Joyce's classic "rites of passage" story, relates a young Dublin boy's initiation into the world of reality, as he moves from childhood innocence and romanticism into the brutal world of experience and adulthood. The daily practices or *risks* Lawrence Ferlinghetti expresses in his poem "Constantly Risking Absurdity" address both ritual and initiation; while the speaker's routine represents rituals, the world of danger—figurative and literal life and death—demands *constant* initiations.

RHETORIC AT WORK

Of particular interest in the following essays, short stories, and poems embodying some aspect of a ritual or initiation will be the cause–effect relationship between words and structures. Examine the authors' diction carefully as you read through the literary works in this chapter and record words that suggest specific cause-and-effect relationships in your writing log. For instance, words like *because* or *since* may denote definite causal relationships (I ate *because* I was hungry; I sang out loud as I walked to the store *since* nobody was around). Review your list of words during the editing stage of writing your own essays. Words indicating a cause–effect relationships can often add precision to your written expression.

A Checklist for Writing about *Initiations and Rituals*

1. Am I writing about an initiation, a ritual, or both?
2. What is the point of my paper? How do I arrive at it? What lead-in sentences do I use in my introduction to "hook" the interest of my readers?
3. Do I clarify all cause–effect relationships in my essay? Do I avoid faulty cause–effect relationships?
4. How are my ideas unified, working to argue or explain a specific thesis?
5. Is it clear how an effect or chain of effects followed a cause? Do I show how a multiple chain of causes can create one or multiple effects?
6. How do I use a variety of detailed descriptions to illustrate the true nature of an initiation, rite, or ritual?
7. To what extent does my rhetorical style reinforce my thesis?
8. Do I make sufficient use of time transitions to clarify the order of events in a ritual activity or initiation rite?

✳

The Call to Adventure

Joseph Campbell

A native of New York, Joseph Campbell served as Professor of Literature
and Mythology at Sarah Lawrence College from 1934 to 1972. Jungian
psychology, as well as Eastern and Western mysticism, greatly influenced
Campbell's work. A prolific mythologist, Campbell wrote numerous
books including *The Hero with a Thousand Faces* (1947), *The Masks of God:
Primitive Mythology* (1959), *The Masks of God: Occidental Mythology* (1964),
The Masks of God: Creative Mythology (1968), *The Flight of the Wild Gander*
(1972), *Myths to Live By* (1972), *The Mythic Image,* (1974), *The Way of Animal
Powers* (1983), *The Inner Reaches of Outer Space* (1986), and *The Power of
Myth* (1988). In the following essay, "The Call to Adventure," Campbell
explains the first stage in the heroic journey, illustrating his points with
allusions to folktales and myths from around the world.

1   "Long long ago, when wishing still could lead to something, there lived a
king whose daughters all were beautiful, but the youngest was so beautiful
that the sun itself, who had seen so many things, simply marveled every
time it shone on her face. Now close to the castle of this king was a great
dark forest, and in the forest under an old lime tree a spring, and when the
day was very hot, the king's child would go out into the wood and sit on
the edge of the cool spring. And to pass the time she would take a golden
ball, toss it up and catch it; and this was her favorite plaything.

2   "Now it so happened one day that the golden ball of the princess did not
fall into the little hand lifted into the air, but passed it, bounced on the
ground, and rolled directly into the water. The princess followed it with her
eyes, but the ball disappeared; and the spring was deep, so deep that the
bottom could not be seen. Thereupon she began to cry, and her crying became louder and louder, and she was unable to find consolation. And while
she was lamenting in this way, she heard someone call to her: 'What is the
matter, Princess? You are crying so hard, a stone would be forced to pity
you.' She looked around to see where the voice had come from, and there
she beheld a frog, holding its fat, ugly head out of the water. 'Oh, it's you,
old Water Plopper,' she said. 'I am crying over my golden ball, which has
fallen into the spring.' 'Be calm; don't cry,' answered the frog. 'I can surely
be of assistance. But what will you give me if I fetch your toy for you?'
'Whatever you would like to have, dear frog,' she said; 'my clothes, my
pearls and jewels, even the golden crown that I wear.' The frog replied, 'Your
clothes, your pearls and jewels, and your golden crown, I do not want; but

if you will care for me and let me be your companion and playmate, let me sit beside you at your little table, eat from your little golden plate, drink from your little cup, sleep in your little bed: if you will promise me that, I will go straight down and fetch your golden ball.' 'All right,' she said. 'I promise you anything you want, if you will only bring me back the ball.' But she thought: 'How that simple frog chatters! There he sits in the water with his own kind, and could never be the companion of a human being.'

3   "As soon as the frog had obtained her promise, he ducked his head and sank, and after a little while came swimming up again; he had the ball in his mouth, and tossed it on the grass. The princess was elated when she saw her pretty toy. She picked it up and scampered away. 'Wait, wait,' called the frog, 'take me along; I can't run like you.' But what good did it do, though he croaked after her as loudly as he could? She paid not the slightest heed, but hurried home, and soon had completely forgotten the poor frog—who must have hopped back again into his spring."[1]

4   This is an example of one of the ways in which the adventure can begin. A blunder—apparently the merest chance—reveals an unsuspected world, and the individual is drawn into a relationship with forces that are not rightly understood. As Freud has shown,[2] blunders are not the merest chance. They are the result of suppressed desires and conflicts. They are ripples on the surface of life, produced by unsuspected springs. And these may be very deep—as deep as the soul itself. The blunder may amount to the opening of a destiny. Thus it happens, in this fairy tale, that the disappearance of the ball is the first sign of something coming for the princess, the frog is the second, and the unconsidered promise is the third.

5   As a preliminary manifestation of the powers that are breaking into play, the frog, coming up as it were by miracle, can be termed the "herald"; the crisis of his appearance is the "call to adventure." The herald's summons may be to live, as in the present instance, or, at a later moment of the biography, to die. It may sound the call to some high historical undertaking. Or it may mark the dawn of religious illumination. As apprehended by the mystic, it marks what has been termed "the awakening of the self."[3] In the case of the princess of the fairy tale, it signified no more than the coming of adolescence. But whether small or great, and no matter what the stage or grade of life, the call rings up the curtain, always, on a mystery of transfiguration—a rite, or moment, of spiritual passage, which, when complete, amounts to a dying and a birth. The familiar life horizon has been outgrown; the old concepts, ideals, and emotional patterns no longer fit; the time for the passing of a threshold is at hand.

6   Typical of the circumstances of the call are the dark forest, the great tree, the babbling spring, and the loathly, underestimated appearance of the carrier of the power of destiny. . . .

---

[1]*Grimms' Fairy Tales*, No. 1, "The Frog King."
[2]Sigmund Freud, *The Psychopathology of Everyday Life* (Standard Ed., VI; orig. 1901).
[3]Evelyn Underhill, *Mysticism, A Study in the Nature and Development of Man's Spiritual Consciousness* (New York: E. P. Dutton and Co., 1911).

7 ...The herald or announcer of the adventure, therefore, is often dark, loathly, or terrifying, judged evil by the world; yet if one could follow, the way would be opened through the walls of day into the dark where the jewels glow. Or the herald is a beast (as in the fairy tale), representative of the repressed instinctual fecundity within ourselves, or again a veiled mysterious figure—the unknown.

8 The story is told, for example, of King Arthur, and how he made him ready with many knights to ride ahunting. "As soon as he was in the forest, the King saw a great hart afore him. This hart will I chase, said King Arthur, and so he spurred the horse, and rode after long, and so by fine force he was like to have smitten the heart; whereas the King had chased the hart so long, that his horse lost his breath, and fell down dead; then a yeoman fetched the King another horse. So the King saw the hart embushed, and his horse dead; he set him down by a fountain, and there he fell in great thoughts. And as he sat so, him thought he heard a noise of hounds, to the sum of thirty. And with that the King saw coming toward him the strangest beast that ever he saw or heard of; so the beast went to the well and drank, and the noise was in the beast's belly like unto the questyng of thirty couple hounds; but all the while the beast drank there was no noise in the beast's belly: and therewith the beast departed with a great noise, whereof the King had great marvel."[4]

9 Or we have the case—from a very different portion of the world—of an Arapaho girl of the North American plains. She spied a porcupine near a cottonwood tree. She tried to hit the animal, but it ran behind the tree and began to climb. The girl started after, to catch it, but it continued just out of reach. "Well!" she said, "I am climbing to catch the porcupine, for I want those quills, and if necessary I will go to the top." The porcupine reached the top of the tree, but as she approached and was about to lay hands on it, the cottonwood tree suddenly lengthened, and the porcupine resumed its climb. Looking down, she saw her friends craning up at her and beckoning her to descend; but having passed under the influence of the porcupine, and fearful for the great distance between herself and the ground, she continued to mount the tree, until she became the merest speck to those looking from below, and with the porcupine she finally reached the sky.[5] . . .

10 Whether dream or myth, in these adventures there is an atmosphere of irresistible fascination about the figure that appears suddenly as guide, marking a new period, a new stage, in the biography. That which has to be faced, and is somehow profoundly familiar to the unconscious—though unknown, surprising, and even frightening to the conscious personality— makes itself known; and what formerly was meaningful may become strangely emptied of value: like the world of the king's child with the sudden disappearance into the well of the golden ball. Thereafter, even though the hero returns for a while to his familiar occupations, they may be found

---

[4]Malory, *Le Morte d'Arthur*, I. xix.
[5]George A. Dorsey and Alfred L. Kroeber, *Traditions of the Arapaho* (Field Columbia Museum, Publication 81, Anthropological Series, Vol. V; Chicago, 1903).

unfruitful. A series of signs of increasing force then will become visible, until—as in the following legend of "The Four Signs," which is the most celebrated example of the call to adventure in the literature of the world—the summons can no longer be denied.

11   The young prince Gautama Sakyamuni, the Future Buddha, had been protected by his father from all knowledge of age, sickness, death, or monkhood, lest he should be moved to thoughts of life renunciation; for it had been prophesied at his birth that he was to become either a world emperor or a Buddha. The king—prejudiced in favor of the royal vocation—provided his son with three palaces and forty thousand dancing girls to keep his mind attached to the world. But these only served to advance the inevitable; for while still relatively young, the youth exhausted for himself the fields of fleshly joy and became ripe for the other experience. The moment he was ready, the proper heralds automatically appeared:

12   "Now on a certain day the Future Buddha wished to go to the park, and told his charioteer to make ready the chariot. Accordingly the man brought out a sumptuous and elegant chariot, and, adorning it richly, he harnessed to it four state horses of the Sindhava breed, as white as the petals of the white lotus, and announced to the Future Buddha that everything was ready. And the Future Buddha mounted the chariot, which was like to a palace of the gods, and proceeded toward the peak.

13   " 'The time for the enlightenment of the prince Siddhartha draweth nigh,' thought the gods; 'we must show him a sign': and they changed one of their number into a decrepit old man, broken-toothed, gray haired, crooked and bent of body, leaning on a staff, and trembling, and showed him to the Future Buddha, but so that only he and the charioteer saw him.

14   "Then said the Future Buddha to the charioteer, 'Friend, pray, who is this man? Even his hair is not like that of other men.' And when he heard the answer, he said, 'Shame on birth, since to every one that is born old age must come.' And agitated in heart, he thereupon returned and ascended his palace.

15   " 'Why has my son returned so quickly?' asked the king.

16   " 'Sire, he has seen an old man,' was the reply; 'and because he has seen an old man, he is about to retire from the world.'

17   " 'Do you want to kill me, that you say such things? Quickly get ready some plays to be performed before my son. If we can but get him to enjoying pleasure, he will cease to think of retiring from the world.' Then the king extended the guard to half a league in each direction.

18   "Again on a certain day, as the Future Buddha was going to the park, he saw a diseased man whom the gods had fashioned; and having again made inquiry, he returned, agitated in heart, and ascended his palace.

19   "And the king made the same inquiry, and gave the same order as before; and again extending the guard, placed them for three quarters of a league around.

20   "And again on a certain day, as the Future Buddha was going to the park, he saw a dead man whom the gods had fashioned; and having again made inquiry, he returned, agitated in heart, and ascended his palace.

21   "And the king made the same inquiry and gave the same orders as before; and again extending the guard placed them for a league around.

22   "And again on a certain day, as the Future Buddha was going to the park, he saw a monk, carefully and decently clad, whom the gods had fashioned; and he asked his charioteer, 'Pray, who is this man?' 'Sire, this is one who has retired from the world'; and the charioteer thereupon proceeded to sound the praises of retirement from the world. The thought of retiring from the world was a pleasing one to the Future Buddha."[6]

23   The first stage of the mythological journey—which we have designated the "call to adventure"—signifies that destiny has summoned the hero and transferred his spiritual center of gravity from within the pale of his society to a zone unknown. This fateful region of both treasure and danger may be variously represented: as a distant land, a forest, a kingdom underground, beneath the waves, or above the sky, a secret island, lofty mountaintop, or profound dream state; but it is always a place of strangely fluid and polymorphous beings, unimaginable torments, superhuman deeds, and impossible delight. The hero can go forth of his own volition to accomplish the adventure, as did Theseus when he arrived in his father's city, Athens, and heard the horrible history of the Minotaur; or he may be carried or sent abroad by some benign or malignant agent, as was Odysseus, driven about the Mediterranean by the winds of the angered god, Poseidon. The adventure may begin as a mere blunder, as did that of the princess of the fairy tale; or still again, one may be only casually strolling, when some passing phenomenon catches the wandering eye and lures one away from the frequented paths of man. Examples might be multiplied, ad infinitum, from every corner of the world.

Writing Log/Journal Assignment

What *call to adventure* have you or someone you know had lately? Write a few paragraphs about your *call*—as well as your subsequent adventure—in your journal.

Individual and Collaborative Considerations

1. According to Campbell, what is the *call to adventure?*
2. Campbell's first three paragraphs are devoted to retelling the story of "The Frog King," and it is not until the fourth paragraph that you understand *why*. Assess the advantages and disadvantages of Campbell's break from a more traditional essay structure.
3. Typical circumstances usually accompany the *call to adventure;* list some of them.
4. Literally, what is the *herald?* What might the herald represent?

[6]Henry Clark Warren, *Buddhism in Translations* (Harvard Oriental Studies, 3) Cambridge: Harvard UP, 1896.

5. How did Gautama Sakyamuni, the Future Buddha, experience the *call to adventure?* How does Campbell illustrate the *call to adventure* with concrete allusions to folktales and myths?

Writing Activities

1. The voyage of the hero typically consists of (a) *separation* from the known world (this stage includes the call to adventure); (b) *initiation* into the world of unknown experiences, where the hero encounters and does battle with personal dragons; and (c) *return*, where the hero comes back to the known world, bringing a boon or a greater truth. Analyze someone in the last century in terms of his or her heroic journey—heroic quest if you will (e.g., Martin Luther King, Jr., his quest being civil rights).
2. In what three ways might a person receive the *call to adventure?* In an imitation of Campbell's essay, illustrate the three ways a person might receive the call, drawing on folktales and myths he *did not* mention in his essay.

✷

Superstitious Minds

Letty Cottin Pogrebin

Born in 1939 in New York City, Letty Cottin Pogrebin is one of the founding editors of *Ms.* magazine and has been a columnist for the *Ladies Home Journal*, a writer for *Time* magazine, and an editor for *Newsweek*. She has written several books including *How to Make the System Work for the Working Woman* (1975), *Stories for Free Children* (1982), *Family Politics* (1983), *Among Friends* (1987), and *Debra, Golda, and Me: A Jewish Feminist Memoir* (1991). "Superstitious Minds" originally appeared in the February 1988 issue of *Ms.* Pogrebin's essay approaches the perpetuation of superstitions as part of her matrilineal heritage; superstitions had always given her mother "a means of imposing order on a chaotic system."

1   I am a very rational person. I tend to trust reason more than feeling. But I also happen to be superstitious—in my fashion. Black cats and rabbits' feet hold no power for me. My superstitions are my mother's superstitions, the amulets and incantations she learned from *her* mother and taught me.

2   I don't mean to suggest that I grew up in an occult atmosphere. On the contrary, my mother desperately wanted me to rise above her immigrant

ways and become an educated American. She tried to hide her superstitions, but I came to know them all: Slap a girl's cheeks when she first gets her period. Never take a picture of a pregnant woman. Knock wood when speaking about your good fortune. When ready to conceive, eat the ends of bread if you want to have a boy. Don't leave a bride alone on her wedding day.

3   When I was growing up, my mother often would tiptoe in after I seemed to be asleep and kiss my forehead three times, making odd noises that sounded like a cross between sucking and spitting. One night I opened my eyes and demanded an explanation. Embarrassed, she told me she was exorcising the "Evil Eye"—in case I had attracted its attention that day by being especially wonderful. She believed her kisses could suck out any envy or ill that those less fortunate may have directed at her child.

4   By the time I was in my teens, I was almost on speaking terms with the Evil Eye, a jealous spirit that kept track of those who had "too much" happiness and zapped them with sickness and misery to even the score. To guard against this mischief, my mother practiced rituals of interference, evasion, deference, and above all, avoidance of situations where the Evil Eye might feel at home.

5   This is why I wasn't allowed to attend funerals. This is also why my mother hated to mend my clothes while I was wearing them. The only garment one should properly get sewn *into* is a shroud. To ensure that the Evil Eye did not confuse my pinafore with a burial outfit, my mother insisted that I chew a thread while she sewed, thus proving myself very much alive. Outwitting the Evil Eye also accounted for her closing the window shades above my bed whenever there was a full moon. The moon should only shine on cemeteries, you see; the living need protection from the spirits.

6   Because we were dealing with a deadly force, I also wasn't supposed to say any words associated with mortality. This was hard for a twelve-year-old who punctuated every anecdote with the verb "to die," as in "You'll die when you hear this!" or "If I don't get home by ten, I'm dead." I managed to avoid using such expressions in the presence of my mother until the day my parents brought home a painting I hated and we were arguing about whether it should be displayed on our walls. Unthinking, I pressed my point with a melodramatic idiom: "That picture will hang over my dead body!" Without a word, my mother grabbed a knife and slashed the canvas to shreds.

7   I understand all this now. My mother emigrated in 1907 from a small Hungarian village. The oldest of seven children, she had to go out to work before she finished the eighth grade. Experience taught her that life was unpredictable and often incomprehensible. Just as an athlete keeps wearing the same T-shirt in every game to prolong a winning streak, my mother's superstitions gave her a means of imposing order on a chaotic system. Her desire to control the fates sprung from the same helplessness that makes the San Francisco 49ers' defensive more superstitious than its offensive team. Psychologists speculate this is because the defense has less control; they don't have the ball.

8   Women like my mother never had the ball. She died when I was fifteen, leaving me with deep regrets for what she might have been—and a growing understanding of who she was. *Superstitious* is one of the things she was. I wish I had a million sharp recollections of her, but when you don't expect someone to die, you don't store up enough memories. Ironically, her mystical practices are among the clearest impressions she left behind. In honor of this matrilineal heritage—and to symbolize my mother's effort to control her life as I in my way try to find order in mine—I knock on wood and I do not let the moon shine on those I love. My children laugh at me, but they understand that these tiny rituals have helped keep my mother alive in my mind.

9   A year ago, I awoke in the night and realized that my son's window blinds had been removed for repair. Smiling at my own compulsion, I got a bed sheet to tack up against the moonlight and I opened his bedroom door. What I saw brought tears to my eyes. There, hopelessly askew, was a blanket my son, then eighteen, had taped to his windows like a curtain.

10   My mother never lived to know David, but he knew she would not want the moon to shine upon him as he slept.

Writing Log/Journal Assignment

Write freely about superstitious practices or rituals you or people you have observed go through without necessarily thinking about them (e.g., knocking on wood). What do you think would be an appropriate definition for the word "superstition" in the twenty-first century?

Individual and Collaborative Considerations

1. What do you imagine Pogrebin wants to establish with the first two sentences, "I am a very rational person. I tend to trust reason more than feeling," in her essay?
2. How would you characterize Pogrebin's essay? Is it formal or informal, and what qualities led you to your conclusion? How is the level of formality—or informality—appropriate to her essay's content?
3. Who or what was "the Evil Eye"? Why was Pogrebin not allowed to go to funerals, and why did she have to stand up when her mother mended her clothes?
4. What did superstitions offer the author's mother? What do superstitions offer Pogrebin? Explain the significance—if any—of superstitions in the relationship she had with her mother. In what way does her mother live on through superstitions?
5. Analyze the sentence, "Women like my mother never had the ball." What is the author "figuratively" implying about her mother?

Writing Activities

1. Do you recall any superstitions handed down to you by your parents or relatives? If so, what were they? Do you ignore the superstitions or respect them? Why or why not? Prewrite briefly on this topic to gauge your inner feelings on it. Then write an essay defending an original thesis about superstitions.
2. Compare and contrast the superstitions and beliefs of two or more cultures. You might, for instance, devote an entire paper to superstitions about the moon, demonstrating that the beliefs from many different cultures have uncanny resemblances.

❊

Spirit Woman

Paula Gunn Allen

Paula Gunn Allen, a well-known Laguna (Sioux) and Lebanese poet, novelist, and essayist, has written many works touching on themes relevant to the Native American experience. Her works include *The Woman Who Owned the Shadows* (1983), *The Sacred Hoop: Recovering the Feminine in American Indian Traditions* (1986), *Spider Woman's Granddaughters: Traditional Tales and Contemporary Writings by Native American Women* (1989), and *Grandmothers of the Light: A Medicine Woman's Source Book* (1992). With rich allusions to Native American folklore, Allen paints a picture of the double women—the women who never married but held power. These women who were not mothers were sisters, "born of the same mind, the same spirit."

1 "Sister. Sister, I am here."

2 Ephanie opened her eyes. Looked around. Saw someone, shadowy, at the bottom of her bed.

3 "I have come to tell you a story. One that you have long wanted to hear."

4 Ephanie saw that the shadowy form was a woman whose shape slowly focused out of the swirl of vapor she was cloaked in. She saw that the woman was small. There was something of bird, a hawk perhaps, about her. Her eyes gleamed in a particular way, like no shine Ephanie had ever seen. The woman was dressed in the old way and her hair was cut traditionally, so that it fell in a straight line from crown to jaw. The sides formed perfect square corners on either side. Straight bangs fell over her forehead, almost

to her eyebrows in the ancient arrangement that signified the arms of the galaxy, the Spider. It was another arrangement of the four corners that composed the Universe, the four days of sacredness that women remembered in their bodies' blood every month.

5   The woman wore a white, finely woven manta and shawl, each richly embroidered in fine black wool with geometrical patterns that told the story of the galaxy. Ephanie recognized only the spider among the symbols embroidered there. She saw the woman's thick, snowy buckskin leggings, wrapped perfectly around her calves. She raised herself to a sitting position and with her hand made the sign of sunrise, the gesture of taking a pinch of corn pollen between fingers and thumb, then opening them as though to let the pollen free.

6   The spirit woman began to speak, chanting her words in a way that seemed so familiar, that brought Ephanie near tears.

7   "In the beginning time, in the place of Sussistinaku, The Spider, Old Woman, placed the bundles that contained her sisters Uretsete and Naotsete, the women who had come with her from the center of the galaxy to this sun. She sang them into life. She established the patterns of this world. The pattern of the singing, of the painting she made to lay the spirit women upon, the pattern of placing the bundles that contained their forms, of the signs that she made, was the pattern she brought with her, in her mind. It is the pattern of the corners, their turning, their multidimensional arrangings. It is the sign and the order of the power that informs this life and leads back to Shipap. Two face outward, two inward, the sign of doubling, of order and balance, of the two, the twins, the doubleminded world in which you have lived," she chanted.

8   And in the living shadows that swirled around the spirit woman's face, Ephanie saw moving patterns that imaged what the woman was saying. Saw the corners lying flat like on paper, then taking on dimensions, like in rooms as on the outside of boxes and buildings, then combining and recombining in all of their dimensions, forming the four-armed cross, ancient symbol of the Milky Way, found on rocks and in drawings of every land. Saw the square of glossy, deeply gleaming blackness that was the door to the place of the Spider. Saw held within it the patterned stars, the whirling suns, the deep black brilliance of the center of the sun. Saw the perfect creation space from which earth and her seven sisters had sprung at the bidding of the Grandmothers, long ago so far, before time like a clock entered and took hold.

9   She understood the combinations and recombinations that had so puzzled her, the One and then the Two, the two and then the three, the three becoming the fours, the four splitting, becoming two and two, the three of the beginning becoming the three-in-one. One mother, twin sons; two mothers, two sons; one mother, two sons. Each. First there was Sussistinaku, Thinking Woman, then there was She and two more: Uretsete and Naotsete. Then Uretsete became known as the father, Utset, because Naotsete had become pregnant and a mother, because the Christians would not understand and

killed what they did not know. And Iyatiku was the name Uretsete was known by, she was Utset, the brother. The woman who was known as father, the Sun. And Utset was another name for both Iyatiku and Uretsete, making three in one. And Naotsete, she with more in her bundle, was the Woman of the Sun, after whom Iyatiku named her first daughter Sun Clan, alien and so the combinations went on, forming, dissolving, doubling, splitting, sometimes one sometimes two, sometimes three, sometimes four, then again two, again one. All of the stories formed those patterns, laid down long before time, so far.

10   The One was the unity, the source, Shipap, where Naiya Iyatiku lived. The two was the first splitting of the one, the sign of the twins, the double-woman, the clanmother-generation. From whom came all the forms of spirit and of matter as they appear on earth and in earth's heavens. Which could only come into being in time, the counting, pulsating, repetitive, cycling beat, held in its four coordinating patterns by the power of the three who become seven in all the tales eventually. The forms of flame. The dark flame. The gold flame. The flame of white. The Grandmother flame. The sister flame. The flame of the sun. The fire of flint. The fire of corn. The fire of passion, of desire. The flame of longing. The flame of freedom. The flame of vision, of dream.

11   In the patterns before her eyes, within her mind, that pulsed and flowed around and through her, Ephanie found what she so long had sought. The patterns flowed like the flowings of her life, the coming out and the going in, the entering and the leaving, the meeting and gathering, the divisions and separations, how her life, like the stories, told the tale of all the enterings, all the turning away. Waxing and waning, growing and shrinking, birthing and dying, flowering and withering. The summer people and the winter people, that ancient division of the tribe. The inside priestess and the outside priest. The mother who was the center of their relationship to each other and to the people, the things of the earth. What was within went without. What was without, went within. As Kochinnenako returning home stepped four times up the ladder, each time calling, "I am here." And on the fourth step, at her words, her sister had cried with relief. And Kochinnenako vanished, could not therefore return. Ephanie understood that Kochinnenako was the name of any woman who, in the events being told, was walking in the ancient manner, tracing the pattern of the ancient design.

12   Ephanie looked at the face of the spirit woman, eyes drawn there with undeniable force, and saw that powerful, gleaming hawk-beaked face changing, changing, growing old, old, until it was older than time. The face of Old Woman, of hawk, of butterfly, of bee. The face of wolf and spider. The face of old woman coyote. The face of rock and wind and star. The face of infinite, aching, powerful, beloved darkness, of midnight. The face of dawn. The face of red flame. The face of distant star.

13   And from that great distance, the voice was saying. In a whisper that held the echo of starlight in its depth. That a certain time was upon them. That Ephanie would receive a song.

14   "The time of ending is upon the Indian. So few, so few are there left. So many being killed. So many already dead. But do not weep for this. For it is as it should be.

15   "My sister, my granddaughter. A door is closing upon a world, the world we knew. The world we guide and protect. We have ever guarded it. We ever will protect it. But the door closes now. It is the end of our time. We go on to another place, the sixth world. For that is our duty, and our work.

16   "But we will leave behind in this fifth world certain things. We go so that the people will live.

17   "Each spirit has its time and place. And it is a certain spirit, a great one, which calls to us now. We go on. The others come behind us. As we go, they take our place. And when they are ready for the next step, others will replace them. For that is the law of the universe, of the Grandmother. The work that is left is to pass on what we know to those who come after us. It is an old story. One that is often repeated. One that is true.

18   "It isn't whether you're here or there. Whether the people are what you call alive or dead. Those are just words. What you call dead isn't dead. It is a different way of being. And in some cases, in many, the new place, the new way of looking at reality and yourself, is far more valid, far more real, far more vital than the old way.

19   "I am not saying we want to die. Only that one way or another we live. And on another earth, just like this one, in almost the same place as the one you are lying in, talking with me, the world where your room is, where the city you call San Francisco is. I am also in San Francisco. But it is a very different version of the place from the version you inhabit.

20   "Come. See my city. Visit me. I think you will like it here. I think you will be surprised to see that death is not possible. That life and being are the only truth.

21   "Long ago, so far, the people knew this. That was when they could see the person leave the flesh, like you can see someone take off their clothes. They could see the change. Then old Coyote said there would be death. The people would no longer see the whole of the transformation in its entirety. They would only see the body, first vital, then still. So that they would want to go on from where they were. So they would have reason to think. About what life is, about what their flesh is. So they would learn other ways to know, to see. The katsina withdrew so that you would know their true being in yourself. Iyatiku withdrew so you would put her thoughts into your own hearts, and live them as was intended by All That Moves.

22   "The story of the people and the spirits, the story of the earth, is the story of what moves, what moves on, what patterns, what dances, what signs, what balances, so life can be felt and known. The story of life is the story of moving. Of moving on.

23   "Your place in the great circling spiral is to help in that story, in that work. To pass on to those who can understand what you have learned, what you know.

24   "It is for this reason you have endured. That you have tried to understand. When you give away what is in your basket, when what you have given takes root, when it dances, it sings on the earth. Give it to your sister, Teresa. The one who waits. She is ready to know.

25   "The stories of the old ones, of Utset, Iyatiku and Naotsete, of corn sister and sun sister and of the Spider, shadow sister, is just that. Each gives over what she has and goes on.

26   "Pass it on, little one. Pass it on. That is the lesson of the giveaways that all the people honor. That is the story of life here where we are and where you are. It is all the same. Grow, move, give, move. That is why they are always leaving. And always coming home. Why it is so that every going out is a coming in. Why every giving is a getting. Every particle in creation knows this. And only the human beings grieve about it. Because only the human beings have forgotten how to live.

27   "Jump.

28   "Fall.

29   "Little sister, you have jumped. You have fallen. You have been brave, but you have misunderstood. So you have learned. How to jump. How to jump. How to fall. How to learn. How to understand.

30   "We are asking you to jump again. To fall into this world like the old one, the one you call Anciena, sky woman, jumped, fell, and began in a world that was new."

31   And the corners grew endless to fill the room. To surround Ephanie and the woman who sat near her on the bed. They grew larger, somehow brighter but with no more light than before, growing, filled, filling her mind and her eyes, her body and her heart with dreams.

32   And she dreamed. About the women who had lived, long ago, hame haa. Who had lived near caves, near streams. Who had known magic far beyond the simple charms and spells the moderns knew. Who were the Spider. The Spider Medicine Society. The women who created, the women who directed people upon their true paths. The women who healed. The women who sang.

33   And she understood. For those women, so long lost to her, whom she had longed and wept for, unknowing, were the double women, the women who never married, who held power like the Clanuncle, like the power of the priests, the medicine men. Who were not mothers, but who were sisters, born of the same mind, the same spirit. They called each other sister. They were called Grandmother by those who called on them for aid, for knowledge, for comfort, for care.

34   Who never used their power to coerce. Who waited patient, weaving, silent. Who acted when called on. Who disappeared. Who never abused. Who never allowed themselves to be abused. Who sang.

35   And in the dream she opened her eyes. Hearing a bird sing. She looked out of her window. Believing she was home, in Guadalupe, that the golden

sun was in the window, that the tall trees were singing to the birds, that the birds were singing to the trees.

36   She sat up, gazing at the window. From which foggy light streamed. She brushed back her untamed hair with a strong, thin hand. The turquoise ring on her finger shone, dully it gleamed. She saw a white, hand-woven shawl, heavily embroidered with black and white designs lying crumpled on the bottom of the bed. She stared at it for a moment, hearing the birds, hearing a chant in her mind, feeling it throbbing at her throat, feeling the drum resonant and deep in her chest. She leaned forward and reached for the shawl. Wrapped it around her shoulders and chest. She lay back down on the pillow. Eyes wide open she lay. Remembering her dream.

37   Remembering all the wakings of her life. All the goings to sleep. Remembering, humming quietly to herself, in her throat, in her mind she lay. Understanding at last that everything belonged to the wind.

38   Knowing that only without interference can the people learn and grow and become what they had within themselves to be. For the measure of her life, of all their lives, was discovering what she, they, were made of. What she, they, could do. And what consequences their doing created, and what they would create of these.

39   And remembered the voice of the woman, who sat in the shadows and spoke, saying "There are no curses. There are only descriptions of what creations there will be."

40   And in the silence and the quieting shadows of her room, in her bed surrounded by books and notebooks and silence and dust, she thought. And the spiders in the walls, on the ceiling, in the corners, beneath the bed and under the chair began to gather. Their humming, quiet at first, grew louder, filling all of the spaces of the room. Their presence grew around her. She did not move.

41   And around her the room filled with shadows. And the shadows became shapes. And the shapes became women singing. Singing and dancing in the ancient steps of the women, the Spider. Singing they stepped, slowly, in careful balance of dignity, of harmony, of respect. They stepped and they sang. And she began to sing with them. With her shawl wrapped around her shoulders in the way of the women since time immemorial, she wrapped her shawl and she joined the dance. She heard the singing. She entered the song.

I am walking	Alive
Where I am	Beautiful
I am still	Alive
In Beauty	Walking
I am	Entering
Not alone	

Writing Log/Journal Assignment

In your journal, write about an influential person's voice you remember hearing at some point in your life. What remains vivid and clear about the experience, and what is fuzzy, "in the shadows," disrupted by noise?

Individual and Collaborative Considerations

1. Who were the *double women*? Describe some of their characteristics.
2. Why did the Spirit Woman come to Ephanie? What did she wish to share?
3. What duty did the Spirit Woman give Ephanie?
4. Describe Ephanie's dream. What does she see? Whom does she meet?
5. What lesson does Ephanie ultimately learn? What does she do in recognition of her true self at the end of the narrative?

Writing Activities

1. Write an essay detailing how the appearance of the Spirit Woman in Allen's story initiates what Joseph Campbell would refer to as "The Call to Adventure." Explain Ephanie's adventure or experience in terms of Campbell's heroic journey (a journey can be spiritual).
2. Explain a story or aspect of your culture that you have passed on—or will pass on—to your own children (and they to their children) as a means of preserving the best of the past in the present. How will your experience resemble Ephanie's charge from the Shadow Woman? What will you both hope to accomplish?

※

Just Lather, That's All

Hernando Téllez

Hernando Téllez (1908–1966) was born in Bogotá, Colombia, and lived there most of his life, actively involved in the city's literary and journalistic life. Téllez was designated the consul in Marseilles, France, but he returned to Colombia shortly before World War II and took up the post of subdirector of the publication *El Liberal*. A senator from 1944 to 1947, Téllez was appointed ambassador to UNESCO in Paris in 1959. In addition to his editorial and diplomatic activities, Téllez published *The Restless of the World* (1943), *Bagatelas* (1944), *Diario* (1946), *Lights in the Woods* (1946), *Ashes in the Wind and Other Stories* (1950), and *In the Name of Confession* (1966).

He said nothing when he entered. I was passing the best of my razors back and forth on a strop. When I recognized him I started to tremble. But he didn't notice. Hoping to conceal my emotion, I continued sharpening the razor. I tested it on the meat of my thumb, and then held it up to the light. At that moment he took off the bullet-studded belt that his gun holster dangled from. He hung it up on a wall hook and placed his military cap over it. Then he turned to me, loosening the knot of his tie, and said, "It's hot as hell. Give me a shave." He sat in the chair.

I estimated he had a four-day beard. The four days taken up by the latest expedition in search of our troops. His face seemed reddened, burned by the sun. Carefully, I began to prepare the soap. I cut off a few slices, dropped them into the cup, mixed in a bit of warm water, and began to stir with the brush. Immediately the foam began to rise. "The other boys in the group should have this much beard, too." I continued stirring the lather.

"But we did all right, you know. We got the main ones. We brought back some dead, and we've got some others still alive. But pretty soon they'll all be dead."

"How many did you catch?" I asked.

5   "Fourteen. We had to go pretty deep into the woods to find them. But we'll get even. Not one of them comes out of this alive, not one."

He leaned back on the chair when he saw me with the lather-covered brush in my hand. I still had to put the sheet on him. No doubt about it, I was upset. I took a sheet out of a drawer and knotted it around my customer's neck. He wouldn't stop talking. He probably thought I was in sympathy with his party.

"The town must have learned a lesson from what we did the other day," he said.

"Yes," I replied, securing the knot at the base of his dark, sweaty neck.

"That was a fine show, eh?"

10   "Very good," I answered, turning back for the brush. The man closed his eyes with a gesture of fatigue and sat waiting for the cool caress of the soap. I had never had him so close to me. The day he ordered the whole town to file into the patio of the school to see the four rebels hanging there, I came face to face with him for an instant. But the sight of the mutilated bodies kept me from noticing the face of the man who had directed it all, the face I was now about to take into my hands. It was not an unpleasant face, certainly. And the beard, which made him seem a bit older than he was, didn't suit him badly at all. His name was Torres. Captain Torres. A man of imagination, because who else would have thought of hanging the naked rebels and then holding target practice on certain parts of their bodies? I began to apply the first layer of soap. With his eyes closed, he continued, "Without any effort I could go straight to sleep," he said, "but there's plenty to do this afternoon." I stopped the lathering and asked with a feigned lack of interest: "A firing squad?" "Something like that, but a little slower." I got on with the job of lathering his beard. My hands started trembling again. The man

could not possibly realize it, and this was in my favor. But I would have preferred that he hadn't come. It was likely that many of our faction had seen him enter. And an enemy under one's roof imposes certain conditions. I would be obliged to shave that beard like any other one, carefully, gently, like that of any customer, taking pains to see that no single pore emitted a drop of blood. Being careful to see that the little tufts of hair did not lead the blade astray. Seeing that his skin ended up clean, soft, and healthy, so that passing the back of my hand over it I couldn't feel a hair. Yes, I was secretly a rebel, but I was also a conscientious barber, and proud of the preciseness of my profession. And this four-days' growth of beard was a fitting challenge.

I took the razor, opened up the two protective arms, exposed the blade and began the job, from one of the sideburns downward. The razor responded beautifully. His beard was inflexible and hard, not too long, but thick. Bit by bit the skin emerged. The razor rasped along, making its customary sound as fluffs of lather mixed with bits of hair gathered along the blade. I paused a moment to clean it, then took up the strop again to sharpen the razor, because I'm a barber who does things properly. The man, who had kept his eyes closed, opened them now, removed one of his hands from under the sheet, felt the spot on his face where the soap had been cleared off, and said, "Come to the school today at six o'clock." "The same thing as the other day?" I asked horrified. "It could be better," he replied. "What do you plan to do?" "I don't know yet. But we'll amuse ourselves." Once more he leaned back and closed his eyes. I approached him with the razor poised. "Do you plan to punish them all?" I ventured timidly. "All." The soap was drying on his face. I had to hurry. In the mirror I looked toward the street. It was the same as ever: the grocery store with two or three customers in it. Then I glanced at the clock: two-twenty in the afternoon. The razor continued on its downward stroke. Now from the other sideburn down. A thick, blue beard. He should have let it grow like some poets or priests do. It would suit him well. A lot of people wouldn't recognize him. Much to his benefit, I thought, as I attempted to cover the neck area smoothly. There, for sure, the razor had to be handled masterfully, since the hair, although softer, grew into little swirls. A curly beard. One of the tiny pores could be opened up and issue forth its pearl of blood. A good barber such as I prides himself on never allowing this to happen to a client. And this was a first-class client. How many of us had he ordered shot? How many of us had he ordered mutilated? It was better not to think about it. Torres did not know that I was his enemy. He did not know it nor did the rest. It was a secret shared by very few, precisely so that I could inform the revolutionaries of what Torres was doing in town and of what he was planning each time he undertook a rebel-hunting excursion. So it was going to be very difficult to explain that I had him right in my hands and let him go peacefully—alive and shaved.

The beard was now almost completely gone. He seemed younger, less burdened by years than when he had arrived. I suppose this always happens with men who visit barber shops. Under the stroke of my razor Torres was being rejuvenated—rejuvenated because I am a good barber, the best in the town, if I may say so. A little more lather here, under his chin, on his Adam's apple, on this big vein. How hot it is getting! Torres must be sweating as much as I. But he is not afraid. He is a calm man, who is not even thinking about what he is going to do with the prisoners this afternoon. On the other hand, I, with this razor in my hands, stroking and restroking this skin, trying to keep blood from oozing from these pores, can't even think clearly. Damn him for coming, because I'm a revolutionary and not a murderer. And how easy it would be to kill him. And he deserves it. Does he? No! What the devil! No one deserves to have someone else make the sacrifice of becoming a murderer. What do you gain by it? Nothing. Others come along and still others, and the first ones kill the second ones and they the next ones and it goes on like this until everything is a sea of blood. I could cut this throat just so, zip! zip! I wouldn't give him time to complain and since he has his eyes closed he wouldn't see the glistening knife blade or my glistening eyes. But I'm trembling like a real murderer. Out of his neck a gush of blood would spout onto the sheet, on the chair, on my hands, on the floor. I would have to close the door. And the blood would keep inching along the floor, warm, ineradicable, uncontainable, until it reached the street, like a little scarlet stream. I'm sure that one solid stroke, one deep incision, would prevent any pain. He wouldn't suffer. But what would I do with the body? Where would I hide it? I would have to flee, leaving all I have behind, and take refuge far away, far, far away. But they would follow until they found me. "Captain Torres' murderer. He slit his throat while he was shaving him—a coward." And then on the other side, "The avenger of us all. A name to remember. (And here they would mention my name.) He was the town barber. No one knew he was defending our cause."

And what of all this? Murderer or hero? My destiny depends on the edge of this blade. I can turn my hand a bit more, press a little harder on the razor, and sink it in. The skin would give way like silk, like rubber, like the strop. There is nothing more tender than human skin and blood is always there, ready to pour forth. A blade like this doesn't fail. It is my best. But I don't want to be a murderer, no sir. You came to me for a shave. And I perform my work honorably. . . . I don't want blood on my hands. Just lather, that's all. You are an executioner and I am only a barber. Each person has his own place in the scheme of things. That's right. His own place.

Now his chin had been stroked clean and smooth. The man sat up and looked into the mirror. He rubbed his hands over his skin and felt it fresh, like new.

15 "Thanks," he said. He went to the hanger for his belt, pistol and cap. I must have been very pale: my shirt felt soaked. Torres finished adjusting the buckle, straightened his pistol in the holster and after automatically smoothing down his hair, he put on the cap. From his pants pocket he took out several coins to pay me for my services. And he began to head toward the door. In the doorway he paused for a moment, and turning to me he said:

"They told me that you'd kill me. I came to find out. But killing isn't easy. You can take my word for it." And he headed on down the street.

Writing Log/Journal Assignment

Write a brief character sketch of both Captain Torres and the barber. In what way are they the same? How are they different? What sort of descriptive words and phrases did you use to distinguish the two men?

Individual and Collaborative Considerations

1. How does the author develop the relationship between the barber and Captain Torres?
2. What would the barber like to do and why?
3. Analyze how the action or plot of the story clarifies the rather nebulous title, "Just Lather, That's All."
4. While engaged in the ritual act of shaving a customer, the narrator goes through an entirely different ritual in his mind. What moral and ethical victory does he ultimately win at the end of the "ritual drama" staged in his imagination?
5. Explain the irony of the final paragraph. What might Captain Torres' comments suggest about his character? Is he a happy, a disturbed, or a tortured individual?

Writing Activities

1. Téllez's barber is unwilling to become initiated into the world of Captain Torres, whose identity is forever clouded between murderer and hero. Write an essay about a situation similar to but different from the one the barber faced, explaining how and why you also were unwilling to become an initiate into a new world of experiences (e.g., gangs, cliques, cults, political groups).
2. In a well-developed paper, illustrate how you might use a common ritual practice—such as shaving an individual—as a pretense for accomplishing an entirely different objective (e.g., *accidentally* cutting someone's throat). What prevents you from following through with your ulterior motive?

※

Araby

James Joyce

Though born in Dublin, Ireland, James Joyce became a self-imposed exile from his native land, living on the continent in Trieste, Zürich, and Paris for half of his life. Ironically, he wrote exclusively about Ireland while so far away from it. Through his experimentation with the "stream of consciousness" technique of writing, Joyce won many admirers, and he became one of the major influences in Western literature during the early twentieth century. In addition to *Chamber Music*, a volume of poetry, Joyce also wrote *No Exit*, a play; he gained attention and respect mostly for his fiction, however: *Dubliners* (1914), *Portrait of an Artist As a Young Man* (1916), *Ulysses* (1922), and *Finnegans Wake* (1939). Joyce's characters were usually drawn from a wide spectrum of Dublin life: politicians, servants, young people, and complacent members of the middle class. His perception of the great spiritual waste during his times became one of his favorite themes in his writings. As in "Araby," a rite-of-passage tale, many of Joyce's stories were structured around epiphanies—sudden revelations of the true nature of characters or situations through a specific event or action.

N orth Richmond Street, being blind, was a quiet street except at the hour when the Christian Brothers' School set the boys free. An uninhabited house of two storeys stood at the blind end, detached from its neighbours in a square ground. The other houses of the street, conscious of decent lives within them, gazed at one another with brown imperturbable faces.

The former tenant of our house, a priest, had died in the back drawing room. Air, musty from having been long enclosed, hung in all the rooms, and the waste room behind the kitchen was littered with old useless papers. Among these I found a few paper-covered books, the pages of which were curled and damp: *The Abbot*, by Walter Scott, *The Devout Communicant* and *The Memoirs of Vidocq*. I liked the last best because its leaves were yellow. The wild garden behind the house contained a central apple-tree and a few straggling bushes under one of which I found the late tenant's rusty bicycle pump. He had been a very charitable priest; in his will he had left all his money to institutions and the furniture of his house to his sister.

When the short days of winter came dusk fell before we had well eaten our dinners. When we met in the street the houses had grown sombre. The space of sky above us was the colour of ever-changing violet and towards it the lamps of the street lifted their feeble lanterns. The cold air stung us and we played till our bodies glowed. Our shouts echoed in the silent street. The career of our play brought us through the dark muddy lanes behind the houses where we ran the gauntlet of the rough tribes from the cottages, to the back doors of the dark dripping gardens where odours arose from the ashpits, to the dark odorous stables where a coachman smoothed and combed the horse or shook music from the buckled harness. When we returned to the street light from the kitchen windows had filled the areas. If my uncle was seen turning the corner we hid in the shadow until we had seen him safely housed. Or if Mangan's sister came out on the doorstep to call her brother in to his tea we watched her from our shadow peer up and down the street. We waited to see whether she would remain or go in and, if she remained, we left our shadow and walked up to Mangan's steps resignedly. She was waiting for us, her figure defined by the light from the half-opened door. Her brother always teased her before he obeyed and I stood by the railings looking at her. Her dress swung as she moved her body and the soft rope of her hair tossed from side to side.

Every morning I lay on the floor in the front parlour watching her door. The blind was pulled down to within an inch of the sash so that I could not be seen. When she came out on the doorstep my heart leaped. I ran to the hall, seized my books and followed her. I kept her brown figure always in my eye and, when we came near the point at which our ways diverged, I quickened my pace and passed her. This happened morning after morning. I had never spoken to her, except for a few casual words, and yet her name was like a summons to all my foolish blood.

5   Her image accompanied me even in places the most hostile to romance. On Saturday evenings when my aunt went marketing I had to go to carry some of the parcels. We walked through the flaring streets, jostled by drunken men and bargaining women, amid the curses of labourers, the shrill litanies of shop-boys who stood on guard by the barrels of pigs' cheeks, the nasal chanting of street-singers, who sang a *come-all-you* about O'Donovan Rossa, or a ballad about the troubles in our native land. These noises converged in a single sensation of life for me: I imagined that I bore my chalice safely through a throng of foes. Her name sprang to my lips at moments in strange prayers and praises which I myself did not understand. My eyes were often full of tears (I could not tell why) and at times a flood from my heart seemed to pour itself out into my bosom. I thought little of the future. I did not know whether I would ever speak to her or not or, if I spoke to her, how I could tell her of my confused adoration. But my body was like a harp and her words and gestures were like fingers running upon the wires.

One evening I went into the back drawing-room in which the priest had died. It was a dark rainy evening and there was no sound in the house. Through one of the broken panes I heard the rain impinge upon the earth, the fine incessant needles of water playing in the sodden beds. Some distant lamp or lighted window gleamed below me. I was thankful that I could see so little. All my senses seemed to desire to veil themselves and, feeling that

I was about to slip from them, I pressed the palms of my hands together until they trembled, murmuring: *"O love! O love!"* many times.

At last she spoke to me. When she addressed the first words to me I was so confused that I did not know what to answer. She asked me was I going to *Araby*. I forgot whether I answered yes or no. It would be a splendid bazaar, she said she would love to go.

"And why can't you?" I asked.

While she spoke she turned a silver bracelet round and round her wrist. She could not go, she said, because there would be a retreat that week in her convent. Her brother and two other boys were fighting for their caps and I was alone at the railings. She held one of the spikes, bowing her head towards me. The light from the lamp opposite our door caught the white curve of her neck, lit up her hair that rested there and, falling, lit up the hand upon the railing. It fell over one side of her dress and caught the white border of a petticoat, just visible as she stood at ease.

10   "It's well for you," she said.

"If I go," I said, "I will bring you something."

What innumerable follies laid waste my waking and sleeping thoughts after that evening. I wished to annihilate the tedious intervening days. I chafed against the work of school. At night in my bedroom and by day in the classroom her image came between me and the page I strove to read. The syllables of the word *Araby* were called to me through the silence in which my soul luxuriated and cast an Eastern enchantment over me. I asked for leave to go to the bazaar on Saturday night. My aunt was surprised and hoped it was not some Freemason affair. I answered few questions in class. I watched my master's face pass from amiability to sternness; he hoped I was not beginning to idle. I could not call my wandering thoughts together. I had hardly any patience with the serious work of life which, now that it stood between me and my desire, seemed to me child's play, ugly monotonous child's play.

On Saturday morning I reminded my uncle that I wished to go to the bazaar in the evening. He was fussing at the hallstand, looking for the hat-brush, and answered me curtly:

"Yes, boy, I know."

15   As he was in the hall I could not go into the front parlour and lie at the window. I left the house in bad humour and walked slowly towards the school. The air was pitilessly raw and already my heart misgave me.

When I came home to dinner my uncle had not yet been home. Still it was early. I sat staring at the clock for some time and, when its ticking began to irritate me, I left the room. I mounted the staircase and gained the upper part of the house. The high cold empty gloomy rooms liberated me and I went from room to room singing. From the front window I saw my companions playing below in the street. Their cries reached me weakened and indistinct and, leaning my forehead against the cool glass, I looked over at the dark house where she lived. I may have stood there for an hour, seeing nothing but the brown-clad figure cast by my imagination, touched discreetly by the lamplight at the curved neck, at the hand upon the railings and at the border below the dress.

When I came downstairs again I found Mrs. Mercer sitting at the fire. She was an old garrulous woman, a pawnbroker's widow, who collected used stamps for some pious purpose. I had to endure the gossip of the tea-table. The meal was prolonged beyond an hour and still my uncle did not come. Mrs. Mercer stood up to go: she was sorry she couldn't wait any longer, but it was after eight o'clock and she did not like to be out late, as the night air was bad for her. When she had gone I began to walk up and down the room, clenching my fists. My aunt said:

"I'm afraid you may put off your bazaar for this night of Our Lord."

At nine o'clock I heard my uncle's latchkey in the halldoor. I heard him talking to himself and heard the hallstand rocking when it had received the weight of his overcoat. I could interpret these signs. When he was midway through his dinner I asked him to give me the money to go to the bazaar. He had forgotten.

20   "The people are in bed and after their first sleep now," he said.

I did not smile. My aunt said to him energetically:

"Can't you give him the money and let him go? You've kept him late enough as it is."

My uncle said he was very sorry he had forgotten. He said he believed in the old saying: "All work and no play makes Jack a dull boy." He asked me where I was going and, when I had told him a second time he asked me did I know *The Arab's Farewell to His Steed*. When I left the kitchen he was about to recite the opening lines of the piece to my aunt.

I held a florin tightly in my hand as I strode down Buckingham Street towards the station. The sight of the streets thronged with buyers and glaring with gas recalled to me the purpose of my journey. I took my seat in a third-class carriage of a deserted train. After an intolerable delay the train moved out of the station slowly. It crept onward among ruinous houses and over the twinkling river. At Westland Row Station a crowd of people pressed to the carriage doors; but the porters moved them back, saying that it was a special train for the bazaar. I remained alone in the bare carriage. In a few minutes the train drew up beside an improvised wooden platform. I passed out on to the road and saw by the lighted dial of a clock that it was ten minutes to ten. In front of me was a large building which displayed the magical name.

25   I could not find any sixpenny entrance and, fearing that the bazaar would be closed, I passed in quickly through a turnstile, handing a shilling to a weary-looking man. I found myself in a big hall girdled at half its height by a gallery. Nearly all the stalls were closed and the greater part of the hall was in darkness. I recognized a silence like that which pervades a church after a service. I walked into the centre of the bazaar timidly. A few people were gathered about the stalls which were still open. Before a curtain, over which the words Café *Chantant* were written in coloured lamps, two men were counting money on a salver. I listened to the fall of the coins.

Remembering with difficulty why I had come I went over to one of the stalls and examined porcelain vases and flowered tea-sets. At the door of the stall a young lady was talking and laughing with two young gentlemen. I remarked their English accents and listened vaguely to their conversation.

"O, I never said such a thing!"

"O, but you did!"

"O, but I didn't!"

30 "Didn't she say that?"

"Yes. I heard her."

"O, there's a . . . fib!"

Observing me the young lady came over and asked me did I wish to buy anything. The tone of her voice was not encouraging; she seemed to have spoken to me out of a sense of duty. I looked humbly at the great jars that stood like eastern guards at either side of the dark entrance to the stall and murmured:

"No, thank you."

35 The young lady changed the position of one of the vases and went back to the two young men. They began to talk of the same subject. Once or twice the young lady glanced at me over her shoulder.

I lingered before her stall, though I knew my stay was useless, to make my interest in her wares seem the more real. Then I turned away slowly and walked down the middle of the bazaar. I allowed the two pennies to fall against the sixpence in my pocket. I heard a voice call from one end of the gallery that the light was out. The upper part of the hall was now completely dark.

Gazing up into the darkness I saw myself as a creature driven and derided by vanity; and my eyes burned with anguish and anger.

Writing Log/Journal Assignment

Write a journal entry about a place you would like to go to because of its promise of change, renewal, or relief from your day-to-day lifestyle.

Individual and Collaborative Considerations

1. How does the young boy feel about living in Dublin? What future does it promise him?
2. Is the narrator a realist or a romantic? What details in the story help to form your opinion?
3. Why does Araby, the bazaar, become so important to the boy? What does it represent?
4. In your opinion, is the young boy infatuated with Mangan's sister or actually in love with her? What might she represent? (Note his descriptions of her; are they fanciful or realistic?)

5. How does Joyce's figurative language complement the protagonist's worldview before his epiphany at the bazaar?

Writing Activities

1. Compose an essay tracing how Joyce's use of light and dark imagery and religious symbolism reinforce the notion that Dublin is the "center of paralysis" and in need of renewal. How does he seek deliverance from Dublin? In what way does he attempt to escape "the center of paralysis"?
2. Write an essay showing how the intensity and importance you placed on an event became all the more meaningful to you due to your plans and expectations—only to leave you disappointed or disillusioned when the true nature of the event became known to you. Wherever possible, relate your experience to the experience of the boy in "Araby."

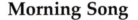

Morning Song

Sylvia Plath

A Massachusetts native, Sylvia Plath attended Smith College. Though her education was interrupted when she suffered a nervous breakdown, she returned to Smith and graduated in 1955. Plath's traumatic experiences provided the basis of her well-known novel *The Bell Jar* (1963), a book she published under the pseudonym Victoria Lewis. Her poetic works include *The Colossus* (1962), *Ariel* (1966), *Crossing the Water* (1971), *Winter Trees* (1972), and *Collected Poems* (1981), which received a Pulitzer Prize. Plath's other works include a collection of prose writings, *Johnny Panic and the Bible of Dreams* (1977); her correspondences, *Letters Home* (1975); and her journals, *Journals* (1982). As demonstrated in the following poem, "Morning Song," Plath's verse was characterized by stark, vivid, often disturbing imagery.

> Love set you going like a fat gold watch.
> The midwife slapped your footsoles, and your bald cry
> Took its place among the elements.
>
> Our voices echo, magnifying your arrival. New statue.
> In a drafty museum, your nakedness
> Shadows our safety. We stand round blankly as walls.

5

I'm no more your mother
Than the cloud that distills a mirror to reflect its own slow
Effacement at the wind's hand.

10   All night your moth-breath
Flickers among the flat pink roses. I wake to listen:
A far sea moves in my ear.

One cry, and I stumble from bed, cow heavy and floral
In my Victorian nightgown
15   Your mouth opens clean as a cat's. The window square

Whitens and swallows its dull stars. And now you try
Your handful of notes;
The clear vowels rise like balloons.

Writing Log/Journal Assignment

Wake up early some morning and record all the sights, sounds, and smells you usually do not notice during daylight hours.

Individual and Collaborative Considerations

1. The opening line of Plath's poem, "Love set you going like a fat gold watch," offers a curious image. Why does the speaker set the young body ticking like a watch—a mechanical act—rather than lovingly creating a new life?
2. Locate the definition of *oxymoron* in your dictionary. Then explain how "bald cry" functions as an *oxymoron* in Plath's poem.
3. Are there any words reflecting the speaker's love for her infant in the poem? If so, what are they? If not, why do you imagine the poet avoided such language?
4. What does the image "cow heavy" suggest about the speaker?
5. In the final few lines of the poem, "And now you try / Your handful of notes; / The clear vowels rise like balloons," why might the infant's cries "rise like balloons"?

Writing Activities

1. What causes parents to bond with their children? What are some of the results of a parent–child relationship where bonding does not take place? Devise a thesis and write an essay persuading your readers to share your point of view on the merits of *bonding*.
2. Write an essay in which you define either *parental duty* or *parental nurturing*. A variation of this assignment would be an essay comparing and contrasting the effects of growing up in a household where parents view raising children as a *duty* rather than a *loving, nurturing* experience.

Constantly Risking Absurdity

Lawrence Ferlinghetti

Poet and publisher Lawrence Ferlinghetti was born in New York in 1919,
but it was through his residence in San Francisco that he became associated with Allen Ginsberg, Gary Snyder, Jack Kerouac, and the Beat movement—a bohemian movement against the folkways and mores of
established society in general. His City Lights Bookshop in San Francisco,
California, became the center for many writers during the late 1950s. Ferlinghetti's own works include *Pictures of the Gone World* (1955), *A Coney Island of the Mind* (1958), *Starting from San Francisco* (1961), *After the Cries of
the Birds* (1967), *The Secret Meaning of Things* (1969), *Tyrannus Nix* (1969),
Open Eye, Open Heart (1973), *Who Are We Now?* (1976), and *Endless Night*
(1981). Shocking, experimental language often characterizes Ferlinghetti's
poetry though his verse remains fully accessible to his readers. In "Constantly Risking Absurdity," Ferlinghetti compares how both a poet and a
trapeze artist ritually face and accept the dangers associated with their
skills on a daily basis.

Constantly risking absurdity
          and death
    whenever he performs
        above the heads
5   of his audience
the poet like an acrobat
      climbs on rime
      to a high wire of his own making
and balancing on eyebeams
10   above a sea of faces
    paces his way

      to the other side of day
  performing entrechats
      and sleight-of-foot tricks
15 and other high theatrics
      and all without mistaking
    any thing
      for what it may not be

  For he's the super realist
20   who must perforce perceive
    taut truth

before the taking of each stance or step
in his supposed advance
toward that still higher perch
25   where Beauty stands and waits
with gravity
to start her death-defying leap

And he
a little charleychaplin man
30   who may or may not catch
her fair eternal form
spreadeagled in the empty air
of existence

Writing Log/Journal Assignment

Explore why people tend to be fascinated by the circus—especially its acrobatic performers like tight-rope walkers and trapeze artists, forever engaged in dangerous ritual practices. (How is missing a trapeze in midair like
writing a bad poem?)

Individual and Collaborative Considerations

1. Discuss Ferlinghetti's word choice in his poem. Why do you think he
   selected words with multiple meanings?
2. How does the typography—the way lines in the poem are organized and
   indented—reflect the poem's theme?
3. In your opinion, what is "super reality"?
4. Why does Ferlinghetti equate a poet to an acrobat? What ritual do both
   go through every day?
5. Who was Charley Chaplin? What sort of reader response does the speaker
   seem to expect with his reference to Chaplin?

Writing Activities

1. Write an essay defining what you think a poet is. How does your personal
   definition compare/contrast to Ferlinghetti's definition of a poet?
2. Construct an essay where you dared to risk absurdity. What was the
   situation, why did you take the risk, and what was the outcome? Would
   you repeat the risk? Why or why not?

Rockaway

Katharine Harer

Katharine Harer was born in Oakland, California, in 1949. She studied at San Francisco State University and at the University of Nevada at Reno. She has worked with the California Poets in The Schools Program since 1978 as a poet-teacher and as Executive Director, and she has been a California Arts Council Poet in Residence at two San Francisco high schools. Harer currently teaches English and Creative Writing at Skyline Community College in San Bruno. In 1995, Harer won the Slipstream Annual Poetry Award, resulting in the publication of *Hubba Hubba*, a collection of her poems. Harer's poetry has been published in numerous magazines and anthologies, as well as in three small-press collections: *Spring Cycle, In These Bodies*, and *The Border*. Her most recent works appear in *onthebus* and *Calyx*, literary magazines, and she has published prose poems titled *The Party Train*, an anthology. In the following poem, Harer relates her observation of the rituals surfers go through. From the moment they arrive at the ocean until they come out of the water and "stand dripping by their cars," the surfers cannot take their eyes off the water. When asked about the poem, Harer noted the surfers' "depth of concentration seemed to be at the heart of their existence."

> They stare at the ocean as if they're
> looking for something a certain curl a
> ripple a break in the lacy
> foam that unravels from the
> 5 hearts of waves
>
> Slowly they undo their pants
> all the while looking out beyond
> themselves pull their wet suits on
> carefully like women easing
> 10 nylons over their legs all
> without looking away
> chests bare and soft
> the rubber suit flapping at
> their waists they savor every step
> 15 that takes them towards the waves
>
> Some run like children
> boards strapped to their wrists
> others walk a slow, jagged line
> disappearing and reappearing

20 patiently stroking the water
    slipping inside the crashing
    and coming out whole skimming
    the thunder slick as glass
    for as long as it lets them

25 When they come in
    and stand dripping by their cars
    faces calm from the tossing
    and riding hair tangled
    a salty wet glaze on their skin
30 when you think they'd had enough
    of water
    their eyes are still
    searching the waves.

Writing Log/Journal Assignment

Observe someone or something that seems to be engaged in a ritual act of some sort for an extended period of time and then jot down what you see or think you see in your journal.

Individual and Collaborative Considerations

1. How does Harer structure her poem?
2. Describe the tone of Harer's poem. Does it capture the mood of a speaker totally mesmerized by her immediate surroundings and the people in it? Why or why not?
3. What common rituals do the surfers in "Rockaway" observe and how do their rituals differ?
4. Which image in "Rockaway" resonates or stays with you the longest? Why?
5. What is the effect of occasional images running on to each other in "Rockaway"?

Writing Activities

1. Write an essay where your compare and contrast the surfers' rituals at the ocean in "Rockaway" to the mother's observances at home in "Superstitious Minds."
2. Return to the Writing Log/Journal Assignment following "Rockaway" and use your impressions of someone or something engaged in a ritual act as a starting point for an analytical essay. You might, for instance, brainstorm your journal entry (or use any other prewriting method that works for you) and write a tentative thesis for an essay that shows readers

what you initially felt about a ritual act (narrative) to why, in retrospect, you felt as you did (analysis).

ADDITIONAL TOPICS AND ISSUES FOR WRITING AND RESEARCH

1. A recent news segment claimed that teenagers who smoke cigarettes are eighteen percent more likely to commit suicide than nonsmokers. How accurate do you imagine that information is? Are you knowledgeable of people who have become cigarette smokers? Are they more prone to personal violence than your other friends? What cause–effect relationships between smoking and depression (leading to suicide) did you uncover? Write about your findings in a formal essay.

2. Write an essay in which you expose a campaign rally for a political candidate for what it really is: a ritual. What is the procedure for a campaign rally? Who speaks first and what is done? How does a rally usually conclude?

3. Take a holiday familiar to your culture and write an essay explaining its significance to an audience that knows nothing about it. Within your essay, you will want to mention details pertaining to traditional practices (e.g., exchanging gifts or lighting fireworks).

4. What ritual customs do you observe when you greet elders and loved ones? Where did each custom originate and when? Do you imagine your own children will carry on the customs and traditions that have been an important part of your life? Write an essay arguing for the preservation of customs and rituals.

5. Have you ever listened to two people argue about the same issue day after day and never reach a solution? If so, write a paper where you liken the repetitive nature of the "predictable argument" to a ritual.

6. How might any courting practice be considered a ritual? In a well-developed essay, illustrate this or a related position on courting practices, drawing most of your examples from direct experience as well as through your observation of others around you.

7. How has joining the army, navy, air force, marines, or coast guard become an initiation into adulthood for many Americans? Fully demonstrate your thesis on this subject with facts and statistics drawn from recent surveys and studies—followed by commentary and analysis.

8. At what point in your life does free choice become a matter of obligation and responsibility? Explain your thesis based on this question with reference to "rites of passage" and stages of human development.

9. In an expository essay, offer your hypothesis explaining what motivates people to develop and maintain hobbies often completely unrelated to their vocations in life. What do hobbies offer people? (Since you know the effect of a hobby is an ongoing interest in it, your paper will probably want to focus on the immediate and contributory causes for hobbies.)

10. Analyze how and why voter registration and presidential elections are all part of a perpetual ritual, a ritual to make the masses feel empowered although, in reality, the elite electoral college still makes the final decisions.

Starting Points for Research

Initiations	Rituals
• Table manners	• Animal behavior
• Business world: dog-eat-dog	• Cults
• Confirmation (political/religious)	• Chinese rites
• Communion (primitive/modern practice)	• Malabar rites
• Coronations	• Ecclesiastical
• Fraternities and sororities	• Traditions
• Greek letter societies	• Manners and customs
• Hazing	• Mysteries
• Initiations in literature	• Birth customs
• Initiations into trades	• Rites of spring
• Mythological rites of passage	• Funeral rites and ceremonies
• Political initiations (also, protocol)	• Exorcism
• Puberty rites	• Fasts and feasts
• Religious initiations	• Incantations
Buddhism	• Marriage customs and rites
Christianity	• Mourning customs
Hinduism	• Last meal before execution
Islam	• Ceremonial objects
Judaism	• Memorial rites and ceremonies
Shamanism	• Rain-making rites
• Rites and ceremonies	• Religious services industry
• Secret societies	• Taboos
• Voyage of the hero	• Public worship
• Youth dedications	• Liturgies
• Scapegoats	• Ritual calendar
• Ordinations	• Ritual dances
• Natural Disasters	• Foot washing

13

Art and Aesthetics

The beginning of all art:
a song when planting a rice field
in the country's inmost part.
MATSUO BASHO

Essays

Susan Sontag   Beauty

•

Neil Postman   Euphemism

•

Fiction

Hermann Hesse   The Brahmin's Son

•

Junichiro Tanizaki   The Tattooer

•

Rabindranath Tagore   The Artist

•

Poetry

Pablo Neruda   The Word

•

X. J. Kennedy   Nude, Descending a Staircase

•

Ezra Pound   Salutation

In a "Statement on Aesthetics, Poetics, Kinetics," poet Al Young said, "Singing, playing, dancing, painting, sculpting, acting, laughing, crying, winning, hurting, writing—all these are ways of reaching out and they all come back down to that basic touch, a way of seeing, a way of saying: 'I live in the world too and this is my way of being here with you.' " Art might be aptly defined as the active craft of creating "beautiful" things such as paintings, poems, musical tunes, embroidered clothes, stained glass windows, fine jewelry, and sculptures. Although the old saying that "beauty is in the eye of the beholder" is often indisputable, it is difficult to confuse *beauty* with something disturbing, outlandish, or offensive. *Beautiful things* are attractive to most people—not repulsive.

Authors' values are frequently expressed through aesthetics. You might define aesthetics as a branch of philosophy devoted to a theory of "the beautiful and the fine arts in literature" (*Webster's*). An aesthetic can also refer to specific individuals who build a superior appreciation of beauty, of art, and of their spiritual existence. A definition provides only a point of departure in comprehending aesthetics. Your sense of art and aesthetics will play a large role in your life preference for one type of shoe, one kind of movie, one style of architecture, and so forth, over another.

The aesthetically pleasing or disturbing forms of art are experienced daily through the senses: *sights* from mass media such as magazine photographs, graffiti, and billboard images; *sounds* around us including conversations, musical compositions, and sirens; *smells* ranging from flower fragrances and perfumes to car exhaust.

The selections in this chapter offer a look into art or aesthetics from many perspectives. Susan Sontag begins to examine aesthetics at its most basic level in her essay titled "Beauty." As Neil Postman indicates in "Euphemism," using words effectively is an art form in itself. Nonetheless, he is concerned when "euphemizing information" interferes with clear expression, making an art form something devious or dangerous. Pablo Neruda's poem "The Word" quite literally is a celebration of the word—elevated to an art form.

In search of beauty and truth, Junichiro Tanizaki approaches art and aesthetics in "The Tattooer" from both a visual and a psychological perspective. On the literal side, Seikichi finds the canvas for his masterpiece: the skin of a beautiful woman who met "various qualifications of character as well as appearance." On the psychological side, there is a definite role reversal taking place. Siddhartha pursues aesthetic principles in Hermann Hesse's "The Brahmin's Son" from a different point of view. He seeks a higher meaning in life than being "the Brahmin's son," and so he leaves home to live as an aesthetic—one of the Samanas.

Where do the arts rate among the ever-changing social structures in the modern world? What is and is not a practical use of time? Rabindranath Tagore presents a familiar theme of personal gratification versus monetary gains in "The Artist." Readings about art and aesthetics are certainly not limited to selections collected under that heading. Remember that the definition of art is relative and your response to it is frequently subjective. In "Salutation," Ezra Pound salutes those with simple lives and simple needs (a living aesthetic). "Nude, Descending a Staircase" by X. J. Kennedy represents a natural, pure act "in nature's own," marred only by those peeking *behind the stairs*. Here you may argue whether the poet was attempting to capsulate a moment of truth and beauty or to present an aesthetic. In any case, the literature in this chapter seeks more to elicit your response to art or aesthetics than to present a narrow definition of either.

RHETORIC AT WORK

To use words "artistically" might imply artificiality to some people who prefer plain diction to explain or argue material over diction filled with fanciful conceits and figurative language. On the other hand, word use need not be flowery to be effective. By capitalizing on the aesthetic qualities of denotation and connotation, you are certainly bringing your writing to

---

A Checklist for Writing about *Art and Aesthetics*

1. What am I examining in my writing assignment? Will I discuss some aspect of art, the concept of aesthetics, or a combination of the two?
2. Did I provide a definition of art or aesthetics early in my paper?
3. How does an analysis of aesthetics develop my thesis? What do I want my reader to realize?
4. What sort of examples or allusions did I offer to illustrate the concepts set forth in my essay? How do they appeal to a wide audience with diverse opinions about the nature of art and aesthetics?
5. Does figurative language help to convey the more abstract or ineffable aspects of my topic? How? Why? When? Where?
6. How did I use reader associations made through denotation and connotation to bring my writing to another level?
7. Did I consider the role of feelings, imagination, and subjective reality when I wrote my thesis? How? When? Where?
8. What conclusions did I reach? Did I place my major discussion points into perspective with my thesis? Have I achieved what I set out to do?
9. Did my final sentence leave something memorable in my readers' minds? What was it?

another level, using words to "artistically" express meaning through association. As you read through the forthcoming literary works, take a moment once in a while to underline instances where the denotation or connotation of words influences your response to the material. What was it about the author's diction that made the piece striking and memorable? What would have been lost if the author had used a plain style, void of words with connotations inferring meaning?

✳

Beauty

Susan Sontag

Born in New York City in 1933, Susan Sontag was educated at the University of California, the University of Chicago, Harvard University, and St. Anne's College of Oxford University. After the publication of *Against Interpretation, and Other Essays* (1966), Sontag established herself as a major social critic in America. Although she is best known for her nonfiction, she has written two novels, *The Benefactor* (1964) and *Death Kit* (1967), numerous short stories, and several screenplays. Over the years, she has also been a frequent contributor to *Harper's* and *Atlantic* magazines. Sontag's reputation as the "Dark Lady of American Literature" can be witnessed in many of her works: *Trip to Hanoi* (1969), *Styles of Radical Will* (1969), *On Photography* (1976), *Illness As Metaphor* (1977), and *Under the Sign of Saturn* (1980). The following essay, "Beauty," was originally titled "Woman's Beauty: Put-Down or Power-Source?" and published in *Vogue* magazine in 1975.

1 For the Greeks, beauty was a virtue: a kind of excellence. Persons then were assumed to be what we now have to call—lamely, enviously—*whole* persons. If it did occur to the Greeks to distinguish between a person's "inside" and "outside," they still expected that inner beauty would be matched by beauty of the other kind. The well-born young Athenians who gathered around Socrates found it quite paradoxical that their hero was so intelligent, so brave, so honorable, so seductive—and so ugly. One of Socrates' main pedagogical acts was to be ugly—and teach those innocent, no doubt splendid-looking disciples of his how full of paradoxes life really was.

2 They may have resisted Socrates' lesson. We do not. Several thousand years later, we are more wary of the enchantments of beauty. We not only split off—with the greatest facility—the "inside" (character, intellect) from

the "outside" (looks); but we are actually surprised when some one who is beautiful is also intelligent, talented, good.

3   It was principally the influence of Christianity that deprived beauty of the central place it had in classical ideals of human excellence. By limiting excellence (*virtus* in Latin) to *moral* virtue only, Christianity set beauty adrift— as an alienated, arbitrary, superficial enchantment. And beauty has continued to lose prestige. For close to two centuries it has become a convention to attribute beauty to only one of the two sexes: the sex which, however Fair, is always Second. Associating beauty with women has put beauty even further on the defensive, morally.

4   A beautiful woman, we say in English. But a handsome man. "Handsome" is the masculine equivalent of—and refusal of—a compliment which has accumulated certain demeaning overtones, by being reserved for women only. That one can call a man "beautiful" in French and in Italian suggests that Catholic countries—unlike those countries shaped by the Protestant version of Christianity—still retain some vestiges of the pagan admiration for beauty. But the difference, if one exists, is of degree only. In every modern country that is Christian or post-Christian, women *are* the beautiful sex—to the detriment of the notion of beauty as well as of women.

5   To be called beautiful is thought to name something essential to women's character and concerns. (In contrast to men—whose essence is to be strong, or effective, or competent.) It does not take someone in the throes of advanced feminist awareness to perceive that the way women are taught to be involved with beauty encourages narcissism, reinforces dependence and immaturity. Everybody (women and men) knows that. For it is "everybody," a whole society, that has identified being feminine with caring about how one *looks*. (In contrast to being masculine—which is identified with caring about what one *is* and *does* and only secondarily if at all, about how one *looks*.) Given these stereotypes, it is no wonder that beauty enjoys, at best, a rather mixed reputation.

6   It is not, of course, the desire to be beautiful that is wrong but the obligation to be—or to try. What is accepted by most women as a flattering idealization of their sex is a way of making women feel inferior to what they actually are—or normally grow to be. For the ideal of beauty is administered as a form of self-oppression. Women are taught to see their bodies in *parts*, and to evaluate each part separately. Breasts, feet, hips, waistline, neck, eyes, nose, complexion, hair, and so on—each in turn is submitted to an anxious, fretful, often despairing scrutiny. Even if some pass muster, some will always be found wanting. Nothing less than perfection will do.

7   In men, good looks is a whole, something taken in at a glance. It does not need to be conformed by giving measurements of different regions of the body, nobody encourages a man to dissect his appearance, feature by feature. As for perfection, that is considered trivial—almost unmanly. Indeed, in the ideally good-looking man a small imperfection or blemish is considered positively desirable. According to one movie critic (a woman) who is a declared Robert Redford fan, it is having that cluster of skin-colored moles on one

cheek that saves Redford from being merely a "pretty face." Think of the depreciation of women—as well as of beauty—that is implied in that judgment.

8   "The privileges of beauty are immense," said Cocteau. To be sure, beauty is a form of power. And deservedly so. What is lamentable is that it is the only form of power that most women are encouraged to seek. This power is always conceived in relation to men; it is not the power to do but the power to attract. It is a power that negates itself. For this power is not one that can be chosen freely—at least not by women—or renounced without social censure.

9   To preen, for a woman, can never be just a pleasure. It is also a duty. It is her work. If a woman does real work and even if she has clambered up to a leading position in politics, law, medicine, business, or whatever—she is always under pressure to confess that she still works at being attractive. But in so far as she is keeping up as one of the Fair Sex, she brings under suspicion her very capacity to be objective, professional, authoritative, thoughtful. Damned if they do—women are. And damned if they don't.

10   One could hardly ask for more important evidence of the dangers of considering persons as split between what is "inside" and what is "outside" than that interminable half-comic, half-tragic tale, the oppression of women. How easy it is to start off by defining women as caretakers of the surfaces, and then to disparage them (or find them adorable) for being "superficial." It is a crude trap, and it has worked for too long. But to get out of the trap requires that women get some critical distance from that excellence and privilege which is beauty, enough distance to see how much beauty itself has been abridged in order to prop up the mythology of the "feminine." There should be a way of saving beauty *from* women—and *for* them.

Writing Log/Journal Assignment

Explain your intuitive or scholastic knowledge of "feminism." Then, briefly respond to the author's assertion that "it does not take someone in the throes of advanced feminist awareness to perceive that the way women are taught to be involved with beauty encourages narcissism, reinforces dependence and immaturity."

Individual and Collaborative Considerations

1. Sontag begins her essay offering a historical perspective on the concept of "beauty." What purpose does this serve? To what extent do you find her strategy effective?

2. This essay first appeared in *Vogue* magazine in 1975 under the title "Woman's Beauty: Put-Down or Power-Source?" How does the title indicate the focus of the essay? For whom was this article initially intended? How might the new title, "Beauty," appeal to or draw in a wider audience?

3. How does Sontag argue that the desire to be beautiful is fine but the "obligation" to be beautiful is wrong? Do you agree with her reasoning?
4. According to Sontag, what specific associations do people in modern society make with individuals who are identified as (1) masculine or (2) feminine?
5. In what way might beauty be considered a form of power and for whom?

Writing Activities

1. Review your writing log/journal entry for this essay. Then expand your brief response to Sontag's assertion that "the way women are taught to be involved with beauty encourages narcissism, reinforces dependence and immaturity" into a well-reasoned essay—supported with specific, concrete examples. (Hint: The major discussion points in your paper might be narcissism, dependence, and immaturity. Though Sontag identifies these qualities herself, your original examples will breathe fresh life into her argument and strengthen it!)
2. Go through advertisements for "beauty aids" in a variety of magazines. How are women portrayed in these ads? How are men depicted? Do cosmetic companies attempt to be politically correct by using ugly men and unattractive women to sell their products? After synthesizing your findings, prewrite with focus on the topic of "the future of men and beauty aids." Next, construct a thesis with an argumentative edge to focus your discussion points. Finally, develop your speculative thesis and argue your points based on the sort of "beauty aids" men are presently encouraged to buy. Make sure you explain how and why the male attitude towards "beauty aids" may change from unnecessary to important as we move into the twenty-first century. (Consider: Is America the land of the young? If so, what must one do to look young?)

※

Euphemism

Neil Postman

A critic, communications theorist, and writer, Neil Postman achieved recognition for his essays and books advocating radical reforms in education. A contributor to the *Atlantic* and *The Nation*, Postman also is the author of *Crazy Talk, Stupid Talk: How We Defeat Ourselves by the Way We Talk and What to Do about It* (1976), *Teaching As a Conserving Activity* (1980), *The Disappearance of Childhood* (1982), *Amusing Ourselves to Death: Public Discourse in the Age of Show Business* (1985), and *Conscientious Objections* (1988). In addition, he coauthored several books, including *Linguistics: A Revolution in Teaching* (1966) and *Teaching As a Subversive Activity* (1969). In the following essay, he discusses the value of using euphemisms in speaking and writing, considering their political as well as their linguistic implications.

1 **A** euphemism is commonly defined as an auspicious or exalted term (like "sanitation engineer") that is used in place of a more down-to-earth term (like "garbage man"). People who are partial to euphemisms stand accused of being "phony" or of trying to hide what it is they are really talking about. And there is no doubt that in some situations the accusation is entirely proper. For example, one of the more detestable euphemisms I have come across in recent years is the term "Operation Sunshine," which is the name the U.S. Government gave to some experiments it conducted with the hydrogen bomb in the South Pacific. It is obvious that the government, in choosing this name, was trying to expunge the hideous imagery that the bomb evokes and in so doing committed, as I see it, an immoral act. This sort of process—giving pretty names to essentially ugly realities—is what has given euphemizing such a bad name. And people like George Orwell have done valuable work for all of us in calling attention to how the process works. But there is another side to euphemizing that is worth mentioning, and a few words here in its defense will not be amiss.

2 To begin with, we must keep in mind that things do not have "real" names, although many people believe that they do. A garbage man is not "really" a "garbage man," any more than he is really a "sanitation engineer." And a pig is not called a "pig" because it is so dirty, nor a shrimp a "shrimp" because it is so small. There are things, and then there are the names of things, and it is considered a fundamental error in all branches of semantics to assume that a name and a thing are one and the same. It is true, of course, that a name is usually so firmly associated with the thing it denotes that it is extremely difficult to separate one from the other. That is why, for example, advertising is so effective. Perfumes are not given names like "Bronx Odor," and an automobile will never be called "The Lumbering Elephant." Shakespeare was only half right in saying that a rose by any other name would smell as sweet. What we call things affects how we will perceive them. It is not only harder to sell someone a "horse mackerel" sandwich than a "tuna fish" sandwich, but even though they are the "same" thing, we are likely to enjoy the taste of tuna more than that of the horse mackerel. It would appear that human beings almost naturally come to *identify* names with things, which is one of our more fascinating illusions. But there is some substance to this illusion. For if you change the names of things, you change how people will regard them, and that is as good as changing the nature of the thing itself.

3   Now, all sorts of scoundrels know this perfectly well and can make us love almost anything by getting us to transfer the charm of a name to whatever worthless thing they are promoting. But at the same time and in the same vein, euphemizing is a perfectly intelligent method of generating new and useful ways of perceiving things. The man who wants us to call him a "sanitation engineer" instead of a "garbage man" is hoping we will treat him with more respect than we presently do. He wants us to see that he is of some importance to our society. His euphemism is laughable only if we think that he is not deserving of such notice or respect. The teacher who prefers us to use the term "culturally different children" instead of "slum children" is euphemizing, all right, but is doing it to encourage us to see aspects of a situation that might otherwise not be attended to.

4   The point I am making is that there is nothing in the process of euphemizing itself that is contemptible. Euphemizing is contemptible when a name makes us see something that is not true or diverts our attention from something that is. The hydrogen bomb kills. There is nothing else that it does. And when you experiment with it, you are trying to find out how widely and well it kills. Therefore, to call such an experiment "Operation Sunshine" is to suggest a purpose for the bomb that simply does not exist. But to call "slum children" "culturally different" is something else. It calls attention, for example, to legitimate reasons why such children might feel alienated from what goes on in school.

5   I grant that sometimes such euphemizing does not have the intended effect. It is possible for a teacher to use the term "culturally different" but still be controlled by the term "slum children" (which the teacher may believe is their "real name"). "Old people" may be called "senior citizens," and nothing might change. And "lunatic asylums" may still be filthy, primitive prisons though they are called "mental institutions." Nonetheless, euphemizing may be regarded as one of our more important intellectual resources for creating new perspectives on a subject. The *attempt* to rename "old people" "senior citizens" was obviously motivated by a desire to give them a political identity, which they not only warrant but which may yet have important consequences. In fact, the fate of euphemisms is very hard to predict. A new and seemingly silly name may replace an old one (let us say, "chairperson" for "chairman") and for years no one will think or act any differently because of it. And then, gradually, as people begin to assume that "chairperson" is the "real" and proper name (or "senior citizen" or "tuna fish" or "sanitation engineer"), their attitudes begin to shift, and they will approach things in a slightly different frame of mind. There is a danger, of course, in supposing that a new name can change attitudes quickly or always. There must be some authentic tendency or drift in the culture to lend support to the change, or the name will remain incongruous and may even appear ridiculous. To call a teacher a "facilitator" would be such an example. To eliminate the distinction between "boys" and "girls" by calling them "childpersons" would be another.

6   But to suppose that such changes never "amount to anything" is to un-
derestimate the power of names. I have been astounded not only by how
rapidly the name "blacks" has replaced "Negroes" (a kind of euphemizing
in reverse) but also by how significantly perceptions and attitudes have
shifted as an accompaniment to the change.

7   The key idea here is that euphemisms are a means through which a culture
may alter its imagery and by so doing subtly change its style, its priorities,
and its values. I reject categorically the idea that people who use "earthy"
language are speaking more directly or with more authenticity than people
who employ euphemisms. Saying that someone is "dead" is not to speak
more plainly or honestly than saying he has "passed away." It is, rather, to
suggest a different conception of what the event means. To ask where the
"shit house" is, is no more to the point than to ask where the "restroom" is.
But in the difference between the two words, there is expressed a vast difference in one's attitude toward privacy and propriety. What I am saying is
that the process of euphemizing has no moral content. The moral dimensions
are supplied by what the words in question express, what they want us to
value and to see. A nation that calls experiments with bombs "Operation
Sunshine" is very frightening. On the other hand, a people who call "garbage
men" "sanitation engineers" can't be all bad.

Writing Log/Journal Assignment

Do you know people who tend to use many euphemistic words or phrases?
How often do you substitute a mild (euphemistic) expression for a
harsh one?

Individual and Collaborative Considerations

1. To what extent do you agree with the statement "we must keep in mind
   that things do not have 'real' names, although many people believe that
   they do. A garbage man is not 'really' a 'garbage man,' any more than he
   is really a 'sanitation engineer' "? Why does Postman claim that the significance of names and titles needs to be kept in perspective?
2. How does Postman's introductory paragraph immediately involve you
   with his topic? Explain the strategic function of his initial paragraph as
   you see it.
3. What was "Operation Sunshine"? Why does Postman mention it?
4. Evaluate the vividness and strength of Postman's examples.
5. Why does Postman claim that euphemizing has "no moral content"?

Writing Activities

1. Take a position on "political correctness," and argue that (1) it is unjustly
   confused with euphemism *or* (2) despite some good intent, a good part

of "political correctness" amounts to little more than euphemizing names, addresses, and concepts without really addressing problems or changing attitudes.

2. Do you agree with Postman's belief "that euphemisms are a means through which a culture may alter its imagery and by so doing subtly change its style, its priorities, and its values"? In a fully developed essay, justify your position, including fresh supporting evidence and reasoning.

※

The Brahmin's Son

Hermann Hesse

Hermann Hesse was brought up in a missionary household in India, and it was thought he would study for the ministry. Although he went through a religious crisis, fleeing the Maulbronn seminary in 1892, he remained quasi-religious most of his life. His works often suggest a romantic faith that reconciliation, whether it is psychoanalysis, meditation, drugs, or fantasy, is possible, especially in situations that cannot be solved by logic. Hesse's first novel, *Peter Camenzind* (1904), was followed by *Beneath the Wheel* (1906), *Demian* (1919), *Siddhartha* (1922), *Steppenwolf* (1927), *Narcissus and Goldmund* (1930), and *Journey to the East* (1932). His next novel, *Magister Ludi* (1943), appeared eleven years later and won him the Nobel Prize for literature in 1946. In "The Brahmin's Son," Hesse's protagonist, Siddhartha, begins an ascetic lifestyle—a spiritual existence in search of greater truth and beauty.

In the shade of the house, in the sunshine on the river bank by the boats, in the shade of the sallow wood and the fig tree, Siddhartha, the handsome Brahmin's son, grew up with his friend Govinda. The sun browned his slender shoulders on the river bank, while bathing at the holy ablutions, at the holy sacrifices. Shadows passed across his eyes in the mango grove during play, while his mother sang, during his father's teachings, when with the learned men. Siddhartha had already long taken part in the learned men's conversations, had engaged in debate with Govinda and had practiced the art of contemplation and meditation with him. Already he knew how to pronounce Om silently—this word of words, to say it inwardly with the intake of breath, when breathing out with all his soul, his brow radiating the glow of pure spirit. Already he knew how to recognize Atman within the depth of his being, indestructible, at one with the universe.

There was happiness in his father's heart because of his son who was intelligent and thirsty for knowledge; he saw him growing up to be a great learned man, a priest, a prince among Brahmins.

There was pride in his mother's breast when she saw him walking, sitting down and rising: Siddhartha—strong, handsome, supple-limbed, greeting her with complete grace.

Love stirred in the hearts of the young Brahmins' daughters when Siddhartha walked through the streets of the town, with his lofty brow, his king-like eyes and his slim figure.

5   Govinda, his friend, the Brahmin's son, loved him more than anybody else. He loved Siddhartha's eyes and clear voice. He loved the way he walked, his complete grace of movement; he loved everything that Siddhartha did and said, and above all he loved his intellect, his fine ardent thoughts, his strong will, his high vocation. Govinda knew that he would not become an ordinary Brahmin, a lazy sacrificial official, an avaricious dealer in magic sayings, a conceited worthless orator, a wicked sly priest, or just a good stupid sheep amongst a large herd. No, and he, Govinda, did not want to become any of these, not a Brahmin like ten thousand others of their kind. He wanted to follow Siddhartha, the beloved, the magnificent. And if he ever became a god, if he ever entered the All-Radiant, then Govinda wanted to follow him as his friend, his companion, his servant, his lance bearer, his shadow.

That was how everybody loved Siddhartha. He delighted and made everybody happy.

But Siddhartha himself was not happy. Wandering along the rosy paths of the fig garden, sitting in contemplation in the bluish shade of the grove, washing his limbs in the daily bath of atonement, offering sacrifices in the depths of the shady mango wood with complete grace of manner, beloved by all, a joy to all, there was yet no joy in his own heart. Dreams and restless thoughts came flowing to him from the river, from the twinkling stars at night, from the sun's melting rays. Dreams and a restlessness of the soul came to him, arising from the smoke of the sacrifices, emanating from the verses of the Rig-Veda, trickling through from the teachings of the old Brahmins.

Siddhartha had begun to feel the seeds of discontent within him. He had begun to feel that the love of his father and mother, and also the love of his friend Govinda, would not always make him happy, give him peace, satisfy and suffice him. He had begun to suspect that his worthy father and his other teachers, the wise Brahmins, had already passed on to him the bulk and best of their wisdom, that they had already poured the sum total of their knowledge into his waiting vessel; and the vessel was not full, his intellect was not satisfied, his soul was not at peace, his heart was not still. The ablutions were good, but they were water; they did not wash sins away, they did not relieve the distressed heart. The sacrifices and the supplication of the gods were excellent—but were they everything? Did the sacrifices give happiness? And what about the gods? Was it really Prajapati who had created the world? Was it not Atman, He alone, who had created it? Were not the gods forms created like me and you, mortal, transient? Was it therefore good and right, was it a sensible and worthy act to offer sacrifices to the gods? To whom else should one offer sacrifices, to whom else should one pay honor, but to Him, Atman, the Only One? And where was Atman to be found, where did He dwell, where did His eternal heart beat, if not within the Self, in the innermost, in the eternal which each person carried within him? But where was this Self, this innermost? It was not flesh and bone, it was not thought or consciousness. That was what the wise men taught. Where, then, was it? To press towards the Self, towards Atman—was there another way that was worth seeking? Nobody showed the way, nobody knew it—neither his father, nor the teachers and wise men, nor the holy songs. The Brahmins and their holy books knew everything, everything; they had gone into everything—the creation of the world, the origin of speech, food, inhalation, exhalation, the arrangement of the senses, the acts of the gods. They knew a tremendous number of things—but was it worthwhile knowing all these things if they did not know the one important thing, the only important thing?

Many verses of the holy books, above all the Upanishads of Sama-Veda, spoke of this innermost thing. It is written: "Your soul is the whole world." It says that when a man is asleep, he penetrates his innermost and dwells in Atman. There was wonderful wisdom in these verses; all the knowledge of the sages was told here in enchanting language, pure as honey collected by the bees. No, this tremendous amount of knowledge, collected and preserved by successive generations of wise Brahmins could not be easily overlooked. But where were the Brahmins, the priests, the wise men, who were successful not only in having this most profound knowledge, but in experiencing it? Where were the initiated who, attaining Atman in sleep, could retain it in consciousness, in life, everywhere, in speech and in action? Siddhartha knew many worthy Brahmins, above all his father—holy, learned, of highest esteem. His father was worthy of admiration; his manner was quiet and noble. He lived a good life, his words were wise; fine and noble thoughts dwelt in his head—but even he who knew so much, did he live in bliss, was he at peace? Was he not also a seeker, insatiable? Did he not go continually to the holy springs with an insatiable thirst, to the sacrifices, to books, to the Brahmins' discourses? Why must he, the blameless one, wash away his sins and endeavor to cleanse himself anew each day? Was Atman then not within him? Was not then the source within his own heart? One must find the source within one's own Self, one must possess it. Everything else was seeking—a detour, error.

10   These were Siddhartha's thoughts; this was his thirst, his sorrow. He often repeated to himself the words from one of the Chandogya-Upanishads. "In truth, the name of Brahman is Satya. Indeed, he who knows it enters the heavenly world each day." It often seemed near—the heavenly world—but never had he quite reached it, never had he quenched the final thirst. And among the wise men that he knew and whose teachings he enjoyed, there

was not one who had entirely reached it—the heavenly world—not one who had completely quenched the eternal thirst.

"Govinda," said Siddhartha to his friend, "Govinda, come with me to the banyan tree. We will practice meditation."

They went to the banyan tree and sat down, twenty paces apart. As he sat down ready to pronounce the Om, Siddhartha softly recited the verse:

> "Om is the bow, the arrow is the soul,
> Brahman is the arrow's goal
> At which one aims unflinchingly."

When the customary time for the practice of meditation had passed, Govinda rose. It was now evening. It was time to perform the evening ablutions. He called Siddhartha by his name; he did not reply. Siddhartha sat absorbed, his eyes staring as if directed at a distant goal, the tip of his tongue showing a little between his teeth. He did not seem to be breathing. He sat thus, lost in meditation, thinking Om, his soul as the arrow directed at Brahman.

Some Samanas once passed through Siddhartha's town. Wandering ascetics, they were three thin worn-out men, neither old nor young, with dusty and bleeding shoulders, practically naked, scorched by the sun, solitary, strange and hostile—lean jackals in the world of men. Around them hovered an atmosphere of still passion, of devastating service, of unpitying self-denial.

15   In the evening, after the hour of contemplation, Siddhartha said to Govinda: "Tomorrow morning, my friend, Siddhartha is going to join the Samanas. He is going to become a Samana."

Govinda blanched as he heard these words and read the decision in his friend's determined face, undeviating as the released arrow from the bow. Govinda realized from the first glance at his friend's face that now it was beginning. Siddhartha was going his own way; his destiny was beginning to unfold itself, and with his destiny, his own. And he became as pale as a dried banana skin.

"Oh, Siddhartha," he cried, "will your father permit it?"

Siddhartha looked at him like one who had just awakened. As quick as lightning he read Govinda's soul, read the anxiety, the resignation.

"We will not waste words, Govinda," he said softly. "Tomorrow at daybreak I will begin the life of the Samanas. Let us not discuss it again."

20   Siddhartha went into the room where his father was sitting on a mat made of bast. He went up behind his father and remained standing there until his father felt his presence. "Is it you, Siddhartha?" the Brahmin asked. "Then speak what is in your mind."

Siddhartha said: "With your permission, Father, I have come to tell you that I wish to leave your house tomorrow and join the ascetics. I wish to become a Samana. I trust my father will not object."

The Brahmin was silent so long that the stars passed across the small window and changed their design before the silence in the room was finally broken. His son stood silent and motionless with his arms folded. The father, silent and motionless, sat on the mat, and the stars passed across the sky. Then his father said: "It is not seemly for Brahmins to utter forceful and angry words, but there is displeasure in my heart. I should not like to hear you make this request a second time."

The Brahmin rose slowly. Siddhartha remained silent with folded arms.

"Why are you waiting?" asked his father.

25 "You know why," answered Siddhartha.

His father left the room displeased and lay down on his bed.

As an hour passed by and he could not sleep, the Brahmin rose, wandered up and down and then left the house. He looked through the small window of the room and saw Siddhartha standing there with his arms folded, unmoving. He could see his pale robe shimmering. His heart troubled, the father returned to his bed.

As another hour passed and the Brahmin could not sleep, he rose again, walked up and down, left the house and saw the moon had risen. He looked through the window. Siddhartha stood there unmoving, his arms folded; the moon shone on his bare shinbones. His heart troubled, the father went to bed.

He returned again after an hour and again after two hours, looked through the window and saw Siddhartha standing there in the moonlight, in the starlight, in the dark. And he came silently again, hour after hour, looked into the room, and saw him standing unmoving. His heart filled with anger, with anxiety, with fear, with sorrow.

30 And in the last hour of the night, before daybreak, he returned again, entered the room and saw the youth standing there. He seemed tall and a stranger to him.

"Siddhartha," he said, "why are you waiting?"

"You know why."

"Will you go on standing and waiting until it is day, noon, evening?"

"I will stand and wait."

35 "You will grow tired, Siddhartha."

"I will grow tired."

"You will fall asleep, Siddhartha."

"I will not fall asleep."

"You will die, Siddhartha."

40 "I will die."

"And would you rather die than obey your father?"

"Siddhartha has always obeyed his father."

"So you will give up your project?"

"Siddhartha will do what his father tells him."

45 The first light of day entered the room. The Brahmin saw that Siddhartha's knees trembled slightly, but there was no trembling in Siddhartha's face; his eyes looked far away. Then the father realized that Siddhartha could no longer remain with him at home—that he had already left him.

The father touched Siddhartha's shoulder.

"You will go into the forest," he said, "and become a Samana. If you find bliss in the forest, come back and teach it to me. If you find disillusionment, come back, and we shall again offer sacrifices to the gods together. Now go, kiss your mother and tell her where you are going. For me, however, it is time to go to the river and perform the first ablution."

He dropped his hand from his son's shoulder and went out. Siddhartha swayed as he tried to walk. He controlled himself, bowed to his father and went to his mother to do what had been told to him.

As, with benumbed legs, he slowly left the still sleeping town at daybreak, a crouching shadow emerged from the last hut and joined the pilgrim. It was Govinda.

50   "You have come," said Siddhartha and smiled.

"I have come," said Govinda.

Writing Log/Journal Assignment

Write a brief narrative about a time when you were dissatisfied with someone or something in your life.

Individual and Collaborative Considerations

1. Who are the Brahmins?
2. What hope did Siddhartha's father have for him?
3. Why is Siddhartha unhappy? To what does he aspire?
4. Who is Govinda and what role does he play in Hesse's story?
5. What trial or ordeal must Siddhartha go through before he receives his father's blessing?

Writing Activities

1. Argue how maintaining or pursuing a particular lifestyle is "aesthetic." Begin your essay with a definition of terms (how you are using the word "aesthetic"). Then defend your thesis with careful reasoning and exemplification. Since your essay is likely to be theoretical—and thereby abstract or difficult to conceptualize—provide concrete representative examples whenever possible.
2. Write a persuasive essay convincing your readers that they would be far better off working for a nonprofit (humanitarian) group like the Peace Corps or the United Nations Relief Agency than having a high-paying job and all the material "creature comforts" imaginable. To begin, list the pros and cons of each job. Next, consider the pros in terms of aesthetic merit.

※

The Tattooer

Junichiro Tanizaki

Junichiro Tanizaki, 1886–1965, is viewed by many literary critics as the most brilliant Japanese novelist of the twentieth century, yet his writings often make Western readers uncomfortable. To appreciate this subtle and complex writer, it may be helpful to focus on the following points: (1) Tanizaki always includes carefully chosen details, often based on historical research, to create the illusion of a vivid realism—however, his stories are fantasies; (2) Tanizaki masterfully presents an "alternate world" in which the usual socially acceptable values are reversed. Some of these reversals include power versus weakness, kindness versus cruelty, masculinity versus femininity, beauty versus ugliness. It is also interesting to note that Tanizaki referred to himself as a feminist and that he was inspired throughout his career by the greatest writer in Japanese history, Lady Murasiki Shikib. As in the following story, Tanizaki frequently presents a role reversal in his stories, with women gaining positions of power and dominance over men. His works include *Some Prefer Nettles* (1928), *The Makioka Sisters* (1948–1949), *The Key* (1956), and *The Diary of a Mad Old Man* (1961).

It was an age when men honored the noble virtue of frivolity, when life was not such a harsh struggle as it is today. It was a leisurely age, an age when professional wits could make an excellent livelihood by keeping rich or well-born young gentlemen in a cloudless good humor and seeing to it that the laughter of Court ladies and geisha was never stilled. In the illustrated romantic novels of the day, in the Kabuki theater, where rough masculine heroes like Sadakuro and Jiraiya were transformed into women—everywhere beauty and strength were one. People did all they could to beautify themselves, some even having pigments injected into their precious skins. Gaudy patterns of line and color danced over men's bodies.

Visitors to the pleasure quarters of Edo preferred to hire palanquin bearers who were splendidly tattooed; courtesans of the Yoshiwara and the Tatsumi quarter fell in love with tattooed men. Among those so adorned were not only gamblers, firemen, and the like, but members of the merchant class and even samurai. Exhibitions were held from time to time; and the participants, stripped to show off their filigreed bodies, would pat themselves proudly, boast of their own novel designs, and criticize each other's merits.

There was an exceptionally skillful young tattooer named Seikichi. He was praised on all sides as a master the equal of Charibun or Yatsuhei, and the skins of dozens of men had been offered as the silk for his brush. Much of the work admired at the tattoo exhibitions was his. Others might be more noted for their shading, or their use of cinnabar, but Seikichi was famous for the unrivaled boldness and sensual charm of his art.

Seikichi had formerly earned his living as an ukiyoye painter of the school of Toyokuni and Kunisada, a background which, in spite of his decline to the status of a tattooer, was evident from his artistic conscience and sensitivity. No one whose skin or whose physique failed to interest him could buy his services. The clients he did accept had to leave the design and cost entirely to his discretion—and to endure for one or even two months the excruciating pain of his needles.

5   Deep in his heart the young tattooer concealed a secret pleasure, and a secret desire. His pleasure lay in the agony men felt as he drove his needles into them, torturing their swollen, blood-red flesh; and the louder they groaned, the keener was Seikichi's strange delight. Shading and vermilioning—these are said to be especially painful—were the techniques he most enjoyed.

When a man had been pricked five or six hundred times in the course of an average day's treatment and had then soaked himself in a hot bath to bring out the colors, he would collapse at Seikichi's feet half dead. But Seikichi would look down at him coolly. "I dare say that hurts," he would remark with an air of satisfaction.

Whenever a spineless man howled in torment or clenched his teeth and twisted his mouth as if he were dying, Seikichi told him: "Don't act like a child. Pull yourself together—you have hardly begun to feel my needles!" And he would go on tattooing, as unperturbed as ever, with an occasional sidelong glance at the man's tearful face. But sometimes a man of immense fortitude set his jaw and bore up stoically, not even allowing himself to frown. Then Seikichi would smile and say: "Ah, you are a stubborn one! But wait. Soon your body will begin to throb with pain. I doubt if you will be able to stand it. . . . ."

For a long time Seikichi had cherished the desire to create a masterpiece on the skin of a beautiful woman. Such a woman had to meet various qualifications of character as well as appearance. A lovely face and a fine body were not enough to satisfy him. Though he inspected all the reigning beauties of the Edo gay quarters he found none who met his exacting demands. Several years had passed without success, and yet the face and figure of the perfect woman continued to obsess his thoughts. He refused to abandon hope.

One summer evening during the fourth year of his search Seikichi happened to be passing the Hirasei Restaurant in the Fukagawa district of Edo, not far from his own house, when he noticed a woman's bare milk-white foot peeping out beneath the curtains of a departing palanquin. To his sharp eye, a human foot was as expressive as a face. This one was sheer perfection. Exquisitely chiseled toes, nails like the iridescent shells along the shore at Enoshima, a pearl-like rounded heel, skin so lustrous that it seemed bathed in the limpid waters of a mountain spring—this, indeed, was a foot to be nourished by men's blood, a foot to trample on their bodies. Surely this was the foot of the unique woman who had so long eluded him. Eager to catch a glimpse of her face, Seikichi began to follow the palanquin. But after pursuing it down several lanes and alleys he lost sight of it altogether.

10 Seikichi's long held desire turned into passionate love. One morning late the next spring he was standing on the bamboo-floored veranda of his home in Fukagawa, gazing at a pot of *omoto* lilies, when he heard someone at the garden gate. Around the corner of the inner fence appeared a young girl. She had come on an errand for a friend of his, a geisha of the nearby Tatsumi quarter.

"My mistress asked me to deliver this cloak, and she wondered if you would be so good as to decorate its lining," the girl said. She untied a saffron-colored cloth parcel and took out a woman's silk cloak (wrapped in a sheet of thick paper bearing a portrait of the actor Tojaku) and a letter. The letter repeated his friend's request and went on to say that its bearer would soon begin a career as a geisha under her protection. She hoped that, while not forgetting old ties, he would also extend his patronage to this girl.

"I thought I had never seen you before," said Seikichi, scrutinizing her intently. She seemed only fifteen or sixteen, but her face had a strangely ripe beauty, a look of experience, as if she had already spent years in the gay quarter and had fascinated innumerable men. Her beauty mirrored the dreams of the generations of glamorous men and women who had lived and died in this vast capital, where the nation's sins and wealth were concentrated.

Seikichi had her sit on the veranda, and he studied her delicate feet, which were bare except for elegant straw sandals. "You left the Hirasei by palanquin one night last July, did you not?" he inquired.

"I suppose so," she replied, smiling at the odd question. "My father was still alive then, and he often took me there."

15 "I have waited five years for you. This is the first time I have seen your face, but I remember your foot. . . . Come in for a moment, I have something to show you."

She had risen to leave, but he took her by the hand and led her upstairs to his studio overlooking the broad river. Then he brought out two picture scrolls and unrolled one of them before her.

It was a painting of a Chinese princess, the favorite of the cruel Emperor Chou of the Shang Dynasty. She was leaning on a balustrade in a languorous pose, the long skirt of her figured brocade robe trailing halfway down a flight of stairs, her slender body barely able to support the weight of her gold crown studded with coral and lapis lazuli. In her right hand she held a large wine cup, tilting it to her lips as she gazed down at a man who was about to be tortured in the garden below. He was chained hand and foot to a hollow copper pillar in which a fire would be lighted. Both the princess and her victim—his head bowed before her, his eyes closed, ready to meet his fate—were portrayed with terrifying vividness.

As the girl stared at this bizarre picture her lips trembled and her eyes began to sparkle. Gradually her face took on a curious resemblance to that of the princess. In the picture she discovered her secret self.

"Your own feelings are revealed here," Seikichi told her with pleasure as he watched her face.

20   "Why are you showing me this horrible thing?" the girl asked, looking up at him. She had turned pale.

"The woman is yourself. Her blood flows in your veins." Then he spread out the other scroll.

This was a painting called "The Victims." In the middle of it a young woman stood leaning against the trunk of a cherry tree: she was gloating over a heap of men's corpses lying at her feet. Little birds fluttered about her, singing in triumph; her eyes radiated pride and joy. Was it a battlefield or a garden in spring? In this picture the girl felt that she had found something long hidden in the darkness of her own heart.

"This painting shows your future," Seikichi said, pointing to the woman under the cherry tree—the very image of the young girl. "All these men will ruin their lives for you."

"Please, I beg of you to put it away!" She turned her back as if to escape its tantalizing lure and prostrated herself before him, trembling. At last she spoke again. "Yes, I admit that you are right about me—I *am* like that woman. . . . So please, please take it away."

25   "Don't talk like a coward," Seikichi told her, with his malicious smile. "Look at it more closely. You won't be squeamish long."

But the girl refused to lift her head. Still prostrate, her face buried in her sleeves, she repeated over and over that she was afraid and wanted to leave.

"No, you must stay—I will make you a real beauty," he said, moving closer to her. Under his kimono was a vial of anesthetic which he had obtained some time ago from a Dutch physician.

The morning sun glittered on the river, setting the eight-mat studio ablaze with light. Rays reflected from the water sketched rippling golden waves on the paper sliding screens and on the face of the girl, who was fast asleep. Seikichi had closed the doors and taken up his tattooing instruments, but for a while he only sat there entranced, savoring to the full her uncanny beauty. He thought that he would never tire of contemplating her serene mask-like face. Just as the ancient Egyptians had embellished their magnificent land with pyramids and sphinxes, he was about to embellish the pure skin of this girl.

Presently he raised the brush which was gripped between the thumb and last two fingers of his left hand, applied its tip to the girl's back, and, with the needle which he held in his right hand, began pricking out a design. He felt his spirit dissolve into the charcoal-black ink that stained her skin. Each drop of Ryukyu cinnabar that he mixed with alcohol and thrust in was a drop of his life blood. He saw in his pigments the hues of his own passions.

30   Soon it was afternoon, and then the tranquil spring day drew toward its close. But Seikichi never paused in his work, nor was the girl's sleep broken. When a servant came from the geisha house to inquire about her, Seikichi turned him away, saying that she had left long ago. And hours later, when the moon hung over the mansion across the river, bathing the houses along the bank in a dream-like radiance, the tattoo was not yet half done. Seikichi worked on by candlelight.

    Even to insert a single drop of color was no easy task. At every thrust of his needle Seikichi gave a heavy sigh and felt as if he had stabbed his own heart. Little by little the tattoo marks began to take on the form of a huge black-widow spider; and by the time the night sky was paling into dawn this weird, malevolent creature had stretched its eight legs to embrace the whole of the girl's back.

    In the full light of the spring dawn boats were being rowed up and down the river, their oars creaking in the morning quiet; roof tiles glistened in the sun, and the haze began to thin out over white sails swelling in the early breeze. Finally Seikichi put down his brush and looked at the tattooed spider. This work of art had been the supreme effort of his life. Now that he had finished it his heart was drained of emotion.

    The two figures remained still for some time. Then Seikichi's low, hoarse voice echoed quaveringly from the walls of the room:

    "To make you truly beautiful I have poured my soul into this tattoo. Today there is no woman in Japan to compare with you. Your old fears are gone. All men will be your victims."

35   As if in response to these words a faint moan came from the girl's lips. Slowly she began to recover her senses. With each shuddering breath, the spider's legs stirred as if they were alive.

    "You must be suffering. The spider has you in its clutches."

    At this she opened her eyes slightly, in a dull stare. Her gaze steadily brightened, as the moon brightens in the evening, until it shone dazzlingly into his face.

    "Let me see the tattoo," she said, speaking as if in a dream but with an edge of authority to her voice. "Giving me your soul must have made me very beautiful."

    "First you must bathe to bring out the colors," whispered Seikichi compassionately. "I am afraid it will hurt, but be brave a little longer." "I can bear anything for the sake of beauty." Despite the pain that was coursing through her body, she smiled.

40   "How the water stings! . . . Leave me alone—wait in the other room! I hate to have a man see me suffer like this!"

    As she left the tub, too weak to dry herself, the girl pushed aside the sympathetic hand Seikichi offered her, and sank to the floor in agony, moaning as if in a nightmare. Her disheveled hair hung over her face in a wild tangle. The white soles of her feet were reflected in the mirror behind her.

    Seikichi was amazed at the change that had come over the timid, yielding girl of yesterday, but he did as he was told and went to wait in his studio.

About an hour later she came back, carefully dressed, her damp, sleekly combed hair hanging down over her shoulders. Leaning on the veranda rail, she looked up into the faintly hazy sky. Her eyes were brilliant; there was not a trace of pain in them.

"I wish to give you these pictures too," said Seikichi, placing the scrolls before her. "Take them and go."

"All my old fears have been swept away—and you are my first victim!" She darted a glance at him as bright as a sword. A song of triumph was ringing in her ears.

45 "Let me see your tattoo once more," Seikichi begged.

Silently the girl nodded and slipped the kimono off her shoulders. Just then her resplendently tattooed back caught a ray of sunlight and the spider was wreathed in flames.

Writing Log/Journal Assignment

Think of someone with whom you would like to reverse roles—and why. Have you ever felt powerless? Have you ever fantasized about what you would do if you could change places with someone who has power over you? Write a brief description of this fantasy role reversal.

Individual and Collaborative Considerations

1. What happens to the young woman in "The Tattooer" when she looks at the two pictures? What do you think she means when she says, "All my fears have been swept away"?
2. In the story, what does the black widow spider symbolize?
3. In small groups, discuss the possibility of *unconscious* fears with your peers. Do our cultural values force us to repress even the awareness of some of our fears? Are women in your group aware of being afraid of the power and domination of men? Are the men in your group aware of being afraid of the sexual power of women?
4. If you were ever able to create a magnificent work of art like Seikichi, what would you create and why? What would the piece of artwork mean to you?
5. Do you or does anyone you know have a tattoo? If so, what is the story behind the tattoo? What did you or the person you know decide to get as a tattoo?

Writing Activities

1. Write an essay about a work of art (a painting, a piece of sculpture, a selection of music, an etching, a drawing) you consider very beautiful.

Explain in detail why the work appeals to you and what its symbolic meaning (if any) is.

2. Write an essay about a fear you would like to overcome—or a fear you overcame. (What procedure would you or did you follow to eliminate your respective fear?) Your essay may be either serious or humorous.

✳

The Artist

Rabindranath Tagore

Rabindranath Tagore was born in Calcutta in 1861 and was raised in a household of performance artists: painters, musicians, actors. Tagore, quite an artist in his own right, was an accomplished musician, a cherished painter, and a prolific writer. He published over sixty volumes of poetry, twenty-four plays, eight novels, and eight short-story collections. Some of his best-known works in the Western world include his collection of lyric poetry, *Song Offerings* (1909), and his major philosophical work based on ideas from sacred Hindu writings, *Sadhana: The Realization of Life* (1913). Tagore's poetic accomplishments made him internationally famous; in 1913, Tagore won the Nobel Prize for literature and two years later he was knighted. After the Amritsar Massacre—an event where British troops suppressed an Indian demonstration, Tagore renounced the honor of knighthood. In "The Artist," Tagore contrasts Chunilal and Satyabati's appreciation and indulgence in art and aesthetics to Govinda's obsession with money and practicality.

Govinda came to Calcutta after graduation from high school in Mymensingh. His widowed mother's savings were meager, but his own unwavering determination was his greatest resource. "I will make money," he vowed, "even if I have to give my whole life to it." In his terminology, wealth was always referred to as *pice*. In other words he had in mind a very concrete image of something that could seen, touched, and smelled; he was not greatly fascinated with fame, only with the very ordinary *pice*, eroded by circulation from market to market, from hand to hand, the tarnished *pice*, and *pice* that smells of copper, the original form of Kuvera, who assumes the assorted guises of silver, gold, securities, and wills, and keeps men's minds in a turmoil.

After traveling many tortuous roads and getting muddied repeatedly in the process, Govinda had now arrived upon the solidly paved embankment of his wide and free-flowing stream of money. He was firmly seated in the manager's chair at the MacDougal Gunnysack Company. Everyone called him MacDulal.

When Govinda's lawyer-brother, Mukunda, died, he left behind a wife, a four-year-old son, a house in Calcutta, and some cash savings. In addition to this property there was some debt; therefore, provision for his family's needs depended upon frugality. Thus his son, Chunilal, was brought up in circumstances that were undistinguished in comparison with those of the neighbors.

Mukunda's will gave Govinda entire responsibility for this family. Ever since Chunilal was a baby, Govinda had bestowed spiritual initiation upon his nephew with the sacred words: "Make money."

5   The main obstacle to the boy's initiation was his mother, Satyabati. She said nothing outright; her opposition showed her behavior. Art had always been her hobby. There was no limit to her enthusiasm for creating all sorts of original and decorative things from flowers, fruits and leaves, even food-stuffs, from paper and cloth cutouts, from clay and flour, from berry juices and the juices of other fruits, from *jaba-* and *shiuli-* flower stems. This activity brought her considerable grief, because anything unessential or irrational has the character of flash floods in July: it has considerable mobility, but in relation to the utilitarian concerns of life it is like a stalled ferry. Sometimes there were invitations to visit relatives; Satyabati forgot them and spent the time in her bedroom with the door shut, kneading a lump of clay. The relatives said, "She's terribly stuck-up." There was no satisfactory reply to this. Mukunda had known, even on the basis of his bookish knowledge, that value judgements can be made about art too. He had been thrilled by the noble connotations of the word "art," but he could not conceive of its having any connection with the work of his own wife.

This man's nature had been very equable. When his wife squandered time on unessential whims, he had smiled at it with affectionate delight. If anyone in the household made a slighting remark, he had protested immediately. There had been a singular self-contradiction in Mukunda's makeup; he had been an expert in the practice of law, but it must be conceded that he had had no worldly wisdom with regard to his household affairs. Plenty of money had passed through his hands, but since it had not preoccupied his thoughts, it had left his mind free. Nor could he have tyrannized over his dependents in order to get his own way. His living habits had been very simple; he had never made any unreasonable demands for the attention or services of his relatives.

Mukunda had immediately silenced anyone in the household who cast an aspersion upon Satyabati's disinterest in housework. Now and then, on his way home from court, he would stop at Radhabazar to buy some paints, some colored silk and colored pencils, and stealthily he would go and arrange them on the wooden chest in his wife's bedroom. Sometimes, picking up one of Satyabati's drawings, he would say, "Well, this one is certainly very beautiful."

One day he had held up a picture of a man, and since he had it upside down, he had decided that the legs must be a bird's head. He had said, "Satu, this should be framed—what a marvelous picture of a stork!" Mukunda had gotten a certain delight out of thinking of his wife's art work as child's play, and the wife had taken a similar pleasure in her husband's judgment of art. Satyabati had known perfectly well that she could not hope for so much patience so much indulgence, from any other family in Bengal. No other family would have made way so lovingly for her overpowering devotion to art. So, whenever her husband had made extravagant remarks about her painting, Satyabati could scarcely restrain her tears.

One day Satyabati lost even this rare good fortune. Before his death her husband had realized one thing quite clearly: the responsibility for his debt-ridden property must be left in the hands of someone astute enough to skillfully steer even a leaky boat to the other shore. This is how Satyabati and her son came to be placed completely under Govinda's care. From the very first day Govinda made it plain to her that the *pice* was the first and foremost thing in life. There was such profound degradation in his advice that Satyabati would shrink with shame. Nevertheless, the worship of money continued in diverse forms in their daily life. If there had been some modesty about it, instead of such constant discussion, it wouldn't have been so bad. Satyabati knew in her heart that all of this lowered her son's standard of values, but there was nothing to do but endure it. Since those delicate emotions endowed with uncommon dignity are the most vulnerable, they are very easily hurt or ridiculed by rude or insensitive people.

10   The study of art requires all sorts of supplies. Satyabati had received these for so long without even asking that she had felt no reticence with regard to them. Amid the new circumstances in the family she felt terribly ashamed to charge all these unessential items to the housekeeping budget. So she would save money by economizing on her own food and have the supplies purchased and brought in secretly. Whatever work she did was done furtively, behind closed doors. She was not afraid of a scolding, but the stares of insensitive observers embarrassed her.

Now Chuni was the only spectator and critic of her artistic activity. Gradually he became a participant. He began to feel its intoxication. The child's offense could not be concealed, since it overflowed the pages of his notebook onto the walls of the house. There were stains on his face, on his hands, on the cuffs of his shirt. Indra, the king of the gods, does not spare even the soul of a little boy in the effort to tempt him away from the worship of money.

On the one hand the restraint increased, on the other hand the mother collaborated in the violations. Occasionally the head of the company would take his office manager, Govinda, along on business trips out of town. Then the mother and son would get together in unrestrained joy. This was the absolute extreme of childishness! They drew pictures of animals that God has yet to create. The likeness of the dog would get mixed up with that of the cat. It was difficult to distinguish between fish and fowl. There was no way to preserve all these creations; their traces had to be thoroughly oblit-erated before the head of the house returned. Only Brahma, the Creator, and Rudra, the Destroyer, witnessed the creative delight of these two persons; Vishnu the heavenly Preserver, never arrived.

The compulsion for artistic creation ran strong in Satyabati's family. There was an older nephew, Rangalal, who rose overnight to fame as an artist. That is to say the connoisseurs of the land roared with laughter at the unortho-doxy of his art. Since their stamp of imagination did not coincide with his, they had a violent scorn for his talent. But curiously enough, his reputation thrived upon disdain and flourished in this atmosphere of opposition and mockery. Those who imitated him most took it upon themselves to prove that the man was a hoax as an artist, that there were obvious defects even in his technique.

This much-maligned artist came to his aunt's home one day, at a time when the office manager was absent. After persistent knocking and shoving at the door he finally got inside and found that there was nowhere to set foot on the floor. The cat was out of the bag.

15 "It is obvious," said Rangalal, "that the image of creation has emerged anew from the soul of the artist; this is not random scribbling. He and that god who creates form are the same age. Get out all the drawings and show them to me."

Where should they get the drawings? That artist who draws pictures all over the sky in myriad colors, in light and shadow, calmly discards his mists and mirages. Their creations had gone the same way. With an oath Rangalal said to his aunt, "From now on, I'll come and get whatever you make."

There came another day when the office manager had not returned. Since morning the sky had brooded in the shadows of July; it was raining. No one monitored the hands of the clock and no one wanted to know about them. Today Chuni began to draw a picture of a sailing boat while his mother was in the prayer room. The waves of the river looked like a flock of hungry seals just on the point of swallowing the boat. The clouds seemed to cheer them on and float their shawls overhead, but the seals were not conventional seals, and it would be no exaggeration to say of the clouds: "Light and mist merge in the watery waste." In the interests of truth it must be said that if boats were built like this one, insurance companies would never assume such risks. Thus the painting continued; the sky-artist drew fanciful pictures, and inside the room the wide-eyed boy did the same.

No one realized that the door was open. The office manager appeared. He roared in a thunderous voice, "What's going on?"

The boy's heart jumped and his face grew pale. Now Govinda perceived the real reason for Chunilal's examination errors in historical dates. Mean-while the crime became all the more evident as Chunilal tried unsuccessfully to hide the drawing under his shirt. As Govinda snatched the picture away, the design he saw on it further astonished him. Errors in historical dates would be preferable to this. He tore the picture to pieces. Chunilal burst out crying.

20   From the prayer room Satyabati heard the boy's weeping, and she came running. Both Chunilal and the torn pieces of the picture were on the floor. Govinda went on enumerating the reasons for his nephew's failure in the history examination and suggesting dire remedies.

Satyabati had never said a word about Govinda's behavior toward them. She had quietly endured everything, remembering that this was the person on whom her husband had relied. Now her eyes were wet with tears, and shaking with anger, she said hoarsely, "Why did you tear up Chuni's picture?"

Govinda said, "Doesn't he have to study? What will become of him in the future?"

"Even if he becomes a beggar in the street," answered Satyabati, "he'll be better off in the future. But I hope he'll never be like you. May his pride in his God-given talent be more than your pride in *pices*. This is my blessing for him, a mother's blessing."

"I can't neglect my responsibility," said Govinda. "I will not tolerate this. Tomorrow I'll send him to a boarding school; otherwise, you'll ruin him."

25   The office manager returned to the office. The rain fell in torrents and the streets flowed with water.

Holding her son's hand, Satyabati said, "Let's go, dear."

Chuni said, "Go where, Mother?"

"Let's get out of this place."

The water was knee-deep at Rangalal's door. Satyabati came in with Chunilal. She said, "My dear boy, you take charge of him. Keep him from the worship of money."

Writing Log/Journal Assignment

Write a short paragraph giving your definition of an artist. Just what makes a person "artistic"? Is being artistic simply a frame of mind or dexterity with the hands? After you write your paragraph, briefly describe a time in your life when you felt particularly artistic—when you illustrated your own definition.

Individual and Collaborative Considerations

1. How does Govinda refer to wealth? Exactly what does his terminology refer to?
2. In what way does Govinda bestow "spiritual initiation" upon his nephew? What sacred words does he use?
3. What is Satyabati's hobby? Explain your answer in detail. How does Chunilal share the love of her hobby?

4. Compare and contrast Govinda and Rangalal. What system of values does each man live by? What is aesthetically meaningful to each?
5. In the final paragraph, why is it significant that "the water was knee-deep at Rangalal's door" (the place where Satyabati and Chunilal came to live)?

Writing Activities

1. Consider Tagore's line "Since their stamp of imagination did not coincide with his, they had a violent scorn for his talent" and apply it outside the context of his story. How often do people, regardless of their social class or occupations in life, criticize others simply because their "imaginations" or "beliefs" differ? Prewrite on this topic and arrive at a tentative thesis (make sure your thesis has an argumentative edge). Then prewrite again, generating as many supporting examples drawn from real life as you can. Finally, organize your material into a persuasive essay.
2. Compare and contrast the human benefits of spiritual (aesthetic) wealth and monetary acumen. Provide concrete, verifiable examples illustrating the major benefits you select to compare or contrast and ultimately draw a conclusion based on your findings.

The Word

Pablo Neruda

Born Ricardo Neftali Reyes, Pablo Neruda (1904–1973) won the Nobel Prize for literature in 1971 "for a poetry that with the action of an elemental force brings alive a continent's destiny and dreams." A career diplomat, when his mentor, Federico García Lorca, was executed for sympathizing with the Republican side in the Spanish Civil War, Neruda became politically active. Social issues became thematically important in his work, even after he was forced to flee his homeland, Chile, and live out his life in Argentina. The preeminent Chilean poet's efforts are numerous to say the least; twenty-nine volumes of poetry have been translated into eighty different languages, and his surrealistic, symbolic, and visionary writing have changed the style of modern Latin American poetry. Neruda is best known for *Twenty Love Poems and a Song of Despair* (1924) and *General Song* (1950), a collection of poetry that includes his great poem, "The Heights of Machu Picchu," *Fully Empowered* (1962), and *Memoirs* (1974). The following poem accentuates Neruda's reverence for words.

The word
was born in the blood,
grew in the dark body, beating,
and flew through the lips and the mouth.
Farther away and nearer
still, still it came
from dead fathers and from wandering races,
from lands that had returned to stone
weary of their poor tribes,
because when pain took to the roads
the settlements set out and arrived
and new lands and water reunited
to sow their word anew.

And so, this is the inheritance—
this is the wavelength which connects us
with the dead man and the dawn
of new beings not yet come to light.

Still the atmosphere quivers
with the initial word
dressed up
in terror and sighing.
It emerged
from the darkness
and until now there is no thunder
that rumbles yet with all the iron
of that word,
the first
word uttered—
perhaps it was only a ripple, a drop,
and yet its great cataract falls and falls.
Later on, the word fills with meaning.
It remained gravid and it filled up with lives.
Everything had to do with births and sounds—
affirmation, clarity, strength,
negation, destruction, death—
the verb took over all the power
and blended existence with essence
in the electricity of its beauty.

Human word, syllable, combination
of spread light and the fine art of the silversmith,
hereditary goblet which gathers
the communications of the blood—
here is where silence was gathered up
in the completeness of the human word

45   and, for human beings, not to speak is to die—
      language extends even to the hair,
      the mouth speaks without the lips moving—
      all of a sudden the eyes are words.

      I take the word and go over it
50   as though it were nothing more than a human shape,
      its arrangements awe me and I find my way
      through each variation in the spoken word—
      I utter and I am and without speaking I approach
      the limit of words and the silence.

55   I drink to the word, raising
      a word or a shining cup,
      in it I drink
      the pure wine of language
      or inexhaustible water,
60   maternal source of words,
      and cup and water and wine
      give rise to my song
      because the verb is the source
      and vivid life—it is blood,
65   blood which expresses its substance
      and so implies its own unwinding—
      words give glass-quality to glass, blood to blood,
      and life to life itself.

Writing Log/Journal Assignment

Summarize Neruda's poem in a paragraph or so. Then freewrite about "words." How do you use them? Where? With whom?

Individual and Collaborative Considerations

1. Discuss the way Neruda uses personification in this poem.
2. Look back over your summary of the poem and make an outline of its progression (from birth to toast).
3. How do the first four lines set the tone for the poem?
4. Why does Neruda "drink to the word"?
5. To what does Neruda compare the "word"? What artistic and aesthetic connections does he seem to make with words?

Writing Activities

1. In a fashion similar to Neruda's, write a narrative essay beginning with the *birth* of something, continuing with its growth, and concluding with reasons why you *toast* its existence.

2. Write an essay analyzing the communicative power of the use of words or musical notes. Present concrete examples of the ways words or musical notes manifest themselves in modern society as well as the ways people respond to them.

※

Nude, Descending a Staircase

X. J. Kennedy

X. J. Kennedy is a highly acclaimed poet, scholar, college professor, and critic. His *An Introduction to Poetry* text is presently in its eighth edition and *An Introduction to Fiction* now in its fifth edition; both texts tend to blend a sense of humor, style, and earnest, demystifying poetry and prose for an audience with limited exposure to the genres. Kennedy has also edited *Literature: An Introduction to Fiction, Poetry, and Drama*; this text is also in its fifth edition. His following poem blends concrete imagery and active verbs to describe a singular act, a woman descending a staircase, collecting her set of motions as she reaches the last step.

> Toe upon toe, a snowing flesh,
> A gold of lemon, root and rind,
> She sifts in sunlight down the stairs
> With nothing on. Nor on her mind.
>
> We spy beneath the banister
> A constant thresh of thigh on thigh—
> Her lips imprint the swinging air
> That parts to let her parts go by.
>
> One-woman waterfall, she wears
> Her slow descent like a long cape
> And pausing, on the final stair
> Collects her motions into shape.

Writing Log/Journal Assignment

To the best of your recollection, jot down a moment in your life when you took particular notice of the fact that a picture or statue of a person you were looking at was without clothes.

Individual and Collaborative Considerations

1. Who is the speaker in the poem? How old do you imagine the speaker is? How did you reach your conclusion?
2. Does the poet offer any clues as to the gender of the speakers (note the use of the plural first-person pronoun "we")? Would it matter? Explain why or why not.
3. Kennedy's twelve-line poem conveys a particular moment in verse. Paraphrase his poem in a paragraph or two.
4. What do you associate with a waterfall? How is Kennedy's description of the woman as a "One-woman waterfall" an effective figurative description? What other images did you find particularly memorable in "Nude, Descending a Staircase"?
5. How would you characterize the woman in the poem? How do you think the speaker(s) views her?

Writing Activities

1. How is Kennedy's poem an example of both art in its purest form and aesthetics? Construct an original thesis derived from your response to this question, supporting your position with historical, literary, and contemporary examples, as well as persuasive reasoning.
2. Reflect on something risqué, provocative, or uninhibited you did on the spur of the moment. How did you feel? What did you do? Next, ask a close friend or relative to watch you as you attempt to consciously repeat your former action. Make a note of what you did or did not do "the second time around." Finally, write an essay analyzing the difference between spontaneous and premeditated actions, possibly showing how the latter can lead to self-consciousness, guilt, embarrassment, shame, and so on.

✳

Salutation

Ezra Pound

Born in the United States, Ezra Pound spent a good deal of his life in Europe. Many people have called Pound the father of "modern poetry." Though such paternal recognition among fellow poets may be disputable, Pound definitely was at the heart of the modern literary movement in the twentieth century. Pound surrounded himself with the leading young poets of the day like Robert Frost, Rabindranath Tagore, and T. S. Eliot, as well as older poets like William Butler Yeats. In addition, he was a founder of the Imagists, a group of American and English poets who believed in artistic value of modern life and wished to use the precise language of common speech to "create new rhythms," and he assisted countless contemporaries like James Joyce publish their work. Pound's poetic works include *Provenca* (1910), *Cantzoni* (1911), *Lustra* (1916), *Hugh Selwyn Mauberley* (1920), *Personae* (1926), and *Selected Poems* (1926). In 1970, his *Cantos*, which tended to be rather esoteric, full of recondite theories, finally were collected. *The Literary Essays* (1954) offered a collection of much of his prose work and featured an introduction by T. S. Eliot. Pound also translated several texts, such as *Confucian Dialects* (1951) and *The Classic Anthology* (1954).

O generation of the thoroughly smug
    and thoroughly uncomfortable,
I have seen fishermen picnicking in the sun,
I have seen them with untidy families,
5   I have seen their smiles full of teeth
    and heard ungainly laughter
And I am happier than you are,
And they are happier than I am;
And the fish swim in the lake
10   and do not even own clothing.

Writing Log/Journal Assignment

In either prose or verse, write a brief "salutation" to someone or something important in your life. You might use Pound's poem as well as Pablo Neruda's "The Word" as examples.

Individual and Collaborative Considerations

1. What is a "salutation"? Why do you think Pound uses the word as the title of his poem? In what way is or is it not appropriate?
2. Identify the theme of "Salutation."
3. What words and phrases help to establish the tone here? How do you picture the speaker? Does he seem to have a negative "attitude" to you?
4. How does Pound rely on his powers of personal observation? What made his observations vivid, if not memorable?
5. Explain how the last four lines in "Salutation" place its theme into Pound's desired perspective. What is he saying about modern society?

Writing Activities

1. Write an essay defining your interpretation of "happiness." What enables some people to be happy while other people are miserable? Is happiness an elusive quality fictitiously presented in television comedies and in dime store novels? In the body of your paper, illustrate the rather abstract concept of *happiness* with as many concrete examples as you can.
2. Are you materialistic? Write an essay explaining either how your life would improve if you had all the material possessions you wanted, *or* how you could "let go" of your present attachment to material objects. To convince your audience of your thesis, be sure to answer the question "why?"

ADDITIONAL TOPICS AND ISSUES FOR WRITING AND RESEARCH

1. Write an essay in which you reverse roles with another person. Use descriptive details to convey the emotional depth and significance of your role.
2. Select an artist, alive or dead, whose work you admire and write a brief expository essay explaining verifiable and probable influences behind his or her work. Why do some artists paint or sculpt statues with religious themes? Why did Andy Warhol paint Campbell's Soup cans?
3. Compare and contrast a situation you encountered through "the eyes of innocence" to the same situation viewed through the "eyes of experience." What conclusions can you draw about human nature?
4. If you could redecorate where you live—and you had an unlimited budget—what changes would you make? What criteria or basis would you use in determining the design for your new environment?
5. Freewrite on the topic of dances. What conclusions can you draw about most dances? From your freewriting, move on to a structured essay wherein you compare and contrast two types of dance, such as ballet and ballroom dancing, bearing a specific ultimate purpose in mind.
6. Go to a museum or the library and research the arts and crafts of an unfamiliar culture. What patterns, themes, and motifs occur time and again? Write an essay explaining the values that appear to motivate the art of your chosen culture.
7. Critique the aesthetics of a group of pictures of your own choice.
8. Write a paper satirizing some aspect of modern art, popular culture, fashionable clothing, chic television commercials, and so on. In order for your paper to "work," you will have to exercise control over your material (use satire rather than a series of sarcastic remarks), as well as to distinguish between what you say to point out *human folly* and what you really mean.

9. Construct an essay in which you explain how the art of a particular culture or civilization "speaks to you." What does it say and how? Perhaps your selection is related to a specific artistic or aesthetic movement. If so, what is it, and how does it further influence your identification with the art?

10. Compare and contrast *Japanese scrolls* such as those for *The Tale of Genji* by Murasaki Sikibu and medieval *illuminated manuscripts* like *The Canterbury Tales* by Geoffrey Chaucer.

Starting Points for Research

Art

- Air art
- Art nouveau
- Art deco
- Anamorphic art
- Commercial art
- Costume
- Courtroom art
- Cubism
- Drawing
- Ballet
- Etching
- Ethnic art
- Graphic art
- Homosexuality and art
- Human figure in art
- Illumination of books and manuscripts
- Jewelry
- Occidental art
- Western art
- Primitive art
- Visual arts
- Iconography
- Fine arts
- Lithography
- Animal paintings
- Antiques
- Architecture
- Collage
- Gems/precious stones
- Feminism and art
- Folk art

Aesthetics

- Art appreciation
- Avant-garde (aesthetics)
- Classicism
- Dancing—philosophy
- Dentistry (aesthetics)
- Dilettantism
- Environment (aesthetics)
- Feminine/masculine
- Fantastic, the (aesthetics)
- Choreography
- Form
- Style
- Harmony (aesthetics)
- Grotesque
- Futurism (art)
- Idealism in art
- Indians of North America
- Lettrism
- Kitsch
- Music—theory
- Moving pictures (aesthetics)
- Decadence
- Plastic surgery (aesthetics)
- Beauty—the beautiful
- Taste (aesthetics)
- Music and architecture
- Originality (aesthetics)
- Picturesque, the
- Poetry
- Post-impressionism
- Rhythm

Starting Points for Research (continued)

Art

- Stained glass (glass art)
- Art and literature
- Art and motion pictures
- Art and music
- Art and mythology
- Art and nuclear warfare
- Art and ethnopsychology
- Art and photography
- Art metal work
- Art museums
- Art restoration
- Art treasures in war
- Reproductions
- Limited edition
- Religious influence on art
  Christian
  Islamic
  Jewish
  Hindu
  Buddhist
- Idols and images
- Reformation and art
- Rococo art
- Photo-realism
- Neoplasticism (aesthetics)
- Vorticism
- Erotic art
- Art Brut
- Paper stretching
- Unfinished works of art
- Idealism in art
- Art therapy
- Classical art
- Gothic art
- Art colonies
- Artists
- Mass media and art
- Medicine and art
- Miniature paintings
- Mosaics
- Mural painting and decoration
- Mobiles (sculptures)

Aesthetics

- Art for art's sake
- Positivist aesthetics
- Medieval aesthetics
- Romanian aesthetics
- Russian aesthetics
- Greek aesthetics
- Spanish aesthetics
- Scottish aesthetics
- Sri Lankan aesthetics
- Swedish aesthetics
- Tamil aesthetics
- Turkmen aesthetics
- Ukrainian aesthetics
- Aesthetics in the Bible
- Drama (aesthetics)
- Fiction (aesthetics)
- Comedy
- Tragedy
- Utopian
- Anti-Utopian
- Ut pictura poesis
  (aesthetics)
- Aesthetic criticism
- Romanticism
- Furniture (aesthetics)
- Landscapes
- Aesthetic pleasure
- Aesthetic language
- Taste in art (aesthetics)
- Preference in food
- Preference in entertainment
- Bad taste / good taste
- Food presentations
- Taste in music
- Philosophy of art
- Philosophy of dance
- Philosophy of music
- Science (aesthetics)
- Spectacular, the (aesthetics)
- Sublime, the
- Truth (aesthetics)
- Ugliness

Starting Points for Research *(continued)*

Art

- Mysticism and art
- Censorship and art
- Audiovisual arts
- Painting (oils, watercolors, acrylics)
- Naturalism
- Ceramics/pottery
- Sculpture
- Posters
- Art collectors
- Art patrons
- Extraterrestrial influences on art
- Art forgeries
- Mutilation, defacement of art
- Surrealism
- Expressionism in art
- Spatialism
- Themes and motifs
- Abstract art
- Apocalyptic art
- Ancient art
- Art, twentieth century
- Dadaism
- Concrete art
- Conceptual art
- Body art (tattoos)
- Private art collections
- Constructivism
- Art and industry
- Art and dancing
- Art and anthropology

Aesthetics

- Architecture
- Visual
- Audio
- Aesthetic realism
- Aesthetic objects
- Aesthetic movements
- Aesthetic philosophy
- Aesthetic/psychic distance
- Religious aesthetics
- African aesthetics
- European aesthetics
- Asian aesthetics
- Aztec aesthetics
- Mayan aesthetics
- Byzantine aesthetics
- Comparative aesthetics
- Indic aesthetics
- Canadian aesthetics
- Chinese aesthetics
- English aesthetics
- French aesthetics
- German aesthetics
- Hungarian aesthetics
- Italian aesthetics
- Japanese aesthetics
- Javanese aesthetics
- Korean aesthetics
- Lithuanian aesthetics
- Marxist aesthetics
- Democratic aesthetics
- Communist aesthetics

14

City and Country: Urban, Suburban, and Rural

A peasant's child
Husking the rice, pauses
To look at the moon.
MATSUO BASHO

Essays

Tom Wolfe   O Rotten Gotham—Sliding Down into the Behavioral Sink

•

Annie Dillard   Living Like Weasels

•

Piri Thomas   Puerto Rican Paradise

•

Fiction

Flannery O'Connor   Good Country People

•

Garrison Keillor   Pontoon Boat

•

Poetry

Claude McKay   Subway Wind

•

Margaret Atwood   The City Planners

•

Quincy Troupe   Impressions of Chicago; For Howlin' Wolf

The juxtaposition of city and country probably takes you back to your childhood, where the story of the city mouse and the country mouse suggests that everyone has an expected niche in society. Such a view would not be tolerated today, since it does not offer individuals any chance for social or economic mobility. Rather than focus on the issue of change, however, this chapter will examine people, places, and things within the context of an immediate social environment.

There are many unhealthy sights and sounds associated with the city. "Subway Wind" by Claude McKay takes you "Far down, down through the city's great gaunt gut" where rushing gray trains—subways—bear "the weary wind." Tom Wolfe paints a bleak picture of city life in "O Rotten Gotham—Sliding Down into the Behavioral Sink," a look into overcrowding and its effects on people in general and society as a whole. "The City Planners" by Margaret Atwood vividly portrays the unwholesome "sanities" and insane faces of these planners whose values are not the same as community members'. Quincy Troupe offers yet another look at city life in "Impressions of Chicago; For Howlin' Wolf," noting how the wind cuts across the lake "slicing white foam from the tips / of delicate water fingers," and how south side Chicago children often "dance in & out of the traffic" barefoot among slivers of glass that never seem to cut their feet.

"Pontoon Boat" gives you a glimpse of Garrison Keillor's fictitious community of Lake Wobegon. Much of his humor in this narrative centers around how people respond when they are "out of their element" (familiar social environment).

The perceived goodness of rural areas and wilderness areas and the unavoidable evils of urban squalor are common views people hold of the country and the city, views that have resurfaced in dynamic ways from time to time during the course of history. From romantic visions of Native Americans living off the land, to communes in the 1960s, to peaceful country homes for retirement, coexisting with nature in an untainted environment definitely has had a positive appeal. Does the country really have all the good things in life and the city all the bad? At what point does the country become infected or impure? Industry and pollution are the most obvious offenders here, but individuals who are representative of self-serving acts might also be identified.

The Bible salesman in Flannery O'Connor's "Good Country People" presents an ironic look at the truisms of character types. Mrs. Hopewell thinks he is simple because he comes from the country and is therefore untainted by the city. Mrs. Freeman, by contrast, whom Mrs. Hopewell also identifies as a "good country person," is not fooled by outer appearances. Here lies the ultimate irony of Mrs. Hopewell's acceptance of stereotypes and facades.

Different settings also provide an opportunity to examine lifestyles and ideas. Despite his parents' nostalgia about Puerto Rico, "Puerto Rican Paradise," by Piri Thomas suggests the real paradise to be found in life is within the family; his life on the streets certainly did not change much when his father finally got employment at an airplane factory. In contrast, in her essay, "Living Like Weasels," Annie Dillard says, "I would like to learn, or remember, how to live." She wants to experience the mindless purity of "living in the physical senses . . . without bias or motive."

Suburbia seems a magnificent compromise between city and country living. Living in the suburbs takes one away from the hustle and bustle of busy city streets, heavy traffic, and close living quarters. In the suburbs, houses are not built inches apart, and usually, suburban homes have front and back yards. The suburbs are also close to other things formerly offered by the big city: convenience stores, employment, entertainment, shopping malls, and schools. There is a catch, however. For suburban development to continue, rural areas—including forests and farmlands—have to be sacrificed. The fact that earth is becoming polluted by the human race—from the country, cities, and suburbia—is more than simply an idea popularized by ecologists. Plant and animal life forms now face extinction at a pace a thousand times faster than normal. Thus, though immediate social environments differ, they also have something in common: certain social impact by human beings, which means change is unavoidable even when undesirable.

RHETORIC AT WORK

After reading through each literary work, go back and write down instances of comparative and superlative word use. How did these further the writer's purpose? Did they clarify a point or place it into perspective? Also consider how various forms of figurative language, such as metaphors and similes, offer writers a means for comparing things. To what extent do the comparatives you discover deal with stereotypes? Make two lists, one with the heading of stereotypes and the other with the heading of reality types. Place as many stereotypes of people or places in the country, the city, or suburbia on the list as you can. In the second column, explain how or why the person or place has been stereotyped.

**A Checklist for Writing about *City and Country:*
*Urban, Suburban, and Rural***

1. How do I address different social environments? Who or what am I comparing or contrasting? If I am not writing a comparative essay, who or what am I describing, defining, or explaining?
2. Do I support my thesis? Are my examples descriptive, varied, and representative of what I contend about city, country, or suburban life or do I rely on a single example to do the job?
3. Do concrete nouns and active verbs bring my descriptions of urban, suburban, or rural settings to life?

4. What do I emphasize when discussing individuals from a particular social background? Have I avoided stereotypes?
5. Is my use of comparative language clear and consistent? Have I eliminated careless spelling errors (writing *then* when I mean *than*) that misdirect my readers?
6. Does my language appeal to the senses? Do I enable my readers to see the pollution filling in the city, hear birds singing in the country, or smell charcoal burning from barbecue pits in the suburbs?
7. What techniques do I use in order to *fine-tune* my introductory and concluding paragraphs? As a result, do my sentences flow smoothly into each other? Does my introduction contain a "hook" and my conclusion a "clincher" sentence?

✱

O Rotten Gotham—Sliding Down into the Behavioral Sink

Tom Wolfe

Tom Wolfe, a graduate of Washington and Lee University, as well as Yale where he earned his doctorate, worked for several years as a reporter—first for *The Washington Post* and later for the *New York Herald Tribune*. A regular contributor to such magazines as the *New Yorker* and *Esquire,* his collections of articles and other books include *The Kandy-Kolored Tangerine-Flake Streamline Baby* (1965), *The Electric Kool-Aid Acid Test* (1968), *Radical Chic and Mau-Mauing the Flak Catchers* (1970), *New Journalism* (1973), *The Painted Word* (1975), *The Right Stuff* (1977), *In Our Time* (1980), *Underneath the I-Beams: Inside the Compound* (1981), *From Bauhaus to Our House* (1981), *The Purple Decades: A Reader* (1984), and *Bonfire of the Vanities* (1986). "O Rotten Gotham—Sliding Down into the Behavioral Sink," an essay examining the cause-and-effect relationships of overcrowding in cities, was originally published in *The Pump House Gang* (1968).

1   **I** just spent two days with Edward T. Hall, an anthropologist, watching thousands of my fellow New Yorkers short-circuiting themselves into hot little twitching death balls with jolts of their own adrenalin. Dr. Hall says it is overcrowding that does it. Overcrowding gets the adrenalin going, and the adrenalin gets them hyped up. And here they are, hyped up, turning bilious, nephritic, queer, autistic, sadistic, barren, batty, sloppy, hot-in-the-pants, chancred-on-the-flankers, leering, pulling, numb—the usual in New

York, in other words, and God knows what else. Dr. Hall has the theory that overcrowding has already thrown New York into a state of behavioral sink. Behavioral sink is a term from ethology, which is the study of how animals relate to their environment. Among animals, the sink winds up with a "population collapse" or "massive die-off." O rotten Gotham.

2   It got to be easy to look at New Yorkers as animals, especially looking down from some place like a balcony at Grand Central at the rush hour Friday afternoon. The floor was filled with the poor white humans, running around, dodging, blinking their eyes, making a sound like a pen full of starlings or rats or something.

3   "Listen to them skid," says Dr. Hall.

4   He was right. The poor old etiolate animals were out there skidding on their rubber soles. You could hear it once he pointed it out. They stop short to keep from hitting somebody or because they are disoriented and they suddenly stop and look around, and they skid on their rubber-soled shoes, and a screech goes up. They pour out onto the floor down the escalators from the Pan-Am Building, from 42nd Street, from Lexington Avenue, up out of subways, down into subways, railroad trains, up into helicopters—

5   "You can also hear the helicopters all the way down here," says Dr. Hall. The sound of the helicopters using the roof of the Pan-Am Building nearly fifty stories up beats right through. "If it weren't for this ceiling"—he is referring to the very high ceiling in Grand Central—"this place would be unbearable with this kind of crowding. And yet they'll probably never 'waste' space like this again."

6   They screech! And the adrenal glands in all those poor white animals enlarge, micrometer by micrometer, to the size of cantaloupes. Dr. Hall pulls a Minox camera out of a holster he has on his belt and starts shooting away at the human scurry. The Sink!

7   Dr. Hall has the Minox up to his eye—he is a slender man, calm, fifty-two years old, young-looking, an anthropologist who has worked with Navajos, Hopis, Spanish-Americans, Negroes, Trukese. He was the most important anthropologist in the government during the crucial years of the foreign aid program, the 1950s. He directed both the Point Four training program and the Human Relations Area Files. He wrote *The Silent Language* and *The Hidden Dimension*, two books that are picking up the kind of "underground" following his friend Marshall McLuhan started picking up about five years ago. He teaches at the Illinois Institute of Technology, lives with his wife, Mildred, in a high-ceilinged town house on one of the last great residential streets in downtown Chicago, Astor Street; he has a grown son and daughter, loves good food, good wine, the relaxed, civilized life—but comes to New York with a Minox at his eye to record!—perfect—The Sink.

8   We really got down in there by walking down into the Lexington Avenue line subway stop under Grand Central. We inhaled those nice big fluffy fumes of human sweat, urine, effluvia, and sebaceous secretions. One old female human was already stroked out on the upper level, on a stretcher,

with two policemen standing by. The other humans barely looked at her. They rushed into line. They bellied each other, haunch to paunch, down the stairs. Human heads shone through the gratings. The species North European tried to create bubbles of space around themselves, about a foot and a half in diameter—

9   "See, he's reacting against the line," says Dr. Hall.

10 —but the species Mediterranean presses on in. The hell with bubbles of space. The species North European resents that, this male human behind him presses forward toward the booth . . . *breathing* on him, he's disgusted, he pulls out of the line entirely, the species Mediterranean resents him for resenting it, and neither of them realizes what the hell they are getting irritable about exactly. And in all of them the old adrenals grow another micrometer.

11 Dr. Hall whips out the Minox. Too perfect! The bottom of The Sink.

12 It is the sheer overcrowding, such as occurs in the business sections of Manhattan five days a week and in Harlem, Bedford-Stuyvesant, southeast Bronx every day—sheer overcrowding is converting New Yorkers into animals in a sink pen. Dr. Hall's argument runs as follows: all animals, including birds, seem to have a built-in inherited requirement to have a certain amount of territory, space, to lead their lives in. Even if they have all the food they need, and there are no predatory animals threatening them, they cannot tolerate crowding beyond a certain point. No more than two hundred wild Norway rats can survive on a quarter acre of ground, for example, even when they are given all the food they can eat. They just die off.

13 But why? To find out, ethologists have run experiments on all sorts of animals, from stickleback crabs to Sika deer. In one major experiment, an ethologist named John Calhoun put some domesticated white Norway rats in a pen with four sections to it, connected by ramps. Calhoun knew from previous experiments that the rats tend to split up into groups of ten to twelve and that the pen, therefore, would hold forty to forty-eight rats comfortably, assuming they formed four equal groups. He allowed them to reproduce until there were eighty rats, balanced between male and female, but did not let it get any more crowded. He kept them supplied with plenty of food, water, and nesting materials. In other words, all their more obvious needs were taken care of. A less obvious need—space—was not. To the human eye, the pen did not even look especially crowded. But to the rats, it was crowded beyond endurance.

14 The entire colony was soon plunged into a profound behavioral sink. "The sink," said Calhoun, "is the outcome of any behavioral process that collects animals together in unusually great numbers. The unhealthy connotations of the term are not accidental: a behavioral sink does act to aggravate all forms of pathology that can be found within a group."

15 For a start, long before the rat population reached eighty, a status hierarchy had developed in the pen. Two dominant male rats took over the two end sections, acquired harems of eight to ten females each, and forced the

rest of the rats into the two middle pens. All the overcrowding took place in the middle pens. That was where the "sink" hit. The aristocrat rats at the end grew bigger, sleeker, healthier, and more secure the whole time.

16   In The Sink, meanwhile, nest building, courting, sex behavior, reproduction, social organization, health—all of it went to pieces. Normally, Norway rats have a mating ritual in which the male chases the female, the female ducks down into a burrow and sticks her head up to watch the male. He performs a little dance outside the burrow, then she comes out, and he mounts her, usually for a few seconds. When The Sink set in, however, no more than three males—the dominant males in the middle sections—kept up the old customs. The rest tried everything from satyrism to homosexuality or else gave up on sex altogether. Some of the subordinate males spent all their time chasing females. Three or four might chase one female at the same time, and instead of stopping at the burrow entrance for the ritual, they would charge right in. Once mounted, they would hold on for minutes instead of the usual seconds.

17   Homosexuality rose sharply. So did bisexuality. Some males would mount anything—males, females, babies, senescent rats, anything. Still other males dropped sexual activity altogether, wouldn't fight and, in fact, would hardly move except when the other rats slept. Occasionally, a female from the aristocrat rats' harems would come over the ramps and into the middle sections to sample life in The Sink. When she had had enough, she would run back up the ramp. Sink males would give chase up to the top of the ramp, which is to say, to the very edge of the aristocratic preserve. But one glance from one of the king rats would stop them cold and they would return to The Sink.

18   The slumming females from the harems had their adventures and then returned to a placid, healthy life. Females in The Sink, however, were ravaged, physically and psychologically. Pregnant rats had trouble continuing pregnancy. The rate of miscarriages increased significantly, and females started dying from tumors and other disorders of the mammary glands, sex organs, uterus, ovaries, and Fallopian tubes. Typically, their kidneys, livers, and adrenals were also enlarged or diseased or showed other signs associated with stress.

19   Child-rearing became totally disorganized. The females lost the interest or the stamina to build nests and did not keep them up if they did build them. In the general filth and confusion, they would not put themselves out to save offspring they were momentarily separated from. Frantic, even sadistic competition among the males was going on all around them and rendering their lives chaotic. The males began unprovoked and senseless assaults upon one another, often in the form of tail-biting. Ordinarily, rats will suppress this kind of behavior when it crops up. In The Sink, male rats gave up all policing and just looked out for themselves. The "pecking order" among males in The Sink was never stable. Normally, male rats set up a three-class structure. Under the pressure of overcrowding, however, they broke up into all sorts of unstable subclasses, cliques, packs—and constantly

pushed, probed, explored, tested one another's power. Anyone was fair game, except for the aritocrats in the end pens.

20   Calhoun kept the population down to eighty, so that the next stage, "population collapse" or "massive die-off," did not occur. But the autopsies showed that the pattern—as in the diseases among the female rats—was already there.

21   The classic study of die-off was John J. Christian's study of Sika deer on James Island in the Chesapeake Bay, west of Cambridge, Maryland. Four or five of the deer had been released on the island, which was 280 acres and uninhabited, in 1916. By 1955 they had bred freely into a herd of 280 to 300. The population density was only about one deer per acre at this point, but Christian knew that this was already too high for the Sikas' inborn space requirements, and something would give before long. For two years the number of deer remained 280 to 300. But suddenly, in 1958, over half the deer died; 161 carcasses were recovered. In 1959 more deer died and the population steadied at about 80.

22   In two years, two-thirds of the herd had died. Why? It was not starvation. In fact, all the deer collected were in excellent condition, with well-developed muscles, shining coats, and fat deposits between the muscles. In practically all the deer, however, the adrenal glands had enlarged by fifty percent. Christian concluded that the die-off was due to "shock following severe metabolic disturbance, probably as a result of prolonged adrenocortical hyperactivity. . . . There was no evidence of infection, starvation, or other obvious cause to explain the mass mortality." In other words, the constant stress of overpopulation, plus the normal stress of the cold of the winter, had kept the adrenalin flowing so constantly in the deer that their systems were depleted of blood sugar and they died of shock.

23   Well, the white humans are still skidding and darting across the floor of Grand Central. Dr. Hall listens a moment longer to the skidding and darting noises, and then says, "You know, I've been on commuter trains here after everyone has been through one of these rushes, and I'll tell you, there is enough acid flowing in the stomachs in every car to dissolve the rails underneath."

24   Just a little invisible acid bath for the linings to round off the day. The ulcers the acids cause, of course, are the one disease people have already been taught to associate with the stress of city life. But overcrowding, as Dr. Hall sees it, raises a lot more hell with the body than just ulcers. In everyday life in New York—just the usual, getting to work, working in massively congested areas like 42nd Street between Fifth Avenue and Lexington, especially now that the Pam-Am Building is set in there, working in cubicles such as those in the editorial offices at Time-Life, Inc., which Dr. Hall cites as typical of New York's poor handling of space, working in cubicles with low ceilings and, often, no access to a window, while construction crews all over Manhattan drive everybody up the Masonite wall with air-pressure generators with noises up to the boil-a-brain decibel level, then rushing to get home, piling into subways and trains, fighting for time and for space,

the usual day in New York—the whole now-normal thing keeps shooting jolts of adrenalin into the body, breaking down the body's defenses and winding up with the work-a-daddy human animal stroked out at the breakfast table with his head apoplexed like a cauliflower out of his $6.95 semispread Pima-cotton shirt, and nosed over into a plate of No-Kloresto egg substitute, signing off with the black thrombosis, cancer, kidney, liver, or stomach failure, and the adrenals ooze to a halt, the size of eggplants in July.

25   One of the people whose work Dr. Hall is interested in on this score is Rene Dubos at the Rockefeller Institute. Dubos's work indicates that specific organisms, such as the tuberculosis bacillus or a pneumonia virus, can seldom be considered "the cause" of a disease. The germ or virus, apparently, has to work in combination with other things that have already broken the body down in some way—such as the old adrenal hyperactivity. Dr. Hall would like to see some autopsy studies made to record the size of adrenal glands in New York, especially of people crowded into slums and people who go through the full rush-hour-work-rush-hour cycle every day. He is afraid that until there is some clinical, statistical data on how overcrowding actually ravages the human body, no one will be willing to do anything about it. Even in so obvious a thing as air pollution, the pattern is familiar. Until people can actually see the smoke or smell the sulphur or feel the sting in their eyes, politicians will not get excited about it, even though it is well known that many of the lethal substances polluting the air are invisible and odorless. For one thing, most politicians are like the aristocrat rats. They are insulated from The Sink by practically sultanic buffers—limousines, chauffeurs, secretaries, aides-de-camp, doormen, shuttered houses, high-floor apartments. They almost never ride subways, fight rush hours, much less live in the slums or work in the Pam-Am Building.

Writing Log/Journal Assignment

Write a journal entry explaining your philosphy about the present cause and effects of overcrowding in major American cities.

Individual and Collaborative Considerations

1. What is Dr. Hall's theory about New York City's overcrowding?
2. To what extent do you find Wolfe's diction (word choice) effective and persuasive?
3. As described by ethologist John Calhoun, what is the "behavioral sink"?
4. The entire colony of Dr. Calhoun's rats fell into a behavioral sink; what were some of their symptoms?
5. What does Dr. Calhoun believe must be done to avoid the behavioral sink and its consequences, such as the collapse of culture? Do you agree with his analogy that most politicians are like aristocratic rats?

Writing Activities

1. Wolfe wrote about the behavioral sink in 1968. Now, more than twenty-five years later, there has been ample time to reconsider "autopsy studies made to record the size of adrenal glands in New York, especially of people crowded into slums and people who go through the full rush-hour-work-rush-hour cycle every day." After reviewing the studies made during the past twenty-five years, write an essay affirming Dr. Hall's and Wolfe's position on the behavioral sink *or* argue that substantial changes have been made over the last quarter of a century to reduce overpopulation and overcrowding.

2. Compare and contrast conditions in New York City during 1968 to similar conditions present in world societies today. In what way do modern societies contain specific qualities and characteristics of the "behavioral sink"?

✳

Living Like Weasels

Annie Dillard

Pulitzer Prize–winning author Annie Dillard is a poet and essayist whose works include *Pilgrim at Tinker Creek* (1974), *Holy the Firm* (1977), *Teaching a Stone to Talk* (1982), and *Encounters with Chinese Writers* (1984). She also has written *Tickets for a Prayer Wheel* (1974), a volume of poetry. Nature, love, and God are among her favorite writing subjects. In *Living by Fiction* (1983), a book about writing, Dillard states, "I approach fiction, and the world, and these absurdly large questions, as a reader, and a writer, and a lover."

1 **A** weasel is wild. Who knows what he thinks? He sleeps in his underground den, his tail draped over his nose. Sometimes he lives in his den for two days without leaving. Outside, he stalks rabbits, mice, muskrats, and birds, killing more bodies than he can eat warm, and often dragging the carcasses home. Obedient to instinct, he bites his prey at the neck, either splitting the jugular vein at the throat or crunching the brain at the base of the skull, and he does not let go. One naturalist refused to kill a weasel who was socketed into his hand deeply as a rattlesnake. The man could in no way pry the tiny weasel off, and he had to walk half a mile to water, the weasel dangling from his palm, and soak him off like a stubborn label.

2   And once, says Ernest Thompson Seton—once, a man shot an eagle out of the sky. He examined the eagle and found the dry skull of a weasel fixed by the jaws to his throat. The supposition is that the eagle had pounced on the weasel and the weasel swiveled and bit as instinct taught him, tooth to neck, and nearly won. I would like to have seen that eagle from the air a few weeks or months before he was shot: was the whole weasel still attached to his feathered throat, a fur pendant? Or did the eagle eat what he could reach, gutting the living weasel with his talons before his breast, bending his beak, cleaning the beautiful airborne bones?

3   I have been reading about weasels because I saw one last week. I startled a weasel who startled me, and we exchanged a long glance.

4   Twenty minutes from my house, through the woods by the quarry and across the highway, is Hollins Pond, a remarkable piece of shallowness, where I like to go at sunset and sit on a tree trunk. Hollins Pond is also called Murray's Pond; it covers two acres of bottomland near Tinker Creek with six inches of water and six thousand lily pads. In winter, brown-and-white steers stand in the middle of it, merely dampening their hooves; from the distant shore they look like miracle itself, complete with miracle's nonchalance. Now, in summer, the steers are gone. The water lilies have blossomed and spread to a green horizontal plane that is terra firma to plodding blackbirds, and tremulous ceiling to black leeches, crayfish, and carp.

5   This is, mind you, suburbia. It is a five-minute walk in three directions to rows of houses, though none is visible here. There's a 55 mph highway at one end of the pond, and a nesting pair of wood ducks at the other. Under every bush is a muskrat hole or a beer can. The far end is an alternating series of fields and woods, fields and woods, threaded everywhere with motorcycle tracks—in whose bare clay wild turtles lay eggs.

6   So. I had crossed the highway, stepped over two low barbed-wire fences, and traced the motorcycle path in all gratitude through the wild rose and poison ivy of the pond's shoreline up into high grassy fields. Then I cut down through the woods to the mossy fallen tree where I sit. This tree is excellent. It makes a dry, upholstered bench at the upper, marshy end of the pond, a plush jetty raised from the thorny shore, between a shallow blue body of water and a deep blue body of sky.

7   The sun had just set. I was relaxed on the tree trunk, ensconced in the lap of lichen, watching the lily pads at my feet tremble and part dreamily over the thrusting path of a carp. A yellow bird appeared to my right and flew behind me. It caught my eye; I swiveled around—and the next instant, inexplicably, I was looking down at a weasel, who was looking up at me.

8   Weasel! I'd never seen one wild before. He was ten inches long, thin as a curve, a muscled ribbon, brown as fruitwood, soft-furred, alert. His face was fierce, small and pointed as a lizard's; he would have made a good arrowhead. There was just a dot of chin, maybe two brown hairs' worth, and then

the pure white fur began that spread down his underside. He had two black eyes I didn't see, any more than you see a window.

9   The weasel was stunned into stillness as he was emerging from beneath an enormous shaggy wild rose bush four feet away. I was stunned into stillness twisted backward on the tree trunk. Our eyes locked, and someone threw away the key.

10   Our look was as if two lovers, or deadly enemies, met unexpectedly on an overgrown path when each had been thinking of something else: a clearing blow to the gut. It was also a bright blow to the brain, or a sudden beating of brains, with all the charge and intimate grate of rubbed balloons. It emptied our lungs. It felled the forest, moved the fields, and drained the pond; the world dismantled and tumbled into that black hole of eyes. If you and I looked at each other that way, our skulls would split and drop to our shoulders. But we don't. We keep our skulls. So.

11   He disappeared. This was only last week, and already I don't remember what shattered the enchantment. I think I blinked, I think I retrieved my brain from the weasel's brain, and tried to memorize what I was seeing, and the weasel felt the yank of separation, the careening splashdown into real life and the urgent current of instinct. He vanished under the wild rose. I waited, motionless, my mind suddenly full of data and my spirit with pleadings, but he didn't return.

12   Please do not tell me about "approach-avoidance conflicts." I tell you I've been in that weasel's brain for sixty seconds, and he was in mine. Brains are private places, muttering through unique and secret tapes—but the weasel and I both plugged into another tape simultaneously, for a sweet and shocking time. Can I help it if it was a blank?

13   What goes on in his brain the rest of the time? What does a weasel think about? He won't say. His journal is tracks in clay, a spray of feathers, mouse blood and bone: uncollected, unconnected, loose-leaf, and blown.

14   I would like to learn, or remember, how to live. I come to Hollins Pond not so much to learn how to live as, frankly, to forget about it. That is, I don't think I can learn from a wild animal how to live in particular—shall I suck warm blood, hold my tail high, walk with my footprints precisely over the prints of my hands?—but I might learn something of mindlessness, something of the purity of living in the physical senses and the dignity of living without bias or motive. The weasel lives in necessity and we live in choice, hating necessity and dying at the last ignobly in its talons. I would like to live as I should, as the weasel lives as he should. And I suspect that for me the way is like the weasel's: open to time and death painlessly, noticing everything, remembering nothing, choosing the given with a fierce and pointed will.

15   I missed my chance. I should have gone for the throat. I should have lunged for that streak of white under the weasel's chin and held on, held on

through mud and into the wild rose, held on for a dearer life. We could live under the wild rose wild as weasels, mute and uncomprehending. I could very calmly go wild. I could live two days in the den, curled, leaning on mouse fur, sniffling bird bones, blinking, licking, breathing musk, my hair tangled in the roots of grasses. Down is a good place to go, where the mind is single. Down is out, out of your ever-loving mind and back to your careless senses. I remember muteness as a prolonged and giddy fast, where every moment is a feast of utterance received. Time and events are merely poured, unremarked, and ingested directly, like blood pulsed into my gut through a jugular vein. Could two live that way? Could two live under the wild rose, and explore by the pond, so that the smooth mind of each is as everywhere present to the other, and as received and as unchallenged, as falling snow?

16   We could, you know. We can live any way we want. People take vows of poverty, chastity, and obedience—even of silence—by choice. The thing is to stalk your calling in a certain skilled and supple way, to locate the most tender and live spot and plug into that pulse. This is yielding, not fighting. A weasel doesn't "attack" anything; a weasel lives as he's meant to, yielding at every moment to the perfect freedom of single necessity.

17   I think it would be well, and proper, and obedient, and pure, to grasp your one necessity and not let it go, to dangle from it limp wherever it takes you. Then even death, where you're going no matter how you live, cannot you part. Seize it and let it seize you up aloft even, till your eyes burn out and drop; let your musky flesh fall off in shreds, and let your very bones unhinge and scatter, loosened over fields, over fields and woods, lightly, thoughtless, from any height at all, from as high as eagles.

Writing Log/Journal Assignment

Write a journal entry describing an "idealized" world where you would live like other animals in burrows, caves, or trees.

Individual and Collaborative Considerations

1. The opening paragraph sets up the rest of the essay. What information does it give you? How does this information guide you through the essay?
2. How does Dillard describe the weasel?
3. Dillard says that when she and the weasel gazed at each other, their eyes locked and it was as if someone had thrown away the key: "Our look was as if two lovers, or deadly enemies, met unexpectedly." Explain what she is trying to convey by her allusion to two "lovers or deadly enemies."
4. What do you find most interesting about a weasel? What does Dillard claim we can learn from it?

5. "A weasel doesn't 'attack' anything; a weasel lives as he's meant to, yielding at every moment to the perfect freedom of single necessity." How does this behavior contrast with the way people behave?

Writing Activities

1. Of all nature's animals, which one intrigues you most and why? Do the animal's actions ennoble it? How? Might human beings learn something about "ideal behavior" from your animal's natural instinct or habits? If so, what? After you thoroughly examine the possibilities of your topic, prewrite to achieve some sort of focus (a thesis), and assemble your information into an essay. Like Dillard, entitle your essay after the animal of your choice (e.g., weeping like crocodiles).
2. Compare and contrast the difference between exercising freedom of choice and acting upon necessity in a well-written, thoroughly supported essay.

✳

Puerto Rican Paradise

Piri Thomas

Puerto Rican American Piri Thomas was born in Spanish Harlem, and he began his writing career while serving time in prison for armed robbery. Today, Thomas remains active on the lecture circuit. His works include *Down These Mean Streets* (1967), *Savior, Savior Hold My Hand* (1972), *Seven Times Long* (1974), and *The View from El Barrio* (1978).

1 **P**oppa didn't talk to me the next day. Soon he didn't talk much to anyone. He lost his night job—I forget why, and probably it was worth forgetting— and went back on home relief. It was 1941, and the Great Hunger called Depression was still down on Harlem.

2 But there was still the good old WPA. If a man was poor enough, he could dig a ditch for the government. Now Poppa was poor enough again.

3 The weather turned cold one more time, and so did our apartment. In the summer the cooped-up apartments in Harlem seem to catch all the heat and improve on it. It's the same in the winter. The cold, plastered walls embrace that cold from outside and make it a part of the apartment, till you don't

know whether it's better to freeze out in the snow or by the stove, where four jets, wide open, spout futile, blue-yellow flames. It's hard on the rats, too.

4   Snow was falling. "My *Cristo*," Momma said, "*qué frío*. Doesn't that landlord have any *corazón?*[1] Why don't he give more heat?" I wondered how Pops was making out working a pick and shovel in that falling snow.

5   Momma picked up a hammer and began to beat the beat-up radiator that's copped a plea from so many beatings. Poor steam radiator, how could it give out heat when it was freezing itself? The hollow sounds Momma beat out of it brought echoes from other freezing people in the building. Everybody picked up the beat and it seemed a crazy, good idea. If everybody took turns beating on the radiators, everybody could keep warm from the exercise.

6   We drank hot cocoa and talked about summertime. Momma talked about Puerto Rico and how great it was, and how she'd like to go back one day, and how it was warm all the time there and no matter how poor you were over there, you could always live on green bananas, *bacalao*,[2] and rice and beans. "*Dios mío*," she said, "I don't think I'll ever see my island again."

7   "Sure you will, Mommie," said Miriam, my kid sister. She was eleven. "Tell us, tell us all about Porto Rico."

8   "It not Porto Rico, it's Puerto Rico," said Momma.

9   "Tell us, Moms," said nine-year-old James, "about Puerto Rico."

10   "Yeah, Mommie," said six-year-old José.

11   Even the baby, Paulie, smiled.

12   Moms copped that wet-eyed look and began to dream-talk about her *isla verde*,[3] Moses' land of milk and honey.

13   "When I was a little girl," she said, "I remember the getting up in the morning and getting the water from the river and getting the wood for the fire and the quiet of the greenlands and the golden color of the morning sky, the grass wet from the *lluvia*[4] . . . Ai, Dios, the *coquís*[5] and the *pajaritos*[6] making all the *música* . . . "

14   "Mommie, were you poor?" asked Miriam.

15   "*Sí, muy pobre*, but very happy. I remember the hard work and the very little bit we had, but it was a good little bit. It counted very much. Sometimes when you have too much, the good gets lost within and you have to look very hard. But when you have a little, then the good does not have to be looked for so hard."

16   "Moms," I asked, "did everybody love each other—I mean, like if everybody was worth something, not like if some weren't important because they were poor—you know what I mean?"

---

[1]heart
[2]codfish
[3]green island
[4]rain
[5]small treetoads
[6]little birds

17   *"Bueno hijo,* you have people everywhere who, because they have more, don't remember those who have very little. But in Puerto Rico those around you share *la pobreza*[7] with you and they love you, because only poor people can understand poor people. I like *los Estados Unidos,* but it's sometimes a cold place to live—not because of the winter and the landlord not giving heat but because of the snow in the hearts of the people."

18   "Moms, didn't our people have any money or land?" I leaned forward, hoping to hear that my ancestors were noble princes born in Spain.

19   "Your grandmother and grandfather had a lot of land, but they lost that."

20   "How come, Moms?"

21   "Well, in those days there was nothing of what you call *contratos,*[8] and when you bought or sold something, it was on your word and a handshake, and that's the way your *abuelos*[9] bought their land and then lost it."

22   "Is that why we ain't got nuttin' now?" James asked pointedly.

23   "Oh, it—"

24   The door opened and put an end to the kitchen yak. It was Poppa coming home from work. He came into the kitchen and brought all the cold with him. Poor Poppa, he looked so lost in the clothes he had on. A jacket and coat, sweaters on top of sweaters, two pairs of long johns, two pairs of pants, two pairs of socks, and a woolen cap. And under all that he was cold. His eyes were cold; his ears were red with pain. He took off his gloves and his fingers were stiff with cold.

25   *"Cómo está?"*[10] said Momma. "I will make you coffee."

26   Poppa said nothing. His eyes were running hot frozen tears. He worked his fingers and rubbed his ears, and the pain made him make faces. "Get me some snow, Piri," he said finally.

27   I ran to the window, opened it, and scraped all the snow on the sill into one big snowball and brought it to him. We all watched in frozen wonder as Poppa took that snow and rubbed it on his ears and hands.

28   "Gee, Pops, don't it hurt?" I asked.

29   *"Sí,* but it's good for it. It hurts a little first, but it's good for the frozen parts."

30   I wondered why.

31   "How was it today?" Momma asked.

32   "Cold. My God, ice cold."

33   *Gee,* I thought, *I'm sorry for you, Pops. You gotta suffer like this.*

34   "It was not always like this," my father said to the cold walls. "It's all the fault of the damn depression."

35   "Don't say 'damn,'" Momma said.

36   "Lola, I say 'damn' because that's what it is—*damn.*"

37   And Momma kept quiet. She knew it was "damn."

[7]poverty
[8]contracts
[9]grandparents
[10]How are you?

38   My father kept talking to the walls. Some of the words came out loud, others stayed inside. I caught the inside ones—the damn WPA, the damn depression, the damn home relief, the damn poorness, the damn cold, the damn crummy apartments, the damn look on his damn kids, living so damn damned and his not being able to do a damn thing about it.

39   And Momma looked at Poppa and at us and thought about her Puerto Rico and maybe being there where you didn't have to wear a lot of extra clothes and feel so full of damns, and how when she was a little girl all the green was wet from the *lluvias.*

40   And Poppa looking at Momma and us, thinking how did he get trapped and why did he love us so much that he dug in damn snow to give us a piece of chance? And why couldn't he make it from home, maybe, and keep running?

41   And Miriam, James, José, Paulie, and me just looking and thinking about snowballs and Puerto Rico and summertime in the street and whether we were gonna live like this forever and not know enough to be sorry for ourselves.

42   The kitchen all of a sudden felt warmer to me, like being all together made it like we wanted it to be. Poppa made it into the toilet and we could hear everything he did, and when he finished, the horsey gurgling of the flushed toilet told us he'd soon be out. I looked at the clock and it was time for "Jack Armstrong, the All-American Boy."

43   José, James, and I got some blankets and, like Indians, huddled around the radio digging the All-American Jack and his adventures, while Poppa ate dinner quietly. Poppa was funny about eating—like when he ate, nobody better bother him. When Poppa finished, he came into the living room and stood there looking at us. We smiled at him, and he stood there looking at us.

44   All of a sudden he yelled, "How many wanna play 'Major Bowes' Amateur Hour'?"

45   "Hoo-ray! Yeah, we wanna play," said José.

46   "Okay, first I'll make some taffy outta molasses, and the one who wins first prize gets first choice at the biggest piece, okay?"

47   "Yeah, hoo-ray, *chevere.*"

48   "Gee, Pops, you're great, I thought, *you're the swellest, the bestest Pops in the whole world, even though you don't understand us too good.*

49   When the candy was all ready, everybody went into the living room. Poppa came in with a broom and put an empty can over the stick. It became a microphone, just like on the radio.

50   "Pops, can I be Major Bowes?" I asked.

51   "Sure, Piri," and the floor was mine.

52   "Ladies and gentlemen," I announced, "tonight we present 'Major Bowes' Amateur Hour," and for our first number—"

53   "Wait a minute, son, let me get my ukelele," said Poppa. "We need music."

54   Everybody clapped their hands and Pops came back with his ukelele.

55   "The first con-tes-tant we got is Miss Miriam Thomas."

56   "Oh no, not me first, somebody else goes first," said Miriam, and she hid behind Momma.

57   "Let me! Let me!" said José.

58   Everybody clapped.

59   "What are you gonna sing, sir?" I asked.

60   "Tell the people his name," said Poppa.

61   "Oh yeah. Presenting Mr. José Thomas. And what are you gonna sing, sir?"

62   I handed José the broom with the can on top and sat back. He sang well and everybody clapped.

63   Everyone took a turn, and we all agreed that two-year-old Paulie's "gurgle, gurgle" was the best song, and Paulie got first choice at the candy. Everybody got candy and eats and thought how good it was to be together, and Moms thought that it was wonderful to have such a good time even if she wasn't in Puerto Rico where the grass was wet with *lluvia*. Poppa thought about how cold it was gonna be tomorrow, but then he remembered tomorrow was Sunday and he wouldn't have to work, and he said so and Momma said "*Sí*," and the talk got around to Christmas and how maybe things would get better.

64   The next day the Japanese bombed Pearl Harbor.

65   "My God," said Poppa. "We're at war."

66   "*Dios mío*," said Momma.

67   I turned to James. "Can you beat that," I said.

68   "Yeah," he nodded. "What's it mean?"

69   "What's it mean?" I said. "You gotta ask, dopey? It means a rumble is on, and a big one, too."

70   I wondered if the war was gonna make things worse than they were for us. But it didn't. A few weeks later Poppa got a job in an airplane factory. "How about that?" he said happily. "Things are looking up for us."

71   Things *were* looking up for us, but it had taken a damn war to do it. A lousy rumble had to get called so we could start to live better. I thought, *How do you figure this crap out?*

72   I couldn't figure it out, and after a while I stopped thinking about it. Life in the streets didn't change much. The bitter cold was followed by the sticky heat; I played stickball, marbles, and Johnny-on-the-Pony, copped girls' drawers and blew pot. War or peace—what difference did it really make?

Writing Log/Journal Assignment

Write a journal entry about activities your family used to do together or things you wish your family had done together. Where would these activities take place and under what conditions?

Individual and Collaborative Considerations

1. Why is Thomas' father having so much difficulty getting a job?
2. What do you find ironic about needing to be incredibly poor in order to get a government job digging ditches?
3. Explain the significance of Major Bowes' Amateur Hour. How did it help the family to *bond* during hard times?
4. On the Sunday following their Major Bowes' Amateur Hour, what happened? Why are the circumstances surrounding the ultimate employment of Thomas' father rather ironic?
5. Reflect on the entire story once again; exactly where is the "Puerto Rican Paradise"?

Writing Activities

1. Create an original thesis and argue how and why World War II provided employment in munitions plants for many people hurt by the depression. One direction you might take would be a comparative study of war and its needs in the 1940s in contrast to subsequent wars the United States was involved in. Did the Korean War, the Vietnam War, and the Gulf War help to strengthen the United States' economy? How? Why? Why not?
2. Do some research on business practices leading up to the stock market crash in 1929. Then write an essay analyzing what you perceive as the major sociological and economical reasons for the stock market crash and the ensuing depression. (Make sure you narrow your focus here; entire books have been written on this subject.)

❋

Good Country People

Flannery O'Connor

Flannery O'Connor wrote mostly tales about the southern part of the United States, and her novels and short stories frequently deal with grotesques. Her many novels include *Wise Blood* (1952) and *The Violent Bear It Away* (1960). Her collected short stories appeared as *A Good Man Is Hard to Find* (1955), *Everything That Rises Must Converge,* (1965), and *Complete Stories* (1971). In his essay "Flannery O'Connor: Satan Comes to Georgia," V. S. Pritchett wrote "the essence of Flannery O'Connor's vision is that she sees terror as a purification—unwanted, of course; it is never the sadomasochist's intended indulgence. The moment of purification may actually destroy; it will certainly show someone change" as vividly illustrated by Hulga and the Bible salesman in "Good Country People." O'Connor died of lupus, an incurable disease where the natural antibodies in the immune system attack the body itself.

Besides the neutral expression that she wore when she was alone, Mrs. Freeman had two others, forward and reverse, that she used for all her human dealings. Her forward expression was steady and driving like the advance of a heavy truck. Her eyes never swerved to left or right but turned as the story turned as if they followed a yellow line down the center of it. She seldom used the other expression because it was not often necessary for her to retract a statement, but when she did, her face came to a complete stop, there was an almost inperceptible movement of her black eyes, during which they seemed to be receding, and then the observer would see that Mrs. Freeman, though she might stand there as real as several grain sacks thrown on top of each other, was no longer there in spirit. As for getting anything across to her when this was the case, Mrs. Hopewell had given it up. She might talk her head off. Mrs. Freeman could never be brought to admit herself wrong on any point. She would stand there and if she could be brought to say anything, it was something like, "Well, I wouldn't of said it was and I wouldn't of said it wasn't," or letting her gaze range over the top kitchen shelf where there was an assortment of dusty bottles, she might remark, "I see you ain't ate many of them figs you put up last summer."

They carried on their most important business in the kitchen at breakfast. Every morning Mrs. Hopewell got up at seven o'clock and lit her gas heater and Joy's. Joy was her daughter, a large blonde girl who had an artificial leg. Mrs. Hopewell thought of her as a child though she was thirty-two years old and highly educated. Joy would get up while her mother was eating and lumber into the bathroom and slam the door, and before long, Mrs. Freeman would arrive at the back door. Joy would hear her mother call, "Come on in," and then they would talk for a while in low voices that were indistinguishable in the bathroom. By the time Joy came in, they had usually finished the weather report and were on one or the other of Mrs. Freeman's daughters, Glynese or Carramae, Joy called them Glycerin and Caramel. Glynese, a redhead, was eighteen and had many admirers; Carramae, a blonde, was only fifteen, but already married and pregnant. She could not keep anything in her stomach. Every morning Mrs. Freeman told Mrs. Hopewell how many times she had vomited since the last report.

Mrs. Hopewell liked to tell people that Glynese and Carramae were two of the finest girls she knew and that Mrs. Freeman was a *lady* and that she was never ashamed to take her anywhere or introduce her to anybody they might meet. Then she would tell how she had happened to hire the Freemans in the first place and how they were a godsend to her and how she had had them four years. The reason for her keeping them so long was that they were not trash. They were good country people. She had telephoned the man whose name they had given as a reference and he had told her that Mr. Freeman was a good farmer but that his wife was the nosiest woman ever to walk the earth. "She's got to be into everything," the man said. "If she don't get there before the dust settles, you can bet she's dead, that's all. She'll want to know all your business. I can stand him real good," he had said, "but me nor my wife neither could have stood that woman one more minute on this place." That had put Mrs. Hopewell off for a few days.

She had hired them in the end because there were no other applicants but she had made up her mind beforehand exactly how she would handle the woman. Since she was the type who had to be into everything, then, Mrs. Hopewell had decided, she would not only let her be into everything, she would *see to it* that she was into everything—she would give her the responsibility of everything, she would put her in charge. Mrs. Hopewell had no bad qualities of her own but she was able to use other people's in such a constructive way that she never felt the lack. She had hired the Freemans and she had kept them four years.

5   Nothing is perfect. This was one of Mrs. Hopewell's favorite sayings. Another was: that is life! And still another, the most important, was: well, other people have their opinions too. She would take these statements, usually at the table, in a tone of gentle insistence as if no one held them but her, and the large hulking Joy, whose constant outrage had obliterated every expression from her face, would stare just a little to the side of her, her eyes icy blue, with the look of someone who has achieved blindness by an act of will and means to keep it.

When Mrs. Hopewell said to Mrs. Freeman that life was like that, Mrs. Freeman would say, "I always said so myself." Nothing had been arrived at by anyone that had not first been arrived at by her. She was quicker than Mrs. Freeman. When Mrs. Hopewell said to her after they had been on the place a while, "You know, you're the wheel behind the wheel," and winked, Mrs. Freeman had said, "I know it. I've always been quick. It's some that are quicker than others."

"Everybody is different," Mrs. Hopewell said.

"Yes, most people is," Mrs. Freeman said.

"It takes all kinds to make the world."

10   "I always said it did myself."

The girl was used to this kind of dialogue for breakfast and more of it for dinner; sometimes they had it for supper too. When they had no guest they ate in the kitchen because that was easier. Mrs. Freeman always managed to arrive at some point during the meal and to watch them finish it. She would stand in the doorway if it were summer but in the winter she would stand with one elbow on top of the refrigerator and look down on them, or she would stand by the gas heater, lifting the back of her skirt slightly. Occasionally she would stand against the wall and roll her head from side to side. At no time was she in any hurry to leave. All this was very trying on Mrs.

Hopewell but she was a woman of great patience. She realized that nothing is perfect and that in the Freemans she had good country people and that if, in this day and age, you get good country people, you had better hang onto them.

She had had plenty of experience with trash. Before the Freemans she had averaged one tenant family a year. The wives of these farmers were not the kind you would want to be around you for very long. Mrs. Hopewell, who had divorced her husband long ago, needed someone to walk over the fields with her; and when Joy had to be impressed for these services, her remarks were usually so ugly and her face so glum that Mrs. Hopewell would say, "If you can't come pleasantly, I don't want you at all," to which the girl, standing square and rigid-shouldered with her neck thrust slightly forward, would reply, "If you want me, here I am—LIKE I AM."

Mrs. Hopewell excused this attitude because of the leg (which had been shot off in a hunting accident when Joy was ten). It was hard for Mrs. Hopewell to realize that her child was thirty-two now and that for more than twenty years she had had only one leg. She thought of her still as a child because it tore her heart to think instead of the poor stout girl in her thirties who had never danced a step or had any *normal* good times. Her name was really Joy but as soon as she was twenty-one and away from home, she had had it legally changed. Mrs. Hopewell was certain that she had thought and thought until she had hit upon the ugliest name in any language. Then she had gone and had the beautiful name, Joy, changed without telling her mother until after she had done it. Her legal name was Hulga.

When Mrs. Hopewell thought the name, Hulga, she thought of the broad blank hull of a battleship. She would not use it. She continued to call her Joy to which the girl responded but in a purely mechanical way.

15   Hulga had learned to tolerate Mrs. Freeman who saved her from taking walks with her mother. Even Glynese and Carramae were useful when they occupied attention that might otherwise have been directed at her. At first, she had thought she could not stand Mrs. Freeman for she had found that it was not possible to be rude to her. Mrs. Freeman would take on strange resentments and for days together she would be sullen but the source of her displeasure was always obscure; a direct attack, a positive leer, ugliness to her face—these never touched her. And without warning one day, she began calling her Hulga.

She did not call her that in front of Mrs. Hopewell who would have been incensed but when she and the girl happened to be out of the house together, she would say something and add the name Hulga to the end of it, and the big spectacled Joy-Hulga would scowl and redden as if her privacy had been intruded upon. She considered the name her personal affair. She had arrived at it first purely on the basis of its ugly sound and then the full genius of its fitness had struck her. She had a vision of the name working like the ugly sweating Vulcan who stayed in the furnace and to whom, presumably, the goddess had to come when called. She saw it as the name of her highest creative act. One of her major triumphs was that her mother had not been able to turn her dust into Joy, but the greater one was that she had been able to turn it herself into Hulga. However, Mrs. Freeman's relish for using the name only irritated her. It was as if Mrs. Freeman's beady steel-pointed eyes had penetrated far enough behind her face to reach some secret fact. Something about her seemed to fascinate Mrs. Freeman and then one day Hulga realized that it was the artificial leg. Mrs. Freeman had a special fondness for the details of secret infections, hidden deformities, assaults upon children. Of diseases, she preferred the lingering or incurable. Hulga had heard Mrs. Hopewell give her the details of the hunting accident, how the leg had been literally blasted off, how she had never lost consciousness. Mrs. Freeman could listen to it any time as if it had happened an hour ago.

When Hulga stumped into the kitchen in the morning (she could walk without making the awful noise but she made it—Mrs. Hopewell was certain—because it was ugly-sounding), she glanced at them and did not speak. Mrs. Hopewell would be in her red kimono with her hair tied around her head in rags. She would be sitting at the table, finishing her breakfast and Mrs. Freeman would be hanging by her elbow outward from the refrigerator, looking down at the table. Hulga always put her eggs on the stove to boil and then stood over them with her arms folded, and Mrs. Hopewell would look at her—a kind of indirect gaze divided between her and Mrs. Freeman—and would think that if she would only keep herself up a little, she wouldn't be so bad looking. There was nothing wrong with her face that a pleasant expression wouldn't help. Mrs. Hopewell said that people who looked on the bright side of things would be beautiful even if they were not.

Whenever she looked at Joy this way, she could not help but feel that it would have been better if the child had not taken the Ph.D. It had certainly not brought her out any and now that she had it, there was no more excuse for her to go to school again. Mrs. Hopewell thought it was nice for girls to go to school to have a good time but Joy had "gone through." Anyhow, she would not have been strong enough to go again. The doctors had told Mrs. Hopewell that with the best of care, Joy might see forty-five. She had a weak heart. Joy had made it plain that if it had not been for this condition, she would be far from these red hills and good country people. She would be in a university lecturing to people who knew what she was talking about. And Mrs. Hopewell could very well picture her there, looking like a scarecrow and lecturing to more of the same. Here she went about all day in a six-year-old skirt and a yellow sweat shirt with a faded cowboy on a horse embossed on it. She thought this was funny; Mrs. Hopewell thought it was idiotic and showed simply that she was still a child. She was brilliant but she didn't have a grain of sense. It seemed to Mrs. Hopewell that every year she grew less like other people and more like herself—bloated, rude, and squint-eyed. And she said such strange things! To her own mother she had said—without warning, without excuse, standing up in the middle of a meal with her face purple and her mouth half full—"Woman! do you ever look inside? Do you ever look inside and see what you are *not*? God!" she had cried sinking down again and staring at her plate, "Malebranche was right: we are not our own light. We are not our own light!" Mrs. Hopewell had no idea to this day what brought that on. She had only made the remark, hoping Joy would take it in, that a smile never hurt anyone.

The girl had taken the Ph.D. in philosophy and this left Mrs. Hopewell at a complete loss. You could say, "My daughter is a nurse," or "My daughter is a schoolteacher," or even, "My daughter is a chemical engineer." You could not say, "My daughter is a philospher." That was something that had ended with the Greeks and Romans. All day Joy sat on her neck in a deep chair, reading. Sometimes she went for walks but she didn't like dogs or cats or birds or flowers or nature or nice young men. She looked at nice young men as if she could smell their stupidity.

20   One day Mrs. Hopewell had picked up one of the books the girl had just put down and opening it at random, she read, "Science, on the other hand, has to assert its soberness and seriousness afresh and declare that it is concerned solely with what-is. Nothing—how can it be for science anything but a horror and a phantasm? If science is right, then one thing stands firm: science wishes to know nothing of nothing. Such is after all the strictly scientific approach to Nothing. We know it by wishing to know nothing of Nothing." These words had been underlined with a blue pencil and they worked on Mrs. Hopewell like some evil incantation in gibberish. She shut the book quickly and went out of the room as if she were having a chill.

This morning when the girl came in, Mrs. Freeman was on Carramae. "She thrown up four times after supper," she said, "and was up twice in the night after three o'clock. Yesterday she didn't do nothing but ramble in the bureau drawer. All she did. Stand up there and see what she could run up on."

"She's got to eat," Mrs. Hopewell muttered, sipping her coffee, while she watched Joy's back at the stove. She was wondering what the child had said to the Bible salesman. She could not imagine what kind of a conversation she could possibly have had with him.

He was a tall gaunt hatless youth who had called yesterday to sell them a Bible. He had appeared at the door, carrying a large black suitcase that weighted him so heavily on one side that he had to brace himself against the door facing. He seemed on the point of collapse but he said in a cheerful voice. "Good morning, Mrs. Cedars!" and set the suitcase down on the mat. He was not a bad looking young man though he had on a bright blue suit and yellow socks that were not pulled up far enough. He had prominent face bones and a streak of sticky-looking brown hair falling across his forehead.

"I'm Mrs. Hopewell," she said.

25   "Oh!" he said, pretending *to* look puzzled but with his eyes sparkling, "I saw it said 'The Cedars' on the mailbox so I thought you was Mrs. Cedars!" and he burst out in a pleasant laugh. He picked up the satchel and under

cover of a pant, he fell forward into her hall. It was rather as if the suitcase had moved first, jerking him after it. "Mrs. Hopewell!" he said and grabbed her hand. "I hope you are well!" and he laughed again and then all at once his face sobered completely. He paused and gave her a straight earnest look and said, "Lady, I've come to speak of serious things."

"Well, come in," she muttered, none too pleased because her dinner was almost ready. He came into the parlor and sat down on the edge of a straight chair and put the suitcase between his feet and glanced around the room as if he were sizing her up by it. Her silver gleamed on the two sideboards; she decided he had never been in a room as elegant as this.

"Mrs. Hopewell," he began, using her name in a way that sounded almost intimate, "I know you believe in Chrustian service."

"Well yes," she murmured.

"I know," he said and paused, looking very wise with his head cocked on one side, "that you're a good woman. Friends have told me."

30 Mrs. Hopewell never liked to be taken for a fool. "What are you selling?" she asked.

"Bibles," the young man said and his eye raced around the room before he added, "I see you have no family Bible in your parlor, I see that is the one lack you got!"

Mrs. Hopewell could not say, "My daughter is an atheist and won't let me keep the Bible in the parlor." She said, stiffening slightly, "I keep my Bible by my bedside." This was not the truth. It was in the attic somewhere.

"Lady," he said, "the word of God ought to be in the parlor."

"Well, I think that's a matter of taste," she began. "I think . . ."

35 "Lady," he said, "for a Chrustian, the word of God ought to be in every room in the house besides in his heart. I know you're a Chrustian because I can see it in every line of your face."

She stood up and said, "Well, young man, I don't want to buy a Bible and I smell my dinner burning."

He didn't get up. He began to twist his hands and looking down at them, he said softly, "Well lady, I'll tell you the truth—not many people want to buy one nowadays and besides, I know I'm real simple. I don't know how to say a thing but to say it. I'm just a country boy." He glanced up into her unfriendly face. "People like you don't like to fool with country people like me!"

"Why!" she cried, "good country people are the salt of the earth! Besides, we all have different ways of doing, it takes all kinds to make the world go 'round. That's life!"

"You said a mouthful," he said.

40 "Why, I think there aren't enough good country people in the world!" she said, stirred. "I think that's what's wrong with it!"

His face had brightened. "I didn't introduce myself," he said. "I'm Manley Pointer from out in the country around Willohobie, not even from a place, just from rear a place."

"You wait a minute," she said. "I have to see about my dinner." She went out to the kitchen and found Joy standing near the door where she had been listening.

"Get rid of the salt of the earth," she said, "and let's eat."

Mrs. Hopewell gave her a pained look and turned the heat down under the vegetables. "I can't be rude to anybody," she murmured and went back into the parlor.

45   He had opened the suitcase and was sitting with a Bible on each knee. "You might as well put those up," she told him. "I don't want one."

"I appreciate your honesty," he said. "You don't see any more real honest people unless you go way out in the country."

"I know," she said, "real genuine folks!" Through the crack in the door she heard a groan.

"I guess a lot of boys come telling you they're working their way through college," he said, "but I'm not going to tell you that. Somehow," he said, "I don't want to go to college. I want to devote my life to Chrustian service. See," he said, lowering his voice, "I got this heart condition. I may not live long. When you know it's something wrong with you and you may not live long, well then, lady . . ." He paused, with his mouth open, and stared at her.

He and Joy had the same condition! She knew that her eyes were filling with tears but she collected herself quickly and murmurered, "Won't you stay for dinner? We'd love to have you!" and was sorry the instant she heard herself say it.

50   "Yes mam," he said in an abashed voice, "I would sher love to do that!"

Joy had given him one look on being introduced to him and then throughout the meal had not glanced at him again. He had addressed several remarks to her which she had pretended not to hear. Mrs. Hopewell could not understand deliberate rudeness, although she lived with it, and she felt she had always to overflow with hospitality to make up for Joy's lack of courtesy. She urged him to talk about himself and he did. He said he was the seventh child of twelve and that his father had been crushed under a tree when he himself was eight years old. He had been crushed very badly, in fact, almost cut in two and was practically not recognizable. His mother had got along the best she could by hard working and she had always seen that her children went to Sunday School and that they read the Bible every evening. He was now nineteen years old and he had been selling Bibles for four months. In that time he had sold seventy-seven Bibles and had the promise of two more sales. He wanted to become a missionary because he thought that was the way you could do most for people. "He who losest his life shall find it," he said simply and he was so sincere, so genuine and earnest that Mrs. Hopewell would not for the world have smiled. He prevented his peas from sliding onto the table by blocking them with a piece of bread which he later cleaned his plate with. She could see Joy observing sidewise how he handled his knife and fork and she saw too that every few minutes, the boy would dart a keen appraising glance at the girl as if he were trying to attract her attention.

After dinner Joy cleared the dishes off the table and disappeared and Mrs. Hopewell was left to talk with him. He told her again about his childhood and his father's accident and about various things that had happened to him. Every five minutes or so she would stifle a yawn. He sat for two hours until finally she told him she must go because she had an appointment in town. He packed his Bibles and thanked her and prepared to leave, but in the doorway he stopped and wrung her hand and said that not on any of his trips had he met a lady as nice as her and he asked if he could come again. She had said she would always be happy to see him.

Joy had been standing in the road, apparently looking at something in the distance, when he came down the steps toward her, bent to the side with his heavy valise. He stopped where she was standing and confronted her directly. Mrs. Hopewell could not hear what he said but she trembled to think what Joy would say to him. She could see that after a minute Joy said something and that then the boy began to speak again, making an excited gesture with his free hand. After a minute Joy said something else at which the boy began to speak once more. Then to her amazement, Mrs. Hopewell saw the two of them walk off together, toward the gate. Joy had walked all the way to the gate with him and Mrs. Hopewell could not imagine what they had said to each other, and she had not yet dared to ask.

Mrs. Freeman was insisting upon her attention. She had moved from the refrigerator to the heater so that Mrs. Hopewell had to turn and face her in order to seem to be listening. "Glynese gone out with Harvey Hill again last night," she said. "She had this sty."

55 "Hill," Mrs. Hopewell said absently, "is that the one who works in the garage?"

"Nome, he's the one that goes to chiropractor school," Mrs. Freeman said. "She had this sty. Been had it two days. So she says when he brought her in the other night he says, 'Lemme get rid of that sty for you,' and she says, 'How?' and he says, 'You just lay your self down acrost the seat of that car and I'll show you.' So she done it and he popped her neck. Kept on a-popping it several times until she made him quit. This morning," Mrs. Freeman said, "she aint' got no sty. She ain't got no traces of a sty."

"I never heard of that before," Mrs. Hopewell said.

"He ast her to marry him before the Ordinary," Mrs. Freeman went on, "and she told him she wasn't going to be married in no *office*."

"Well, Glynese is a fine girl," Mrs. Hopewell said. "Glynese and Carramae are both fine girls."

60 "Carramae said when her and Lyman was married Lyman said it sure felt sacred to him. She said he wouldn't take five hundred dollars for being married by a preacher."

"How much would he take?" the girl asked from the stove.

"He said he wouldn't take five hundred dollars," Mrs. Freeman repeated.

"Well we all have work to do," Mrs. Hopewell said.

"Lyman said it just felt more sacred to him," Mrs. Freeman said. "The doctor wants Carramae to eat prunes. Says instead of medicine. Says them cramps is coming from pressure. You know where I think it is?"

65   "She'll be better in a few weeks," Mrs. Hopewell said.

"In the tube," Mrs. Freeman said. "Else she wouldn't be as sick as she is." Hulga had cracked her two eggs into a saucer and was bringing them to the table along with a cup of coffee that she had filled too full. She sat down carefully and began to eat, meaning to keep Mrs. Freeman there by questions if for any reason she showed an inclination to leave. She could perceive her mother's eye on her. The first round-about question would be about the Bible salesman and she did not wish to bring it on. "How did he pop her neck?" she asked.

Mrs. Freeman went into a description of how he had popped her neck. She said he owned a '55 Mercury but that Glynese said she would rather marry a man with only a '36 Plymouth who would be married by a preacher. The girl asked what if he had a '32 Plymouth and Mrs. Freeman said what Glynese had said was a '36 Plymouth.

Mrs. Hopewell said there were not many girls with Glynese's common sense. She said what she admired in those girls was their common sense. She said that reminded her that they had had a nice visitor yesterday, a young man selling Bibles. "Lord," she said, "he bored me to death but he was so sincere and genuine I couldn't be rude to him. He was just good country people, you know," she said, "—just the salt of the earth."

"I seen him walk up," Mrs. Freeman said, "and then later—I seen him walk off," and Hulga could feel the slight shift in her voice, the slight insinuation, that he had not walked off alone, had he? Her face remained expressionless but the color rose into her neck and she seemed to swallow it down with the next spoonful of egg. Mrs. Freeman was looking at her as if they had a secret together.

70   "Well, it takes all kinds of people to make the world go 'round," Mrs. Hopewell said. "It's very good we aren't all like."

"Some people are more alike than others," Mrs. Freeman said.

Hulga got up and stumped, with about twice the noise that was necessary, into her room and locked the door. She was to meet the Bible salesman at ten o'clock at the gate. She had thought about it half the night. She had started thinking of it as a great joke and then she had begun to see profound implications in it. She had lain in bed imagining dialogues for them that were insane on the surface but that reached below to depths that no Bible salesman would be aware of. Their conversation yesterday had been of this kind.

He had stopped in front of her and had simply stood there. His face was bony and sweaty and bright, with a little pointed nose in the center of it, and his look was different from what it had been at the dinner table. He was gazing at her with open curiosity, with fascination, like a child watching a new fantastic animal at the zoo, and he was breathing as if he had run a great distance to reach her. His gaze seemed somehow familiar but she could

not think where she had been regarded with it before. For almost a minute
he didn't say anything. Then on what seemed an insuck of breath, he whispered, "You ever ate a chicken that was two days old?"

The girl looked at him stonily. He might have just put this question up
for consideration at the meeting of a philosophical association. "Yes," she
presently replied as if she had considered it from all angles.

75   "It must have been mighty small!" he said triumphantly and shook all
over with little nervous giggles, getting very red in the face, and subsiding
finally into his gaze of complete admiration, while the girl's expression remained exactly the same.

"How old are you?" he asked softly.

She waited some time before she answered. Then in a flat voice she said,
"Seventeen."

His smiles came in succession like waves braking on the surface of a little
lake. "I see you got a wooden leg," he said. "I think you're brave. I think
you're real sweet."

The girl stood blank and solid and silent.

80   "Walk to the gate with me," he said. "You're a brave sweet little thing
and I liked you the minute I seen you walk in the door."

Hulga began to move forward.

"What's your name?" he asked, smiling down on the top of her head.

"Hulga," she said.

"Hulga," he murmured, "Hulga. Hulga. I never heard of anybody name
Hulga before. You're shy, aren't you, Hulga?" he asked.

85   She nodded, watching his large red hand on the handle of the giant valise.

"I like girls that wear glasses," he said. "I think a lot. I'm not like these
people that a serious thought don't ever enter their heads. It's because I
may die."

"I may die too," she said suddenly and looked up at him. His eyes were
very small and brown, glittering feverishly.

"Listen," he said, "don't you think some people was meant to meet on
account of what all they got in common and all? Like they both think serious
thoughts and all?" He shifted the valise to his other hand so that the hand
nearest her was free. He caught hold of her elbow and shook it a little. "I
don't work on Saturday," he said. "I like to walk in the woods and see what
Mother Nature is wearing. O'er the hills and far away. Pic-nics and things.
Couldn't we go on a pic-nic tomorrow? Say yes, Hulga," he said and gave
her a dying look as if he felt his insides about to drop out of him. He had
even seemed to sway slightly toward her.

During the night she had imagined that she seduced him. She imagined
that the two of them walked on the place until they came to the storage barn
beyond the two back fields and there, she imagined, that things came to such
a pass that she very easily seduced him and that then, of course, she had to
recken with his remorse. True genius can get an idea across even to an inferior mind. She imagined that she took his remorse in hand and changed it

into a deeper understanding of life. She took all his shame away and turned it into something useful.

90   She set off for the gate at exactly ten o'clock, escaping without drawing Mrs. Hopewell's attention. She didn't take anything to eat, forgetting that food is usually taken on a picnic. She wore a pair of slacks and a dirty white shirt, and as an afterthought, she had put some Vapex on the collar of it since she did not own any perfume. When she reached the gate no one was there.

She looked up and down the empty highway and had the furious feeling that she had been tricked, that he had only meant to make her walk to the gate after the idea of him. Then suddenly he stood up, very tall, from behind a bush on the opposite embankment. Smiling, he lifted his hat which was new and wide-brimmed. He had not worn it yesterday and she wondered if he had bought it for the occasion. It was toast-colored with a red and white band around it and was slightly too large for him. He stepped from behind the bush still carrying the black valise. He had on the same suit and the same yellow socks sucked down in his shoes from walking. He crossed the highway and said, "I knew you'd come!"

The girl wondered acidly how he had known this. She pointed to the valise and asked, "Why did you bring your Bibles?"

He took her elbow, smiling down on her as if he could not stop. "You can never tell when you'll need the word of God, Hulga," he said. She had a moment in which she doubted that this was actually happening and then they began to climb the embankment. They went down into the pasture toward the woods. The boy walked lightly by her side, bouncing on his toes. The valise did not seem to be heavy today; he even swung it. They crossed half the pasture without saying anything and then, putting his hand easily on the small of her back, he asked softly, "Where does your wooden leg join on?"

She turned an ugly red and glared at him and for an instant the boy looked abashed. "I didn't mean you no harm," he said. "I only meant you're so brave and all. I guess God takes care of you."

95   "No," she said, looking forward and walking fast, "I don't even believe in God."

At this he stopped and whistled. "No!" he exclaimed as if he were too astonished to say anything else.

She walked on and in a second he was bouncing at her side, fanning with his hat. "That's very unusual for a girl," he remarked, watching her out of the corner of his eye. When they reached the edge of the wood, he put his hand on her back again and drew her against him without a word and kissed her heavily.

The kiss, which had more pressure than feeling behind it, produced that extra surge of adrenaline in the girl that enables one to carry a packed trunk out of burning house, but in her, the power went at once to the brain. Even before he released her, her mind, clear and detached and ironic anyway, was regarding him from a great distance, with amusement but with pity. She had never been kissed before and she was pleased to discover that it was an unexceptional experience and all a matter of the mind's control. Some people might enjoy drain water if they were told it was vodka. When the boy, looking expectant but uncertain, pushed her gently away, she turned and walked on, saying nothing as if such business, for her, were common enough.

He came along panting at her side, trying to help her when he saw a root that she might trip over. He caught and held back the long swaying blades of thorn vine until she had passed beyond them. She led the way and he came breathing heavily behind her. Then they came out on a sunlit hillside, sloping softly into another one a little smaller. Beyond, they could see the rusted top of the old barn where the extra hay was stored.

100   The hill was sprinkled with small pink weeds. "Then you ain't saved?" he asked suddenly, stopping.

The girl smiled. It was the first time she had smiled at him at all. "In my economy," she said, "I'm saved and you are damned but I told you I didn't believe in God."

Nothing seemed to destroy the boy's look of admiration. He gazed at her now as if the fantastic animal at the zoo had put its paw through the bars and given him a loving poke. She thought he looked as if he wanted to kill her again and she walked on before he had the chance.

"Ain't there somewheres we can sit down sometime?" he murmured, his voice softening toward the end of the sentence.

"In that barn," she said.

105   They made for it rapidly as if it might slide away like a train. It was a large two-story barn, cool and dark inside. The boy pointed up the ladder that led into the loft and said, "It's too bad we can't go up there."

"Why can't we?" she asked.

"Yer leg," he said reverently.

The girl gave him a contemptuous look and putting both hands on the ladder, she climbed it while he stood below, apparently awestruck. She pulled herself expertly through the opening and then looked down at him and said, "Well, come on if you're coming," and he began to climb the ladder, awkwardly bringing the suitcase with him.

"We won't need the Bible," she observed.

110   "You never can tell," he said, panting. After he had got into the loft, he was a few seconds catching his breath. She had sat down in a pile of straw. A wide sheath of sunlight, filled with dust particles, slanted over her. She lay back against a bale, her face turned away, looking out the front opening of the barn where hay was thrown from a wagon into the loft. The two pink-speckled hillsides lay back against a dark ridge of woods. The sky was cloudless and cold blue. The boy dropped down by her side and put one arm under her and the other over her and began methodically kissing her face, making little noises like a fish. He did not remove his hat but it was pushed far enough back not to interfere. When her glasses got in his way, he took them off of her and slipped them into his pocket.

The girl at first did not return any of the kisses but presently she began to and after she had put several on his cheek, she reached his lips and remained there, kissing him again and again as if she were trying to draw all the breath out of him. His breath was clear and sweet like a child's and the kisses were sticky like a child's. He mumbled about loving her and about knowing when he first seen her that he loved her, but the mumbling was like the sleepy fretting of a child being put to sleep by his mother. Her mind, throughout this, never stopped or lost itself for a second to her feelings. "You aint' said you loved me none," he whispered finally, pulling back from her, "You got to say that."

She looked away from him off into the hollow sky and then down at a black ridge and then down farther into what appeared to be two green swelling lakes. She didn't realize he had taken her glasses but this landscape could not seem exceptional to her for she seldom paid any close attention to her surroundings.

"You got to say it," he repeated. "You got to say you love me."

She was always careful how she committed herself. "In a sense," she began, "if you use the word loosely, you might say that. But it's not a word I use. I don't have illusions. I'm one of those people who see *through* to nothing."

115 The boy was frowning. "You got to say it. I said it and you got to say it," he said.

The girl looked at him almost tenderly. "You poor baby," she murmured. "It's just as well you don't understand," and she pulled him by the neck, face-down, against her. "We are all damned," she said, "but some of us have taken off our blindfolds and see that there's nothing to see. It's a kind of salvation."

The boy's astonished eyes looked blankly through the ends of her hair. "Okay," he almost whined, "but do you love me or don'tcher?"

"Yes," she said and added, "in a sense. But I must tell you something. There mustn't be anything dishonest between us." She lifted his head and looked him in the eye. "I am thirty years old," she said. "I have a number of degrees."

The boy's look was irritated but dogged. "I don't care," he said. "I don't care a thing what all you done. I just want to know if you love me or don'tcher?" and he caught her to him and wildly planted her face with kisses until she said, "Yes, yes."

120 "Okay then," he said, letting her go. "Prove it."

She smiled, looking dreamily out on the shifty landscape. She had seduced him without even making up her mind to try. "How?" she asked, feeling that he should be delayed a little.

He leaned over and put his lips to her ear. "Show me where your wooden leg joins on," he whispered.

The girl uttered a sharp little cry and her face instantly drained of color. The obscenity of the suggestion was not what shocked her. As a child she had sometimes been subject to feelings of shame but education had removed the last traces of that as a good surgeon scrapes for cancer; she would no more have felt it over what he was asking than she would have believed in his Bible. But she was as sensitive about the artificial leg as a peacock about his tail. No one ever touched it but her. She took care of it as someone else would his soul, in private and almost with her own eyes turned away. "No," she said.

"I known it," he muttered, sitting up. "You're just playing me for a sucker."

125   "Oh no no!" she cried. "It joins on at the knee. Only at the knee. Why do you want to see it?"

The boy gave her a long penetrating look. "Because," he said, "it's what makes you different. You ain't like anybody else."

She sat staring at him. There was nothing about her face or her round freezing-blue eyes to indicate that this had moved her; but she felt as if her heart had stopped and left her mind to pump her blood. She decided that for the first time in her life she was face to face with real innocence. This boy, with an instinct that came from beyond wisdom, had touched the truth about her. When after a minute, she said in a hoarse high voice, "All right," it was like surrendering to him completely. It was like losing her own life and finding it again, miraculously, in his.

Very gently he began to roll the slack leg up. The artificial limb, in a white sock and brown flat shoe, was bound in a heavy material like canvas and ended in an ugly jointure where it was attached to the stump. The boy's face and his voice were entirely reverent as he uncovered it and said, "Now show me how to take it off and on."

She took it off for him and put it back on again and then he took it off himself, handling it as tenderly as if it were a real one. "See!" he said with a delighted child's face. "Now I can do it myself!"

130   "Put it back on," she said. She was thinking that she would run away with him and that every night he would take the leg off and every morning put it back on again. "Put it back on," she said.

"Not yet," he murmured, setting it on its foot out of her reach. "Leave it off for a while. You got me instead."

She gave a little cry of alarm but he pushed her down and began to kiss her again. Without the leg she felt entirely dependent on him. Her brain seemed to have stopped thinking altogether and to be about some other function that it was not very good at. Different expressions raced back and forth over her face. Every now and then the boy, his eyes like two steel spikes, would glance behind him where the leg stood. Finally she pushed him off and said, "Put it back on me now."

"Wait," he said. He leaned the other way and pulled the valise toward him and opened it. It had a pale blue spotted lining and there were only two Bibles in it. He took one of these out and opened the cover of it. It was hollow and contained a pocket flask of whiskey, a pack of cards, and a small blue box with printing on it. He laid these out in front of her one at a time in an evenly-spaced row, like one presenting offerings at the shrine of a goddess. He put the blue box in her hand. THIS PRODUCT TO BE USED ONLY FOR THE PREVENTION OF DISEASE, she read, and dropped it. The boy was unscrewing the top of the flask. He stopped and pointed, with a smile, to the deck of cards. It was not an ordinary deck but one with an obscene picture on the back of each card. "Take a swig," he said, offering her the bottle first. He held it in front of her, but like one mesmerized, she did not move.

Her voice when she spoke had an almost pleading sound. "Aren't you," she murmured, "aren't you just good country people?"

135   The boy cocked his head. He looked as if he were just beginning to understand that she might be trying to insult him. "Yeah," he said, curling his lip slightly, "but it ain't held me back none. I'm as good as you any day in the week."

"Give me my leg," she said.

He pushed it farther away with his foot. "Come on now, let's begin to have us a good time," he said coaxingly. "We ain't got to know one another good yet."

"Give me my leg!" she screamed and tried to lunge for it but he pushed her down easily.

"What's the matter with you all of a sudden?" he asked, frowning as he screwed the top on the flask and put it quickly back inside the Bible. "You just a while ago said you didn't believe in nothing. I thought you was some girl!"

140   Her face was almost purple. "You're a Christian!" she hissed. "You're a fine Christian! You're just like them all—say one thing and do another. You're a perfect Christian, you're . . ."

The boy's mouth was set angrily. "I hope you don't think," he said in a lofty indignant tone, "that I believe in that crap! I may sell Bibles but I know which end is up and I wasn't born yesterday and I know where I'm going!"

"Give me my leg!" she screeched. He jumped up so quickly that she barely saw him sweep the cards and the blue box into the Bible and throw the Bible into the valise. She saw him grab the leg and then she saw it for an instant slanted forlornly across the inside of the suitcase with a Bible at either side of its opposite ends. He slammed the lid shut and snatched up the valise and swung it down the hole and then stepped through himself.

When all of him had passed but his head, he turned and regarded her with a look that no longer had any admiration in it. "I've gotten a lot of interesting things," he said. "One time I got a woman's glass eye this way. And you needn't to think you'll catch me because Pointer ain't really my name. I use a different name at every house I call at and don't stay nowhere long. And I'll tell you another thing, Hulga," he said, using the name as if he didn't think much of it, "you ain't so smart. I been believing in nothing ever since I was born!" and then the toast-colored hat disappeared down the hole and the girl was left, sitting on the straw in the dusty sunlight. When she turned her churning face toward the opening, she saw his blue figure struggling successfully over the green speckled lake.

Mrs. Hopewell and Mrs. Freeman, who were in the back pasture, digging up onions, saw him emerge a little later from the woods and head across the meadow toward the highway. "Why, that looks like that nice dull young man that tried to sell me a Bible yesterday," Mrs. Hopewell said, squinting. "He must have been selling them to the Negroes back in there. He was so simple," he said, "but I guess the world would be better off if we were all that simple."

145 Mrs. Freeman's gaze drove forward and just touched him before he disappeared under the hill. Then she returned her attention to the evil-smelling onion shoot she was lifting from the ground. "Some can't be that simple," she said. "I know I never could."

Writing Log/Journal Assignment

In your journal or writing log, examine any programmed notions you might have about people who come from a particular part of the United States. You might, for instance, identify and define examples of *good city people, trustworthy farmers, typical fishermen,* and so on.

Individual and Collaborative Considerations

1. List some of Mrs. Hopewell's sayings. Why are they so important to her and how do they give us insight into her character?
2. How highly educated is Hulga? Why is she living at home in the country instead of using her education and securing a job teaching at a college in a city?
3. What is Hulga's interest in the Bible salesman?
4. What is the role of deception and role reversals in O'Connor's story?
5. At the end of the story Mrs. Hopewell comments that "He [the Bible salesman] was so simple" and that "the world would be better off if we were all that simple." Explain the irony and insight into "good country people" of Mrs. Freeman's reply, "Some can't be that simple . . . I know I never could." Remember, like the Bible salesman, Mrs. Freeman and her daughters are also "good country people" according to Mrs. Hopewell.

Writing Activities

1. Hulga draws unnecessary notice to her false leg by stomping around the house with it. Write an essay in which you explain the many ways people draw attention to themselves in society and the possible reasons for doing so. In Hulga's case, for instance, why would she want to call undue attention to her imperfection—her false leg?

2. Write an essay demonstrating how our perception of people, places, events, and objects can be greatly influenced by our immediate environment. You may want to allude to "Good Country People" in your essay to establish common ground with your readers (assume your audience has read the story) before moving on to your original supporting materials.

✳

Pontoon Boat

Garrison Keillor

Born in 1942, author and humorist Garrison Keillor began his successful writing and broadcasting career after graduating from the University of Minnesota. Keillor received nationwide attention for his radio program, *Prairie Home Companion,* broadcast every Saturday evening on National Public Radio. His printed works include *Happy to Be Here* (1982), *Lake Wobegon Days* (1985), *Leaving Home: A Collection of Lake Wobegon Stories* (1987), *We Are Still Married* (1989), and *WLT: A Radio Romance* (1992). Keillor offers audiences a rarefied style of homespun humor, frequently distinguished by tongue-in-cheek remarks, understatement, and irony.

It has been a quiet week in Lake Wobegon. It's been hot and dry, and everyone was extremely touchy, so when you walked in the Chatterbox for lunch and sat at the counter and got your cup of coffee and looked at the menu and finally ordered what you have every day anyway, a bowl of chili and a grilled cheese, and turned to Ed on your left and were set to say something, you hesitated. Even to say, "Boy, she's a hot one," might start something. So you make it a question and ask, "Say, I wonder how hot she's supposed to get today anyway?" And he says, "How the hell should I know? What? You think I sit listening to the damn radio all morning?"

That's how hot it was. So hot you didn't dare ask, and no rain, but muggy so the dust sticks to your face. It doesn't seem fair for the Midwest, the nation's icebox, to be the nation's oven too. It's like living in the Arctic but spending your summers at Death Valley. Even at the Sidetrack Tap, where men sit in air-cooled comfort in dim light and medicate themselves against anger and bitterness, they were touchy too.

It's so good to step out of a hot dirty day into a cool tavern and hold a bottle of Wendy's but two or three Wendy's later, it's so awful to go back out. After an hour in the dark, the sunlight hits you like a two-by-four, and the beer in your head heats up, the yeast grows, the brain rises. When a man on a hot day who's enjoyed an hour of fellowship gets up to leave, he knows he has dug a hole for himself.

The portly gent in the cool dark behind the bar, Wally, recently bought a boat, a twenty-six foot pontoon boat with a green-striped canopy, a thirty-six horsepower outboard, four lawn chairs, and a barbecue grill, which arrived Sunday by flatbed truck and was put in the water off Art's fishing dock. It was christened the *Agnes D.* after his mother. He and Evelyn took a maiden voyage in the twilight. It was cool out there under the canopy, with a nice breeze off the lake. Wally stood at the tiny wheel amidships, wearing a white skipper cap. His ship was only a piece of plywood, twenty-six by twelve, on two steel pontoons, but to him, standing, steering it, it was majestic. He wanted to hang lights on it from bow to stern, on port (left) and starboard (right) sides. He gunned it. "Not so fast," Evelyn said, "you don't have to drive the boat so fast."

5   "My love," he said, "you do not *drive* a boat. You drive *a car*. You *sail* a boat. And when you *sail* a boat, you need to find out what she's got under the hood." She'd never heard him talk like that.

He didn't talk like that in the Sidetrack—he didn't want anyone to think he was showing off—so when guys asked what was this they heard about him buying a boat, Wally frowned, he shook his head, he said, "Yeah, I don't know. I got a deal on it from a guy I know, but I tell you, it's a headache. Insurance and the upkeep and worrying about the thing—did you know that if some fellows stole my boat to commit crimes with, if they got hurt I could be liable? It's true! But you and the wife oughta come out with us some evening. Wouldn't that be something? We could grill up some steaks, have a beer. . . ."

He invited about a hundred couples aboard the *Agnes D.* in three days. An occupational hazard of being a tavern owner is that you have an awful lot of extremely close friends, men who've become very intimate and told you confidential things they wouldn't even tell their close friends, so that makes you their closest friend, although you barely know their name.

When he invited Mayor Clint Bunsen to come for a cruise, Clint said, "You know what you ought to do? There's a bunch of Lutheran ministers coming through on a tour Friday, we oughta give them a boat ride so they get a nice look at town."

How and why twenty-four Lutheran ministers were touring rural Minnesota is a long digression that I'd rather skip, dear reader. People are so skeptical, they force a storyteller to spend too much time on the details and not enough on the moral, so I'll just say that the five-day tour, "Meeting the Pastoral Needs of Rural America," was organized by an old seminary pal of Pastor Ingqvist's, the Reverend J. Peter Larson, who called him in April and said, "You know what our problem is, we're so doggone theological we can't see past the principles to the people, and the people are hurting, so I'm organizing a tour of a hundred ministers to go and look at rural problems and I want to visit Lake Wobegon in mid-July."

10   Fine, said David Ingqvist, who forgot about it until, last Sunday, his wife, Judy, said, "What's this on the calendar for Friday? 'Tour / Larson / here'?"

"Oh that," he said. "Well," he said, "I was meaning to discuss that with you," he said. "It's some Luteran ministers coming through town and I thought we could have them over for a picnic supper in the backyard."

"How many?" she said.

"I don't know exactly, but certainly no more than a hundred."

"Well, I think your best bet would be wieners. You probably just want to boil them. Maybe you could get someone to make you some potato salad."

15   Rural problems was what Pete wanted to see, but you can't take a crowd of ministers around to someone's house and point to him and say, "There's one. He's in trouble. I don't give him long. No sir. He's headed down the chute." Clint Bunsen thought it was strange. If a minister visits, you hide your problems, and shine up your children and put them through their paces. And you talk about other people's problems. But he agreed to talk to them about municipal affairs, and then he got the brilliant idea of the boat trip. When they arrived, tired and hot and dusty at five o'clock on Thursday, that was the plan: boat trip, speech on board and roasted wienies, and fellowship at the Ingqvists' (four gallons of wine, $4.39 apiece).

They got off the bus and Clint thought: *Ministers.* Men in their forties mostly, a little thick around the middle, thin on top, puffy hair around the ears, some fish medallions, turtleneck pullovers, earth tones. Hush Puppies; but more than dress, what set them apart was the ministerial eagerness, more eye contact than you were really looking for, a longer handshake, and a little more affirmation than you needed. "Good to see you, glad you could be here, nice of you to come, we're very honored," they said to him, although they were guests and he was the host.

"Down this way! Let's go! Down to the lake!" Pastor Ingqvist wore yellow Bermuda shorts and sunglasses. "It's been an incredible trip," Pete said. "Really amazing." They strolled down from Bunsen Motors, down the alley behind Ralph's, and along the path between Mrs. Mueller's yard and Elmer and Myrtle's. Myrtle's cat lay in a limb of an apple tree, its long gray tail hung down and twitched at the tip. Mrs. Mueller's cat sat in the shade of an old green lawn chair, its gaze set on the birdbath. "I tell you," Pete said, "I really feel we've gotten an affirmation of Midwestern small-town values as something that's tremendously viable in people's lives. But there's a dichotomy between the values and the politics that is really critical at this point. It's a fascinating subject."

Wally had gone all out. The *Agnes D.* was hung with two strings of Christmas lights, the kind that twinkle on and off. He had laid in five cases of pop, a keg of beer, and enough hamburger patties to feed the freshman class. The twenty-four men trooped up the plank and on deck, and she sank lower and lower in the water. Clint was the last aboard. He thought, "I'm not sure about this." But how do you tell some ministers to get off? The Church invites us all, the concept of "That's enough for now" isn't part of Lutheran teaching, so Clint stepped lightly aboard, trying not to put all his weight on it, and felt water slosh in his shoe.

The boat was riding low, no doubt about it. Wally thought, "I'm not sure about this," but he didn't want to sound worried like an amateur. A true sailor would be hearty. He yelled, "Cast off the bow line!," and Pastor Ingqvist leaned over to cast off, and the *Agnes D.* tilted to starboard. Wally gunned the engine, she righted herself, and off they went, at about four mph, with little waves lapping at the sides, so low in the water that to people on shore it looked like a miracle.

20   One problem with twenty-four men on a twenty-six-foot boat is that in the Midwest we need to stand about twenty-eight inches or more from each other, otherwise we get headaches. With the steering post, lawn chairs, motor, canopy, pop cases, barbecue grill, and card table, there wasn't room. Men herded forward and to the sides; there was clearing of throats and "Excuse me"s as twenty-four men edged away from each other and into each other, and that was before the coals got hot.

Wally poured half a can of lighter fluid on them and lit them just before departure. As the heat rose, ministers standing near the grill edged away toward the bow. There were too many Lutherans squeezed into too small a space, and the barbecue shooting up sparks and men ducking and edging—Wally thought, "If we'd just get up more speed I'll bet that bow would come up a little."

Pete was saying to Pastor Ingqvist, "Dave, I don't have the answers, but I think that all of us will come out of this with a feeling of unity of concern," but David was feeling his own concern: they were sinking and he didn't know how to mention it in a way that wouldn't seem negative. Wally at the wheel, calling, "Steady as she goes!," and twenty-four nervous ministers in earth tones and suede shoes edging, shifting, herding, trying to be good listeners and share concerns as the fire got hotter and hotter, driving them toward the bow, which was sinking, but all of them trying to keep a good positive attitude, and then Dave said, "Somebody put out the fire! We're sinking!"

Five men took their beer cups and leaned over to dip up water and the *Agnes D.* tipped. The left front pontoon went under and the *Agnes D.* stopped dead in the water and turned to port. They had reached the edge of the laws of physics. They lurched to the starboard side and both pontoons went under and there—in full view of town—the boat pitched forward and dumped some ballast: eight Lutheran ministers in full informal garb took their step for total immersion.

As the boat sank, they slipped over the edge to give their lives for Christ, but in only five feet of water. It's been a hot dry summer.

25   Eight went over, and then the *Agnes D.* came up again, a little, and the survivors grabbed to hold on, but then the grill tipped over and they turned

to see hundreds of burning coals sliding down the deck toward them—the Book of Revelation come to life!—and they plunged overboard like a load of hay bales. The *Agnes D.*'s bow rose, and Wally turned to Clint hanging on to the canopy and said, "I think I got her under control now."

The ministers stood perfectly still in the water and didn't say much at all. Five feet of water, and some of them not six feet tall, so their faces were upraised to the bright blue sky. They didn't dare walk for fear of dropoffs, their clothes were to heavy to swim in, and they couldn't call for help because their voices were too deep and mellow. So they stood, faces upturned, in prayerful apprehension. Twenty-four ministers standing up to their smiles in water, chins up, trying to understand this experience and its deeper meaning.

Clint's little nephew Brian waded out to them. "It's not deep this way," he said. He stood about fifteen feet away, a little boy up to his waist. They followed him out single file, twenty-four dripping clergy, their clothes hanging heavy as millstones, but still looking interested, concerned, eager to get on to the next item on the agenda. It was fellowship at Pastor Ingqvist's home, but he was still aboard the *Agnes D.* with Wally and Clint, so they sat down in a circle under the trees to await further directions.

Writing Log/Journal Assignment

Have you ever been particularly proud of a possession? If so, what was it? If not, what *would be* your most cherished possession? Write a journal entry explaining how you do or would "show off" your prized possession to others.

Individual and Collaborative Considerations

1. Comment on the conversational diction and tone of Keillor's piece.
2. How many couples did Wally invite to his pontoon boat in three days? What might this reveal about his character?
3. Read sections of Keillor's piece out loud in small groups. How tightly is the entire piece structured? That is, how easy is it to move from one point to the next with perfect clarity? What devices add cohesion to his tale?
4. In what way does Keillor's use of understatement add to the home-spun flavor of this story?
5. What makes Keillor's story amusing?

Writing Activities

1. Write an essay describing an event allowed to reach the point of absurdity merely because those involved were unwilling to admit their limitations

(lack of knowledge, lack of skill, lack of experience). To achieve a calm, relaxed tone—perhaps to mask your uncertainty about the situation—use understatement as Keillor did in "Pontoon Boat."

2. Construct a paper satirizing the folly of people from your hometown or present residence. Employ a conversational tone in your paper, as if you were organizing material for an oral presentation rather than an essay.

※

Subway Wind

Claude McKay

Claude McKay (1889–1948) was the child of peasant farmers in Jamaica. His first two volumes of poetry, *Songs of Jamaica* (1912) and *Constab Ballads* (1912), were published before he moved to the United States. After attending college in Alabama and Kansas, he went north and settled in New York City where he wrote poetry. McKay became one of the most radical African American writers of the Harlem Renaissance, and he constantly fought accepted norms in society that any one group of individuals could "confine" another. McKay's volumes of poetry include *Spring in New Hampshire* (1920) and *Harlem Shadows: The Poems of Claude McKay* (1922). He also wrote three novels: *Home to Harlem* (1928), *Banjo—A Story without a Plot* (1929), and *Banana Bottom* (1933)— in addition to a collection of short stories—*GingerTown* (1932).

Far down, down through the city's great gaunt gut
    The gray train rushing bears the weary wind;
In the packed cars the fans the crowd's breathe cut,
    Leaving the sick and heavy air behind.
5 And pale-cheeked children seek the upper door
    to give their summer jackets to the breeze;
Their laugh is swallowed in the deafening roar
    Of captive wind that moans for fields and seas;
Seas cooling warm where native schooners drift
10   Through sleepy waters, while gulls wheel and sweep,
Waiting for windy waves the keels to lift
    Lightly among the islands of the deep;
Islands of lofty palm trees blooming white
    That lend their perfume to the tropic sea,
15 Where fields lie idle in the dew-drenched night,
    And the Trades float above them fresh and free.

Writing Log/Journal Assignment

Describe what it is like to pass through a tunnel in a subway car or an automobile.

Individual and Collaborative Considerations

1. List some of the visual images McKay creates with words.
2. In what way does McKay use personification in his poem? Why is it effective? When might personification enhance your own method of written communication?
3. McKay mentions several types of wind in his poem, beginning with the "weary" subway wind. Where do the other winds he cites come from, and where are they going?
4. How does McKay use words appealing to the five senses? In what way do they further the purpose of his poem?
5. The latter part of the poem contains a lot of water imagery (the sea, dew, waves). What might such imagery represent? How does this water imagery contrast with the subway wind presented at the beginning of the poem?

Writing Activities

1. Using personification, write an essay describing the relationship between nature and a human creation such as a city, a farm house, a coliseum, or a castle.
2. Write a descriptive essay of a major industrial complex, a shopping mall, a college campus, a ghetto, a resort, or a luxury ocean liner. To give yourself a sense of purpose or direction, prewrite on your selected topic to determine what you want to say about it.

※

The City Planners

Margaret Atwood

A native of Canada, Margaret Atwood received her college education at the University of Toronto and Radcliffe. She has written many volumes of award-winning poetry and fiction, including *Double Persephone* (1961), *The Circle Game* (1967), *Procedures for Underground* (1970), and *Power Politics* (1972). In addition to her short fiction, essays, and literary scripts, Atwood also distinguished herself as a novelist in *The Edible Woman* (1969), *Surfacing* (1972), *Life before Man* (1979), and *The Handmaid's Tale* (1986). Atwood's achievements also include compiling *The Oxford Book of Canadian Verse* (1982). She likes to compare writing to telling jokes and riddles because they all require "the same mystifying build-up, the same surprising twist, the same impeccable sense of timing." There is a dual nature to many of her poems—comic yet grim—and they frequently deal with the destructive nature of human relationships and alienation.

Cruising these residential Sunday
streets in dry August sunlight;
what offends us is
the sanities:

5   the houses in pedantic rows, the planted
sanitary trees, assert
levelness of surface like a rebuke
to the dent in our car door.
No shouting here, or

10   shatter of glass; nothing more abrupt
than the rational whine of a power mower
cutting a straight swath in the discouraged grass.
But through the driveways neatly
sidestep hysteria

15   by being even, the roofs will display
the same slant of avoidance to the hot sky,
certain things:
the smell of spilled oil a faint

sickness lingering in the garages,

20   a splash of paint on brick surprising as a bruise,
a plastic hose poised in a vicious
coil; even the too-fixed state of the wide windows

give momentary access to
the landscape behind or under

25   the future cracks in the plaster

when the houses, capsized, will slide
obliquely into the clay seas, gradual as glaciers
that right now nobody notices.

That is where the City Planners

30   with the insane faces of political conspirators
are scattered over unsurveyed
territories, concealed from each other
each in his own private blizzard;

35   guessing directions, the sketch
transitory lines rigid as wooden borders
on a wall in the white vanishing air

tracing the panic of suburb
order in a bland madness of snows.

Writing Log/Journal Assignment

Write a journal entry detailing observations you have made while traveling through the city, country, or suburbs.

Individual and Collaborative Considerations

1. Specifically, who are the City Planners? Does Atwood apply the phrase literally, figuratively, or both in her poem? Please justify your answer.
2. What do you imagine will be the literal and symbolic future of Atwood's city? Why?
3. How does Atwood's use of images in her poem project the essence of city life she wants readers to remember?
4. Where is the real madness in "The City Planners"?
5. Select three or four instances of figurative language in Atwood's poem. Analyze your selection explaining what the poem would gain or lose by replacing figures of speech with literal language. Be specific.

Writing Activities

1. Compare and contrast life in the city to life in the country. Before you begin to write, you may want to make a list of "sanities" found in each.
2. Write a comparative analysis on the theme of *alienation* and *emptiness* as portrayed in Atwood's "The City Planners" and Ray Bradbury's "There Will Come Soft Rains" (pp. 565–571).

❋

Impressions of Chicago; For Howlin' Wolf

Quincy Troupe

An award-winning poet, Quincy Troupe is an equally distinguished prose stylist. His works include *Embryo* (1972), *Snake-Back Solos* (1979), and *Skulls along the River* (1984). In addition to his poetry collections, Troupe collaborated with Miles Davis in *Miles: The Autobiography* (1989), edited *Giant Talk, A Third-World Anthology*, and wrote *The Inside Story of TV's "Roots"* with David L. Wolper. Currently, Troupe is a professor in the literature program at the University of California, San Diego, and he is writing *The Footman's Chronicles*, a novel based on growing up in St. Louis with his father. Troupe published *Weather Reports* in 1991 and *Avalanche*, his fifth book of poetry in 1996. *Soundings*, a collection of his essays, is also forthcoming. A versatile artist, Troupe also made a CD and recorded a tape titled *Root Doctor* (1994) wherein he read his own poems, accompanied by legendary jazz and blues guitarist Phil Upchurch. The title of the following poem from *Weather Reports* provides two important textual clues: (1) the subject matter (impressions of Chicago's "southside streets") and (2) Howlin' Wolf, the person for whom the poem is written.

1.

    the wind blade cutting in
    & out, swinging in over the lake
    slicing white foam from the tips
    of delicate water fingers
5   dancing & weaving
    under the sunken light, night
    & this wind blade was so sharp & cold
    it'd cut a pole-legged mosquito into fours
    while a hungry child slept down wind from some chittlins
10   slept within the cold blues of a poem that was formin
    & we came in the sulphuric night drinkin old crow
    while a buzzard licked its beak atop the head of tricky dick nixon
    while gluttonous daly ate hundreds of pigs that were his ego
    while daddy-o played bop on the box
15   came to the bituminous breath of chicago
    howlin with three-million voices of pain

    & this was the music;
    the kids of chicago have eyes that are older
                than the deepest pain the the world
20   & they run with bare feet over south side streets
    shimmering with slivers of glass
    razors that never seem to cut their feet;
    they dance in & out of the traffic
    between carhorns
25   the friday night smells of fish
    barbecue & hog maws, the scoobedoo sounds
    blues sounds of bo didley

2.

these streets belong to the dues payers
to the blues players drinkin rot gut whiskey on satdaynight
30   muddy waters & the wolfman howlin smokestack lightin
how many more years down in the bottom
no place to go moanin for my baby
a spoonful of evil
back door man
35   all night long how many more years
down in the bottom built for comfort

Writing Log/Journal Assignment

Write your own "impressions" about a city in either verse (poetic format) or prose. Include details appealing to the senses.

Individual and Collaborative Considerations

1. Characterize the mood of Troupe's poem. (How does his word choice contribute to the tone of the poem?)
2. Names like Bo Diddley and Muddy Waters appear throughout the poem; how do they contribute or relate to Troupe's theme? How are allusions to Mayor Daly and Richard Nixon relevant?
3. The poem is divided into two parts. Why do you imagine Troupe set his material apart in this manner? What is specifically different about the two parts?
4. Images abound in Troupe's poem. Which words in particular paint "mental pictures" for you?
5. What does the speaker's major impression of Chicago seem to be? What action or instrument appears again and again in the poem?

Writing Activities

1. Describe a city or area that seems to be inescapably associated with a certain style of music. You might use your journal entry as a starting point for ideas—"impressions."
2. Argue that a particular city is the best or the worst place in the world to live and work. Dedicate or address your writing to a specific person in essay or letter format. Include plenty of concrete details and images. Try to enable your reader to feel, hear, smell, and see the environment around you.

ADDITIONAL TOPICS AND ISSUES
FOR WRITING AND RESEARCH

1. What are the advantages and disadvantages of suburban development? Construct a persuasive essay outlining its benefits to prospective home-owners, small businesses, and local government.

2. Compare and contrast two species of dogs, two types of cars, or two people employed by the same company and doing the same job.

3. Contrast your present style of living to that which you intend to enjoy in the immediate future. What changes do you plan to make in your social life, at your residence, and with your friends?

4. Evaluate a comedian's routine you have seen at a comedy club or on one of the many comedy channels on television today. Was the comedian funny? Why or why not? How would you classify the comedian's humor? What audience does the comedian appeal to: working-class adults? suburban audiences? country audiences? Ultimately assess whether you think the comedian will have a limited or extended appeal to the American public.

5. Using the theme of appearance versus reality, write a paper in which you compare the portrayal of a city or a part of the country in a film with your firsthand knowledge of the respective location. Ultimately determine if the film was true to life, filming scenes as they really are, or merely a fictitious treatment of an area.

6. Write an extended comparison—analogy—that explains how and why the perception of life in the city is different from yet similar to life in the country, in industrialized nations as well as developing countries. How might you compare the complex, impersonal atmosphere of a large city to that of an industrialized nation? In what way might life in the country be similar to life in a developing country—unpolluted by technology and industry? Make sure you clearly state your thesis and arrive at some sort of conclusion based on your analogy.

7. Write a humorous essay wherein you explain how to become the head of a large company or firm. Where are you from? The city, the country, or a suburban area? Who will get hurt as you rise to power? How will you deal with those you will manage who, like yourself, are trying to advance to the top of the corporate ladder and have their eyes on your job? (You might conclude your essay with some remarks detailing how you will maintain the position you now hold.)

8. In today's society, as much or more money is appropriated for new prisons as is given to the education of our children. What do you think? Does the United States need new prisons more than it needs new schools and resources for education? Perhaps you believe both are needed. Take a position on this topic and construct a well-reasoned argumentative essay. Draw some of your supporting points from recent news articles to increase the credibility and strength of your argument.

9. Analyze the appeal of two political candidates or two job prospects

based on their background (city person versus country person). Take the biases each stereotype carries into careful consideration. Does wealth have anything to do with one's credibility as a quintessential country person or city slicker?

10. How might you argue that suburban youths are insulated from "real life"? Before you begin to defend your thesis, make sure you provide readers with a careful definition of the terms.

Starting Points for Research

Urban and Suburban

- Suburban churches
- City churches
- Suburban crimes
- Suburban homes
- Suburban life
- Suburban newspapers
- Suburban schools
- Growth in cities and suburbs
- Municipal powers and services
- Subways
- Local transit
    Underground railroads
    Elevated railways
    Automatic train control
- City planning
- Metroplitan areas
- Urban–rural migration
- Urban agriculture
- Urban crime
- Urban community development
- Urban dialects
- Urban ecology
- Urban economics
- Urban flora and fauna
- Urban folklore
- Urban homesteading
- Urban hydrology
- Urban noise
- Urban pests
- Urban poor
- Urban renewal
- Urban schools
- Urban sociology
- Urban youth

Rural

- Rural churches
- Rural aged
- Rural architecture
- Rural bishops
- Rural charities
- Rural newspapers
- Rural life
- Rural clinics
- Rural crimes
- Rural rehabilitation
- Radio in rural development
- Rural health services
- High schools
- Rural industry
- Rural community development
- Social history
- Rural journalism
- Rural libraries
- Manpower policy
- Mental health services
- Rural police
- Rural poor
- Rural poor in art
- Rural flora and fauna
- Rural folktales
- Rural roads
- Rural sewage
- Rural telephones
- Rural–urban migration
- Small family farms
- Cooperate farms
- Women in agriculture
- Rural sociology
- Rural youth

15

Multiple Communities, Multiple Perspectives

"In a Café"
I watched a man in a café fold a slice of bread
as if he were folding a birth certificate or looking
at the photograph of a dead lover.
RICHARD BRAUTIGAN

Essays

Richard Rodriguez Aria

•

Barbara Ehrenreich The Warrior Culture

•

Ishmael Reed America: The Multinational Society

•

Fiction

Louise Erdrich Fleur

•

Ryunosuke Akutagawa In a Grove

•

Ray Bradbury There Will Come Soft Rains

•

Poetry

Paul Laurence Dunbar We Wear the Mask

•

Elizabeth Bishop The Moose

In a way, this chapter, "Multiple Communities, Multiple Perspectives," brings you back to the first section, "Identity," in chapter 5 of *Thresholds*. Today the word *community* has come to mean many things. In its most basic sense, a community refers to people living in the same locality; a community can also be individuals sharing a similar set of values, beliefs, occupations, heritage, creeds, or tastes in music. Individuals are not limited to a single community; it would be a rarity if they were! People respond to and cross over from one community to another with different levels of comfort—different feelings of belonging.

In Louise Erdrich's short story "Fleur," for instance, Fleur is an outcast, an unfortunate victim of hearsay and circumstance, and she is never really allowed to become part of any community for long. In contrast, Richard Rodriguez's "Aria" examines the borders and boundaries of being part of multiple communities. His membership in at least two communities corresponds to the languages he uses: Spanish—Español, his "private language," at home, and English, his "public language," at school and work. Paul Laurence Dunbar points out that some communities are preferential in "We Wear the Mask." The plural first-person pronoun *we* in the poem spoke for African Americans who suffered but said nothing because speaking did no good.

A discussion of communities quite naturally invites an examination of cultures ranging from the status quo to religious cults, as well as a search for shared values, interests, and perceptions. Closely inspecting patriarchal traits of American society in "The Warrior Culture," for instance, Barbara Ehrenreich demonstrates the undeniable fact that the United States is a *warrior culture*. Ishmael Reed takes a different approach to communities and culture. In "America: The Multinational Society," he says that modern American society contains a "blurring of cultural styles"—overlapping communities. A higher rate of exchange now exists among cultures than ever before (although tabloid news would have everyone believe just the opposite). This leads him to conclude that the future of the United States will be "a place where the cultures [communities] of the world crisscross" rather than just conflict. Perspectives frequently differ. Elizabeth Bishop's poem "The Moose" looks at a collection of people from diverse communities with different reasons for taking the bus; all, however, are fascinated by the *moose*, a symbol of something not in the realm of their immediate experience and something they are not likely to forget. The moose provides all passengers with a common focal point—short as that may be—and in that moment all communities overlap recognizably.

Multiple perspectives result from observing and assessing topics or issues through a lens influenced by various social and cultural value systems. Thus, people view themselves—and the actions around them—differently. Ryunosuke Akutagawa shows how this can happen in his short story "In a Grove." Therein three people confess to a murder and four other people testify as to what took place. The very fact that three people confess to committing the crime causes a reader to stop and carefully examine each person's possible motivation for so doing.

The theme of nature versus technology is very common in twentieth-century literature, and the extent to which the two communities can compatibly overlap is questioned daily. Which is more important: preserving natural resources and wildlife or moving forward technologically and scientifically? Both, of course, are desirable, but there comes a point when one must be prioritized above the other. In Ray Bradbury's short story "There Will Come Soft Rains," readers are led from a fully automated house—the product of a technologically developed society—to the utter wasteland surrounding the home, all that remains of an *advanced civilization*. Ironically, the homeowner's favorite poem in Bradbury's story is Sara Teasdale's poem "There Will Come Soft Rains," which celebrates the ultimate triumph of nature and its creatures over modern society and humankind.

RHETORIC AT WORK

The communities mentioned in chapter 15, the last chapter of readings in *Thresholds*, differ in scope, setting, and purpose. In the following and final Rhetoric at Work activity, carefully consider the point of view of each piece of literature. Who is doing the speaking? What is the purpose of the respec-

---

**A Checklist for Writing about *Multiple Communities,
Multiple Perspectives***

1. Am I defining my terms carefully? How will my readers know whom or what I am referring to at all times? What contextual clues do I provide?
2. How has the diverse nature of my audience determined the breadth of examples I used to substantiate discussion points in my essay?
3. Do I represent multiple perspectives on my topic or issue? In what way is my supporting evidence representative rather than selective?
4. How might illustration and classification be appropriate strategies for categorizing and dividing topics about multiple communities and multiple perspectives?
5. How do I use sentence variety to maintain reader interest in my writing?
6. What revision and editing techniques do I use to add style to my prose? Do I condense and combine wordy structures and vary my sentence patterns?
7. How do I bring my essay to a satisfying, definitive conclusion?

tive essay, short story, or poem, and how does *point of view* reinforce the author's objective? Once again, your concern with rhetoric will be diction. In many respects, you have come full circle—back to when your concern with annotations might have been primarily to determine meaning. Now, however, you will want to approach literary works on a different level.

Thoroughly annotate each selection in this chapter, paying particular attention to *concrete imagery* and *tone*. A response to the first paragraph of Ryunosuke Akutagawa's "In a Grove" might be as follows:

Text	Annotations
"Yes, sir. Certainly, it was I who found the body. This morning, as usual, I went to cut my daily quota of cedars, when I found the body in a grove in a hollow in the mountains. The exact location? About 150 meters off the Yamashina stage road. It's an out-of-the-way grove of bamboo and cedars."	IMAGERY: body (corpse), cedars (trees), grove (group of trees or lesser plants), hollow (cavity or sunken area), bamboo (plant) TONE: matter-of-fact, business-like

※

Aria

Richard Rodriguez

A San Francisco native, Richard Rodriguez is the son of Mexican immigrants. His articles frequently appear in *Change, The American Scholar*, and *The Saturday Review*. His works include *Hunger of Memory* (1982), which relates the conflict of ethnic identification and American cultural assimilation, and *Days of Obligation: An Argument with My Mexican Father* (1992). The following essay, "Aria," taken from *Hunger of Memory*, discusses what it is like to be caught between two cultures with two languages when growing up. Contrary to the beliefs held by many proponents of bilingualism, Rodriguez believes it is essential to move from the "private language" of home to the "public language" of school and work in order for minority groups to achieve social mobility.

1 **I** remember to start with that day in Sacramento—a California now nearly thirty years past—when I first entered a classroom, able to understand some fifty stray English words.

2 The third of four children, I had been preceded to a neighborhood Roman Catholic school by an older brother and sister. But neither of them had revealed very much about their classroom experiences. Each afternoon they returned, as they left in the morning, always together, speaking in Spanish as they climbed the five steps of the porch. And their mysterious books, wrapped in shopping-bag paper, remained on the table next to the door, closed firmly behind them.

3 An accident of geography sent me to a school where all my classmates were white, many the children of doctors and lawyers and business executives. All my classmates certainly must have been uneasy on that first day of school—as most children are uneasy—to find themselves apart from their families in the first institution of their lives. But I was astonished.

4 The nun said, in a friendly but oddly impersonal voice, 'Boys and girls, this is Richard Rodriguez.' (I heard her sound out: *Rich-heard Road-ree-guess*.) It was the first time I had heard anyone name me in English. 'Richard,' the nun repeated more slowly, writing my name down in her black leather book. Quickly I turned to see my mother's face dissolve in a watery blur behind the pebbled glass door.

5 Many years later there is something called bilingual education—a scheme proposed in the late 1960s by Hispanic-American social activists, later endorsed by a congressional vote. It is a program that seeks to permit non-English-speaking children, many from lower-class homes, to use their family language as the language of school. (Such is the goal its supporters announce.) I hear them and am forced to say no: It is not possible for a child—any child—ever to use his family's language in school. Not to understand this is to misunderstand the public uses of schooling and to trivialize the nature of intimate life—a family's 'language.'

6 Memory teaches me what I know of these matters; the boy reminds the adult. I was a bilingual child, a certain kind—socially disadvantaged—the son of working-class parents, both Mexican immigrants.

7 In the early years of my boyhood, my parents coped very well in America. My father had steady work. My mother managed at home. They were nobody's victims. Optimism and ambition led them to a house (our home) many blocks from the Mexican south side of town. We lived among *gringos* and only a block from the biggest, whitest houses. It never occurred to my parents that they couldn't live wherever they chose. Nor was the Sacramento of the fifties bent on teaching them a contrary lesson. My mother and father were more annoyed than intimidated by those two or three neighbors who tried initially to make us unwelcome. ('Keep your brats away from my sidewalk!') But despite all they achieved, perhaps because they had so much to achieve, any deep feeling of ease, the confidence of 'belonging' in public was withheld from them both. They regarded the people at work, the faces in crowds, as very distant from us. They were the others, *los gringos*. That term was interchangeable in their speech with another, even more telling, *los americanos*.

8   I grew up in a house where the only regular guests were my relations. For one day, enormous families of relatives would visit and there would be so many people that the noise and the bodies would spill out to the backyard and front porch. Then, for weeks, no one came by. (It was usually a salesman who rang the doorbell.) Our house stood apart. A gaudy yellow in a row of white bungalows. We were the people with the noisy dog. The people who raised pigeons and chickens. We were the foreigners on the block. A few neighbors smiled and waved. We waved back. But no one in the family knew the names of the old couple who lived next door; until I was seven years old, I did not know the names of the kids who lived across the street.

9   In public, my father and mother spoke a hesitant, accented, not always grammatical English. And they would have to strain—their bodies tense— to catch the sense of what was rapidly said by *los gringos*. At home they spoke Spanish. The language of their Mexican past sounded in counterpoint to the English of public society. The words would come quickly, with ease. Conveyed through those sounds was the pleasing, soothing, consoling reminder of being at home.

10   During those years when I was first conscious of hearing, my mother and father addressed me only in Spanish; in Spanish I learned to reply. By contrast, English (*inglés*), rarely heard in the house, was the language I came to associate with *gringos*. I learned my first words of English overhearing my parents speak to strangers. At five years of age, I knew just enough English for my mother to trust me on errands to stores one block away. No more.

11   I was a listening child, careful to hear the very different sounds of Spanish and English. Wide-eyed with hearing, I'd listen to sounds more than words. First, there were English (*gringo*) sounds. So many words were still unknown that when the butcher or the lady at the drugstore said something to me, exotic polysyllabic sounds would bloom in the midst of their sentences. Often the speech of people in public seemed to me very loud, booming with confidence. The man behind the counter would literally ask, 'What can I do for you?' But by being so firm and so clear, the sound of his voice said that he was a *gringo*; he belonged in public society.

12   I would also hear then the high nasal notes of middle-class American speech. The air stirred with sound. Sometimes, even now, when I have been traveling abroad for several weeks, I will hear what I heard as a boy. In hotel lobbies or airports, in Turkey or Brazil, some Americans will pass, and suddenly I will hear it again—the high sound of American voices. For a few seconds I will hear it with pleasure, for it is now the sound of *my* society— a reminder of home. But inevitably—already on the flight headed for home—the sound fades with repetition. I will be unable to hear it anymore.

13   When I was a boy, things were different. The accent of *log gringos* was never pleasing nor was it hard to hear. Crowds at Safeway or at bus stops would be noisy with sound. And I would be forced to edge away from the chirping chatter above me.

14   I was unable to hear my own sounds, but I knew very well that I spoke English poorly. My words could not stretch far enough to form complete

thoughts. And the words I did speak I didn't know well enough to make into distinct sounds. (Listeners would usually lower their heads, better to hear what I was trying to say.) But it was one thing for *me* to speak English with difficulty. It was more troubling for me to hear my parents speak in public: their high-whining vowels and guttural consonants; their sentences that got stuck with 'eh' and 'ah' sounds; the confused syntax; the hesitant rhythm of sounds so different from the way the *gringos* spoke. I'd notice, moreover, that my parents' voices were softer than those of *gringos* we'd meet.

15   I am tempted now to say that none of this mattered. In adulthood I am embarrassed by childhood fears. And, in a way, it didn't matter very much that my parents could not speak English with ease. Their linguistic difficulties had no serious consequences. My mother and father made themselves understood at the county hospital clinic and at government offices. And yet, in another way, it mattered very much—it was unsettling to hear my parents struggle with English. Hearing them, I'd grow nervous, my clutching trust in their protection and power weakened.

16   There were many times like the night at a brightly lit gasoline station (a blaring white memory) when I stood uneasily, hearing my father. He was talking to a teenaged attendant. I do not recall what they were saying, but I cannot forget the sounds my father made as he spoke. At one point his words slid together to form one word—sounds as confused as the threads of blue and green oil in the puddle next to my shoes. His voice rushed through what he had left to say. And, toward the end, reached falsetto notes, appealing to his listener's understanding. I looked away to the lights of passing automobiles. I tried not to hear anymore. But I heard only too well the calm, easy tones in the attendant's reply. Shortly afterward, walking toward home with my father, I shivered when he put his hand on my shoulder. The very first chance that I got, I evaded his grasp and ran on ahead into the dark, skipping with feigned boyish exuberance.

17   But then there was Spanish. *Español:* my family's language. *Español:* the language that seemed to me a private language. I'd hear strangers on the radio and in the Mexican Catholic church across town speaking in Spanish, but I couldn't really believe that Spanish was a public language, like English. Spanish speakers, rather, seemed related to me, for I sensed that we shared—through our language—the experience of feeling apart from *los gringos.* It was thus a ghetto Spanish that I heard and I spoke. Like those whose lives are bound by a barrio, I was reminded by Spanish of my separateness from *los otros, los gringos* in power. But more intensely than for most barrio children—because I did not live in a barrio—Spanish seemed to me the language of home. (Most days it was only at home that I'd hear it.) It became the language of joyful return.

18   A family member would say something to me and I would feel myself specially recognized. My parents would say something to me and I would feel embraced by the sounds of their words. Those sounds said: *I am speaking*

with ease in Spanish. I am addressing you in words I never use with los gringos. *I recognize you as someone special, close, like no one outside. You belong with us. In the family.*

19   (*Ricardo.*)

20   At the age of five, six, well past the time when most other children no longer easily notice the difference between sounds uttered at home and words spoken in public, I had a different experience. I lived in a world magically compounded of sounds. I remained a child longer than most; I lingered too long, poised at the edge of language—often frightened by the sounds of *los gringos,* delighted by the sounds of Spanish at home. I shared with my family a language that was startingly different from that used in the great city around us.

21   For me there were none of the gradations between public and private society so normal to a maturing child. Outside the house was public society; inside the house was private. Just opening or closing the screen door behind me was an important experience. I'd rarely leave home all alone or without reluctance. Walking down the sidewalk, under the canopy of tall trees, I'd warily notice the—suddenly—silent neighborhood kids who stood warily watching me. Nervously, I'd arrive at the grocery store to hear there the sounds of the *gringo*—foreign to me—reminding me that in this world so big, I was a foreigner. But then I'd return. Walking back toward our house, climbing the steps from the sidewalk, when the front door was open in summer, I'd hear voices beyond the screen door talking in Spanish. For a second or two, I'd stay, linger there, listening. Smiling, I'd hear my mother call out, saying in Spanish (words): 'Is that you, Richard?' All the while her sounds would assure me: *You are home now; come closer; inside. With us.*

22   '*Si,*' I'd reply.

23   Once more inside the house I would resume (assume) my place in the family. The sounds would dim, grow harder to hear. Once more at home, I would grow less aware of that fact. It required, however, no more than the blurt of the doorbell to alert me to listen to sounds all over again. The house would turn instantly still while my mother went to the door. I'd hear her hard English sounds. I'd wait to hear her voice return to soft-sounding Spanish, which assured me, as surely as did the clicking tongue of the lock on the door, that the stranger was gone.

24   Plainly, it is not healthy to hear such sounds so often. It is not healthy to distinguish public words from private sounds so easily. I remained cloistered by sounds, timid and shy in public, too dependent on voices at home. And yet it needs to be emphasized: I was an extremely happy child at home. I remember many nights when my father would come back from work, and I'd hear him call out to my mother in Spanish, sounding relieved. In Spanish, he'd sound light and free notes he never could manage in English. Some nights I'd jump up just at hearing his voice. With *mis hermanos* I would come running into the room where he was with my mother. Our laughing (so deep was the pleasure!) became screaming. Like others who know the pain of

public alienation, we transformed the knowledge of our public separateness and made it consoling—the reminder of intimacy. Excited, we joined our voices in a celebration of sounds. *We are speaking now the way we never speak out in public. We are alone—together,* voices sounded, surrounded to tell me. Some nights, no one seemed willing to loosen the hold sounds had on us. At dinner, we invented new words. (Ours sounded Spanish, but made sense only to us.) We pieced together new words by taking, say, an English verb and giving it Spanish endings. My mother's instructions at bedtime would be lacquered with mock-urgent tones. Or a word like *si* would become, in several notes, able to convey added measures of feeling. Tongues explored the edges of words, especially the fat vowels. And we happily sounded that military drum roll, the twirling roar of the Spanish *r*. Family language: my family's sounds. The voices of my parents and sisters and brother. Their voices insisting: *You belong here. We are family members. Related. Special to one another. Listen!* Voices singing and sighing, rising, straining, then surging, teeming with pleasure that burst syllables into fragments of laughter. At times it seemed there was steady quiet only when, from another room, the rustling whispers of my parents faded and I moved closer to sleep.

Writing Log/Journal Assignment

Do you have a private language you use with your friends and associates and a public language you use with everyone else? Briefly describe your two languages in your journal. If you have no "private" language, what do you imagine your "private" language would be like?

Individual and Collaborative Considerations

1. How does Rodriguez distinguish between his "private" language and his "public" language?
2. What is a *gringo?* What did Rodriguez associate with *gringos?*
3. Why did Rodriguez conclude he spoke English poorly when he was a child?
4. Describe or characterize the style of Rodriguez's prose. What devices enable him to vividly convey his information?
5. In what way is Rodriguez's essay a story of sounds? How and why is the title of the essay, "Aria," appropriate to the subject matter? What is an aria?

Writing Activities

1. Compare and contrast Rodriguez's dilemma in "Aria" to Mai's situation in T. T. Nhu's "Becoming American Is a Constant Cultural Collision"

(pp. 92–94). How do both address the issue of culture clashes? To what extent do Richard and Mai resolve their respective "clashes" and how?

2. Formulate and analyze a thesis about your experience with alienation from a mainstream culture (if such a thing still exists!). Your alienation may have stemmed from language barriers, gender inequities, racial discrimination, unfamiliar customs, or religious intolerance.

※

The Warrior Culture

Barbara Ehrenreich

Born in 1941, Barbara Ehrenreich is a frequent contributor to magazines like *Time, Mother Jones,* and *Ms.,* and she has written regular columns for the latter two. Politics and issues revolving around mass media are constant targets of her prose. Her works include *The Hearts of Men: American Dreams and the Flight from Commitment, Fear of Failing: The Inner Life of the Middle Class,* and *The Worst Years of Our Lives.* The following essay appeared as the back-page column in *Time* magazine on October 15, 1990. At the time, Americans were busy debating whether or not to declare war on Iraq. (War began three months later.)

1 In what we like to think of as "primitive" warrior cultures, the passage to manhood requires the blooding of a spear, the taking of a scalp or head. Among the Masai of eastern Africa, the North American Plains Indians and dozens of other pretechnological peoples, a man could not marry until he had demonstrated his capacity to kill in battle. Leadership too in a warrior culture is typically contingent on military prowess and wrapped in the mystique of death. In the Solomon Islands a chief's importance could be reckoned by the number of skulls posted around his door, and it was the duty of the Aztec kings to nourish the gods with the hearts of human captives.

2 All warrior peoples have fought for the same high-sounding reasons: honor, glory or revenge. The nature of their real and perhaps not conscious motivation is a subject of much debate. Some anthropologists postulate a murderous instinct, almost unique among living species, in human males. Others discern a materialistic motive behind every fray: a need for slaves, grazing land or even human flesh to eat. Still others point to the similarities between war and other male pastimes—the hunt and outdoor sports—and suggest that it is boredom, ultimately, that stirs men to fight.

3   But in a warrior culture it hardly matters which motive is most basic. Aggressive behavior is rewarded whether or not it is innate to the human psyche. Shortages of resources are habitually taken as occasions for armed offensives, rather than for hard thought and innovation. And war, to a warrior people, is of course the highest adventure, the surest antidote to malaise, the endlessly repeated theme of legend, song, religious myth and personal quest for meaning. It is how men die and what they find to live for.

4   "You must understand that Americans are a warrior nation." Senator Daniel Patrick Moynihan told a group of Arab leaders in early September, one month into the Middle East crisis. He said this proudly, and he may, without thinking through the ugly implications, have told the truth. In many ways, in outlook and behavior the U.S. has begun to act like a primitive warrior culture.

5   We seem to believe that leadership is expressed, in no small part, by a willingness to cause the deaths of others. After the U.S. invasion of Panama, President Bush exulted that no one could call him "timid": he was at last a "macho man." The press, in even more primal language, hailed him for succeeding in an "initiation rite" by demonstrating his "willingness to shed blood."

6   For lesser offices too we apply the standards of a warrior culture. Female candidates are routinely advised to overcome the handicap of their gender by talking "tough." Thus, for example, Dianne Feinstein has embraced capital punishment, while Colorado senatorial candidate Josie Heath has found it necessary to announce that although she is the mother of an eighteen-year-old son, she is prepared to vote for war. Male candidates in some of the fall contests are finding their military records under scrutiny. No one expects them, as elected officials in a civilian government, to pick up a spear or a sling and fight. But they must state, at least, their willingness to have another human killed.

7   More tellingly, we are unnerved by peace and seem to find it boring. When the cold war ended, we found no reason to celebrate. Instead we heated up the "war on drugs." What should have been a public-health campaign, focused on the persistent shame of poverty, became a new occasion for martial rhetoric and muscle flexing. Months later, when the Berlin Wall fell and communism collapsed throughout Europe, we Americans did not dance in the streets. What we did, according to the networks, was change the channel to avoid the news. Nonviolent revolutions do not uplift us, and the loss of mortal enemies only seems to leave us empty and bereft.

8   Our collective fantasies center on mayhem, cruelty and violent death. Loving images of the human body—especially of bodies seeking pleasure or expressing love—inspire us with the urge to censor. Our preference is for warrior themes: the lone fighting man, bandoliers across his naked chest, mowing down lesser men in gusts of automatic-weapon fire. Only a real war seems to revive our interest in real events. With the Iraqi crisis, the networks report, ratings for news shows rose again—even higher than they were for Panama.

9   And as in any primitive warrior culture, our warrior elite takes pride of place. Social crises multiply numbingly—homelessness, illiteracy, epidemic disease—and our leaders tell us solemnly that nothing can be done. There is no money. We are poor, not rich, a debtor nation. Meanwhile, nearly a third of the federal budget flows, even in moments of peace, to the warriors and their weaponmakers. When those priorities are questioned, some new "crisis" dutifully arises to serve as another occasion for armed and often unilateral intervention.

10   Now, with Operation Desert Shield, our leaders are reduced to begging foreign powers for the means to support our warrior class. It does not seem to occur to us that the other great northern powers—Japan, Germany, the Soviet Union—might not have found the stakes so high or the crisis quite so threatening. It has not penetrated our imagination that in a world where the powerful, industrialized nation-states are at last at peace, there might be other ways to face down a pint-size Third World warrior state than with massive force of arms. Nor have we begun to see what an anachronism we are in danger of becoming: a warrior nation in a world that pines for peace, a high-tech state with the values of a warrior band.

11   A leftist might blame "imperialism"; a right-winger would call our problem "internationalism." But an anthropologist, taking the long view, might say this is just what warriors do. Intoxicated by their own drumbeats and war songs, fascinated by the glint of steel and the prospect of blood, they will go forth, time and again, to war.

Writing Log/Journal Assignment

How does America's love of violent sports reflect the value system of a *warrior culture?* Record your responses to this question in your journal or writing log.

Individual and Collaborative Considerations

1. For what "high-sounding reasons" have warrior people fought?
2. How did the press exult former President Bush's Panama invasion? What did Bush prove?
3. What examples does Ehrenreich cite from recent history to illustrate her claim that the United States is a warrior culture? Since this article was published on October 15, 1990, what *current* examples can you think of to add to her list?
4. From what point of view does Ehrenreich write? Liberal, conservative, or neither? Why might her point of view be important?
5. What constitutes your favorite leisure reading material, television programs, and movies? Do they contain what Ehrenreich refers to as adventure, "mayhem, cruelty and violent sex"? Is she correct in her convictions? Explain.

Writing Activities

1. Write an argument of refutation, disproving Ehrenreich's thesis that the United States is a *warrior culture*. In the same manner as Ehrenreich, draw representative examples from recent history to defend your discussion points.
2. Using similar techniques to those in Ehrenreich's essay, write a paper with one of these titles: The High Technology Culture, The Party Culture, The Apathetic Culture, or The Politically Correct Culture. Essentially, you are substituting "warrior" for another, somewhat controversial characteristic you identify with American culture. Select your supporting evidence from recent news articles to add credibility and currency to your argument.

※

America: The Multinational Society

Ishmael Reed

Born in 1938, Ishmael Reed is a native of Buffalo, New York. A prolific writer, Reed has explored his talents in many genres. He writes verse, songs, plays, essays, and novels. Additionally, Reed produces television shows and works as a publisher and a magazine editor. Reed's fiction is often marked by surrealism, fantasy, and satire. His award-winning works include the novels *The Free Lance Pall Bearers* (1967), *Mumbo Jumbo* (1978), *The Terrible Twos* (1982), and *Restless Eyeballing* (1986); several volumes of verse like *Catechism of D Neoamerican Hoodoo* (1970) and *Conjure* (1972); and the essay collections *Shrovetide in New Orleans* (1979) and *Writin' Is Fightin'* (1988)—the source of the following essay.

1   At the annual Lower East Side Jewish Festival yesterday, a Chinese woman ate a pizza slice in front of Ty Thuan Duc's Vietnamese grocery store. Beside her a Spanish-speaking family patronized a cart with two signs: "Italian Ices" and "Kosher by Rabbi Alper." And after the pastrami ran out, everybody ate knishes.

(New York Times, 23 June 1983)

2   On the day before Memorial Day, 1983, a poet called me to describe a city he had just visited. He said that one section included mosques, built by the Islamic people who dwelled there. Attending his reading, he said, were large

numbers of Hispanic people, forty thousand of whom lived in the same city. He was not talking about a fabled city located in some mysterious region of the world. The city he'd visited was Detroit.

3   A few months before, as I was leaving Houston, Texas, I heard it announced on the radio that Texas's largest minority was Mexican American, and though a foundation recently issued a report critical of bilingual education, the taped voice used to guide the passengers on the air trams connecting terminals in Dallas Airport is in both Spanish and English. If the trend continues, a day will come when it will be difficult to travel through some sections of the country without hearing commands in both English and Spanish; after all, for some western states, Spanish was the first written language and the Spanish style lives on in the western way of life.

4   Shortly after my Texas trip, I sat in an auditorium located on the campus of the University of Wisconsin at Milwaukee as a Yale professor—whose original work on the influence of African cultures upon those of the Americas has led to his ostracism from some monocultural intellectual circles—walked up and down the aisle, like an old-time southern evangelist, dancing and drumming the top of the lectern, illustrating his points before some serious Afro-American intellectuals and artists who cheered and applauded his performance and his mastery of information. The professor was "white." After his lecture, he joined a group of Milwaukeeans in a conversation. All of the participants spoke Yoruban, though only the professor had ever traveled to Africa.

5   One of the artists told me that his paintings, which included African and Afro-American mythological symbols and imagery, were hanging in the local McDonald's restaurant. The next day I went to McDonald's and snapped pictures of smiling youngsters eating hamburgers below paintings that could grace the walls of any of the country's leading museums. The manager of the local McDonald's said, "I don't know what you boys are doing, but I like it," as he commissioned the local painters to exhibit in his restaurant.

6   Such blurring of cultural styles occurs in everyday life in the United States to a greater extent than anyone can imagine and is probably more prevalent than the sensational conflict between people of different backgrounds that is played up and often encouraged by the media. The result is what the Yale professor, Robert Thompson, referred to as a cultural bouillabaisse, yet members of the nation's present educational and cultural Elect still cling to the notion that the United States belongs to some vaguely defined entity they refer to as "Western civilization," by which they mean, presumably, a civilization created by the people of Europe, as if Europe can be viewed in monolithic terms. Is Beethoven's Ninth Symphony, which includes Turkish marches, a part of Western civilization, or the late nineteenth- and twentieth-century French paintings, whose creators were influenced by Japanese art? And what of the cubists, through whom the influence of African art changed modern painting, or the surrealists, who were so impressed with the art of the Pacific Northwest Indians that, in their map of North America, Alaska dwarfs the lower forty-eight in size?

7   Are the Russians, who are often criticized for their adoption of "Western" ways by Tsarist dissidents in exile, members of Western civilization? And what of the millions of Europeans who have black African and Asian ancestry, black Africans having occupied several countries for hundreds of years? Are these "Europeans" members of Western civilization, or the Hungarians, who originated across the Urals in a place called Greater Hungary, or the Irish, who came from the Iberian Peninsula?

8   Even the notion that North America is part of Western civilization because our "system of government" is derived from Europe is being challenged by Native American historians who say that the founding fathers, Benjamin Franklin especially, were actually influenced by the system of government that had been adopted by the Iroquois hundreds of years prior to the arrival of large numbers of Europeans.

9   Western civilization, then, becomes another confusing category like Third World, or Judeo-Christian culture, as man attempts to impose his small-screen view of political and cultural reality upon a complex world. Our most publicized novelist recently said that Western civilization was the greatest achievement of mankind, an attitude that flourishes on the street level as scribbles in public restrooms: "White Power," "Niggers and Spics Suck," or "Hitler was a prophet," the latter being the most telling, for wasn't Adolph Hitler the archetypal monoculturalist who, in his pigheaded arrogance, believed that one way and one blood was so pure that it had to be protected from alien strains at all costs? Where did such an attitude, which has caused so much misery and depression in our national life, which has tainted even our noblest achievements, begin? An attitude that caused the incarceration of Japanese-American citizens during World War II, the persecution of Chicanos and Chinese Americans, the near-extermination of the Indians, and the murder and lynchings of thousands of Afro-Americans.

10   Virtuous, hardworking, pious, even though they occasionally would wander off after some fancy clothes, or rendezvous in the woods with the town prostitute, the Puritans are idealized in our schoolbooks as "a hardy band" of no-nonsense patriarchs whose discipline razed the forest and brought order to the New World (a term that annoys Native American historians). Industrious, responsible, it was their "Yankee ingenuity" and practicality that created the work ethic. They were simple folk who produced a number of good poets, and they set the tone for the American writing style, of lean and spare lines, long before Hemingway. They worshiped in churches whose colors blended in with the New England snow, churches with simple structures and ornate lecterns.

11   The Puritans were a daring lot, but they had a mean streak. They hated the theater and banned Christmas. They punished people in a cruel and inhuman manner. They killed children who disobeyed their parents. When they came in contact with those whom they considered heathens or aliens, they behaved in such a bizarre and irrational manner that this chapter in the American history comes down to us as a late-movie horror film. They exter-

minated the Indians, who taught them how to survive in a world unknown to them, and their encounter with the calypso culture of Barbados resulted in what the tourist guide in Salem's Witches' House refers to as the Witchcraft Hysteria.

12 The Puritan legacy of hard work and meticulous accounting led to the establishment of a great industrial society; it is no wonder that the American industrial revolution began in Lowell, Massachusetts, but there was the other side, the strange and paranoid attitudes toward those different from the Elect.

13 The cultural attitudes of that early Elect continue to be voiced in everyday life in the United States: the president of a distinguished university, writing a letter to the *Times,* belittling the study of African civilizations; the television network that promoted its show on the Vatican art with the boast that this art represented "the finest achievements of the human spirit." A modern uptempo state of complex rhythms that depends upon contacts with an international community can no longer behave as if it dwelled in a "Zion Wilderness" surrounded by beasts and pagans.

14 When I heard a schoolteacher warn the other night about the invasion of the American educational system by foreign curriculums, I wanted to yell at the television set, "Lady, they're already here." It has already begun because the world is here. The world has been arriving at these shores for at least ten thousand years from Europe, Africa, and Asia. In the late nineteenth and early twentieth centuries, large numbers of Europeans arrived, adding their cultures to those of the European, African, and Asian settlers who were already here, and recently millions have been entering the country from South America and the Caribbean, making Yale Professor Bob Thompson's bouillabaisse richer and thicker.

15 One of our most visionary politicians said that he envisioned a time when the United States could become the brain of the world, by which he meant the repository of all of the latest advanced information systems. I thought of that remark when an enterprising poet friend of mine called to say that he had just sold a poem to a computer magazine and that the editors were delighted to get it because they didn't carry fiction or poetry. Is that the kind of world we desire? A humdrum homogenous world of all brains but no heart, no fiction, no poetry; a world of robots with human attendants bereft of imagination, of culture? Or does North America deserve a more exciting destiny? To become a place where the cultures of the world crisscross. This is possible because the United States is unique in the world: The world is here.

Writing Log/Journal Assignment

Brainstorm the word *multinational* and write your own definition of the term in your journal.

Individual and Collaborative Considerations

1. In what way does Reed defend his concept of a multinational society within the context of the essay?
2. How and why is the United States a multicultural society?
3. Describe the tone of Reed's essay.
4. What appeals to *ethos* (ethics), *pathos* (emotions), and *logos* (logic—especially induction) does Reed make throughout his essay?
5. How does Reed structure his essay? In what way does all his information lead to his general conclusion?

Writing Activities

1. In a fully supported essay, argue the extent to which you agree with Reed's conclusion that North America deserves the exciting destiny of becoming "a place where cultures of the world crisscross. This is possible because the United States is unique in the world: The world is here."
2. If you disagree with Reed's conclusion, write a paper hypothesizing when and where the *cultures of the world* will *crisscross*. Use several similes (comparisons using "like" or "as") to compare concrete characteristics from existing societies to societies you predict in the future. (You may want to limit the focus of your essay to one existing society and one predicted society.)

❋

Fleur

Louise Erdrich

Of Chippewa and German American descent, Louise Erdrich is both a poet and a novelist and frequently writes about the Native American experience. Many of her stories have appeared in such magazines as *Esquire, Chicago, Paris Review, Antaeus, Georgia Review, Redbook, Ms.*, and *Frontiers*. Erdrich's published works include *Jacklight* (1984) and *Baptism of Desire* (1989), collections of poetry, and several novels: *Love Medicine* (1984), *The Beet Queen* (1986), and *Tracks* (1988). In 1992, Erdrich published *The Crown of Columbus*, a novel she coauthored with her husband Michael Dorris. Erdrich's newest novel, *The Bingo Palace*, was published in 1994, and she is currently putting together a collection of her essays. The following story, "Fleur," appears as it was originally published by *Esquire* magazine in 1986. Later, the story was reworked as one of the chapters in *Tracks* (1988).

The first time she drowned in the cold and glassy waters of Lake Turcot, Fleur Pillager was only a girl. Two men saw the boat tip, saw her struggle in the waves. They rowed over to the place she went down, and jumped in. When they dragged her over the gunwales, she was cold to the touch and stiff, so they slapped her face, shook her by the heels, worked her arms back and forth, and pounded her back until she coughed up lake water. She shivered all over like a dog, then took a breath. But it wasn't long afterward that those two men disappeared. The first wandered off, and the other, Jean Hat, got himself run over by a cart.

It went to show, my grandma said. It figured to her, all right. By saving Fleur Pillager, those two men had lost themselves.

The next time she fell in the lake, Fleur Pillager was twenty years old and no one touched her. She washed onshore, her skin a dull dead gray, but when George Many Women bent to look closer, he saw her chest move. Then her eyes spun open, sharp black riprock, and she looked at him. "You'll take my place," she hissed. Everybody scattered and left her there, so no one knows how she dragged herself home. Soon after that we noticed Many Women changed, grew afraid, wouldn't leave his house, and would not be forced to go near water. For his caution, he lived until the day that his sons brought him a new tin bathtub. Then the first time he used the tub he slipped, got knocked out, and breathed water while his wife stood in the other room frying breakfast.

Men stayed clear of Fleur Pillager after the second drowning. Even though she was good-looking, nobody dared to court her because it was clear that Misshepeshu, the waterman, the monster, wanted her for himself. He's a devil, that one, love-hungry with desire and maddened for the touch of young girls, the strong and daring especially, the ones like Fleur.

5 Our mothers warn us that we'll think he's handsome, for he appears with green eyes, copper skin, a mouth tender as a child's. But if you fall into his arms, he sprouts horns, fangs, claws, fins. His feet are joined as one and his skin, brass scales, rings to the touch. You're fascinated, cannot move. He casts a shell necklace at your feet, weeps gleaming chips that harden into mica on your breasts. He holds you under. Then he takes the body of a lion or a fat brown worm. He's made of gold. He's made of beach moss. He's a thing of dry foam, a thing of death by drowning, the death a Chippewa cannot survive.

Unless you are Fleur Pillager. We all knew she couldn't swim. After the first time, we thought she'd never go back to Lake Turcot. We thought she'd keep to herself, live quiet, stop killing men off by drowning in the lake. After the first time, we thought she'd keep the good ways. But then, after the second drowning, we knew that we were dealing with something much more serious. She was haywire, out of control. She messed with evil, laughed at the old women's advice, and dressed like a man. She got herself into some half-forgotten medicine, studied ways we shouldn't talk about. Some say she kept the finger of a child in her pocket and a powder of unborn rabbits in a leather thong around her neck. She laid the heart of an owl on her tongue so she could see at night, and went out, hunting, not even in her own body. We know for sure because the next morning, in the snow or dust, we followed the tracks of her bare feet and saw where they changed, where the claws sprang out, the pad broadened and pressed into the dirt. By night we heard her chuffing cough, the bear cough. By day her silence and the wide grin she threw to bring down our guard made us frightened. Some thought that Fleur Pillager should be driven off the reservation, but not a single person who spoke like this had the nerve. And finally, when people were just about to get together and throw her out, she left on her own and didn't come back all summer. That's what this story is about.

During that summer, when she lived a few miles south in Argus, things happened. She almost destroyed that town.

When she got down to Argus in the year of 1920, it was just a small grid of six streets on either side of the railroad depot. There were two elevators, one central, the other a few miles west. Two stores competed for the trade of the three hundred citizens, and three churches quarreled with one another for their souls. There was a frame building for Lutherans, a heavy brick one for Episcopalians, and a long narrow shingled Catholic church. This last had a tall slender steeple, twice as high as any building or tree.

No doubt, across the low, flat wheat, watching from the road as she came near Argus on foot, Fleur saw that steeple rise, a shadow thin as a needle. Maybe in that raw space it drew her the way a lone tree draws lightning. Maybe, in the end, the Catholics are to blame. For if she hadn't seen that sign of pride, that slim prayer, that marker, maybe she would have kept walking.

10   But Fleur Pillager turned, and the first place she went once she came into town was to the back door of the priest's residence attached to the landmark church. She didn't go there for a handout, although she got that, but to ask for work. She got that too, or the town got her. It's hard to tell which came out worse, her or the men or the town, although the upshot of it all was that Fleur lived.

The four men who worked at the butcher's had carved up about a thousand carcasses between them, maybe half of that steers and the other half pigs, sheep, and game animals like deer, elk, and bear. That's not even mentioning the chickens, which were beyond counting. Pete Kozka owned the place, and employed Lily Veddar, Tor Grunewald, and my stepfather, Dutch James, who had brought my mother down from the reservation the year before she disappointed him by dying. Dutch took me out of school to take her place. I kept house half the time and worked the other in the butcher shop, sweeping floors, putting sawdust down, running a hambone across the street to a customer's bean pot or a package of sausage to the corner. I was a good one to have around because until they needed me, I was invisible. I blended into the stained brown walls, a skinny, big-nosed girl with staring eyes. Because I could fade into a corner or squeeze beneath a shelf, I knew everything, what the men said when no one was around, and what they did to Fleur.

Kozka's Meats served farmers for a fifty-mile area, both to slaughter, for it had a stock pen and chute, and to cure the meat by smoking it or spicing it in sausage. The storage locker was a marvel, made of many thicknesses of brick, earth insulation, and Minnesota timber, lined inside with sawdust and vast blocks of ice cut from Lake Turcot, hauled down from home each winter by horse and sledge.

A ramshackle board building, part slaughterhouse, part store, was fixed to the low, thick square of the lockers. That's where Fleur worked. Kozka hired her for her strength. She could lift a haunch or carry a pole of sausages without stumbling, and she soon learned cutting from Pete's wife, a string-thin blonde who chain-smoked and handled the razor-sharp knives with nerveless precision, slicing close to her stained fingers. Fleur and Fritzie Kozka worked afternoons, wrapping their cuts in paper, and Fleur hauled the packages to the lockers. The meat was left outside the heavy oak doors that were only opened at 5:00 each afternoon, before the men ate supper.

Sometimes Dutch, Tor, and Lily ate at the lockers, and when they did I stayed too, cleaned floors, restoked the fires in the front smokehouses, while the men sat around the squat cast-iron stove spearing slats of herring onto hardtack bread. They played long games of poker or cribbage on a board made from the planed end of a salt crate. They talked and I listened, although there wasn't much to hear since almost nothing ever happened in Argus. Tor was married, Dutch had lost my mother, and Lily read circulars. They mainly discussed about the auctions to come, equipment, or women.

15   Every so often, Pete Kozka came out front to make a whist, leaving Fritzie to smoke cigarettes and fry raised doughnuts in the back room. He sat and played a few rounds but kept his thoughts to himself. Fritzie did not tolerate him talking behind her back, and the one book he read was the New Testament. If he said something, it concerned weather or a surplus of sheep stomachs, a ham that smoked green or the markets for corn and wheat. He had a good-luck talisman, the opal-white lens of a cow's eye. Playing cards, he rubbed it between his fingers. That soft sound and the slap of cards was about the only conversation.

Fleur finally gave them a subject.

Her cheeks were wide and flat, her hands large, chapped, muscular. Fleur's shoulders were broad as beams, her hips fishlike, slippery, narrow. An old green dress clung to her waist, worn thin where she sat. Her braids were thick like the tails of animals, and swung against her when she moved, deliberately, slowly in her work, held in and half-tamed, but only half. I could tell, but the others never saw. They never looked into her sly brown eyes or noticed her teeth, strong and curved and very white. Her legs were bare, and since she padded around in beadwork moccasins they never saw that her fifth toes were missing. They never knew she'd drowned. They were blinded, they were stupid, they only saw her in the flesh.

And yet it wasn't just that she was a Chippewa, or even that she was a woman, it wasn't that she was good-looking or even that she was alone that made their brains hum. It was how she played cards.

Women didn't usually play with men, so the evening that Fleur drew a chair up to the men's table without being so much as asked, there was a shock of surprise.

20   "What's this," said Lily. He was fat, with a snake's cold pale eyes and precious skin, smooth and lily-white, which is how he got his name. Lily had a dog, a stumpy mean little bull of a thing with a belly drum-tight from eating pork rinds. The dog liked to play cards just like Lily, and straddled his barrel thighs through games of stud, rum poker, vingt-un.[1] The dog snapped at Fleur's arm that first night, but cringed back, its snarl frozen, when she took her place.

"I thought," she said, her voice soft and stroking, "you might deal me in."

There was a space between the heavy bin of spiced flour and the wall where I just fit. I hunkered down there, kept my eyes open, saw her black hair swing over the chair, her feet solid on the wood floor. I couldn't see up on the table where the cards slapped down, so after they were deep in their game I raised myself up in the shadows, and crouched on a sill of wood.

I watched Fleur's hands stack and ruffle, divide the cards, spill them to each player in a blur, rake them up and shuffle again. Tor, short and scrappy, shut one eye and squinted the other at Fleur. Dutch screwed his lips around a wet cigar.

"Gotta see a man," he mumbled, getting up to go out back to the privy. The others broke, put their cards down, and Fleur sat alone in the lamplight that glowed in a sheen across the push of her breasts. I watched her closely, then she paid me a beam of notice for the first time. She turned, looked straight at me, and grinned the white wolf grin a Pillager turns on its victims, except that she wasn't after me.

25   "Pauline there," she said, "how much money you got?"

We'd all been paid for the week that day. Eight cents was in my pocket.

"Stake me," she said, holding out her long fingers. I put the coins in her palm and then I melted back to nothing, part of the walls and tables. It was a long time before I understood that the men would not have seen me no matter what I did, how I moved. I wasn't anything like Fleur. My dress hung loose and my back was already curved, an old woman's. Work had roughened me, reading made my eyes sore, caring for my mother before she died had hardened my face. I was not much to look at, so they never saw me.

When the men came back and sat around the table, they had drawn together. They shot each other small glances, stuck their tongues in their

---

[1]Vingt-un—twenty-one, a card game.

cheeks, burst out laughing at odd moments, to rattle Fleur. But she never minded. They played their vingt-un, staying even as Fleur slowly gained. Those pennies I had given her drew nickels and attracted dimes until there was a small pile in front of her.

Then she hooked them with five-card draw, nothing wild. She dealt, discarded, drew, and then she sighed and her cards gave a little shiver. Tor's eye gleamed, and Dutch straightened in his seat.

30   "I'll pay to see that hand," said Lily Veddar.

Fleur showed, and she had nothing there, nothing at all.

Tor's thin smile cracked open, and he threw his hand in too.

"Well, we know one thing," he said, leaning back in his chair, "the squaw can't bluff."

With that I lowered myself into a mound of swept sawdust and slept. I woke up during the night, but none of them had moved yet, so I couldn't either. Still later, the men must have gone out again, or Fritzie come out to break the game, because I was lifted, soothed, cradled in a woman's arms and rocked so quiet that I kept my eyes shut while Fleur rolled me into a closet of grimy ledgers, oiled paper, balls of string, and thick files that fit beneath me like a mattress.

35   The game went on after work the next evening. I got my eight cents back five times over, and Fleur kept the rest of the dollar she'd won for a stake. This time they didn't play so late, but they played regular, and then kept going at it night after night. They played poker now, or variations, for one week straight, and each time Fleur won exactly one dollar, no more and no less, too consistent for luck.

By this time, Lily and the other men were so lit with suspense that they got Pete to join the game with them. They concentrated, the fat dog sitting tense in Lily Veddar's lap, Tor suspicious, Dutch stroking his huge square brow, Pete steady. It wasn't that Fleur won that hooked them in so, because she lost hands too. It was rather that she never had a freak hand or even anything above a straight. She only took on her low cards, which didn't sit right. By chance, Fleur should have gotten a full or flush by now. The irritating thing was she beat with pairs and never bluffed, because she couldn't, and still she ended up each night with exactly one dollar. Lily couldn't believe, first of all, that a woman could be smart enough to play cards, but even if she was, that she would then be stupid enough to cheat for a dollar a night. By day I watched him turn the problem over, his hard white face dull, small fingers probing at his knuckles, until he finally thought he had Fleur figured out as a bit-time player, caution her game. Raising the stakes would throw her.

More than anything now, he wanted Fleur to come away with something but a dollar. Two bits less or ten more, the sum didn't matter, just so he broke her streak.

Night after night she played, won her dollar, and left to stay in a place that just Fritzie and I knew about. Fleur bathed in the slaughtering tub, then slept in the unused brick smokehouse behind the lockers, a windowless place tarred on the inside with scorched fats. When I brushed against her skin I noticed that she smelled of the walls, rich and woody, slightly burnt. Since that night she put me in the closet I was no longer afraid of her, but followed her close, stayed with her, became her moving shadow that the men never noticed, the shadow that could have saved her.

August, the month that bears fruit, closed around the shop, and Pete and Fritzie left for Minnesota to escape the heat. Night by night, running, Fleur had won thirty dollars, and only Pete's presence had kept Lily at bay. But Pete was gone now, and one payday, with the heat so bad no one could move but Fleur, the men sat and played and waited while she finished work. The cards sweat, limp in their fingers, the table was slick with grease, and even the walls were warm to the touch. The air was motionless. Fleur was in the next room boiling heads.

40   Her green dress, drenched, wrapped her like a transparent sheet. A skin of lakeweed. Black snarls of veining clung to her arms. Her braids were loose, half-unraveled, tied behind her neck in a thick loop. She stood in steam, turning skulls through a vat with a wooden paddle. When scraps boiled to the surface, she bent with a round tin sieve and scooped them out. She'd filled two dishpans.

"Ain't that enough now?" called Lily. "We're waiting." The stump of a dog trembled in his lap, alive with rage. It never smelled me or noticed me above Fleur's smoky skin. The air was heavy in my corner, and pressed me down. Fleur sat with them.

"Now what do you say?" Lily asked the dog. It barked. That was the signal for the real game to start.

"Let's up the ante," said Lily, who had been stalking this night all month. He had a roll of money in his pocket. Fleur had five bills in her dress. The men had each saved their full pay.

"Ante a dollar then," said Fleur, and pitched hers in. She lost, but they let her scrape along, cent by cent. And then she won some. She played unevenly, as if chance was all she had. She reeled them in. The game went on. The dog was stiff now, poised on Lily's knees, a ball of vicious muscle with its yellow eyes slit in concentration. It gave advice, seemed to sniff the lay of Fleur's cards, twitched and nudged. Fleur was up, then down, saved by a scratch. Tor dealt seven cards, three down. The pot grew, round by round, until it held all the money. Nobody folded. Then it all rode on one last card and they went silent. Fleur picked hers up and blew a long breath. The heat lowered like a bell. Her card shook, but she stayed in.

45   Lily smiled and took the dog's head tenderly between his palms.

"Say, Fatso," he said, crooning the words, "you reckon that girl's bluffing?"

The dog whined and Lily laughed. "Me too," he said, "let's show." He swept his bills and coins into the pot and then they turned their cards over.

Lily looked once, looked again, then he squeezed the dog up like a fist of dough and slammed it on the table.

Fleur threw her arms out and drew the money over, grinning that same wolf grin that she'd used on me, the grin that had them. She jammed the bills in her dress, scooped the coins up in waxed white paper that she tied with string.

"Let's go another round," said Lily, his voice choked with burrs. But Fleur opened her mouth and yawned, then walked out back to gather slops for the one big hog that was waiting in the stock pen to be killed.

The men sat still as rocks, their hands spread on the oiled wood table. Dutch had chewed his cigar to damp shreds, Tor's eye was dull. Lily's gaze was the only one to follow Fleur. I didn't move. I felt them gathering, saw my stepfather's veins, the ones in his forehead that stood out in anger. The dog had rolled off the table and curled in a knot below the counter, where none of the men could touch it.

Lily rose and stepped out back to the closet of ledgers where Pete kept his private stock. He brought back a bottle, uncorked and tipped it between his fingers. The lump in his throat moved, then he passed it on. They drank, quickly felt the whiskey's fire, and planned with their eyes things they couldn't say out loud.

When they left, I followed. I hid out back in the clutter of broken boards and chicken crates beside the stock pen, where they waited. Fleur could not be seen at first, and then the moon broke and showed her, slipping cautiously along the rough board chute with a bucket in her hand. Her hair fell, wild and coarse, to her waist, and her dress was a floating patch in the dark. She made a pig-calling sound, rang the tin pail lightly against the wood, froze suspiciously. But too late. In the sound of the ring Lily moved, fat and nimble, stepped right behind Fleur and put out his creamy hands. At his first touch, she whirled and doused him with the bucket of sour slops. He pushed her against the big fence and the package of coins split, went clinking and jumping, winked against the wood. Fleur rolled over once and vanished in the yard.

The moon fell behind a curtain of ragged clouds, and Lily followed into the dark muck. But he tripped, pitched over the huge flank of the pig, who lay mired to the snout, heavily snoring. I sprang out of the weeds and climbed the side of the pen, stuck like glue. I saw the sow rise to her neat, knobby knees, gain her balance, and sway, curious, as Lily stumbled forward. Fleur had backed into the angle of rough wood just beyond, and when Lily tried to jostle past, the sow tipped up on her hind legs and struck, quick and hard as a snake. She plunged her head into Lily's thick side and snatched a mouthful of his shirt. She lunged again, caught him lower, so that he grunted in pained surprise. He seemed to ponder, breathing deep. Then he launched his huge body in a swimmer's dive.

The sow screamed as his body smacked over hers. She rolled, striking out with her knife-sharp hooves, and Lily gathered himself upon her, took her foot-long face by the ears and scraped her snout and cheeks against the trestles of the pen. He hurled the sow's tight skull against an iron post, but instead of knocking her dead, he merely woke her from her dream.

She reared, shrieked, drew him with her so that they posed standing upright. They bowed jerkily to each other, as if to begin. Then his arms swung and flailed. She sank her black fangs into his shoulder, clasping him, dancing him forward and backward through the pen. Their steps picked up pace, went wild. The two dipped as one, box-stepped, tripped each other. She ran her split foot through his hair. He grabbed her kinked tail. They went down and came up, the same shape and then the same color, until the men couldn't tell one from the other in that light and Fleur was able to launch herself over the gates, swing down, hit gravel.

The men saw, yelled, and chased her at a dead run to the smokehouse. And Lily too, once the sow gave up in disgust and freed him. That is where I should have gone to Fleur, saved her, thrown myself on Dutch. But I went stiff with fear and couldn't unlatch myself from the trestles or move at all. I closed my eyes and put my head in my arms, tried to hide, so there is nothing to describe but what I couldn't block out, Fleur's hoarse breath, so loud it filled me, her cry in the old language, and my name repeated over and over among the words.

The heat was still dense the next morning when I came back to work. Fleur was gone but the men were there, slack-faced, hung over. Lily was paler and softer than ever, as if his flesh had steamed on his bones. They smoked, took pulls off a bottle. It wasn't noon yet. I worked awhile, waiting shop and sharpening steel. But I was sick, I was smothered. I was sweating so hard that my hands slipped on the knives, and I wiped my fingers clean of the greasy touch of the customers' coins. Lily opened his mouth and roared once, not in anger. There was no meaning to the sound. His boxer dog, sprawled limp beside his foot, never lifted its head. Nor did the other men.

They didn't notice when I stepped outside, hoping for a clear breath. And then I forgot them because I knew that we were all balanced, ready to tip, to fly, to be crushed as soon as the weather broke. The sky was so low that I felt the weight of it like a yoke. Clouds hung down, witch teats, a tornado's green-brown cones, and as I watched one flicked out and became a delicate probing thumb. Even as I picked up my heels and ran back inside, the wind blew suddenly, cold, and then came rain.

60 Inside, the men had disappeared already and the whole place was trembling as if a huge hand was pinched at the rafters, shaking it. I ran straight through, screaming for Dutch or for any of them, and then I stopped at the heavy doors of the lockers, where they had surely taken shelter. I stood there a moment. Everything went still. Then I heard a cry building in the wind, faint at first, a whistle and then a shrill scream that tore through the walls and gathered around me, spoke plain so I understood that I should move, put my arms out, and slam down the great iron bar that fit across the hasp and lock.

Outside, the wind was stronger, like a hand held against me. I struggled forward. The bushes tossed, the awnings flapped off storefronts, the rails of porches rattled. The odd cloud became a fat snout that nosed along the earth and sniffled, jabbed, picked at things, sucked them up, blew them apart, rooted around as if it was following a certain scent, then stopped behind me at the butcher shop and bored down like a drill.

I went flying, landed somewhere in a ball. When I opened my eyes and looked, stranger things were happening.

A herd of cattle flew through the air like giant birds, dropping dung, their mouths opened in stunned bellows. A candle, still lighted, blew past, and tables, napkins, garden tools, a whole school of drifting eyeglasses, jackets on hangers, hams, a checkerboard, a lampshade, and at last the sow from behind the lockers, on the run, her hooves a blur, set free, swooping, diving, screaming as everything in Argus fell apart and got turned upside down, smashed, and thoroughly wrecked.

Days passed before the town went looking for the men. They were bachelors, after all, except for Tor, whose wife had suffered a blow to the head that made her forgetful. Everyone was occupied with digging out, in high relief because even though the Catholic steeple had been torn off like a peaked cap and sent across five fields, those huddled in the cellar were unhurt. Walls had fallen, windows were demolished, but the stores were intact and so were the bankers and shop owners who had taken refuge in their safes or beneath their cash registers. It was a fair-minded disaster, no one could be said to have suffered much more than the next, at least not until Fritzie and Pete came home.

65 Of all the businesses in Argus, Kozka's Meats had suffered worst. The boards of the front building had been split to kindling, piled in a huge pyramid, and the shop equipment was blasted far and wide. Pete paced off the distance the iron bathtub had been flung—a hundred feet. The glass candy case went fifty, and landed without so much as a cracked pane. There were other surprises as well, for the back rooms where Fritzie and Pete lived were undisturbed. Fritzie said the dust still coated her china figures, and upon her kitchen table, in the ashtray, perched the last cigarette she'd put out in haste. She lit it up and finished it, looking through the window. From there, she could see that the old smokehouse Fleur had slept in was crushed to a reddish sand and the stockpens were completely torn apart, the rails stacked helter-skelter. Fritzie asked for Fleur. People shrugged. Then she asked about the others and, suddenly, the town understood that three men were missing.

There was a rally of help, a gathering of shovels and volunteers. We passed boards from hand to hand, stacked them, uncovered what lay beneath the pile of jagged splinters. The lockers, full of the meat that was Pete and Fritzie's investment, slowly came into sight, still intact. When enough room was made for a man to stand on the roof, there were calls, a general urge to hack through and see what lay below. But Fritzie shouted that she wouldn't allow it because the meat would spoil. And so the work continued, board by board, until at last the heavy oak doors of the freezer were revealed and people pressed to the entry. Everyone wanted to be the first, but since it was my stepfather lost, I was let go in when Pete and Fritzie wedged through into the sudden icy air.

Pete scraped a match on his boot, lit the lamp Fritzie held, and there the three of us stood still in its circle. Light glared off the skinned and hanging carcasses, the crates of wrapped sausages, the bright and cloudy blocks of lake ice, pure as winter. The cold bit into us, pleasant at first then numbing. We must have stood there a couple of minutes before we saw the men, or more rightly, the humps of fur, the iced and shaggy hides they wore, the bearskins they had taken down and wrapped around themselves. We stepped closer and tilted the lantern beneath the flaps of fur into their faces. The dog was there, perched among them heavy as a doorstop. The three had hunched around a barrel where the game was still laid out, and a dead lantern and an empty bottle, too. But they had thrown down their last hands and hunkered tight, clutching one another, knuckles raw from beating at the door they had also attacked with hooks. Frost stars gleamed off their eyelashes and the stubble of their beards. Their faces were set in concentration, mouths open as if to speak some careful thought, some agreement they'd come to in each other's arms.

Power travels in the bloodlines, handed out before birth. It comes down through the hands, which in the Pillagers were strong and knotted, big, spidery, and rough, with sensitive fingertips good at dealing cards. It comes through the eyes, too, belligerent, darkest brown, the eyes of those in the bear clan, impolite as they gaze directly at a person.

In my dreams, I look straight back at Fleur, at the men. I am no longer the watcher on the dark sill, the skinny girl.

70   The blood draws us back, as if it runs through a vein of earth. I've come home and, except for talking to my cousins, live a quiet life. Fleur lives quiet too, down on Lake Turcot with her boat. Some say she's married to the waterman, Misshepeshu, or that she's living in shame with white men or windigos, or that she's killed them all. I'm about the only one here who ever goes to visit her. Last winter, I went to help out in her cabin when she bore the child, whose green eyes and skin the color of an old penny made more talk, as no one could decide if the child was mixed blood or what, fathered in a smokehouse, or by a man with brass scales, or by the lake. The girl is bold, smiling in her sleep, as if she knows what people wonder, as if she hears the old men talk, turning the story over. It comes up different every time and has no ending, no beginning. They get the middle wrong too. They only know that they don't know anything.

Writing Log/Journal Assignment

Write about a natural disaster (flood, earthquake, hurricane) you have witnessed.

Individual and Collaborative Considerations

1. Erdrich opens her story with the sentence: "The first time she drowned in the cold and glassy waters of Lake Turcot, Fleur Pillager was only a girl." In what way is this line similar to a *lead-in sentence* in an essay?
2. List some nature images or animal metaphors Erdrich uses to describe Fleur. What is peculiar or extraordinary about Fleur?
3. How are names symbolic or ironic in the story?
4. Why do you think Fleur moves from one community to another? How do the residents of the respective communities view Fleur and why?
5. Pauline is referred to as a "moving shadow that the men never noticed." Does she ever change? What makes her relationship with Fleur special?

Writing Activities

1. Prewrite, focusing on the words *gossip* and *hearsay*. Then freewrite about what it means to be a *victim*. Finally, devise a thesis that says something about people who are *victims* of *gossip* and *hearsay*. Defend your thesis with information cited from readings as well as personal experience and observations. (Distinguish between verifiable facts and hearsay information early in your essay.)
2. Have you ever known the sort of people who seem to "make things happen" whether they are at work or play (e.g., igniting peer productivity at work or sparking a dead party to life at play)? Brainstorm this topic to gather as many examples of people who "seem" to make things happen as you can. Then take a position and write an essay persuading your reader that some people possess extraordinary power or that the powers people "seem" to exert over their environment are only as real as others imagine them to be.

In a Grove
(Yabu no Naka)

Ryunosuke Akutagawa

Ryunosuke Akutagawa became one of Japan's first internationally famous modern authors. One of his best-known works, *Rashomon*, appeared in 1915, but received little notice at the time. Thereafter, his career improved. He had a string of successful publications, engaged in teaching, and also began collecting art. When Akutagawa lost his art collection in the 1923 Tokyo fire, he was devastated. From that period in his life onward he was plagued by poor mental and physical health. In 1927, he took his own life rather than watch himself deteriorate any further. In the West, Akutagawa is probably best known for his short stories such as "The Hell Screen," "In a Grove," and "The Nose." The following short story, "In a Grove," beautifully illustrates Akutagawa's favorite belief that there are no "simple truths."

THE TESTIMONY OF A WOODCUTTER QUESTIONED BY A HIGH POLICE COMMISSIONER

Yes, sir. Certainly, it was I who found the body. This morning, as usual, I went to cut my daily quota of cedars, when I found the body in a grove in a hollow in the mountains. The exact location? About 150 meters off the Yamashina stage road. It's an out-of-the-way grove of bamboo and cedars.

The body was lying flat on its back dressed in a bluish silk kimono and a wrinkled headdress of the Kyoto style. A single sword-stroke had pierced the breast. The fallen bamboo-blades around it were stained with bloody blossoms. No, the blood was no longer running. The wound had dried up, I believe. And also, a gad-fly was stuck fast there, hardly noticing my footsteps.

You ask me if I saw a sword or any such thing?

No, nothing, sir. I found only a rope at the root of a cedar near by. And . . . well, in addition to a rope, I found a comb. That was all. Apparently he must have made a battle of it before he was murdered, because the grass and fallen bamboo-blades had been trampled down all around.

5 "A horse was near by?"

No, sir. It's hard enough for a man to enter, let alone a horse.

THE TESTIMONY OF A TRAVELING BUDDHIST PRIEST QUESTIONED BY A HIGH POLICE COMMISSIONER

The time? Certainly, it was about noon yesterday, sir. The unfortunate man was on the road from Sekiyama to Yamashina. He was walking toward Sekiyama with a woman accompanying him on horseback, who I have since learned was his wife. A scarf hanging from her head hid her face from view. All I saw was the color of her clothes, a lilac-colored suit. Her horse was a sorrel with a fine mane. The lady's height? Oh, about four feet five inches. Since I am a Buddhist priest, I took little notice about her details. Well, the man was armed with a sword as well as a bow and arrows. And I remember that he carried some twenty odd arrows in his quiver.

Little did I expect that he would meet such a fate. Truly human life is as evanescent as the morning dew or a flash of lightning. My words are inadequate to express my sympathy for him.

THE TESTIMONY OF A POLICEMAN QUESTIONED BY A HIGH POLICE COMMISSIONER

The man that I arrested? He is a notorious brigand called Tajomaru. When I arrested him, he had fallen off his horse. He was groaning on the bridge at Awataguchi. The time? It was in the early hours of last night. For the record, I might say that the other day I tried to arrest him, but unfortunately he escaped. He was wearing a dark blue silk kimono and a large plain sword. And, as you see, he got a bow and arrows somewhere. You say that this bow and these arrows look like the ones owned by the dead man? Then Tajomaru must be the murderer. The bow wound with leather strips, the black lacquered quiver, the seventeen arrows with hawk feathers—these were all in his possession I believe. Yes, sir, the horse is, as you say, a sorrel with a fine mane. A little beyond the stone bridge I found the horse grazing by the roadside, with his long rein dangling. Surely there is some providence in his having been thrown by the horse.

Of all the robbers prowling around Kyoto, this Tajomaru has given the most grief to the women in town. Last autumn a wife who came to the mountain back of the Pindora of the Toribe Temple, presumably to pay a visit, was murdered, along with a girl. It has been suspected that it was his doing. If this criminal murdered the man, you cannot tell what he may have done with the man's wife. May it please your honor to look into this problem as well.

THE TESTIMONY OF AN OLD WOMAN QUESTIONED BY A HIGH POLICE COMMISSIONER

Yes, sir, that corpse is the man who married my daughter. He does not come from Kyoto. He was a samurai in the town of Kokufu in the province of Wakasa. His name was Kanazawa no Takehiko, and his age was twenty-six. He was of a gentle disposition, so I am sure he did nothing to provoke the anger of others.

My daughter? Her name is Masago, and her age is nineteen. She is a spirited, fun-loving girl, but I am sure she has never known any man except Takehiko. She has a small, oval, dark-complected face with a mole at the corner of her left eye.

Yesterday Takehiko left for Wakasa with my daughter. What bad luck it is that things should have come to such a sad end! What has become of my daughter? I am resigned to giving up my son-in-law as lost, but the fate of my daughter worries me sick. For heaven's sake leave no stone unturned to find her. I hate that robber Tajomaru, or whatever his name is. Not only my son-in-law, but my daughter . . . (Her later words were drowned in tears.)

TAJOMARU'S CONFESSION

I killed him, but not her. Where's she gone? I can't tell. Oh, wait a minute. No torture can make me confess what I don't know. Now things have come to such a head, I won't keep anything from you.

15   Yesterday a little past noon I met that couple. Just then a puff of wind blew, and raised her hanging scarf, so that I caught a glimpse of her face. Instantly it was again covered from my view. That may have been one reason; she looked like a Bodhisattva. At that moment I made up my mind to capture her even if I had to kill her man.

Why? To me killing isn't a matter of such great consequence as you might think. When a woman is captured, her man has to be killed anyway. In killing, I use the sword I wear at my side. Am I the only one who kills people? You, you don't use your swords. You kill people with your power, with your money. Sometimes you kill them on the pretext of working for their good. It's true they don't bleed. They are in the best of health, but all the same you've killed them. It's hard to say who is a greater sinner, you or me. (An ironical smile.)

But it would be good if I could capture a woman without killing her man. So, I made up my mind to capture her, and do my best not to kill him. But it's out of the question on the Yamashina stage road. So I managed to lure the couple into the mountains.

It was quite easy. I became their traveling companion, and I told them there was an old mound in the mountain over there, and that I had dug it open and found many mirrors and swords. I went on to tell them I'd buried the things in a grove behind the mountain, and that I'd like to sell them at a low price to anyone who would care to have them. Then . . . you see, isn't greed terrible? He was beginning to be moved by my talk before he knew it. In less than half an hour they were driving their horse toward the mountain with me.

When he came in front of the grove, I told them that the treasures were buried in it, and I asked them to come and see. The man had no objection—he was blinded by greed. The woman said she would wait on horseback. It was natural for her to say so, at the sight of a thick grove. To tell you the truth, my plan worked just as I wished, so I went into the grove with him, leaving her behind alone.

20   The grove is only bamboo for some distance. About fifty yards ahead there's a rather open clump of cedars. It was a convenient spot for my purpose. Pushing my way through the grove, I told him a plausible lie that the treasures were buried under the cedars. When I told him this, he pushed his

laborious way toward the slender cedar visible through the grove. After a while the bamboo thinned out, and we came to where a number of cedars grew in a row. As soon as we got there, I seized him from behind. Because he was a trained, sword-bearing warrior, he was quite strong, but he was taken by surprise, so there was no help for him. I soon tied him up to the root of a cedar. Where did I get a rope? Thank heaven, being a robber, I had a rope with me, since I might have to scale a wall at any moment. Of course it was easy to stop him from calling out by gagging his mouth with fallen bamboo leaves.

When I disposed of him, I went to his woman and asked her to come and see him, because he seemed to have been suddenly taken sick. It's needless to say that this plan also worked well. The woman, her sedge hat off, came into the depths of the grove, where I led her by the hand. The instant she caught sight of her husband, she drew a small sword. I've never seen a woman of such violent temper. If I'd been off guard, I'd have got a thrust in my side. I dodged, but she kept on slashing at me. She might have wounded me deeply or killed me. But I'm Tajomaru. I managed to strike down her small sword without drawing my own. The most spirited woman is defenseless without a weapon. At least I could satisfy my desire for her without taking her husband's life.

Yes, . . . without taking his life. I had no wish to kill him. I was about to run away from the grove, leaving the woman behind in tears, when she frantically clung to my arm. In broken fragments of words, she asked that either her husband or I die. She said it was more trying than death to have her shame known to two men. She gasped out that she wanted to be the wife of whichever survived. Then a furious desire to kill him seized me. (Gloomy excitement.)

Telling you in this way, no doubt I seem a crueler man than you. But that's because you didn't see her face. Especially her burning eyes at that moment. As I saw her eye to eye, I wanted to make her my wife even if I were to be struck by lightning. I wanted to make her my wife . . . this single desire filled my mind. This was not only lust, as you might think. At that time if I'd had no other desire than lust, I'd surely not have minded knocking her down and running away. Then I wouldn't have stained my sword with his blood. But the moment I gazed at her face in the dark grove, I decided not to leave there without killing him.

But I didn't like to resort to unfair means to kill him. I untied him and told him to cross swords with me. (The rope that was found at the root of the cedar is the rope I dropped at the time.) Furious with anger, he drew his thick sword. And quick as thought, he sprang at me ferociously, without speaking a word. I needn't tell you how our fight turned out. The twenty-third stroke . . . please remember this. I'm impressed with this fact still. Nobody under the sun has ever clashed swords with me twenty strokes. (A cheerful smile.)

When he fell, I turned toward her, lowering my blood-stained sword. But to my great astonishment she was gone. I wondered to where she had run away. I looked for her in the clump of cedars. I listened, but heard only a groaning sound from the throat of the dying man.

As soon as we started to cross swords, she may have run away through the grove to call for help. When I thought of that, I decided it was a matter of life and death to me. So, robbing him of his sword, and bow and arrows, I ran out to the mountain road. There I found her horse still grazing quietly. It would be a mere waste of words to tell you the later details, but before I entered town I had already parted with the sword. That's all my confession. I know that my head will be hung in chains anyway, so put me down for the maximum penalty. (A defiant attitude.)

The Confession of a Woman Who Has Come to the Shimizu Temple

That man in the blue silk kimono, after forcing me to yield to him, laughed mockingly as he looked at my bound husband. How horrified my husband must have been! But no matter how hard he struggled in agony, the rope cut into him all the more tightly. In spite of myself I ran stumblingly toward his side. Or rather I tried to run toward him, but the man instantly knocked me down. Just at that moment I saw an indescribable light in my husband's eyes. Something beyond expression . . . his eyes make me shudder even now. That instantaneous look of my husband, who couldn't speak a word, told me all his heart. The flash in his eyes was neither anger nor sorrow . . . only a cold light, a look of loathing. More struck by the look in his eyes than by the blow of the thief, I called out in spite of myself and fell unconscious.

In the course of time I came to, and found that the man in blue silk was gone. I saw only my husband still bound to the root of the cedar. I raised myself from the bamboo-blades with difficulty, and looked into his face but the expression in his eyes was just the same as before.

Beneath the cold contempt in his eyes, there was hatred. Shame, grief, and anger . . . I didn't know how to express my heart at that time. Reeling to my feet, I went up to my husband.

30   "Takejiro," I said to him, "since things have come to this pass, I cannot live with you. I'm determined to die, . . . but you must die, too. You saw my shame. I can't leave you alive as you are."

This was all I could say. Still he went on gazing at me with loathing and contempt. My heart breaking, I looked for his sword. It must have been taken by the robber. Neither his sword nor his bow and arrows were to be seen in the grove. But fortunately my small sword was lying at my feet. Raising it over head, once more I said, "Now give me your life. I'll follow you right away."

When he heard these words, he moved his lips with difficulty. Since his mouth was stuffed with leaves, of course his voice could not be heard at all. But at a glance I understood his words. Despising me, his look said only,

"Kill me." Neither conscious nor unconscious, I stabbed the small sword through the lilac-colored kimono into his breast.

Again at this time I must have fainted. By the time I managed to look up, he had already breathed his last—still in bonds. A streak of sinking sunlight streamed through the clump of cedars and bamboos, and shone on his pale face. Gulping down my sobs, I untied the rope from his dead body. And . . . and what has become of me since I have no more strength to tell you. Anyway I hadn't the strength to die. I stabbed my own throat with the small sword, I threw myself into a pond at the foot of the mountain, and I tried to kill myself in many ways. Unable to end my life, I am still living in dishonor. (A lonely smile.) Worthless as I am, I must have been forsaken even by the most merciful Kwannon. I killed my own husband. I was violated by the robber. Whatever can I do? Whatever can I . . . I . . . (Gradually, violent sobbing.)

The Story of the Murdered Man, As Told through a Medium

After violating my wife, the robber, sitting there, began to speak comforting words to her. Of course I couldn't speak. My whole body was tied fast to the root of a cedar. But meanwhile I winked at her many times, as much as to say "Don't believe the robber." I wanted to convey some such meaning to her. But my wife, sitting dejectedly on the bamboo leaves, was looking hard at her lap. To all appearances, she was listening to his words. I was agonized by jealousy. In the meantime the robber went on with his clever talk, from one subject to another. The robber finally made his bold brazen proposal. "Once your virtue is stained, you won't get along well with your husband, so won't you be my wife instead? It's my love for you that made me be violent toward you."

35   While the criminal talked, my wife raised her face as if in a trance. She had never looked so beautiful as at that moment. What did my beautiful wife say in answer to him while I was sitting bound there? I am lost in space, but I have never thought of her answer without burning with anger and jealousy. Truly she said, . . . "Then take me away with you wherever you go."

This is not the whole of her sin. If that were all, I would not be tormented so much in the dark. When she was going out of the grove as if in a dream, her hand in the robber's, she suddenly turned pale, and pointed at me tied to the root of the cedar, and said, "Kill him! I cannot marry you as long as he lives." "Kill him!" she cried many times, as if she had gone crazy. Even now these words threaten to blow me headlong into the bottomless abyss of darkness. Has such a hateful thing come out of a human mouth ever before? Have such cursed words ever struck a human ear, even once? Even once such a . . . (A sudden cry of scorn.) At these words the robber himself turned pale. "Kill him," she cried, clinging to his arms. Looking hard at her, he answered neither yes or no . . . but hardly had I thought about his answer before she had been knocked down into the bamboo leaves. (Again a cry of scorn.) Quietly folding his arms, he looked at me and said, "What will you do with her? Kill her or save her? You have only to nod. Kill her?" For these words alone I would like to pardon his crime.

While I hesitated, she shrieked and ran into the depths of the grove. The robber instantly snatched at her, but he failed even to grasp her sleeve.

After she ran away, he took up my sword, and my bow and arrows. With a single stroke he cut one of my bonds. I remember his mumbling, "My fate is next." Then he disappeared from the grove. All was silent after that. No, I heard someone crying. Untying the rest of my bonds, I listened carefully, and I noticed that it was my own crying. (Long silence.)

I raised my exhausted body from the root of the cedar. In front of me there was shining the small sword which my wife had dropped. I took it up and stabbed it into my breast. A bloody lump rose to my mouth, but I didn't feel any pain. When my breast grew cold, everything was as silent as the dead in their graves. What profound silence! Not a single bird-note was heard in the sky over this grave in the hollow of the mountains. Only a lonely light lingered on the cedars and mountains. By and by the light gradually grew fainter, till the cedars and bamboo were lost to view. Lying there, I was enveloped in deep silence.

40   Then someone crept up to me. I tried to see who it was. But darkness had already been gathering round me. Someone . . . that someone drew the small sword softly out of my breast in its invisible hand. At the same time once more blood flowed into my mouth. And once and for all I sank down into the darkness of space.

Writing Log/Journal Assignment

Is there anything in your family history that has never been resolved? What is it about family dynamics that makes the truth difficult to express? Your journal entry here may consist of no more than a *prewriting* exercise on the topic: *family history.*

Individual and Collaborative Considerations

1. Who committed murder? Why?
2. What does Akutagawa seem to imply about *truth?*
3. What did the people who confessed to the murder have to gain from their testimonies?
4. How do our egos often prevent individuals from perceiving the truth accurately?
5. What might be Akutagawa's strategic purpose for structuring his story as a series of interviews and confessions rather than a continuous narrative presented from one point of view?

Writing Activities

1. Research an unsolved crime and come up with a hypothesis followed by careful reasoning and evidence, pointing to the probable perpetrator of the crime.
2. Given the same set of circumstances as another person's (e.g., an automobile accident or a robbery), analyze what caused you to *witness* the event differently. Pay attention to specific details.

❋

There Will Come Soft Rains

Ray Bradbury

Ray Bradbury began his career publishing short stories in pulp magazines, but by 1945 he earned the respect of his peers and became known as a serious author of fiction, drama, and poetry. Today, his name is synonymous with science fiction and fantasy. Bradbury's collections include *Dark Carnival* (1947), *The Martian Chronicles* (1950), *The Illustrated Man* (1951), *The Golden Apples of the Sun* (1953), *October Country* (1955), *A Meditation for Melancholy* (1959), *R Is for Rocket, S Is for Space* (1962), *Any Friend of Nicholas Nickleby's Is a Friend of Mine* (1968), and *I Sing the Body Electric* (1969). His novels are also well known: *Fahrenheit 451* (1953), *Dandelion Wine* (1957), and *Something Wicked This Way Comes* (1962). Among Bradbury's plays are *The Wonderful Ice Cream Suit* (1965), *The Halloween Tree* (1968), and *Pillar of Fire* (1975), as well as film scripts like *Moby Dick* (1954). His poems appear in *When Elephants Last in the Dooryard Blossomed* (1973) and *Where Robot Men and Robot Women Run Round in Robot Towns* (1977).

In the living room the voice-clock sang, *Tick-tock, seven o'clock, time to get up time to get up, seven o'clock!* as if it were afraid that nobody would. The morning house lay empty. The clock ticked on repeating and repeating its sounds into the emptiness. *Seven-nine, breakfast time, seven-nine!*

In the kitchen the breakfast stove gave a hissing sigh and ejected from its warm interior eight pieces of perfectly browned toast, eight eggs sunnyside up, sixteen slices of bacon, two coffees, and two cool glasses of milk.

"Today is August 4, 2026," said a second voice from the kitchen ceiling, "in the city of Allendale, California." It repeated the date three times for memory's sake. "Today is Mr. Featherstone's birthday. Today is the anniversary of Tilita's marriage. Insurance is payable, as are the water, gas, and light bills."

Somewhere in the walls, relays clicked, memory tapes glided under electric eyes.

5   *Eight-one, tick-tock, eight-one o'clock, off to school, off to work, run, run, eight-one!* But no doors slammed, no carpets took the soft tread of rubber heels. It was raining outside. The weather box on the front door sang quietly: "Rain, rain, go away; rubbers, raincoats for today. . . ." And the rain tapped on the empty house, echoing.

Outside, the garage chimed and lifted its door to reveal the waiting car. After a long wait the door swung down again.

At eight-thirty the eggs were shriveled and the toast was like stone. An aluminum wedge scraped them into the sink, where hot water whirled them down a metal throat which digested and flushed them away to the distant sea. The dirty dishes were dropped into a hot washer and emerged twinkling dry.

Nine-fifteen, sang the clock, *time to clean.*

Out of warrens in the wall, tiny robot mice darted. The rooms were acrawl with the small cleaning animals, all rubber and metal. They thudded against chairs, whirling their mustached runners, kneading the rug nap, sucking gently at hidden dust. Then, like mysterious invaders, they popped into their burrows. Their pink electric eyes faded. The house was clean.

10   *Ten o'clock.* The sun came out from behind the rain. The house stood alone in a city of rubble and ashes. This was the one house left standing. At night the ruined city gave off a radioactive glow which could be seen for miles.

Ten-fifteen. The garden sprinklers whirled up in golden founts, filling the soft morning air with scatterings of brightness. The water pelted window-panes, running down the charred west side where the house had been burned evenly free of its white paint. The entire west face of the house was black, save for five places. Here the silhouette in paint of a man mowing a lawn. Here, as in a photograph, a woman bent to pick flowers. Still farther over, their images burned on wood in one titanic instant, a small boy, hands flung into the air; higher up, the image of a ball, and opposite him a girl, hands raised to catch a ball which never came down.

The five spots of paint—the man, the woman, the children, the ball— remained. The rest was a thin charcoaled layer.

The gentle sprinkler rain filled the garden with falling light.

Until this day, how well the house had kept its peace. How carefully it had inquired, "Who goes there? What's the password?" and, getting no answer from lonely foxes and whining cats, it had shut up its windows and drawn shades in an old-maidenly preoccupation with self-protection which bordered on a mechanical paranoia.

15   It quivered at each sound, the house did. If a sparrow brushed a window, the shade snapped up. The bird, startled, flew off! No, not even a bird must touch the house!

The house was an altar with ten thousand attendants, big, small, servicing, attending, in choirs. But the gods had gone away, and the ritual of the religion continued senselessly, uselessly.

Twelve noon.

A dog whined, shivering, on the front porch.

The front door recognized the dog voice and opened. The dog, once huge and fleshy, but now gone to bone and covered with sores, moved in and through the house, tracking mud. Behind it whirred angry mice, angry at having to pick up mud, angry at inconvenience.

20   For not a leaf fragment blew under the door but what the wall panels flipped open and the copper scrap rats flashed swiftly out. The offending dust, hair, or paper, seized in miniature steel jaws, was raced back to the burrows. There, down tubes which fed into the cellar, it was dropped into the sighing vent of an incinerator which sat like evil Baal in a dark corner.

The dog ran upstairs, hysterically yelping to each door, at last realizing, as the house realized, that only silence was here.

It sniffed the air and scratched the kitchen door. Behind the door, the stove was making pancakes which filled the house with a rich baked odor and the scent of maple syrup.

The dog frothed at the mouth, lying at the door, sniffing, its eyes turned to fire. It ran wildly in circles, biting at its tail, spun in a frenzy, and died. It lay in the parlor for an hour.

Two o'clock, sang a voice.

25   Delicately sensing decay at last, the regiments of mice hummed out as softly as blown gray leaves in an electrical wind.

Two-fifteen.

The dog was gone.

In the cellar, the incinerator glowed suddenly and a whirl of sparks leaped up the chimney.

Two thirty-five.

30   Bridge tables sprouted from patio walls. Playing cards fluttered onto pads in a shower of pips. Martinis manifested on an oaken bench with egg-salad sandwiches. Music played.

But the tables were silent and the cards untouched.

At four o'clock the tables folded like great butterflies back through the paneled walls.

Four-thirty.

The nursery walls glowed.

35   Animals took shape: yellow giraffes, blue lions, pink antelopes, lilac panthers cavorting in crystal substance. The walls were glass. They looked out upon color and fantasy. Hidden films clocked through well-oiled sprockets, and the walls lived. The nursery floor was woven to resemble a crisp, cereal meadow. Over this ran aluminum roaches and iron crickets, and in the hot still air butterflies of delicate red tissue wavered among the sharp aroma of animal spoor! There was the sound like a great matted yellow hive of bees within a dark bellows, the lazy bumble of a purring lion. And there was the patter of okapi feet and the murmur of a fresh jungle rain, like other hoofs, falling upon the summer-starched grass. Now the walls dissolved into

distances of parched weed, mile on mile, and warm endless sky. The animals drew away into thorn brakes and water holes.

It was the children's hour.

Five o'clock. The bath filled with clear hot water.

Six, seven, eight o'clock. The dinner dishes manipulated like magic tricks, and the study a *click.* In the metal stand opposite the hearth where a fire now blazed up warmly, a cigar popped out, half an inch of soft gray ash on it, smoking, waiting.

Nine o'clock. The beds warmed their hidden circuits, for nights were cool here.

40   *Nine-five.* A voice spoke from the study ceiling:

"Mrs. McClellan, which poem would you like this evening?"

The house was silent.

The voice said at last, "Since you express no preference, I shall select a poem at random." Quiet music rose to back the voice. "Sara Teasdale." As I recall, favorite . . .

> There will come soft rains and the smell of the ground,
> And swallows circling with their shimmering sound;
>
> And frogs in the pools singing at night,
> And wild plum trees in tremulous white;
>
> Robins will wear their feathery fire,
> Whistling their whims on a low fence-wire;
>
> And not one will know of war, not one
> Will care at last when it is done.
>
> Not one would mind, neither bird nor tree,
> If mankind perished utterly;
>
> And Spring herself, when she woke at dawn
> Would scarcely know that we were gone.

The fire burned on the stone hearth and the cigar fell away into a mound of quiet ash on its tray. The empty chairs faced each other between the silent walls, and the music played.

45   At ten o'clock the house began to die.

The wind blew. A falling tree bough crashed through the kitchen window. Cleaning solvent, bottled, shattered over the stove. The room was ablaze in an instant!

"Fire!" screamed a voice. The house lights flashed, water pumps shot water from the ceilings. But the solvent spread on the linoleum, licking, eating, under the kitchen door, while the voices took it up in chorus: "Fire, fire, fire!"

The house tried to save itself. Doors sprang tightly shut, but the windows were broken by the heat and the wind blew and sucked upon the fire.

The house gave ground as the fire in ten billion angry sparks moved with flaming ease from room to room and then up the stairs. While scurrying water rats squeaked from the walls, pistoled their water, and ran for more. And the wall sprays let down showers of mechanical rain.

50 But too late. Somewhere, sighing, a pump shrugged to a stop. The quenching rain ceased. The reserve water supply which had filled baths and washed dishes for many quiet days was gone.

The fire crackled up the stairs. It fed upon Picassos and Matisses in the upper halls, like delicacies, baking off the oily flesh, tenderly crisping the canvases into black shavings.

Now the fire lay in beds, stood in windows, changed the colors of drapes! And then, reinforcements.

From attic trapdoors, blind robot faces peered down with faucet mouths gushing green chemical.

55 The fire backed off, as even an elephant must at the sight of a dead snake. Now there were twenty snakes whipping over the floor, killing the fire with a clear cold venom of green froth.

But the fire was clever. It had sent flame outside the house, up through the attic to the pumps there. An explosion! The attic brain which directed the pumps was shattered into bronze shrapnel on the beams.

The fire rushed back into every closet and felt of the clothes hung there.

The house shuddered, oak bone on bone, its bared skeleton cringing from the heat, its wire, its nerves revealed as if a surgeon had torn the skin off to let the red veins and capillaries quiver in the scalded air. Help, help! Fire! Run, run! Heat snapped mirrors like the first brittle winter ice. And the voices wailed Fire, fire, run, run, like a tragic nursery rhyme, a dozen voices, high, low, like children dying in a forest, alone, alone. And the voices fading as the wires popped their sheathings like hot chestnuts. One, two, three, four, five voices died.

In the nursery the jungle burned. Blue lions roared, purple giraffes bounded off. The panthers ran in circles, changing color, and ten million animals, running before the fire, vanished off toward a distant steaming river. . . .

60 Ten more voices died. In the last instant under the fire avalanche, other choruses, oblivious, could be heard announcing the time, playing music, cutting the lawn by remote control mower, or setting an umbrella frantically out and in the slamming and opening front door, a thousand things happening, like a clock shop when each clock strikes the hour insanely before or after the other, a scene of maniac confusion, yet unity; singing, screaming, a few last cleaning mice darting bravely out to carry the horrid ashes away! And one voice, with sublime disregard for the situation, read poetry aloud in the fiery study, until all the film spools burned, until all the wires withered and the circuits cracked.

The fire burst the house and let it slam flat down, puffing out skirts of spark and smoke.

In the kitchen, an instant before the rain of fire and timber, the stove could be seen making breakfasts at a psychopathic rate, ten dozen eggs, six loaves of toast, twenty dozen bacon strips, which, eaten by fire, started the stove working again, hysterically hissing!

The crash. The attic smashing into kitchen and parlor. The parlor into cellar, cellar into sub-cellar. Deep freeze, armchair, film tapes, circuits, beds, and all like skeletons thrown in a cluttered mound deep under.

Smoke and silence. A great quantity of smoke.

65   Dawn showed faintly in the east. Among the ruins, one wall stood alone. Within the wall, a last voice said, over and over again and again, even as the sun rose to shine upon the heaped rubble and steam:

"Today is August 5, 2026, today is August 5, 2026, today is . . ."

Writing Log/Journal Assignment

Write the title of Bradbury's story (and Teasdale's poem) on the top of a piece of paper and meditate on it for a minute or two. Then, in either poetry or verse, write about something you feel directly responds to "There Will Come Soft Rains."

Individual and Collaborative Considerations

1. At what point in the story does it become apparent to you that some great catastrophe has occurred?
2. Who or what is the protagonist in this story? Who or what is the antagonist?
3. When did you realize you were reading a futuristic story? What techniques did the author use to draw you into his story?
4. How does Bradbury spark your imagination? Explain how his appeal to one's sense of sound helps create atmosphere appropriate to the occasion and setting.
5. Many of Bradbury's paragraphs begin with a time reference. How does this affect reader perception of the information that follows? In what way do these references provide coherence and move the story along?

Writing Activities

1. What is your personal definition of "science fiction"? In a well-developed essay, show how and why "There Will Come Soft Rains" exemplifies your definition and clarifies your reader's conception of that form of fiction. You might want to ask yourself, "What are the qualities of science fiction?"

2. Do some research on nuclear holocausts. Rent a film like *The Day After* or watch some footage of the effects of atomic radiation on the survivors of Hiroshima or Nagasaki (after World War II). Then write a descriptive essay detailing what an imaginative city (in your own mind) would look like following nuclear destruction. To sharpen some of your descriptions, you might allude to either Bradbury's story or your visual references.

We Wear the Mask

Paul Laurence Dunbar

Although he lived only thirty-four years, Dunbar became Black America's first nationally known poet, was a popular reader of his verse in both the United States and England, and held a job at the Library of Congress. His literary output was incredible in spite of the fact that he had a debilitating illness. The best of Dunbar's earliest poetry was collected and published as *Lyrics of Lowly Life* (1896). Between 1896 and 1906, the year of his death, Dunbar wrote and published four novels: *The Uncalled* (1896), *The Love of Landry* (1900), *The Fanatics* (1901), and *The Sport of the Gods* (1902); three volumes of verse: *Lyrics of the Hearthside* (1899), *Lyrics of Love and Laughter* (1903); four collections of short stories; and a musical play: *Uncle Eph's Christmas* (1900). He referred to his poetry written in standard American English, such as "We Wear the Mask," as "major" poems and poetry written in dialect as "minor." Although both his "major" and "minor" poetry were well received, Dunbar is best known today for his verse written in standard American English.

> We wear the mask that grins and lies,
> It hides our cheeks and shades our eyes—
> This debt we pay to human guile;
> With torn and bleeding hearts we smile,
> And mouth with myriad subtleties.
>
> Why should the world be over-wise,
> In counting all our tears and sighs?
> Nay, let them only see us, while
>   We wear the mask.

5

10   We smile, but, O great Christ, our cries
        To thee from tortured souls arise.
        We sing, but oh the clay is vile
        Beneath our feet, and long the mile;
        But let the world dream otherwise,
15   We wear the mask.

Writing Log/Journal Assignment

Have you or a friend of yours ever "worn a mask" or a false face? What were you hiding? How successful were you?

Individual and Collaborative Considerations

1. Go back through the poem and identify words reflecting pain and humility—both hidden by "the mask."
2. What is "human guile"? Why would anyone owe a "debt" to it?
3. Dramatically read the poem aloud. What is the dominant tone of "We Wear the Mask"?
4. What does the speaker mean by the lines, "Why should the world be over-wise, / In counting all our tears and sighs?"
5. What helps Dunbar's poem build intensity during the third (and final) stanza?

Writing Activities

1. Have you ever experienced prejudice and oppression? Compose an essay titled "I Wore the Mask," explaining how and why you felt compelled by social pressures or fear to adopt a false guise. After focusing in on your thesis, try developing your paper by blending narration with cause and effect.
2. It is very common to hear the expression that "every person wears many different hats," depending on the situation (especially in the business world). Write an essay defending or attacking such a concept, using specific, contemporary examples and careful analysis.

The Moose

Elizabeth Bishop

A Vassar graduate in 1934, Elizabeth Bishop spent many years of her life in Brazil and published several of her colloquial poems in *North and South* (1946). These and additional poems were later reprinted as *North and South—A Cold Spring,* for which she received a Pulitzer Prize (1955). Bishop's other works include *Brazil* (1962), *Questions of Travel* (1965), *Complete Poems,* which won the National Book Award (1969), *Geography III* (1976), *That Was Then* (1980), and the posthumously published *Collected Prose.* Bishop's verse tends to be full of vivid images and figurative language and has influenced the work of her friends, Robert Lowell and Randell Jarrell, and many other poets in the twentieth century.

From narrow provinces
of fish and bread and tea,
home of the long tides
where the bay leaves the sea
5   twice a day and takes
the herrings long rides,

where if the river
enters or retreats
in a wall of brown foam
10   depends on if it meets
the bay coming in,
the bay not at home;

where, silted red,
sometimes the sun sets
15   facing a red sea,
and others, veins the flats'
lavender, rich mud
in burning rivulets;

on red, gravelly roads,
20   down rows of sugar maples,
past clapboard farmhouses
and neat, clapboard churches,
bleached, ridged as clamshells,
past twin silver birches,

25   through late afternoon
a bus journeys west,
the windshield flashing pink,
pink glancing off metal,
brushing the dented flank
30   of blue, beat-up enamel;

down hollows, up rises,
and waits, patient, while
a lone traveller gives
kisses and embraces
35   to seven relatives
and a collie supervises.

Goodbye to the elms,
to the farm, to the dog.
The bus starts. The light
40   grows richer; the fog,
shifting, salty, thin,
comes closing in.

Its cold, round crystals
form and slide and settle
45   in the white hens' feathers,
in gray glazed cabbages,
on the cabbage roses
and lupins like apostles;

the sea peas cling
50   to their wet white string
on the whitewashed fences;
bumblebees creep
inside the foxgloves,
and evening commences.

55   One stop at Bass River.
Then the Economies—
Lower, Middle, Upper;
Five Islands, Five Houses,
where a woman shakes a tablecloth
60   out, after supper.

A pale flickering. Gone.
The Tantramar marches
and the smell of salt hay.
An iron bridge trembles
65   and a loose plank rattles
but doesn't give way.

On the left, a red light
swims through the dark:
a ship's port lantern.
70   Two rubber boots show,
illuminated, solemn.
A dog gives one bark.

A woman climbs in
with two market bags,
75   brisk, freckled, elderly.
"A grand night, Yes, sir,
all the way to Boston."
She regards us amicably.

Moonlight as we enter
80   the New Brunswick woods,
hairy, scratchy, splintery;
moonlight and mist
caught in them like lamb's wool
on brushes in a pasture.

85   The passengers lie back.
Snores. Some long sighs.
A dreamy divagation
begins in the night,
a gentle, auditory,
90   slow hallucination. . . .

In the creakings and noises,
an old conversation
—not concerning us,
but recognizable, somewhere,
95   back in the bus:
Grandparents' voices

uninterruptedly
talking, in Eternity:
names being mentioned,
100   things cleared up finally;
what he said, what she said,
who got pensioned;

deaths, deaths, and sicknesses;
the year he remarried;
105   the year (something) happened.
She died in childbirth.
That was the son lost
when the schooner foundered.

He took to drink. Yes.
She went to the bad.
When Amos began to pray
even in the store and
finally the family had
to put him away.

"Yes . . ." that peculiar
affirmative. "Yes . . ."
A sharp, indrawn breath,
half groan, half acceptance,
that means "Life's like that.
We know *it* (also death)."

Talking the way they talked
in the old featherbed,
peacefully, on and on,
dim lamplight in the hall,
down in the kitchen, the dog
tucked in her shawl.

Now, it's all right now
even to fall asleep
just as on all those nights.
—Suddenly the bus driver
stops with a jolt,
turns off his lights.

A moose has come out of
the impenetrable wood
and stands there, looms, rather,
in the middle of the road.
It approaches; it sniffs at
the bus's hot hood.

Towering, antlerless,
high as a church,
homely as a house
(or, safe as houses).
A man's voice assures us
"Perfectly harmless . . ."

Some of the passengers
exclaim in whispers,
childishly, softly,
"Sure big creatures."
"It's awful plain."
"Look! It's a she!"

110
115
120
125
130
135
140 .
145
150

Taking her time,
she looks the bus over,
grand, otherworldly.
Why, why do we feel
55   (we all feel) this sweet
sensation of joy?

"Curious creatures,"
says our bus driver,
rolling his *r's*.
60   "Look at that, would you."
Then he shifts gears.
For a moment longer,

by craning backward,
the moose can be seen
65   on the moonlit macadam;
then there's a dim
smell of moose, an acrid
smell of gasoline.

Writing Log/Journal Assignment

Think about a time in your life when you went on a vacation, immigrated from another country to the United States, or moved from one part of the United States to another and reconstruct the events leading up to your departure, your trip itself, and your arrival at your destination.

Individual and Collaborative Considerations

1. What do the first four stanzas in "The Moose" set up? That is, what do they describe and why?
2. How does Bishop's use of vivid imagery re-create the spirit of her subject: the journey in general and the moose in particular?
3. Who might the "lone traveller" in stanza 6 symbolize? Apart from seven relatives—in stanza 7, to what is the "lone traveller" saying "goodbye"?
4. How do Bishop's allusions to several unrelated conversations capture the atmosphere of a bus journey?
5. Why do you imagine the moose appears out of "nowhere" at the end of the poem? How does it relate to people on a journey to "somewhere"? Why do you think Bishop titled her poem "The Moose" instead of "The Bus"?

Writing Activities

1. Write a narrative essay detailing your encounter with the sights and sounds of a *community* different from your own. Consider all of the *curious*

creatures, people, places, and things you observe. How and why are they new, fascinating, or terrifying? Attempt to enable your readers to feel, smell, hear, and visualize what you do through careful word selection.

2. Analyze your writing log/journal assignment. What thesis would epitomize your feelings about the movement from one place to another? (Perhaps you would like to focus on only the departure or the arrival.) After determining a thesis statement, write an analytical essay that examines your theme in detail. Support your essay with examples drawn from your writing log/journal assignment (and other personal experiences), observations you have made of others, and readings.

ADDITIONAL TOPICS AND ISSUES FOR WRITING AND RESEARCH

1. Go back to Richard Brautigan's poem, "In a Café," and glance over your annotations. Freewrite about your conception of the type of man who would "fold a slice of bread/as if he were folding a birth certificate or looking at the photograph of a dead lover." Write an essay arguing how either activity might be considered interaction with identity or belonging. Draw on thoughts and ideas presented in your freewriting to help justify and support your thesis.

2. In a thoroughly documented paper, examine the metaphor of "family" as it relates to youth groups, gangs, clichés, sororities, and fraternities today. What did the family unit traditionally offer? Why do you imagine so many "surrogate families" have evolved through the ages?

3. Research how unions (limit your focus here) have assisted their members in the fight for reasonable, safe working conditions; fair, competitive salaries; and good opportunities for upward social mobility.

4. Write an essay explaining the meaning of the words *progress* and *change* in modern society. Support your definition and claims with a variety of evidence, including firsthand interviews or testimonies from people who have witnessed change for over three quarters of a century.

5. Compare and contrast two communities (figurative or literal), focusing on the advantages and disadvantages of belonging to them. Reach some definite conclusions based on your examination of both communities.

6. Convince your readers that the future of small, independent businesses is or is not secure in the United States. Begin your persuasive essay by making a survey of the independent or "family" businesses in your area. These may include grocery stores, restaurants, small-scale electronics firms, and farms. Then, contrast your findings to the size and power of corporate conglomerates.

7. Argue for a larger role for minorities, especially recent immigrants (women in particular), in the workplace.

8. Glance over a photograph and prewrite about it. What images, topics, or issues did your prewriting activity generate? Take one of them and

construct a thesis about it. Then write an essay fully defending your thesis.

9. Write an essay explaining what it is like to be a member of a learning community in college. Who or what are some of the people, places, and things you must put up with? How do the advantages outweigh the disadvantages of belonging to the community?

10. In a well-reasoned essay that also appeals to the emotions, persuade your readers that introducing young children to elderly people in rest homes can be a healthy, eye-opening, memorable experience.

Starting Points for Research

Multiple Communities, Multiple Perspectives

- Kissing customs
- Drinking on television
- Community colleges
- Detention camps
- Juvenile delinquency
- Cable television
- Community-based correction centers
- Community centers
- Schools as social centers
- Youth centers
- Movements
- Welfare councils
- Community development
    Regional
    Economic assistance
    Communications and rural development
    Factories—location
    Federal aid
    Fundamental education
    Mass media in community development
    Television in community development
    Women in community development
    Youth volunteers in community development
    City planning
- Community libraries
- Community forests
- Community gardens
- Leadership
- Human ecology
- Community music

- Newspapers
- Television stations
- Community property
- Community psychology
- Community theater
- Rehabilitation programs
- Comparative religions
- Comparative morphology
- Multilingual societies
- Monolingual societies
- Cults
- The workplace
- Drinking customs
- Community churches
- Native American reservations
- Hospitals and community
- Community antenna television
- Community art projects
- Halfway houses
- Community chests
- Mosques as social centers
- Unions
- Multinationalism
- Community health services

The Research Paper

16

Research

The nature of a research paper may vary from instructor to instructor. Some believe a research paper starts with a hypothesis and moves towards a thorough study of the topic or issue. The results of your research will usually validate or disprove a tentative hypothesis. In this sort of research paper, you will gather, read, and synthesize a good deal of research before you begin the writing process. Lauren Radkins offers an example of such a research paper in "Health and Cultural Traditions" at the end of chapter 17. Other professors consider a research paper any essay applying *parenthetical citations* and including a list of *works cited*. The sample student essay in part 1 of *Thresholds*, "Disparity and the Wild Woman Archetype," presents an excellent example of a paper with documented sources—sometimes called a "limited research paper." Both forms of research require you to use the library and other resources to collect data and information supporting or refuting your thesis. Starting points for investigation and research have been provided at the end of each thematic chapter in *Thresholds*.

THE RESEARCH PROCESS

Traditional practice suggests *brainstorming* a list of topics or issues appropriate for research—topics or issues you would like to know more about. After generating a list of topics, go back and ask yourself questions like these:

> Why am I interested in this topic? What do I want or expect to get out of my research? What is my attitude towards each topic on my list? How might my attitude cloud objectivity? Where will I be able to locate the most current information on my topic? The library, Public Records Office, ERIC? An online computer information service or network?

Like any other essay you write, your research paper should limit its scope. A narrowly focused thesis will help you to offer a thorough treatment of a subject within an allotted time period and, perhaps, a prescribed length. Your questions will enable you to narrow your list of possible essay topics. Thus, a research paper on modern filmmakers might be narrowed to women and the cinema in the 1990s; a paper on the United States and government elections could eventually focus on the art of political smear campaigns.

Whether you take and enter a topic generated from one of your lists or begin your research with one of the suggested Starting Points for Research that appear at the end of each thematic chapter, locating what others have written about your topic will further refine your focus and influence the direction you wish to take when developing a tentative thesis. The sample student research paper at the end of chapter 17 provides a case in point. After reading several selections on initiations and rituals in chapter 12, Lauren Radkins, a nursing student, began prewriting by brainstorming a word very important to her, *medicine,* as well as *social change.* Following a series of prewriting activities, Radkins arrived at a preliminary focus—a tentative thesis—for her research paper: medicine as ritual. From there, she began to do some research on holistic medicine, something she had always wanted to know more about.

Once you have selected a topic, the next step is to locate information on or about your tentative hypothesis or area of research. Traditional resources include bibliographies, abstracts, encyclopedias, and indexes to related books, articles, and electronic media. The *Readers' Guide to Periodical Literature,* for instance, indexes the contents of magazines and journals and is often a good place to begin your general research. Specialized indexes such as *The Applied Science and Technology Index* (science and technology), the *MLA International Bibliography* (language and literature), *Social Science Index* (social sciences), or the *Index to Legal Periodicals* (law) are also quite useful when researching subjects in a particular discipline.

In addition to *hard copy* indexes, abstracts, bibliographies, and encyclopedias, as the twenty-first century approaches, electronic media is becoming more and more accessible in public and college libraries throughout America. Online databases, CD-ROM, Central Information Systems, and electronic catalogs and indexes are just a few resources now available for researching, locating, and verifying information. Specific electronic reference works including the *Directory of Electronic Journals, Newsletters, and Academic Discussion Lists, The Internet Directory,* and *The Internet Complete Reference*—just to name a few of them—expedite the research process. Consult with a librarian to determine which databases are available to you and how to access them.

Assuming you are connected to a computer service or network, it is now possible to do much of your research at home. Radkins used both traditional and electronic research methods and indexes when she researched material for "Health and Cultural Traditions." She began her exploration by going through a "key word" search at the college online catalog, and later, since she was familiar with how to locate electronic media, she accessed databases on her home computer. As a result of her research, she found herself expanding the projected parameters of her paper on holistic medicine. She noticed an inseparable relationship between holistic healing and cultural traditions in medicine; the traditional therapeutic practices, meditation, herbal remedies, shaman intermediaries, and folk medicines of diverse cultures all became relevant to her topic.

USING ONLINE CATALOGS AND INDEXES

Online computer card catalogs, which are accessed through various *research engines,* will differ from service to service, but their basic function remains the same: locating specifically defined materials. The most useful function of electronic catalogs is the *key word* search. The key word search allows you to (1) *type* in a general topic like *art;* (2) *browse* through all available information on it; (3) *limit* the scope of your search on *art* by asking questions to further define what you are looking for (a specific artist, a medium of artistic expression, or an artistic movement); and (4) *identify* the most recent information on your subject (references appear in reverse chronological order in online catalogs and indexes). The research engines in online catalogs also permit you to locate works by author, title, subject, or words in the title/subject (e.g., surrealism and movies). The following diagram is a detailed example of the first screen for an online catalog. Press "N" for new search and start with the screen as illustrated:

```
            WELCOME TO THE
        ALL STATE UNIVERSITY
          LIBRARY CATALOG
    You may search for library materials
          by any of the following:

        A>      Author
        T>      Title
        S>      Subject
        W>      Words in Title or Subject

        C>      Call Number

        R>      Reserve Lists
        V>      View Your Loan Record
        L>      Library Information

    Choose one [A, T, S, W, C, R, V, L].

    For assistance, ask the reference librarian.
```

After you select one of the search keys, you will enter the next screen. By following directions on subsequent screens, you will find the location and call number of the material you need.

TAKING NOTES

As you begin to locate and read what others have to say about your subject, you will want to keep a record of who said what, when, and where (source material, publisher, year of publication, page number) for future reference and possible acknowledgment if you use information gleaned from another author in your own paper. Some instructors like you to write out a 3-by-5-inch note card for each source you locate. The thinking behind this procedure is that you will be able to organize and reorganize the sequence in which the notes will appear in your research paper. Then, you can organize the note cards alphabetically when preparing your list of works cited. With modern technology, however, this traditional practice has been frequently replaced with services provided by word processing and computer software programs.

Your word processor is also an excellent place to write out notes on resource materials. Your notes about primary or secondary resource materials should include especially significant quotes, summaries of sections of a work, or paraphrases of another author. Regardless of what type of notes you take, you will always want to follow them with information such as the author, book or article title, publisher, date or year of publication, and page number for later reference. Detailed notes and documentation information will be useful when you integrate and acknowledge other authors' opinions into your own writings.

DIRECT QUOTATIONS, PARAPHRASES, AND SUMMARIES

Research papers will undoubtedly contain a combination of quotations, paraphrases, and summaries. Direct quotations are the exact words of an author and must be copied exactly as they are written. Use direct quotations either when an author has expressed something so well it adds clarity and momentum to your own writing, or when you find it difficult to paraphrase material. However, do not expect your reader to reach the same insights you express with a quotation. Add commentary and analysis, placing the quotation into proper perspective with your discussion point or thesis.

Paraphrasing, the act of reconstructing another's ideas in your own words, should not be undervalued. You paraphrase when you use *loose translations* of thoughts, or when you attempt to restate a complex topic or issue using different diction (word choice) and form (prose instead of verse, perhaps) than the original literary work. In fact, to maintain a balanced level of diction in your research paper, whenever possible, paraphrase information with appropriate parenthetical citations to acknowledge your source material.

Unlike paraphrases, which tend to be as long as their source materials, summaries capsulate information, expressing the big picture briefly and concisely. For this reason, accuracy is very important when you summarize main points in the arguments or ideas of others. Summaries also efficiently and effectively present evidence in a research paper because they are easy to subordinate to your controlling idea and, therefore, do not often become an end in themselves. The following examples may help to clarify the distinction between quoted material, paraphrases, and summaries:

QUOTATION:	*What's in a name? That which we call a rose By any other word would still smell as sweet. (Romeo and Juliet 4.1)*
PARAPHRASE:	Names cannot define or change the authentic nature of people, places, or things.
SUMMARY:	Names are not definitions.

INTRODUCING QUOTATIONS

Introductory word groups prior to quotations provide clarity and coherence between your sentences. Just as lead-in sentences move smoothly into the thesis of an essay, introductory remarks flow into quotations. Consider the following examples:

> **As Robin Fadden observed,** *"disobedient women* reinforce the idea that, wherever the spirit of this Wild Woman is being restricted or enslaved, women must strike out at the enemy which attacks them, and protect themselves from becoming a forgotten myth."

> **In her essay, "Disparity and the Wild Woman Archetype," Robin Fadden noted,** *"disobedient women* reinforce the idea that, wherever the spirit of this Wild Woman is being restricted or enslaved, women must strike out at the enemy which attacks them, and protect themselves from becoming a forgotten myth."

Without such lead-ins, direct quotations seem stilted, abrupt, and confusing, while paraphrases of another's words may be indistinguishable from your own thoughts. For effectiveness, vary your method of introducing quotations. Also notice how the way you introduce a quotation can change an author's relationship to it. Above, Robin Fadden *observed* and *noted* the information in her quotation. You might have introduced the same quotation saying:

According to Robin Fadden ... ,
Robin Fadden argued that ... ,
Robin Fadden said it best ... ,
As Robin Fadden said ... and so on.

Colons and semicolons, along with forms of *end punctuation* like question marks and exclamation points, must be analyzed in context to determine their proper placement in a quotation. If such punctuation marks are part of the quoted material, then put them *inside* the quotation marks *before* the citation. On the other hand, when question marks and exclamation points serve to punctuate an entire sentence, place them outside the quotation marks *after* the citation.

> How should one respond to the call to adventure when "destiny has summoned the hero and transferred his spiritual center of gravity from within the pale of his society to a zone unknown" (Campbell 58)?

ORGANIZING INFORMATION

At this stage in writing a research paper there are several views on what is the best way to organize your material. Some instructors will insist that you write out a detailed outline before you begin to draft your paper; other instructors will suggest that you keep an evolving *scratch outline,* one that can change direction as a result of research. During the writing process, it is advisable to use the evolving outline. Rigidly structuring an outline before drafting a paper can put you in a position of writing to fit an outline instead of organizing material to argue and demonstrate a thesis. An outline is important since it provides you with tentative direction, but the very nature of research leads to discoveries; these discoveries might modify your tentative thesis and rightfully so. Do not simply write without reorganizing successive drafts. (See chapter 2 for a further discussion on outlining and organizing materials.)

DRAFTING THE RESEARCH PAPER

Draft the research paper as you would any other essay, remembering that your first draft will essentially place your ideas and information down on paper. Successive drafts will refine your thesis and reorganize material. As you revise your drafts, read for parts of your paper that are rather thin on support. These sections are usually easy to identify because they tend to support discussion points with generalities instead of specific, verifiable evidence or they lack a strong sense of reasoning. To strengthen such parts in your paper, consult your authoritative sources and add expert testimony to what you say. You might paraphrase your source or use a direct quotation followed by commentary and analysis.

In addition to your grammatical, mechanical, and stylistic concerns when you edit various drafts of your research paper, pay particular attention to MLA documentation. Did you use parenthetical references to acknowledge the words and ideas of others? Did you supply enough information in the parenthetical references so that your readers can easily identify them in the list of works cited?

17

Documenting Sources

There is one crucial reason for documenting sources accordingly when you write. If you use sources and do not acknowledge their authors, you are *plagiarizing* information. That is, you are claiming another person's words or ideas as your own. Plagiarizing material is the same as *stealing*. Besides, resource materials are usually written by experts on specific topics or issues. Therefore, proper documentation will usually strengthen the legitimacy of your discussion points. (It is important to have an expert on your side when you argue about a controversial issue!)

Although documenting sources always is important, citing your resource materials is particularly crucial when constructing a research paper. As your readers consider the facts, figures, reasoning, synthesis, and conclusions in your paper, they may want to verify your sources and, perhaps, read more about your paper's topic. Paraphrasing material does not eliminate the need to cite a parenthetical reference either. There are two basic parts when documenting primary and secondary resource materials: (1) *parenthetical references* (in-text notes) and (2) a *works cited* list (complete publishing information at the end of the text).

PARENTHETICAL REFERENCES

In 1984, the big change in documentation was the elimination of traditional footnotes that had appeared at the end of an essay or the bottom of a page. How do parenthetical references differ from traditional footnotes? For one, the numbering system for footnotes is not used. Another way traditional footnotes differ from parenthetical references is their placement in a written work: parenthetical references directly follow quoted or acknowledged sources.

When Should I Use Parenthetical References?

Use parenthetical references
- Any time you refer to another person's ideas or writings;
- When using information that is not common knowledge;
- After direct quotations; or
- When directly referring to part of a source.

What Do My Parenthetical References Tell My Readers?

Your parenthetical footnote informs readers of the author's last name so you can locate it in the alphabetically arranged entries in your works cited list. Your parenthetical footnote also indicates the page number or numbers where your reference can be located and verified.

Where Should I Place Parenthetical References?

Your parenthetical footnote will usually appear at the end of your sentence, directly after quotation marks but before end punctuation such as a period.

EXAMPLE: "A 'hacker' refers to an unorthodox, yet talented, professional computer programmer" **(Meyer 22).**

How Should I Structure a Parenthetical Reference?

- Usually, the author's last name and the page number will provide your readers with enough information to locate the piece in your works cited.

EXAMPLE: Luck is associated with all of the circumstances surrounding each person, including illness and health **(Lipson 50–54).**

- If you have already mentioned the author's name in your text, all you need to do is to place the page number or numbers in parentheses.

EXAMPLE: As Barbara Berg suggested in <u>The Crisis of the Working Mother</u>, the 1970s women believed in the myth of the "superwoman" **(29).**

- When you use two or more works by the same author, include (1) the author's last name; (2) the title of the text; and (3) page number or numbers.

EXAMPLE: **(Erdrich, <u>Tracks</u> 119–23)** distinguished from

                 (Erdrich, <u>Love Medicine</u> 119–23)

- If you have two authors with the same last name, eliminate confusion or ambiguous references by including initials or writing out the entire name for each author.

EXAMPLE: **(M. Layton 78)** or **(Michelle Layton 78)** to distinguish

           works by **(T. Layton 248)** or **(Tyrone Layton 248)**

Again, materials appearing in your works cited should be arranged *alphabetically,* and clearly delineated in your parenthetical reference for easy location. The above two authors would appear as follows.

> Layton, Michelle. Pteronon. 3rd edition. New York: New
>   Directions, 1994.
> Layton, Tyrone. "William Blake's Mythology." North
>   Western Humanities Quarterly 4 (1989): 471–92.

Why Is a Complete List of Works Cited Important to the Effective Use of Parenthetical References?

Your works cited list offers readers specific information whereby they may read more about your subject or validate your source. When books, for instance, are revised and appear in new additions, page numbers often change. Also, a complete list of works cited provides readers with all the information necessary for them to find the same edition of the text used when citing quotations. Additionally, acknowledging information, including the author, publisher, and/or publication might strengthen the credibility of your sources. For instance, if you write a paper explaining that aliens from outer space live in every corner of the earth, and use *Star* or *National Enquirer* to corroborate your claims, not too many people will take you seriously.

HINTS:
- Lead your reader into a quotation; maintain a clear context for your parenthetical references.

- Follow quotations with a quotation mark, place the parenthetical reference in parenthesis, and then place the end punctuation *after* the parenthetical references.

- Try to work information you might have placed in an endnote into your text.

ENDNOTES

Although parenthetical references eliminate much of the work formerly associated with documentation (e.g., counting lines, locating notes), you will occasionally want to use endnotes for (1) citing material not necessarily directly related to your discussion at hand but still illuminating or (2) indicating three or more authors at once. An endnote is a number immediately following a word, phrase, sentence, or paragraph that corresponds to a number on a list with the heading *Notes* placed in between the end of your text—before the works cited list. Each endnote should be typed consecutively and double spaced. As a general rule of thumb, make all notes in a research paper *endnotes* unless you are specifically instructed to do otherwise. Vera Nazarov used several notes to insure reader understanding in her research paper titled "Classicism in Eighteenth and Twentieth Century Music: An Analysis of Continuity in Musical Style." Her notes offered readers interesting, though not contextually relevant, information about her discussion of classical music.

Nazarov 7

Notes

[1]Unlike the development, in which the music could modulate to just about any key as long as the progression was logical, the key changes in the exposition of classical music were quite rigid. If the work was in a major key, the bridge must modulate to the dominant key. If the work was in a minor key, the bridge must modulate to the relative major. See Wellesz and Fredrick 112–114.

[2]If the work was in a minor key, the second theme, as stated above, would have modulated to the relative major key. However, in the recapitulation it is not considered proper to significantly change the thematic material, which would happen were you to play the second theme in the home key (it would be minor rather than major). Therefore it is necessary to transpose it to the parallel major, which is a major scale beginning on the same note as the original minor key, whereas the relative major has the same key signature as the original key: for example, C major and A minor both have no sharps or flats whereas C minor has three flats.

WORKS CITED

At the end of your documented research paper, place a works cited list. Since a *bibliography* literally refers to a "listing of books," to place resource materials—which may include interviews, television shows, statistics, and telephone calls—under such a heading would be inappropriate. Information crucial to completing an entry in your works cited list will depend on the sort of material you are gathering. Generally speaking, take note of the following types of information you will need for thorough documentation (or get a computer printout of them). Then, structure the material in your works cited list using the appropriate format as illustrated below:

BOOKS:	Author. Title of the book—<u>underlined</u>. Edition if applicable. City of publication: Publisher, the year of publication.
JOURNALS AND MAGAZINES:	Author. Title of article, short story, or review—*in quotation marks*. Journal title—<u>underlined</u>. Volume number. Date (in parentheses): pages.
NEWSPAPERS:	Author. Article—*in quotation marks*. Newspaper title—<u>underlined</u>, date (day, month, year): Section: page number.
PAMPHLETS:	Author (if indicated). Title of pamphlet—<u>underlined</u>. City of publication: sponsoring organization, year.
INTERVIEWS:	Name of the person interviewed. Topic of discussion—*in quotation marks*. Interviewer, date of interview. City (location could be important—especially if interviewing a disaster victim).
FILMS AND VIDEOS:	Title—<u>underlined</u>. Director. Distributor, year.

In contrast to printed sources, *online databases* are constantly updated and corrected. An article published on July 22, 1993, might contain some significant changes by the time someone accesses it on April 19, 1996. Therefore, your works cited entry for an online source will often contain both dates. Additionally, a citation for an online source should indicate the publication medium and the name of your computer service or network. The additional materials you cite from *online databases* should be structured as follows:

COMPUTER SERVICES:	Author's Name. Article/material accessed—*in quotation marks*. Other publication information for printed sources. Source title or database—<u>underlined</u>. Publication date. Online. Computer service. Access date.
COMPUTER NETWORK:	Author's name. Article or document title—*in quotation marks*. Journal, magazine, newsletter, or conference—<u>underlined</u>. Identifying numbers (volume, issue). Publication year or date (in parentheses). Number of pages or paragraphs (when provided) or *n. pag.* for "no pagination." Online. Computer network. Access date.

ELECTRONIC TEXT:	Author's name. Text title—underlined. City of publication: publisher, publication date. Online. Repository of the electronic text. Computer network. Access date.
CD-ROM AND PORTABLE DATABASES:	Author's name (if provided). Material used—*in quotation marks*. Product or database title—underlined. Publication medium (diskette, CD-ROM, magnetic tapes). Vendor's or publisher's name (if relevant). Year of publication.

Sample Works Cited

1. Book with one author:
Cartiér, Xam Wilson. Be-Bop, Re-Bop. New York: Ballantine, 1974.

2. Book with two authors:
Brown, Robert, and Conrad S. Leedom. Bootheels: American Westerns.
New York: Random, 1996.

3. A translation:
Cervantes, Saavedra Miguel de. The Adventures of Don Quixote.
Trans. J. L. Steinburg. Toronto: Little, Brown, 1989.

4. A book that has three or more authors, has gone through several editions, and is one of a several volumes in a set:
Speiller, Kevin G., et al. The History of England, 5th ed. 2 vols. Vol 1.
New York: Macmillan, 1984.

5. A work in more than one volume:
Richardson, Samuel. Clarissa; or, the History of a Young Lady. 4 vols.
London: Everyman, 1967.

6. A poem in an anthology:
Hughes, Langston. "Harlem (A Dream Deferred)." The Bedford
Introduction to Literature. Ed. Michael Meyes. New York: St.
Martin's, 1987. 797.

7. A short story or essay in an anthology:
Téllez, Hernando. "Just Lather, That's All." Contemporary Latin
American Authors. New York: Ballantine, 1974. 209–14.

8. A play in an anthology:
Wilson, August. Fences. Types of Drama: Plays and Essays. Ed. Sylvia
Barnet et al. New York: Scott Foresman, 1989. 695–733.

9. A foreword, introduction, preface, or afterword:
Le Guin, Ursula. Introduction. The Book of Fantasy. Ed. Jorge Luis
Borges. New York: Caroll & Graf, 1976. 9–12.

10. An edition of an author's work:
Miller, Arthur. Death of a Salesman. 2nd edition. New York: Viking,
1949.

11. **A magazine article:**
Croce, Arlene. "Dancing." The New Yorker 25 Jan. 1996: 73–75.

12. **A scholarly journal:**
Jones, Judith Patterson. "Shifting Modes and Plural Visions: The
Modernity of Thomas More's History of King Richard III." The
Indiana Social Studies Quarterly 1 (1982): 57–69.

13. **A newspaper article:**
Nhu, T. T. "The Children Who Won't Eat Their Meat." San Jose
Mercury News 24 July 1994, sec. H: 1.

14. **A lecture:**
Zimmerman, Seth. "A Journey through Dante's Inferno." Evergreen
Valley College, San Jose, California. 7 Oct. 1995.

15. **An encyclopedia:**
"American Literature." Collier's Encyclopedia. 1996 ed.

16. **An interview:**
Hernandez, Xiormara. Personal interview. "Modern Mass Media and
Murder Trials." 9 Jan. 1995.

17. **Computer network:**
Brahmer, Linda. "What's Thought Got to Do with It?" Computer
Underground Digest 2.7 (1991): n. pag. Online. Internet. 2 June
1996.

18. **Electronic text:**
Sinclair, Robbie. Dominion of Machinery. Ed. Colleen Annice. Fort
Worth: Harcourt, 1994. Online. Evergreen Coll. Lib. Internet. 12
May 1995.

19. **Computer service:**
King, Taran. "Phrack Worlds News Special Edition." Phrack
Magazine. 28 July 1987. Phrack Magazine Online. Online. AOL. 1
Jan. 1996.

20. **Computer software:**
GlobalFax OCR. Diskette. Sunnyvale: Global Village Communication,
1993.

21. **CD-ROM:**
"It's All Relative." Comedy Central. CD-ROM. Burbank: Time Warner
Interactive Group. 1994.

22. **Films:**
The Joy Luck Club. Dir. Wayne Wang. Prod. Oliver Stone. Screenplay
by Amy Tan and Ronald Bass. Buena Vista Pictures, 1993.

23. **Videotapes:**
Batman. Dir. Tim Burton. Perf. Jack Nicholson, Kim Basinger, and
Michael Keaton. Warner Brothers Home Video Inc., 1989.

24. Recordings:

Keillor, Garrison. "Pontoon Boat." <u>More News from Lake Wobegon:</u>
<u>Faith</u>. Audiotape. HighBridge Company HBP 18204, 1989.

Sometimes your instructors will want you to annotate your list of works cited. Usually, the annotation provides a brief overview and evaluation of your book, article, pamphlet, interview, video conference, and so on; here, you might alert your reader to the best sources for further reading. Your annotations may also be helpful when you quickly refresh your memory on your supporting or source materials during various drafts of your composition.

TIPS:
1. Trust in your own judgment and write original annotations for your materials. Your instructor—like yourself—has access to the sort of annotations offered by many of the computer catalogs!
2. Annotate an article, story, essay, poem, or other source as soon as you read the material. Follow the same procedure for interviews, electronically reproduced media (i.e., information systems, CD-ROM), television shows, or radio broadcasts. You can always revise and sharpen your annotations at another date, but you may not be as lucky in capturing the power or spirit of the moment.

Sample Annotated Works Cited

Annotated Works Cited

Bolen, Jean Shinoda. <u>Goddess in Everywoman: A New</u>
<u>Psychology of Women</u>. New York: Harper, 1984. Dr.
Bolen takes a look at goddesses from Greek mythology,
their Jungian psychological types, and their archetypal
roles.

- - -. <u>Gods in Everyman: A New Psychology of Men's Lives</u>.
New York: Harper, 1989. Bolen examines Greek gods as
cultural images of the various male archetypes, offering
a lucid male psychology.

Gulley, Rosemary Ellen. <u>Moonscapes: A Celebration of Lunar</u>
<u>Astronomy, Magic, Legend, and Lore</u>. New York:
Prentice–Hall, 1991. Gulley's book offers a balanced,
readable account of all aspects of "lunar lore." In
addition to a look at astronomers, their theories, and
their discoveries—past and present—Gulley discusses

myths, rites, mysticism, moon magic, and creatures influenced by the moon.

Hill, Geoffrey. Illuminating Shadows: The Mythic Power of Film. Boston: Shambbala, 1992. This is a book-length study of film as a vehicle for mythology. Hill claims that the cinema (movie theaters) are the modern-day equivalent to tribal dreamhouses.

Kendall, Paul Murray. Richard the Third. New York: Anchor, 1965. Kendall's book is an excellent biography of the life and reign of the "historical" Richard III. It provides interesting, objective information regarding the death of the two princes, Edward IV's marriage to Elizabeth Woodville, Richard's defamation, and the rise of the "Tudor Myth." While "fascinating" in its own right, Kendall's book does little more than suggest how Shakespeare's perception of Richard III was a product of the "Tudor Myth," popular when he wrote The Tragedy of Richard III.

Landreath, Helen. Dear Dark Head: An Intimate Story of Ireland. New York: Wittlessey House, 1956. This book is a fine collection of folktales and legends indigenous to Ireland. Beginning with "Nueda of the Silverhand," the author carries her readers through the tale of "Deirdre of the Sorrows," "Cormac MacArt and Tara," "Grainne and Diarmuid," and the coming of "St. Patrick," just to name a few. Through the flash of steel, the warmth of love, the tragedy of loss, and the eventual impact of Christianity, Landreath skillfully illuminates the colorful history and cultural richness of the Irish race.

Neider, Josephine. "War and Human Progress in Italy." Butte Historical Quarterly 10 (Winter 1980): 45–61. Though Neider explores many of the gaps present in Renaissance "military history," her arguments concerning gunpowder and firearms in the sixteenth century are occasionally suspect. While Neider does make a case that human progress resulted from internal strife and external wars in Europe, Italian history seems to play a secondary role in her analysis.

Tenenti, Alberto. Piracy and the Decline of Venice: 1568–1619. Trans. Janet and Brian Pullman. London:

Longmans, 1987. In addition to being a study of Venetian economic problems, this book explains the rise of the "Atlantic" maritime powers at the expense of the Mediterranean merchants. The atrocities committed by the pirates upon innocent travelers are explained in depth. Ultimately, Tenenti draws some interesting conclusions about the flexibility of Venetian government and society.

Valdez, Lupeta. "Watsonville, California, during the 1989 Earthquake." Personal interview. 25 Oct. 1989. During my interview with Valdez, she recounted the destruction caused by the October 17, 1989, earthquake in Watsonville. In addition to detailing what happened to the older buildings in town, she discussed the hardships that she and her family faced as the city slowly recovered from the natural disaster. Valdez's recollection of the makeshift, post-earthquake town— tents and old trailers—was particularly vivid and memorable.

Research Essay Evaluation Checklist

+ Excellent   / Good   √√ Needs Work

Rhetoric
  Effective introduction (good lead-in / crisp thesis)   ———
  Clear, consistent focus on a central idea (unity)   ———
  Consistent flow of reasoning   ———
  Specific details and examples to support the main idea   ———
  Integration of quoted material   ———
  Sufficient commentary following quoted material   ———
  Satisfying, appropriate (logical) conclusion   ———

Style/Diction
  Effective word choice (avoid using jargon or clichés)   ———
  Honest and clear tone or voice   ———
  Syntax (word order)   ———
  Clear expression (avoid wordiness)   ———
  Use of concrete nouns and active verbs   ———

Editing
  Grammar / spelling   ———
  Mechanics / punctuation   ———
  Format (essay structure)   ———

Documentation/Research
  Parenthetical references   ———
  List of works cited   ———
  Annotated list of works cited (when applicable)   ———
  Variety of resource materials (when applicable)   ———

Sample Student Research Paper: "Health and Cultural Traditions"

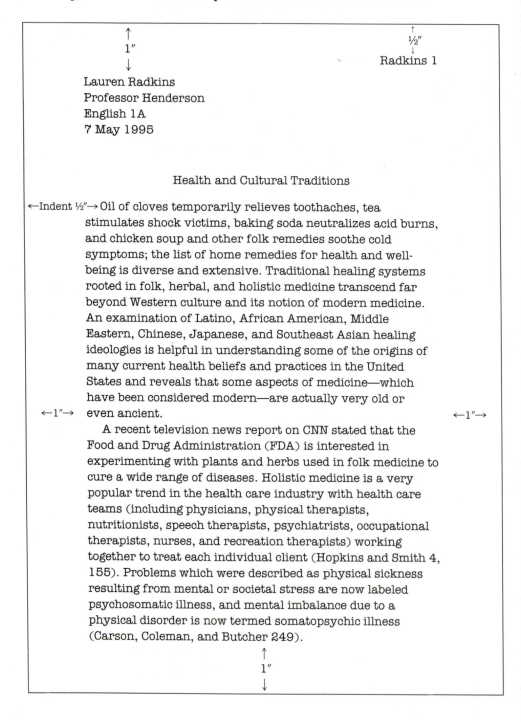

↑
1″
↓

½″
↓

Radkins 1

Lauren Radkins
Professor Henderson
English 1A
7 May 1995

Health and Cultural Traditions

←Indent ½″→ Oil of cloves temporarily relieves toothaches, tea
stimulates shock victims, baking soda neutralizes acid burns,
and chicken soup and other folk remedies soothe cold
symptoms; the list of home remedies for health and well-
being is diverse and extensive. Traditional healing systems
rooted in folk, herbal, and holistic medicine transcend far
beyond Western culture and its notion of modern medicine.
An examination of Latino, African American, Middle
Eastern, Chinese, Japanese, and Southeast Asian healing
ideologies is helpful in understanding some of the origins of
many current health beliefs and practices in the United
States and reveals that some aspects of medicine—which
have been considered modern—are actually very old or
←1″→ even ancient.   ←1″→
     A recent television news report on CNN stated that the
Food and Drug Administration (FDA) is interested in
experimenting with plants and herbs used in folk medicine to
cure a wide range of diseases. Holistic medicine is a very
popular trend in the health care industry with health care
teams (including physicians, physical therapists,
nutritionists, speech therapists, psychiatrists, occupational
therapists, nurses, and recreation therapists) working
together to treat each individual client (Hopkins and Smith 4,
155). Problems which were described as physical sickness
resulting from mental or societal stress are now labeled
psychosomatic illness, and mental imbalance due to a
physical disorder is now termed somatopsychic illness
(Carson, Coleman, and Butcher 249).

↑
1″
↓

↑
1″
↓

↑
½″
↓
Radkins 2

There is nothing new, however, about psychosomatic or somatopsychic illnesses and their cures. Latinos recognized the benefits of "curanderismo," a healing art, long ago: "With origins in pre-Columbian times and influenced by sixteenth-century Spanish health care traditions, curanderismo uses herbs, ritual, prayer, music, dance, and massage to cure people" (Lopez 26). As Renaldo Maduro further explains in "Curanderismo and Latin Views of Disease and Curing," the folk healing system Latinos call "curanderismo" is based on their beliefs about the <u>causes</u> and <u>cures</u> of diseases.

Eight major philosophical premises underlie a coher-ent curing worldview of Latino patients: disease or ill-ness may follow (1) strong emotional states (such as rage, fear, envy, or mourning of painful loss); or (2) being out of balance or harmony with one's environ-ment; (3) a patient is often the innocent victim of ma-levolent forces; (4) the soul may become separated from the body (loss of soul); (5) cure requires the par-
←Indent ½″→ ticipation of the entire family; (6) the natural world is not always distinguishable from the supernatural; (7) sickness often serves the social function, through in-creased attention and rallying of the family around a patient, of reestablishing a sense of belonging (reso-cialization); and (8) Latinos respond better to an open interaction with their healer. (64)

Practitioners of "curanderismo" view their health and well-being holistically. Since they believe that the mind cannot be separated from the body, it makes sense that any intense emotions can affect the body by causing illness. A fever is an example of an imbalance because it is a deviation from normal body temperature. People are not blamed for their illnesses because tradition passes on the belief that the illness is an attack from within the environment by an evil spirit or angry saint. When a sickness is thought to have resulted from a person's soul being separated from the body, the physician's primary concern is to treat the soul because it is the true being of that person (64–69).

↑
1″
↓

↑
1"
↓

↑
½"
↓

Radkins 3

In curing an illnesses brought on by emotional, environmental, spiritual, or social causes, there is much more to consider than simply getting a prescription from the doctor (too often the procedure in Western medicine). The family participates in the healing process through their support and reassurance; this is very important because a great deal of interdependence exists among family members in the Latino community. To cure illnesses caused by the soul leaving the body, the traditional healer practicing "curanderismo" would use supernatural means such as sacrifice, penance, prayer, and magic. Cultural change among Latinos often results in a great deal of stress which is treated through resocialization into the community. Therefore to treat the patient successfully, the modern, science-based physician must have a connection to the sacred nature of healing, and he or she should allow the patient to actively participate in the healing process (64–69).

Among the folklore and traditional medical practices of many African Americans is the belief that illness is believed to result from either "natural" or "unnatural" causes. A "natural" illness may be caused by one's own immediate environment (too hot or too cold), an improper diet, and social conditions which create conditions causing changes in the blood. "Unnatural illnesses are the result of witchcraft and reflect conflict in the social network" (Maston 16). Blood is thought to have certain characteristics that need to be kept in balance for a person to remain healthy. An example of this would be if the blood was too thin and left a person susceptible to disease. There is a belief that there are forces in the environment that can be gathered and used to inflict illness upon a specific person (this type of illness would be considered unnatural). Thus, many traditional folk remedies for illness among many African Americans focus a great deal on the preventive measures that should be taken to avoid "natural" and "unnatural" illnesses (60–61).

African Americans have been advocates for several aspects of naturopathic medicine, especially preventive medicine, for hundreds of years—partly out of tradition and sometimes out of necessity. Naturopathic medicine, itself, only has been around for about a hundred years, and yet, in

←1"→

←1"→

↑
1"
↓

addition to Africa, the "philosophy and healing approaches used in naturopathic medicine in the West are similar to those that have been practiced for hundreds of years in other countries such as Ayurveda in India and traditional Chinese Medicine" ("Naturopathic Medicine"). The African Amercan cultural respect for preventative medicine entails living life in moderation, resting, and eating healthily. True to the holistic philosophies and practices of patient and healer, beliefs are extremely important to the traditional African American healing art. To prevent any "unnatural" illnesses, for instance, one should also act in a proper manner spiritually, bodily, and socially; this is meant to avoid angering God or people in the community who may choose to punish this person for his or her behavior (Maston 65).

Since Middle Easterners customarily have believed that their fate is in the hands of God, divine punishment is considered an important factor in the cause of illness. The "evil eye," food, herbs, temperature variances, evil spirits, and bad luck are also considered valid etiologies of disease. Good fortune is thought to provoke jealousy in others who through their feelings of envy are given the power to cause illness, accidents, and other misfortunes laid upon the lucky person or family. Middle Easterners and their traditional health care systems share theories and ideologies about food, temperature, and evil spirit causation of disease with Latinos and African Americans. Interestingly, the health care traditions in medicine for all these cultures look beyond immediate, short-term cures to good health in order to maximize their wellness—holistically. For practitioners of most types of folk medicine, "rather than defining health as the absence of disease, health is defined as the presence of wellness" ("Holistic Medicine"). The concept of wellness in the Middle East considers all aspects of the "whole" person, and the belief that luck is associated with all of the circumstances surrounding each person, including illness and health, is consistent with such ideology (Lipson and Meleis 50–54).

Traditional healing practices from Asian countries have also contributed to what some hail as modern medical

↑
1″
↓

practices. Acupuncture from China, for instance, is a technique for "curing disease, relieving pain, or bringing about partial ANESTHESIA by inserting needles into the body at specific points" (<u>Dictionary of Cultural Literacy</u>). The Chinese use acupuncture to liberate the "Qui" (also called "Chi"), which roughly translates as "energy" (there really is no equivalent word for "Qui" in Western society). The "Qui" or life force is a form of electromagnetic energy which the Chinese believe all living things share in common, and encompass all significant activities in life—mental, physical, spiritual, and emotional ("Acupressure" Par. 4).

The "Qui" circulates throughout the body along "meridians" and "special pathways," and if it remains balanced and flows evenly throughout the body, a person will stay in an optimum state of health and well-being. However, accumulations of acids in the muscle tissues or blockages in the pathways "cause stagnation of blood and stiffness throughout the body. Stiffness creates abnormal pressure on nerves, blood, and lymph nodes. In turn, the functioning of the skeletal system and internal organs are also abnormally affected" ("Acupressure" Par. 6). By stimulating the key
←1″→ pressure points in one's body, acupuncture not only diffuses   ←1″→
acids from muscle tissues, but also removes blockages in the "Qui" or life force.

In the twentieth century, physical therapists, occupational therapists, and others owe a great deal to the Japanese technique of acupressure—a counterpart to Chinese acupuncture. For over five thousand years, the Japanese have used acupressure, and as with acupuncture, acupressure tends to stimulate electromagnetic energy—the life force called "Qui" by the Chinese and "Ki" by the Japanese. Simply put, the system of acupressure deals with various "message techniques and therapies that are used to stimulate the body's own healing powers" ("Acupressure" Par. 1). The massage techniques may vary from the application of light to medium pressure by one's fingers and hands (and occasionally one's elbows, knees, and feet) to "key points in the body" which are identical to the pressure points in Chinese acupuncture ("Acupressure" Par. 2).

For the most part, the Japanese culture views illness as a

↑
1″
↓

↑
1″
↓

disruption of harmony. The mind and body are considered inseparable, and if an illness occurs, it is often believed to have resulted from societal stress.

Neither in "intimate" nor "ritual" communication should one express negative feelings and there is, therefore, usually no acceptable time to verbalize such feelings. Beliefs derived from Buddhism reinforce ←Indent ½″→ this situation because high priority is given to inductive and intuitive learning rather than to deductive analysis and it is also thought that verbal statements cannot possibly express the complexity and changeable nature of one's inner self. (Lock 27)

The main concern of Japanese patients pertains to the restoration of their previous societal role—a balanced self (25–27). This need for balance corresponds with the Chinese concept of yin and yang, the "dark passive" and "light active" principles that govern the universe. When there is an imbalance between the yin and yang, illness may occur. Support systems such as ties to family and community additionally are thought to protect a person from disease. ←1″→ Japanese patients resort to the use of medication only to   ←1″→ help them adjust to their illness and return their physical balance. By normalizing physical order through acupuncture and meditation, they believe that their emotional harmony will also be returned and their "Ki" will flow freely throughout their bodies. Even though patients are unable to avoid illness, since they choose to adjust to the disorder, they are still productive (25–30).

There are many types of acupressure systems now being used by physicians and therapists in the Western world:

1. Acupressure "First Aid": A symptom-based approach that focuses on acupressure points for the temporary relief of common problems such as headaches and menstrual cramps.
←Indent ½″→ 2. Acu-yoga: Whole-body yogic stretches and postures that activate points and meridian channels.
3. Do-In: Self-acupressure massage of points and muscles that also includes breathing exercises [a technique often used in the West for Lamaze—natural childbirth], movement, and stretching.

↑
1″
↓

Radkins 7

4. Jin Shin: A pattern of prolonged holding (one to five minutes) of key acupressure points along the meridians. ("Acupressure" Pars. 15–18)

Although acupressure is still viewed by some individuals as "unconventional medicine," it may be only a matter of time before even they must consider its merits. Presently, the Japanese Ministry of Health and Welfare recognizes acupressure as an "acceptable medical practice" and the Chinese, in addition to acupuncture, "have also used acupressure for centuries" ("Acupressure" Par. 13). The mind–body connection, as addressed through both Eastern healing arts, a synergy of energy, is but another face of the "total" treatment for an ailment.

The traditional healing arts of Southeast Asia might also be placed by some under the heading of "unconventional medicine." For the many peasant people of Southeast Asia, health is dependent upon their natural environment; their method of treatment for an illness often involves herbal medications, dermabrasive procedures, or the intake of certain foods. "The primary system prevailing among these peasant people is here called natural medicine, in contrast to the supernatural medicine of the hill people" (Muecke 837). Medicine is inseparable from religion to the people in the hills of Laos, and sickness is believed to be caused by the gods. Shamans are necessary to intermediate for the patient and hopefully convince the gods to cure the illness.

The shamans in folk medicine, regardless whether they are in Asia or in North and South America, continue to cause Western eyes to raise an incredulous eyebrow. How can a shaman or witch doctor heal? What good is superstition in modern medical practice? Perhaps such questions are best addressed with counter queries: Why do people in Western society allow exorcisms to purge evil spirits (or beliefs) from the soul? Why do doctors sometimes prescribe placebos for their patients? What do patients think will happen if they embrace such a prescription from a modern physician? To ignore a part of a culture's traditional healing practices may be to limit the whole, and this is where folk remedies for illness may be light-years away from the quantifiable data of research in Western medicine. Holistic healing or "holism is a way of thinking, a way of being. In health care, it is a way of viewing the mind and body as a living system that is influenced by many factors including environment, diet, society and family, philosophical outlook, attitude, family history of disease, cultural beliefs, behavior, and personal history" ("Holistic Medicine").

There are very complex reasons behind what people often view as superstitions and myths, and we are now rediscovering many treatments used in folk medicine, both holistic and herbal, which have been scientifically proven— or finally acknowledged—to promote healing. Medical doctors and psychiatrists will undoubtedly continue to serve millions of people in the United States yearly. Still, the number of people who look for alternatives to "standard Western medical practices" to address illnesses and disease grows daily. From holistic healing methods, traditional therapeutic practices, and meditation to herbal remedies, shaman intermediaries, and folk medicine, many of these health beliefs and practices in the United States that have been upheld by Latinos, African Americans, Middle Easterners, Chinese, Japanese, and Southeast Asians have gained Western recognition and approval. Traditional healing arts are no longer subject to ridicule or passed off as superstition. More than ever before, people seek a balance in their lives. The "holistic approach [of healing] is more and more what people may be looking for as modern medicine becomes more specialized and to many people, alienating" (Lopez 27). Hopefully, physicians and holistic practitioners will work toward incorporating modern with traditional medical practices and possibly create a comprehensive health care system that can look beyond statistics and serve people's "whole" medical needs: mentally, physically, spiritually, and emotionally.

↑
1″   ½″
↓   ↓

Works Cited

"Acupressure." Health ResponseAbility Systems (1993): 18
   pars. Online. Internet. 22 Feb. 1995.
Carson, Robert C., et al. Abnormal Psychology and Modern
   Life. 11th ed. New York: Scott Foresman, 1990.
Dictionary of Cultural Literacy. Ed. E. D. Hirsch, Jr., Joseph
   F. Kett and James Trefil. New York: Houghton, 1993.
   Online. BITNET. 9 Feb. 1995.
Hopkins, Helen, and Helen Smith, eds. Occupational Therapy.
   7th ed. Pennsylvania: Lippincott, 1963.
"Holistic Medicine." Health ResponseAbility Systems (1993):
   13 pars. Online. Prodigy. 6 Mar. 1995.
←1″→ Lipson, Juliene G., and Afaf I. Meleis. "Issues in Health Care   ←1″→
   of Middle Eastern Patients." The Western Journal of
   Medicine (1983): 50–57.
Lock, Margaret. "Japanese Responses to Social Change—
   Making the Strange Familiar." The Western Journal of
   Medicine (1983): 25–30.
Lopez, Christina. "Curanderismo." Intercambios. (Winter
   1990): 26–27.
Maduro, Renaldo. "Curanderismo and the Latin View of
   Disease and Curing." The Western Journal of Medicine
   (1983): 64–70.
Maston, Claire. "African-Americans: Forerunners of
   Preventative Medicine." Health Now 9.7 (1994): 59–68.
Muecke, Marjorie. "In Search of Healers—Southeast Asian
   Refugees in the American Health Care System." The
   Western Journal of Medicine (1993): 835–40.
"Naturopathic Medicine." Health ResponseAbility Systems
   (1993): 26 pars. Online. Internet. 22 Feb. 1995.

↑
1″
↓

A Glossary of Literary and Rhetorical Terms

Allegory   A narrative in which all of the elements are symbolic. Some contemporary allegories include George Orwell's *Animal Farm* and William Golding's *Lord of the Flies*.

Allusion   A term used when making reference to a famous literary, historical, or social figure or event. Alluding to the Kennedy administration in the White House as "Camelot" conjures up visions of Arthurian romances and "the once and future king" who will return to unite a troubled country.

Analogy   An extended comparison where an unfamiliar topic is explained by noting its similarity to something familiar.

Analysis   To come to a conclusion about something through close inspection and observation. Analysis often includes separating a topic or an issue into smaller parts in order to reach a more thorough understanding of the whole.

Anecdote   A short story used to illustrate a point.

Antagonist   The antagonist is a character in drama or fiction who rivals or opposes the central character (protagonist) in a work. The antagonist need not always be a person; in fiction like Jack London's "To Build a Fire," nature itself functions as the antagonist in the story.

Archetypes   Controlling paradigms or metaphors for the human experience—both mind and body—frequently represented in art, literature, dreams, and ritual. Psychologists like Carl Jung have seen the value in exploring archetypes since "to understand an archetype is to recognize a pattern of behavior, and possibly how to relate or deal with it."

Audience   The readers that writers address (friends, professors, public servants, relatives). Writers must consider whether their audience knows little or a lot about a topic, as well as whether it would be best to present material formally or informally.

Brainstorming   Solving a problem individually or collectively by considering or rejecting ideas. In a composition, a writer uses brainstorming to generate topics for research papers and essays in general.

Cause and Effect   A rhetorical strategy that explains "why" in a composition. There are frequently multiple causes to a single effect, and a single cause can have multiple effects. Furthermore, an effect is not caused by a previously occurring event just because the first event occurred before it in time. Just because a musician receives a speeding ticket on the way to a concert does not mean the concert *caused* the speeding ticket. Cause-and-effect relationships in writing are very common! In fact, simply using words such as "because," "since," and "therefore" indicate causal relationships.

Cliché   A trite, tired, unimaginative use of language. Example: I am *as hungry as a horse.* Unless readers have seen a hungry horse, this statement—as familiar as it sounds—will probably not project a visual image to them.

Coherence   The smooth integration and flow of ideas within sentences and paragraphs.

Colloquialisms   Informal expressions, somewhere between slang and formal expressions. Colloquialisms are acceptable in speech but not desirable in formal writing.

Comparison and Contrast   A rhetorical strategy that sorts out differences and notes similarities between people, places, and things. Comparison and contrast is not an end in itself, however. Instead, it is a means to an end. There would be little point in comparing two kinds of food unless I wanted to reach some conclusion, such as which food was healthier, which food was the better buy for the money, or which food was the more satisfying. In successful comparative papers, authors often exhaustively research the differences and the similarities between items. Then and only then can they fully justify the conclusions.

Complex Sentence   A sentence structure consisting of an independent clause and one or more dependent clauses. An *independent* clause, which contains a subject, a verb, and a complete thought, and could be punctuated as a complete sentence, becomes *dependent* when preceded by a subordinate conjunction (a dependent word). Subordinate conjunctions include words like these:

after	because	during	since	whenever
although	before	even though	though	wherever
among	beyond	except	until	while
as	despite	if	when	without

Independent Clause: *The butcher mixed up some pork sausages.*
Dependent Clause: *After the butcher mixed up some pork sausages, . . .*

Obviously, the dependent clause above would be a sentence fragment if punctuated with a period after *sausages.* The subordinating conjunction "after" makes the entire clause dependent on an independent clause for completion. In a complete complex sentence, a dependent clause might read something like this:

> *After the butcher mixed up some pork sausages, he placed them in a meat locker.*

Whenever a dependent clause opens a sentence, follow it with a comma.

> EXAMPLE: *Since Javier designed his own house,* nobody told him it was ugly.

A dependent clause at the end of the sentence needs no punctuation because the *subordinate conjunction* clarifies its relationship to the preceding independent clause.

EXAMPLE: A concert pianist, Patrick performed in every major metropolitan city in the United States *before he retired in Hilo, Hawaii.*

Compound Sentence   A sentence consisting of two or more independent clauses (complete sentences) into a single structure by separating the two independent clauses with (1) a comma and a coordinating conjunction, (2) a semicolon, or (3) a semicolon and an adverbial conjunction.

Compound/Complex Sentence   A sentence structure consisting of at least two independent clauses and one or more dependent clauses. The clauses need not appear in any particular order to qualify as compound / complex, although compound / complex sentences which open with a dependent clause should be followed by a comma. Back-to-back independent clauses should be punctuated with (1) a comma and one of the seven coordinating conjunctions, (2) a semicolon, or (3) a semicolon followed by an adverbial conjunction and a comma.

Independent Clause
EXAMPLE: Maxine and Phillipe rented an apartment in downtown Chicago

Dependent Clause
because Maxine worked at the Civic Center, and

Independent Clause
Phillipe sold tickets at Soldier Field.

Dependent Clause
EXAMPLE: If Dana Stout becomes the new University President,

Independent Clause
the student body will gain an enthusiastic supporter, and

Independent Clause
the faculty will have an administrator interested in education.

Concrete/Abstract Words   As a general rule, *concrete words* may stand by themselves and be understood because they are perceived through the five senses: touch, taste, sight, smell, and sound. For instance, a person can touch, see, and smell a flower; therefore, the word *flower* is concrete.

Abstract words define ideas, concepts, and attitudes (love, hate, ethical, indifference, honesty, pride) and tend to be interpreted subjectively.

Connotation   The meanings or implications associated with a particular word beyond its literal definition.

Coordinating Conjunctions   Joining words. There are seven—and only seven—coordinating conjunctions: *and, but, for, or, nor, so, yet.* When you write and revise your work, you will frequently use such words to indicate the equal importance but varying relationship between words or clauses. Your comma and coordinating conjunction function as a single unit to correctly punctuate two complete thoughts into a single sentence.

EXAMPLE: The campsite filled with mosquitoes at dusk, *so* we built a fire out of green wood and lit several coils of bug repellent.

Definition   A brief exposition designed to explain the meaning of a term or concept. Sometimes an author will spend an entire essay defining a term; Susan Sontag's "Beauty" clearly illustrates this point, beginning with an historical reference to Greece. The rhetorical strategy of definition limits a focus, narrows a topic, clarifies a point of view, or establishes a frame of reference. If key terms are carefully defined, both the writer and the reader will stay focused on the controlling idea or thesis of an essay and avoid digressions and misunderstandings.

Denotation   The literal or standard dictionary definition of a word, understood without emotional influences or associations.

Diction   An author's word choice. High diction consists of elevated or elaborate speech, formal language, and, quite often, polysyllabic words. Diction also deals with word usage (concrete/abstract expressions, denotation/connotation, colloquialisms).

Division and Classification   A rhetorical strategy that takes the subject and breaks it down into smaller, more comprehensible units. In the process, writers consider subject matter from diverse points of view until they have found the most appropriate categories for divisions. After dividing the subject matter into smaller units, writers will then be free to examine each point in detail. Division and classification are probably some of the most familiar methods of essay development. Most material in an essay outline or the table of contents in a book, for instance, has been divided and classified.

Documentation   Acknowledging primary and secondary sources of information through "parenthetical references" and a list of works cited.

Doublespeak   A verbal smoke screen that covers up or masks unpleasant facts and details (e.g., referring to soldiers shot by their own infantry as *victims of friendly fire*).

Evidence   In fiction, evidence often takes on the face of clues or information which motivates an action or resolves a mystery. In nonfiction, facts and examples support and thereby prove the validity of what you claim.

Evidence can take the form of personal experience, observations of others, professional testimonies, and authoritative studies (readings).

Figures of Speech Figurative language adds variety to literary works by referring to people, places, and things in a nonliteral sense. The most common forms of figures of speech include the use of metaphor, simile, hyperbole, and personification. (Figurative language is discussed in detail in chapter 4.)

Idioms The use of words unique to a particular group or language. Idiomatic expressions are often neither grammatical or logical, but they are "understood" when used (e.g., "hitting the bottle," which literally means "to strike a bottle" but idiomatically refers to drinking liquor). Idioms are difficult or impossible to translate into another language.

Illustration Showing rather than telling a reader what statements and claims mean is one of the chief functions of illustration and example. When illustrating discussion points, writers will use concrete examples from their personal experiences, observations, and readings. By using plenty of representative examples to illustrate and support what is said, writers validate their premises and help readers to visualize discussion points by showing—not just telling.

Imagery Concrete expressions that appeal to the *five* senses, often employing the use of figurative speech to produce mental pictures.

Irony Irony is a matter of indirection. *Verbal irony* exists when the opposite of what was intended is expressed. *Situational irony* results when the opposite of what was expected takes place, leaving those involved powerless. *Dramatic irony* places characters in a state of ignorance, while you, the reader or viewer, are aware of what is about to take place.

Metaphor A figurative comparison without the use of *like* or *as*. For instance, a simile would state: "The ballroom dancers floated across the floor like butterflies." A metaphor would simply state: "The ballroom dancers were butterflies, floating across the floor." (See the expanded discussion of figurative language in chapter 4.)

Mood The mood is the emotional or emotional-intellectual attitude that an author takes towards a work (e.g., gloomy, optimistic, pessimistic, cheerful).

Parallelism Constructing word groups into consistent, balanced patterns, using the same grammatical forms. Parallelism offers an excellent rhetorical scheme for condensing material using an economy of words. To achieve parallel structure, arrange your information into similar grammatical constructions, balancing a noun with a noun, a verb with a verb, an adjective with an adjective (e.g., *Bright, intelligent, and ambitious,* Xiomara won every academic honor at the university). The possibilities for condensing paragraphs and sentences are endless, and the results of your efforts will not go unrewarded.

Paraphrase Putting someone else's writings or ideas into your own words.

Persona Literally speaking, a persona is "a mask" and is used in the form of a character or voice as the speaker of an essay or short story. An author's persona may change to suit his/her audience. Frequently, the attitudes of the persona differ from those of the author.

Personification Giving human characteristics and attributes to inanimate objects (boats, cans, trees) and nonhuman animals (horses, cats, owls).

Plot The sequence of events or story line in a dramatic work, a piece of fiction, as well as some verse. As Aristotle put it, plot is "the imitation of an action" and also "the arrangement of the incidents."

Point of View The perspective from which an essay or story is written. In formal writing, point of view is expressed in *first person*, wherein the author uses the pronoun "I," and *third person*, which is a more objective form of writing, wherein the writer uses "he," "she," or "it" as the narrator. Point of view may also refer to an author's attitude towards his or her subject matter.

Process Analysis A rhetorical strategy that answers the question "how" in composition. There are two basic types of process analysis essays: informative process analysis, which shows how something happens or how something has occurred (the evolution of life according to both Charles Darwin and the Bible), and directive process analysis, which indicates "how to do" something (how to drive a tractor, how to make good first impressions).

Prose A general term applied to all forms of writing that do not follow any regular rhythmic pattern (such as poetry).

Protagonist The main character in a fictional or dramatic work.

Satire An attack on human vices and follies. It ridicules people, places, and things for amusement—ideally to correct behavior or to improve attitudes and bring about necessary change.

Setting The social or historical or geographic background in fiction or drama. Setting may also include seasons, locations (e.g., city office or farm house) and occasions (a birthday, the Mardi Gras, Independence Day).

Simile A comparative figure of speech using "like" with nouns and "as."

> EXAMPLE: Elton looked *like* a railway conductor.
> EXAMPLE: The crowd surged forward *as* violently *as* the raging seas.

Simple Sentences Sentence constructions with a basic subject–verb core: *bees sting, people speak, wood floats, airplanes fly*. Granted, two-word sentences are not very common, and most simple sentences contain direct and indirect objects or complements.

> EXAMPLE: *The motorcycle roared down the street, expelling dark clouds of smoke and exhaust.*

Stripped of additional information regarding what the motorcycle did, the subject–verb core reads "The motorcycle roared." A complete thought in a simple sentence may contain a compound (more than one) subject, a compound verb, or both a compound subject and compound verb.

Compound Subject and *Single Verb*

EXAMPLE: Skip and Lindo *learned* how to play golf during the summer.

Single Subject and Compound Verb

EXAMPLE: *Shelia* read Toni Morrison's *Sula* and wrote a lecture on it.

Compound Subject and *Compound Verb*

EXAMPLE: Annice, Tara, and Penelope *drove* to Monterey, *saw* Coco Taylor at the annual Blues Festival, and *stayed* at the Holiday Inn.

Speaker   In a story or a poem, the speaker is the narrator, providing the point of view from which something is experienced. In addition to narrating a literary work, the speaker may present privileged information—insights that come from his or her sphere of knowledge.

Strategy   Plan of action or method used for approaching, analyzing, and writing about a topic or an issue.

Summary   Condensation of another author's work into a shorter composition. A summary of a literary piece may help to grasp a firm sense of "the whole."

Syntax   The arrangement of words in a sentence.

Thesis   The main or controlling idea of an essay.

Tone   The tone of a literary work projects the writer's attitude towards his or her subject through the use of carefully selected words (diction).

Topic Sentence   Much like a thesis, though not as broad, a topic sentence is the main idea of a paragraph. A topic sentence usually leads off a paragraph, and the sentences that follow should support the point with specific facts and details in order to provide unity for the paragraph.

Transitions   Words or word groups that assist a writer or a speaker in moving from one point to the next. Some common transitions include *after, before, therefore, however, moreover, nevertheless, thus.*

Understatement   Intentionally undervaluing or overplaying something to create emphasis.

Unity   A writer unifies a piece of nonfiction by making a point—usually the thesis or topic sentence—and sticking to the controlling idea he or she has established without digressing from that major discussion point. In other words, paragraphs should stick to supporting the thesis in a paper, and sentences should back up the topic sentence in paragraphs to unify your writing.

Voice   There are two voices—active and passive. In the active voice the subject *does* the acting (e.g., The actress read her lines), and in the passive voice the subject *receives* the action of the verb (e.g., The lines were read by the actress).

Literary Credits

Akutagawa, Ryunosuke. "In a Grove" (*Yabu no Naka*) Reprinted from *Rahsomon and Other Stories* by Ryunosuke Akutagawa, translated by Takashi Kojima, with the permission of Liveright Publishing Corporation.

Allen, Paula Gunn. "Spirit Women." From *The Woman Who Owned the Shadows* by Paula Gunn Allen. Copyright © 1983 by Paula Gunn Allen. Reprinted with permission from Aunt Lute Books.

Allen, Woody. "The Kugelmass Episode." From *Side Effects* by Woody Allen, Copyright © 1977 by Woody Allen. Reprinted by permission of Random House, Inc.

Allende, Isabel. "Out Secret." Reprinted with the permission of Simon & Schuster from *The Stories of Eva Luna* by Isabel Allende, translated from the Spanish by Margaret Sayers Peden. Copyright © 1989 by Isabel Allende. English translation copyright © 1991 by Macmillan Publishing Company.

Atwood, Margaret. "The City Planners." From *The Circle Game* by Margaret Atwood. Copyright © 1966 by Margaret Atwood. Reprinted with the permission of Stoddart Publishing Company Limited.

Bambara, Toni Cade. "Blues Ain't No Mockin Bird." From *Gorilla, My Love* by Toni Cade Bambara. Copyright © 1971 by Toni Cade Bambara. Reprinted by permission of Random House, Inc.

Baraka, Amiri. "Ka 'Ba." From *Black Magic Poetry* by Amiri Baraka. Copyright © 1969 by Amiri Baraka. Reprinted with permission of Sterling Lord Literistic, Inc.

Basho, Matsuo. From *Matsuo Basho.* Reprinted with permission of Kodansha American, Inc.

Bishop, Elizabeth. "The Moose." From *The Complete Poems 1927–1979* by Elizabeth Bishop. Copyright © 1979, 1983 by Alice Helen Methfessel. Reprinted by permission of Farrar, Straus & Giroux, Inc.

Boyle, Kay. "Astronomer's Wife." From *Life Being the Best & Other Stories* by Kay Boyle. Copyright © 1988 by Kay Boyle. Reprinted by permission of New Directions Publishing Corporation.

Bradbury, Ray. "There Will Come Soft Rains." Originally published in *Collier's,* 1950. Copyright © 1950, renewed 1977 by Ray Bradbury. Reprinted by permission of Don Congdon Associates, Inc.

Brautigan, Richard. "In a Café." From *The Pill Versus the Springhill Mine Disaster* by Richard Brautigan. Copyright © 1968. Reprinted by permission of Ianthe Brautigan Swensen.

Britt, Susanne. "Love and Hate." From *A Writer's Rhetoric* by Susanne Britt. Copyright © 1988 by Harcourt Brace & Company. Reprinted by permission of the publisher.

Campbell, Joseph. "The Call to Adventure." From *The Hero with a Thousand Faces* by Joseph Campbell. Copyright © 1979 by Princeton University Press. Reprinted by permission of Princeton University Press.

Camus, Albert. "The Myth of Sisyphus." From *The Myth of Sisyphus and Other Essays* by Albert Camus, translated by Justin O'Brien. Copyright © 1955 by Alfred A. Knopf, Inc. Reprinted by permission of the publisher.

Cisneros, Sandra. "The Monkey Garden." From *The House on Mango Street* by Sandra Cisneros. Copyright © 1984 by Sandra Cisneros. Published by Vintage Books, a division of Random House, Inc., New York, and in hardcover by Alfred A. Knopf 1994. Reprinted by permission of the Susan Bergholtz Literary Agency.

Cohen, Leonard. "Queen Victoria." Written by Leonard Cohen. Copyright © 1973 by Leonard Cohen Stranger Music, Inc. Used by permission of the author. All rights reserved.

Cortázar, Julio. "Axolotl." From *End of the Game and Other Stories* by Julio Cortázar, translated by Paul Blackburn. Copyright © 1967, 1963 by Random House, Inc. Reprinted by permission of Pantheon Books, a division of Random House, Inc.

Higashi, Rose Anna. "Thoughts of a Gambler's Lover." Copyright © 1986 by Rose Anna Higashi. Used by permission of the author.

Housman, A. E. "To An Athlete Dying Young." From *The Collected Poems of A. E. Housman.* Copyright © 1939, 1940 Holt, Rinehart & Winston, Inc. Copyright © 1967 Robert E. Symons. Copyright © 1965 Henry Holt & Co., Inc. Reprinted by permission of Henry Holt & Co., Inc.

Hughes, Langston. "On The Road." From *Laughing to Keep from Crying* by Langston Hughes. Copyright © 1952 by Langston Hughes. Copyright renewed by George Houston Bass in 1980. Used by permission of Harold Ober Associates Incorporated.

Issa. *The Year of My Life: A Translation of Issa's 'Oraga Hura.'* Translated by Nobuyuki Yuasa. Copyright © 1972 by The Regents of the University of California. Used by permission of the University of California Press.

Jackson, Shirley. "The Lottery." From *The Lottery* by Shirley Jackson. Copyright © 1948, 1949 by Shirley Jackson. Copyright © renewed 1976, 1977 by Lawrence Hyman, Barry Hyman, Mrs. Sarah Webster and Mrs. Joanne Schnurer. Reprinted by permission of Farrar, Straus & Giroux, Inc.

Jeffers, Robinson. "To The Stone-cutters." From *Selected Poems* by Robinson Jeffers. Copyright © 1924 and renewed 1953 by Robinson Jeffers. Reprinted by permission of Random House, Inc.

Joyce, James. "Araby." From *Dubliners* by James Joyce. Copyright © 1916 by B. W. Huebach, Inc. Definitive text Copyright © 1967 by Estate of James Joyce. Used by permission of Viking Penguin, a division of Penguin Books USA Inc.

Kawabata, Yasunari. "The Pomegranate." From *Contemporary Japanese Literature* by Howard Hibbett, editor. Copyright © 1977 by Alfred A. Knopf Inc. Reprinted by permission of the publisher.

Keillor, Garrison. "Pontoon Boat." From *Leaving Home* by Garrison Keillor. Copyright © 1987 by Garrison Keillor. Used by permission of Viking Penguin, a division of Penguin Books USA Inc.

Kennedy, X. J. "Nude Descending a Staircase." From *Nude Descending a Staircase* by X. J. Kennedy. Copyright © 1961 by X. J. Kennedy. Reprinted by permission of Curtis, Brown Ltd.

Kingston, Maxine Hong. "No Name Woman." From *The Woman Warrior* by Maxine Hong Kingston. Copyright © 1975, 1976 by Maxine Hong Kingston. Reprinted by permission of Alfred A. Knopf, Inc.

Lakoff, George. "Metaphor and War." From *Express,* February 22, 1991. Copyright © 1991 by George Lakoff. Reprinted by permission of the author.

Lawrence, D. H. "The Horse Dealer's Daughter." From *Complete Short Stories of D. H. Lawrence* by D. H. Lawrence. Copyright © 1922 by Thomas B. Seltzer, Inc., renewed © 1950 by Frieda Lawrence. Used by permission of Viking Penguin, a division of Penguin Books USA Inc.

Le Guin, Ursula. "Introduction to *The Book of Fantasy* by Jorge Luis Borges." Copyright © 1986 by Ursula K. Le Guin. Reprinted by permission of the author and the author's agent, Virginia Kidd.

Levertov, Denise. "Pleasures." From *Collected Earlier Poems 1940–1960* by Denise Levertov. Copyright © 1959 by Denise Levertov. Reprinted by permission of New Directions Publishing Corporation.

Lockett, Reginald. "When They Came to Take Him." Copyright © 1993 by Reginald Lockett. "When They Came to Take Him" appeared in a slightly different form in "Appeal to Reason," 1982. Reprinted by permission of the author.

Lu, The. "Nightmare." From *A Thousand Years of Vietnamese Poetry*, Nguyen Ngoc Bich, translator. Copyright © 1975 by Alfred A. Knopf. Reprinted by permission of The Asia Society.

Malcolm X. "Homemade Education." From *The Autobiography of Malcolm X* by Malcolm X with the assistance of Alex Haley. Copyright © 1964 by Alex Haley and Malcolm X and copyright © 1965 by Alex Haley and Betty Shabazz. Reprinted by permission of Random House, Inc.

Malamud, Bernard. "The Magic Barrel." From *The Magic Barrel* by Bernard Malamud. Copyright © 1958 and renewed © 1986 by Bernard Malamud. Reprinted by permission of Farrar, Straus & Giroux, Inc.

Index